MW00609236

"Many Christians are unprepared to answer the postmodern notion that truth is unknowable and hence ultimately unimportant. That premise refutes itself, of course, but for those already steeped in existential and postmodern ways of thinking, self-defeating propositions are standard fare, and even the simplest truths can seem elusive. Persuading those who love darkness and revel in contradiction can be quite a challenge. Dr. John Feinberg is uniquely qualified to untangle the knots of modern and postmodern thought, pointing us to a better way of understanding truth in the clear light of Scripture. This is an extremely helpful study."

John MacArthur, Pastor, Grace Community Church, Sun Valley, California

"John Feinberg meets the challenge of modern skepticism head on, with the full confidence that Christianity is rational and defensible in the marketplace of ideas. Your mind will be stretched and your faith strengthened when you read this book."

Erwin W. Lutzer, Senior Pastor, The Moody Church, Chicago, Illinois

"Dr. Feinberg, a well-respected philosopher and theologian, has written a rigorous and learned work. The first two sections give a careful prolegomena to apologetics, emphasizing epistemology and apologetic method—subjects that are all too often ignored or glossed over in works on apologetics. He then applies his apologetic method to some of the most important questions in apologetics. The attentive reader will be richly rewarded."

Douglas Groothuis, Professor of Philosophy, Denver Seminary; author, *Christian Apologetics*

"John Feinberg's book is an insightful, thoughtful, and thorough analysis of the modern and postmodern mindsets and a guide on how to engage them. In addition to astute treatments of traditional apologetical themes, such as the Gospels' reliability and religious pluralism, this volume incisively engages skepticism, truth, and knowledge quite unlike the standard texts in apologetics. Carefully argued yet quite readable, Feinberg's book has much to offer the expert, the novice, and those in between."

Paul Copan, Pledger Family Chair of Philosophy and Ethics, Palm Beach Atlantic University

"John Feinberg is one of today's most accomplished Christian scholars. Having written on ethics, the doctrine of God, and on the problem of evil, he here turns his attention to apologetics in a modern *and* postmodern world. *Can You Believe It's True?* manages to make a large and complex body of material accessible. In Feinberg's rendering, truth is neither irrational nor strictly modern (foundational), but *biblical*. Both theoretically solid and ultimately practical, this book will contribute enormously to showing how Christian faith is reasonable, credible, and pertinent to our confused world."

William Edgar, Professor of Apologetics, Westminster Theological Seminary, Philadelphia

Can You Believe It's True?

Can You Believe It's True?

Christian Apologetics in a Modern and Postmodern Era

John S. Feinberg

CROSSWAY

WHEATON, ILLINOIS

Can You Believe It's True? Christian Apologetics in a Modern and Postmodern Era

Copyright © 2013 by John S. Feinberg

Published by Crossway
   1300 Crescent Street
   Wheaton, Illinois 60187

Cover design: Simplicated Studio

First printing 2013

Printed in the United States of America

Unless otherwise noted, Scripture quotations are from *The New American Standard Bible®*. Copyright © The Lockman Foundation 1960, 1962, 1963, 1968, 1971, 1972, 1973, 1975, 1977. Used by permission.

Scripture quotations marked KJV are from the *King James Version* of the Bible.

Hardcover ISBN: 978-1-4335-3900-8
PDF ISBN: 978-1-4335-3901-5
Mobipocket ISBN: 978-1-4335-3902-2
ePub ISBN: 978-1-4335-3903-9

Library of Congress Cataloging-in-Publication Data

Feinberg, John S., 1946-
 Can you believe it's true? : Christian apologetics in a modern and postmodern era / John S. Feinberg.
  pages cm
 Includes bibliographical references and index.
 ISBN 978-1-4335-3900-8
 1. Apologetics. 2. Philosophy, Modern.
3. Postmodernism. I. Title.
BT1103.F45 2013
239—dc23   2012047649

Crossway is a publishing ministry of Good News Publishers.

SH		22	21	20	19	18	17	16	15	14	13
15	14	13	12	11	10	9	8	7	6	5	4	3	2	1

In Memory of
Paul David Feinberg
Great Theologian and Ethicist
Great Defender of the Faith
Best Brother
Best Friend

Contents

Preface

Though I have taught apologetics for many years to graduate students, I hadn't actually planned on writing this book. Most of my attention academically has been occupied with systematic theology and ethics. Of course, I am greatly interested in apologetics, but to write a text would require covering a number of diverse issues. In addition, in recent decades, many outstanding works in Christian apologetics have been published, so I thought those were sufficient. And, my brother Paul was planning to write an apologetics text. Though it would have been a different book from this in various ways, I didn't sense an urgent need for there to be two apologetics textbooks written by two Feinbergs.

So, what happened? I changed my mind more than a decade ago, because I saw truth being relentlessly attacked both by nonbelievers and even by some who call themselves Christians. And, I didn't see much of an answer to the onslaught of epistemological relativism, especially in the most virulent and deadly forms of postmodern skepticism about truth and reason.

But truth matters enormously—if there is no such thing as absolute truth, or if none of us can know what it is, then many of us are wasting our lives in a futile pursuit of it and deluding others and ourselves into thinking that we are leading them to find truth. So, even though this book is usable as a general text in apologetics, the greatest burden and passion of the book is to defend the notions that there is truth, humans can find it, and we can "know that we know" what is true. Not only are these ideas presented, but detailed arguments and explanations are offered to support these views.

In order to accomplish such a goal, it is necessary to understand the times in which we live and the reasons that so many of our contemporaries are not only convinced that we can't know absolute truth, but are quite comfortable with that conclusion. Though many in our day have capitulated to the beguilement of postmodern skepticism about reason, knowledge, and truth, there are still many who hold some form of modern epistemology. Many moderns, like postmoderns, are skeptical about the truth of Christianity, but not because they believe it is impossible to know what is true. They just don't think there is enough evidence to support Christianity as true. Thus, the first major section of the book presents both modern and postmodern forms of skepticism, and offers detailed answers to both. I begin the book this way, because unless it can be established that there is such a thing as truth and that humans can know what it is, there is little sense in talking about the best way to defend the truth of Christianity (or any other beliefs).

After answering reasons for skepticism about religious beliefs in general and Christianity in particular, the book turns in part 2 to consider several methods of defending Christian truth that have been prevalent among Christian apologists during at least the last century (some have been around much longer). The third part of the book turns to Christian evidences. Originally, I had planned to cover all of the major areas that Christian apologists have traditionally defended with arguments and evidences. However, as earlier chapters and the pages piled up, it became clear that to cover all areas of Christian evidences would result in a book much too long. So, I decided to limit my coverage to just a few issues, and to use the chapters in part 3 to illustrate the methodology I had presented as my own approach through the first two parts of the book.

Undoubtedly, some will be unhappy that I didn't cover their topic of special interest. In particular, some won't be pleased that I didn't do a chapter on the existence of God. I didn't include such a chapter, in part because I have elsewhere presented in detail traditional arguments for God's existence,[1] and I wanted to cover some issues I haven't previously defended in print. There are other reasons for this decision that you will see as you read my comments on methods of defending Christian truth. So, if I didn't defend a doctrine you had wanted, I apologize, but please remember that while I have tried to present the strongest case possible for each tenet of the faith I defend, I am also using part 3 of this book to illustrate the methodology worked out in the earlier parts of the book.

There are a number of people who have been very helpful in producing this book, and I want to acknowledge them. First, a word of thanks is due to Crossway for its willingness to publish the book, and for its patience in waiting for me to finish it. I am grateful to Marvin Padgett, who saw to it that the book was contracted by Crossway. In addition, Allan Fisher has been most supportive as I have worked on the book, and his advice on what to include and what to omit has been very helpful and is greatly appreciated. As always, I am indebted to the extraordinary editorial skills of Bill Deckard; in my experience, no other press has an editor who can match Bill's expertise.

In addition, I have been helped by a variety of student assistants with the gathering of bibliography. Some have also read portions of an earlier draft of the manuscript and made helpful comments. In particular, I want to thank Shawn Bawulski, Todd Saur, Ike Miller, and Jessica Wilson.

One other person has been enormously helpful. My dear friend and colleague Harold A. Netland is a tremendously gifted apologist/philosopher of religion and an exceptional teacher. Harold read and commented on the whole manuscript. In addition, we have had a number of conversations about the book and its various topics. I found all of his counsel greatly helpful, and have tried to accommodate all of his suggestions. The book is significantly better because of his input, and so I am very grateful to him. Errors that still remain are, of course, my responsibility, not Harold's.

Then, I must say a word about my brother Paul, in whose memory this volume is dedicated. Soon after I decided to write this book I also decided to dedicate it to Paul. I had hoped that he would get to see it, but sadly, rather unexpectedly he went to be with the Lord some eight years ago. Throughout my life, Paul was a great encouragement to me about everything. In my judgment (and that of many others), he was also a brilliant theologian and philosopher/apologist. His clear and cogent stand for Christ and for the truth of Christianity has been and remains a great source of inspiration to all who knew him. And, his clear and loving voice in defense of truth is greatly missed by all who knew and loved him! I can't say that Paul would agree with everything in this book, but I know he would be pleased to find that this project is finally finished! In his memory this volume is lovingly dedicated.

Today truth, especially Christian truth, is under attack seemingly from all quarters. As you read this book, I trust that you will be convinced that there is truth, and that we can know what it is. Even more, I hope that you will see that Christianity is truth, truth you can believe. May God grant us knowledge and faith to see this, and may he give us strength and courage to take an unwavering stand for the truth!

John S. Feinberg
July 2012

PART ONE

The Question of Truth

Chapter 1

Introduction

The great twentieth-century philosopher Bertrand Russell was once asked what he would say if, after he died, contrary to his expectations, he found himself standing before God and God asked him why he hadn't believed in God. Russell replied that he would say, "Not enough evidence, God! Not enough evidence!"[1] Russell believed, in the words of W. K. Clifford, that "it is always wrong, everywhere, and for anyone to believe anything upon insufficient evidence."[2] Russell further believed that our world doesn't contain enough evidence for God's existence for anyone to believe in him. As Clifford wrote about beliefs based on insufficient evidence, it is our duty "to guard ourselves from such beliefs as from a pestilence."[3]

Implicit in what Russell and Clifford said is a belief that it is rational to hold only beliefs supported by evidence. There is also an implicit faith in our ability to gather accurately (by observation of the world and by reflection on observed data and on principles of reasoning) and to evaluate accurately the quality of various purported evidences in support of an idea. Reason can be trusted to tell us what to believe and what to reject about the world around us.

Somewhat later in the twentieth century a very different perspective on the search for truth by compiling evidences arose. Willard Van Orman Quine, espousing the view that what we know and understand is a product of the communities in which we were raised, wrote the following:

> The totality of our so-called knowledge or beliefs, from the most casual matters of geography and history to the profoundest laws of atomic physics or even of pure mathematics and logic, *is a man-made fabric* which

impinges on experience only along the edges. Or, to change the figure, total science is like a field of force whose boundary conditions are experience. A conflict with experience at the periphery occasions readjustments in the interior of the field. Truth values have to be redistributed over some statements. Re-evaluation of some statements entails re-evaluation of others, because of their logical interconnections. . . . But the total field is so underdetermined by its boundary conditions, experience, that there is much latitude of choice as to what statements to re-evaluate in the light of any single contrary experience. *No particular experiences are linked with any particular statements in the interior of the field*, except indirectly through considerations of equilibrium affecting the field as a whole[4] (italics mine).

These are remarkable claims! If all our concepts are man-made, then the world is not simply mirrored on our mind through sense perception, allowing us objectively to read off the results. Nor do our observations and reasoning "see things as they are." What we claim to know is actually an interconnected web of beliefs that touch reality, experience, only at the borders of that web. But, note that Quine says that the total field of our knowledge is underdetermined by experience. This means that experience and our contact with it are such that there simply is insufficient evidence from experience for us to know which beliefs are true or false or whether our whole perspective on the world is right or wrong.

The problem of deciding which views are correct is further exacerbated by the fact that different cultures have their own constructions of reality which are not the same as another culture's. As Diogenes Allen explains about the most radical current approaches to epistemology,

We not only construct the world, so that all knowledge, value, and meaning are relative to human beings, as Idealists since Kant have argued, but now the radical conclusion is drawn that there is no reality that is *universally* constructed because people in different periods of history and in different societies construct it differently. There is no definitive procedure or universal basis to settle disputes in the natural sciences, in ethics, and in the interpretation of literature. Every domain of inquiry and every value is relative to a culture and even to subcultures.[5]

In short, there is no absolute truth, or if there is, no one is in a position to know what it is. If so, what is the point of marshaling evidences in support of a belief?

As is clear from comparing the comments of Russell and Clifford, on the one hand, and those of Quine and Allen, on the other, something very significant has changed. Sometimes in philosophy it takes a long time for entrenched ideas to change; at other times change seems to come rather quickly. Shortly after the middle of the twentieth century, philosophers made some major changes in their assessment of reason's abilities to know the world aright. Doubts about whether there is such a thing as absolute truth (and whether, if so, anyone is in a position to discover it) became the norm. In addition, philosophers raised serious doubts about whether some set of beliefs should be seen as foundational to all other beliefs and hence relatively or even totally immune from all attack. Of course, there have always been some skeptics about the mind's abilities to "get things right," even in Western cultures that shared a basic commitment to Christianity. There were, for example, skeptics in Augustine's era, and he addressed the issues they repeatedly raised. In addition, there was widespread skepticism about knowledge and religion in the sixteenth and seventeenth centuries, and it became even more vocal in later centuries.[6] In our day skepticism seems to be the predominant attitude toward knowledge, not just among trained philosophers but among ordinary, everyday people.

These more recent beliefs about reason's inadequacies involve what scholars call a move from a modern to a postmodern understanding of our world. While it is safe to say that not everyone has made this switch, evidences of the postmodern mind-set becoming increasingly entrenched are too numerous to deny. We cannot merely say these are views relegated to ivory-tower academics who need something to think and write about in order to justify their salaries. In many areas of life, we find that various postmodern themes have trickled down into everyday life among "ordinary" people. Some believe this flirtation with things postmodern will be short-lived, for when one understands its contours, its most radical expressions, and its ultimate implications, one realizes that no one can or does live consistently with such a mind-set. I am not a prophet, so I cannot predict how long postmodern thinking will last, but I do know that many non-academics with whom we rub shoulders every day are very much captivated by some of postmodernity's most fundamental themes. Hence, in constructing a strategy for defending Christianity, if we are to challenge nonbelievers who are postmodern in their outlook, we must take postmodern themes seriously. Of course, not everyone has completely abandoned the modern mind-set, and thus, we must also think of how to defend the Christian faith to people of that persuasion.

At this point you may be interested but uncertain about how to proceed, because you are not quite sure about what modernity and postmodernity are and how they differ. Rather than first present a set of ideas associated with each perspective, let me introduce you to these understandings of reality through two imaginary conversations which will illustrate them.

Let us imagine first a conversation between two university students that takes place sometime between 1955 and 1969. One student is a nonbeliever working within the modern mind-set. Let us call him Modern Joe, or MO JOE for short. The second participant knows Christ as his personal Savior. Let us call him Joe Christian, or JOE C for short. JOE C is quite concerned about the spiritual condition of his university friends and acquaintances, and so he witnesses to them whenever possible. Let's listen to this imaginary conversation between MO JOE and JOE C:

> JOE C: I'm really glad we could get together for coffee today, Mo Joe.

> MO JOE: Thanks for the invite. I'm always open for free coffee. What did you want to talk about?

> JOE C: I wanted to talk to you about spiritual matters.

> MO JOE: Spiritual matters? I don't believe in ghosts! Is that what you mean?

> JOE C: No, I'm talking about what you think about God and whether you have a relationship with him. Specifically, I want to share with you what's called "the four spiritual laws."

> MO JOE: Joe C, I didn't know you were into some religious cult. Mind control and all that. Oh, well, I guess everyone has a right to do his own thing. But that's not for me.

> JOE C: Mo Joe, I understand your concerns, but I'm not into any cult. I am concerned, though, about what you think about God and where you're planning to spend eternity.

> MO JOE: Oh, brother! I'll spend it where everyone else does. Planted six feet under in some cemetery. Reason and experience

tell us that death ends it all—period! So, you'd better plan to enjoy yourself while you're here, because there's no second chance once you're dead and gone.

JOE C: That's an interesting philosophy, Mo Joe. I'd like to share a different one with you that I've found very meaningful. It's based on God's Word, the Bible, and it involves those four spiritual laws. The first law says that God loves you and has a wonderful plan for your life.

MO JOE: Hold on, Joe C. Your so-called first law contains a lot of unproved assumptions, and I don't think you can prove any of them.

JOE C: Uhm, can I go on to the second law?

MO JOE: Not so fast! We need first to identify those unproved assumptions in your first law, and you need to give me some evidence why I should believe them. Without sufficient evidence, I can't believe anything, even if it is something others find helpful. Let me point out those unproved assumptions I was talking about. For example, your first law assumes that there is a God, but offers no proof. I think we can explain everything in our universe by an appeal to natural laws and evolution. Don't you know that science tells us everything we need to know to get along in our world? There's no need to appeal to the supernatural. Anyway, I only believe what's provable through reason and the five senses.

JOE C: That's a very interesting theory, Mo Joe. Are you saying that human reason and sense perception never make mistakes?

MO JOE: No, Joe C. Reason and sense perception aren't infallible, but that doesn't mean they don't work at all. There is a real world outside of our minds, and through our reason and sense perception we are able to understand that world correctly most of the time. When we're wrong, others with the same intellectual equipment can steer us in the right direction. Joe C, I'm not a skeptic about knowing anything. I'm just skeptical when someone wants me to believe something without evidence.

JOE C: But, Mo Joe, I'll bet you do believe in things you can't confirm by reason or experience through the five senses. For example, I bet you believe there's such a thing as love.

21

MO JOE: Sure, but I can feel what love is like. And, I can see love's results when I look at a newlywed couple, for example. So, it's not so invisible as you suggest. Anyway, speaking of love, you said your God is a loving God. That's another unproved assumption. If God is so loving, why do terrible things happen in our world? Murders, disease, wars, famines? No, I can't believe in a loving God, when so many evil things happen. If God really does care about all this, then he must be powerless to do anything about it. And, if that's so, then he's no God after all.

JOE C: I agree that those problems are hard to explain, but they aren't impossible to answer. Anyway, Mo Joe, answer me one question: If there is no God, why does anything ever go right in our world?

MO JOE: That's easy. Natural laws run our world. Our universe is all a product of chance, but once it got here, it keeps running according to natural laws. There's plenty of evidence that this is how things work; hence I don't see that it's rational to postulate a supernatural being who keeps our world running. If you want me to believe otherwise, you need to present enough evidence to support your belief. As for me, I trust what reason and my senses teach me about the world, and they don't show me that there's a God. If you want to believe in such things, that's your business, but I'm not going to be so irresponsible as to believe what can't be proved!

JOE C: But that's my point. Who runs the natural laws and keeps things going according to those laws?

MO JOE: I don't know. Maybe Mother Nature. Maybe not. But why do we have to have an explanation for everything? Things just run by natural laws in our universe. That's a fact, and that's all there is to it. But we're digressing. Your so-called spiritual law not only says God is loving. It says he loves me and has a plan for my life. There you go again. More unproved assumptions.

JOE C: What do you mean?

MO JOE: I mean that if you knew what's been going on in my life, you wouldn't say God loves me. My life is a mess, and no one steps in to help, least of all your supposed God. If there is a God and he loves me, he sure has a funny way of showing it.

JOE C: No one is guaranteed exemption from all problems in life, Mo Joe. As bad as things are now for you, they might be worse if not for God's loving hand in your life. Besides, he showed his love for you by sending Christ to die for you.

MO JOE: I don't need Christ or anyone else to die for me. I need help with living—you know, paying bills, staying well, and the like. No, there's little evidence of a God of love in my life. In addition, you say that God has a plan for my life. There's another unproved assumption. Even if God does care about our world, what's the proof that he can act in history or that he does? History is going nowhere, and so is my life. Neither has any meaning.

JOE C: Christ would give meaning to your life, if you'd let him.

MO JOE: I'm sorry, but how can someone who's dead bring meaning to my life? I know you believe God has this great plan for my life, but how can that be? And even if he does, I repeat that nowhere do we see God's hand in history. Evidently he's locked out of this world, if he even exists in the first place.

JOE C: Actually, he's acting all around us all the time. If you only had the faith to see his hand!

MO JOE: Yeah, that's what you Christians always say. I'm still waiting to see the hard evidence to support your claims. As for me, I believe what I can touch, see, smell, and the like, and what appears reasonable to me.

JOE C: How sad that you feel that way. There's so much more to life with Christ at its center.

MO JOE: Joe C, that may be fine for you, but not for me. You utter all these pious-sounding phrases, but what do they mean? I think what you're talking about amounts to nothing, since you can't prove a thing you say. You know, the logical positivists warned us about people like you. You go around using theological and religious language as though you are making meaningful claims about the world. But you aren't. Logical positivism has shown us that unless we know how to verify a sentence, what it asserts is meaningless. Since no one knows how to verify theological and religious propositions, all of them are meaningless, and what they talk about is probably nonexistent. By the way, that includes your first spiritual law (and probably all the others as well).

JOE C: My, you have thought a lot about this! Have you ever considered the claims of Christ?

MO JOE: No, nor those of Muhammad, Buddha, or anyone else. Why should I? I consider seriously only what I can touch, feel, et cetera. Things that run by natural laws. Which reminds me, Joe C. You've been talking about spiritual laws. What sort of thing is a spiritual law? Is it some law that controls my driving? Is it a law passed by Congress? Is it something like the law of gravity? Is it a law about spirits? I have no idea of what you are talking about, and I doubt that you know what it means either. Just points up the problems I was mentioning about religious and theological language.

JOE C: Well, Mo Joe, I'd really like to talk to you more about all of this, but I have a class in a few minutes. Can we get together and talk about this some other time?

MO JOE: Sure, talk is cheap, and I'm always happy to have someone buy me coffee. But next time, bring evidence to support what you're saying! Have a good class, Joe C. See you later.

If you went to a secular university or college during the 1960s or before, I'm sure you can identify with this conversation. You've probably run into some "Mo Joes" before. For those of us who were undergraduates during those years, it is easy to think at first that on university campuses today little has changed about basic outlooks on life and the world. But a closer look at academia and, more broadly, at popular culture shows that there has been a major shift in the way many people see the world. That different approach is the postmodern point of view, and our second imaginary conversation illustrates it.

Imagine that this conversation takes place at a secular university somewhere between 1995 and 2002. It involves a Christian—again, let us call him Joe Christian, or Joe C for short—and a nonbeliever. Let's call the nonbeliever Postmodern Joe, or Pomo Joe for short. They meet one afternoon and the following conversation ensues:

JOE C: Hi, Pomo Joe. I'm glad we could sit down and talk together. I've been wanting to talk with you about your spiritual life.

POMO JOE: My spiritual life? Cool! Have you found a good way to channel into the spirit world? Or do you just know a really good psychic? I've been trying to contact my grandparents who died a few years ago, but I'm having some trouble. I don't know whether I'm just not good at making the connection or whether they've been reincarnated again as someone or something else. Maybe you could shed some light on that.

JOE C: Well, not exactly. I had something else in mind. I wanted to talk with you about Christ and Christianity.

POMO JOE: Fine, but what's to talk about? I'm already a Christian, and I'm a Muslim, a Buddhist, and a Hindu. You know, all religions are really saying the same thing. It's all one.

JOE C: Not quite. There are some differences. But we'll get to that in a bit. I just wanted to share with you something of how much Christianity means to me and to tell you about what is called the four spiritual laws.

POMO JOE: Very interesting, Joe C. Whatever works for you. But each of us has to find our own truth wherever we can. Now about these spiritual laws. I thought religion was a personal matter between you and your God. Are you saying our government is making this a matter of public policy by passing laws? That violates the separation of church and state guaranteed by the US Constitution! That's just so-o-o-o politically incorrect!

JOE C: No, no, Pomo Joe. No one would dare ignore the separation of church and state. These laws are just principles that cover the spiritual realm. I can see you're confused a bit, so why don't I just tell you the first law. That will illustrate my point. The first law says God loves you and has a wonderful plan for your life.

POMO JOE: Oh, so that's what you're getting at. Well, of course, she loves me! I see her and feel her all around me. She's present in the baby's smile, in a sunset, in a gentle breeze, and I see her in the faces of all my friends. God's in all of us, you know. So, I can agree with what you say, but I didn't know that was what you meant by a spiritual law.

JOE C: Pomo, I'm afraid we're talking about two different things. I must not be making myself clear. I'm referring to the Judeo-Christian God. He created all things, he's moral governor of the universe, he knows we are all sinners, and he sent Christ to die to save us from our sins. All of these truths fit together very logically, and they show us a God of great grace.

POMO JOE: Oh, now I see where you're coming from. Logical, huh? Whose logic are you talking about? Western Aristotelian logic? Man, don't you know that such a way of thinking controls Western thought forms and institutions? But there's no reason that we should believe that's the right way to think. Not everything works by reason and logic. And anyway, reason and logic aren't even close to infallible. I don't trust either; I've found that it's better to go with my heart! Oh, and by the way, the God you're describing—there's a whole history of horrible things that have been done in his name. Why, the very way your Bible is written discriminates against women, the poor, and other minorities! The Christian outlook on things has really controlled many societies, including ours, for the last two thousand years, but it's not the only way to look at things. In fact, we need to examine all of our concepts and all of our institutions and get rid of things that incorporate prejudices against people. In other words, we really need to reconstruct a whole new picture of reality. Don't you know that belief in your God is totally out of touch with current times?

JOE C: I think the Judeo-Christian God is very relevant to our day. And, as I was saying, he loves you and has a wonderful plan for your life.

POMO JOE: Does he also love gays and lesbians, or does he exclude certain groups from the dialogue table?

JOE C: God loves everybody. That doesn't mean he's always happy about everything we do. But he does love us all.

And he showed that love by sending Christ to die for
our sins.

POMO JOE: What sins? The only sin I can see is being a bigot and
discriminating against people because of things they have
no control over. Besides, I think Christ was a very loving
person, but I don't get why you think he's so important.
There are many roads to God. Each one of us is traveling
down our own road, but we'll all get there.

JOE C: Christ is more than you suggest. He said, "I am the way,
and the truth, and the life; no one comes to the Father but
through me."

POMO JOE: Are you sure Christ said that? Man, I didn't know he was
so narrow in his thinking! So, Christ thinks he's the truth,
does he?

JOE C: He is the truth. I know that for a fact.

POMO JOE: Joe C, you're amazing. How can anyone know something
like that for a fact? All of us view things from our own
perspective. Our subjectivity makes it impossible to know
exactly what's true. All we can do is get together and
share experiences with one another. You know, talk about
what feels right and works for us. But what works for you
may not work for me. You know, everyone has an element
of truth in their belief system, even if we don't know
which beliefs are true.

JOE C: Pomo, I hate to tell you this, but you just contradicted
yourself. If we can't know which of our beliefs are true
and which aren't, how can you be sure that your belief
that everyone's beliefs contain some truth is true itself? Do
you see the problem?

POMO JOE: There you go again, Joe C, with your Western logic-
chopping! Who's to say what's contradictory? And, why
is it a problem to be contradictory unless you worship
Aristotelian logic? Surely that's not the only way to think.
One thing more, Joe C. Did your God have to take a logic
course from Aristotle in order to figure out how we humans think so he could talk to us?

JOE C: Of course not. God knows everything.

POMO JOE: But, then, why do you think God restricts herself only to Western logical thought forms? We need to see that God is bound to no culture or mind-set. Incidentally, I'm troubled by something else you said. Did you mean that Christ is the only way to God?

JOE C: That's what Christ said, and I believe it.

POMO JOE: Let me say this very clearly. You arrogant, bigoted snob! Where do you come off acting as though you have a corner on the market of truth? Who do you think you are, saying there's only one way to God? I suppose you also believe that all people of other religions and of times before Christ are just going to hell if they don't see things your way. Well, if that's so, at least we won't have to put up with people like you. You can have your so-called heaven. You and your redneck bigoted friends are not welcome at the dialogue table. There's no room at the table for those who think their views are absolute truth. There isn't any such thing, or if there is, none of us is in a position to know what it is! Anyway, who wants to believe in a God who would torment people forever just because they didn't think Christ was someone special? You know, your God doesn't have a very good track record. You say he's all-loving and all-powerful, but he didn't stop the Holocaust. And now you want me to believe that there will be an eternal holocaust for those who aren't Christians? No, thanks. Boy, are you out of step with the times!

JOE C: I'm sorry you feel this way. There are reasonable, convincing answers to your questions, if you'd let me tell you. But let me just say, I'm telling you these things because I care about you, not because I want to exclude you and see you punished.

POMO JOE: But what you're telling me is just your opinion—one among many. You've got to learn to be more tolerant of other people and their ideas. And you really have a problem with pride—thinking that you, of all people, know what's true, and you don't even realize that it makes sense only if you buy into your Western logic-chopping mind-set. No, Joe C. I like you—I even sense God's presence in you—but until you come down off your high horse, there's really nothing for us to talk about and no basis for us to have a relationship. You don't want dialogue. You want to instruct me. Thanks, but no thanks.

JOE C: But, Pomo, this isn't just my opinion. If it were, you'd be right that I'm just too arrogant. No, Pomo, I'm telling you what God himself says.

POMO JOE: Whoa, Joe C! When did God ever say that about herself? Where are you getting this stuff?

JOE C: I'm just telling you what Jesus said. It's recorded in the Bible.

POMO JOE: The Bible??!!! Oh, brother! Don't you know that people have made the Bible say anything they want it to say? Yeah, the key thing when I read any book, including the Bible (though I haven't read it), is to see what it says to me. But, then, that's just my take on it. Yours may be different. Besides, why should we listen to your holy book, instead of the Koran or other religious books? You know, Joe C, I think I see your problem. You are treating the Bible as if it's God's Word. You think it sets down God's marching orders for the world—orders that must be followed or we're in trouble. That's not what the Bible is. It's just a human attempt to express mythologically the sense that there's a cosmic force out there to which all of us can attune ourselves. But you'd find the same stuff in any other religion's holy book.

JOE C: Well, Pomo, I can see that we really have many disagreements. I'd sure like to talk to you further about which views are right and which are wrong.

POMO JOE: Well, nobody's views are right or wrong—absolutely. Each person just works out what feels right from his or her perspective, and goes with that until something that works better comes along. I'm happy to talk with you about things that work for you, so long as you get rid of this idea that your views are absolute truth and you can prove them right. Your views are just a product of your social context. You know, life experiences you've had. You're just like everyone else in that respect. So, we can continue to dialogue, if it's a real discussion. But if you're going to preach at me, forget it! OK?

JOE C: Well, at least you're willing to talk. I'll see you later.

Even brief reflection on these two conversations should convince anyone that some significant things have changed. In upcoming chapters, I plan to describe and interact more fully with the perspectives of modern and postmodern epistemology, but even now we can note some basic things about each.

Mo Joe is fairly clearly an atheist. As the discussion proceeds, it is also evident that his idea of God is that of the traditional Judeo-Christian God. However, it is also obvious that he believes *that* God doesn't exist. In addition, for Mo Joe, even if God did exist, it is dubious that he does or even could act in the world. Of course, lack of evidence of God acting is only part of the evidentially impoverished case for God. The existence of evil in our world and Mo Joe's assessment that history in general and his life in particular are meaningless and going nowhere are further signs that there is no God.

None of this seems terribly troublesome to Mo Joe, because even without God he can know the world around him. Mo Joe trusts human reason, sense experience, and logic to tell him what is true and believable. Hence, he is adamant that no one should accept any belief without sufficient evidence. Though he doesn't describe what would count as sufficient evidence, he is certain that there isn't enough evidence to support belief in God's existence. Mo Joe's reliance on reason is evident throughout this conversation. He analyzes everything Joe C says (see, for example, his handling of the meaning of Joe C's first spiritual law), demands that Joe C define his terms, and refuses to believe anything for which he is certain there isn't enough evidence.

What we have in Mo Joe is a young man who is intellectually rigorous about everything, and that rigor leads him to conclude several important things. One is that the world operates in accord with natural laws and is explainable in naturalistic terms. Thus, he sees no need to appeal to the supernatural to explain anything. He also believes there is a world external to the mind, and he believes that humans can know that world. So, there is truth for all of us; whether Mo Joe thinks it is absolute truth is unclear, but he definitely believes there is truth. One can also assume that he thinks of truth in terms of a correspondence of our words to our world, and he also believes that it is possible to gain objective knowledge of the world around us. One also senses that he puts a lot of trust in science's ability to explain our world, and that that is so because science deals objectively with the tangible, physical universe.

In sum, Mo Joe is typical of modernity's trust in reason, logic, and sense experience to help us understand our world. Since this intellectual equipment works so well, in his judgment, he won't believe anything that fails to meet reason's demands for sufficient proof. In his judgment, a naturalistic worldview is more than adequate for understanding the world, so there is no need to invoke God to explain anything. Hence, Mo Joe has little or no use for religion and God, and doesn't find that unsettling at all. Of course, without God there can be no direction or meaning to history other than the meaning each of us gives our personal history, but Mo Joe is more than willing to accept the human condition.

In contrast, Pomo Joe distrusts reason and is quite negative toward logic and Western ways of thinking in general. This is so not just because Western thought forms have been used to discriminate against minorities and those out of power. His basic objection to reason and traditional ways of knowing is that they assume that humans can and do know objective truth about our world. Pomo strongly disagrees, because each of us has his own way of thinking, which has arisen from our past experiences and the linguistic communities in which we were raised. Moreover, given human finitude, it is impossible to know enough to be sure that "we really know." It is better to admit that our finitude and subjectivity make it impossible for anyone to do any more than offer his or her perspective on the world. Of course, no one has an absolute perspective (nor can there be absolute truth), so the proper response to other ways of thinking is to listen to them, dialogue with and learn from them, and be tolerant of them. It also goes without saying that truth, in the sense of our language corresponding to states of affairs in the world, is not possible. Hence, it is wisest to follow paths that have "worked" for us or for others, and to follow our heart rather than our head.

We might think that such skepticism about knowledge would make it harder for Pomo Joe to believe in God than for Mo Joe to do so. However, just the opposite is the case. Since there is no longer a requirement that there must be sufficient evidence to warrant belief in anything, and since there is no absolute knowledge but rather a plethora of views from varying perspectives, who is to say that there is no God? Some have found such an idea useful and so they have believed. Pomo probably adopts Mo Joe's basic naturalistic viewpoint, but clearly that isn't the whole story. Pomo does believe in God; of course, it's little like the God of the Judeo-Christian tradition. Though it is not true of all postmoderns who believe in God, Pomo sounds like he's adopted a conception of God in tune with New Age and radical feminist thinking. Moreover, it is clear that he would be offended by any attempt to evangelize him (or anyone else) to believe in a more traditional God, because he believes that all religions are basically the same. He is especially scornful of religious exclusivists who believe not only that theirs is the only right religion but also that any dissenters will spend eternity in hell. How intolerant and discriminatory such views are!

In sum, Pomo Joe is not a rigorous, disciplined thinker, and that is fine with him because logic and reason (and faith in them) are misguided and only lead us back to the perspective we held in the first place. The most that any of us can know is how we see things from our own perspective, but everyone's perspective is shaped by countless experiences and presuppositions that make objective, absolute knowledge impossible. The best we can do is share our views with others and learn from what has worked for them. Since traditional ways of thinking have been discriminatory and have marginalized those who aren't already in power, we must be suspicious of any accounts of reality that empower a few and discard the many. Rather, we must be tolerant of all people and all viewpoints, for who among us can say with certainty that any single approach to reality is "correct?"

Clearly, these are two significantly different approaches to knowledge, reason, and living in our world. As we shall see, it is hard to imagine someone committed to postmodern values living in a way that is consistent with his or her views. That might lead us to believe that postmodernism (at least as it relates to epistemology, the area of philosophy that deals with the nature of knowledge and belief) is and will be a short-lived phenomenon. Whether or not that is so, many readers can affirm that many postmodern themes and attitudes are well entrenched in contemporary society. But there are still many whose understanding of knowledge and rationality are much closer to the central epistemological tenets of modernity. Hence, we must fashion an apologetic that appeals to as many people as possible, regardless of their allegiance to modernity, postmodernity, or a combination of both.

So, how should we proceed, and what is this book mostly about? First and foremost, this is a book about truth. Truth continues to be under attack in our day, seemingly from every quarter, and I haven't found particularly satisfying the responses I read and hear. So, before we address anything else, we must address the issue of truth. In the first section of the book I begin with a chapter describing modern and postmodern epistemology. Both approaches cast doubt about Christianity as true, and both offer their own reasons for being skeptical about absolute truth of any sort. After describing these different epistemologies, I then turn to address postmodern skepticism, and then modern skepticism. I follow this order, because postmodern skepticism is the most radical, and if its concerns cannot be met, then there is little reason to bother with modern skepticism. But I argue in chapters 3–6 that both forms of skepticism can be answered, and I present what I find to be the most cogent answers.

In chapter 3, on postmodern skepticism, I address the basic question of why anyone has to be logical, beginning with a description of the many different issues that question can raise, and then I answer each objection. Chapter 4 contains a substantial discussion of whether objectivity in intellectual (or nonintellectual) pursuits is possible or whether we are all doomed to hold nothing we haven't already learned and held. I also address perspectivism, part of the concern about objectivity and subjectivity, but not exactly identical to it.

Chapters 5 and 6 address concerns raised by modern skepticism. Of course, moderns may ask some of the same questions as postmoderns, and hence the issues and answers offered in chapters 3 and 4 are relevant to moderns as well. But, specifically, moderns still believe in reason and truth, and so it is worth asking how one might go about proving something to be true. In chapter 6 I also discuss the relation of truth to certainty and evidence, and one of the underlying concerns is how, if one were to marshal evidence for a belief, one would know if the defense was successful.

My conclusion from the first major portion of the book is that there is truth, we can demonstrate that something is true, and we can be certain that we have done so. In other words, both postmodern and modern skeptical concerns can be answered. Hence, there is reason to do apologetics (and any other intellectual enterprise that aims to find truth), and reason for the book to continue. In the second major part of this book I turn to several ways of defending Christian truth. In particular, I focus on three that have been the most prominent and influential over the last century or so. Chapters address Reformed Epistemology, presuppositionalism, and Christian evidentialism. While my own approach is a variety of evidentialism, the nature of my approach is such that it takes things of value from the other approaches.

From my description so far of what I intend to do in this book, readers can easily see that it is not a book devoted to presenting Christian evidences for every tenet of the faith. The first two sections of the book, dealing with various methodological issues, primarily address theoretical issues and suggest how I might defend the faith. But amidst the theory there is nothing quite like concrete illustrations of how my method of defending any belief or system of beliefs works, in order for readers to see the answers to theoretical questions (from parts 1 and 2) in action.

Because I am most concerned to make the points about truth that you will read in the upcoming pages, and because coverage of evidences for every major tenet of the Christian faith would result in a text much too long, I have chosen to offer a defense of only four key issues. Some may find it odd that one of those issues is not the existence of God. However, I don't hold a methodology that requires one to prove God's existence before anything else can be addressed. In addition, in our era it has again become fashionable for many people to believe in some sort of God, so I'm not sure that rehearsing the traditional arguments for God's existence would be of great value. For those who don't believe in God, it would be of some value to offer those arguments, but as I have explained elsewhere,[7] I don't find any of them to be lock-sure proofs. For those who would like to pursue this issue further, I suggest that Alvin Plantinga's and William Lane Craig's coverage of the traditional arguments are most capable resources.[8] Also greatly impressive is Craig's chapter in *Reasonable Faith* on the futility of life without God.[9]

The topics for which I do present evidences are crucial to defending Christianity. The problem of evil is one of the strongest objections to belief in anything like the Christian God, and we must have answers to it. Then, since the greatest source of evidence for Christianity is Scripture, early in one's defense of the faith there needs to be a defense of Scripture's reliability. Specifically, I address the reliability of the Gospels, four independent accounts of the life, ministry, death, and resurrection of Christ. Of course, at some point in defending Christianity, the resurrection of Christ must be established as true. If Christ has not been raised, it seems pointless to argue for much else that Christianity claims about God and his relation to human beings. Finally, we live in a time of great intellectual, moral, and spiritual relativism. As a result, it is taken as supremely narrow-minded to think that only one religion is the way to God. All religions are thought to be adequate vehicles to a relationship with God, and anyone who says otherwise is thought to be fully out of touch with the reality of our times. Hence, my final chapter of "evidences" addresses religious pluralism.

In each portion of this book, an underlying theme is that truth matters. Even more, there is truth and it can be known. While it can be quite comfortable to argue that no one can know the truth, but only what is true for them, this is actually a very dangerous thing to believe. It is dangerous because all of us have to live in the real world. Thinking that everyone's version of reality is fine may sound attractive, but there is a real God with real demands on our life. Ignoring him and his demands may "work" for a while, but sooner or later we must leave our fantasy world, abandon all of our clever intellectual doctrines that allow us to do just exactly whatever makes us feel good while believing there is no accountability for anything we do, and face reality.

And then all of us, sooner than we might suspect, have to face eternity! In our day, it is very fashionable for people to believe that a loving God would never judge anyone for eternity with anything like hell. Others find it comforting to believe that physical death ends everything—there is no afterlife, so regardless of what we have done in this life, we needn't worry about some eternal punishment.

These two stories are only some of the many ways our contemporaries have deluded themselves into thinking that they can think and do whatever they want and never be held accountable. But truth does matter! And in a day when so many seem so sure that there is no absolute truth, it is right to ask how, then, they can be so sure that their "story" about eternity is correct! If you make a mistake on some of your beliefs, the consequences will be minimal. But if your beliefs about eternity are wrong, that is a mistake that will last forever and can never be undone! Truth matters, so you'd better find a truth you can believe in. The aim of this book is to help you see how to find and know truth, in hopes that you will also see that there is no hope for time or eternity outside of Jesus Christ. He is the most important truth, and he is definitely truth you can trust!

Chapter 2

Modernity and Postmodernity

In chapter 1, I briefly introduced both modernity and postmodernity. In this chapter my concern is to describe in more detail the elements of each which are especially significant for philosophy of religion and apologetics. While it is tempting to describe modern and postmodern themes in "neat, unrelated, and distinct packages," we must remember that history seldom fits our characterizations in which each thing clearly belongs to one era but not another. Describing things so that everything fits in tidy self-contained packages may be helpful conceptually to understand the major thrusts of a given movement, but intellectual history is often much messier. That is, though for the sake of conceptual clarity we may want to distinguish certain trends as modern and others as postmodern, the truth is that over the last five to six hundred years in Western thought, various "modern" and "postmodern" emphases have been present to one degree or another. For example, there have always been epistemological skeptics, and on the contemporary scene there are still many who do not have the distrust in reason that is so frequently associated with postmodernity.

While keeping what has just been said in mind, I still believe it is helpful to describe major themes which, even if present at various times during the last six hundred years, are typically associated with the conceptual model of either modernity or postmodernity. Though modernity and postmodernity have been used as labels for a series of diverse items which conjointly offer a basic intellectual and cultural outlook on reality, my focus is the epistemologies of each.[1]

Though there is room for debate,[2] broadly speaking, the modern era in a significant sense began with René Descartes (1596–1650) in philosophy and with Galileo and Isaac Newton in science. The period continued into the nineteenth-century rationalism and scientism that still influence our own times.[3] But many different intellectual trends have been present during the modern era. For example, modernity is sometimes equated with the Enlightenment, but the two are not identical. Though modernity is often dated as starting in the 1600s, the historical Enlightenment was at its apex during the eighteenth and early nineteenth centuries. During Descartes's lifetime, the great empiricist philosophers Thomas Hobbes (1588–1679) and John Locke (1632–1704) were also alive. They, like other empiricists, rejected Cartesian rationalism. In addition, rationalism was not embraced by many key Enlightenment thinkers. It is also worth noting that from a mere historical standpoint the life of David Hume (1711–1776) coincided with the French Enlightenment. Hume, though known for both his empiricism and his skepticism, is considered by some to be the prototypical Enlightenment figure.[4]

Even so, it is possible to describe basic epistemological themes associated with modernity, but I begin with a general description of modernity as a whole. One writer characterizes modernity as a "belief in reason and progress."[5] Thomas Jovanovski adds that modernity is committed to foundationalism, essentialism, and realism, and also tends to see Western culture as the norm or ideal for what other cultures should strive to be.[6] Clinton Collins cites an article by Vaclav Havel (then president of Czechoslovakia) that appeared in March 1992 in *The New York Times*. Collins notes that Havel "called for a change of attitudes, away from the arrogance of typically modern beliefs in a humanism that dominates the natural universe, a scientific method that generates objective knowledge and assures unlimited progress, and advancing technology that can overcome the problems that are the byproduct of earlier technologies."[7] And Jared Hiebert characterizes the key themes of modernity as objectivity, metanarratives, the independent human, and absolute truth.[8]

THEMES IN MODERN EPISTEMOLOGY

Modern epistemology addresses a variety of issues, and not all modern thinkers have agreed on those key issues. Nonetheless, I propose that the place to begin is with René Descartes and his search for a secure foundation for knowledge.

Human Consciousness and Certain Knowledge

Many affirm that the modern period (at least philosophically) began with Descartes. The premodern era before Descartes was one of tradition and authority. Various ideas were deemed correct, and working within the tradition of those ideas, one held them. Moreover, governmentally and ecclesiastically, it was also an age of authority. Descartes was born on the eve of the Reformation. The Roman Catholic Church fundamentally told people what was correct to believe, and if one was a Christian, one followed that without question. Governments were absolutist, and common people had little choice but to do what leaders demanded.

Philosophers working within the Western tradition were often also theologians. The point of philosophy was not primarily to prove God's existence (though we find a lot of that in thinkers like Anselm and Aquinas), but to understand one's faith (*fides quaerens intellectum*, "faith seeking understanding," Anselm's motto). Within Western cultures committed to the basics of the Judeo-Christian worldview, God was, so to speak, the starting point of philosophy. If proofs were to be offered for his existence, that was one of the first things done in philosophical and theological writings (see, for example, Aquinas's *Summa Theologiae*). Of course there were skeptics, but it was unwise to voice such sentiments if one wished to remain alive.

During the modern era and into the postmodern era, skepticism has increased. That is, even if the percentage of a given population that is skeptical about God has remained relatively constant (and that is debatable), at very least, skeptics have become increasingly vocal about disbelief in God and in absolute knowledge and truth.

Surely Descartes, who seems to have been a devout Roman Catholic, did not espouse religious skepticism, and it would be unfair to blame him as "the cause" of growing skepticism about God and knowledge that we find in both the modern and postmodern eras. Even so, epistemology took a significant turn with Descartes. Like others of his day, he had believed many things without questioning their truthfulness. But what if these beliefs were false, or at least questionable? Descartes reasoned that one's beliefs must be based on far firmer ground than on beliefs that had always been assumed as true but never demonstrated to be so. Hence, he concluded that he must call into question everything he believed so as to see whether it could be supported by evidence and argument. But support with some evidence that made a belief's truthfulness less than certain wasn't sufficient. Descartes reasoned that he had a right to hold only those beliefs which could not reasonably be doubted because they were supported by conclusive arguments and evidence. So, Descartes set out to ascertain whether there was anything he claimed to know that could not reasonably be doubted. If there was something of this sort, it would serve as the basis or foundation upon which to build everything else he knew.

This must not be misunderstood. Descartes's search for certainty did not mean he had rejected belief in God or in divine revelation. Rather, he wanted to see what reason, unaided by revelation, could derive as a foundation to secure whatever he believed. Descartes's search for certainty eventually led him to conclude that only one thing could not reasonably be doubted. It made no sense to doubt his own existence as a thinking thing, for in the moment that he doubted it, he proved its truth. Nonexistent things do nothing at all, including doubting their own existence. Of course, this indubitable "I" did not include his body, for one could always be deceived about whether one was actually embodied. But the immaterial part of human nature, with its ability to think, could not be doubted.

As a result, Descartes deemed the *cogito, ergo sum* ("I think, therefore I am") the one indubitable truth from which to build knowledge in any and every field. Of course, the *cogito* is true for each person only in reference to herself or himself. So, Descartes was still troubled about how to justify all other beliefs he held. He eventually came to a rationalistic conclusion that if he had a clear and distinct idea of something, this idea must be true of the world. But how could one be sure that when one thought one was having a clear and distinct idea of something, that was really so? This question led Descartes to formulate his version of the ontological argument for God's existence. If God exists, Descartes reasoned, he would ensure that whenever I think I am having a clear and distinct idea of something, I really am. Hence, not only the foundation but also the superstructure of knowledge would be secure.

The details of Descartes's ontological argument needn't detain us, but two points should be clear. First, Descartes's "intellectual project" can hardly be seen as a rejection of belief in God or in revelation. Indeed, without the existence of God as a certainty, Descartes believed that his other beliefs could not be sustained.

But a second point is also crucial. With Descartes, epistemology moved front and center in philosophy. No longer could beliefs just be accepted on religious authority, tradition, or any other authority. There had to be indubitable evidence for what one believed. And, of course, human consciousness plays a crucial role in structuring and certifying whatever is true.

For Descartes, one's knowledge of the world grew through clear and distinct ideas of things. For empiricists like Locke and Hume, appeal to sense data from ordinary experience was the key. But in both cases, attaining knowledge involves a subject-object relation; i.e., human consciousness is the subject, the knower, which attempts to ascertain what is true of the world (the object). The two are distinct, and hence the subject can with disinterested objectivity "read off" things that are true of the world (the object). Human consciousness takes the role of sitting in judgment of what is true in regard to reality.

This emphasis on human consciousness only became heightened with Immanuel Kant (1724–1804). Prior to Kant, the mind was deemed as fundamentally passive in the knowing process. Sense data from the external world came to it through the sensory organs. Those organs might distort the data, and that was thought to explain why, for example, two people looking at the same thing might report seeing things differently, but this account still portrayed the mind as basically passive. The mind was viewed, to use contemporary philosopher Richard Rorty's metaphor, as the mirror of nature. Kant disagreed about the mind being totally passive, and argued that not only does the world act upon the mind (through the senses), but the mind, in virtue of various concepts inherent in it (the Kantian categories), is also active. The mind structures the sense data and then makes a judgment about what is perceived. In light of this two-way process, Kant proposed his famous distinction between things-in-themselves and things-as-they-appear-to-us. He argued that while things really exist outside of our mind, no one can experience them as they are in themselves. Things which are not objects of our knowledge (including things-in-themselves) Kant labeled noumena. Things as they appear to us he called phenomena.[9]

Despite Kant's claim that the mind is active in the knowing process, one doesn't sense in Kant's writings that this meant that he thought we couldn't know about things in the world outside the mind. Though no one could know noumena, neither Kant nor other thinkers of his time thought that humans have little hope of knowing phenomena and of agreeing with others about what they were experiencing. Hence, even with the Kantian position that mind and object are active in relation to each other, the basic view seemed to be that the data of the world come into the mind basically unmediated, and hence the mind can still be seen to function basically as the mirror of nature.

Hence, with Kant, the trend begun by Descartes of structuring the world from one's own consciousness continued. Human consciousness as active, not passive, becomes even more important. After Kant, philosophers have increasingly emphasized the mind's action in understanding reality. In addition, Kant, like other modern philosophers, was concerned to ground knowledge ultimately in certain foundational beliefs, but unlike Descartes, the key for him was empirical data.[10] Throughout the rest of the modern era, the emphasis on empirical data as the key to knowledge remains. This is true for contemporary theology and also in philosophical critiques of theology.

In sum, the notion that our understanding of the world stems from human consciousness's structuring of the world is crucial to the modern era. Of course, with the role given human consciousness, if either human reason or sensory organs malfunction, human beings are in serious trouble in respect to knowing and living in their world. During the modern era, many thinkers were quite optimistic about the mind's ability to "get things right" in its search for knowledge. As we shall see later, many postmoderns significantly disagree.

Foundationalism, Metanarratives, and Truth

Because human minds can misinterpret and misrepresent data, we might think that the emphasis on the subject's role in the acquisition of knowledge would only make it more difficult to secure a certain foundation for knowledge, but the modern mentality said otherwise. Reason was deemed capable of grasping and interacting correctly with the world, and it was held that this was true for all people. Just as Descartes wanted to find an indubitable foundation on which to base his knowledge, so others after him thought this was both necessary and possible. A universal perspective on reality was possible through reason, and belief in everyone's ability to find the truth made it possible in every discipline of study to know truth and error and to convince others, if one thought their views were wrong.

The picture of knowledge and rationality just described normally incorporated a theory of knowledge known as foundationalism. However, there are two distinct senses in which the term foundationalism is used by both moderns and postmoderns. The first refers to epistemological foundationalism, and there are various versions of it. In general, according to this theory of knowledge, beliefs are justified in terms of other beliefs, which ultimately are supported by beliefs that need no justification, because they are self-evidently true (such foundational beliefs are called basic beliefs; beliefs that need support from other beliefs are called non-basic beliefs). Because of modernity's belief in reason's ability to support and confirm beliefs as true or false, thinkers claimed that it is rational to hold a belief only if one does so on the basis of sufficient evidence, arguments, or reasons for the belief.[11] Descartes's concern to believe only what cannot reasonably be doubted is clearly incorporated in this notion.

Of course, the next question is what counts as sufficient evidence, argument, or reasons for belief? How does one know that one has a right to hold a given belief? Foundationalism provides the answer. As Laurence Bonjour explains, there are at least three basic kinds of foundationalism: strong foundationalism, moderate foundationalism, and weak foundationalism. Only the first claims that basic beliefs are indubitable and absolutely certain. To one degree or another, the other forms of foundationalism do not hold that basic beliefs are indubitable and absolutely certain.[12] Strong or classical foundationalism (which has been the predominant theory of knowledge within the modern era) claims that a belief has sufficient support if it is supported by evidences and arguments that are ultimately supported by (inferred from) beliefs that are properly basic. A properly basic belief is a belief that is either self-evident (like "all bachelors are unmarried men"), evident to the senses (e.g., one has an experience of a red object), or incorrigible, i.e., something that it would make no sense to doubt (like the *cogito*).[13]

Whereas for Descartes, the ultimate foundation was something rational, the empiricists emphasized sense impressions as the source of the most basic beliefs that form the foundations of our knowledge. Kant combined both rational (the mind's categories that allow it to structure reality) and empirical (data from observation) as foundational. For Kant the only truths about the world that are deemed objects of knowledge are truths that can be known through the senses. Despite the mind's activity in interacting with the world, there was great optimism about an individual's ability to know rightly what is true or false. As David Griffin explains, the basic epistemological doctrine of the modern world is sensate empiricism, according to which knowledge of the world beyond ourselves comes exclusively through sense perception.[14] Moderns have generally held that the data that come into the mind do so directly, either unmediated or mediated by something that does not so distort the data as to result in the person misjudging what is being perceived.

But what if a belief is not about a matter of pure reason (e.g., "round squares do not exist") nor is open to sense perception? Kant said that things-in-themselves are not objects of sense perception, but neither are values and moral judgments, the world as a whole, nor God. All of these are noumena, not phenomena, and as such, they are not objects of knowledge. As a result, Kant claimed to put an end to metaphysics, for the subjects normally discussed in that discipline are beyond empirical investigation.[15] However, this didn't mean for Kant that there is no God. Kant believed it necessary to posit the existence of God, but he did so as a grounding for morality. So God exists, according to Kant, but his existence is not a matter of knowledge; it is a postulate of practical reason.

If the only beliefs that qualify as knowledge are ones supported ultimately by foundational beliefs that are self-evident, evident to the senses, or incorrigible, it seemed to many moderns that the beliefs most capable of being justified are the beliefs of science. In fact, among the logical atomists and logical positivists of the late nineteenth and early twentieth century (and many others who followed their general empiricist emphasis), there was a desire to purify language, insofar as possible, of talk that is not empirically verifiable. If this were done, then our language would be basically the language of science, i.e., whatever is open to verification by empirical observation. The logical positivists, however, were more negative than Kant toward things he called noumena. For the positivists, if an assertion isn't in principle verifiable by empirical means (for it to be in principle verifiable, one would have to be able to state verification procedures), the claim is deemed nonsense, and that of which it speaks is considered nonexistent. This meant that talk of morals and of God is nonsense, and they do not exist.[16]

Ludwig Wittgenstein (1889–1951) was a contemporary of the logical positivists. His early philosophy as set forth in his *Tractatus-Logico-Philosophicus* presented a portrait of the world and language that was not unlike that of the logical positivists. Though the positivists appreciated Wittgenstein's work, he did not deem himself one of them. Nonetheless, he did hold that unless language pictures objects and states of affairs in the world, it is meaningless. If language is about something unobservable in the world, it should not be spoken. Unlike the positivists, however, Wittgenstein didn't conclude that things that were unsayable (because incapable of empirical verification) did not exist. Rather, such things are not objects of knowledge, and so should not be spoken of at all.[17]

There is a second sense of foundationalism that also applies to modern thinking. In various discussions, foundationalism refers to some set of beliefs that is deemed the ultimate reference point for everything else one believes. As such, they have a privileged status in a person's conceptual grid (i.e., his or her overall worldview). While other individual ideas and even other worldviews are open to and frequently subject to critique and revision, a particular set of ideas that is foundational for a given individual (or even a whole society) is not open to critique and revision, nor does the one who holds them sense any need to offer evidential support that these views are correct. For example, the Judeo-Christian perspective and the Bible itself have been the very foundation of Western societies and cultures. Though there have always been skeptics about the biblical worldview, for much of the last two thousand years the biblical perspective has been, so to speak, the presupposition of Western cultures. It goes without saying as well that a worldview that is foundational in this second sense tells the story of how to understand reality and how to structure societies. As such, it legitimizes certain groups of people as those who ought to have power and control in society, and excludes others. This sort of foundationalism is, for postmoderns, anathema!

This second kind of foundationalism goes together with what is called a metanarrative. A narrative (as used in this discussion) is a story that tells a given group of people or a culture how things are and how they should be done. A metanarrative is a larger story (i.e., it encompasses more aspects of reality) that undergirds and supports individual narratives. And then there are grand metanarratives, which present a whole worldview. That grand metanarrative is deemed the ultimate reference point against which any particular idea or set of ideas, particular practice or set of practices, is to be judged. I can illustrate these different types of narratives and metanarratives easily enough. For example, evangelical Christians typically believe in heaven and hell. Depending on one's response and relation to Christ, one will wind up either in heaven or in hell when he dies. Evangelicals, therefore, reject the ideas that at death humans will be totally annihilated, that at death only those who know Christ as personal Savior will be given immortality while the rest are annihilated, or that at death all will be given heaven because a loving God could never punish any of his creatures forever.

These beliefs about heaven and hell, however, presuppose a larger story. That story involves beliefs that humans are sinners, Christ is the God-man, Christ died on Calvary to pay for our sins, and those who by faith turn from their sin and accept Christ as personal Savior will have a personal relationship with him. These beliefs form the metanarrative out of which the particular Christian narrative about heaven and hell comes. But we can also identify a grand metanarrative out of which beliefs about Christ, sin, and salvation grow. It is the story of our universe as created and sustained by the God of the Scriptures. As sovereign, he also has the right to institute a system of moral governance in this universe and to demand that his creatures be subject to his moral standards. This grand metanarrative of ours as a theistic universe with God as moral governor undergirds both Judaism and Christianity. From this most fundamental narrative, Christians move to the doctrine of the Trinity and the doctrine of the incarnation of Christ as the God-man. Christians further add biblical teaching about the relation of human beings to God as moral judge. Typically, they appeal to the fall of the human race into sin and our continued sinfulness as the basis of our need for a redeemer. At that point in Christian thinking, the Christian story about God, Christ, and humanity in its sinfulness can be linked together to present the Christian doctrine of salvation. Part of the plan of salvation involves each person's eternal destiny, and that, of course, is the signal for Christians to offer their teaching on heaven and hell.

The preceding description is just an example of various narratives and metanarratives and their relation to one another; there are many other metanarratives. My reason for introducing this should now be clear. A set of ideas or a worldview that is foundational (in the second sense of foundationalism) to one's thinking and action is clearly a metanarrative—perhaps even a grand metanarrative. Moderns in general have little aversion to any type of foundationalism, including those types which employ metanarratives. As we shall see, however, postmoderns reject all forms of foundationalism and are incredulous about all metanarratives.[18]

Realism, Objectivity, and Truth

How can moderns be so sanguine about reason's ability to know the world aright? And how can they be sure that sense perception actually allows us to have contact with the world outside the mind? These are questions not only about the intellectual and sensory equipment with which humans are born, but also about whether there is a real world outside our minds and whether humans, with our "equipment," can get at the actual world, assuming that there is one external to the mind.

In reply, I note initially that moderns are invariably realists. A realist is "someone who thinks that there is an *objective, mind-independent reality* to be known, and that the beliefs that we come to hold about the world represent (or fail to represent) the world 'as it is'."[19] Thus, with respect to persons and objects, insofar as such persons and objects exist, they do so independently of our thought, language, and experience.[20] An anti-realist holds just the opposite view.

In spite of believing in realism, and even if realism is correct, what hope is there that we can know how things actually are in the world? Won't our conceptual grid with its presuppositions and preferences get in the way of our seeing things correctly? Moderns reply that it is possible to connect to the world around us and to know it accurately because the mind can function objectively.[21] We must be careful, however, to understand what this does and does not mean. It does not mean that we can know the world as a thing-in-itself. To know some object without at least some involvement of the knower is impossible. Nor does it mean that we must revert to a pre-Kantian epistemology that sees the mind as a passive mirror. We can grant with Kant that both subject and object are active in the knowing process. Nor does objectivity mean that humans' presuppositions, preferences, and experiences cannot get in the way of their seeing the world aright.

Sometimes we do allow those preferences to guide our observations and rational reflections so that we misidentify what we are seeing or hearing and misunderstand the concepts we are handling. What moderns mean by saying that objective knowledge is possible is that it is possible to identify and set aside our biases and preferences so that when we observe the world or reflect on concepts and arguments, we can know them aright. The fact that our mind with its conceptual grid is involved does not make it inevitable that we treat data unfairly or that we make intellectual judgments about matters of fact arbitrarily or based solely on emotion rather than reason.

Moderns believe that there are brute facts which are not theory-laden by our preferences and theories. There is the "given" world about us, that is, the world as it is apart from anything we think or sense about it. So the nature of the world won't "get in the way" of our attaining accurate knowledge of it. Moreover, despite our past experiences and the cultures and contexts in which we were raised, it is still possible to set presuppositions aside, observe the world around us, and without bias intruding, make accurate judgments about what we are seeing. So, human minds need not "get in the way" of attaining accurate knowledge. Moreover, these mental capacities belong to all humans, not to just a few, and the world is observable by all. Hence, if someone misidentifies an object or event in the world or is mistaken in what he or she believes, enough evidence for or against a viewpoint is available to all, so that we can correct our mistakes with the help of others.

For moderns, then, objectivity is possible, and is most clearly seen in science. The fact that science works with data of the tangible world and uses an observational method that everyone can use to confirm or disconfirm scientific conclusions seems to guarantee objectivity. Of course, errors are still possible, and given the demand to justify beliefs ultimately by beliefs that are self-evident, evident to the senses, or incorrigible, it was granted that some might hold beliefs that are not justifiable by such criteria. But the predominant mood through much of the modern period has been that it is possible to be objective in our handling of data and to know what is true of our world.

With these beliefs about knowledge, it follows that moderns believe there is truth, and for them the predominant theory of truth is the correspondence theory. According to this theory, propositional truth is a relation between language and our world. What we say about the world is said to correspond to or match what is true of the world. Moreover, moderns believe it is possible to know what is true by means of our rational and sensory faculties, and this is so for all people.

Any human being can use his or her intellectual faculties to reach a correct conclusion about our world. And what is correct in one person's judgment will be correct according to others. We don't need to think of truth as relative to each person's perspective, for we all can know the same truth. Hence, it makes sense to talk about absolute truth, i.e., propositions that are true for all people at all times. This is not to say that we are absolutely certain about everything we know, but only that absolute truth is possible and that many of us do know things that are absolutely true. Of course, to hold that there is absolute truth and that we can know it must be understood against the backdrop of a foundationalist theory of knowledge. That is, if there are many propositions that are true in a correspondence sense of truth, that also means that those claims we deem true must and do meet foundationalist criteria for proper basicality. Hence, many things we believe about our world are either basic beliefs or are non-basic beliefs which are ultimately supported by basic beliefs.

Theory of Meaning and Essentialism

Nancey Murphy and James McClendon argue that a further characteristic of modern epistemology is its emphasis on a representational or referential theory of language. According to such theories, words and sentences (or for some theories, the proposition a sentence is about[22]) refer to objects, actions, and events. Their meaning is what they refer to. For example, the meaning of the word 'Parthenon' (i.e., what the word refers to) is the building, known as the Parthenon, which is situated atop the Acropolis in Athens, Greece. Typically, the referential theory in question considers that meaning invariant. Hence, it is possible to talk about the "essence" of the meaning of a given word, and one can draw clear boundaries between the meanings of different words. As Murphy and McClendon show, this sort of theory also fits very nicely with a theory of knowledge that says beliefs are to be justified in terms of more basic beliefs. Beliefs can be shown true by seeing that the things they refer to are true of the world.

But what happens with this sort of theory if a sentence doesn't name or picture something empirically observable? Does the sentence have any meaning? While theories like the logical positivists' verification theory of meaning concluded that such sentences are meaningless, not every theory agreed. Some philosophers of language argued that those sentences do have meaning, but not a meaning that refers to some object or state of affairs in the world. Rather, these sentences express either the speaker's emotional reaction or intentions to act in a certain way.[23] For example, "God is love" does not refer to anything that can be verified by empirical observation, but it is still meaningful. On an emotivist account of language it might mean nothing more than "I like God" or "I think God is nice." Another "expressivist" theory of language is what R. B. Braithwaite calls a conative theory. In this case, the sentence expresses the utterer's intention to act a certain way. Thus, "God is love" might mean that the speaker intends to act in a loving, agapeistic way.[24]

The main point for our purposes, however, is that for many moderns, their theory of meaning was referential in nature. Such a theory fits with modern views about our ability to connect to the world, treat data objectively, and determine what is invariably true for all people at all times.

THEMES IN POSTMODERN EPISTEMOLOGY

While many moderns trust reason and believe in absolute truth that is discoverable by objective reflection on data from sense perception as well as from *a priori* reasoning, some postmoderns also espouse some of these views. However, postmodern epistemology in its most well-known forms offers a different perspective on knowledge. Actually, the term 'postmodernity' has been attached to many different trends in various fields like art and architecture,[25] literary criticism and interpretation, epistemology, politics, etc. It goes without saying that in each of these fields there are varieties of postmodern viewpoints. When it comes to postmodern epistemology in its more radical forms, perhaps a good place to begin is Jean-François Lyotard's claim about postmodernity in general that "simplifying to the extreme, I define postmodern as incredulity toward metanarratives."[26] David Griffin's characterization of some major philosophical themes of the most negative forms of postmodernism is also helpful. He writes,

> Philosophical postmodernism is inspired variously by pragmatism, physicalism, Ludwig Wittgenstein, Martin Heidegger, and Jacques Derrida

and other recent French thinkers. By the use of terms that arise out of particular segments of this movement, it can be called *deconstructive* or *eliminative postmodernism*. It overcomes the modern worldview through an anti-worldview: it deconstructs or eliminates the ingredients necessary for a worldview, such as God, self, purpose, meaning, a real world, and truth as correspondence. While motivated in some cases by the ethical concern to forestall totalitarian systems, this type of postmodern thought issues in relativism, even nihilism. It could also be called *ultramodernism*, in that its eliminations result from carrying modern premises to their logical conclusions.[27]

This description is most apt for deconstructive postmodernism, but it hints at several themes that are broadly true of the postmodern mood. These statements by Lyotard and Griffin are very helpful, but we must say more.[28] Of course between the seventeenth and nineteenth centuries there were many epistemological skeptics, and while skeptics and relativists have become more vocal in the late twentieth century and the new millennium, it would be wrong to think such epistemological trends stem only from the middle of the twentieth century onward. As noted in introducing modernity, intellectual trends and labels don't always fit into neatly defined historical eras. Even so, we can distinguish various trends in postmodern epistemology. While some in our day are still ensconced in a modern epistemological mind-set, and while some more moderate postmoderns seem very much like moderns in their epistemology, we can still distinguish certain themes in postmodern epistemology in some of its more radical forms.

POSTMODERN EPISTEMOLOGY

Skepticism about Reason

As we saw when discussing modern epistemology, Descartes searched for an indubitable truth upon which to build knowledge. He believed that the *cogito* is that one certain truth, and proceeded from that foundational truth to structure a worldview of propositions he believed were certainly true. Postmoderns roundly reject Descartes's claims to certain knowledge, but they go even further. Postmoderns are in general very skeptical about reason. On the one hand, they doubt that humans are in a position to know what is true of reality outside the mind. Kant distinguished between things-in-themselves and things-for-us, that is, things as they appear to us, but at least he and many after him believed that we can know things as they appear to us, and that the way they appear to us gives an accurate reflection of the world external to the mind. Postmoderns agree that we can't know things-in-themselves, but further believe that we should be skeptical about whether our knowledge claims accurately reflect the world around us. As we shall see, there is reason to doubt that sense perception is accurate. On the other hand, even if one thinks humans can get in touch with the world outside their minds, that in no way guarantees the correct handling of the information that floods into their minds through the senses. We might misidentify what we think we are seeing, or we might rationally infer from information that comes to us things about reality that just aren't warranted or true.[29]

Anti-Realism

So, postmoderns are skeptical about whether our mental and sensory equipment function properly. But this is not the only reason postmoderns are suspicious of claims to know how things "really are" in the world. Even if humans were much less inclined to mishandle data that the mind collects, that still wouldn't allow us to know the world as it is, for it is dubious that any of us has contact with the world as it is independent of our minds. That is, postmoderns are typically anti-realists. To repeat Michael Murray's description, a realist is "someone who thinks that there is an *objective, mind-independent reality* to be known, and that the beliefs that we come to hold about the world represent (or fail to represent) the world 'as it is'."[30] An anti-realist, then, is someone who holds just the opposite. That is, as Keith Yandell says about anti-realism with respect to persons and objects, such anti-realism is "the view that insofar as there are persons and physical objects, there [sic; should be "they"] are dependent on our experience, thought and language."[31] Though one might be a realist or anti-realist in regard to some things but not all, "contemporary anti-realists typically are anti-realists about everything."[32] This is certainly the case for many postmoderns.[33]

Language as Constitutive of Reality

But why should there be so much skepticism about human ability to know the world around us? And why, in particular, would postmoderns think that we have so little, if any, contact with the world outside of our minds? And what do such views mean about our understanding of what truth is, whether we can know it, and whether there is any such thing as absolute truth? The answers to all of these and like questions take us in a dramatically different direction from that taken by modern epistemology.

To begin to answer these questions, we must remind ourselves of what has happened in Western philosophy over the last three hundred or so years. For a long time Western philosophers viewed the mind as relatively passive in the acquisition of knowledge of persons, objects, and states of affairs in the world outside the mind. Sensory data were thought to flood into the mind through the senses and were represented on the mind much as a mirror reflects the images before it. Gradually, philosophers grew to recognize that sense perception wasn't infallible. For example, if two people looked at a stick that was standing in a lake or river, both might see it as a bent stick, both might perceive it as straight, or each might see it differently than the other did. Even if both agreed, once the stick was removed from the water, they might discover that neither of them was correct in identifying what they saw. Despite these facts about sense perception, philosophers still held a rather positive view of the mind's ability to grasp reality aright as it was "mirrored" on the mind.

With the philosophy of Immanuel Kant, a major shift occurred in our understanding of the mind's interaction with the world. Kant argued that the acquisition of knowledge was not merely a matter of the object being mirrored on the passive mind. Rather, both subject and object are active in the knowing process. As data enter the mind through the senses, the mind, in virtue of various transcendental categories inherent in it, makes judgments about what the person sees. It decides what sort of thing presents itself to the knower, what its size and shape are, how many objects are before it, and whether and how the various objects causally interact with one another and even with the knower. Kant argued that though everyone is born with these transcendental (i.e., not in the empirical world itself but inherent to each person's mind) categories, one must still use one's intellectual equipment to learn various concepts, and once a concept is learned, it can be used to identify a specific object the person perceives.

The point is easy enough to illustrate. No one is born with the concepts of a dog, a cat, a cow, a horse, a chair, etc., imprinted on their minds. Instead, using the intellectual and perceptual equipment we all have, we are ready to interact with the world. As we interact, we see many things we don't understand. Typically, a family member will point to a family pet and say, "That's a dog." When the child plays with the neighborhood children, some of those children will have a cat. The first child, using the concept of a dog that he has learned, may point to the neighbor's cat and call it a dog. Undoubtedly, those who hear this will correct the child and point out some key differences between dogs and cats.

In this way, any given individual acquires concepts of any number of objects, events, actions, etc. Those concepts become parts of the person's noetic structure. Given this conceptual grid, the person, in virtue both of the Kantian categories and of the acquired concepts of various things, is now ready to confront the world and make judgments about what she experiences. Because she has the concepts of dogs, cats, and many other things, when she encounters a cat she has never seen before, she identifies it as a cat, not a dog, a rabbit, a rodent, or a goldfish (she knows those concepts, too).[34]

Kant also distinguished between things-in-themselves and things as they appear to us. We can never know things as they are in themselves, but only as they appear to us. Now, given Kantian doctrines about how subject and object relate and function in the knowing process, plus his avowal that we can know things only as they appear to us, one might be inclined to think that Kant and his followers were quite skeptical about the mind's ability to know, learn, and persuade others that reality matches what they perceive it to be. However, this was not the case initially.

Many Western philosophers after Kant, though agreeing that both mind and object are active in the knowing relation, were still rather optimistic about the mind's ability to know the world aright. The picture of the mind as the mirror of nature was so ingrained in philosophical thinking that it was very hard to jettison. But it was only a matter of time until philosophers really began to take seriously the implications of Kantian epistemology.

Richard Rorty's *Philosophy and the Mirror of Nature* was a very influential book in moving philosophers to embrace the implications of the mind's not passively being the mirror of nature. Rorty argued that for several hundred years after Descartes, philosophy has been held captive by this picture of knowledge that holds that various ideas are represented on that mirror (the mind), and then the individual compares those ideas with the world outside the mind. By these empirical and rational processes, one can ultimately support one's beliefs and so provide a foundation for knowledge.

But Rorty argues that this is just not how the mind works. He explains the thesis of his work as follows:

> It is pictures rather than propositions, metaphors rather than statements, which determine most of our philosophical convictions. The picture which holds traditional philosophy captive is that of the mind as a great mirror, containing various representations—some accurate, some not— and capable of being studied by pure, nonempirical methods. Without the notion of the mind as mirror, the notion of knowledge as accuracy of representation would not have suggested itself. Without this latter notion, the strategy common to Descartes and Kant—getting more accurate representations by inspecting, repairing, and polishing the mirror, so to speak—would not have made sense.[35]

It is this picture, according to Rorty, that must be rejected. But what does one put in its place? If the world isn't just "given" to each of us in its pristine objectivity and then mirrored upon our minds, how do we contact reality outside our minds, and construct an accurate view of the world around us? Postmodern skepticism answers that we don't touch the world around us unmediated by anything between our minds and the world. Rather, it is through our language that we construct our understanding of the world. And we do not first contact the world and then apply our language to it. Rather, we bring our language with us whenever we confront the world. As noted above, without concepts of some things already formed, we couldn't identify particular instances of the thing designated by the concept when we encounter one of them. But if that is so, then we bring our language with us on every occasion of interacting with the world. Of course, it is crucial to remember that our concepts and the very language we use to convey them are embedded in our social context. That is, we are all members of some linguistic community, and each community has not only its own language but also its own culture, etc. Moreover, in addition to having lived in a given linguistic community, each of us has had our own specific experiences as we grew up and then went about our business as adults. Our linguistic community, our conceptual grid, and our past experiences influence how we understand our world and interact with things around us. And, according to postmoderns, it is impossible for us to set aside all of our presuppositions, preferences, etc., and just see the world as it is. In essence, it is our language that constitutes our view of the world.

Of course, there are many different languages in our world today, and each construction of reality will incorporate the nuances of the language and culture that are specific to each language, but not to all.[36]

In our day, it is truly disconcerting to see how widespread is the notion that we construct through our language the world as we know it. Perhaps you have seen the motion picture *The Matrix*. This is an overtly postmodern movie, one that is immensely popular among many of our contemporaries. Those who have seen it will undoubtedly remember what the matrix is. Early in the film we see video footage of various contemporary American cities. We are familiar with these photos, so we believe that the video just pictures things as they are. However, we are then told that the matrix is in fact humans' construction of the world and reality around us as we know it. The message is clear: what we are seeing in the film is not objective reality but rather a certain portrait of contemporary life constructed by human beings. We aren't told that the matrix is not the same as how things really are, but throughout the film that is the repeated impression we are given, especially by the video sequences that show the characters in burned out buildings and land that is laid waste, sequences that make it clear that such portraits aren't portraits of the matrix. If that is so, and if the matrix is the world as we have mentally constructed it, the implication seems clear enough that the scenes of demolished and ruined cities and landscapes are what is actually real.

One might wonder, however, why anyone would understand language in this way. In addition to what has already been said about the role of the mind and its conceptual grid (which of course involves language), the answer also involves a particular theory of *how* words and sentences mean, i.e., a theory of meaning. As we saw when discussing modernity, many moderns basically hold the view Rorty calls the mind as the mirror of nature, and they believe that it is possible to contact and know what is happening in the world outside the mind. We noted as well that typical of modernity is some theory of meaning that is heavily, if not exclusively, referential in nature. And that makes sense, because if we are able to contact objective reality and know what is true of it, we should be able to represent in our language what is mirrored on our mind about the world. Hence, individual words attach to various objects, events, and actions in our world, and those things in the world are the meaning of our words. Sentences typically describe states of affairs in our world, and those states of affairs, as referents to our various sentences about the world, are the meaning of those sentences. With such a theory of meaning, the meaning of individual words and sentences is deemed to be invariant. Hence, it is possible to state "the essence," so to speak, of a word's meaning.

Postmoderns have a decidedly different account of meaning. Many of them take their cue from the later philosophy of Ludwig Wittgenstein. However, it is safe to say that what they have done with Wittgenstein's doctrines goes beyond what he said and likely held as his own view. In his earlier work (represented by the *Tractatus-Logico-Philosophicus*), Wittgenstein held a strongly referential theory of meaning. However, he later came to see that language is much more complex than any referential theory would suggest. In his *Philosophical Investigations* Wittgenstein argued that words (and even sentences) are used in so many different ways in various contexts that it is impossible to state *the* meaning of a given term. Rather, what a word, phrase, or sentence means depends on how it is used in a given situation.

Wittgenstein's theory of meaning, as incorporated and defended in his later works, involves two main things. First, he saw language as a complex of language-games. A language-game is a complete way of doing one kind of activity or another. As such it involves both linguistic and non-linguistic behavior. A given language-game covers a particular way people use language to do one thing or another; hence a language-game is a "form of life" (a way that humans do a given activity).[37] Hence, we can talk about the language-games of science, philosophy, literature, theology, and religious expression. Each language-game is governed by its own rules and has its own criteria and test for truth (if truth is a matter at issue in a given language-game). For Wittgenstein these language-games are logically independent of one another, so, for example, the test for truth in one language-game (as well as the procedures for discovering truth in that game) is not necessarily the same as in another language-game.[38] For example, criteria of truth and procedures for determining true or false propositions in the language-game of mathematics are significantly different from those used in a physical science like biology or botany. While various language-games may have a "family" resemblance to other games, each is logically distinct.

As to how many language-games there are, Wittgenstein claimed that they are innumerable, and their number is not constant, for there are always new ways that language can be used in one context or another to communicate.[39] In light of this notion of language as a complex of language-games, a purely referential theory of meaning seems inadequate. Indeed, Wittgenstein saw things that way and hence proposed a use theory of meaning. According to this theory, the meaning of any word or sentence is a function of its use in a language-game. Words are to be compared to tools in a toolbox, and any given tool can be used to do a number of different things. Similarly, words have this multiple function.[40] Given the flexibility of what words may mean, there can be no talk of the "essence" of a word's meaning, as though the word referred only and always to one thing alone. Wittgenstein also granted that how a word is used may change from time to time. Certain uses may come into existence, while others go out of use. It is purely a matter of social convention as to which uses of a word will be acceptable at a given time and in a specific culture. Think, for example, of the phenomenon of slang. Uses of language in slang go in and out of style; moreover, the linguistic community over time learns which uses of a term are intended as slang and which are not. To illustrate this point, consider the many uses of the English word 'head' in the following sentences: "Go to the head of the class and write your answer on the chalkboard"; "Sally was named valedictorian, because she was the head of her graduating class"; "If you're ever in a jam, count on Jim for help, because he will always keep a cool head under fire"; "My head hurts from trying to read my book without enough light on it"; "You should meet my friend Joe; I'm sure you'd like him, because he's a real cool head." I could go further, but I think the point is clear enough. There are many ways to use language, and some of these uses of the word 'head' are in vogue now and others aren't. Language's meaning is not invariant.

Now, it is very interesting to see how many postmoderns have picked up ideas from Wittgenstein's views on meaning and applied them to their own use. Postmoderns, rejecting any referential theory of meaning according to which words represent things in our world, have adopted a use theory of meaning but have taken it to mean that words point only to other words, not to the world. They also affirm that word meaning is a product of the conventions of the linguistic community involved and hence can be changed at the whim and wish of the community. Some postmoderns have even concluded that how a community uses words and sentences is a matter of arbitrary choice.

In adopting such a stance, postmoderns have gone beyond what Wittgenstein actually held. It is true that the way language is used in various circumstances is largely a matter of societal conventions, but Wittgenstein never said that because of this, the choice of which words to use to say one thing or another is totally arbitrary. More importantly, however, he never rejected the referential element of language. Though he claimed that words and sentences could be used in various language-games to mean different things, still in each instance a word, phrase, or sentence did refer to something in the world beyond our language. It's just that the word, phrase, or sentence didn't forever have to refer to one and only one thing. Such a theory is clearly a use theory of meaning, but even a use theory says more than that language refers only to other language and never gets us to the world. Nonetheless, many postmoderns have thought that a use theory of meaning had to remove entirely any reference and representation beyond language.

As to Wittgenstein's concept of language as a complex of language-games, postmoderns have adopted much of what Wittgenstein held, but even here they have somewhat gone beyond him. Postmoderns have especially focused on the logical independence of each language-game and the claim that each language-game has its own rules and procedures. Accordingly, some language-games might talk about truth, but it is truth according to the kind of language-game involved, and hence not necessarily truth in the sense of language matching our world. Moreover, the nature of some language-games is such that they don't involve truth at all. For example, Wittgenstein held that religious language-games are not games in which one makes assertions of facts that are testable in one way or another. Hence, it cannot be legitimate to ask whether a religion's doctrines are true or not (in a correspondence sense), or to ask which religion is "the true religion." Religious claims can be used to state one's preference for a certain kind of activity (e.g., "It's a sin to steal" doesn't assert that stealing something is actually morally wrong; it just shows that the one who makes such a claim doesn't like stealing—or more to the point, being robbed), one's intentions to act in a certain way, or even one's sense of being at peace and feeling safe in the world because of one's picture of the world as run by an all-loving God (having such a feeling of security doesn't arise, however, because of constructing an evidential case which proves that one's theistic worldview matches what is true of our world).[41]

Postmoderns find especially attractive the notion that each language-game has its own rules and procedures, and defines truth in its own way. They have moved beyond such claims, however, to argue that these Wittgensteinian doctrines support their claim that there is no such thing as absolute truth. Rather, what is true and how truth is even defined varies from person to person and from language-game to language-game. Moreover, there just isn't some "super" language-game which governs all other language-games and defines a sense of truth that applies to all language-games. There is only a multiplicity of language-games, and truth is relative to each game. Though it might seem that such a conclusion about truth is an inevitable result of Wittgenstein's teachings about language-games, I think this is an instance where postmoderns have gone beyond Wittgenstein. If asked, Wittgenstein might have agreed with the way postmoderns use his notion of language-games, but he certainly doesn't say in his *Philosophical Investigations* that his views make truth entirely relative. There are places in the *Investigations* where he talks about certainty and notes that one can have certainty both in the language-games of math and logic as well as in other language-games that deal more directly with empirical reality.[42] Moreover, while language-games that deal with matters of empirical reality such as science do have their own procedures and criteria for truth, Wittgenstein nowhere suggests that we should be skeptical about most scientific or historical propositions taken to be true, just because they are part of one language-game and not of all or even of many. In both the *Investigations* and his *On Certainty*, there is plenty of evidence that he believed that there are many propositions that are certainly true and make no sense to doubt. And he held that this was so not just for some people at one time and place in history, but for all. Yes, such propositions come from a particular language-game which is distinct from others, but in cases where the language-game allows one to make assertions about reality (i.e., statements about matters of fact), Wittgenstein never says that such claims are not or cannot be true in a correspondence sense of truth or that only people from one linguistic community should think such claims are true. So, in taking Wittgenstein's concept of language as a complex of language-games as evidence for the complete relativity of truth, I think postmoderns have gone well beyond the views presented in Wittgenstein's writings.

Objectivity, Subjectivity, and Truth

In light of what postmoderns say about the mind's construction of reality and the other doctrines discussed in the previous section, it comes as no surprise that postmoderns thoroughly reject the claim that one can know the world objectively and hence as it truly is. In fact, one of the complications that makes it dubious that there can be any objective knowledge about the world is the likelihood that humans cannot "get to that world," that is, see the world apart from our presuppositions and preferences which we all bring to our observation of the world. The point here is not simply Kant's claim that we cannot know things-in-themselves. Rather, even granting that we must know things as they appear to us, the postmodern claim is that our conceptual grid, which incorporates all our past experiences, presuppositions, and preferences, guarantees that we are distanced too far from the world to know whether the way we are seeing it has any similarity to the way it is. Kant believed that even though we could know things only as they appeared to us, the way they appeared was not likely so markedly different from the way they actually are that our knowledge claims are typically wrong. Postmoderns are far more pessimistic about this than Kant and other moderns.

Willard Van Orman Quine helps us to understand why postmoderns are so skeptical about our mind's and sensory organs' abilities to have contact with the world around us (and hence skeptical that our language can really match the way things are in the world). In his groundbreaking "Two Dogmas of Empiricism," Quine rejected the idea that all meaningful discourse can be translated or reduced into language about immediate experience. This cannot be done with individual words or even whole sentences. Instead, the whole fabric of our knowledge confronts "the tribunal of experience." This does not mean, however, we have the ability to compare our beliefs objectively with experience to see if they match. Rather, Quine, as quoted in chapter 1 of this book, wrote that "The totality of our so-called knowledge or beliefs, from the most casual matters of geography and history to the profoundest laws of atomic physics or even of pure mathematics and logic, *is a man-made fabric* which impinges on experience only along the edges. . . . No *particular experiences are linked with any particular statements in the interior of the field*, except indirectly through considerations of equilibrium affecting the field as a whole"[43] (italics mine).

If all our language is man-made, then the world is not simply mirrored on our minds, allowing us objectively to read off the results. Nor do our observations and reasoning "see things as they are." What we claim to know is actually an interconnected web of beliefs that touch reality, experience, only at the borders of that web. But, our knowledge is underdetermined by experience. That is, experience and our contact with it are such that there simply isn't enough evidence from experience for us to know which beliefs are true or false or whether our whole perspective on the world is right or wrong.

Quine very clearly rejects the "myth of the given," the idea that the world is just there for us as a set of brute, theory-neutral facts which we can objectively know. Instead, what we see is our structuring of reality from the perspective of our own conceptual grid. Regardless of how distant or close the world is relative to our minds, postmoderns agree that we cannot know it objectively. As Jared Hiebert explains,

> Knowledge and reality are not absolute, ordered and objective but are constructed. We create the world in which we live by forming our own concepts of reality, truth and knowledge. Nothing is fixed and definitively identifiable because we do not have an anchor point from which we can objectively view our world and by which we can structure our world. We can only view our world from the structures that we have brought to it.[44]

John Macquarrie contends that this lack of objectivity is especially evident in disciplines such as history. He thinks the quest for the historical Jesus is a good example of this. Despite the nineteenth century and later, and the late-twentieth-century quest for facts about the historical Jesus, Macquarrie affirms that "the 'objective facts' can never be fully established. . . . In fact we can never get beyond reports, and even the earliest gospel (Mark) was written more than thirty years after the crucifixion, and must itself have had its origin in earlier reports, most or even all of them unwritten. So we must ask, 'Is there anything except interpretation of interpretations . . . ?'"[45]

While MacQuarrie fears that matters of historical fact can't be objectively known, he doubts that many postmoderns hold views (like those of George Berkeley) in regard to the natural sciences that material things are in fact only ideas in our minds (Berkeley's claim was "to be is to be perceived").[46] MacQuarrie is probably correct, but we must not misunderstand the point. While postmoderns are not likely to adopt Berkeley's form of idealism, that doesn't mean that they think science is still dedicated to objectivity and is the one discipline that achieves it. In fact, one of the important elements in getting philosophers and other academicians (as well as ordinary people) to discard modern epistemology in favor of postmodern epistemology is the attack during the twentieth century on the objectivity of science. Today, many philosophers of science, for example, contend that science is just as fraught with theory-ladenness and subjectivity as anything else we purport to know.

One of the important elements in the attack on science's objectivity came from philosopher of science Thomas Kuhn. In the late 1960s and early 1970s Kuhn published *The Structure of Scientific Revolutions*. He argued that despite the widely held belief that science (of all disciplines) operates with pristine objectivity and no bias in handling data, that is not so. According to Kuhn, there are no theory-neutral observations and no brute facts in our world that await our objective inspection. Instead, scientists' observations are colored by their conceptual framework, a framework that comes from their life situation, training as scientists, and knowledge of current scientific theory. No matter how hard a scientist tries to put presuppositions aside, it is impossible to do so. Inevitably, observations of data are shaped by the scientist's language, concepts, training, and experience.[47]

Kuhn distinguished what he called normal science and revolutionary science. Once a scientific paradigm like Newtonian physics is accepted, scientists work within that paradigm to explain the phenomena and data of the world. Their observations and conclusions are governed by the reigning theory. This sort of science is normal science. On the other hand, as scientists work within a paradigm, they notice certain data and concepts that don't quite fit the prevailing theory. At some point, anomalies with the current paradigm become so hard to overcome that it is scrapped in favor of a new paradigm. The switch, Kuhn argued, does not come from a long-reasoned process that deductively or inductively yields the new view, but instead comes suddenly, almost like a conversion experience. This is revolutionary science, and once the revolution ends, normal science works within the new paradigm.[48]

In early years after Kuhn's proposal appeared, there were many critics,[49] but in recent decades, despite lingering criticism, Kuhn's basic claim that all observation and reasoning are theory-laden has been widely accepted.

The implications of such views are devastating to the notion of objective knowledge. If even science cannot know or be trusted to tell us the truth about the world, what hope is there of finding truth (let alone convincing anyone of it) in more abstract disciplines?[50]

From what I have already described in this and previous sections, postmoderns' understanding of truth likely comes as no surprise. The correspondence theory of truth has been the predominant notion of truth throughout the history of Western philosophy. According to this view, truth or falsity is a property of sentences that assert something about the world. If what the speaker or writer says about the world matches the way things are in the world, then the sentence is true in that it corresponds to the world. If what the sentence affirms does not match what we find in the world, the sentence is false. All of this makes an abundant amount of sense, and upon minimal reflection it seems clear that ordinary language presupposes the correspondence theory of truth. That is, what we attempt to do in our daily verbal interactions with others is say things that match what has happened or is true of the world.

All of this likely seems rather obvious, so it may at first seem a bit puzzling to hear that postmoderns typically reject the correspondence theory of truth. However, when we hear the reasons for doing so, their rejection becomes more understandable. Postmoderns reject the correspondence theory of truth for a variety of reasons. For one thing, all of us bring our conceptual grid with all of its presuppositions and preferences to the acquisition of knowledge. Those preferences are shaped by our experiences and by the linguistic community(ies) in which we were raised and have lived. As we learned from Kant, the mind is not passive in the knowing process. Given each person's background and conceptual grid, it is understandable that each will have his or her own perspective on any given topic, with no way to decide which perspective actually matches the way things in our world are. Douglas Groothuis describes the situation as postmoderns see it: "Our access to the territory of reality is through our language, which acts as a map. But we cannot check the map against the territory, since we can know nothing outside our language. Thus, language becomes a kind of prison of signifiers that can never connect with the signified outside of itself."[51]

Reading this, one might respond that this makes sense when dealing with abstract concepts, but not when dealing with claims about the material, tangible world. Don't we, when reporting what we see, hear, touch, etc., come directly in contact with the world and, hence, experience it as it really is? If so, then why can't we talk about our language as corresponding to reality? James Danaher explains why the suppositions embodied in these questions are wrong. He explains that while it is true that each person has both intellectual and sensory equipment, "such equipment allows us to form language and ideas that reflect the perspectival nature of our experience."[52]

But don't the brute facts of material reality confront each person equally? That is, aren't the brute facts universally available to all? Danaher replies that while they are universally available, that doesn't mean that all of us will understand them in the same way. Each of us has his or her own perspective, and that impacts how we judge what we experience in the world around us.[53] If this is so in relation to our judgments about what we experience in the physical world, how much more is there room for misunderstanding when we reflect upon abstract concepts!

Put a bit differently, the correspondence theory of truth seems to necessitate that the knower's mind has direct contact with the world outside the mind and doesn't distort anything it perceives. But, for that to be true, the mind would have to function as a passive mirror upon which sensory data are directly imprinted, unmediated by any conceptual framework with its presuppositions and preferences. But Kant taught us that the mind is not passive in the knowing process. Moreover, we can further see that our intellectual equipment allows us freedom to make judgments about what we experience and gives us the ability to make alternate concepts. It is that freedom of judgment and ability to create alternate concepts that "accounts for the different perspectival, historical, and cultural conceptualization of our experience."[54] Once and for all, the metaphor of the mind as passive mirror must be discarded. Danaher summarizes the situation as follows:

> although there might be the possibility of a correspondence (inexact as it may be) between our ideas and the brute facts of the physical world, once those ideas of the brute facts are conceptualized, and organized into an understanding, there is no longer anything for them to correspond to. The physical world of raw experience only contains individual facts and no concepts to which our concepts might correspond. Thus, today the truth of our conceptual reality is often established on the basis of how well a

certain conceptualization of the world offers a coherent picture of the world and/or how well a particular conceptualization yields the pragmatic consequences we value.[55]

In light of these considerations, what do postmoderns believe about truth? From the preceding description, it is very clear that for them there can be no such thing as absolute truth, or if there is, no one is in a position to know what it is. Rather, each of us is left to his or her perspective, and we have no way to tell whose perspective is closer to or further from what is actually the case in our world. There just isn't any "God's-eye" perspective that allows us to judge, among finite perspectives, which one is closest to the truth. It would be wonderful if we could judge which of our claims match our world and which don't, but truth as correspondence simply is unavailable to us.

As a result, postmoderns typically adopt some form of the coherence theory of truth, the pragmatic theory of truth, or a combination of both. According to the former, what is true is the set of sentences that fit together without contradicting one another (think here of Quine's picture of an interconnected web of beliefs that may require readjusting some of its components for sake of logical consistency). According to the latter, what is true is what offers the most workable results when believed. Earlier pragmatists held that truth as correspondence was possible, but thought that for something to be true it should do more than just tell us that; it should guide us to beliefs and actions that have the most desirable results.[56] Postmodern pragmatists disagree about the matter of correspondence, for we cannot know what matches the world. The best each of us can do is choose beliefs that seem to work for him or her.[57]

Anti-foundationalism, Rejection of Grand Metanarratives, and Perspectivism

One of the hallmarks of postmodern thinking is its rejection of foundationalism. In fact much of what I have described in the previous sections presupposes a rejection of foundationalism. Foundationalism is to be abandoned in at least two distinct respects. First, there is the rejection of epistemological foundationalism. Here Brian Trainor is very helpful in explaining why a foundation for knowledge was deemed necessary. Prior to Descartes's methodological doubt with a view to finding an indubitable truth from which to build knowledge, medieval thinking saw a connectedness between "Reason" and "Nature." "'Nature' was understood or experienced as an ordering, enveloping, unifying process which assigned to each species, including the human, its proper place in the natural or divine—but, at any rate intelligible—scheme of things."[58] Reasoning was typically understood as a way to participate in the "life" of an all-encompassing "Nature." With Descartes reason became disconnected, unhinged from the cosmic order, which order is no longer seen as intrinsically rational.[59] Trainor explains the result as follows:

> The medieval view is decisively rejected: the modernist attitude is to regard the view that Divine Reason percolates through the entire cosmic order, (including the reasoning of man* as an integral part of that order) as unscientific and unsustainable, as no more indeed than a relic of medieval anthropomorphism that deserves to perish in an age of scientific enlightenment. The cost is high, however, for the 'real' cosmic order of medieval thought, an order of interconnected essences and real kinds, becomes replaced under the banner of enlightenment and scientific progress with the modernist mathematical universe of matter-in-motion inhabited by Galileo, Descartes and Hobbes. At any rate, from its inception, when it set 'reason' adrift in the universe, a virtually constant feature of modernity has been its attempt to find some kind of secure foundation for human thought, or to somehow come to grips with its declared absence.[60]

In describing modernity, I presented the basic notion of foundationalism. Epistemological foundationalism, especially in its classical form, has come under increasing attack over the last thirty to forty years. A major complaint is that if classical foundationalism's criteria for proper basicality are accepted, then foundationalism should be rejected. Classical foundationalism held that beliefs must be supportable ultimately by beliefs that are either self-evident, evident to the senses, or incorrigible. But none of these three criteria is either self-evident, evident to the senses, or incorrigible, nor are they supported by other more basic beliefs that meet those requirements. Hence, no one should adopt foundationalism.

In place of foundationalism, postmoderns most typically adopt a coherentist theory of knowledge. Whereas foundationalism portrays knowledge as a building or a pyramid which ultimately rests on indubitable foundations, according to coherentism, beliefs still must be justified by other beliefs, but no beliefs are more basic than any other. Nor are any beliefs directly in touch with experience outside the mind in a way that would confirm them as self-evident or indubitable. This is especially so if one agrees with Quine's claim that no particular experiences are linked with *any particular statements* (beliefs) within the web of our beliefs. Hence, we are free to reevaluate any statement we like and make adjustments in other statements for the sake of logical consistency in the "overall story" we tell, but that does not mean we are in a position to know or prove that the whole story (or even individual statements within it) match(es) the world. Instead of portraying knowledge as a building, knowledge is now described as a web or net of interconnected beliefs. Such a view is often called a "holistic" theory of knowledge.[61]

Postmoderns also reject foundationalism in a second sense. The term 'foundationalism' is often used to refer to any belief, set of beliefs, or worldview which is taken to be beyond critique. A foundational set of beliefs (in this sense) is typically assumed true and not necessarily demonstrated as such, but all other beliefs are judged in light of their conformity or lack thereof to the foundational viewpoint. As noted in the previous section, all human knowledge is deemed as time- and culture-bounded. No one has a "God's-eye" view of the nature of reality. Moreover, if it is really impossible to contact the external world unmediated by our conceptual grid with its presuppositions, it stands to reason that none of us is in a position to show that her or his view is the "correct" one. And if that is the case, then no viewpoint can be foundational in the second sense defined in this paragraph. No viewpoint can be beyond critique or have privileged status. This is so whether we are talking about a whole worldview or specific elements within a given position.

If one rejects foundationalism in this second sense, one implicitly agrees that no religion, no worldview, and no concept is better than any other in telling us the nature of the world around us. Individual ideas or whole systems of thought can be judged only as to how well they fit or don't fit with the basic understanding of reality a given person holds. If all of this is so, then the only reasonable approach to life is to be tolerant of all people and all points of view. There is no point in trying to defend one's religion as better than others, nor is there any need to try to convert others to a given religion. All that we can talk about is how our religion has met our own needs, if it has, but then everyone else can offer a similar testimony, regardless of which religion they espouse. No religion or worldview has privileged status as exempt from critique and as governing everything else we think.

Rejecting foundationalism in this second sense seems to make witnessing for Christ and defending the Christian faith inappropriate, unwelcome, and useless. It also seems to lead to nihilism, where anything or nothing can be believed. Many trace such a rejection of foundationalism back to Nietzsche, and fear that if we agree we will fall prey to the nihilism that many believe is central to Nietzsche's philosophy. While it is appropriate to trace anti-foundationalism in this second sense to Nietzsche, and while he does speak of nihilism, some have argued that Nietzsche didn't embrace nihilism himself. Rather, he used the fear of nihilism as grounds for the "Overman" to make his own rules and impose his own point of view on reality. Ken Gemes is helpful in relation to these issues; he writes,

> Now Nietzsche, as postmodernists rightly observe, is a destroyer of all kinds of foundationalisms. They are right to interpret this as the force behind Nietzsche's madman's proclamation of the death of God. . . . It is not simply the Christian world-view that is at stake here but all notions of an external authority that might provide some ultimate guarantor of beliefs. But postmodernists are wrong to take this rejection of the notion of an external, transcendent authority as a rejection of all authority. The postmodern rejection of all authority, all principle of order among the competing modes of representation, presents the very Nihilism that Nietzsche predicts, and warns against, as a natural result of the defeat of dogmatism. For Nietzsche there is still room for an immanent authority, an authority that comes from within.[62]

Regardless of one's views about Nietzsche's philosophy, the point is rather clear. No viewpoint is "the" legitimizing viewpoint which isn't open to review and critique. The implications of this point are quite significant, for societies throughout history have taken some worldview as the most basic understanding of reality and have structured the various aspects of life as a society governed by this fundamental viewpoint. Now we are told by postmoderns that there is no place for such grand, overarching "stories" around which society should be lived. As quoted from Lyotard at the outset of our discussion on postmodernity, "simplifying to the extreme, I define postmodern as incredulity toward metanarratives."[63] A metanarrative is a story about reality that is used to legitimize a particular way of thinking and acting. Lyotard argues that in premodern societies there were conventions about who would tell the story and who must listen. Of course, this allowed those in power to repeat the account of reality that kept them in power. In the modern era, there are still narratives, but they must be legitimized. For moderns, science legitimizes and verifies the account of reality offered. This seems to free people from the authoritarian oppression of the premodern, but what actually happens is that science depends on a narrative of its own, a certain story about how we attain, verify, and falsify beliefs. Lyotard argues that this metanarrative, too, is authoritarian, and must be rejected. What takes its place? Lyotard answers that there is no grand narrative, no big picture that makes sense of everything. There are only our individual narratives, our individual perceptions of reality as we see it.[64]

Clearly, each language-game and each society has its own metanarratives. In fact it is normal and to be expected that any society will "tell its story" of why social, political, religious, etc., aspects of life are structured the way they are in that particular society. Postmoderns, therefore, do not reject metanarratives completely. Rather, they reject any grand narrative, a story that attempts to give an account of all of reality and to legitimize that account as correct. And, they also reject any lesser metanarrative that anyone or any group would treat as foundational (and hence uncontestable) to the way some aspect of life is carried out in a particular society.

In light of what has been said about anti-realism, anti-objectivity, the notion of truth, etc., the rejection of grand narratives and of lesser narratives that are given a privileged position should surprise no one. Moreover, it fits extremely well with the perspectivism that typifies postmodern thinking. That is, since none of us has access to absolute truth (assuming that there is such a thing), we are necessarily left to hold our particular perspective on the world. And, of course, that perspective is simply one of many different "takes" on reality. No individual perspective is "the" correct one; at most we can say that a given perspective fits better or worse with what we have found to be the best way to conduct our lives in this world. As such it is "true" for us, but not true absolutely![65]

Relativism, Hermeneutics of Suspicion, and Deconstruction

From what I have already described, it should be very clear that postmodernism involves a commitment to relativism (or as Henriksen calls it, "plurality"). Henriksen agrees with German philosopher Wolfgang Welsch that plurality or relativism is the key issue in postmodernity. It stems from the recognition that "there is no neutral, commonly valid or acceptable description of the world."[66] These are all familiar themes, and relativism does logically follow from postmodern acceptance of such themes as anti-realism; anti-foundationalism; rampant subjectivity without the possibility of objective, absolute truth; and the construction of one's worldview on the basis of one's conceptual grid as formed by his or her language community, life experiences, and presuppositions.

Henriksen offers two points of elaboration from Welsch and adds a third himself. First, Welsch distinguishes plurality at the surface and "the deep and basic plurality that is rooted in what he calls *basic differences*."[67] The point is that some things that appear to be different at first glance, at a closer look turn out to be variations on the same thing. An example would be various Christian denominations and churches which have some surface differences, but at root have more in common than not. On the other hand, while there are some similarities between Christianity, Judaism, and Islam (all three are monotheistic religions), at a deeper level there are some basic differences that would make unity between any or all of them impossible. Views which are at root genuinely different engender what Welsch calls hard pluralism. Of this type of pluralism, Henriksen explains that it "is the pluralism that has no hope of being reconciled, a pluralism that, if you try to overcome it, will imply the violation of the identity of that which you try to reconcile."[68]

Welsch's second point in elaborating the results of this relativism or plurality is that since there are many different ways of understanding our world and various perspectives from which to understand it, each person should resist the temptation to stick with only one way of making sense of reality. Instead, we should "constantly try to overcome, criticise, make more complete and transcend what is given, by moving towards something new. The past and the given have no inherent and final normativity, nothing that *secures* its authority in the contemporary cultural situation."[69]

Henriksen thinks Welsch's definition of postmodernity is fine as far as it goes, but Henriksen thinks something further should be added. There is another side to plurality which Henriksen identifies with the following thesis:

> All cultural expressions contribute to the articulation—and thereby the construction—of those parts of reality that only exist due to our

understanding, i.e., the cultural sphere. Hence, the articulation of culture (in the wide sense of the word) constitutes the reality that is articulated. *The cultural reality appears as a construction by humans.*[70]

Henriksen notes that an implication of this added thesis leads us to see that "none of our expressions of self-understanding need to be what they are, and that they could be otherwise. . . . As long as we can construct otherwise, we will have plurality."[71] When one combines Welsch's and Henriksen's insights, Henriksen believes it becomes easier to understand some key postmodern themes. He shows the relation to six key postmodern notions.

First, postmodernism's rejection of a common human rationality fits with the insight that "we reconstruct different forms of rationality according to specific interests, needs and concerns."[72] It is just impossible to get beyond the fact that each of us lives in and is conditioned by his or her own culture, which has its own way of interpreting things and communicating about the world. Second, the previous point also implies "that contingency and contextuality are a corollary of the lack of common rationality."[73] From one society to the next, nothing has to be the way it is; social understanding and conventions could be different than they are at any given time and place. Third, the contextual nature of our understanding of reality also implies perspectivism. As Henriksen explains, "since we have different concerns, interests, etc., these also give us the perspectives by which we construct our pictures of the world and the patterns of meaning we need."[74]

Points one through three above lead to the realization that we must accept relativism, even when and if it yields conflicting, disturbing, and contradicting viewpoints. Since all viewpoints are contingent and don't encompass everything, it follows that each needs to be supplemented by other constructions of reality.[75] Henriksen adds a fifth point, to the effect that the constructive nature of reason and understanding "leads to a reflexivity that affirms how nothing can be taken at face value, but must be seen also as a part of a larger cultural current of which it is a part."[76] Finally, when we recognize that our cultures are our own constructions, we realize as well that we also have the possibility, if we so choose, "to reconstruct patterns, constructions, rationalities in the light of other insights, thereby not only contributing to the multiplicity of constructions . . . , but also amplifying the experience of plurality and contingency."[77] Hence, relativism should not be feared or rejected, but rather embraced. Given our limited perspectives, we really have no other choice, but it is a path we should gladly accept rather than decrying the possibility that, with relativism, no one really knows what line of thought or action is correct (if "correct" means absolutely true for all people at all times and places).[78]

If relativism is the order of the day, then any institution, any document, any system of thought that claims to be (or to be founded on) absolute truth must be suspect. For example, postmoderns who are feminists often remind us that Western cultures have been built on the foundation of the Judeo-Christian Scriptures. Those Scriptures present a world order in which men are in charge and women are excluded from power. Since the Bible claims to be divinely inspired, it is often argued that putting men in positions of power in the home, society, and the church is the expressed will of God in Scripture, and hence societies can be constructed to please God only when they are centered on male supremacy.

But if postmoderns are right about every culture at all times constructing their societies from their own perspective, then no society can claim to have absolute truth. Moreover, the various books of the Bible are to be seen merely as expressing the perspectives of the writers who wrote them and the cultures that formed those writers. Hence, the biblical perspective has no more right to be preeminent than the views of any other culture at any other time.

If all of this is so, then not only is Scripture not the inspired Word of God, but it needs to be read with a healthy dose of suspicion. Using what is called the hermeneutics of suspicion, we cannot take things in Scripture at face value. When reading the various commands of Scripture, for example, with each injunction we must always ask *cui bono*—to whose good or benefit was this written?[79] When we use the hermeneutics of suspicion in reading Scripture or any other formative document of a culture (e.g., the United States Constitution or the Declaration of Independence), we see that these documents are not so benign as they may seem. Rather, they have been constructed so as to empower certain members of society and exclude others. And they should be read as such, rather than being treated as divine revelation or anything else that would exempt them from critique and revision. The suspicion we should bring to the reading of any text should also be applied to our understanding of social institutions and structures. Someone or some group put these institutions and structures together so as to legitimize the empowerment that some members of society have and the discrimination that excludes others who are different from having any power or say.

None of this should surprise anyone, especially in light of postmodernism's anti-foundationalist rejection of any viewpoint as exempt from critique because of its alleged absolute authority. And, if relativism and perspectivism are the proper approaches to life in our day, then we must be suspicious about any written or oral statement, as well as any institution, that claims to offer the "correct" account of how societies and cultures should be organized. But how exactly should we exercise the hermeneutics of suspicion? Should we doubt and reject everything, ultimately embracing nihilism and anarchy? Postmoderns answer that we should use the hermeneutics of suspicion as part of an overall process called deconstruction.

The name most associated with deconstructionism is Jacques Derrida (1930–2004), a French philosopher. The term 'deconstruction' seems odd at first glance, but that is because it is actually the combination of two terms, 'destruction' and 'construction.' Derrida and his followers urge us to deconstruct all texts, all narratives, and all institutions. That is, analyze them by "taking them apart" to see the motivation behind the particular form in which we find them. When you do so, you will see that while these texts, etc. reveal a certain order of things, at the same time they hide that which is different or other. In so hiding the other, they exclude it. Hence, the question noted above, *cui bono*—to whose benefit?—is a helpful tool to bring to the interpretation of texts, narratives, etc. It presupposes that something has been hidden and excluded as well as that which is stated more plainly in the text.

Taking a text apart, however, is only half the "assignment." We need to reconstruct the text and its meaning in a way that takes seriously those excluded and includes them. Hence, deconstruction involves both a tearing down and a building up (destruction and construction). And since the viewpoint apparent on the surface of the text is only one of potentially limitless perspectives on the issues with which the text deals, it is good that we don't absolutize one reading of the text, but rather seek for other ways to understand the text.

Hearing this, you may be troubled by a key question hermeneuts should and do discuss. How can we look for alternate readings of a text when whoever wrote the text intended to say one specific thing? Mustn't we give the author(s) his, her, or their due? A key postmodern theme is that authors must be detached from the texts they have written. It is dubious that we can know what an author intended to say. Even if he states his intentions in the text, that statement, as part of the text, must itself be interpreted, and is open to a variety of interpretations. We simply aren't in a position to know what he intended to say. Perhaps even he did not fully understand everything he had in mind when he wrote it, spoke it, etc. Moreover, any text is ambiguous and capable of various interpretations that depend on the exegete's interaction with the text, an interaction that can never be objective and so see things as they really are.[80] To offer only one interpretation as "the" meaning of the text is to miss the point about ambiguity, but it is also to adopt the same foundationalist, objectivist, absolutist notions of knowledge and truth that postmoderns believe they have already discredited. When such absolutist readings of texts, institutions, etc., are adopted, they empower some and exclude others from power. Hence, even the way we treat certain ideas, institutions, texts, etc., involves a kind of violence that excludes the "other." Language is powerful; properly handling it allows us to open ourselves and our societies to the excluded, the others, and thereby to produce a more just society. Hence, all ideas, theories, texts, institutions, etc., need to be deconstructed and then reconstructed so as to give ear to the different possible ways of seeing things.

John MacQuarrie offers a helpful summary of these ideas as he discusses the meaning of two of Derrida's key terms, 'deconstruction' and '*differance*.' He writes,

> According to Derrida, descriptions, histories, theories etc. need to be taken apart, because language is riddled by ambiguities. The logical analyst's plea that each word should have only one meaning is impossible to obey. As Derrida says more than once, we live after the Tower of Babel. Every text has a plurality of meanings as soon as it is put into words, and from that point on there are different interpretations. But if that is the negative side of deconstruction, it points to an affirmative task. The work of deconstruction prevents closure, and room is left for new interpretations. Our language never quite coincides with what is talked about. The language overflows, it has an excess of meanings and connotations. Its failure to coincide with what is talked about is called *differance*, a neologism which combines two distinguishable meanings of the French verb

differer, 'to differ' and 'to defer'. Every text calls for re-writing, and this goes on indefinitely, always with *differance*. . . . Deconstruction forbids closure and there will always be new deferrals.[81]

If one encounters someone committed to these most extreme forms of postmodern thinking on truth and knowledge, is any attempt to convince them of the accuracy of the Christian worldview futile? Those of us who went to college when modern epistemology reigned supreme on university campuses know how difficult it was for Christianity to get a hearing. Christian beliefs were dismissed as hopelessly naive, at least in part because nonbelievers were convinced there was no way to support such beliefs with adequate evidence.

As a postmodern mind-set has been adopted by many, Christians find it a bit easier to be heard by nonbelievers. After all, if no one can know absolute truth and can only tell their own story about how their beliefs have helped them live life, then perhaps even a Christian perspective can be helpful to some struggling to find their way in this world. But Christians should take little comfort in being heard, because if they even remotely intimate that Christianity is truth for all, they will be dismissed as intolerant and naive, just as their forebears were when they attempted to convince moderns that there is sufficient evidence to warrant belief in Christianity.

So, how should a Christian address a non-Christian (modern or postmodern)? Is traditional apologetics dead? Should we forget about truth, acknowledge some form of modern or postmodern skepticism, and resort to nothing more than telling our personal narratives and hope that what we say will "resonate" with our listeners? Sadly, there are some in our day who seem to think this is the only way forward in attempting to reach a nonbelieving world.

But I disagree. In the next chapters I address the various issues raised by postmodern and modern forms of skepticism. As readers will see, I believe there are answers to both, even as I believe there is truth and a way to find it. I do not believe the appropriate response to skepticism is to lay down our apologetic ammunition and merely regale nonbelievers with our stories. Not all will agree with what I offer, but before you reject my answers to postmodern and modern skepticism, at the very least let me sit at the "dialogue table," and listen (as open-mindedly as you can) to what I say!

Chapter 3

Answers to Postmodern Skepticism (I)

In the preceding chapters we have seen two different types of epistemological skepticism. These different kinds of skepticism actually raise two different sets of issues when applied to religious belief. On the one hand, they raise what Alvin Plantinga calls *de facto* issues, issues about whether religious beliefs (Christian ones in particular) are true. In addition, skepticism raises what Plantinga labels *de jure* issues, questions about whether religious believers in general and Christians in particular can be rational, justified, and warranted in holding their religious beliefs.

As we shall see in the second section of this book (on ways of defending Christian truth), most forms of Christian apologetics (presuppositionalism and Christian evidentialism) over the last century or so have occupied themselves with *de facto* questions. In contrast, we shall also see that Alvin Plantinga's Reformed Epistemology is most concerned to address *de jure* issues. He is specifically concerned to answer the skeptical claim that no one has a right to believe in God (and more specifically in Christian theism), because there simply isn't adequate evidence to support such belief. All of this will become clearer when we discuss various ways of defending the Christian faith, but I raise the *de jure*/*de facto* distinction now, because it is a helpful way to understand what exactly modern and postmodern skeptics are complaining about when they reject Christianity.

In reflecting on postmodern beliefs about truth (as described in chapter 2), it should be clear that the most radical forms of postmodern skepticism would not find meaningful (let alone interesting) questions about whether Christian beliefs are true. Moreover, the claim that one only has a right to believe things supported by adequate evidence is nowhere to be found in *post*modern epistemology; it is clearly a concern of *modern* epistemology. In fact, both *de facto* and *de jure* issues about religious belief seem to be the concerns only of *modern* epistemology.

The preceding paragraphs may disturb readers, for clearly, the major Christian approaches (over the last century at least) to apologetics all presuppose a modern mind-set and attempt to defend Christianity by meeting modern epistemology's requirements. None of them is addressed to peculiarly postmodern concerns. One can reply that postmodern epistemology is a passing fancy and hence isn't something Christian apologists should worry about or attempt to answer. In my judgment, that response is a major mistake. Even if one thinks postmodern epistemology is a transient perspective which is losing or will lose ground in academia, there are still many academics who have imbibed it totally, and if we want to reach such people with the gospel, we must address their postmodern epistemology.

Beyond that, when one moves from academia to popular culture, the situation is all the more troubling. For here we see many people who have adopted a rather hefty dose of postmodern epistemology at its skeptical strongest, even if they don't know it. The general cultural drift toward tolerance for all ideas and for political correctness because no one can decisively show that any given perspective on reality is likely true—in an absolute sense, i.e., true for all people at all times—is pervasive in our day. While most of our contemporaries could not define "postmodern epistemology" nor could they offer much of an argument to support it, they clearly have adopted many of its key notions. And even if academia in the future moves toward a less skeptical view of knowledge, that doesn't mean popular culture will be aware of that shift, let alone know the arguments that pushed academics to abandon postmodern skepticism.

In light of these things, I believe Christian apologists must address postmodern epistemology, and they need to do more than just describe it—they need to refute it! But, you may wonder, how can we do this when the major Christian approaches to apologetics currently available and in use to one degree or another over the last century are aimed at answering modern epistemology's objections to religious belief, not at postmodern concerns?

I believe that the appropriate tools and weapons for addressing post-modern concerns are already in our hands. We just need to clarify the issues postmoderns are raising, and then answer them one by one. In what follows, I intend to do just that.

POSTMODERNISM AND *DE JURE* AND *DE FACTO* ISSUES

Does postmodern epistemology address *de jure* or *de facto* issues? Is the answer ultimately my point in raising this distinction? These are very interesting and, I think, important questions, for their answers underscore how badly out of step with the main insights of Western philosophy down through the centuries postmodern epistemology actually is. As suggested above, the short answer to these questions is that postmoderns won't likely answer either *de jure* or *de facto* questions about Christianity or any other worldview or interpretation of reality. Why this is so, however, must be explained, for it will help us see the enormity of the hurdles we must overcome to make headway in persuading postmoderns to look at Christianity seriously.

In general, we can say that postmoderns wouldn't be inclined to answer questions of either a *de jure* or a *de facto* nature, because they would see such questions as stemming from modern epistemology. As can be seen from chapter 2, there is little hope of holding both modern and postmodern epistemology at the same time without incorporating enormous contradictions into one's belief system. Though some postmoderns may not be bothered by holding contradictory views, that doesn't mean they don't see that modern and postmodern epistemologies contradict one another. I don't see postmodern epistemologists holding the main tenets of modern epistemology, and I think this is so at least in part because even postmoderns can and do recognize a contradiction when they see it!

But specifically why do postmoderns reject *de jure* and *de facto* questions altogether? As to the former, postmoderns might reject them for any of three possible reasons. *De jure* questions ask about the rationality and justifiableness of religious beliefs. One way postmoderns, with their healthy skepticism about human reason's ability to get things right, might respond is that we shouldn't waste time on discussions about what is rational or irrational to hold. Even to engage seriously in such a conversation requires one first to believe that it is possible for there to be rational belief, regardless of how "rationality" is defined. Since many postmoderns are dubious about what rationality is and whether humans can be rational in any traditional philosophic or non-philosophic sense of that term, it is understandable that they might have little time for questions about the rationality of religious or any other beliefs.

Postmoderns who do think it makes sense to talk about whether beliefs are rational may offer a second objection to *de jure* questions. For them, to say that a religious believer is rational in his or her belief may mean nothing more than that he or she is holding what seems good and useful to them. Such a claim in no way commits anyone to believe in truth as correspondence or in absolute truth, but it at least allows us to use the terms 'rational' and 'rationality' in everyday (if not also in academic philosophic) parlance. The view just described in no way contradicts any major tenet of postmodern epistemology, so postmoderns could respond to *de jure* questions in this way and give away nothing significant to their main epistemological commitments. Of course, Christian apologists are interested in a lot more than whether one finds a particular belief useful. If apologetics is only about whether Christianity is a useful set of ideas, then there is no need for books, including this one, whose intent is to support Christianity as true in a correspondence sense of 'true.' Given postmodern epistemology, neither Christianity nor any other religion can be shown to be true in a correspondence sense of 'true,' so why waste time trying to prove that Christianity is rational in that sense?

Finally, postmoderns might reject *de jure* questions because they believe questions about warrant, rationality, and the like cannot be answered, because it is impossible to offer acceptable definitions of such notions. In *Warrant: The Current Debate*, Plantinga made the point quite clearly and forcefully that he found no univocal definition for these terms as he did his research for writing his trilogy.[1] Though Plantinga, by the end of his trilogy, does offer rather precise definitions of these terms, that doesn't mean everyone, believer and unbeliever alike, agrees with those definitions. Hence, a postmodern might say that while he might like to address *de jure* questions, he cannot do so because those questions are about issues and concepts that are just too ambiguous for any of us to offer decisive answers to them. Or a postmodern might agree that we can define these concepts in an acceptable way, but also hold that human intellectual equipment and the human condition with respect to knowledge simply don't allow us to test a set of beliefs for their rationality in any way that would decisively determine whether the beliefs are or aren't rational.

As to postmodern unwillingness to engage *de facto* questions, the reason is rather obvious. Given postmodern epistemology, either there is no such thing as the truth of the matter in regard to whether religious beliefs are absolutely true, or there *are* such things as absolutely true religious beliefs but humans are in no position to know what those beliefs are. Hence, while there would undoubtedly be value to answers about Christianity's truth, there is no way to answer such questions decisively for all people.

A REMINDER ABOUT POSTMODERN SKEPTICISM

In light of the preceding, how should we handle postmodern epistemological concerns, given that postmoderns reject the very questions epistemologists have traditionally addressed and prefer to discuss other issues altogether? At the outset, we should note that in contrast to modern skepticism, postmodern skepticism is much more critical of reason's and sense perception's ability to find the truth. In fact, for postmoderns there is no absolute truth to be found. All humans have a finite intellect, and our worldview is formed by our basic experiences, biases, and linguistic communities, so the best anyone can do is offer his or her perspective on issues. People living at other times and places in history will see things from a different perspective. No mere human is able to discover what is true of our universe at all times and places. Such a "God's-eye view" that defines absolute truth just isn't available to mere mortals.

From the preceding, it also follows that postmoderns deny that knowledge can be acquired objectively. This is true of things learned both from sense perception and from pure reason alone. What I believe I see and hear is affected by my prejudices, assumptions, and biases. The mind is not passive during sense perception so that the world is mirrored on it like a snapshot, representing the world exactly as it is. Moreover, everyone knows how much presuppositions guide and govern our reasoning. Religious believers find arguments for God's existence and answers to various problems of evil compelling, while nonbelievers are unmoved by such arguments. Subjectivity rules supreme, especially when the knower is not disinterested and has an emotional stake in what is studied and thought.

So, the most vigorous forms of postmodern skepticism doubt that there is truth and objectivity, but postmoderns have another complaint. Postmoderns complain that the problem historically (especially in Western cultures) with traditional philosophy and theology and with their use of reason is that they presuppose certain things about how we should interact with and think about our world. Specifically, we often hear that we think what we do about God, the world, etc. because we have bought into certain ways of thinking about the world. The most skeptical postmoderns complain about assumptions undergirding these methods. Western philosophy and theology presuppose that reason is to be used in accord with rules of logic and argument that go back at least as far as the ancient Greeks. As a result, Christians in Western cultures value beliefs and systems of belief that are not self-contradictory, not guilty of various fallacies of reasoning, and that are held on the basis of other beliefs which can be verified either through sense perception or reason. But why should anyone embrace those ways of thinking? Aren't the worldviews and methods of thinking of non-Western cultures just as valid as those of Western cultures?

In sum, postmodern skeptics embrace perspectivism (no human has absolute truth, true for all people at all times and places), reject reason as the ultimate arbiter of all things, reject objectivity in the knowing process, and most fundamentally, ask why we must be logical (in accord with principles and procedures of Western logic) in our approach to the world. As already noted in this chapter, skepticism of this sort rejects as useless and misguided discussions that are about—to use Plantinga's terms—both *de jure* and *de facto* issues.

So, how should we proceed in addressing postmodern skepticism? It seems that the most fundamental postmodern complaints begin with a radical rejection of reason that is evident in the question of why we have to be logical. As we shall soon see, this complaint actually encompasses a number of different objections that must be answered. Once those issues are addressed, we must then turn to the matter of objectivity and subjectivity in the knowing process. If objectivity in any significant sense cannot be upheld, then of course, there can be no talk of absolute truth and no 'proving' of one's views as correct in any traditional sense of 'proof.' That is, even if everyone really does "have to be logical," that won't much matter if no one can get beyond his or her own perspective on things. There is no point in offering argument and evidence for one's views, if nothing conclusive can be proved about *any* viewpoint. If reason and sense perception simply can't be trusted to "get things right" (whatever "getting it right" even means), then what's the point of any intellectual endeavor, including apologetics?

In the rest of this chapter, I want to address the following major issue: why do we have to be logical? In chapter 4, I shall address whether it is possible for the knowing process to be objective enough so that learners can find the truth and convince others of it.

Suppose, as I shall argue, that we do have to be "logical" and that objectivity is possible. What follows from that? It is at that point that modern concerns come most to the forefront. Many moderns deny that there is sufficient evidence to justify holding religious beliefs. Moreover, even if one can show that holding religious beliefs is warranted, that doesn't prove those beliefs are true. Of course, this raises a question that must be addressed whether one is dealing with religious beliefs or any other kind of beliefs. If one holds a belief about history, science, philosophy, or religion, how would one go about demonstrating that the belief is true? And if we can talk about truth, what about certainty? Must a belief be absolutely certain (and what does that even mean?) in order for a believer to have sufficient evidence to hold it? How does evidence relate to the truth and certainty of a proposition? How would you know what kind of evidence is needed, for example, to support Christ's resurrection as true, and what quantity of such evidence is required? Questions about truth, certainty, evidence, and proof will be the focus of later chapters.

One final word of explanation before turning specifically to postmodern skepticism. Questions about logic, objectivity, and absolute truth will be handled in this and the next chapter, but the answers are important for more than just postmoderns. Moreover, if we can move postmoderns beyond their skepticism about logic and objectivity, then the topics of truth, certainty, and evidence should merit their attention. So, the subjects of this chapter and chapter 4 are also significant for moderns, and the topics of the chapters addressing modern skepticism are important for postmoderns. I place discussions of these topics in their respective chapters because the former seem to arise more from postmodern thinking and the latter are more germane to the mind-set of moderns. I address postmodern concerns first because I believe them to be logically prior to the issues to be handled when addressing modern concerns. That is, discussions about how to prove something and to know when one has done so make little sense if we don't have to follow rules of reason and argument and if it is impossible for any mere human to be objective in studying any topic.

WHY DO WE HAVE TO BE LOGICAL?

There is an objection one often hears from postmoderns in relation to Christianity, other religious views, and more broadly, Western worldviews that are not Christian, Jewish or Muslim. Often when presenting arguments *against* postmodern epistemology, apologists and philosophers make the valid point that if what postmoderns say about no absolute truth and about all viewpoints as purely perspectival (and hence too parochial to satisfy all people) is true, then there is no reason to accept postmodern epistemology. This is so because the tenets of postmodern epistemology, including those just mentioned, are themselves perspectival and hence cannot be absolutely true. So, postmodern epistemology refutes itself; it logically contradicts itself.

This has always seemed to me to be a valid objection. The problem is that too often this is the only objection raised against postmodern epistemology. If this is our only objection, I contend that those who reject postmodern skepticism are in deep trouble. That is so for a number of reasons, but one of the main ones is revealed in the way some postmoderns respond to the objection that their views are self-contradictory and hence illogical. When confronted with this objection, postmoderns may answer that perhaps their views are logically contradictory, but so what? Why do we have to be logical? Moreover, if everyone must be logically consistent in their views, postmoderns may be especially irked because those who make this demand invariably seem to think Western logic sets the rules for everyone. Couldn't there be some other logic, postmoderns may ask, and if so, perhaps that is the logic that binds all of us. Western critics of postmodern epistemology seem oblivious to such possibilities, and postmoderns find that especially disturbing.

If postmoderns answer the complaint that their epistemology is self-refuting by asking why we must be logical, we must first understand the exact nature of the postmodern's question. Though we might think the question about being logical is unambiguous, I contend that it is in fact "shorthand" for a number of different issues. Each issue raises a distinct objection for *anyone* who rejects postmodern skepticism and thinks there is absolute truth that can be known. In what follows, I want to explain the many different things a postmodern may be saying when he or she asks us why we must be logical (and why it must be Western logic, if indeed logic is required). But I must do more; I want to answer each of those objections, for in doing so, I believe that we can refute many of the ideas that move and shape postmodern skepticism and its rejection of Christianity.

Of course, postmoderns may hear our answers and reply that they just don't care about the answers we offer. For example, if the Christian offers a reason and/or argument as to why the law of noncontradiction must be taken seriously, the postmodern may respond that one should take such an argument seriously only if one is impressed by views that assume there is truth and that we can know what that truth is. Those who reject such assumptions may hear our explanation of why we shouldn't ignore the law of noncontradiction, shrug their shoulders, and say, "So what?" or "You have an interesting point, but it doesn't move me at all."

Students often ask what I would say if a postmodern answered my argument with either of these responses. I reply that we can't convince everybody. If we offer a cogent and compelling argument, the postmodern may agree that it is compelling but respond that he doesn't see why anyone must hold beliefs that are cogent and compelling. Hence our argument doesn't impress him at all. In such a case there may be nothing more we can say. Sometimes it is time to stop witnessing and defending Christianity to a particular person and move on to someone who will be more receptive to what we have to say. I make this point to say that the questions I shall address (and especially the answers I offer) aren't guaranteed to convince and convert everyone. However, for those open to reason and argument, there are convincing answers to their questions. But let me begin by listing a number of concerns on postmoderns' minds when they raise the objection about being logical.

When asking why we must be logical, postmoderns may be asking why we must follow the law of noncontradiction. Or they may be asking why we should bother with avoiding the various logical fallacies that one learns about in elementary logic classes. Perhaps instead the complaint is that Westerners don't like the idea that some things in this world are paradoxical or even contradictory; hence they always try to explain everything so as to remove apparent contradictions. Isn't it possible that there really are some things in our world that are genuinely contradictory? Or perhaps the objector's complaint is that there is some other way to learn about our world besides the use of human reason and sense perception. If so, then what is known by these avenues is not all that can be known.

Yet another interpretation of the complaint about logic is that Westerners typically assume that propositions are either true or false rather than a combination of both, and that's a problem. Here the point is not that we don't know whether a proposition is true or false, so it seems to be both; rather, the claim is that some things actually are a combination of true and false (partly true) and that we can know that this is so. Finally, this question about being logical may intend to assert that there is no reason why we should agree that we should only believe things for which we have evidences and arguments.

Clearly, this is a mixed bag of issues, and the postmodern may intend to raise any or all of them. What can we say in response to each objection?

Why do we have to follow the law of noncontradiction? In essence, this objection asks why it is a problem to incorporate logical contradictions in our conceptual schemes, writing, and speech. Answers to such questions involve a fundamental ontological point about our world and two basic points about language (all of them so far as I can ascertain) as it connects to our world. Hence, the linguistic points presuppose the ontological one. If I am right, this issue about the law of noncontradiction is not really about Western logic versus other ways of thinking. Let me explain.

Throughout human history people have come from various backgrounds and cultures, and have lived at various times and places. Nonetheless, all of them have lived on Planet Earth in the one universe we all know. But what are things like in our world? Has anyone ever actually met someone who was at one and the same time both a bachelor and a married man? Are there objects on Planet Earth which are at once both totally round and totally square? Is it possible for someone at one and the same moment in history to be driving an automobile in metropolitan Chicago and also getting a suntan while lying on the beach in Miami? Can I meet someone for lunch on June 1, 2012, at exactly 12:15 p.m. (central daylight time) at two physically distinct restaurants, one in Milwaukee and the other in Chicago?

You are probably thinking that such suppositions are absurd impossibilities. And you are right, but the reason you are right has nothing to do with Western logic or any other kind of logic. The questions above ask absurdities, because everyone knows you cannot be in two distinct places at the very same moment, that there is no such thing which at one and the same time is completely round and completely square, and that the normal meanings of the English words 'married' and 'bachelor' are such that no one could literally be both at one and the same moment. What the questions ask is absurd because in our world there just are not logically contradictory states of affairs.

I understand that some may think that some things are genuinely contradictory, such as freedom and determinism. But that reply seriously misunderstands my ontological point. Neither freedom nor determinism are objects, actions, or events, nor are they states of affairs. Certainly, there are concepts whose "fit" with one another may be hard to explain, and so we may think of them as paradoxical or perhaps even contradictory. But my ontological point isn't about concepts or about anyone's ability to reason and explain ideas. My point is about the things in our world—people, animal and plant life, objects, events, actions, and the states of affairs into which those things, actions, and events can be configured. When I awake in the morning, I may be confused about whether it is Sunday or Wednesday, but I know that it cannot be both during the same twenty-four-hour period. If someone asks me to explain the theological difference between justification and sanctification, I may not be able to do so, but that does not mean that I should think that, if I knew the precise definitions of these two concepts, I would see that they really are the same thing.

The ontological point I am making is that in our world, our universe, there just are not contradictory states of affairs, nor can we do something to bring about such things. This isn't so because I was born, raised, and live in the West, whereas if I were from the East, I could find all sorts of examples of contradictory states of affairs. No, there are no married bachelors, round squares, etc., in Asia. This isn't a "Western" thing; it's a thing about being human and living on Planet Earth.

So, the ultimate reason one must follow the law of noncontradiction stems from the nature of reality. But there is more to say than just this, and it rests on two points about language. The first is about how ordinary languages relate to the world. They do so by describing what goes on in it—at least that's how ordinary language intends to function. If I tell you that certain merchandise of highest quality is on sale at a very low price, how will you likely respond? Will you think that I'm just expressing my feelings, concocting a story to entertain you, or simply offering a report of what I am imagining at that moment? Depending on my tone of voice, my mood and body language, you might think that's what I am doing. But ordinarily, when someone makes such claims, they are asserting something that is true of the world. If you were to go to the store that sells the merchandise in question, you would find, presumably, that what is happening at the store matches or corresponds to what I said about it. And this is usually how we employ ordinary language. That is, our language about the world relates to it by corresponding to what happens in the world.

In light of the way we use language to connect to the world, there should be contradictions in our language about the world *only* if the world actually contains contradictory states of affairs. However, as already noted, in the world there are no contradictory states of affairs, so unless we intend to use language in an entirely different way (only to express emotion, etc.), we should not include contradictions in our thinking and speaking, because doing so would misrepresent the world around us. This isn't a "Western" thing; it is a point about the world in which everyone lives and about a major purpose of the languages we speak.

A second point about human languages stems from the first, and from our ontological point. In all languages there is a way to make an assertion, ask a question, state a command, etc. Consider for a moment making an assertion. In every language I know of (and I've asked those who know languages I don't know about this), to make an assertion one affirms/states either that something is the case or that it is not the case. To make an assertion is to say that something is true of the world while other things are excluded. For example, to say "I am present at school today at 1 p.m." says that I am not also at the same moment somewhere else. For anyone, including myself, to understand my assertion, he must implicitly understand the rule of noncontradiction even if he can't state that rule. For example, when I utter the sentence above, I must understand that saying I am at one place means I cannot be at some other place (far removed from where I am) at the same time. If I don't presuppose this point when I speak, then I may in fact be claiming to be several places at once even if I promise to be only at one place at that very moment.

Likewise, for someone to understand what I mean when I promise to be at a given place at a specific time, she must also implicitly understand and use the law of noncontradiction. If she doesn't, she may think I'm claiming that I'll be at two places simultaneously or think I'm just speaking gibberish when I say where I'll be. So, if I don't presuppose the law of noncontradiction when I speak and/or if you don't presuppose it when you interpret what I say, it will be very difficult to know how to respond to me.

Consider another illustration of my point. Suppose I ignore the law of noncontradiction when I ask you a question. Suppose I say, "Tomorrow at 11:30 a.m. I'll be in downtown Nice, France, and in Sydney, Australia—won't you join me for lunch?" My question, of course, implies that I can be at two entirely different places at the same moment, and that's a contradiction. However, having become annoyed by this rule about logical consistency, I decide to ignore it and think differently; hence I ask you the question about meeting me for lunch at two different places at the same time.

How should you answer my question? How could you even know *what* I'm asking you? Since my assertion followed by a question incorporates one contradiction, why couldn't it include another? If I suggest that I'll be in two hugely separated (by geography) places at once, perhaps I am also asking you both to join me for lunch and not to meet me for lunch at that time. Or perhaps I'm not including two contradictions but only the one most apparent. Perhaps as well, since I've freed myself of the responsibility to abide by the law of noncontradiction, what I really intend is to be in Rio de Janeiro tomorrow at 11:30 a.m., and I just figure that I don't even have to mention that in order for you to decide where to meet me. How would you know what I'm really asking, and how could you respond? Likewise, however you might respond, should I or shouldn't I expect you for lunch tomorrow, and if I should, where exactly should I meet you? Answers to such questions would help me (and you) know whether to buy an airline ticket to France, Australia, or Brazil; who in their right mind would buy three airline tickets—one to France, another to Australia, and a third to Brazil—for roughly the same time on exactly the same day? But if I can ignore the law of noncontradiction when I speak, and if you are free to do the same when you listen and respond, how can we communicate, and how can we know what course of action to take in relation to tomorrow's lunch? Communication seems clearly to be jeopardized in a dramatic way, dramatically enough so as to paralyze action—at least any action that could stem from our interchange.[2]

What is critically important about these examples is that I am *not* making points about Western languages *alone* but about the way all languages work. If that were not so, i.e., if, for example, English presupposes the law of noncontradiction but Chinese does not, then when English speakers learn Chinese, they would have to learn not only the rules of the language but also a new understanding of logic and its rules in order to know how to use the new language. But even if we learn the new logic and then, using an interpreter, speak in English to our Chinese friend, how will we know what to say and how to say it, and how will the translator know what to tell our Chinese friend about what we are saying? Talk about "lost in translation"! In this case, how can translation even begin!

As readers surely know, learning a new language such as Chinese or English doesn't involve learning a totally different logic (and hence ignoring, e.g., the law of noncontradiction because the new language does). This point must not be misunderstood. I am not suggesting that beliefs about the world in general (or some worldview in particular) are exactly the same from one language and culture to another. I'm talking about something much more fundamental than the major concepts of one's noetic structure. I'm talking about the most basic rules that govern how to ask a question, how to make an assertion, how to make a command, etc. These are rules which all of us implicitly follow by using language at all—they presuppose *nothing* about one worldview being a more accurate description of reality than other mindsets. They refer instead to the basic ground rules for using language at all, understanding that it is in language that we express our worldview.

If a language did not presuppose the law of noncontradiction, then it would have to tell us how assertions are made in that language or we would not know (in learning the language) that assertions are made in a different way than in Western languages. Hence, in point of fact, everyone presupposes and uses the law of noncontradiction when using language. If not, they need to state how else they can make an assertion in their own language. And of course, if we are to understand what they are saying, we will presuppose the law of noncontradiction when we interpret what they tell us about how to make an assertion in their language. If we are wrong in that assumption, then we won't even be able to understand their instructions about how to assert something in their language! Does anyone really think it is this difficult to learn a language foreign to their mother tongue?

Finally, this objection that says it isn't necessary to use the law of non-contradiction is itself an assertion whose meaningfulness relies upon the law of noncontradiction. That is, no one who hears the objection can understand it if they don't interpret it using rules for making assertions, rules that incorporate the law of noncontradiction itself. In addition, anyone who has understood my discussion of this objection shows that my point about the law of noncontradiction is correct, because I wrote this section presupposing and incorporating the law of noncontradiction in my thinking and writing. That I incorporated the law of noncontradiction as I wrote should surprise no one. That's just how languages work—all of them. It's not just a Western thing!

Why must we avoid committing various logical fallacies such as question begging? If you have ever taken a course on how to reason and about errors in reasoning to avoid, you can identify with this question. Many people would agree that faulty reasoning must be avoided, and that reasoning that incorporates logical fallacies cannot be true.

Unfortunately, some people are so skeptical about reason's abilities that they believe that avoiding errors of reasoning isn't something we can do, so we need to just accept that fact and move on. Others may argue that even though we can identify errors in reasoning, what difference does that make? Even if a piece of reasoning contains a logical fallacy, they ask, couldn't it be helpful, even true in some sense? If someone finds helpful a specific piece of reasoning (in a speech, book, or article, e.g.), then what difference does it make if it contains some errors in reasoning? Surely no one is harmed, is he, when someone includes in his thinking one or more of these fallacies?

While an error in reasoning may damage only a small portion of what one believes rather than invalidating her whole worldview, that doesn't mean anyone should accept such "sloppy" thinking. If the one committing the error thinks that what she says is true in a correspondence sense of 'true,' then she is sadly mistaken, and any conclusions or actions based on the faulty piece of reasoning need to be reconsidered. Even if one works with a pragmatic notion of truth, why should we be optimistic that a set of beliefs really will "work" if it is riddled with logical fallacies? The ultimate issue here, in a sense, is whether one wants to believe (and act in accord with) things that don't match the way the world is. We can choose to live in a *fantasy* world of our own construction, but our fantasy world won't necessarily help us with any challenges and opportunities we face in the real world.

So, avoiding logical fallacies is important in the ways just explained. But it is important in other respects. The objection we are considering assumes that no one will be hurt or suffer damage if we include errors in reasoning in our thinking. I strongly disagree, and I can most easily make my point by offering examples of how people from varying cultures would in fact agree that logically fallacious reasoning can be harmful and is unacceptable. In fact, I contend that they would reject such fallacious reasoning even if they had never heard a formal name or definition of any of the various fallacies. This is so, I believe, at least in part because, again, we are not talking about something that is peculiarly Western, but about something that is peculiarly human. That is, regardless of our ancestry and culture, all of us are human beings and all of us come with the same basic human equipment for learning about our world—a mind that can reason and senses by which we can perceive our world. Through training and practice, some of us more than others develop our abilities to reason, but everyone can do so to some extent. Moreover, even if someone isn't thinking about avoiding fallacious reasoning, in a practical situation he can still recognize that an error in reasoning has been made, even if he can't name or define the specific error. Let me illustrate these points.

Imagine two scientists, one in the United States and another in China. The Chinese scientist invents a kind of fuel that powers rockets ten times faster than any other fuel ever has. This scientist also redesigns rockets so that humans can fly at accelerated speeds without any damage to their physical well-being. In his home country, the scientist gets patents for these inventions so that he will be fairly compensated for any financial gain that comes from his inventions. In addition, he secures the patent rights to this technology as it will be used by other scientists and other nations.

Imagine as well that at the same time a US scientist, independent of the Chinese scientist and his work, makes a similar set of discoveries/inventions but learns that the Chinese scientist beat him to the patent office. The US scientist files a lawsuit against his Chinese counterpart, claiming that because he (the US scientist) made discoveries that are similar to those of the Chinese scientist, the Chinese scientist must have actually copied the US scientist's work. Hence, all financial proceeds should go to the US scientist. The lawsuit goes to trial, and the argument is presented that because both sets of inventions are similar, the work of the Chinese scientist is not his own, but actually is "borrowed" from the US scientist.

Would the Chinese scientist (or his lawyer) buy this line of reasoning? Would the judge or jury (assuming there is a jury in this case) buy this argument? If they do, the Chinese scientist loses the case, and the results aren't harmless financially or otherwise. Surely, however, the Chinese scientist and/or his attorney will point out that just because two people come up with the same idea, that doesn't mean one got it from the other. Moreover, the attorney will argue that this line of reasoning can't be true, because the two scientists never met and never heard of the other's work until each finished his own work.

Now, the US scientist is actually guilty of committing the logical fallacy known as the *post hoc* fallacy, even if neither he nor his Chinese counterpart have ever heard of that fallacy and can't define it. The fallacy in question— *post hoc, ergo propter hoc* ("after this, therefore because of this")—is the error of assuming that because two things are similar, the one happening after the other is caused by the first.

When confronted with this erroneous reasoning, the Chinese scientist will certainly recognize that something is wrong, even if he can't identify or define the logical error. Why? Because reasoning is a function of being human, not of being Western, Chinese, etc. Even if the Chinese scientist had no training in so-called "Western logic," that doesn't mean that when confronted with this piece of sloppy reasoning, he will let it pass and lose the case. This is clearly a case where an error in reasoning (and the decision by those who detect it to ignore it) makes quite a bit of practical difference!

Imagine a second situation. Two people from Kenya who are interested in history are identified as having exceptional intellectual ability. They will surely be leaders in Kenyan society, if only they can get the proper education. An American philanthropist hears about them and agrees to pay for their education all the way to a PhD. One of the Kenyans decides that it would be better to pursue education closer to home, so he attends universities in Kenya. The second goes to the United States for his education.

Both finish and plan to pursue their life work in Kenya, but before they do, they hear that a major US university is looking to hire an African to teach history. The opportunity looks too good to ignore, so both Kenyans apply for the job. Both go through the interview process; both send recommendations and transcripts of their academic work. Finally, the university decides to hire the Kenyan educated in the United States. The other candidate has an impeccable academic record, so he is puzzled by the decision. Not knowing the basis of the decision, he decides to talk to the chairman of the search committee. He asks why he wasn't chosen. The chairman tells him that while both candidates had comparable academic records and both did equally well in the interview, the other candidate was chosen because he was educated in the United States, and everyone knows that a US education is stronger than one from Kenyan universities. In fact, just looking at the two candidates' resumes, the search committee wondered whether it was even worthwhile to interview the one not chosen, because everyone knows that a US education is superior.

Would the candidate not chosen say, "You know, I agree. In fact, I should have withdrawn my application when I realized the other candidate had a US education. I should have seen that I had an inferior education and wouldn't be hired"? I doubt he'd say this. Wouldn't he at least ask how the committee knew his education was inferior? If the answer was that it's just obvious that American universities are superior to African, would he agree? Wouldn't he tell them they have assumed this but haven't proved it? Wouldn't he think they should have based their decision on the interview, especially if they had questions about his abilities and the quality of his education? Wouldn't he say that their process was unfair, because they assumed without proof that he was inferior because of where he had been educated?

Probably, he would raise such objections. Is he wrong, or has he found an error in the search committee's reasoning? Clearly, the latter is the case. He may never have heard the term 'question begging' (assuming as true without proof what you need to prove is true), nor could he define it if asked, but he has certainly recognized that the committee is guilty of it. He wouldn't think such reasoning is acceptable, and he would think this error is significant and needs to be corrected. And, of course, he didn't learn to spot such mistakes from studying in a Western university, because all of his education was in African universities.

What do these examples show? They show that reasoning is a *human* capability, not a Western, European, Asian, or African one. In a concrete situation, all people (as human and as possessing the same kind of intellectual equipment as others) implicitly recognize that certain types of reasoning maneuvers (even if they can't define them or name them) are wrong. If only certain people (people from a certain culture) can recognize and agree that errors in reasoning matter, there is a major problem. The problem is that many of these "rules of reasoning" were first taught by the ancient Greeks. Anyone who thinks ancient Greek culture is the same as or similar to American or European culture in general today is significantly mistaken. So, if you can't think this way or needn't follow such rules of reason unless you come from the culture that "originated" the rules, then no one not raised in ancient Greek culture should be able to understand and appreciate, let alone agree with, the need to avoid these errors in reasoning. If that sounds absurd (and it should), I maintain that it is no more so than saying that non-Westerners don't have to use the same rules for thinking as do Westerners, because the rules are purely culture specific. If these rules were culture relative, rather than a result of being human, the complaint would have some bite. But the rules are *not* simply culture relative, so this objection, whether raised by a postmodern or not, doesn't have the bite some think it has.[3] Unfortunately, too many in our day think this objection is devastating to the value of apt reasoning and hence are bedeviled by it. Don't be fooled—errors in reasoning matter! It's not a Western thing; it's a human thing!

Why can't you see that some things in this world are just paradoxical or even contradictory? Hence it's not always possible to explain everything so as to remove apparent contradictions. There is an element of truth in this objection, but a fundamental error as well. The element of truth is that we can't always explain certain concepts, events, actions, or states of affairs that are paradoxical or appear contradictory. But that doesn't mean there truly are contradictions in our world. Why not?

Here I can be brief since I've already made these points in answering the objection about the law of noncontradiction. The point is about the nature of language and the nature of our world. As to language, the intent of ordinary language (everyday speech) is to reflect accurately states of affairs in our universe. But if that is so, as noted already, then we can allow genuine contradictions in our language only if there are genuinely contradictory states of affairs in our world. And, as I explained above, that just isn't so.

None of this means that there aren't things or states of affairs in our world that *appear* contradictory or paradoxical. For example, how freedom and determinism operate at the same times and places is a very complicated issue. In fact, it is sufficiently so that many people can't see how the two don't contradict each other. There are other examples of things that *appear* contradictory and are very hard to explain.

To claim that two things are genuinely contradictory is a rather robust claim. That claim means that there is no *possible* way both could be true. Anyone who would defend against such contradictions needs only to show a possible way that both items could be true to answer the charge of contradiction. Of course, one should try to give an answer which is a plausible explanation of how they both could be true. But even if one can't *in language* describe how two apparently contradictory items are not so, that still doesn't prove that *in the world* the two items really are contradictory. The burden of proof is certainly on those who think there are such contradictory states of affairs, because our usual observations of the world don't show it to contain contradictory states of affairs.

All of this underscores one of the basic points I'm making, a point that is implicit in the above. That point is that when someone claims there is a contradiction in our world, we must distinguish between our world and our knowledge of our world. No one has shown that there really are contradictory states of affairs, objects, events in our world. That does not, however, mean that our knowledge is such that we can always explain how all things fit together consistently. But neither does our incomplete knowledge prove that there are genuinely contradictory states of affairs in our world.

In sum, we need to be humble about how much we understand about the world around us, but we needn't abandon reasoning for fear that things around us really are a bundle of contradictions so that reasoning and attempting to make sense of things in our world is futile. It may seem "intellectually naive" to some to believe that there are no genuine contradictions in reality, but those people must also live in the real world, not a fantasy one in which there are round squares, etc. And those same people must make decisions in the real world. At the very least, at the point of decision making such people know they can't choose several mutually contradictory options, because "after all, the world may just be a paradoxical place and so we can embrace paradox and apparent contradictions."

There is some way to learn about our world other than through human reason and sense perception. Hence what is known by these avenues is not the only thing to be known or the only way of knowing. We postmoderns know things in ways other than reason and sense perception, and once that is granted, why must we come to the conclusions of those who reject postmodern epistemology? The reply to this objection is quite straightforward. What is proposed *seems* possible, but is it actually true? Let the objector explain what other way of knowing there is, what other equipment we have for learning about ourselves and our world besides the mind and the senses we possess? It is not enough merely to propose that there is another way of knowing; one must explain what it is and how it works, give evidence and argument that there is such an alternate method, and explain how one knows it to be reliable. And, of course, if there is any hope for the rest of us to understand the explanation, the critic needs to offer this information using reason and sense perception. It's hard to imagine what an alternate way of knowing would be or what evidence for it there is. It is even harder to imagine why we should adopt it, since the critic must explain and defend it using the reasoning and sense perception he hopes to replace! If normal ways of knowing really do work to explain this "other way of knowing," then why do we need this different way of knowing? Still, if the critic offers explanation and evidence, then we can evaluate what is said. Otherwise, the critic needs to drop the objection.

Westerners typically assume that propositions are either true or false rather than a combination of both, but why should we think this is so? Here the point isn't that we don't know whether a proposition is true or false, so it seems to be both. Rather, the claim is that some things are actually a combination of true and false (partly true) and that we can know that this is so.

In reply, we must first distinguish between our ideas/concepts and descriptions of things, on the one hand, and the things and states of affairs themselves. It is undoubtedly true that there are many concepts each of us holds that are partially correct and partially incorrect. It is also true that we can't always tell which part of our concepts of things is correct and which is incorrect. But none of that means that things in the world and actual states of affairs in the world are a combination of true and false. In fact, it's hard to know what it would even mean to say that some state of affairs in the world is partly true and partly false. My point fits with what I said above about apparent contradictions and paradoxes. Don't confuse our ideas of things with the way things in our world actually are. The other point is that even in cases where we hold concepts that are partially true and partially false, it is possible through further study, observation, and reflection to correct the mistaken notions so that we hold concepts that are entirely true. If this were not so, it is hard to imagine what the point of study and education would be.

Of course, some might object that what I've said sounds good, but how can we be sure that we can discover what is really true of our world so as to correct our wrong ideas? This objection actually raises at least three issues, as follows: 1) is there such a thing as truth, and if so, are we in a position to find it? 2) does subjectivity reign so thoroughly in our reasoning and sense perception that there is no hope of knowing what is true in the world outside our minds? and 3) even if we have the ability to discover what is true of our world, how certain could any of our conclusions be? Topics 1 and 3 will be handled in chapters dealing with modern skepticism. I plan to address topic 2 in chapter 4. However, assuming that we can handle these three issues so as to uphold truth, what I've said in the previous paragraphs of this part of this chapter answers the objection about some things being partly true and partly false.

Why should we agree that we should only believe things for which we have evidences and arguments? Here several replies seem appropriate. I note first that it seems fairly clear that what we think and believe does govern our actions. Second, I suppose a lot depends on whether you prefer to believe things that match the way the world actually is, or whether you think it is acceptable to believe just any old thing, even things that are based on fantasy rather than fact. Though we may enjoy thinking about, believing in, and even trying to govern our lives in accord with fantasy, at some point we do have to live in the real world. Hence, since what we think does affect how we act, and since we do have to live/act in the real world, it is only natural that we should believe and act in accord with things for whose truth there is evidence.

This should not be misunderstood. I am not saying that we personally must have worked out a line of argument and evidence to "prove" everything we believe. There are many common sense things that all of us believe but for which we have never worked out a line of argument; such things don't need that kind of "proof." Examples of such common sense beliefs about the world are: the world didn't begin to exist just five minutes ago; if you cut off my head, no one can sew it back onto my neck and bring me back to life; there are things that exist outside my mind; etc.

As for beliefs that are not about common sense things, for many of them our "proof" is not a lengthy argument but only that when we try to live in accord with such beliefs, our experience shows that the beliefs are correct (or at least workable). On the other hand, there are beliefs we hold that aren't common sense beliefs and which we don't verify everyday by our experiences. They tend more to be about things that are abstracted from the "nuts and bolts" of everyday living; they aren't always easy to verify or falsify by empirical investigation. But they are significant beliefs—beliefs about the meaning of life, God's existence, morality, etc.—and they do affect the way we look at the world and lead our life. If there is evidence that such beliefs are false (that they don't match our world), why would one want to hold them? At some point all of us must live in the real world! Of course, in some cases there is little evidence that fantasy beliefs are false, but we also don't have evidence that they are true. In such cases, why would we try to live in accord with those beliefs? Having to live in the real world and confront real situations does seem to force one at some point to try to ascertain whether there is any reason to hold such beliefs, other than wishful thinking.

So, in answer to this challenge, I suppose that all of us are welcome to believe anything we want. If we choose, we can try to live in a complete fantasy world. The problem is that we don't actually live in a fantasy world. Trying to apply fantasy beliefs to the real world and seeing that they don't work should eventually convince us that we would be wise to live in accord with beliefs for which there is a rational and/or evidential case. Of course, none of this tells us how much and what kind of evidence is enough, nor does it tell us how to know when we have sufficient evidence. These issues, along with the issues of truth and certainty, form the basis of later chapters.

Chapter 4

Answers to Postmodern Skepticism (II): Objectivity, Subjectivity, and Apologetics

In the previous chapter, I offered reasons for being logical in one's approach to the things we believe. Whether or not any postmodern would agree, after reading my responses, that it is necessary to be logical is not predictable. My uncertainty is not because the answers offered don't really answer the postmodern's objections. Rather, a postmodern skeptic might reply that though what I've been saying makes sense, there is still no room to talk about absolute truth of any point of view or about proving as true or even confirming as most probable any worldview. The reason is that our subjectivity precludes human beings, believers and nonbelievers alike, from knowing the world as it really is and from proving anything conclusively about what we ought to believe. It would be nice to obtain objective truth, but, according to postmodern skeptics, that just isn't possible.

Though it might be tempting to offer explanations of why there is objective truth, truth that humans can know, I suggest that we slow down. My reason is that the issue of objectivity and subjectivity is ambiguous. That is, raising this issue raises potentially a series of distinct philosophical questions, and we must be clear about what those questions are and about the one(s) the postmodern is raising. Moreover, in common parlance as well as in philosophical discussion, the terms 'objective'/ 'objectivity' and 'subjective'/ 'subjectivity' are used in a variety of ways. So, we must begin by clarifying what these terms mean as they relate to the issue(s) involving objectivity that we are to discuss. I propose to begin by defining the terms.

Defining Objectivity and Subjectivity

The terms 'objective' and 'objectivity' have a variety of uses. Someone, for example, might say that her teacher is an objective grader. On another occasion, someone called for jury duty might disqualify himself from a particular case because he knows the defendant, and that makes it impossible to decide objectively whether or not the accused is guilty. Then, someone else might claim that she believes in the objectivity of truth and of moral values and norms, and also affirms that a world objective to our minds exists. Someone else might hold that we cannot know the world around us objectively, because that requires knowing the world as it is in itself, and if we are to know anything about the world, what we know will involve how things in the world appear to us. And, finally, an ethics professor might claim that in determining one's moral duty to others, one must treat others as subjects, not as objects.

The different senses of 'objective', 'objectivity', 'object' (and their counterparts 'subjective', 'subjectivity', 'subject') illustrate the point that these terms do not have an invariant meaning. Depending on the context, they may be used to say some things that are very distinct from other uses of the terms. I suspect that most of us have heard the terms used in the ways represented by the sentences in the previous paragraph. Still, we may not be entirely clear as to the exact sense of each use, so let me offer some help.

Saying that a teacher is an objective grader means she is fair and unbiased in her grading. She doesn't assign grades on the basis of her emotional response to students but on rational grounds, and she is impartial to all. If a student defends some claim, the teacher will evaluate the student's work on the basis of whether the student's arguments meet the requirements of reason and argument for a rationally acceptable case.

Then, the withdrawal from jury service mentioned above uses 'objective' in a related but distinct sense. The person who refuses to serve does so because he knows that jurors should be fair, unbiased, and open-minded to all evidence. He is concerned that he can't be fair, because he has a "connection" to the defendant. Thus, he can't hear the evidence in a detached, uninvolved way; he has a personal stake in this case because he knows the defendant well.

The person avowing belief in objective truth and the objectivity of moral values and norms is using the terms in yet a different sense. Believing in objective truth means that one believes that some things outside of the mind are true of the world around us. They don't depend for their existence on whether we or anyone else knows them. Water in its liquid form gets things wet, even if the person thinking or uttering that thought has no contact with water. As applied to morality, a claim to believe in the objectivity of moral rules means that moral judgments like 'murder is wrong' are true, not because we as individuals or corporate society have decided that murder is immoral. Rather by the very nature of things, apart from anything we may think about it, murder is wrong.

Similarly, to say that there is an objective world outside of our minds is to reject idealism in its various forms and accept some form of realism. A realist believes that when she observes a tree, a lake, or other people and their actions, they really exist outside of her mind. As a result, whether she observes those things or not, they exist, and they do so as more than concepts in anyone's mind. In contrast, an idealist claims that what we observe and think are our ideas about things. For some idealists, concepts are all that exist; the things of which they conceive do not exist outside of our minds. For others there is a world external to the mind, but for any of a variety of reasons (depending on the specific idealist thinker) we do not have contact with the world. Sense perception is connected to the world, but even so, it is not the world we see or hear directly but rather concepts derived from our sensory experiences.

The sentence about knowing the world as it is in itself relates to what I have been saying about the objective world, but it goes further. In this case, it is assumed not only that there is a world outside the mind, but also that one must distinguish between that world as it appears to us and the world as it is in itself. This distinction, of course, goes back to Kant's distinction between the thing-in-itself and the thing as it appears to us. The latter is an object of knowledge, i.e., we can know things about the world around us as they appear to us. The world in itself is the world apart from any knowing person. Obviously, the world apart from the knowing subject or person is something we cannot know. Still, this fact doesn't make it impossible to speak intelligibly about things-in-themselves.

Then, the ethics teacher's claim that people must be treated as subjects and not objects means that they must be deemed to be persons, capable, as are we, of interacting with other persons and the world. Persons must not be treated as things (objects in that sense). Mere objects don't think, act, or interact with others. They don't have a point of view or a mind and will capable of making choices and implementing them. They are commodities, not persons, so the way we treat them must be different from the way we handle persons.

In sum, we have seen 'objective' and 'objectivity' used in the following senses: 1) fair, unbiased, based on reason rather than emotion, impartial; 2) disconnected and disinterested;[1] 3) true of the world outside our minds and not depending for existence on anyone's thinking of it;[2] 4) as it is apart from any knowing subject; and 5) things, not persons.

In addition to these different senses of objectivity, there are several other notions of objectivity that have been proposed by various thinkers. Most of these notions actually focus on how objectivity is to be obtained, rather than offering an entirely different sense of objectivity from the five mentioned above. Let me offer five examples.

First, Peter Kosso offers a notion of objectivity that we may call objectivity as epistemic independence. Kosso refers to Israel Scheffler's *Science and Subjectivity*[3] as his starting point. Scheffler claims that evidence, for example, is objective "if its gathering is independent of that for which it serves as evidence."[4] As Kosso notes, scientists may have this kind of objectivity at several points in their work: 1) observation of data, in that any given observation claim can be tested against the empirical facts of observation; 2) the independence of sensory systems as a physical kind of independence, so that what we sense through our senses need not have any impact on what we think we are hearing, tasting, or smelling; and 3) epistemic independence between theories.[5] Kosso's paper is an extended discussion of *how* to do science so that the results will be considered epistemically independent and hence objective.

H. E. Longino also writes about objectivity in science. He distinguishes the objectivity of scientific method and the objectivity of individual practitioners of science. The objectivity of scientific method relates to whatever logical and systematic procedures science relies upon in accepting a theory and incorporating it into the larger body of scientific knowledge. As Longino notes, individual practitioners of science aren't necessarily working objectively just because they follow standard scientific procedures; it is possible to follow those procedures and interject personal preferences into the research to a point that those preferences color what the scientist observes and concludes.[6]

Despite the possibility that subjectivity might mar the work of a scientist, something about the way scientists do science fosters objectivity—scientists don't work in isolation from the whole scientific community, and their work is public. That is, the empirical data with which scientists work is available to all, and so are the theories that are constructed and tested. This means there is an intersubjectivity involved in the way science is done that fosters objectivity. Longino recognizes that these factors don't mean that scientists' conclusions are infallible. But the intersubjectivity of scientific inquiry raises significantly the likelihood that scientists are not simply reading the data, etc., in light of their own scientific preferences.[7]

Mark Bevir offers a notion of objectivity closely related to Longino's, but it is more explicit about how such objectivity is to be achieved. Bevir writes specifically about the work of historians. It is always possible that a particular historical interpretation may be wrong for any number of reasons, including the fact that empirical data that would confirm or disconfirm a theory are simply unavailable to the historian. That concern plus the fact that historians' presuppositions can impact their interpretation of an event might seem to make objectivity in any sense impossible. Bevir disagrees and explains that an objective historical interpretation "is one we select in a process of comparison with other interpretations using rational criteria."[8] His suggestion is quite close to objectivity as intersubjectivity presented by Longino, but Bevir adds that "objectivity arises from criticizing and comparing rival webs of interpretations in terms of agreed facts."[9] What counts as agreed facts? Bevir answers that "a fact is a piece of evidence which nearly everyone in a given community would accept as true. . . . Facts entail observations, and because observations stick to the world, facts too must attach themselves to the world. . . . Facts typically are observations embodying categories based on the recognition of similarities and differences between particular cases."[10]

Amartya Sen is the proponent of a fourth notion of objectivity, called positional objectivity. As Sen explains, the typical concept of objectivity holds that various observers would make the same observations, regardless of their physical location, when viewing the same thing. Their personal makeup, the kind of person they are, and their position geographically would make no difference. In contrast, Sen argues that many observations we make depend upon our position. If I'm a quarter of a mile away from an oncoming train, it will look very small, whereas someone viewing the train from fifty feet will think it is quite large.[11]

Thus, observation of physical objects is not invariant, but Sen claims that even our beliefs about nonphysical things are position-dependent. For example, Julius Caesar's belief that Brutus wasn't planning to kill him depended on what he knew about himself, about Brutus, and about the situation in the Roman government. That is, *given the information and knowledge he had*, he didn't mistrust Brutus. Of course, Caesar was wrong, but his belief depended on his position. However, that his belief was wrong didn't mean that Caesar wasn't objective in holding it. One can hold a false belief objectively, in Sen's position-dependent sense of 'objective'.[12]

This may seem odd because normally we associate true beliefs with objectivity and objective beliefs with truth. What, then, is this position-dependent objectivity (positional objectivity) of which Sen speaks? Sen doesn't offer a precise definition, but we can do so. For an observation of a physical object to be positionally objective means anyone else observing the same thing under similar or identical conditions would report seeing roughly the same thing.

What is true of observing physical objects is also true of beliefs. Anyone, for example, in Caesar's position, having the information he had before Brutus killed him, would be expected to believe that Brutus wasn't planning to kill him. The same is true of beliefs about abstract concepts. Whatever someone with a given set of arguments and evidence would conclude, for example, about the nature of freedom is the positionally objective belief about freedom, assuming that others under the same or similar conditions would conclude the same thing about freedom.[13]

A final sense of objectivity comes from Fred D'Agostino. This notion is objectivity as transcendence. D'Agostino explains that two main features of human experience motivate attempts to fashion ideas of objectivity.

Each human being is enmeshed in a particular time, place, culture, and language. If we could adopt a perspective that encompasses everything by means of transcending it all, that would address the problem of our limited perspectives. A second motivation behind ideas of objectivity is a search for an authoritative basis for our social practices. Regardless of how a particular culture does things, there is always the question of why things should be done that way and not another. At one time in Western cultures, the church played that authority role, and societies were structured and functioned according to what the church said. In more recent centuries, Western cultures have made *reason* the ultimate authority of how things should be done in individual societies. Of course, the use of reason by various cultures has not resulted in uniform institutions and ways of doing things. In part this is so because each culture is stuck in its own time- and culture-bounded perspective.[14]

One answer to these problems—generally speaking, the dominant one in Western cultures—has been to understand objectivity as transcendence. What is to be transcended is every particular perspective so that the result is a "God's-eye view"—or in Thomas Nagel's terms, "a view from nowhere" (i.e., a perspective that is tied to no particular perspective and hence sees and understands everything at once). As D'Agostino says of this notion, "Objectivity . . . is *transcendence*; our beliefs or values are objectively valid when they are or would be endorsed from a perspective . . . which transcends the particularities, biases, and contingencies of our own egocentric perspectives."[15]

According to D'Agostino, this notion of objectivity seems to undergird much of the history of Western cultures, but mere humans cannot attain such objectivity. So D'Agostino champions conversation. That is, the way to attain objectivity is not to run from what is foreign, but to seek other perspectives and to converse with people who hold them. Clearly, this elaborates a *method* of finding "objectivity" of the sort envisioned more than it offers a *definition* of objectivity.

From the preceding discussion it should be clear that objectivity has many different definitions. The five notions of objectivity originally set forth have their corollaries in five notions of subjectivity. Those five senses of subjectivity are: 1) unfair, biased, based on emotion or whim rather than on reason and evidence, partial; 2) interrelated and deeply committed to and involved with some person or thing; 3) true of the worldview constructed in our minds and dependent upon the knower for its existence as a concept or concepts, without existence in the world outside the mind; 4) known only as it appears or seems to the knower; impossible to know apart from the knowing subject; and 5) focusing on persons, not things. In addition, readers can easily identify counterpart meanings of subjectivity for the other five senses of objectivity.

So, What's the Problem?

In the preceding pages, I have detailed different senses of objectivity and subjectivity. As you read, you must have thought, "So what exactly is the problem of objectivity and subjectivity the writer has in mind?" This is a fair question, and I answer it now.

From the preceding discussion at least three distinct issues can be identified. The first has to do with the issue of realism vs. anti-realism (or, if preferred, idealism). Though this is an extremely important topic in metaphysics, and though I hold realism, I don't intend to defend realism against anti-realism in this book. I am not certain that one needs to defend realism in order to defend Christianity, but even if so, that is a complication to be handled elsewhere.

There are, however, two other crucial issues involving objectivity and subjectivity. The first involves two different senses of objectivity and subjectivity. It should be obvious that no one can know something without personal involvement of their own mind. That is, nothing can be known apart from a knower who knows it. Of course, the knower doesn't approach learning with a mind that is a blank and empty slate. All of us bring our experiences, our ideas, our culture, etc., to the knowing process, and this raises a very important question. Since all of us must be subjective in the sense of our mind being involved in acquiring knowledge, does that mean that it is inevitable that we will also be subjective in the sense that prior knowledge and experience will cause us to handle intellectual issues, along with their arguments and evidences, in a biased and unfair way? Or is it possible that although our minds are personally involved in the study of every topic, we can still handle matters in a fair and unbiased way? Can we free ourselves enough from our presuppositions to see something other than what we already believe? If we are inevitably doomed to see ultimately only what we already hold, then how can anyone really know that what she thinks is true actually matches the world around her? How can we ever convince someone who doesn't already hold our views? If there aren't good answers to these questions, there seems to be little reason to do apologetics, especially if we hoped to use apologetics to change minds and lead people to Christ.

Suppose that despite being personally involved, it is possible to handle issues, evidences, and arguments in a fair way. There still seems to be a major problem confronting anyone who thinks there is absolute truth and also believes he can make a convincing case for Christianity as true. That problem is perspectivism, as previously described. No matter how open-minded and fair we are with ideas and evidences, we cannot escape our time-boundedness and culture-boundedness. It is hard to hold ideas you have never heard of, and it is hard to escape holding ideas that reflect your time and place in history. So, no matter how fairly someone interacts with arguments and evidences, he still cannot know, for instance, "things as they really are." No mere human has a God's-eye view. So, how can we really know what is true absolutely, and what is the point of any discussion with anyone who thinks their views are the only correct ones? In light of perspectivism, how can you reasonably say not only that Christianity is right but also that it is the only true religion? Evangelical Christians think Christ is the only way to God, but that suggests to many nonbelievers that Christians just don't get the point that all of us are trapped in our own perspectives, or, worse yet, that Christians do know this but arrogantly believe that their views and their perspective are the only right ones. How can we get beyond being bound by our own perspectives?

The Problem of Theory-ladenness. For a long time in Western philosophy, the mind was thought to be basically passive in the acquisition of knowledge. This was especially the view about knowledge obtained through sense perception. Philosophers knew that sometimes our senses work in less than optimum circumstances and that our ability to see, hear, etc., can diminish over time. Thus, sense perception might in some instances distort what we think we perceive. Still, it was assumed that sense perception works well most of the time, and that what enters the mind through the senses is accurately mirrored on the mind. To use Richard Rorty's metaphor, the mind was considered to be the mirror of nature.[16] The basic task for anyone was

109

thought to be to make whatever moderate adjustments of the image in the mirror that are needed. One could then "read off" the results and know accurately what is happening in the world outside the mind.

All of this seemed right until, as noted previously, Immanuel Kant introduced his Copernican Revolution in philosophy. Kant argued that it is not just the object of knowledge that acts upon a basically passive mind, but the mind also is active in the knowing process. What one comes to know (through empirical observation or otherwise) is a result of the interplay between mind and world, subject and object. One of the first conceptual implications of this new way of understanding how people come to believe and know was Kant's distinction between what he labeled *noumenal objects* and *phenomenal objects*. If the world around us is not simply mirrored on our passive but receptive minds, but our understanding of it also depends on the faculties of the mind interacting with data from outside the mind and making a judgment as to what is perceived through the senses or apprehended through reason, then it seemed to Kant that what we actually know about the world around us is how things appear to us (*phenomena*). What we cannot know is the nature of things-in-themselves (such things Kant called *noumena*). Kant also included in the group of *noumena* things that are not available to the senses, such as the propositions of ethics, metaphysics, and theology. Perhaps the things of which those propositions speak actually exist, but Kant reasoned that they could not be objects of knowledge.

In spite of these beliefs, Kant still was basically positive about the mind's ability to learn and know. Kant believed that reason and sense perception function well enough much of the time so that we can in a basically accurate way know many things about the world around us. From Kant's day onward there have, of course, been some epistemological skeptics. It wasn't until after the midpoint of the twentieth century, however, that many turned from optimism about the mind's ability to know truth to a postmodern skepticism about truth. In a way these skeptics have simply taken Kant's doctrine about the mind being active, not passive, in the knowing process to its logical conclusion. Many in our day argue that, indeed, the mind is very active in the acquisition of knowledge, and an involved mind is not a blank slate. What we think about any new idea, argument, or evidence relies on a mind that is heavily influenced by previous and current experiences and by ideas we already know and believe.

Put simply, everyone has presuppositions about the nature of reality. These assumptions, though one has likely never made a case for their truth, result from our beliefs, our experiences in life, the time and culture in which we live, and the linguistic community in which we were raised and continue to live. When one learns a language, more than just vocabulary and grammar are embedded in one's mind. A whole way of looking at and functioning in the world is also learned. Our conceptual grid, the whole set of our beliefs about the world which have been acquired in the ways mentioned, impacts the way we understand and evaluate new ideas, arguments, and evidences. It is unrealistic and naive, we are told, to think that this conceptual grid won't influence our thoughts and actions. The mind simply is not a passive mirror.

This view that our conceptual framework impacts our understanding of what we hear, see, and think is not just a general claim about knowledge. It also applies to the various kinds of things we believe. Think, for example, of beliefs based on sense perception. We understand that the mind is not a passive mirror on which sense data from the world are imprinted like a snapshot of whatever objects confront us. The problem is not just that our senses may be weak or that they may distort things that are sensed because of the circumstances in which we sense them (e.g., a straight stick which is partially in and partially out of water may appear bent). The problem is that our mind is active in the process of sense perception. The mind makes judgments about the size, shape, smell, feel, etc., of what we are sensing. Based on prior experiences and beliefs the mind concludes that one is seeing, hearing, etc., one thing or another. But if the sense data do not themselves form the beliefs we have about what we are experiencing, and if, instead, our mind evaluates and reaches a conclusion about what we are sensing, how can we be sure that we really hear, see, etc., what we think we do? It seems that we can't, skeptics tell us. No one can simply "turn off" his whole conceptual grid when he has these sensory experiences, so no one can be sure that his beliefs about the observable world are correct.

If presuppositions govern and impact the outcome of what we hold as observation claims, how much more must this be so for propositions we believe about things that are not observable through our senses! Beliefs about love, freedom, knowledge itself, the existence of God, or the immaterial soul are not confirmable through sense experience. These beliefs are abstractions from the tangible world. Surely, our conceptual grid will influence what we think and believe about such concepts. Since everyone's conceptual framework is unique to him or her, how can we possibly hope to see things the way others do? Skeptics believe that we can't set aside our presuppositions and see things as they really are. Thus, it is unthinkable that we could confirm any worldview as correct. There may be absolute truth about the world, but none of us is in a position to know what it is and whether any of our beliefs are absolutely true.

Does the skepticism just described apply to all disciplines of knowledge? Many have believed, and still do, that at least science is the domain of objectivity. But during the last thirty-five to forty years or so, even the objectivity of science has been called into question. The reason is that one simply cannot "turn off" one's conceptual grid when doing science. Though many have held that a good part of what makes science objective is that scientists follow the scientific method of observation, philosophers of science inform us that following this method doesn't guarantee objectivity. At any given time in history, there is a reigning paradigm (a broad conception of some discipline like physics) that governs scientific thought and work. This basic way of seeing things infects even the observation of new data. There are no theory-neutral, brute facts, we are told, ready to be understood with precise accuracy by scientists. What scientists think and even what they observe is theory-laden. That is, the overarching scientific paradigm defines how science understands physics, geology, botany, etc. That basic mind-set influences what scientists understand themselves to be seeing, hearing, etc., as they gather new data. Evolutionists and creationists, for example, agree that there are many fossil remains (what counts as a fossil is sometimes debated, but both creationists and evolutionists can agree that most of the things thought to be fossils are). However, what the existence of these fossils proves about the origins of life on earth is not an item of agreement. Scientists who believe in evolution think the fossils confirm their theory, and those for whom creationism is the governing paradigm think the fossils don't confirm evolution.

According to philosophers of science like Thomas Kuhn, scientists normally work within a given paradigm. Any new data they find are to be synthesized with the accepted theory. Often new data can be made to fit prevailing understanding, but sometimes the data just don't fit. As more anomalies between evidence and theory arise, scientists increasingly become uncomfortable with the prevailing paradigm. At some point the theory fits so poorly with the data that a scientific revolution occurs. The governing scientific paradigm is dropped and a new one is adopted. An example of this sort of scientific revolution is the move from a Newtonian to an Einsteinian understanding of physics. Kuhn and other philosophers of science like Paul Feyerabend explain that this happens in part because Newtonian and Einsteinian physics are incommensurable. It isn't possible to blend the two paradigms together to make a hybrid. They just don't fit together; they have such distinct ways of looking at the world that they often don't even seem to be speaking to the same issues.

Does this mean that scientists believe the new paradigm describes reality "as it *really* is"? Not at all! There have been other paradigm shifts in physics and in other sciences as well. Einsteinian physics is likely not the end of the story. But for now it is the governing paradigm. If this is so not only for physics but for other sciences as well, how can we really know what is absolutely true, scientifically, about our world? Clearly, our subjectivity, including the commitments we have made to a given paradigm, make it impossible to speak of scientific *truth* in an absolute sense. But then, are we just left with competing paradigms that vie for our attention and commitment? Indeed, that is just what Kuhn and Feyerabend say, but they don't see this as problematic. Why not proliferate scientific theories (different ways of looking at the same thing) and bring more people to the dialogue table? The more people engaged in the discussion and the more points of view there are, the closer we come to the truth—of course, no scientist knows *the* truth in relation to his discipline. But if you increase the theories and the scientists, the truth is bound to be in the mix of what they all think—somewhere. At least that's what we are told. Clearly, the biases that corrupt other academic disciplines as practitioners work within their respective fields are present even in science. It's impossible to escape them, even if scientists try to be fair in their investigations and reasoning, and even if that involves submitting to the evaluation and critique of their work by other scientists.

The case for all of thought being riddled by subjectivity (in the sense of bias and presupposition) is only underscored by what we hear from psychology. Psychologists tell us that we have both a conscious and a subconscious mind. Often things that are in our subconscious govern what we consciously think and do. Of course, we aren't aware of this, because it is after all the *sub*conscious mind that is ruling. We are also reminded that what others say and think makes an enormous impact on both our conscious and subconscious mind. Our thoughts and deeds are governed by the opinions and practices of others much more than we know. One example is said to be the morals we adopt. Though we might wish (and even believe) that the moral rules we follow are based on an objective moral law, we are told that isn't so. Many psychologists say the morals we adopt result from pressure to conform to the standards and practices of our family, friends, and culture. But that means that morals are really subjective beliefs of the community, beliefs to which we more or less conform because we want to be accepted and affirmed by those around us.

In addition to the foregoing reasons for questioning the objectivity of intellectual pursuits, skeptics remind us that we are finite in intellect and our sense perception is fallible. The problem isn't that we know there are things we don't know, but we just don't have the intellect to learn all of them. The problem is that our intellectual powers are sufficiently finite that we don't even know how much we don't know. Moreover, we don't have the ability, or at least we don't exercise it when we could, to know when our thinking is wrong or right. Normally, we think we haven't erred, but of course, that is so at least in part because what we already believe significantly influences our evaluation of and adoption or rejection of ideas new to us.

There is another reason to be suspicious about claims to objective knowledge. Postmodern skeptics don't often raise this complaint, but it fits the general tenor of their views. The point is that for many issues that have more than one option, available arguments and evidences for or against the different answers to the topic underdetermine each of those answers. That is, there isn't enough evidence to declare conclusively that any of the opposing views on the issue is correct. This is so in part because one can make a good supporting case for each option. In such cases, whatever view one takes will likely be held as the most probable answer to the question debated, at least as each thinker understands the debate. It is not unlikely that one person will think that 55 percent of the evidence supports his position (call it option A), and only 45 percent of the evidence supports an opposing position (option B). Someone else may agree that the evidence for each position splits 55 percent to 45 percent but think that position B has the stronger evidential support. Because the two debaters believe a strong case can be made for the view they don't hold, observers wonder whether the debaters' probability judgments are correct. When arguments and evidence strongly support opposing positions, there probably isn't enough evidence to support or refute either position conclusively. In such cases, there is reason to suspect that the position one favors stems in part from nonrational factors. For example, perhaps one favors a given view because a favorite teacher, family member, or friend held the same position. Given what psychology tells us about motivations for holding various beliefs and doing various acts, it isn't at all clear that any of us are completely aware of the motivation(s) that incline us to hold the views we do. That being the case, however, isn't it likely that the evaluation of which position is supported by 55 percent and which is affirmed by 45 percent of the evidence will depend on the kind of motivational factors just noted? If so, then our probability judgments in these hard cases are likely to be governed ultimately by subjective factors rather than by "the facts of the case." Of course, this wouldn't matter greatly if the only issues that are underdetermined by the evidence are matters of little significance to us. But that is not so. It is often issues that are most important to us (e.g., does God exist; what rules of morality should we follow; which is the "true" religion?) that have opposing answers both supported by a strong evidential case. If so, the wisest approach to such important questions is to be tolerant of views one does not hold and to avoid holding any position with dogmatism. Adopting an absolutist attitude about one's own views displays either unwarranted arrogance or ignorance of the true status of many of the most important things we believe. Better to be silent, or at least agnostic, about one's views on such matters.

A final reason for thinking theory-ladenness governs our reasoning and decision making is that each person has only a limited perspective on any of reality. I have already raised the problem of perspectivism and intend to discuss it as a distinct issue, but it is also relevant to the theory-ladenness of our observations of and reasoning about the world. As critics of the notion that humans can think objectively remind us, no mere human has a God's-eye view of reality. But then, it seems wisest to recognize that with our limited perspective, the best we can do (and the "most comfortable" thing to do) is adopt positions to which we already give preferential treatment. Critics who deny that human reasoning can escape such subjectivity ask what other real option we have. To think that despite our limited perspective on the world we are still absolutely right in our thinking about God, religion, or morality is, as noted, to be either overly arrogant about or ignorant of what we can actually know.

Responses. These are substantial complaints about the theory-ladenness of all thinking. If they are right, there is little hope to escape subjectivity that would skew our understanding of and reasoning about the world. Moreover, if we cannot successfully answer these claims, there seems little reason to engage in apologetics or any other intellectual pursuits if the point of doing so is to discover truth. If presuppositions and preferences so dominate our thinking that we can't come to any conclusions that we don't already hold, then we are kidding ourselves that we are going to find truth and live in accord with it.

Though many in our day believe that because our subjective preferences get in the way, we really cannot know what is the true picture of reality, I don't think the situation is anywhere near as hopeless as critics of reason and objectivity portray it. Why that is so needs explanation, but before turning to that, I need to clarify views that I am not supporting. First, I am not arguing that no kind of subjectivity is involved as we acquire knowledge and think about the world. Surely, acquiring knowledge involves the intellectual and sensory faculties of the knower. Moreover, I am not maintaining that it is possible so totally to disconnect our conceptual framework and personal feelings about issues we investigate that we can, as totally disconnected and uninvolved observers, think about the world as a whole and about individual conceptual issues. The real question is not whether we can be personally uninvolved in the knowing process. Rather, the key is whether that personal involvement guarantees that inevitably our presuppositions, past and present experiences, and cultural conditioning will introduce so much bias and prejudice into the knowing process that we cannot possibly arrive at truth or convince anyone else of it.

Then, I must emphasize that I am not arguing for a kind of sense perception that involves the human mind as a passive mirror on which is imprinted a snapshot of reality. My point here is not just that I recognize that our senses can be defective or can be forced to function in less than optimal conditions, and so our perceptual beliefs can be wrong. Nor do I think that ideas, as we read, think, and converse with others, become mirrored on our passive mind. My point is that I think Kant is right in arguing that both knower and object of knowledge are active in the knowing process.

And I am not arguing that our reasoning abilities are infallible or that our sense perception never misleads us. Each of us is finite in intellect and ability, and we do err at times. Moreover, though I am not a psychologist, I grant that the human mind is quite complex and that the motivation for holding a point of view or thinking that a particular argument is compelling is often at least in part hidden from our conscious mind. Then, I must add that I am not claiming that all issues are conclusively decidable. I think there are real situations in which we cannot marshall evidence that supports *any* claim more than 50 percent. Our intellects are finite, and in virtue of what we are able to comprehend and learn, the evidence and argument we can assemble in regard to some issues will underdetermine every position we know of. In those cases, we won't be able to prove any view conclusively.

Finally, I also agree that there are times when, try as hard as we might to avoid it, our presuppositions and prejudices do get in the way and lead us into error. What I do maintain is that hindrances to handling evidence and argument objectively (i.e., with fairness, impartiality, and lack of bias and of a hidden agenda) do not make it inevitable that our subjective preferences always win in every debate and difference of opinion. I also maintain that we do have means at our disposal to tone down the impact of our subjective biases as we interact with the world and one another. As a result, I believe that it is possible to know what is really true (in a correspondence sense of 'true') about our world. While the situation of the human intellect's attaining knowledge is not as rosy as modern epistemology at times makes it seem, it is not as hopeless as postmodern skeptics of objectivity claim.

But what leads me to think this is so? I can begin to explain by differentiating propositions about the empirical world from beliefs that don't depend on observation of the material world. I want to argue that it is possible to handle both kinds of propositions with fairness and to arrive at an understanding of what is true about reality, but I begin with observational claims.

Many years ago I read Israel Scheffler's book (entitled *Science and Subjectivity*)[17] on this topic. Though I have small disagreements here and there with Scheffler, I have always thought that his basic approach to the issue, his belief that handling ideas with fairness is possible, and his major arguments in support of his view are correct. In what follows, I rely heavily on Scheffler. The terminology I use and the elaboration of the basic ideas are my own, but I am greatly indebted to Scheffler's work on this topic.

As can be seen from the title of Scheffler's book, his specific concern is whether the study of science is so riddled with subjectivity that we are in no position to say that scientific data, arguments, and conclusions are true in a correspondence sense. However, the epistemological issues he addresses relate to study in any academic discipline, including biblical studies, theology, and apologetics. Thus, his book is very helpful on the topic before us.

Early in Scheffler's book he deals with the question of whether observation of the world can be at all objective. He rehearses various objections to the notion of objectivity, but concludes that it is possible to observe the world, if not with pristine objectivity, in a way that is unbiased enough so that observation claims can be believed as true. At the heart of his explanation is a distinction that I find extremely helpful. Borrowing to some extent from Scheffler's terminology, it is the distinction or difference between having a category scheme and applying that scheme in individual instances.[18] Let me explain.

A category scheme is a set of general ideas—a filing system, so to speak—that allows one to sort individual ideas, objects, deeds, etc. Think, for example, of a sorting system for distributing mail at your job. The one who constructs it may make it so that it has twenty-six separate slots. To each slot is assigned a letter of the alphabet. When mail arrives on a given day, all letters to people whose last name begins with "A" go into the mail slot marked "A", letters sent to people whose last name begins with the letter "B" go into the mail slot marked "B", and so forth all the way through the alphabet. Because the mail distributer understands the category scheme and knows how to read, he or she knows which mail to put in each box.

Of course, this isn't the only possible filing system for distributing mail. Where I work, the category scheme for correspondence assigns a separate box for each professor. Since for many letters of the alphabet, more than one professor's last name starts with that letter, our filing scheme puts the full first and last name of each professor on a distinct box. Then, when mail comes, the one who distributes it looks at the addressee of each letter, finds the box that matches the addressee, and puts the letter in that box. And of course, there are other possible ways to set up a category scheme for distributing mail (e.g., each employee could have a box with a number on it, and the mail distributor would have a list of each person's name with a notation of the number assigned to that person. When a letter arrives, the distributor looks at the name of the addressee, finds the same name on the list, and sees the number that has been assigned to her, finds the box with that number, and puts the mail in that box).

As Scheffler notes, one can construct a category scheme for sorting any number of different things, including ideas about one topic or another. As it turns out, each of us has within our mind a category scheme containing the various concepts we know. All of these concepts make up our conceptual grid, our noetic structure. As we go through life, our category scheme grows as we acquire new knowledge. We don't come from our mother's womb with the concepts of a dog, a cat, a whale, a city, a farm, etc., already imprinted on our mind, nor are more abstract concepts like freedom, love, loyalty, friendship in our minds at birth. As we grow, we learn and incorporate these concepts into our basic understanding of reality. Some concepts we learn by ostensive definition. Mom points to the family cat and tells us, "That's a cat"; we drive by a farm, and Dad points to a cow and says, "That's a cow." Other concepts are clarified when we use them mistakenly. When our first child started to learn about the world, he saw some cats, and we told him they were cats. We pointed out various features of cats, including their nice, soft fur. Our son had also seen various people wear one sort of cap or hat, so he had the basic concept of a hat. And, of course, he knew how Mom and Dad usually looked, including how we looked when wearing a hat. But early on, he didn't quite have each of these concepts as clear as could be. I say this because I remember one cold and wet day when I prepared to leave for work. I decided to use a warm hat. I put on a warm, furry hat. Before I left, my son came to say good-bye. But the moment he saw me, his gaze was fixed on my hat. He pointed to the hat and said, "Kitty." That experience gave my wife and me a good laugh, but it also illustrated that concepts of distinct things have to be learned, and we may need to misapply them and have someone correct our mistake before we truly grasp the concept.

As for concepts of more abstract things, learning them will probably require more time and more experiences. In some cases we may not learn the meaning of a concept like love or freedom until we hear people use the terms 'love' and 'freedom' in a number of different circumstances. Gradually, we get the gist of what the word means (and the meaning of the concept it denotes) and begin to use it. The first few times we use the word, we may misapply it, but someone will likely hear us and point out the error we have made. These methods of learning different concepts are intended to be representative, not exhaustive.

The key point is that we don't come at birth with these concepts already imprinted on our minds. What we have at birth is the basic intellectual equipment given to all human beings (a mind capable of reason, and sense organs) for interacting with the world around them. As we experience new things, our conceptual grid grows. Our conceptual grid is our mind's category scheme or filing system for identifying and organizing the various experiences we have and concepts we learn. Throughout our lives we constantly supplement that basic scheme with new concepts and sharpen our understanding of the concepts already in our minds.

Of course, since we interact with the world using our intellectual equipment along with our specific conceptual grid, we don't come to the task of learning and knowing as an empty mirror with absolutely nothing on our minds. That means that our learning experiences are subjective in the sense that they incorporate us and our conceptual grid as the knowing subject. If we didn't have this sort of subjectivity, it would be very hard to make sense at all of what we observe. The question before us is whether this sort of subjectivity (along with the other sorts of subjectivity that we also have) makes it inevitable that we will be unfair, biased, and prejudicial in our handling of new observations and information. Though many postmoderns would answer affirmatively, Scheffler disagrees, and I think he is right. But this brings me to the other part of the distinction.

All of us have our own category scheme for interacting with the world. Those who are professional scientists have many more concepts of scientific things than the rest of us, and those concepts help them greatly to make sense of the data they observe and the conclusions they draw. But having a category scheme isn't the same thing as applying it in individual instances. A scientist has the concepts of various objects (or perhaps even of various chemical reactions he might observe in an upcoming experiment), and he may even have a strong preference for some of the objects and reactions he might see as opposed to others that could be identified when the experiment is done. When he actually does the experiment and watches what happens, is it impossible for him to identify what he is seeing as anything other than the objects or reactions he likes most? That is, when he goes to apply his category scheme (his conceptual grid) to a specific set of data involved in a particular experiment, is he inevitably doomed to misunderstand and misidentify what he observes?

The answer to such questions is clearly no. The scientist isn't doomed to get things wrong unless the actual results match the ideas and outcomes he most prefers. Typically, before doing a scientific experiment the scientist will identify his own presuppositions about what might be the result of the experiment. He does this so that he puts himself on notice that when he observes the upcoming experiment, he must be careful to look closely at the experiment and its results as determinative of what he concludes about what he has observed. Because of his personal preferences in the matter, he will likely check and recheck the conclusions from the experiments to be as certain as he can that he isn't imposing his preferences on the experiment so that he can see nothing other than what he wants to see. Of course, there are times when what is observed does match our preferred concepts, but in such cases, the scientist will likely check and recheck his reasoning to be sure that what he sees is in fact an instance of the ideas, objects, etc., he prefers.

There is a further safeguard against the scientist reading the data totally through the lens of his preferences. In cases where the phenomenon is observable by the senses, the materials the scientist works with are all public. And there are other scientists working in his field who can do the experiment themselves and see the results, and they can also check the reasoning of the first scientist. So long as they have expertise in the area of science involved in the experiment, and so long as there is no evidence that they are trying to fool the scientist who first did the experiment or that they are insincere in their reports, and even though each of these scientists comes to observe the experiment with his or her own conceptual grid with its preferences, it is possible for all of them to set presuppositions aside and see what actually is happening before them. The fact that the data are public for anyone to see and the fact that a number of scientists can corroborate or disprove the results given by the scientist who first performed the experiment serve as safeguards against the experiment being handled in a biased way. Not only can these scientists identify their own presuppositions prior to doing the experiment, but they must also ground their conclusion in specific aspects of the data before them. They cannot reach a conclusion and support it with nothing tangible in the experiment and expect their colleagues to agree with them. None of these safeguards makes it impossible to err, but they help to identify mistakes and remove them.

What I am saying about observation in science is also true of observation claims in other academic disciplines and in ordinary life. Data to confirm or disconfirm our observation claims are public and are available to anyone who cares to examine them. None of this means that it is impossible to be mistaken, but only that there are ways to guard against error.

Some may respond that this cannot be so once we remember Kant's distinction between things-in-themselves and things as they appear to us. The true nature of some tangible things can be camouflaged to fool us, but that is not the point of Kant's distinction. Rather, even when we detect efforts to conceal the true nature of a given object, for example, we still can't see the object as it is apart from our perceiving it. And so, the argument goes, we can't really be sure that we understand the exact nature of whatever we are observing.

Though this line of argument may impress some, I have never found it very compelling. Moreover, I think it is dubious that Kant ever used this distinction to sanction skepticism about knowing anything in the material world. My main concern, however, is why we should imagine that things as they are in themselves are significantly different from what they are as they appear to us. Let me illustrate this point. Consider first the incident recorded in the Old Testament book of 1 Samuel which involved King Saul taking a sword and falling on it (1 Sam. 31:4). Undoubtedly, Saul believed that the sword was made of some solid metal, he believed that it was sharp, and that it could be used to pierce one's body. Depending on what part of the body was pierced, the result would likely be the death of the person being attacked. Wouldn't it have been odd, however, if Saul had paused before he fell on the sword and thought to himself, "I suppose that I perhaps shouldn't do this because my intent is to kill myself, but this sword may not do the deed. It looks solid and sharp, but that's just how it appears to me. Maybe as it is in itself, it's made of jello or pudding [please grant me the suspension of your disbelief; I know there was no such thing as jello in Saul's day]. Perhaps I should try some other way to kill myself. I'd look awfully silly if I fell on this sword and it collapsed in a sticky, runny mess. I should be skeptical about whether in itself this is really a sword."

Should Saul seriously entertain such doubts? Does he really have grounds for doubting that he knows the truth about the nature of this sword? Of course not. Granted, the sword in itself does have one important difference from the sword as one views it; as it is in itself, it is unviewed. But that just isn't a difference that makes any difference in what we think of the sword and how we might use it. Is it really very probable that what we think the sword is like, as we view it, is contrary to the true nature of the sword in itself? Of course not. If Saul wants to commit suicide by falling on his sword, he shouldn't hesitate out of uncertainty that it might not actually have the qualities swords are thought to possess.

Consider another illustration. For as long as I can remember, I have had a left hand. I've found it useful for any number of tasks. I have supposed that it could be used to do such deeds, and as I've watched my left hand, I've seen it do a number of things. Of course, I've never seen my left hand as it is in itself, because as it is in itself must by definition be something unseen by anyone. Since I've never seen it as it is in itself (I'm not talking about what's there if you cut open my skin; a doctor could amputate my left hand so that we could see what lies beneath the skin, but that still wouldn't be seeing my hand as it is in itself), should I think to myself—"I should be careful about what I do today. I'm supposed to teach a class, and I know how in the past I've used my left hand to help me do that. But since I can't see my hand as it is in itself, perhaps while I'm teaching, my left hand will start singing the "Hallelujah Chorus" from Handel's *Messiah*. I know this sounds crazy, but since I can't see my hand as it is in itself, perhaps it actually contains a voice box and can sing. So, I need to be on guard at all times for what my left hand might do." Should I seriously entertain such doubts? Of course not, and if I did, you should think seriously about getting me to a psychiatrist!

I trust that my point is clear enough. Though we can't know things as they are in themselves, we shouldn't think that they are so dramatically different from what they appear to be so that we really know very little if anything about them.

Let me return to the distinction between having a category scheme and applying it. My point, in agreement with Scheffler, is that having a category scheme does not determine into which slot each item I'm sorting will go. It is possible to have our mind with our particular conceptual grid engaged in acquiring knowledge without its being certain and guaranteed that we will treat evidence and argument in accord with our personal biases. Let me illustrate this point.

At a very early age, I learned that there are cats and dogs in the world. In learning that, I of course acquired the concepts of a dog and a cat. If neither of those *concepts* was firmly in place in my noetic structure and a cat walked into a room where I was, I would have no idea of what that moving furry-looking thing was. I need a filing system that has "slots" labeled "dog" and "cat" in order for me to identify it as one or the other animal when I see it.

Now as it turns out, I have a strong preference for dogs. I don't hate cats, but I have very few positive thoughts about them. I have owned a dog, but never a cat—I can't imagine myself ever owning a cat. They are just too aloof and independent, and their actions are too unpredictable and mysterious for me to like them very much. Suppose I was teaching a class, and into the classroom walked a cat. Would the fact that I strongly prefer dogs over cats *force* me to identify the cat in my class as a dog? That is rather unlikely, and even if I should at first say that the animal is a dog, all the evidence that it's a cat is public. If I'm really determined to identify the animal as a dog, you could point to various features of the animal that show that it's a cat. If the animal made a sound, you could point out that it didn't bark—it meowed. If I'm unbelievably stubborn about this, you could have a geneticist show me the difference between dog DNA and cat DNA. He could then take a DNA sample from the animal in question, analyze it, and show me that it matches the DNA of a cat, not of a dog.

It is certainly possible that I'm right that the animal in question is a dog, even as it is possible that the whole class has agreed to let a dog loose in the class and then each student will affirm that it's actually a cat in an attempt to fool me. But how likely is it that this is so? If my students were trying to trick me, that wouldn't overturn the public evidence to the effect that this is a dog. And before too long there would be public evidence that the class is playing a trick on me. My point is not that human observational powers are infallible, or that in every case of observation it will be perfectly clear as to what is being observed. Sometimes we view something and we are confused about what we see. My point is that this doesn't happen most of the time, and when it does, it is usually rather easy to find evidence (publically available to anyone who observes it) that will help us identify this thing correctly. If what we see is something we have never seen before and something of which we have no concept, it wouldn't be impossible for someone familiar with the thing in question to teach us a new concept and show us how to identify what we are viewing as an instance of that thing.

Hearing the above, a skeptic might reply that he can grant what I have said about observational claims. However, the things we are most likely to debate and disagree about are not things that are observable in any ordinary sense of observation. How will what I have said help us to know whether propositions of Christian theology or ethics, for example, are true? Even if we shouldn't be skeptical about knowing the truth or falsity of observation propositions, none of that helps us assess the accuracy of non-observational claims.

Though it might seem that the way to address the objectivity of non-observational propositions is quite different from the way I have handled observational claims, I disagree. Though the propositions we attempt to confirm are not empirical ones, that doesn't mean no evidence of any sort is relevant to their truth or falsity. Moreover, there may be observational claims that do support the proposition in question, even if only indirectly. For example, it is granted that no human saw Christ rising from the grave. If someone had seen this, it isn't clear that he or she would have observed what went on to make him come back to life (i.e., the means or mechanism for performing this act isn't visible to human observers, even if they were present in the tomb when the event occurred). However, there are eyewitness reports from people who were present at the crucifixion that Jesus actually died, and after the resurrection, there were other eyewitness accounts of people who said they saw Jesus alive. Surely that counts as empirical, observational evidence, though of course such evidence is unrepeatable while a scientific experiment can be observed by anyone who cares to do so. Still, just because the crucifixion, resurrection, and post-resurrection appearances of Christ cannot be repeated, that does not mean that people didn't really observe Jesus die and/or that they didn't see him alive later, after his burial.

From these comments about Christ's resurrection, we should see that there is observational evidence that relates to it. Undoubtedly there are other relevant arguments and evidences for the resurrection which are not empirically observable. How does all of this relate to the problem of objectivity we are treating in this chapter? It relates just as my comments on observational sentences do. That is, in order for anyone to understand what we are talking about when we mention the resurrection of Christ, there are certain concepts that must be part of that person's conceptual grid. They include at least the concept of the physical death and burial of a human being. They also include the concept of resurrection from the dead (if someone doesn't have this concept as part of her conceptual grid, it is not difficult to teach it to her), along with the knowledge that such an event hardly ever happens. In the sixty-six books of the Bible, some instances of resurrection from the dead are recorded, but not a lot. And outside of resurrections mentioned in Scripture, one would be hard pressed to find an account of any other resurrections. So, most people have as part of their conceptual grid (their category scheme) the notion that people who die physically stay dead; accounts to the contrary are highly unusual and most likely mistaken.

Though I am a Christian, the items just mentioned about death and the fact that resurrections occur seldom, if at all, are part of my conceptual grid. But does my category scheme, or that of anyone else, inevitably force me to reject accounts of Christ's resurrection without looking at the evidence for it—just because one of my presuppositions is that dead people don't usually rise from the dead? Some people do disbelieve that Christ arose, on the basis of the well-known fact that dead people normally stay dead. But there is no inevitability that those who hear of Christ's resurrection and who examine the evidence for it will conclude that Jesus didn't rise from the dead. Skepticism about resurrections no more forces a person to discount evidence for a resurrection than does one's preference for dogs make one identify a particular cat as a dog, regardless of the evidence to the contrary. There are instances of people who didn't believe in Christ's resurrection and set out to prove it false once and for all. Much to their chagrin, after examining the evidence they were compelled by its conclusiveness to agree that, after all, Christ did rise from the dead. Here I am thinking in particular of Frank Morison and his book on the resurrection entitled *Who Moved the Stone?*[19]

What I am saying is that even if the proposition under consideration is about non-observational things, the same things that make objectivity in the sense of a fair handling of the data a possibility when dealing with observation claims make it a possibility when dealing with non-observational sentences. Evidences for such claims may not be empirical but of a more purely rational nature, or they may be a combination of empirical and non-empirical arguments and evidences. The requirement for confirmation of such propositions is that one's position must be grounded in the evidence, regardless of how much of it there is and how much it proves.[20] The key point for our discussion of objectivity is that our conceptual grid, with all of our preferences and prejudices, does not make it impossible to examine the evidence (along with others doing the same thing) for the claim in question and to come to a conclusion, based on the evidence, that differs from what we first expected and even wanted to be the case.

There is one final issue I want to raise before closing this discussion of subjectivity as theory-ladenness. It is the claim that (as applied to belief and unbelief in God) those who believe in God have an understanding of reality that is incommensurable with that of nonbelievers; their thoughts and deeds are governed by different paradigms. This means that, because people come with different paradigms, what they say about an issue may not at all address what others think and say about it. Hence, it is misguided to think we can by reason and evidence persuade people to drop their worldview and adopt ours. This is so in part because it is not clear that people working within different frameworks can understand what the other is saying.

In response, I note first that Christians and non-Christians indeed hold quite incompatible beliefs. But their viewpoints are not so incommensurable as to render communication impossible. Just as it would be possible to teach Einsteinian physics to Newton (were he alive today), it is possible for nonbelievers to explain their views to believers and vice versa, and it is possible for each side to present evidence for their position that those of opposing views can and do understand. Persuasion is not impossible just because a nonbeliever's paradigm differs from that of the believer. And the reason is not just that the Holy Spirit will help us "get through" to the nonbeliever. It is also that nonbelievers can understand what we say and can evaluate our arguments and evidence with fairness. That doesn't mean they always will or that convincing them will be easy, but it does mean that it is possible to convince them. That being so, apologists are not wrongheaded and don't waste their time when they attempt to defend Christianity to those who don't believe and have a very different worldview than do believers.[21]

Perspectivism and Objectivity. Suppose you agree with what I've said about its being possible to handle issues, evidences, and arguments with fairness (objectively) and to convince others of our views and to be convinced of views not our own. That still doesn't guarantee that we can arrive at truth, because everyone has at best only one perspective on reality. We do not live our lives simultaneously at all times, places, and cultures. At most we can hope to have an accurate understanding of the era in which we live. No doubt, many would like to have a "God's-eye view" of everything, but that isn't available to us. Hence, even if we are objective in that we handle data fairly, we cannot be objective in the sense of having a viewpoint that transcends all lesser perspectives.

Fred D'Agostino is especially helpful in clarifying what is at stake with this kind of objectivity. At least since the Enlightenment era (probably longer in Western thought), there has been a concern for objectivity in the sense of transcendence. As D'Agostino explains, the thought has been that "our beliefs or values are objectively valid when they are or would be endorsed from a perspective . . . which transcends the particularities, biases, and contingencies of our own egocentric perspectives."[22] Were one to achieve such a transcendent perspective, the great value would be that this perspective "insures against *parochialism* and confers *authority* on our beliefs and values."[23] Should one achieve such a perspective, it would allow that person to make authoritative pronouncements that could arbitrate controversies over diverse opinions.[24] As D'Agostino writes, "the key to the transcendental conception of objectivity is the idea of a *securely privileged* perspective, one which is not tied to and therefore is not compromised by the particularities, biases, and contingencies of our own humdrum perspectives . . .".[25]

According to D'Agostino, there are two broad forms of a transcendental conception of objectivity: absolutism and essentialism. An absolutist approach claims to have a perspective that is basically the same as a "God's-eye view." As a result, it incorporates everything, and claims to be supremely authoritative. There are two basic absolutist positions. One can be labeled *synthetic absolutism*, because it attempts to reach an absolute perspective by combining all lesser ones. The other is *eliminative absolutism*; it reaches for an absolute perspective by eliminating everything, including us (we become as nothing), in lesser perspectives.[26] Of course, it is hard to see how mere humans could achieve either form of absolutism. Having a finite intellect militates against a genuine synthesis of perspectives, and with our limited intellect, it is clear that we couldn't even identify and articulate all perspectives to be synthesized. As to eliminative absolutism, what it requires is impossible for humans to do. How can we possibly strip ourselves of all human characteristics so as to be left with only a transcendental perspective? The very fact that it is *our* minds that would do the required stripping should suggest that we couldn't remove ourselves and our limited perspectives entirely so as to have a genuinely absolute perspective.[27]

The other general approach to attaining a totally transcendent perspective is essentialism. As D'Agostino explains, this approach demands that we transcend only those human characteristics that are contingent, local, and biased, "being guided, in making judgments by the necessary, universal, and unbiased core that remains."[28] In other words, objectivity comes by transcending the features of our situations that are peculiar to them. If we do this, we will identify the core or essence of human nature. To achieve objectivity we need not remove everything true of our situations (an impossible task), for "all that is required is that we reduce ourselves to our essence."[29] In order for this approach to bring genuine objectivity, we would have to grasp accurately the human essence, and do the same with things we observe and think about. But how can we be sure that we have accurately removed the nonessential? Wouldn't we already need to have a transcendental perspective to feel confident that we had properly identified the essences of things?

Moreover, as D'Agostino explains, with an essentialist approach, one might hold either theism or naturalism. If the former, we would presuppose that God made us and the world to be attuned to ourselves and other inhabitants of our world so that we could actually identify the essence of all things. But where is the evidence (biblical or otherwise) that God made all things in this fashion? What happens, instead, if one adopts a naturalistic approach such as Darwinian evolution? Would evolution likely have made us aware of our essence and attuned us to the essence of things in the world? It seems harder to believe that than to believe in creationism.[30]

Having rejected the main forms of a transcendent notion of objectivity, what happens to objectivity? D'Agostino believes that all is not lost, but we must recognize that the approach of transcendence is bankrupt. We should turn instead to conversation. Conversation doesn't remove our individual and limited perspectives; it proposes a way around them so as to gain a perspective that is broader than our narrow ones. D'Agostino explains:

> How . . . are we to guard against (inappropriately) parochial judgments? How are we to attain a perspective which, through its authority, facilitates the resolution of disputes and the coordination of social activities? We are to do so, I believe, "conversationally"—that is, by a process in which each of the individuals involved articulates h/er grounds for judgment, listens to the others articulate their grounds for judgment, offers and responds to objections to these considerations, and so on; the process ending, at least sometimes, in an agreement in judgments which suffices to resolve the dispute or to facilitate the coordination of social action.[31]

Readers will note immediately that D'Agostino's proposal does not solve the problem of perspectivism, understood as a need for a God's-eye view. Certainly, conversation requires examining more than one perspective, but for the same sort of reasons that synthetic absolutism makes little sense (i.e., how could we amass all perspectives of all times and places and then evaluate and synthesize them?), conversation makes little sense. Unless all perspectives join in the conversation (or at least are represented), the most one can say is that the resultant views aren't as parochial as they would be if only one perspective were represented.

The basic problem for objectivity remains; we are all rooted in a given time, place, culture, and language. Whatever is true for us is true from our perspective, or at best with conversation, it is true from several perspectives. This must not be misunderstood. I do not advocate that we should keep our thoughts totally to ourselves and consult no one. As argued when discussing theory-ladenness, one safeguard against simply believing our preferences is that our beliefs and the evidences and arguments for them can be subjected to scrutiny by others, because those arguments and evidences are public for all to assess. So, I believe the various academic disciplines, including theology and philosophy of religion, ought to be done "in community," and I also believe that when that happens there will be conversation of the sort D'Agostino envisions. Those conversations will help us move beyond our presuppositions and preferences. What they won't accomplish is getting us beyond our limited perspective(s). The problem of perspectivism remains.

Responses. The problem of perspectivism will again appear when we deal with religious pluralism. But we can't afford to postpone discussing answers to it now. Unless objectivity in its major senses can be upheld, there is little reason to continue the discussion of defending Christianity at all. So, are there adequate responses to perspectivism as it relates to objectivity? I believe there are, and I think they can be organized around three main points. In what follows, many different points will be made, but they cohere with one of three main emphases.

First, it is true that no mere human holds or even knows all perspectives at once. What I fail to see is why this makes it impossible to know any truth. Aren't there many things we know *that don't rely on having our perspective*, as opposed, for example, to having the perspective of a French revolutionary in the late 1700s, or that of a first-century Jew living in Palestine? I believe there are many such things, but I need to explain my point and argue for it.

I begin with a distinction I shall explain in more detail in the chapter on presuppositionalism. It is the difference between presuppositions of method and presuppositions of content. The former are assumptions about the best way to go about finding out whether any proposition is true. The latter refer to presupposing actual beliefs about the world, including even a whole worldview, without ever subjecting those beliefs to critique or supporting those beliefs by argument and evidence. My concern is with the latter kind of presuppositions. Presupposing the truth of the Christian worldview, even as nonbelievers assume the falsity of Christianity, without offering any argument or evidence for it creates two problems. On the one hand, nonbelievers will see no reason to agree with Christianity, especially if we offer no defense of it but simply urge them to accept it. The other concern is that it is possible to make a case for Christianity using a variety of arguments and evidences to support its truth. If we present such a case, a nonbeliever may still reject our defense, but at least she cannot do so on the grounds that we hold it in blind faith and want her to do the same. If you have evidence to support a belief, even to the point of proving its truth, it is, I believe, always better to present the evidence rather than asking the nonbeliever just to accept Christianity without offering any evidences and arguments for its truth.

So, I don't think it is necessary in defending Christianity to adopt presuppositions of content. On the other hand, it is probably not possible to prove everything we hold, but we should at least offer a defense. Our defense must begin somewhere, and I think we should begin with presuppositions of method, that is, presuppositions about the best way to go about determining whether something is true or false.

In particular, I propose that the best way to determine what is true is to do so by using the intellectual equipment we humans are given. That includes a mind that is capable of reason, and sense organs that make sense perception possible. It goes without saying that some people have greater intellectual powers than others, and even those with the same IQ may differ in their reasoning skills. Moreover, not all sense organs in each person function equally well. Still, humans generally have intellect and reason that can be trained, and senses that function well most of the time, especially when used in circumstances that are optimal in which to operate (e.g., a totally dark room is not a good environment if you are asked to read the last lines on a page in a book). If someone isn't sure about whether this is the equipment we have, or whether there isn't a better way for humans to learn about their world, I would ask him or her to name an alternate method using other faculties and abilities to attain knowledge. It is hard to imagine what such abilities could be, especially since even to understand my point and think about alternate methods of knowing, one must use the intellectual equipment already mentioned.

Whether or not one agrees with what I am saying about presuppositions of method, one might still wonder what it has to do with perspectivism. I raise this point about choosing presuppositions of method rather than ones of content, and I make the point about human methods of learning, because I want to add that this intellectual equipment belongs to every human being, regardless of when and where (geographically and culturally) they have lived. In other words, human intellectual equipment belongs to all people, regardless of their perspective. We also noted in chapter 3 things about our world and about how all languages work and what that means *for everyone* about certain laws of logic. Hence, while a person from Asia or Africa may try to support a given belief by recounting a story that illustrates a belief, and a Westerner from Europe or North America may be more inclined to support a given belief by offering an argument with premises that lead to a conclusion, all of these people use the same intellectual equipment and follow the same basic rules of language and logic. Moreover, they must think enough alike so that it is possible to teach them (and for them to learn) about how people of other cultures and times think about the world and support a belief. There are certain ways that intellectual abilities get used in asking a question, making a statement, and supporting a belief. Methods of thinking and learning about the world have a great uniformity among human beings of all times and cultures, despite their differences in culture, language, and worldview.

All of the preceding is meant to say that if you take different people from different times, places, and cultures, it won't be impossible for them to have a conversation and understand one another. Moreover, though they may disagree about which worldview is correct, it is not likely that they will disagree about the methods of investigating such issues and of showing that one side in the debate is supported by substantial arguments while other positions have little or no evidential support.

The reason for belaboring this point about methods of discovering truth is that perspectivists claim that we have no way to decide between different perspectives on reality, which is true. Whatever we say on such matters reflects our own perspective and hence is no better or worse than anyone else's perspective. My response is that this is probably correct if all we have are differing worldviews and everyone starts with presuppositions of content. However, if the method of discovering what is true of reality requires that all of us, regardless of our perspective, use the same intellectual equipment for investigating truth claims, and if all users of the equipment at least implicitly (if not explicitly) generally agree on how to use that equipment to discover truth, then it seems that there is something common to people from very different perspectives that will allow them to learn about, critique, and support various worldviews and individual claims within those worldviews. This must not be misunderstood. I am not saying that by using this equipment there will be agreement on what all of us should believe. Rather I am saying that whatever we conclude is the correct understanding of reality, we will reach those conclusions and talk about them and the evidence supporting them using the exact same intellectual equipment in the same basic ways that our friends from different persuasions use.

In light of what I have been saying, it isn't at all clear that just because we have different perspectives from others, we inevitably will have different beliefs and won't be able to convince one another of our views. The fact that humans have the same basic equipment and ways of using it to determine what is true of the world suggests that we may find it possible to agree on more than we first thought.

Even if you agree with what I have been saying, you may still think we can't talk of absolute truth, because all any of us has is truth from our perspective. But here I must again disagree. There are many things that each of us knows that would be no different, regardless of when and where we lived. For example, I know that my first name is John. Suppose, however, that I was Asian, but there still existed the person John Feinberg. Now just because I would be Asian culturally and linguistically, that wouldn't dictate that everyone in my Asian culture would believe that the first name of this person John Feinberg is really David or Earl. I am not saying that regardless of when and where I lived, I would only ever have John as my first name. If I had lived in Scotland in the eighteenth century, my first name might have been Sean or something entirely different. My point is that the person who I am, living in this current time and culture, has the first name of John, and that is true regardless of when and where anyone else lives, and regardless of what they, considering things from their perspective, might think about my name. If a contemporary Asian were to insist that my first name is really Earl and that anyone living in a contemporary Asian culture would see it that way, I would reply that there is evidence that this is wrong. There are birth certificates; there are also people who have known me all of my life, and other evidences which, if provided, would settle the matter. And it wouldn't be settled by saying that, well, from my perspective my first name is John, but from other perspectives, it's something else!

There are other things that we could know as true, regardless of our perspective. It is difficult, for example, to imagine that propositions of mathematics and logic are perspective relative. Would someone living five centuries ago think that $2 + 2$ does not equal 4? We think it equals 4, but would a person from an earlier time and place think that's just our take on things, but the result might be something else? It's hard to make much sense of such an idea.

I would also contend that various observation statements are true, regardless of one's perspective. I am not suggesting that everything we observe, regardless of our location and the conditions under which we observe it, must be true just as we claim it is. I understand, for example, enough about relativity theory to know that if there is a bolt of lightning that strikes a train, when it strikes and where it strikes can differ for two different observers, one on the train and the other on the ground viewing the train and lightning from a distance.

My point is a much simpler one. It pertains to basic claims about what one observes. As I write this sentence, I am looking at my computer screen. I see black marks on the screen, and I quickly recognize that those marks represent letters in words. I can see that the sentence I'm thinking is represented on the screen as I type. I also note that as I type, I am touching various keys on a keyboard in front of me, and each time I depress a key, I hear a clicking sound. I conclude from all of this, since I have the concepts of a computer and how it works, of typing, and of writing a portion of a book, that I must be working on my forthcoming book on apologetics.

Of course, I may be hallucinating, rather than actually writing. However, there is ample evidence available to me to convince me quickly that I'm not hallucinating. Suppose that we could, via time travel, transport someone living in the fourteenth century AD to my study where I'm working. Undoubtedly, this person would have no concept of a computer, a typewriter, or printing, and wouldn't know what a keyboard is. Still, I can't imagine that he would say my fingers are stroking a dog and that with every stroke the dog barks and it makes black marks on the object in front of me. I think he would understand that the marks are words of some sort, even if he couldn't read. He would also know that the sound made by my touching of the keys on the computer sounds nothing like a dog's bark or the sound of any other animal. I could explain to him (perhaps with difficulty, perhaps not) the concept of a computer, and though he would probably be amazed by what he sees, I think he would come to understand that I am not petting a dog and that I am using an instrument for writing, even though he probably doesn't yet fully understand exactly what a computer is.

Suppose as well that we brought a Muslim living today in Saudi Arabia to my study, and he watched what I was doing. It is hard to imagine that because he is a Muslim he would believe that I'm sitting in front of a piano and playing a song, or that I am watching my pet camels graze on our lawn. If he were to entertain any of those ideas, it would be relatively easy to dissuade him from such notions. When I explain what I'm doing, he wouldn't respond that I think I'm writing because that's the typical

Christian understanding of this activity, but if I were a Muslim I would realize that I'm really doing something quite different. For someone to raise such questions about what I'm doing would not be an example of people from another country and holding another worldview having their own perspective on the world so that no one, including myself, can state truly what I am doing. Rather, we would think such comments likely bespeak some sort of mental disturbance. If my visitor is confused about what I'm doing because he comes from a very primitive part of the world where there is little technology and no computers, that is understandable. But if he knows about computer technology and the like, it is hard to imagine that he will think the computer monitor is a god and that I am worshiping it by stroking it soothingly each time I press a key on the keyboard. If he does entertain such doubts even after getting the explanation, we can teach him more about computers and can get him to abandon his ideas about idol worship. Of course, if we can't, we are then likely dealing with a mental disturbance. Someone with such a disorder does have a distinct perspective on life, but that's not what perspectivists have in mind when they say each of us is locked into our own way of seeing the world!

So, it seems that there are many propositions that we think are true which are true, regardless of one's distinct time, place, culture, and language in history. But what about propositions that involve things that cannot be observed with our sensory equipment? Are they also immune to differences of time and place? If the basic idea of perspectivism makes any sense at all (and it does), it makes its strongest case in regard to propositions of this sort. Propositions about whether someone is in love, whether a society is truly free, whether there is a God or not, whether my avoiding getting into a traffic accident because I was running late is an example of Providence watching over me or just good luck on my part—these are the kinds of claims that even people sharing a similar perspective on the world may disagree about. And, of course, the matters of which these claims speak deal with many of the most important things in life. So, perspectivists do have a point. The question is whether there is no hope of knowing conclusively whether one of these propositions is true or false, regardless of circumstances and situation. I believe we can know the truth about such claims, but I must explain how and why.

My initial point is that there is likely some evidential support for each of these claims. It may not be evidence that one could collect by opening one's eyes or by listening to hear something, but it might be. For example, if I believe that God has greatly blessed me in a number of ways, the claim that the blessings are *from God* won't be directly verifiable or falsifiable. That is, no one, including myself, can see God giving me a blessing when he does. On the other hand, if I say that some of the blessings God has given me are material things, I can take you to my house and show you that these things exist. Regardless of your beliefs about God, you can still see that I have these material things. Of course, the question will still be how I got them. Perhaps you will believe that I just went out and purchased them from my earnings. If instead I purchased them with a monetary gift from someone, especially if that person tells me that God prompted him to give me the money, there should be some evidence that this is true. I can show you the deposit slip for the monetary gift that I put into my checking account. I can even tell you the name of the person who gave it to me, assuming that I know, and he can show you the canceled check that he wrote to me. So, it is possible to establish by empirical evidence that I didn't earn the money but received it as a gift.

Of course, there is still a question about God's role in this. In this case, probably the best I can do is to have the person who gave me the gift explain what prompted him to do so. If the story sounds genuine, you may believe it or you may not. Probably you will want to check out other details involved, such as his circumstances and mine at the time the gift was given. The reason for doing so is that the circumstances may be such that you and I would both conclude that, humanly speaking, there seems to be no way to explain why this gift came from this person at this particular time. Hence, the claim that God moved him to give it to me, and my belief that God used this other person to bless me materially take on greater credibility. In saying that, I am not saying that all of this *proves* that God was involved. But it does lend evidence and support to my belief that he was. We may not have evidence that conclusively settles the issue so that we can say we have "proved" that God was involved, but my belief that he was has greater credibility than if I offer no evidence at all.

But is this sufficient evidence to believe that my claim about God's involvement is correct? I intend to deal with such questions in more detail when I address directly questions of truth, certainty, and evidence. In all honesty, depending on the details of the story, there may not be sufficient evidence to show me or anyone else that my take on God's involvement is true. Of course, we need to ask how the events involved would be interpreted by someone with an atheistic perspective, for example. However he would interpret what has happened, he probably would not include God in the explanation of how this came about. Perhaps he would attribute it to luck, the stars being aligned properly, or whatever. But then we must ask why anyone should believe these alternate explanations, and we should demand to see and hear his evidential support. Without evidential support of atheistic interpretations of what has happened, it is difficult to see why anyone should believe an atheistic interpretation to be probable, or even plausible. I can say, however, that if the atheist attributes my good fortune to luck, part of his defense for this interpretation must include evidence that rather conclusively demonstrates that there even is such a thing as luck, let alone that it was operating when I received the material things in question. Should anyone really believe that providing such evidence would be easy and/or convincing?

What the foregoing shows is that when someone makes a claim (and says it's true) about something that is beyond sense perception, a case must be made for each alternative interpretation of the event, action, etc., in question. Perspectivists may reply that if we try to construct such cases, the most we can expect is that explanations that come from a given perspective will most likely appear to be true when they are supported by "facts" and arguments that presuppose the perspective in question. Hence, making a case for one's interpretation will solve nothing conclusively. I am inclined to agree, if one starts with presuppositions of content. That is, if, without argument and evidence, one just adopts the perspective from which the interpretation of a given event stems, then the case built for the interpretation of the event will likely square with the perspective out of which the explanation arises.

However, we should start instead with presuppositions of method, that is, presuppositions about the best way to go about determining what is true of our world. Those presuppositions are that the intellectual equipment we possess is of a certain nature (in particular, minds that can reason and senses that can perceive the world outside the mind) and that the way such things function involves the laws of logic and argument. Hence, there seems to be something we can all agree on that is not true or false depending on your perspective. Using our intellectual equipment, we must make an evidential case for our interpretation of a given event, and so must those who hold a different interpretation. In some cases there won't be adequate evidence and argument to confirm one interpretation over another. In those cases, one must hold one's views with humility and be open to further argument and evidence. On the other hand, it may be possible to provide appropriate argument and evidence to confirm a claim as true. In the next chapters I want to discuss circumstances in which the required evidence is provided and those in which there isn't enough evidence to confirm a claim as true. For now, suffice it to say that we are not *always* stuck with no way out of our private interpretations when it comes to evaluating the truth or falsity of claims that per se are not observational in nature.

In sum of this first major point, while I grant that each person has a specific perspective that differs from other people's perspectives, that doesn't mean we know nothing as true. Just because our beliefs cohere with our conceptual grid, that does not mean that nothing we believe is true in a correspondence sense of truth. Some things are true, regardless of one's worldview. Other claims may in fact be true but are harder to confirm. That doesn't mean they are not really true or false of our world; it just means that we are not in a position to say conclusively whether they are true or false. We can see that these beliefs fit nicely the worldview of the person holding them, but we may not be able to come any closer to proving a particular belief of this sort to be true or false. That is fine. One doesn't have to prove *everything* conclusively in order to prove *anything* conclusively. And just because what we say comes from our peculiar perspective, that alone doesn't mean it must be false. Using the intellectual equipment with which all people are endowed, and employing it in accord with the rules of reasoning and argument, we can decide and show that certain beliefs are indeed true in a correspondence sense and true for all, not just "true for you or me."

I have a second major point about perspectivism. To a certain extent it is implicit in what I have already said. While it is true that each of us lives at a particular time and place in history and that each has allegiance to a specific culture and language, that doesn't mean that it is impossible to know other perspectives and to incorporate their understanding of the world in our search for truth. For example, none of us lives during the time when

Jesus walked the earth, but that doesn't mean we have no idea whatsoever of the mind-set of people at that time. The Bible helps us understand how people thought at that time and what living conditions were like then. But we don't have to rely solely on the Bible. There are other histories of those times, and there are also archaeological finds that give us further information about life at that time. This is also true of other historical eras. And it is not just our Western culture with its perspective that can be traced through the centuries of history. We can do the same with other cultures, for they too have their history, and we can learn about a culture (including its history) different from ours. It is not just those native to that culture who can and do know its history. Of course, people from another culture can teach us about their culture today and about its history.

Such information can enhance significantly our understanding of other cultures and peoples. Nothing, however, can teach about a given culture like living in it. Though we can't live in multiple cultures at the same time, we can still learn enough about them to broaden our horizon beyond our own perspective and to include their thinking in our consideration of what is the best and most accurate way to understand the world around us.

So, my second major point is that even though we do not and cannot live in all cultures of all times, we are not helpless to understand how others looked at the world and why. And there is no reason that we can't include such information in our reflections about the most accurate understanding of reality. We may still choose to see things according to the perspective with which we began, but that doesn't mean we can't and haven't considered other cultures and perspectives as we grapple with the question of which perspective most closely matches the world around us.

Regardless of your response to my first main points (that 1] despite having different perspectives it still makes sense to say we know many things as true, and that 2] just because we come with a different perspective and from different cultures doesn't mean we can't learn about their way of thinking and incorporate it into our search for truth), critics of theism and Christianity will undoubtedly reject my third point. Still, it is worth making and I believe it is true. Critics of transcendental objectivity complain that no one has a God's-eye view, a view from no specific place alone. As a result, we can see things only from our perspective and talk about what is true for us, given our particular worldview.

In response, I disagree, though this admittedly sounds counterintuitive. I can agree that the only God's-eye view of everything belongs to God himself. But there is a sense in which God's view on many things is available to and known by us. There is information about God and the world available in natural revelation. Since God created the world, it is safe to say that the information available in it in some way or other ultimately stems from God. Thus, we do have a God's-eye view on information available through natural revelation. In addition, we also have Scripture, and it contains, among other things, the words of Christ himself. Of course, Christ is the fullest form of revelation from God that we have. Now, Scripture doesn't discuss every topic from every academic discipline. Some disciplines of study aren't touched by Scripture at all. But it does tell us a great number of things about metaphysics, ethics, anthropology, and so forth. If Scripture is God's Word, in it we do have a God's-eye view of many things. Though we can't grasp every perspective all at once, God does. So whatever he tells us in Scripture isn't subject to the limitations of one perspective or another.

Hearing this, critics will complain that this could be true only if Scripture were God's Word, but why should we believe that? They will also remind us that Scripture was written by various human authors whose perspectives were limited to their time and place. Indeed, I agree that humans were involved in the writing of Scripture. The result is a book with dual authorship, but biblical authors wrote as God the Holy Spirit moved them (2 Pet. 1:19–21). They were not passive secretaries recording dictation, but his superintendence of them did guarantee that what they wrote was what he wanted written and was true in a correspondence sense of 'true'. If the writer wanted to write something the Holy Spirit knew was not true, the Holy Spirit somehow (we don't know the exact method, but we can know that this is so) kept the writer from writing that untruth. Hence, it is reasonable to believe that in Scripture we do get a God's-eye view.

Nonbelievers will undoubtedly ask why anyone should believe any of this about natural and special revelation and God's Word. Such beliefs, they think, come from an evangelical Christian perspective, so there is no reason that they should think those beliefs are true, and even those who hold such views should see them as true only for evangelical Christians. These complaints, however, don't settle the matter; they only bespeak views from people holding non-Christian beliefs. Still, Christians shouldn't just leave matters this way. What is needed is a defense of the reliability of Scripture. And since so much of the evidence for Christianity comes from Scripture, demonstrating the reliability of Scripture needs to come very early in offering an apologetic for Christianity. That in part is why I am including a chapter in this book in defense of the reliability of the Gospels. Other religions with holy books are also required and welcome to defend the reliability of their scriptures. The procedures for evaluating such claims of reliability are not Christian or Buddhist procedures. They are rather the accepted rules (accepted by literary critics, historians, etc., of all stripes) for evaluating the reliability of any literary text.

If indeed the claims of Scripture, including its claim to be God's Word, are true, then we do have access to a God's-eye view. But even without proving Scripture is God's Word, the situation as perspectivists perceive and present it is nowhere near as hopeless with respect to finding truth as they would like us to believe.

In sum, in this chapter we have discussed at length claims that are skeptical about whether disciplines like apologetics can avoid being defeated by various kinds of subjectivity. I have explained why I don't think those objections to objectivity succeed. Even if readers agree that I have answered these major kinds of postmodern objections, that still doesn't offer an apologetic for the truth of Christianity. There is still reason to wonder how one would go about structuring an apologetic for Christianity. What is the strategy for such a defense? How much evidence and what kind of evidence would be needed in order for the defense to succeed? Is it possible to be certain that Christianity is true, and if so, how? However we answer such questions, the further question is how do we know that those answers are correct? These are different questions than the ones asked and answered in this chapter. They are the subject of our next chapters.

Chapter 5

Answers to Modern Skepticism (I)

Postmodern skeptics ask why we must be logical in our reasoning. Even more, they are generally skeptical about the mind's ability to reason accurately. Part of their concern is that subjectivity will get in the way of coming to the truth, and it will make it virtually impossible to convince others that things we believe are true. Those committed to the modern mind-set are concerned about such things, but they are much more positive about reason, sense perception, and objectivity. Still, many moderns doubt that Christianity is true.

In particular, moderns find it hard to believe that there is sufficient evidence (empirical or otherwise) to sustain belief in Christianity. Hence, they typically believe that Christians simply overlook or ignore the dictates of reason and believe anyway. Many nonbelievers know that Christians believe they can defend Christianity as true. They also know that there is some evidence in support of Christianity. They just don't believe there is enough evidence for anyone to believe Christianity is the absolutely correct worldview. Nonbelievers also think there are significant counterarguments to Christianity, so doubting its truth makes sense. Moreover, even if a case can be made for Christianity, it isn't strong enough to believe that Christianity is not only true, but certainly true. For those who believe that one's eternal destiny ultimately rests on whether one's worldview is true or not, these are not questions and criticisms we can simply sweep under the rug. Postmoderns would likely have similar doubts, but even before addressing such issues, they would reject any view that claims to be "the truth" on grounds we saw in the previous chapters.

How should Christians respond to the criticisms that moderns raise? Is there sufficient evidence in support of Christianity to believe it is true? Can we be sure that Christianity is true, or must we add a hefty dose of faith to the meager (in some people's estimation) evidential support available to defend Christian beliefs? And how do believers know when they have offered adequate evidence for Christianity? What amount and sort of evidence would render it certainly true? And, whatever the answers to these questions, how would one know that those answers are correct?

These questions must be addressed. Though some may think it is sufficient to construct an argument that opposing worldviews are false (or at least improbable), that alone won't demonstrate that Christianity is true. Just because I can show, if I can, that a non-Christian perspective is internally inconsistent or that it isn't supported by evidence adequate enough to commend it to anyone for adoption as their worldview, none of that makes a case *in favor of* Christianity. At some point in doing apologetics, one must state the case for Christianity, and it had better be convincing. If not, nonbelievers, though stripped of their worldviews by our attacks on them, will see Christianity as no more believable than their own views. But how should we go about making our case, and how can we know whether we have done so successfully? What would count as a "successful" defense? These questions about truth, certainty, and evidence are the subject matter of this chapter.

What Qualifies as *Sufficient* Evidence?

Many working from the modern mind-set reject Christianity because they think there isn't sufficient evidence to believe it is true. In fact, many moderns hold that it is wrong to believe anything (religious or otherwise) unless there is sufficient evidence to support it. In an upcoming chapter on Reformed Epistemology, we shall discuss in detail two responses to this objection: the classical foundationalist answer and the answer of Alvin Plantinga's Reformed Epistemology. As we shall see, there is ample reason to reject the classical foundationalist answer, and there are good reasons to agree with Plantinga's Reformed Epistemology. But as we shall also see, Plantinga is specifically concerned to support the rationality of one belief:

belief in God. And, his concerns deal more with *de jure* issues (is one warranted in believing in God?) than with *de facto* concerns (is a belief true, and how would we know that?).

In this and the next chapter I want to address *de facto* issues, and I want to answer questions that relate not only to belief in God but also to religious belief in general. In this portion of the chapter, I want specifically to address the *kind* of argument and evidence and the *amount* of it that must be amassed for a believer to think her belief is based on *sufficient* evidence. In discussing those issues, I also intend to outline a strategy for making a case for or against any belief or set of beliefs.

When some proposition (or even a whole worldview like Christianity) is attacked, how should its defenders respond? While it is common to turn immediately to arguments or evidence in support of it, a prior question must be answered before turning to arguments and evidence. Specifically, the first step in defending any view is to clarify exactly what you are defending. In order to do this, you may need to clarify the exact nature of the opponent's attack, or you may need to think through what needs to be proved in order to confirm a given proposition or set of propositions, or you may need to do both. The reason for clarifying the issue under discussion is twofold: 1) you need to think through the *logic* of the issue you are handling (i.e., in order to support a given set of views, you need to clarify what logically needs to be demonstrated first—what is the fundamental concept from which the broader set of propositions stems—and then what follows next, etc.); and 2) if you don't think this through, you may expend much effort gathering arguments and evidences which show that something is true, but the point defended may only be peripheral to the main thing(s) that need evidential support.

Sadly, many thinkers skip this first step and move directly to presenting loads of information which may or may not be relevant to anything that needs support in order to uphold the actual belief under attack. Examples illustrate my point. Suppose someone told you that he believed in evolution and rejected creationism as a myth. Suppose also that you don't ask why he believes in evolution and why he considers creationism false and mythological. Instead, your mind moves to evidences and arguments which are, so to speak, "on the tip of your tongue." These arguments generally seem relevant, but you don't pause long enough to ask what exactly needs to be proved and whether the arguments you are about to present are at all relevant to what should be proved. Suppose that you begin to recite the ontological, cosmological, teleological, and moral arguments for God's existence. Once you present those arguments, you then turn to the question of the literary genre of Genesis 1 and 2, and then you complete your defense by pointing to various geological facts that suggest that at some time in history there was likely a universal flood that covered the whole earth with water.

To respond in these ways would be understandable. Thinking that creationism can be true only if God exists, you offer arguments for his existence. You might even think that evolution can't be true if God exists, for we don't need a naturalistic explanation if a supernatural being exists. Of course, this thought about God and evolution would be challenged by anyone who believed in theistic evolution. Nevertheless, undaunted, you reason that if you can show that the literary genre of Genesis 1 and 2 has something to do with history, then those chapters must offer a historical account of origins, one that leaves out evolution. And, finally, your appeal to geological facts stems from your belief that the Noahic flood comes with the belief in creationism, so if there is geological evidence for a universal flood, then creationism is probably true and there is no need for a theory like evolution to explain the geological facts of Planet Earth.

Though the imagined strategy would be understandable, it is misguided. Arguments for God's existence, if successful, don't disprove evolution, nor do they prove creationism. One could hold theistic evolution, or someone might simply hold a deistic view of God according to which God exists but has little or nothing to do with the universe around him. Arguing for God's existence isn't totally irrelevant, but doing so reveals a lack of understanding of the challenge posed by evolution and of what needs to be argued to make a case *for* creationism, as well as a case *against* evolution.

Then, turning to the literary genre of Genesis 1 and 2 is also of dubious worth. Even if the opponent grants that the account of origins is intended to be historical, this might simply open the door for *theistic* evolution; it wouldn't in itself prove creationism. And, even if Genesis 1 and 2 do not intend to offer a precise history of origins,[1] creationism still might be true, anyway. Neither the case for creationism or against evolution rests on the literary genre of Genesis 1–2. As to offering evidence for a universal flood, many creationists do hold that view, but there are many evangelical creationists who aren't sure whether the Noahic flood was universal or local. Certainly, it is unnecessary, logically speaking, to prove a universal flood in order to prove creation *ex nihilo*. Moreover, even if you could prove that there was a universal flood in the days of Noah, that still wouldn't disprove evolution, nor would it rule out theistic evolution.

I could continue with this example, but I trust the point is clear. The fundamental mistake in the imagined defense is failure to discern what exactly is being attacked, how it needs to be defended, how to make a positive case for the position one holds, and how such a case relates to a case *against* the view one rejects. Imagined arguments and evidences may be very believable, but that doesn't mean they succeed in defending (in the imagined case) creationism and refuting evolution.

Let me offer a second example that underscores the need to identify the exact nature of the attack before offering a defense. Imagine that you are asked to defend miracles. What would be a proper strategy for doing so? There are a number of things one could do, but they are very different responses to the challenge. For example, one might think that the critic is challenging the historicity of one of Jesus's miracles. As a response he might offer a defense of the historical reliability of the Gospels, assuming that if the Gospels are reliable, then the miracle in question, recorded in the Gospels, will have been affirmed as true.

Consider another response. Suppose the nonbeliever grants the historical reliability of the Gospels but doesn't believe there is adequate evidence in the Gospels to support miracles like turning water into wine or the feeding of the five thousand. The Gospel accounts of these miracles don't contain enough information to construct *a defense* that the miracles actually occurred. Surely, what the apologist must do with this challenge is far different from what he should do to defend the historical reliability of the Gospels.

If asked to defend miracles, there is another approach an apologist might take. Here I offer a personal illustration. Some years ago I was asked to write a chapter for a multi-authored book in defense of miracles. Specifically, my task was to write a defense of the incarnation of Jesus. Since the book was intended especially for nonbelievers, it would not suffice merely to cite various scriptures and then say that these passages say it happened, so it did. Nor did I have enough space to write a defense of the historical reliability of the Gospels and then say that since they are reliable and record the incarnation as a historical event, the incarnation must have occurred. And I didn't expect to get very far if I tried to make an evidential case (using Scripture and non-biblical sources) that the incarnation had happened. The reason is that there are few extrabiblical references to the incarnation which would serve as evidence to prove it actually happened. And, the biblical passages that speak of it basically say that it happened; they don't offer much basis for structuring an argument to "prove" that the incarnation occurred.

So what should I do? I remembered that there is one point about the incarnation that nonbelievers attack even before considering any evidence that it happened. Many critics think it is unnecessary to pore over evidence that it occurred, because they think the doctrine is self-contradictory. If so, the doctrine couldn't be true, nor could the event it speaks about have possibly occurred. Now here was something that I could defend, and it would matter to both nonbelievers and believers. As I read complaints against the doctrine, it became clear that many critics don't fully understand what the Christian doctrine actually says. No wonder they think it logically incoherent; if I understood the incarnation as they do, I would agree that it is self-contradictory! It seemed, then, that I first needed to clarify from Scripture and theology just what Christians mean when they say that Jesus, though fully human, is God incarnate. Once the doctrine was clarified, the rest of my defense was consumed with showing how the notion of a God-man could be logically coherent. Of course, that alone won't prove that Jesus is the God-man, but if the very idea of a being who is fully human and fully divine is logically incoherent (and thus impossible to conceive in the way that a round square or a married bachelor are impossible to think of), there is little hope that there ever actually was such a person.

My approach to the incarnation was quite different from other strategies one might use to defend it. However, critics raise an even more fundamental complaint about miracles, and none of the above approaches involves this complaint: the most basic atheistic objection to miracles is that miracles are impossible. There is always a naturalistic explanation of anything, and it is always more believable than a supernaturalistic one, according to these critics. So, the most fundamental thing a nonbeliever may be asking when she asks for a defense of miracles is how it can be *possible* for a miracle to occur. That's a very different request than a request to defend the historical reliability of the Gospels or to offer biblical and non-biblical evidence that a particular miracle occurred.

From these examples it should be clear that much time can be wasted and little ground that nonbelievers care about can actually be defended if we don't at the outset clarify what the critic wants us to prove or defend. If you are not sure what is most troubling to your nonbelieving friend, just ask. In the ensuing conversation you will likely come to understand what needs to be defended. Moreover, I trust that readers can see the value of identifying strategies to defend the doctrine in question and thinking through which strategy will allow one to give the best defense possible.

Once the issue at stake and the best strategy to respond to it are clarified, what kind of arguments and evidences and how many of them should the apologist marshal? Though we frequently think in terms of how many arguments are required to defend a view, something is more important than the number. The crucial issue in building a case is not how much (the *quantity* of) evidence is needed, but what kinds of (the *quality* of) evidence are required. In addressing the quality of evidences needed, apologists should focus on three main items, none of which has anything to do with the quantity of evidence.

Regardless of the argument or evidence the apologist considers, the first thing he or she should ask is whether the argument and/or evidence is true. If the apologist attempts to defend Christianity with loads of arguments and evidence that are false, the nonbeliever may initially be overwhelmed by the amount of evidence offered. However, at some point, the nonbeliever will likely have questions about whether the arguments presented are true. Even if the nonbeliever doesn't raise such questions, we should, because we want not only to hold the right position but to do so for the right reason. No false argument or evidence actually defends the tenet of faith in question. So, the apologist must ask initially whether his evidence is true, and he should also ask how he knows it is true. Exercise some rigor over your own thought processes. If you think an argument is true but later recognize that it is false (or that you can't prove it true), abandon the argument. If your arguments don't convince you, they won't likely convince those who reject your position.

Truthfulness is only one part of deciding on the best arguments. An argument or evidence may be true, but we must also ask whether it is relevant to the issue or viewpoint we are trying to defend. If it isn't relevant, then it isn't a good argument, despite the fact that it is true. Asking this second question simply picks up on our initial point about clarifying the nature of the atheist's attack and what must be proved to answer that attack. A few examples will illustrate this point.

Suppose you want to defend the resurrection of Jesus Christ. You believe that as part of your defense it would be helpful to prove that Jesus actually died. If his tomb is empty several days after his burial, but there is evidence that the crucifixion didn't actually kill him, there is a ready explanation for the empty tomb which requires no miracle whatsoever. So it would be wise to prove that Christ died.

Suppose that to show that Christ really died you noted that the disciples and some of the women saw the tomb where he was placed, and even if they didn't remember the exact tomb, surely Joseph of Arimathea would know it because he owned the tomb. What should we say about this argument? I note first that what it claims about the disciples, the women, and Joseph of Arimathea are all true. Passages in the Gospels support all of these claims. However, it is hard to see exactly how this information proves anything about whether Jesus actually died. The argument is true but irrelevant; so, it isn't a good argument or piece of evidence.

Consider another example. Suppose you were asked to defend the historical reliability of the Gospels. Imagine you respond that the Gospels tell us the truth, because early manuscript evidence of the Gospels shows that the original documents (which predate the manuscripts we have) certainly could have been written by people who were eyewitnesses to the events recorded in the Gospels. You even mention a few existing early manuscripts of parts of the Gospels to show that you are not just imagining this evidence exists.

Now you may think you offered a strong argument to prove the Gospels' reliability, but upon reflection you and/or your nonbelieving friend may sense that something about this argument is "fishy." In particular, your friend may say, "Well, the dates of these manuscripts do suggest that the authors of the original documents could have been eyewitnesses of the events they record. But none of that shows that they told the truth. Maybe they were eyewitnesses but didn't really understand what they were seeing. Or perhaps they did know what was happening (and it wasn't favorable to

Christianity) so they deliberately lied to make Christ and Christianity look as if it were true."

If confronted with that objection, you would hopefully see that you used a bad argument, because your friend's objection makes good sense. What is the problem? The truth of your argument? Not at all! There actually are early manuscripts that help make the case that we know what the original documents said and that they were most likely written by someone who lived when he could have been an eyewitness of the events recorded or could have talked with people who were. Truthfulness isn't the problem with this argument; relevance is! Appealing to manuscript evidence helps us date the original and determine what the original actually said. It doesn't tell us whether the document tells the truth. Since defending the reliability of the Gospels means we defend their truthfulness, the problem with the imagined line of argument is that though true, it doesn't show that the *Gospels* tell the truth.

When asking if an argument or evidence is relevant, regardless of the answer, the apologist should ask himself how he knows. Again, if we "police" our case and weed out the weak arguments, that is better than having the nonbeliever show us our errors.

In addition to asking whether an argument is true or false and whether it is relevant to the specific item being defended, it is important to ask how much (and what) your argument or evidence actually proves. This question, of course, presupposes that the argument is true and relevant. If it isn't, then it won't prove the point you are trying to defend. But even if it is true and relevant, you need to clarify whether you have proved *everything* you need to prove, *some part* of what must be proved (perhaps a major concept, or only a matter that is peripheral to the main issue under consideration), or perhaps *something rather insignificant* to establishing the truth of what you intend to defend. Whatever the answer to how much you have proved, again you should ask how you know that this (whatever it is) is how much you have proved. Let me illustrate the importance of clarifying what you have proved.

Think again about defending the resurrection of Christ. Some apologists think a good argument to show that Jesus really died is that during the trial and before the crucifixion, he was flogged with a flagrum or cat-o'-nine-tails. This Roman means of flogging was brutal, sometimes even disemboweling those who were flogged. Certainly this shows that Jesus must have been dead when they put him in the tomb.

Though this may sound like a strong argument, it involves several different things we must test before we decide to use it and in relation to what. The first is whether or not Jesus was flogged with a flagrum or cat-o'-nine-tails. From what we know of punishment at the hands of the Roman government at that time, a cat-o'-nine-tails was often used for flogging. However, nothing in the Gospels tells us exactly what was used to flog Christ. The passages that speak of his scourging are Mark 15:15, Luke 23:16, 22, and John 19:1. None of them says what was used, nor does any of them say how many lashes he received. Thus, in order to use this argument, one must show that there is extrabiblical evidence that Roman floggings were typically done with a flagrum or cat-o'-nine-tails. One must add that *probably*, therefore, a flagrum was used to flog Jesus (of course, Scripture doesn't say that). So, if Jesus's flogging followed the usual pattern of flogging by the Romans, then Jesus would likely have been in bad shape physically. But all of this is a probability judgment, and one that we can't prove for certain.

Setting aside whether a flagrum was actually used, what does this argument prove? It is relevant to Jesus's physical condition during the ordeal of the trial and crucifixion. However, since the apologist is trying to prove that Jesus really died, this argument clearly doesn't prove that. If Christ's scourging actually killed him, there would have been no need to crucify him; he could have been taken immediately to the tomb. Moreover, if the scourging killed him, the Gospel writers must have been lying when they recorded Christ's words from the cross. No, the most this argument can prove, if it in fact is true, is that Jesus was in a rather weakened condition by the time he was crucified. The scourging didn't kill him, but it helps in part to explain why he died as quickly as he did (so quickly that the centurion didn't need to break his legs to stop him from pushing down on the spikes in his legs to lift himself up to inhale another breath).

Here, then, is an argument whose truth, we must say, is probable at best. It is generally relevant to whether Christ really died. But, even so, it doesn't prove as much as the apologists who use it seem to think it proves. When you realize that it doesn't, you must evaluate whether it's really worth offering. Even if your friend gives you much time to make this argument, it is dubious that it is worth doing so. There are other true arguments, relevant to the point, which actually show that Christ was dead!

Consider another example. Suppose someone tries to defend Scripture's reliability on the grounds that fulfilled prophecies are proof of Scripture's truthfulness. This is an argument many apologists find attractive. Though I agree that evidence of fulfilled prophecies shows that there is something special about this book, I don't think it proves as much as proponents believe it does. In order even to present this argument in a compelling way, the apologist may first need to convince the nonbeliever that the apologist's interpretation of what the prophecy predicts is correct. If the nonbeliever disagrees, he won't agree that it has been fulfilled in the way you claim. However, let's assume that the friend is charitable and agrees with your interpretation of every prophecy you mention. Let's also assume that he agrees that the persons and events you claim fulfill those prophecies actually do. There is still a problem. How many prophecies do you think Scripture contains? I don't know the exact answer, but when you count prophecies of the first *and* second advents, there are many. Even if we believe that every prophecy of things prior to Christ and every prophecy about Christ's first coming has been fulfilled, prophecies concerning the second advent of Christ and beyond (and there are large amounts of them) have not yet been fulfilled.

The problems with this argument are as follows: 1) can I get my friend's agreement with my interpretation of prophecies and my assessment of how many have been fulfilled? 2) if I make the inductive argument that in virtue of all the prophecies that have been fulfilled, there is reason to think unfulfilled prophecies will come to pass as well, such an inductive generalization needs to have more instances of fulfilled prophecy for the nonbeliever to think that the unfulfilled ones will eventually be fulfilled; and 3) even if my nonbelieving friend agrees on items 1 and 2, at most I have shown that there is something very unusual about biblical prophecies of the future (contrary to expectation, they seem to be true); I have proved nothing about all the non-prophetic passages of Scripture. The truthfulness of prophecies, should one grant it, doesn't prove the reliability of non-prophetic passages.

Does the foregoing mean that the argument from fulfilled prophecy is useless? Not at all. If we interpret these prophecies and their fulfillment correctly, that does count for something. It's just that it doesn't prove that all prophecies will be fulfilled or that non-prophetic portions of Scripture are also true.

In sum, in order to know when you have presented adequate or sufficient evidence to support your beliefs, the quantity of arguments and evidences offered will have very little to do with it. First, clarify the issue under discussion and what has to be proved in order to support the belief that you hold. Then, as you begin to choose arguments, ask whether they are true and relevant to what needs to be proved, and then ask how much each argument actually proves. In each case, also ask how you know the argument is true and relevant and proves what you think it does. Twenty arguments for a tenet of the faith which support only a portion of what you need to prove is not sufficient evidence! On the other hand, one argument, for example, that completely removes the possibility that Jesus was still alive when the soldiers took him from the cross, is sufficient evidence to prove that he was dead when laid in the tomb. You may also want to present other confirmative evidences, but that first argument makes the case.

As you reflect on the content of this section, you may still be puzzled. Suppose I do offer arguments that are true and relevant and that support the major ideas and events that need support. Would that mean I had removed any possibility of doubt? Would the belief so defended be absolutely certain, or would there be more evidence and argument needed? In other words, when can one know that he or she has presented a case that meets the requirements of an adequate defense? To those issues we turn next.

TRUTH, CERTAINTY, AND EVIDENCE

In this chapter, we have been addressing modern concerns about sufficient evidence. I have argued that in building a case for or against a belief, sufficient evidence involves at least arguments and evidences that are true and relevant to the issue under consideration, and that one must also be clear about what exactly has been proved by any particular piece of evidence. Even so, at what point have we "made our case" so that the marshaling of argument and evidence can end? Must a case be absolutely certain in order to qualify as true? Unless I am certain about the beliefs I hold and defend, is something more needed to assure myself and my critics that I have offered *sufficient* evidence?

Such questions may at first appear to have simple, straightforward answers. However, looks can be deceiving, and this is a case where there is much more to say than initially meets the eye. The place to begin is with a clear definition of what it means to say something is true. Then we must consider whether something is automatically certain if it is true; that is, what is the relationship between truth and certainty? However, to answer this last question adequately, we must understand the nature of certainty, and I shall present two different types of certainty. Once we clarify the nature of certainty, we can better see the relation between truth and certainty. It will also be clear that the matter of certainty raises the issue of doubt, and various forms of doubt need to be distinguished. Some doubts won't make sense; others will. How this relates to truth and certainty will then be addressed. I maintain that only by treating all of the named issues can we be in a position to make a judgment as to whether we have satisfied the modern's requirement of sufficient evidence.

What Is Truth?

Several major theories of truth are often invoked when speaking of truth. Some have a longer "pedigree" in philosophy than do others, but all have their adherents today. When I speak of truth and theories of truth, I am referring to the truth of propositions or assertions. In John 14:6 Jesus said, "I am the way, and the truth, and the life." Sometimes we refer to an acquaintance by saying, "He is a friend who is true blue." There is, then, a sense in which a person can be true or can be called "the truth," but that is different from the truth of a proposition. My discussion now is about the truth of propositions. What is it about an assertion that makes it true, and even more fundamentally, what do we mean when we say that an affirmation is true?

The theory of truth with the lengthiest pedigree is the correspondence theory of truth. According to it, a sentence is true if what it says about the world is actually so in the world. Truth, then, is a relation between language and the world, and that relation is correspondence. Obviously, claims that relate to some material aspect of the world are easier to confirm as matching the world than are assertions about things that are invisible. But regardless of what the sentence refers to, the correspondence theory of truth says that a sentence is true if what we say in words about the world matches what we find in the world.[2]

Undoubtedly, philosophers and theologians (and ordinary people) would love to hold such a theory, because they would love to be able to see whether there really is a match between word and world. For a long time in Western thought, it was believed that we could make such judgments about our claims. Of course, there have always been skeptics, but they weren't so much skeptical about correspondence being the "right" theory of truth. Their skepticism stemmed from a belief that for one reason or another we simply are not in a position to tell whether our words match the world. In our time, it seems that a large number of philosophers have felt it necessary to abandon the correspondence theory. They believe that the idea of truth and the word "true" are still meaningful, but we just can't understand truth to be what the correspondence theory says it is.

As to why there is so much dissatisfaction with the correspondence theory, the reasons go beyond a mere complaint about sense perception being potentially flawed in any instance. Rather, the concerns are those that I raised in my discussion of objectivity and subjectivity in the chapters on postmodern skepticism. The mind is too active in the knowing process, and it is guided too much by our presuppositions and past experiences for us to think that we can be in touch with reality "out there" beyond our minds. In response, I argued that prejudices do not inevitably lead to errors in judgment about the world. And, though we all come from a particular perspective, that doesn't mean we know nothing correctly. If you adopt a position like the one I took on objectivity and subjectivity, you will likely also grant that though there are various things that can keep us in any given instance from accurately confirming or disconfirming a proposition as true in a correspondence sense, the correspondence theory captures the most fundamental thing we want to know about truth of propositions, and it isn't impossible to discern whether propositions do speak accurately about the world they intend to depict.

Despite arguments to the contrary, many persist in denying that truth as correspondence is available. However, we still think and talk about truth, and so the notion of truth is useful. As a result, critics of the correspondence theory propose that we understand truth differently. Specifically, two other theories of truth are available, and they have become increasingly popular because of the belief that truth as correspondence is unattainable.

The first of those theories is the coherence theory of truth. When this theory originally gained a wide following, it was believed that sentences which expressed what was observed in the world were basically accurate. However, fit with the world isn't the main idea of the coherence theory. Instead, truth as coherence is conceived as a match of words to words. That is, our propositions will either fit with other propositions we hold or they won't. If they fit, that means the propositions do not contradict one another; if they don't fit, then juxtaposing the two will generate a contradiction. Thus, in evaluating the truth of a set of sentences, we must ask whether they form a coherent, noncontradictory set or whether they generate a contradiction. If, for example, one is evaluating the truth (in a coherence sense) of a set of propositions and four fit together without contradiction and a fifth contradicts something about the other four, then the coherent set counts as true and the contradictory sentence is deemed false.

A simple illustration both explains how the coherence theory works when applied to a set of sentences, and also suggests the theory's limitations. Consider the following four sentences: 1) "The present king of France is completely bald on his head and grows no hair on his head at all"; 2) "The present king of France usually wears a nightcap to bed so that his bald head will not be cold during the night"; 3) "The present queen of France kisses the present king of France's bald head each night before they go to bed"; 4) "The royal barber gave the present king of France a haircut and a new hairstyle so that his crown sits firmly on his head without slipping off."

Sentences 1–3 cohere with one another in that nothing in any of those sentences contradicts anything in the other two. On the other hand, sentence 4 seems clearly to contradict 1–3. If we are understanding truth as coherence, then sentences 1–3 must be true, while sentence 4 is false. Of course, there is a problem with the whole set of sentences. Since France does not presently (as I write this) have either a king, queen, or royal barber, none of the four sentences match the world as it actually is. That is, in a correspondence sense, none of the four is true. So, the problem with the coherence theory is that in using it, the best we can do is say that a certain number of sentences don't contradict one another. However, this may amount to nothing more than that we have a logically consistent "system" (the set of four) of error (in a correspondence sense). At one time, this wasn't much of a bother to coherence theorists because they believed that the observational sentences that made up a given set accurately reflected the world around them. Nowadays, few adherents to the coherence theory think this is so. So, it may be that whether we are dealing with observational or non-observational claims, the most we can say is that a given set of those sentences is self-consistent. That doesn't guarantee that they match the world, but it at least shows that the set can't be deemed false on the ground that it contradicts other propositions thought to be true or that the set itself is internally inconsistent.

A third theory of truth is the pragmatic theory of truth. Proponents of this view may also espouse the coherence theory. In its earlier days there were those who also thought we could have truth as correspondence. Their concern was that when we call a proposition "true" we really want to say something more than just that it matches the world. That "more" is to tell us whether or not we can live successfully with the proposition in question. More contemporary theorists agree that truth as correspondence isn't something we can have. So the best we can ask about any claim is whether it is and has proved useful to those who hold it. If this is the criterion of judging whether a belief or belief system is true, I can affirm that for me Christianity is true in this pragmatic sense, while I am also sure that for many atheists they have found their atheism to be very useful in the way they live their lives.

Now there is an intuition at the heart of the pragmatic theory that we can affirm. If something is true in a correspondence and/or coherence sense, we should expect to live and flourish when we live in accord with that claim. On the other hand, if we never ask about the "fit" of the proposition with the world, then the most one can say is that on a given occasion a proposition was helpful and so it was true then. But being true on one occasion or even on many occasions cannot guarantee that it will be useful on others. That is so even if I'm just considering what is "true" for me, let alone what happens when I propose a way to live that I've found useful even if you've never heard of my claims or, if you do know of them, you've never tried to live them out.

I trust that it is clear that if all we have is truth as the pragmatic theory understands it, there can be no discussion of absolute truth in any sense. Moreover, apologetics and evangelism are wrongheaded and futile. The most we can do is tell others that Christianity has worked for us so far. Whether it will be useful in the future and especially in eternity is anybody's guess. For all we know the *truth* of the matter, in a correspondence sense, is that death ends everything; that is, at death we are simply annihilated. Conversely, for all we know the *truth*, in a correspondence sense, is that Christ will return in our lifetime and before too long nonbelievers will stand before him at the Great White Throne Judgment only to be cast subsequently into the lake of fire. Obviously, these two options represent dramatically different destinies. Sadly, with a pragmatic conception of truth, we are simply not in any position to know what will really happen in the future. The best we can do with such futuristic speculation is to adopt one of the two views (or other visions of the future) which we believe will be useful in that it energizes us as we live now.

If pragmatism and/or coherence is the most we can know about "truth," then clearly the proper attitude toward others with different beliefs is tolerance and dialogue. Refutation and defense in apologetics are impossible— at least as traditionally understood to mean showing what is and isn't the case—and conversion when evangelizing is unnecessary. The intellectual grounds upon which so many in our day are rejecting any talk of truth as correspondence in large part relates to objections I raised about objectivity and subjectivity in my responses to postmodern skepticism. Suffice it to say for our purposes that, since I am unconvinced (and believe you should be, too) by the line of argument against logic, reason, and objectivity that we saw in the previous chapters, I believe that truth as correspondence in some sense that actually gets us in touch with the world outside our minds is both the ideal and is attainable.[3]

So, when in this book I speak of truth and the quest for it, I am, unless otherwise indicated, thinking of true claims matching the world outside of our mind. Obviously, this kind of truth is easier to confirm if the matter in question is in some way empirically observable. However, that doesn't mean that nonempirical propositions are unverifiable; it only means that we cannot verify them by direct apprehension of some material state of affairs in the world around us. Of course, since many of the claims of Christianity are about things that are not empirically observable, it will be more challenging to verify them than it is to confirm a belief, for example, that I am seeing a computer screen in front of me as I write this sentence.

If we can speak of truth in a correspondence sense, then there is reason to raise all the questions (raised at the outset of this discussion on truth and certainty) about what certainty is and how it relates to truth. To that topic I now turn.

The Question of Truth

What Is Certainty?

There are several things to say about certainty, but I begin with a distinction that helps clarify what we are talking about. I refer to it as the distinction between *objective certainty* and *subjective certainty*. Sometimes this is referred to as the difference between *certainty* and *certitude*,[4] but regardless of which labels we use, the distinction helps to organize our thoughts about certainty.

When I speak of *objective certainty* I refer to the degree to which one has presented argument and evidence to confirm that a given proposition is true or at least probably true. In other words, objective certainty deals with the "facts of the case" in support of or against any proposition. Here the comments I made earlier in this chapter about clarifying exactly what is under debate and what needs to be proved to support one position or another, and my comments about measuring the quality of arguments and evidences in terms of whether they are true and relevant and how much they prove, are especially relevant. That is, with regard to any belief there is a case to be made for it and against it. That evidential case involves arguments and evidences which support the belief as either true or false. Anyone who knows the rules of reason and argument, including an understanding of various logical fallacies one must avoid, and understands what needs to be proved in order to confirm as true a belief such as the resurrection of Christ will be able to look at the arguments and evidences amassed for and against it and make an assessment of whether the defender or attacker has met the evidential demands of the case. If arguments and evidences that are true and relevant are offered and if they meet the demands of supporting the main tenets of the belief, then we can say that objectively the proposition is certain. As Robert Holyer says of this type of certainty, it "describes a relationship that exists between a proposition and the evidence that supports it. In this sense the problem of certainty is to determine how much or what kind of evidence one must have to be entitled to claim that he is certain."[5]

The objective certainty of a claim is noted in terms of a percentage that indicates how likely it is that the claim is true. If the proposition in question is a matter of math or logic, the claim will be either 100 percent certain or not certain at all. For example, 'married bachelors exist' is not somewhat false and partially true. It is absolutely false. The claim that 2+2=4 is not 98 or 99 percent certain; it is 100 percent certain that this claim is true. If someone challenges its truth, an evidential case can be made for it.

On the other hand, if a proposition is about a matter of fact, philosophers have said that it may be at most 99 percent certain. In this case, they are talking about objective certainty, but why can't such propositions be confirmed by evidence that makes them 100 percent objectively certain? The reason is that the claim in question is about the world outside of the mind. Though it is hard to imagine what an argument would look like that attempted to refute the idea that the sun rose this morning, or one that attempted to do the same about my having two hands and two feet, still it is possible to imagine a situation in which we could be wrong about such things. That doesn't mean that we should worry about whether such things are really true; it's just a way to remind us that we are not infallible nor is our intellect infinite, so it is possible (even if only remotely so) that we are wrong.

In contrast, *subjective certainty* relates to the degree to which we are convinced or persuaded that something is true. It is fundamentally a psychological concept, and it may be based on evidence and our awareness of it, emotion, or a combination of both. Subjective certainty may be seen as the feeling that something is as we think it. As Holyer says, this type of certainty "describes a specific attitude to a proposition—perhaps the feelings and behavior constitutive of feeling sure about it. In this sense, the problems of certainty are these: can we describe this state of mind more exactly? And how is it won, or lost or sustained?"[6]

In addition, it is important to see how objective and subjective certainty relate to each other. Though it is possible for a feeling or conviction that something is true to be based on the objective certainty with which that belief has been confirmed, this does not always happen. Perhaps the person hearing the defense for a belief knows little about argumentation and so doesn't really know how to evaluate the case you have presented. Or perhaps she does know the rules of reason and argument, but there are psychological factors that make it difficult for her to evaluate as sufficient a case you make for a given belief. This is not unusual. For example, someone presented with a case for the resurrection of Christ which, by rules of reason and argument, makes that belief 95 percent objectively certain, may have a family member or friend who has experienced significant tragedy. As a result, he finds it hard to believe in God or anything else related to religion. Though he understands all the arguments and evidence you have presented, he will never be subjectively persuaded that you have proved Christ's resurrection.

Moreover, because of his ill feelings toward God, he can't bring himself to grant that at best you have made a case for the resurrection that makes it even 70 percent objectively certain.

So, subjective certainty may be influenced by objective certainty. The objective certainty of a belief, however, is not determined on the basis of subjective certainty. That is, the degree of objective certainty to which a proposition has been confirmed is determined by the arguments and evidences offered. Are they true and relevant, and do they actually confirm the main things that must be proved in order to confirm objectively that the belief is true? Whether a particular individual believes the case for the objective certainty of a claim to be convincing or persuasive may depend on subjective factors, but those subjective factors don't actually make the objective case more or less *objectively* certain.

We should also add that there are times when a claim has very little, if any, objective certainty, and yet someone believes it anyway. The belief isn't based on the "facts" of the matter; the facts actually disconfirm the belief as false. But for psychological reasons the believer holds on to his belief. Think of some of the beliefs many of us held as young children. We probably believed in Santa Claus and the tooth fairy. We believed not because someone taught us the rules of reason and argument and then offered us a defense of these beliefs that showed them to be objectively certain. Not at all. Moreover, if at that point in our lives, someone had offered evidence that neither Santa Claus nor the tooth fairy exists, we likely would have been troubled, but we might have been so infatuated with the idea that Santa and/or the tooth fairy exist that we would refuse to stop believing. So, sometimes people are convinced that something is true (subjectively certain) in spite of having little evidence for it and in the face of having much evidence against it.

Sadly, there are many who believe that is an apt description of those who believe in God and Christ. Psychologically, we are so in need of there to be a God to ensure that justice will right every wrong done to us and to others (or to accomplish something else) that we ignore all the evidence against these beliefs and become even more determined to believe. There is a rather famous illustration of this point in the writings of Antony Flew. He relates the tale of the invisible gardener as an analogue to how religious believers respond when their beliefs are attacked. Flew asks us to imagine someone who has a garden which he believes is tended by a very special gardener. No one, including the believer, has ever seen this gardener, but he still believes the gardener exists. The fact that no one has seen him may mean that he tends the garden only at night while everyone is sleeping. If you set a guard next to the garden for a whole evening, and the gardener never comes, the believer won't give up his belief. He tells you that the gardener doesn't come every night (perhaps only once a week), but we never know which night he'll come. So the skeptic sets a watch every night for two straight weeks, and the gardener never comes. Still, the believer won't give up his belief. He explains that the gardener actually came; no one saw him because he is invisible. Flew explains that no matter what the objection to the existence of the gardener, the believer will always adjust his beliefs so that nothing can ever count against his belief sufficiently to prove it wrong. Flew argues that when believers make such a "defense" by qualifying their belief to fit whatever objections arise, they are actually holding a belief which has died the death of a thousand qualifications. In such a case, Flew asks, "just how does what you call an invisible, intangible, eternally elusive gardener differ from an imaginary gardener or even from no gardener at all?"[7] Flew suggests that this problem is true of any religious believer who continues to hold his belief, regardless of how much and what sort of counterevidence is presented.

From the preceding it should be clear that objective and subjective certainty are distinct. Though subjective certainty may be based on what is objectively certain, that doesn't always happen. And each of us has cherished beliefs which, from a psychological point of view, we could not abandon without serious damage to our mental health. It is possible that there are times when our subjective conviction of the truth of these beliefs moves us to evaluate as weak an objective case in favor of a proposition which, if true, would mean our "pet" belief(s) could not be true. Nonetheless, objective and subjective certainty are distinct, and when someone begins to speak of the certainty of a given belief, we must initially clarify whether she is thinking of objective certainty, subjective certainty, or both.

This distinction can also be very helpful in reminding us that persuasion is not purely a matter of argument and evidence; it also involves psychological factors over which we may have little or no control. This doesn't mean that we should put together our objective cases for the various tenets of the Christian faith in a haphazard way, because the ultimate persuasion of a person's mind and will is beyond our control. It is true that no one will be argued into the kingdom of God solely on the basis of the brilliance of our objective case for Christianity. It is also true that the type of persuasion we are talking about when we speak of subjective certainty is something that only the Holy Spirit can and does produce in a person. Still, on any occasion the Holy Spirit just may use our case for the objective certainty of a belief as a basis (though not necessarily the only basis) for persuading the nonbeliever to turn to Christ. So, we must present the very best defense we can muster.

Several other points about certainty (objective certainty in particular) are worth noting. One is that when trying to establish the objective certainty of a belief, we must clarify which criteria govern the decision of whether the case we have made renders the belief objectively certain. Let me explain. Often in discussions of certainty you will hear reference to Cartesian certainty. This refers to the work of René Descartes, and especially to his *Meditations*. In this work, Descartes asks how it is that he knows that he knows various things, and he eventually concludes that most of what he knows could reasonably be doubted. Descartes believed that claims to know something should be impervious to doubt. If it makes sense to doubt a belief, then perhaps it is false. In such a case, one wouldn't know whatever the proposition claimed was the case. Because Descartes was uneasy about the thought that much of what he claimed to know could reasonably be doubted, he reasoned that it would be better to base knowledge on truths that are indubitable. So, Descartes thought through the various things he believed, and he found that most of it could reasonably be doubted.

Eventually Descartes concluded that one of his beliefs could not be reasonably doubted. That belief was his famous *cogito, ergo sum* ("I think, therefore I am"). He could not doubt that he, as a thinking thing, existed, because nonexistent things don't do anything, including doubt their own existence. At last he had found one indubitable truth, the foundation upon which to build the rest of his knowledge. But it was a rather small foundation, for if you only know indubitably that you exist, everything else about you can be doubted, and of course, you can't know indubitably that I or anyone else exists. You believe we do, but perhaps some evil demon is tampering with your sense organs, your mind, or both. So, if one had a right to believe only those things one knew indubitably to be true, how could one know anything other than that one existed as a thinking thing?

Descartes proposed that if someone has a clear and distinct idea of something, then it must be true. This criterion has a certain plausibility if the knowledge claim is about something observable in the material world, but Descartes held that this would even be the criterion for knowledge of things that are not about the physical universe. Though this criterion of clear and distinct ideas sounded good, Descartes was still troubled. Even if he thought he was having a clear and distinct idea of something, perhaps he was wrong because an evil demon was tampering with his senses and reason. With respect to either observational claims or non-observational claims, one senses that Descartes would say that if a claim is self-evident, evident to the senses, or incorrigible, then one is right in saying he has a clear and distinct idea of it. Descartes never used that terminology, but it is not hard to imagine someone believing that the only way for sure to satisfy the requirement that one was having a clear and distinct idea was to know it as self-evident, evident to the senses, or incorrigible.

Be that as it may, what about the evil demon, the lingering fly in the epistemological ointment? Descartes believed that there is a way to ensure that if he thought he was having a clear and distinct idea of something, he actually was. As explained in chapter 2, he reasoned that if God exists, God would see to it that when someone thinks she is having a clear and distinct idea of something, she actually is. So, Cartesian demands for certain foundations to knowledge required that Descartes offer a proof for God's existence.

What point, then, am I making by writing of Cartesian certainty? I have mentioned Cartesian certainty for several reasons. One is so that readers will know what it is. Sometimes a reference to Cartesian certainty refers to the requirement of clear and distinct ideas for one to believe that one knows a proposition with objective certainty. Perhaps more frequently when Cartesian certainty is raised, the point is the indubitability that Descartes demanded for his first principle. And, when some philosophers refer to Cartesian certainty, they mean that the requirement of indubitability applies not only to the *cogito*, but to all other beliefs one claims to know.

In an upcoming chapter, we shall discuss classical foundationalism and its criteria of proper basicality (a properly basic belief must be self-evident, evident to the senses, or incorrigible). We shall argue that such criteria are too stringent, even as the notion of clear and distinct ideas is too stringent a requirement for anyone to meet so as to achieve objective certainty. Of course, indubitability is also too strong a requirement, as Descartes himself recognized—he never claimed that one could know any other claim than the *cogito* to be indubitably true.

If so, then there is something further we can learn from these points about Cartesian certainty. It is that once you clarify to yourself and your nonbelieving friend that you need to give an objective case, an apologetic, for Christianity (and your friend needs to give an objective case against it), you still need to designate the standard by which the various arguments and evidences will be judged as to their truth and value in an overall defense. That is, in order to succeed in making an objective case for Christianity (or for one of its tenets), are we to determine that arguments are true if they meet 1) the criteria for Cartesian certainty; or 2) the classical foundationalist criteria of proper basicality; or 3) some other criteria? Implicit in what I have been saying in this and other chapters is a standard that must be met in order to claim that we have succeeded in confirming a proposition as true or in disconfirming it as false, and that standard isn't as stringent as those of Cartesian certainty and classical foundationalism. But more on this matter later. For now I've said enough about Cartesian certainty and how it relates to making a case that a proposition is objectively certain.

A second further point about certainty is its relation to truth. Sometimes the two are thought to be the same (or nearly the same) thing. However, there are significant differences. The most obvious is that *subjective* certainty and truth are not at all the same. As already noted, there are cases where a person is completely persuaded that a belief is true. That is not because they have made a strong case for the belief's truth. In fact, the belief may be known to be false—here think of beliefs in the tooth fairy and Santa Claus. Still, for whatever reasons, the believer cannot jettison the belief. Ideally, we would be strongly convinced of a belief's truth only because of a very strong objective case for its validity. But even when one is subjectively certain that something is true because the objective case made for it is very strong, the objective case (and certainty) is one thing, while subjective certainty, though based on the belief's truth as demonstrated by the objective case for it, is another.

Is *objective* certainty the same as truth? Not necessarily. There are cases where a set of arguments and evidences are presented for the truth of a given belief. Those evidences raise the probability that the belief is true, but suppose they raise the probability to the point of making the belief only 65 percent objectively certain. In such cases we would say the belief is more likely true than not, but given the case in favor of it, we really can't say with confidence that it is true. There are some beliefs, for example, for which one can make only a 52 percent objectively certain case, whereas 48 percent of the evidence favors an opposing view. In such a case, we would be wise not to be dogmatic about which view is true. And then, there are times when a belief is true, but one has insufficient evidence to make a compelling objective case for it. As an example, Christians would most likely say that Jesus is telling the truth when he tells his disciples, "In my Father's house are many mansions: if it were not so, I would have told you. I go to prepare a place for you. And if I go and prepare a place for you, I will come again, and receive you unto myself; that where I am, there ye may be also" (John 14:2–3, KJV). We might even add that we are totally convinced (subjectively certain) that what Jesus says is true. However, the objective case that could be made for it, given the evidence to which we have access, is, if we are honest, not a truly strong one. If we are to make such an objective case, it is more likely that we will find support for the view if we proceed indirectly—for example, we could offer evidence for the truthfulness of the Gospels, and since the passage in question is in the Gospels, it must be true if our objective case in favor of the reliability of the Gospels succeeds.

Clearly, then, the objective certainty of a claim is not identical with its truth. Of course, there are times when a belief is true, and we know that is so because we have gathered together arguments and evidences that show it to be objectively certain and hence true. Even so, the truth of the claim does not depend for its truthfulness on the strength of the objective case made for it. In such cases, the objective certainty and the truth of the claim are closely related. In showing the belief to be objectively true, we come to believe that it is true (or confirm our belief that it is so), but it is still the case that its truth does not depend on the evidence we present for it in order for it to be true. It would be true even if no one knew it or had ever asked about any evidence it has going for it. The truth and the objective certainty of a belief are not the same thing.

A third point about certainty relates specifically to objective certainty. As explained at various points, there are varying degrees of objective certainty that a case for a belief may have. Since the strongest case one can make for a claim of fact is never going to exceed 99 percent objective certainty, and since most cases are somewhat less objectively certain, when we make a case and explain what it tells us about the truth of the proposition in question, we are really making a probability judgment. That is, we reach a conclusion about how likely it is that the claim is true. The stronger the objective case, the greater the dogmatism that is warranted. How do we know the degree to which the case we have offered makes the proposition objectively certain and thus probably true or not? The answer goes back to things discussed in the first part of this chapter. The key isn't the amount of evidence but the quality of the evidence. And evaluation of the quality of the evidence is based on whether it is true and relevant to the issue at hand, and on what exactly the argument and/or evidence proves. If the evidence is true, but much of it is irrelevant to what is really at issue, and/or if the evidence only supports an idea that is at the periphery of what needs to be proved, then our case does not make it very likely that the proposition is true. What percent of objective certainty must attach to the proposition for us to believe that it is probably true? No one can predict in advance of analyzing the issue and the evidential case brought in its favor. But certainly if we and the critic can agree that the evidential case provided raises the probability that the belief is true to 80 percent or better, we are on firm ground, aren't we? Perhaps, but again, whether 80 percent objective certainty is appropriate to feel confident (subjectively certain) that the belief is true will depend on analysis of the issue, the evidence offered for it, the objections against it, and possibly various psychological factors about us that impact whether or not we feel subjectively certain that it is true.

A final word on certainty is that, from what has been said about both objective and subjective certainty, we must, in evaluating the objective case presented for a belief, also speak about doubt. There may be reasons to doubt that the objective case meets the demands of reason and argument. Moreover, there may be reasons to doubt that we should be as subjectively certain (persuaded and convinced) or uncertain as we are. In the next chapter, then, we must address doubt. My main concern is with how doubt relates to the objective certainty of a proposition and whether those doubts can be satisfied and what it is that does so. But I am concerned more generally to deal with the various kinds of doubt and how they relate to the kind of certainty (objective or subjective) in view.

Chapter 6

Answers to Modern Skepticism (II): Doubt and Certainty

At the outset of this discussion I must acknowledge my indebtedness to the later philosophy of Ludwig Wittgenstein. While he devotes a whole work (*On Certainty*) to the topic, his basic approach to it appears in his *Philosophical Investigations*. Much of what I present is as Wittgenstein presented it and, I believe, accurately reflects his thinking. However, I cannot say that everything you will read in this chapter is from Wittgenstein or that he would agree with what I've done with his reflections on certainty. In fact, you will see at various points that I am developing points in ways that he may or may not have affirmed. Nonetheless, my presentation owes its initial impetus and stimulus to Wittgenstein's handling of the topic.

Before turning directly to Wittgenstein's thoughts on doubt and certainty, I must introduce a notion crucial to his whole later philosophy, his concept of a language-game. In his *Philosophical Investigations* Wittgenstein renounced the notion that the way language works is that a given word is tied to the object it names and that connection is invariable. With the rejected view, so long as one knew what might be called the basic "dictionary meaning" of a word, one could understand a given sentence, even if much about it were foreign. Regardless of context and speaker, words were seen as "meaning-invariant."[1]

In his later philosophy Wittgenstein came to see that words don't have an essence that cries out for them to have one and only one meaning, regardless of the context in which they are spoken or written. Rather, words get used in any number of different ways to mean one thing or another, depending on context and the particular use of the word. In short, Wittgenstein came to see language as a complex of what he called language-games or forms of life. A language-game is a complete way of doing a given human activity. As a complete way of engaging in some activity, it incorporates both verbal and nonverbal behavior.[2]

Wittgenstein held that language-games are logically independent of one another. There might be some common terms and ideas that appear in different language-games, but it is their use in a language-game that determines their meaning, not some essential meaning of each word that is in view whenever the term is used.[3] Moreover, even though certain ideas and words might be used similarly in two different language-games, that does not mean the two language-games are identical, i.e., that everything about them is the same. For example, the language-games of history and science use many similar methods, but that doesn't mean the language-games are identical. Nor does it mean that there are some criteria of meaning distinct from all language-games, which different language-games invoke and use identically to "make a move" in the respective language-games.

In addition, because Wittgenstein saw each language-game as logically distinct from all others, and since he saw no criteria independent of all language-games that govern the way things work in each language-game or that allow someone to confirm the winner from among several distinct but competing language-games (e.g., we can speak of the language-game of Christianity, the language-game of Islam, and the language-game of Buddhism—since these are three distinct religions whose claims often contradict those of other religious language-games, it would be helpful if there were a set of criteria independent of all language-games that would allow us to make a judgment about which language-game is the correct one), he believed that all rules and criteria that govern a language-game are internal to it. So, if the language-game allows one to confirm as true or disconfirm as false certain claims, there are rules within each language-game that allow one to make such judgments. What must be remembered, however, is that making such a judgment in one language-game doesn't confirm or disconfirm a similar claim in another language-game. If the similar claim in a different language-game is true, it is so in virtue of the rules and regulations of that language-game.[4]

Given these basics about language-games, we can now turn to what Wittgenstein says about doubt and certainty. One of the many very helpful things about Wittgenstein's handling of this topic is that he distinguishes a variety of types of doubt, and explains which ones make sense and which don't.

Initially, Wittgenstein distinguishes philosophical doubt from doubt in ordinary life. By the former, he means the kind of doubts one might entertain while sitting alone in one's study and musing about some philosophical issue. In such a scenario, one might entertain a doubt about whether the waitress who served him breakfast and the cashier to whom he paid his check were robots rather than real human beings. After all, he might think, one can make some fairly sophisticated robots nowadays. They do many of the things humans do, and a robot as a waitress might save a lot of wear and tear on the actual waitress's feet. Not only that, but whatever tips come in, the human waitress gets those.

Such musings while in one's study are not out of order, nor do they indicate that the person with such thoughts is insane. On the other hand, in a real-life situation, it makes no sense to raise such doubts about others around us. As Wittgenstein writes, "But just try to keep hold of this idea in the midst of your ordinary intercourse with others, in the street, say! Say to yourself, for example: 'The children over there are mere automata; all their liveliness is mere automatism.' And you will either find these words becoming quite meaningless; or you will produce in yourself some kind of uncanny feeling, or something of the sort."[5]

Another situation where doubts one might entertain in the privacy of one's study make no sense in real life has to do with whether other people are actually in pain. Imagine, for example, that you are on your way home one afternoon, and you come upon the scene of an accident. Two cars were involved in the accident, and they are in bad shape, but so are the drivers and passengers. In fact, one man is writhing on the ground in pain. He is holding his right knee and trying to stop the flow of blood from it. Now a philosopher might wonder if that person feels the same way he feels whenever he has that sort of injury. He might even entertain doubts about whether this is a real situation or whether he has just stumbled onto a movie set. That sort of doubt would probably even arise in the mind of a non-philosopher upon seeing what is happening. However, upon looking around, spectators see absolutely no evidence that this is a movie set or that otherwise a number of people just decided to fake a car crash. Everything that meets the eye suggests that this is a real accident. Now in a case such as this, will those philosophically inclined say to themselves, "Still, I wonder if this man really is in pain; does he feel inside the way I do when I am severely injured?" Of course not! As Wittgenstein writes, "If I see someone writhing in pain *with evident cause* [my italics] I do not think: all the same, his feelings are hidden from me."[6] In a real situation like this, we don't pause to philosophize; we call 911 or do whatever else we can to help the victims.

There is a second kind of doubt that Wittgenstein refers to in *Philosophical Investigations* and in *On Certainty*, although the context of each remark is slightly different. I propose that we call this kind of doubt neurotic doubt—this isn't Wittgenstein's term, but I think it is appropriate for what he has in mind. The remark in the *Investigations* comes when Wittgenstein is talking about uses of words and the rules that govern them. He notes that the use of a given word is not "everywhere bounded by rules." He then asks what a game would look like that is everywhere bounded by rules so that there is no room for doubt no matter what one does so long as one follows the rules. In reply he notes that if this is so, then it is also possible to generate an infinite regress of doubts and rules meant to quench doubt. Having made this point, it suggests another to Wittgenstein, and it is at this point that his comments relate to what I am calling neurotic doubt. He picks up the idea of generating rules that remove all doubts, which then suggest another rule for the application of the rule so as to quell further doubts, and so on. He writes,

> But that is not to say that we are in doubt because it is possible for us to *imagine* a doubt. I can easily imagine someone always doubting before he opened his front door whether an abyss did not yawn behind it, and making sure about it before he went through the door (and he might on some occasion prove to be right)—but that does not make me doubt in the same case.[7]

Now assuming that the person in question was born and raised on Planet Earth, if that person entertained doubts about whether he would be swallowed up by a deep hole whenever he set foot outside his house, we would likely say that this person has mental problems. If someone who just arrived from another planet were to raise such a doubt, it would still be a doubt that was ill-raised, but at least we would understand that the doubt doesn't necessarily mean that our interplanetary visitor is mentally ill.

Wittgenstein's comments in *On Certainty* come in a very different sort of context. He notes that certain ideas and beliefs might raise doubts as to their truth. It would be appropriate to offer arguments and evidence to support them or to reject them as false. Wittgenstein in this series of remarks (secs. 69–75) explains that something that rises or falls on evidence is something we can *know*, and it is also something about which we can be *mistaken*. It makes sense to offer grounds for rejecting the belief and to do the same in support of it. On the other hand, there are many things we believe that are so foundational to our way of looking at the world that it would make no sense to doubt them at all. In fact, terms like 'know,' 'evidence,' 'grounds,' 'doubt,' and 'mistake' are not terms that are appropriate to use when talking about such fundamental beliefs. Those terms are appropriate to use when one is considering something that rises or falls on evidence. These foundational beliefs are not of that sort, so if someone were to doubt one of them, we would not take this as a cue to produce argument and evidence to convince the doubter. Rather, we would think such doubts show something radically wrong with the doubter. Wittgenstein writes,

> If my friend were to imagine one day that he had been living for a long time past in such and such a place, etc. etc., I should not call this a *mistake*, but rather a mental disturbance, perhaps a transient one.[8]

He then adds that "Not every false belief of this sort is a mistake."[9] That is, sometimes raising a doubt of this sort can be a mistake—a misreading of the evidence or misunderstanding that the claim is not one that rises or falls on evidence. A young child, for example, who is in the process of developing his understanding of our world might make this sort of mistake. But once we correct the mistake, assuming that the child can and does remember our word of correction, if he raises the same doubt again (even several times in spite of our correcting him), we would begin to wonder whether he was actually mentally disturbed.

So, then, there is a species of doubt that I am labeling *neurotic doubt*. Though there might be a situation or two in which such doubts are understandable and should be taken seriously (the visitor from another planet or the young child with much to learn), most of the time such doubts make no sense to entertain.

At this point, you may be thinking that the types of doubt already mentioned lead us far afield from the task of apologetics. I sympathize with that concern, but think these points are relevant to apologetics. The point is to present a case sufficiently rigorous so as to answer doubting skeptics. Sadly, there are postmoderns and some moderns who are so suspicious of the mind's ability to know anything aright, that they talk as though even the types of claims we've been discussing are ones about which it is legitimate to raise doubts. My further point in raising these issues is to show that, despite protestations that humans really can't know much of anything for a certainty, there are a lot of things that all of us do know, and we shouldn't be ashamed to say so. To entertain such doubts seriously says more about the mental state of the doubter than about whether the claim in question is really knowable and whether we can be certain of its truth.

Wittgenstein's comments about doubts that bespeak a mental disturbance suggest another category of doubts. Actually, he discusses them as distinct cases of doubt, but I think a common thread runs through them. These are doubts that question the very framework of the way we look at reality. They include doubts not about individual claims in one language-game or another; rather they doubt or question the whole language-game or form of life altogether. Some of these doubts are about things which philosophers have often called matters of common sense, but not every doubt in this general category would also be about a matter of common sense. Now all of this needs a good bit of explanation. Let me begin with matters of common sense.

The remarks that make up the text of Wittgenstein's *On Certainty* came from the last year and a half of his life. He died before he had a chance to "polish," edit, and arrange them, so the form of the current work was imposed by the editors who collected his comments. The reflections in this work were spurred on by G. E. Moore's defense of common sense, in which he claimed to *know* a number of propositions for sure. The articles by Moore most directly associated with Wittgenstein's reflections are Moore's

"Proof of the External World" and "Defense of Common Sense." In these essays Moore offers an argument to refute idealism, the belief that there is no world external to the mind (or at least that if there is, it is unknowable).

In Moore's essay in defense of common sense, he argues that there are various propositions of common sense, and all of us know them with the utmost certainty. Beliefs of common sense are beliefs like "There exists at present a living human body which is *my* body," "This body was born at a certain time in the past and has existed continuously ever since, though not without undergoing changes," "Ever since it was born, it has been either in contact with or not far from the surface of the earth," "At every moment since it was born, there have also existed many other things, having shape and size in three dimensions, from which it has been at various distances," "The earth existed for many years before my body was born," etc.[10]

Wittgenstein comments in *On Certainty* extensively about what Moore calls propositions of common sense. Moore claims to know them; Wittgenstein doesn't say that we should doubt them—he is not an idealist. Rather, he is concerned initially about the language we use to talk of these beliefs. He argues that when we talk about knowing or doubting, we are normally talking about things whose truth rises or falls on the basis of argument or evidence. In contrast, beliefs of common sense are not the sort of things anyone has attempted to "prove" by making an evidential case. However, that doesn't mean these propositions are in doubt. Rather, they are absolutely certain for us, because they are totally fundamental to our whole way of thinking and interacting with the world. Ultimately, they reflect the way we act, that is, our form of life. Hence, they don't really rest on grounds or evidence, and so the language of knowing and doubting is out of place. These propositions are even more certain than propositions for which we have presented an extremely well-argued case. Hence, saying "I know" before stating one of these propositions of common sense says nothing more nor less than uttering the proposition without using "I know" at all. Wittgenstein makes these points in a series of comments; let me offer just one series as exemplary:

> "I *know* that I have never been on the moon." . . . I want to say: my not having been on the moon is as sure a thing for me as any grounds I could give for it. (sec. 111)

> And isn't that what Moore wants to say, when he says he *knows* all these things?—But is his knowing it really what is in question, and not rather that some of these propositions must be solid for us? (sec. 112)

> If you are not certain of any fact, you cannot be certain of the meaning of your words either. (sec. 114)[11]

> If you tried to doubt everything you would not get as far as doubting anything. The game of doubting itself presupposes certainty. (sec. 115)[12]

As Wittgenstein says, he doesn't need to give arguments and evidence to be certain he has never been on the moon. Groundlessly, though not therefore erroneously, he knows the truth of this proposition for certain. Some things are just (to use Wittgenstein's terminology) solid for us. Doubt is ruled out. Though Wittgenstein's point about various propositions being foundational for us applies to propositions that are not ones we would label "common sense claims" (e.g., 'I'm in pain' for me is basic when that is the case; I don't need to build an apologetic case for the view before I have a right to say "ouch!"), his point surely includes common sense propositions. Without these propositions being certain, it is hard to know how we could do or think anything. As Wittgenstein says, doubting presupposes certainty, i.e., to use an example from another chapter, it makes no sense for me to wonder whether the cat that walks into a classroom is really a dog unless I already know the concept of a dog, that of a cat, and, even more fundamentally, that of an animal. Surely Descartes, who thought everything was dubitable except the *cogito*, went too far, and surely postmoderns committed to perspectivism go too far when they say that whatever they know, including what we have called propositions of common sense, isn't absolutely true but only true for them.

Something else is also foundational and indubitable: whole language-games—complete forms of life. Wittgenstein is very clear that within any language-game there are various uses of language. In some language-games like history and science, users make claims that they believe are true. Using the rules in a language-game about how to confirm or disconfirm a claim (assuming the language-game is one in which it makes sense to talk of truth and falsity, confirming or disconfirming a claim), it is possible to decide whether a particular claim is true or false. However, what one cannot do is doubt the whole language-game, and then, using criteria for confirmation/

disconfirmation that are independent of all language-games, decide whether or not a given language-game should be eliminated. It is impossible to do this because there are no such rules for determining truth that are external to all language-games. All rules for determining what is true or false come within each language-game. Those rules allow one to judge individual propositions in a language-game, but they don't allow one to judge whether a whole language-game is true or false, and whether it should be kept or removed.

Let me cite two places where Wittgenstein makes this point, and then offer an illustration or two. Toward the end of the *Investigations* Wittgenstein writes about certainty in mathematics. He notes various things that can be confirmed or refuted in the language-game of mathematics. However, he wants to make it clear that this doesn't mean one can reject or even critique the language-game as a whole. He writes that "what has to be accepted, the given, is—so one could say—*forms of life.*"13

In *On Certainty* Wittgenstein discusses knowledge of basic facts about the world, like the fact that water boils and doesn't freeze under certain circumstances. He then asks whether it is possible that we might be wrong about this. Beginning with several rhetorical questions, his answer is emphatically no, but what is most helpful is the reasoning he offers behind the answer. He writes,

> Wouldn't a mistake topple all judgment with it? More: what could stand if that were to fall? Might someone discover something that made us say "It was a mistake"?
>
> Whatever may happen in the future, however water may behave in the future,—we *know* that up to now it has behaved *thus* in innumerable instances.
>
> This fact is fused into the foundations of our language-game.14

Immediately following these remarks, we read,

> You must bear in mind that the language-game is so to say something unpredictable. I mean: it is not based on ground. It is not reasonable (or unreasonable).
>
> It is there—like our life.15

These last comments are especially helpful. They remind us that, as previously noted, Wittgenstein says that terms like 'know' and 'doubt' are appropriate when whether we believe or doubt something depends on the grounds and evidence we have for so doing. But some things are so foundational that we know they are certainly true or false apart from any grounds or evidence one could marshal for or against them. They do not rise or fall on the basis of evidence. Here Wittgenstein says that this is true of whole language-games. They are not subject to "proof" or "refutation"; as forms of the way we live our lives, they are just there.

A couple of examples illustrate this point. Imagine that one morning I am teaching a class. It ends, I pick up my lecture notes, and I begin to walk toward the classroom door. Just as I arrive at the door and reach for the doorknob, one of my students yells, "I doubt it!" Puzzled by this, I turn and ask the student what he meant. He replies that he saw me walk from the podium to the door, and that just isn't the way to move from point "A" to point "B". In order to express his disapproval he yelled "I doubt it!" Increasingly more puzzled, I tell him that I don't know what he means. Did I go too slowly or too quickly? He replies that his doubt isn't about that; rather, his point is that walking at whatever speed just isn't the "right" way for humans to move from one place to another. I reply, "But that's just what humans do. We walk or run. Sometimes we even crawl on our hands and knees, but we use our legs and arms to get from one point to another. There's no room for doubting whether this is the 'right' way for a human to do this; this is simply what we do."

What the imagined student is doing is questioning the very language-game, the form of life we humans live when we change spatial locations. But it makes no sense to question it; it's not as though there is some other alternative that might work well, given human nature as it is. So, what must be accepted is the given, forms of life, as Wittgenstein says.

Another example of this kind of meaningless doubt involves a case where one is looking at an unweaned baby. As we watch, we notice a momentary trace of a smile on the child's face, and we think to ourselves that he must be happy. Wittgenstein asks a question, and responds with another question and then a parenthetical remark: "Are we perhaps over-hasty in our assumption that the smile of an unweaned infant is not a pretence?— And on what experience is our assumption based? (Lying is a language-game that needs to be learned like any other one.)"[16] Wittgenstein imagines that as someone sees the baby smile she thinks to herself, perhaps the baby wants something and knows that if he smiles people might give him what he wants. He's not really happy or positive about onlookers, but he's pretending so that he can get something from them. What Wittgenstein is asking is whether, in a real situation when we are viewing our friends' new baby and the baby smiles, it would be appropriate to raise such a doubt. His answer is that we are over-hasty if we wonder whether the baby is faking a smile. That is so, because a baby at such an early stage of development hasn't learned what lying is, let alone how to do it. To suspect the baby of faking the smile is in effect to reject what we know is true of human development; it is to reject the form of life that is true of a baby's abilities at this stage of life.

Immediately following this remark, Wittgenstein asks:

> Why can't a dog simulate pain? Is he too honest? Could one teach a dog to simulate pain? Perhaps it is possible to teach him to howl on particular occasions as if he were in pain, even when he is not. But the surroundings which are necessary for this behaviour to be real simulation are missing.[17]

The point seems rather clear. Pretending is a rather complex activity that involves various things that one must know and do to pretend. A dog's form of life just isn't such that it would make sense for us to think a dog was really pretending. Similarly, an unweaned baby needs to learn a number of things before there will be a context for it even to understand what pretending is, let alone to do it.[18] To raise the kinds of questions and doubts imagined is to call in question the whole language-game; it is to assume that the language-game is or at least should be different than it is. But such doubts and objections are totally out of place. One doesn't doubt a whole language-game as though it were illegitimate. That would be as wrong-headed as thinking that the baby is faking the smile, the dog knows how to pretend, or that walking from one place to another is the wrong way for a human to move from point "A" to point "B".

So, we have seen that it doesn't make sense to doubt matters of common sense and language-games as a whole. There is a further reason for not doing so, and Wittgenstein makes that point especially clear in *On Certainty*. What is so troublesome with doubts of the sort we are considering is that the beliefs involved are the very foundation of our whole worldview, that is, our whole way of looking at the world. So, to doubt one of those beliefs is not merely to doubt one belief but to call into question the whole conceptual framework we have as humans for interacting with the world. Wittgenstein mentions this point in many sections of *On Certainty*. There are far too many to quote them all, but let me at least offer a sample:[19]

> If someone said to me that he doubted whether he had a body I should take him to be a half-wit. But I shouldn't know what it would mean to try to convince him that he had one. And if I had said something, and that had removed his doubt, I should not know how or why.[20]

> But when does one say of something that it is certain? For there can be dispute whether something *is* certain; I mean, when something is *objectively* certain.

> There are countless general empirical propositions that count as certain for us.

> One such is that if someone's arm is cut off it will not grow again. Another, if someone's head is cut off he is dead and will never live again.

> Experience can be said to teach us these propositions. However, it does not teach us them in isolation: rather, it teaches us a host of interdependent propositions. If they were isolated I might perhaps doubt them, for I have no experience relating to them.[21]

The problem with the "half-wit" who doubts whether he has a body is that his picture of the world, his overall conceptual framework, is very different from ours. That being so, who knows what might convince him that he does have a body? And as Wittgenstein says about why it is so hard to reject beliefs of this sort, we don't learn them in isolation. We learn them as part of an overall way of understanding the world. The ultimate problem with raising the kinds of doubts we've been talking about is not just that they put in question our whole way of understanding reality. It is also that we have no idea of what to put in their place if these beliefs and the picture of reality they paint are rejected. Put another way, we may all be just brains in a vat, but all the "equipment" we have for knowing anything says otherwise. If we really are just brains in a vat, we have no idea of how we'd go about showing that to be so. Hence, certain doubts make no sense. One can, if one wants, make an evidential case to support basic beliefs about the nature of reality, but that's really not necessary. Neither objectively nor subjectively should we doubt them. To be uncertain about such beliefs is likely a mental disturbance.

So far we have considered types of claims which Wittgenstein says make no sense to doubt. I think he is absolutely right about this, and it is important in that it shows that those who think we can know nothing with any kind of assurance are wrong. If they think otherwise, they need to offer an argument as to why their doubts about such propositions don't bespeak a mental disturbance. It is hard to imagine what such an argument could be.

Does the preceding mean that no propositions are appropriate to doubt? Should we just believe anything and everything, regardless of the objective case we could make for it? Wittgenstein does not say this, nor would I. Certainly, there are many claims we say we know, claims about other people, objects, events, and concepts. And for someone to doubt them is not nonsensical. Into this category we would put many claims about the empirical world, about history, about science, and of course, claims about philosophy, theology, and religion. Such beliefs can be supported or attacked by argument and evidence, and those who attack them don't suffer from a mental illness.

What we need to know is how to satisfy such doubts and when to believe that we have done so. My answer borrows from what I have said about evaluating arguments and evidence, but it also comes from things I find in Wittgenstein. I am not suggesting that he would agree with the way I use his ideas. My point is that he does comment on the kind of doubts we are now considering, and I think his comments are helpful. These doubts are legitimate because the proposition(s) in question require(s) evidential support in order for us to believe that they have objective certainty, and it may be that no such evidential case has been offered. Or perhaps the case has been made, but the doubter isn't aware of the arguments and evidence that make the proposition objectively certain.

Suppose someone raises a doubt about the resurrection of Christ. This doubt is not senseless, and I owe it to my enquiring friend to show him the arguments and evidence that lead me to believe that Christ is risen. As I present that evidence, I must first clarify exactly what my friend is challenging and what I must prove, to show that it is highly, objectively certain that Christ is risen. As I present my case, I must evaluate every argument and evidence by the tests I raised earlier in chapter 5: is it true, is it relevant, and how much does it prove? And in all three cases, how do I know? That is, I must be concerned about the quality of my arguments and evidences even more than about the quantity of them.

Now suppose that I have offered an objective case for the resurrection with arguments of the kind required, and yet my friend still isn't satisfied. If this is so because my objective case leaves key elements unsupported, then he should doubt, and I should offer more arguments and evidences to fill in the gaps in my argument. Suppose, however, that he agrees that I have made the objective case, and yet he is still unconvinced. That is, I have made a case that renders it 95 percent objectively certain that Christ arose, and my friend agrees, but he is not subjectively certain. Or suppose that he won't allow himself to agree that an objectively certain case has been offered, so in the face of the types and amounts of arguments required, he wants more evidence.

In response, I must first say that if his uncertainty about the objective case stems from subjective concerns, it may be that no matter how good the objective case, our friend won't accept it as true. Unfortunately, you can't convince everyone. In such cases we must make the best case we can, but then the type of subjective convincing needed must be left to the Holy Spirit.

Suppose, however, that the problem isn't one of subjective uncertainty, but rather that our friend sees all the evidence we've raised and yet isn't convinced that an adequate objective case has been made. He should agree that the objective case is sufficient because the case built satisfies the three tests mentioned. But he's not convinced, because he wants a final argument or evidence that removes all doubt and explains everything he thinks still needs explanation. Suppose, for example, we are discussing the number of eyewitnesses who claimed to see Jesus alive after he died. We note 20 people who claimed to be eyewitnesses, or perhaps we offer even as many as 100 eyewitnesses (the apostle Paul says there were 500 who saw the risen Christ on one occasion). We further offer psychological evidence that suggests conclusively that all of these people were not hallucinating when they claimed to see Christ. In the face of all of this evidence, our friend says this still isn't enough. If there were just five more eyewitnesses, that would remove all doubt. So we mention another five, and he still asks for more.

It is at this point that the doubts no longer make sense. The person who continues such doubt is looking for the final explanation or argument that will supposedly remove all doubt. But the person looking for such an argument does not even know what he is looking for. If he's not satisfied by the series of explanations, arguments, and evidences we offer, what would satisfy him? If he knows, he may realize he already has this "final" explanation or proof. If he doesn't know what it would look like, he probably won't recognize it when he sees it.[22]

But still, can't we be mistaken about the evidence we present and the conclusion we draw from it? Yes, it is possible, but what must be emphasized is that the evidence for many propositions is public. That means it is available to others. They don't have to rely on our say-so; they can check it out. If they examine the evidence and agree with our conclusions (and it is determined that they are giving an honest and sincere report rather than really disagreeing but going along with us to avoid upsetting us), it makes no sense to continue doubting.

This must not be misunderstood. I am not saying we are infallible in our handling of the evidence, or that every proposition can be confirmed so as to be 99 percent objectively certain. Where doubt is in order, there may not be enough evidence for anyone to feel subjectively persuaded. We should hold such ideas more tentatively. But if a case for high objective certainty has been made, then one should not hesitate to feel subjectively certain about it. What percentage of objective certainty must there be before subjective certainty is warranted? As already said, there is no simple way to quantify this. What can be stated is the method to be used in making the case: first clarify what must be proved to make a case, and then offer arguments and evidence that meet the requirements of the three tests already mentioned (is it true, is it relevant, and how much does it prove?). When that procedure is followed and the quality of the evidence warrants believing that objective certainty that warrants subjective certainty has been established, continuing to doubt no longer makes sense.

Having read the above about various types of doubt and certainty, one may still have a question. One might wonder whether we ought to be more subjectively certain about propositions in math and logic than about propositions of history, theology, or the like. In the *Investigations* Wittgenstein offers several remarks that I find very helpful in addressing the degree of certainty one can have about propositions in various language-games. Immediately before the selection I quote below, Wittgenstein discusses whether someone else can know what I intend to do. He argues that it is possible for others to do so, although the basis for their knowing my intentions is not the same as my basis for knowing my intentions. Immediately after these remarks, Wittgenstein turns to address whether one can have an equal amount of certainty about several different matters of fact. He writes,

> I can be as *certain* of someone else's sensations as of any fact. But this does not make the propositions "He is much depressed", "$25 \times 25 = 625$" and "I am sixty years old" into similar instruments. The explanation suggests itself that the certainty is of a different *kind*.—This seems to point to a psychological difference. But the difference is logical!

> "But, if you are *certain*, isn't it that you are shutting your eyes in face of [*sic*] doubt?"—They are shut.

> Am I less certain that this man is in pain than that twice two is four?—Does this shew the former to be mathematical certainty?—'Mathematical certainty' is not a psychological concept.

> The kind of certainty is the kind of language-game.[23]

In the cited portion, Wittgenstein does not use the terms 'objective certainty' and 'subjective certainty,' but I think it isn't hard to tell which he has in mind. Let me make this point by offering an interpretation of the passage quoted.

The comments about being as certain about someone else's sensations as about some mathematical fact refer at least in part to a theme Wittgenstein comments on rather extensively in the *Investigations*. For lack of a better term, let me refer to it as Wittgenstein's *depsychologizing* of private mental states. For a long time philosophers had argued that in order to know what is going on in someone's mind at a given time (for example, to know they were experiencing pain, to know they intended to do a certain action, or even to know what an author intended to say when he wrote an essay), it is necessary somehow to delve into the internal workings of their mind. Since we don't really have access to someone else's private sensations or thoughts, that means, according to some philosophers, that we can never know what they are thinking or feeling, even if they express their thoughts and feelings to us. The only way to be sure about such things, many believed, is to have access to a person's private mental states, and no one has such access except the person who has those mental states.

In contrast, Wittgenstein argued that we must think differently about such things. In order to know what is going on inside of a person's mind, we don't need privileged access to his private states. Rather, everything we need to know is public for anyone to see. Specifically, that involves a person's actions, the expressions on his face, and the words he says in a given situation. Hence, if someone says she has a toothache, I don't need to "get inside her head" to confirm that this is true. When I see her hold her jaw, grimace, and say "Ow, that hurts!" I have all the information I need in order to know what she is feeling. But couldn't she be faking? Of course, but all the evidence that she is faking or that she is genuinely in pain is already present to me and anyone else who might want to know what is actually happening. If she is faking, there will be something she says or does, or something about the situation (perhaps I notice that there are several movie cameras held by people who are watching her—that should make me suspicious) that will show that to us. If she is genuinely in pain, there will be clues in the situation that will show that. So, what we need to do is move our talk about private sensations and mental states out of the inner recesses of the mind, and focus instead on what is public to all of us. In a word, we need to *depsychologize* our thinking about inner mental states.

With this in mind, we are now ready to look at the first paragraph quoted above. I believe that "the kind of certainty I can have about someone else being in pain is as certain as what I have for any fact" refers to subjective certainty. Since objective certainty of a matter of fact can at best be 99 percent, whereas I can be objectively 100 percent certain about a proposition of math or logic, clearly that's not the same certainty. However, if we are thinking instead of subjective certainty, then it is true that I can be as convinced that you are in pain as I am that $2 + 2 = 4$. Wittgenstein then warns us that we dare not think that several different sentences which for us are equally subjectively certain are therefore, to use his words, "the same kind of instrument." For they are not. When it comes to being objectively certain about the three propositions he mentions, it is clear that the rules that govern such claims are different. I know about your inner sensations in a way that is different from my knowledge of my inner sensations and my knowledge of my age. Undoubtedly there will be grounds for my belief about what you are feeling (the public clues mentioned above, like what you say and how you look, for example), whereas my belief about my age is likely groundless. That is, I don't know it by making an evidential case for it and then concluding that I have a right to believe that I am a certain number of years old. That's probably how I will come to believe that you are in pain, but not how I know my private sensations or my age. In addition, the mathematical proposition is a different sort of claim than either of the first two. I don't confirm it by some kind of empirical investigation. If I conclude that it is objectively certain, it will be 100 percent objectively certain, whereas my views about your inner sensations are at most 99 percent objectively certain. And, the procedure I use to confirm whether 25×25 does equal 625 is different from what I would do to convince myself that $2 + 2 = 4$. In the latter case, I would likely know it intuitively. In the former I would most likely need to work the math problem, unless I'm one of those people who has extensively memorized multiplication tables.

The end of the quoted first paragraph is very important to support this interpretation. Wittgenstein says that we are inclined to think the difference between the three sentences is psychological, but it is really logical. Now had Wittgenstein said it is psychological, then I think we'd have to reconsider whether his point about the three sentences isn't in fact about subjective certainty rather than objective certainty. But the fact that he says the difference is logical shows that the point he is making about the three claims is about objective certainty. What is the logical difference to which he points? It is that each one comes from a different language-game, and as he has already said, each language-game has its own rules and procedures, its own methods of demonstrating that a proposition in the language-game is objectively certain or uncertain, and so forth. In the preceding paragraph I explained something of what makes each sentence a "different instrument." If we are really talking about subjective certainty, there is no point to be made about the rules and procedures of each language-game.

Even so, I suggested that the first sentence of the first quoted paragraph is about subjective certainty. Indeed, that is so, and Wittgenstein returns to that topic in the following paragraphs. Of special interest is the third paragraph. It begins with a question. If the question is about objective certainty, then it doesn't entirely make sense. That is so, because we have already granted—and Wittgenstein knows this—that an empirical proposition about someone else's pain can be at best 99 percent objectively certain, whereas a proposition of math is 100 percent objectively certain if it is true.

But surely that's not the point Wittgenstein is making—it's a rather obvious point that many a beginner in philosophy would know. Rather, Wittgenstein is harkening back to the point with which we began—I am not less certain about a matter of empirical fact than I am about a proposition of math and logic. I'm equally certain. But the only way that can be true is if the topic is subjective certainty.

So, I am saying that Wittgenstein wants us to answer the first question of paragraph 3 negatively—"No, I'm equally certain." Let's test this interpretation. Wittgenstein responds to this question with another question: "Does this shew the former to be mathematical certainty?" That is, does this sameness in subjective certainty mean that certainty about someone else's pain is really mathematical certainty? If Wittgenstein is really making a point about objective certainty, then the answer to this second question might be yes, though of course that would be absurd, since we know that Wittgenstein believed that each language-game is logically distinct from all others. He knows that the rules that govern confirmation of propositions of math and logic are not the same as those that govern matters of empirical fact. He knows that objectively one could be 100 percent certain about a proposition of math or logic, but that isn't so for empirical propositions.

So what, then, does Wittgenstein mean? He expects us to answer that the fact that the two types of propositions are equally *subjectively* certain doesn't mean they are from the same language-game. That is, "No, certainty of a proposition about others is not mathematical certainty just because the subjective certainty one has about each claim is the same." Note that the last sentence of paragraph 3, Wittgenstein's comment, confirms my interpretation. He says mathematical certainty isn't a psychological concept. But a person's *psychological* certainty enters the picture only when we are dealing with subjective certainty, not objective certainty. That is, a psychological frame of mind is not about the facts of the case that can be marshaled for and against a belief; it is about the degree to which one is convinced or persuaded that something is true, regardless of the evidential support there is for the proposition's truth. Hence, Wittgenstein's main point in this third paragraph is to say something about subjective certainty, and what he intends to say is that regardless of the language-game, one can be just as subjectively certain about a proposition about a matter of fact as one is about a claim of math and logic.

The final comment—"The kind of certainty is the kind of language-game"—addresses objective certainty. Since one can be just as certain subjectively and have the same state of mind, regardless of whether one is subjectively certain about a claim of math or logic or about a matter of fact, it is then clear that the kind of *subjective* certainty one has in any language-game doesn't depend on the language-game. Hence, Wittgenstein's claim—that the kind of certainty *does* depend on the kind of language-game—must be about objective certainty and how you get it in each language-game, not about subjective certainty. That is, Wittgenstein's comment returns to the point he has been making about the logical difference between language-games.

Having offered my interpretation of this passage, what point for our discussion about doubt and certainty do I want to make? I agree with Wittgenstein that the kind of certainty—objective certainty—depends on the kind of language-game. The language-game of theology is a different sort of game than the language-game of math or logic, or even science. However, there have been (and still are) a number of people who believe that since propositions in theology can never be as certain (objectively) as propositions of math or logic, that means that it will be impossible for anyone ever to offer *sufficient* evidence to support belief in any theology or religion. You can't get 100 percent objective certainty, and usually you can't get 99 percent objective certainty or even 95 percent objective certainty. But then, these critics of religious belief hold that, given the importance of religious beliefs to one's eternal destiny, let alone the matter of how one lives on earth before he steps into eternity, it simply isn't appropriate for someone to embrace any theology or religion when the amount or degree of objective certainty can never be 100 percent, and when it is even unlikely that one can achieve 95 percent objective certainty.

In contrast, my point is that this complaint is to a large degree inappropriate. Why? Because if we call into question every claim that cannot be confirmed to 100 percent objective certainty (or even to 99 percent), we have to conclude that no one really knows anything about history, or science, or even about common sense propositions. And that would, of course, be absurd! But then, if something is less than 100 percent objectively certain because, in the first place, it is a matter of fact, not a matter of logic or math, that shouldn't make anyone believe that he or she has no right to believe that matter of fact. Of course, as the degree of objective certainty a proposition (or propositions) has goes downward, belief in the proposition should become more tentative. And at some point (when the quality of evidence needed to support the proposition as true just isn't there), one shouldn't hold the belief at all.

But there is a further point I want to make, even though Wittgenstein's last sentence—"the kind of certainty is the kind of language-game"—doesn't make this point. Notice that this final claim leaves open the possibility that even though the kind of certainty (objective) depends on the kind of language-game, it doesn't say that the *degree* of *subjective* certainty depends on the kind of language-game. Wittgenstein doesn't need to say that, because he has already in the earlier paragraphs made that point. That was the point, we said, of claiming that one can be just as certain that someone else is in pain as we can be certain that 2 + 2 = 4.

But why am I making this point again? My reason is that there might well be some who would say that, regardless of the degree of objective certainty you could reach in a given language-game such as religion or theology, you would never be justified in being absolutely *subjectively* certain of the truth of religious and theological claims. On the contrary, however, what Wittgenstein has said is that regardless of the language-game, one can be just as subjectively certain about the propositions of theology as of the propositions of math and logic. Now we know that sometimes people are subjectively certain about things that are not true (belief in Santa Claus and the tooth fairy), but of course, that is so because one cannot make much of an objective case for the existence of the tooth fairy or Santa Claus, and a very convincing objective case can be made against their existence. If we simply embrace Christianity (or any other religion) as true and are subjectively convinced it is true without any idea whatsoever of whether there is evidence (of any quality and quantity) to support it, then it is possible that our subjective conviction may be as ill-placed as belief in the tooth fairy or Santa Claus. But it seems to me that this is why an apologetic for the Christian faith is so important. We are not simply taking a leap of faith *in the dark*! Even if we didn't initially embrace Christianity because of the evidential objective case for it, that doesn't mean such a case can't be built. It can be built, and in chapter 5 and in this chapter I am explaining how to do so.

In sum, then, it is illegitimate to reject Christianity simply because the objective case for it can never be better than 99 percent certain, or because you don't have a "right" to be as subjectively certain of its truth as you are of the truth of claims in math and logic. Christian apologists must make the case for Christianity; the fact that it can be at best no more than 99 percent objectively certain no more disqualifies it from acceptance than the fact that propositions of common sense cannot be more than 99 percent objectively certain disqualifies them as unfit for belief. And, if you have a right at all to be subjectively certain that Christianity is true, you have a right to be just as subjectively certain it is true as you are that propositions of math and logic are true. Issues relating to doubt and certainty do not disqualify Christianity as unfit for human consumption!

WHAT ABOUT FOUNDATIONALISM?

In chapters 5 and 6 we have focused on issues raised by modern epistemology as a challenge to Christian faith. I have addressed the matter of "sufficient evidence" from several different angles. Two more issues must be addressed in order to present my fullest understanding of how to respond to the complaint that Christianity isn't supported by sufficient evidence. The first is the matter of foundationalism.

In reading chapter 5 and the previous part of this chapter, readers may have wondered what criteria I am using to decide whether an argument is true and to decide the degree of objective certainty various arguments and evidences produce. Put simply, should we evaluate such things in terms of how well they meet classical foundationalist criteria of proper basicality? If not, then what standard must be met for us to have the right to say that arguments and evidences we present are true?

In the next chapter, I shall discuss Alvin Plantinga's Reformed Epistemology. Here I appeal to what he says about classical foundationalism. Plantinga explains that critics of theism complain that believers do not have a right to maintain belief in God, because there isn't sufficient evidence to support that belief. He also explains that this objection to theism ultimately rests on classical foundationalism. Classical foundationalism distinguishes between basic and non-basic beliefs. Non-basic beliefs are supported by beliefs that either are basic or at least lead us ultimately to basic beliefs. Basic beliefs are supported by the fact that they are either self-evident, evident to the senses, or incorrigible.

Plantinga correctly rejects these criteria for proper basicality, in part because foundationalists' claims about these criteria do not themselves meet the criteria. Of course, if we reject classical foundationalist criteria of proper basicality, that opens the door for people to have warrant to believe in God even if they have never constructed, read, or heard an evidential case for God's existence.

As readers will see in the chapter on Reformed Epistemology, I agree with Plantinga's rejection of classical foundationalism, and I also agree that the mild form of foundationalism he puts in its place successfully addresses the *de jure* challenges to theistic belief. But that isn't the whole story. What about the truth of Christianity, and what criteria are we to use in evaluating whether, in particular, the arguments and evidences we produce to support Christian beliefs provide sufficient evidence that it is true? I have argued that there are true arguments and evidences that support Christian belief to the point that we can be both objectively and subjectively certain that it is true. What I haven't done is state explicitly the criteria that must be met in order for us to consider a belief true. I believe that my answer is implicit in the discussions contained in the chapters on postmodern skepticism and on modern skepticism, including this chapter. But I need to make my answer explicit. Doing so will provide my understanding of what we should do with foundationalism.

First, I note that one could hold either a foundationalist or a coherentist theory of knowledge and make a strong case for the truth of Christianity. A coherentist theory of knowledge holds that beliefs are supported by other beliefs in a person's noetic structure (as is the case with foundationalism), but no belief in one's noetic structure is any more or less basic than any other belief one holds. It is common to say that a foundationalist theory of knowledge portrays knowledge as a pyramid, with beliefs built on top of other beliefs which eventually lead to beliefs that are the foundation of knowledge and rest on nothing else. In contrast, a coherentist theory of knowledge often portrays knowledge as a web of interconnected beliefs, none more or less basic than any other. Now as long as the form of coherentism one holds agrees that we have access to the world outside our minds (as foundationalism typically does), there seems to be no good reason that someone who believes Christianity to be true could not hold a coherentist theory of knowledge, or that she could not make a compelling case for Christianity's truth.

Having said the above, I still find myself in the foundationalist camp. Though I think there are in fact some basic beliefs that meet classical foundationalist criteria for proper basicality, I reject classical foundationalism for the same reasons (to be explained more fully in the next chapter) as Plantinga does. So what would I put in its place? Here it is crucial to remember that my answer focuses on criteria to use when attempting to address the question of whether Christianity is true (the *de facto* issue). For me, the place to start is not so much with a set of basic beliefs but with presuppositions about the best method for determining what is true of the world. As I have argued previously, those assumptions initially involve identifying the intellectual equipment that all of us have been given. We have been given sense organs and minds that can reason. Of course, some people are better at reasoning than others, just as some people have a more acute sense of hearing or vision than others. For those with vision or hearing that is impaired by some physical problem, for example, we live at a time when there are hearing aids, glasses, and contact lenses that can help us with these impaired senses.

Using our minds and senses, we are able to interact with the world around us and with one another. As we do, we begin to learn a variety of concepts. Over time our conceptual framework or noetic structure begins to take shape. As noted in chapter 4, without learning various concepts it would be hard to understand what is happening around us. Of course, it is also likely that we will be especially positive to certain ideas as opposed to others. However, preferences and presuppositions don't guarantee that we can't get things correct, change our minds upon viewing evidence and argument, or convince others of our views. The case for this was made in chapter 4, and I needn't repeat it here.

So, we use the intellectual equipment we are given to interact with the world. In some cases, what we learn doesn't need to be supported by an evidential case for us to believe it. As we saw in our study of Wittgenstein on doubt and certainty, some doubts don't make sense to maintain. On the other hand, others do make sense and need to be satisfied before we can believe with certainty (subjective in this case) the claims in question. As explained in this chapter, our subjective certainty hopefully is based on the objective certainty of the beliefs we hold. That means that there are a number of beliefs for which we must build an objective case; that is, we must present the arguments and evidences that support the beliefs. But how do we know whether we have succeeded in presenting an objectively certain case? Using the intellectual equipment we have been given, we interact with the world around us. We begin by clarifying what exactly the issue before us is and by clarifying what we would need to prove in order to establish the truth of the belief in question. As arguments and evidences are presented, we ask whether they are true and relevant, and how much they prove. As we ask whether the evidence is true, we may find that some of it meets classical foundationalist criteria for proper basicality. If not, that doesn't mean it can't still be true. We marshal the evidence and evaluate it. In the process of doing so, a major help in assuring us that we are "getting it right" is the public nature of much of the evidence. If someone has doubts about our evidence or argument, they are welcome to consider the same data that we studied. If arguments are of a logical nature, others can check to see whether our reasoning has misfired. If arguments are about facts that are empirically observable, others may go and observe the same data we did in coming to an evaluation of what is true and false.

What I am proposing, then, is a mild form of foundationalism, and in chapter 5 and this chapter I am showing how one might use it in addressing *de facto* questions about the truth of one's beliefs. As a foundationalist, I believe that some beliefs rest on other beliefs that are more fundamental to one's worldview. But my main concern is not to identify which beliefs are more fundamental and which are less. Rather, my concern is how to build a case for the truth of *any* belief, regardless of its "position" in one's noetic structure.

As for the truth of some theological and religious claims, it may be hard to build an objective case to support them. But that doesn't mean that we must abandon those beliefs altogether. Rather it shows that we should be considerably less dogmatic about them, because we understand the assets and limitations of the objective case that can be made for those claims, and hence while we are subjectively convinced that the claims are true, the degree of our subjective conviction is not as high as when propositions can be shown to be, for example, 95 percent objectively certain.

What I have also been saying is that if one doesn't think the objective case is strong enough, there is a way to test it out. The arguments and evidences are available to anyone who cares to consider them. Our presuppositions and perspectives don't guarantee that we can't get anything right, can't agree with one another, or can't ever convince someone else of our beliefs. Of course, I am not saying that we are infallible in our knowledge claims or that we can always present a highly objectively certain case. Nor am I saying that every time we present a strong case, we can be sure the nonbeliever will be persuaded. What I am saying, however, is that if one thinks the case for Christianity isn't strong enough to be believable, don't think a stronger objective case is easier to build for a non-Christian worldview. We must be careful that we don't make the requirements for a "successful case" so rigorous that no one has enough evidence for anything to say that it is true. Of course, proving that a strong evidential case can be made for Christianity, strong enough to warrant subjective certainty, depends on presenting and evaluating the evidence for the various tenets of the faith. In the final section of this book, I intend to illustrate how this can be done by presenting a case for several key tenets of the Christian faith.

CONCLUSION

In conclusion, in the chapters addressing postmodern and modern skepticism, I have presented my own approach to answering those points of view. There is a need to explain what is wrong with postmodern and modern epistemology. One must also explain what one would put in their place. It is also necessary to explain the kind of evidential case needed, with this alternate epistemology, to support the truth of any worldview, including Christianity, and how we could know that the case offered actually presented sufficient argument and evidence to believe the views in question.

In this first section of the book, I have argued that there is truth and that it is knowable. Even more, I have explained why it is not wrong to believe, given evidence and argument to support it, in the truth of Christianity. But how, specifically, might one go about defending Christianity as a whole, or some individual tenet of the faith? Christian apologists have not always agreed on this matter, so they have offered different methods and strategies for defending Christian truth. In the next section, I present and evaluate three of the most important approaches to defending Christian truth.

PART TWO

Ways of Defending Christian Truth

Chapter 7

Reformed Epistemology

Now that we have shown that it makes sense to think there is such a thing as truth and that it is possible to know what is true, our discussion turns to how to go about demonstrating the truth of Christianity. We begin with Reformed Epistemology.

Would it be irrational to believe in God if you had little or no evidence for his existence? In such a situation, would you be unjustified and even break rules that are morally reprehensible to break, if you continued to believe in God? Do those who believe in God despite little evidential support and despite significant evidence against his existence (like the evil in our world) sacrifice reason and intellect on the altar of religion?

For much of the last few hundred years the predominant answer to such questions has been yes. In contrast, believers in God might agree that these questions are appropriate, but then add that there *is* sufficient evidence to prove God's existence.

Just as clearly, postmoderns of many varieties would reject these questions as meaningless. This is so because when reason is suspect and when it is believed dubious that we have any unmediated and hence objective contact with the world outside our minds, the idea of marshaling evidence and trying to "demonstrate" the truth of any claim about God's existence is nothing but nonsense. The most we can do is express what seems to be true from our point of view. Of course, our inability to make a convincing evidential case for God's existence doesn't mean he fails to exist. For all postmoderns know, God may exist, but of course, no one can prove that conclusively. So, the questions raised above are wrongheaded and should be rejected.

Though you might think the preceding is the sum total of the discussion, it is not. Over the last two to three decades there has arisen a new approach to religious epistemology. Known as Reformed Epistemology, it has gained a hearing among both Christian and secular philosophers, and has been espoused by many contemporary Christian philosophers. Adherents to Reformed Epistemology would answer the questions at the beginning of this chapter negatively. That is, they believe it is rational to believe in God, even with scant or no evidence at all. Such a believer wouldn't break any epistemic rules (or norms of any sort) if he or she embraced this belief without evidence.

Though such answers may seem impossibly naive, Reformed Epistemology is a rather sophisticated approach to religious belief. It rests on a somewhat subtle and nuanced account of belief formation in general and of the forming of religious beliefs in particular. The ablest proponent of Reformed Epistemology is Alvin Plantinga. Plantinga has expounded this position in a variety of publications. Perhaps his most detailed and well-articulated presentation of Reformed Epistemology is to be found in his "Reason and Belief in God"[1] and in his trilogy: *Warrant: the Current Debate*, *Warrant and Proper Function*, and *Warranted Christian Belief*. These works are the focus of my presentation.

Reformed Epistemology rejects postmodern epistemology, but that doesn't mean it fully embraces modern epistemology as described in my chapter 2. So, what does it do with these epistemologies, and more specifically, what do Reformed Epistemologists believe? Plantinga, in *Warranted Christian Belief*, asserts that this work (and presumably the whole approach of Reformed Epistemology) is a piece of Christian apologetics.[2] How so? Though Reformed Epistemology has been amply criticized, many of the charges leveled against it show that critics haven't really understood the issues of concern to Reformed Epistemologists, nor have they adequately grasped how the views of Reformed Epistemology address those issues. Hence, we must begin by clarifying what Reformed Epistemology intends to address.[3]

REFORMED EPISTEMOLOGY: WHAT'S THE POINT?

I begin with several definitions and distinctions offered by Alvin Plantinga. Especially in his "Reason and Belief in God" and *Warranted Christian Belief*, Plantinga notes that nonbelievers (atheists, agnostics, and even theistic non-Christians) think there is something wrong with believing in God. But what specifically is their complaint, for they may have any number of concerns when they raise this objection?

De Jure vs. *de Facto* Objections to Christian Belief

Plantinga claims that it helps to understand nonbelievers' specific complaint by distinguishing two types of problems related to Christian belief. First, there are objections he labels *de jure* objections, while on the other hand, there are *de facto* concerns. *De jure* objections concern one of three things: epistemic justification, rationality, and/or warrant. These objections ask whether it is "rational, reasonable, justifiable, warranted to accept Christian belief. . . . Or is there something epistemically unacceptable in so doing, something foolish, or silly, or foolhardy, or stupid, or unjustified, or unreasonable, or in some other way epistemically deplorable?"[4]

Of course, in order to answer *de jure* questions one must know what epistemic justification, rationality, and warrant are. As Plantinga shows, these concepts as used in epistemology are notoriously ambiguous. I shall define them shortly, but I must first explain what Plantinga means by saying that there are *de facto* objections one might raise about Christian belief. *De facto* objections to theistic belief claim that it just isn't true. Hence, even if one is *justified* in believing in Christianity, for example, that alone wouldn't mandate that Christianity is true. In fact, there are many *de facto* objections to Christianity. One of the strongest is the problem of evil. Evil in our world, especially in so many varieties and amounts, seems to defeat the notion that any God, let alone the Christian God, exists.

While the problem of evil is perhaps the most frequently heard objection to theism's truth, there are other *de facto* objections. For example, one might believe that Christian doctrines like the Trinity, the deity of Christ, and the hypostatic union of Christ are just not true. So, a Christian might not break any epistemic rules by believing in the Trinity, but that alone is no guarantee that the Trinity is a true account of God's being.[5]

While *de jure* and *de facto* objections are distinct kinds of problems, they may in a given case coincide. For example, Plantinga notes that the facts of evil in our world may do more than simply show that theism is likely false. Evil in our world may also make it irrational to continue believing in God.[6]

In light of the distinction between *de jure* and *de facto* questions, it is easy to see that Plantinga's Reformed Epistemology addresses the *de jure* questions. If readers are unsure about this, at the very end of *Warranted Christian Belief*, Plantinga summarizes what he has done in the book. He notes the various *de jure* questions he has addressed, and concludes that contrary to the claims of nonbelievers there really is no successful *de jure* objection to Christianity. Even so, Plantinga raises a final question: is Christianity true? He affirms that this is a very important question, but it is one that goes "beyond the competence of philosophy." Plantinga thinks Christianity *is* true; he doesn't, however, turn to support its truth. Clearly, he cares about whether Christianity is true, but that is not the focus of his Reformed Epistemology.[7]

Positive vs. Negative Apologetics

Plantinga also notes that one's defense of Christian belief may be an example of either positive or negative apologetics. Negative apologetics involves defending one's beliefs against attack from opponents. The point is to rebut arguments raised against your views, not to offer positive evidence that your beliefs are correct. As such, negative apologetics are basically defensive in nature. Now, it is often true that the best defense is a strong offense, but Plantinga has in mind with negative apologetics a basically defensive stance.[8]

There are many objections to Christianity that require only a negative response. Perhaps the best-known of these is the problem of evil. This objection may be raised in either a logical or an evidential/probabilistic form. According to the former, Christian theism is accused of contradicting itself in virtue of beliefs Christians actually hold. Christians agree that an all-loving, omnipotent God exists, and they also grant that there is evil in our world. Atheists claim that those three claims, taken as a set, are logically inconsistent. Hence, they believe that there is no possible way for all three of these beliefs to be true conjointly. In order to answer this objection to belief in God, believers need not rehearse all the positive evidence for theism (arguments for God's existence, evidence for Scripture's reliability, etc.). Rather, theists need only show a possible way that all three propositions can be true. Doing so rebuts the claim that theism contradicts itself.

The problem of evil is also raised in an evidential form. In that form, atheists do not claim that theism is self-contradictory, but rather that evil is strong evidence against the likelihood or probability that theism is true. Here again, theists need not produce all the positive evidence for theism, but they must instead explain why theism is not improbable in light of evil. They may respond in a number of different ways,[9] but whichever answer they choose, it must explain why the existence of evil in our world is not fatal to any theistic system committed to an omnipotent, omni-benevolent God. Offering such an explanation is engaging in negative or defensive apologetics.[10]

In contrast to negative apologetics, positive apologetics offers positive arguments and evidences for theistic belief. In this case, the nonbeliever's challenge may be nothing more than the request "What leads you to believe in God?" Or a believer may simply want to set forth the positive evidence for belief. Plantinga's discussion of positive apologetics in "Christian Philosophy at the End of the Twentieth Century" focuses on various kinds of arguments for God's existence. They include such traditional arguments as the teleological and moral argument, but Plantinga suggests many others.[11] Presumably, positive apologetics could also be done for any other item of the faith. For example, a believer might assemble the various evidences for the resurrection of Christ. Or she might present the available manuscript evidence that shows that we know what the New Testament when first penned actually said, and then offer positive evidence that what the New Testament says happened actually did.

In regard to this distinction between positive and negative apologetics, Plantinga's Reformed Epistemology is an example of negative apologetics. When the nonbeliever claims that the believer is irrational, unjustified, and/or unwarranted in his or her belief in God, positive apologetics clearly won't work. Suppose in response to the nonbeliever's challenge, I rehearse all the positive arguments for God's existence. The nonbeliever will not likely then respond, "Oh, well, now I see it; any view supported by that kind of evidence must be rational to hold." It is more likely that the nonbeliever knows many of these positive evidences and simply rejects the idea that they are enough to warrant belief. Hence, he holds that it is irrational, etc., for the theist to continue believing.

Knowledge as Justified True Belief

For a long time in Western philosophy, knowledge has been understood as justified true belief. In recent decades that has been challenged for one reason or another, but that definition still remains in common currency, even if it is nuanced in a way that shows that philosophers using that definition have kept abreast of recent developments in epistemology. My concern now is to explain 1) what knowledge as justified true belief means, 2) why that definition is being challenged, and 3) the relevance of all of this to Reformed Epistemology.

The classical notion of knowledge as justified true belief involves several elements. First, the definition relates to propositional knowledge, i.e., knowledge of some matter of fact that is stated in a proposition. Then, a claim to *know* something is much stronger than a claim merely to *believe* it. Hence, what one knows one also believes, but the opposite isn't always the case. Belief is opinion about some matter. If we have little evidence or argument to support the belief, or if there is evidence to show the belief false (even if we don't know that evidence), then the belief doesn't qualify as something we know.

As to truth, a belief may be true and we are aware of that, it may be true and we don't know that, or it may be false and we don't know that to be the case. Presumably, if a belief is false and we know it, we won't continue to believe it. Truth in this discussion is most typically understood in a correspondence sense of truth.

One further item about true belief—to say that a belief must be true in order for one to *know* the proposition in question does not mean that we have actually marshaled the arguments and evidence to build the case for its truth. We may be aware of evidence that shows it to be true, and if we are, that will likely make us hold the belief more firmly and think that we in fact know that the proposition is true. But someone could be said to *know* a proposition so long as it is true, even if he hadn't made the evidential case himself.

However, true belief alone doesn't equal knowledge. The belief must be justified, but it is here that the waters become especially murky. That is unfortunate, as Plantinga notes, because many critics of theism reject belief in God because they think no one is justified in so believing. If justification is necessary to knowledge, and if critics claim that belief in God isn't justified, we must ascertain what epistemic justification is. This is harder than it may at first seem, because the notion of epistemic justification is used in a variety of senses in contemporary epistemology.[12] In *Warrant: The Current Debate* Plantinga isolates five senses in which epistemic justification is understood.

Perhaps the most frequently used notion of epistemic justification is deontological justification. In this sense, one is deemed to have duties and responsibilities with respect to forming and maintaining beliefs. Depending on the exact theory, those duties may vary somewhat, but the main idea is that before one believes a given proposition he must fulfill certain epistemic duties.[13] For example, one shouldn't believe (at least not strongly believe) a proposition for which he has little or no evidence. Likewise, if his reason and sense perception were used to acquire information when he was under the influence of alcohol and/or drugs, he should recognize that such a state doesn't lend toward accurate belief formation, and hence he shouldn't believe in the white elephants or psychedelic mushrooms he thinks he saw when under the influence of drugs or alcohol. If he believes anyway that such things exist, he is being epistemically irresponsible and has failed to meet his duties.

Second, Plantinga notes that there is a rather pervasive linkage in contemporary epistemology of justification and warrant or knowledge. What the exact connection is depends on how one understands warrant (a topic to be discussed in presenting Plantinga's views). For now we can simply note this use. A third sense of justification links it to epistemic internalism. As Plantinga notes, this philosophical notion is also understood in varying ways, but the basic idea of internalism is "that what determines whether a belief is warranted for a person are factors or states in some sense internal to that person; warrant conferring properties are in some way internal to the subject or cognizer."[14] As to the specific way in which those properties are internal to the subject, Plantinga answers that "they are states or conditions of which the cognizer is or can be aware."[15] Not just any states qualify, however, but rather those to which the individual subject has special access. I have no special access to the proposition that leaves change color in autumn, because anyone who isn't blind and lives in a part of the world where leaves do change color in autumn, can know whether that is happening or not on any given day. Instead, the kind of special access Plantinga has in mind may be of the following sorts: by introspection one can see that a given belief has warrant for him; or one is able to determine with certainty whether a given belief has the property that grounds or confers justification; or one knows that the pain he reports to the doctor isn't just something dreamed about last night. In sum, "the internalist holds that a person has some kind of special epistemic access to warrant and the properties that ground it."[16]

With this basic notion of internalism, I note that the third sense of epistemic justification links internalism and justification. What might that link be? Plantinga offers several options: "the believer must have cognitive access to something important lurking in the neighborhood—whether or not he *is* justified, for example, or to the *grounds* of his justification . . . or to the connection between those grounds and the justified belief."[17]

A fourth sense of justification links it with having evidence. In this sense, whether one is justified or not depends on whether the person with the belief has evidence for it, or at least on whether holding the belief at all depends on evidence.[18] With this sense of justification, to be justified in holding a belief would presumably involve the belief being true and the knower being aware of the evidence for its truth. Of course, someone might have evidence for a belief, and in that regard is justified in holding it, and yet it isn't true after all. Often, there is evidence that favors beliefs that are false—obviously, not conclusive evidence, but the cognizer doesn't realize that; she just has evidence supporting the belief and so thinks it is true.

Before moving to another sense of justification, we should note that while justification and evidence may be linked, that doesn't mean that justification and truth always come together. For it is possible that a belief that rests on evidence is true, but we don't know it to be true because we don't know any of the evidence and argument that support it. Moreover, it is also possible to have evidence for a false belief (one doesn't know or even believe it to be false) and hence to be justified in holding it, and yet the belief is false. Consider, for example, the little girl who believes that if she puts her tooth under her pillow at night, the next morning she will find money there which the tooth fairy left. She has never worked out any proof that this is so, but she still believes. Why? Because she has friends who have lost teeth before, placed them under their pillows, and found money there the next morning. Those friends' parents told them about the tooth fairy, and over time their parents have proven to be trustworthy. Similarly, the little girl's parents, also reliable sources, have told her the same story about the tooth fairy. So, she believes in the tooth fairy. Perhaps she has also lost teeth before, and has been "visited" by the tooth fairy, so that is further evidence that there is a tooth fairy. Now in the sense of justification which connects it to evidence, clearly, the little girl is justified in believing in the tooth fairy. However, she believes something that isn't true, as she will later discover. So, saying that justification is tied to evidence doesn't mean the belief so justified must be true. Moreover, it would be wrong to say the little girl *knows* there is a tooth fairy. Her belief, though justified (in the sense of "tied to evidence") isn't true, so she doesn't know it, even if she thinks she does.

Plantinga labels a fifth kind of justification *broad justification*. He says it is difficult to define this, but not impossible. It appears to be a generalization of justification in the deontological sense. This sense of justification involves things going properly from the knowing subject's perspective. But the way the knower's experience is linked to the world is excluded. As Plantinga explains, the knower may be nothing more than a brain in a vat, or he may be someone whose experience is manipulated by a demon so that what he thinks he experiences is actually illusory. Plantinga says that "nevertheless he is justified if everything goes right from there on, so to speak—if, in particular, he reasons aright and forms the appropriate beliefs given the course of his experience."[19] Plantinga adds that there will be different ways in which we can understand "things going right from there on. It could be a matter of forming beliefs responsibly . . . , or in such a way as to properly pursue one's epistemic goals . . . ; it could be a matter of a sort of intrinsic fittingness relating experience and belief . . . ; and it could also be a matter of faculties downstream of experience (reasoning and belief formation, say) *functioning properly*, being subject to no dysfunction."[20]

Plantinga summarizes this discussion by noting that there are various suggestions about what a belief's being justified is:

> being formed responsibly, being reliably produced, being such that the believer has adequate evidence, being formed on the basis of an internally accessible and truth conducive ground, being an evaluation of how well the believer has pursued her epistemic goals, and so on. There is also the connection with knowledge, with internalism, and with evidence.[21]

With so many different notions of epistemic justification, how are we to proceed? Must we choose one? Not really. Rather, the point is to see that the term is used in different senses, and hence when someone says that knowledge is justified true belief, we must try to discover what she means by justification to understand the definition. Moreover, we must also understand the concept of justification in use before we can assess whether someone's claim to know something amounts to their actually *knowing* (not merely believing) what they claim to know. Plantinga himself notes (in *Warranted Christian Belief*) that in his "Reason and Belief in God" (to which we shall turn shortly), the sense of justification involved is justification in its deontological sense.[22]

The point of noting these different senses of epistemic justification is also to recognize that this ambiguity about justification is probably part of why defining knowledge as justified true belief has in recent decades become more controversial than anyone might have suspected. But that isn't the whole story. A further reason for the debate over how to define knowledge stems from a very brief but extremely important paper by Edmund Gettier entitled "Is Justified True Belief Knowledge?" Gettier notes that many have thought that someone *knows* a proposition if the proposition is true, the person in question believes the proposition, and the individual is justified in believing the proposition.[23] Gettier believes this to be incorrect, for a person might in fact be justified in believing a proposition that turned out to be false (think of the little girl and the tooth fairy). He also notes that someone might believe a proposition P which entails proposition Q. If so, and the person deduces Q from P, then she is justified in believing Q.[24]

Gettier next presents examples of cases where justified true belief does not equal knowledge. I offer his first example. Imagine that Smith and Jones both apply for the same job. Smith has strong evidence that the following proposition is true: "Jones is the man who will get the job, and Jones has ten coins in his pocket."[25] The strong evidence Smith has is that the president of the company informed him that Jones would get the job, and Smith counted the coins in Jones's pocket just ten minutes ago. The conjunctive proposition just mentioned entails that "the man who will get the job has ten coins in his pocket."[26]

Gettier then tells us that Smith sees the entailment between the two propositions about who will get hired and how many coins will be in his pocket, so he believes a second proposition, namely, that the man who will get the job has ten coins in his pocket. According to Gettier, Smith is certainly justified in believing this proposition.

But Gettier asks us to imagine next that, unknown to Smith, Smith is the one who will actually get the job, and again, unknown to Smith, he has ten coins in his pocket. The second proposition (Gettier labels it [e]) is then in fact true, Smith believes that (e) is true, and Smith is justified in believing that (e) is true. Still, Smith inferred (e) from the conjunctive proposition about Jones mentioned above (Gettier labels it [d]), and we now know that (d) is false. Jones may have ten coins in his pocket, but contrary to (d), he won't get the job. Clearly, Gettier concludes, Smith does not *know* that (e) is true, because it is true in virtue of the number of coins in his own pocket, a number he does not know, and because he wrongly thinks (e) is true because he believes Jones (who also has ten coins in his pocket) will get the job. Hence, here is a case where justified true belief does not equal knowledge.[27]

What does this discussion of justification and knowledge as justified true belief have to do with Reformed Epistemology? Remember that Plantinga explains that he is concerned to answer the *de jure* objection(s) to belief in God in general and to belief in Christianity in particular. Moreover, Plantinga claims that the *de jure* objection can be stated in terms of justification, rationality, or warrant. We have seen already what justification can mean. Plantinga also shows that there are a number of different notions of rationality one might hold. As to warrant, it also is ambiguous, but Plantinga defines its as "that property—or better, *quantity*—enough of which is what makes the difference between knowledge and mere true belief."[28] Of course, there are various contemporary accounts of what exactly the property (or quantity) warrant is. What they are and which, if any, Plantinga accepts will become clear as we present his views on warranted belief.

Hence, *de jure* objections to theistic belief may be stated so as to incorporate one of these concepts (justification, rationality, warrant). The nonbeliever's complaint might be that belief in God is unjustified, or that believers in God are being irrational in so believing, or that belief in God simply is unwarranted. Plantinga, as we shall see, believes that none of these *de jure* objections succeeds in showing that believers are irresponsible, irrational, foolish, etc., in believing in God. But why would nonbelievers think that belief in God is epistemically unjustified, irrational, or unwarranted? The reason ultimately stems from what Plantinga labels the evidential objection to belief in God. To that objection we turn next.

THE EVIDENTIALIST OBJECTION TO BELIEF IN GOD

Without being overly simplistic, we can say that Reformed Epistemology is a response to evidentialism and what evidentialist critics of theism say about belief in God. But what is evidentialism, and how does it relate to rejecting belief in God? This is a question worth asking, because the term 'evidentialism' has appeared quite frequently in recent *Christian* apologetics.

Many of us first heard the term evidentialism from Christian apologists like John Warwick Montgomery. According to such apologists, there is adequate evidence (rational, empirical, and especially tangible evidence that is historical) to support the major truth claims of Christianity. Moreover, this evidence comes in sufficient quantity and is of a sufficient quality (i.e., it is true, relevant to the tenet being supported, and it does establish as true that which the apologist seeks to defend, not just some inconsequential portion of it) that the Christian apologist can make a successful case for Christianity. By "successful," evidentialists typically mean one which shows that the facts of the case demonstrate the truth of the Christian doctrine being defended. They may also add that the case is strong enough to warrant the subjective conviction (based on objective evidence) that these beliefs are true.

Moreover, Christian evidentialists add that it is not just Christians who can be convinced by marshaling evidence. Rather, the facts themselves are such that anyone acquainted with them, believer or nonbeliever, would agree that they are ample to support the belief in question. Hence, Christian evidentialists believe that there is good reason to offer nonbelievers direct evidence that supports the various tenets of the Christian worldview, because they can understand the arguments and evidence and accept the position espoused by the apologist. Of course, Christian evidentialists add that the Holy Spirit is also involved in convincing nonbelievers of truth, but even if a nonbeliever does not accept Christ upon hearing the defense, she can still understand the arguments and evidence and grant that intellectually the Christian has "made the case."

What I have just described is not what Plantinga and Reformed Epistemologists mean when they speak of evidentialism. Plantinga is referring to a rather long tradition in Western philosophy that goes back at least to John Locke and David Hume, a position that has held sway throughout the modern era with its concept of rationality. In short, evidentialism in general is the view that one should believe only those things for which one has sufficient evidence. As Plantinga shows, Locke held that one should not agree with a proposition unless it is probable with respect to what is certain for that individual.[29] Hence, the proper procedure for determining what to believe is "not entertaining any proposition with greater assurance than the proofs it is built upon warrant."[30]

So Locke was an evidentialist, and as Plantinga shows, with respect to religious belief, Locke believed there *is* sufficient evidence to warrant that belief. Others after Locke also took an evidentialist stance, notably W. K. Clifford, who wrote in his famous essay "The Ethics of Belief," "To sum up: it is wrong always, everywhere, and for anyone to believe anything upon insufficient evidence."[31]

Evidentialism, as Plantinga uses the concept, is the view that "religious belief is rationally acceptable only if there are good arguments for it."[32] The evidentialist *objection* to belief in God is that there isn't sufficient evidence and arguments for holding that belief. Over the last few hundred years, there have been those who dismissed belief in God on such grounds, and on the contemporary scene there are ample examples of philosophers who do the same.[33]

PLANTINGA'S STRATEGY AND RESPONSE TO THE EVIDENTIALIST OBJECTION

In "Reason and Belief in God" Plantinga adopts a particular strategy for addressing the evidentialist objection. In his later works, he incorporates the same basic strategy but offers more details as he elaborates the reasoning behind his claims that belief in God is properly basic, and hence, that theists need not believe in God on the basis of evidence in order to be rational in believing in God. Thus, rather than trying to beat the evidentialist at his own game by showing that there is sufficient evidence for belief in God, Plantinga moves in an entirely different direction, arguing that belief in God doesn't require support by evidence (any evidence) to be rational. If this is so, then the evidentialist objection that says there isn't enough evidence for belief in God is wrongheaded. And, so are theists' attempts to show that belief in God *is* held on sufficient evidence. All of this needs explaining, and I begin with Plantinga's basic strategy and some key definitions.

Plantinga's Strategy in Answering the Evidentialist Objection

In "Reason and Belief in God" Plantinga first argues that both evidentialism and its objection to belief in God ultimately rest on a theory of knowledge called foundationalism. There are various forms of foundationalism, and Plantinga explains that evidentialism rests on what is labeled classical foundationalism.

After clarifying that the evidentialist objection rests on classical foundationalism, Plantinga then attacks that theory of knowledge. If classical foundationalism is incorrect, then both it and the evidentialist objection to religious belief based on it are wrong. If this strategy succeeds, then the attack on belief in God as irrational has been answered. Believing in God is not irrational.

Plantinga, however, does not stop at this point. If classical foundationalism is wrong, Plantinga asks next what we should put in its place, and assesses how belief in God fares in light of this new theory of knowledge. In "Reason and Belief in God," Plantinga offers some hints of what he will put in place of classical foundationalism, but in his trilogy he presents his substitute in all its detail. Plantinga adopts a more moderate form of foundationalism, according to which beliefs that do not meet the demands of classical foundationalism's criteria for proper basicality still turn out to be properly basic and rational to hold.

The final step in Plantinga's strategy is to argue that, given this new theory of knowledge with its own criteria for proper basicality, belief in God is properly basic. This must not be misunderstood, however. Plantinga is not saying that belief in God *is* properly basic for every theist, nor that it *must* be properly basic for anyone. Rather, his point is that many theists come to believe in God in a way that shows that this belief is properly basic for them. And they are totally rational, totally within their epistemic rights and duties, and thoroughly warranted in holding that belief as properly basic. In Plantinga's *Warranted Christian Belief*, he argues that not only belief in God but also belief in the great things of the gospel (Trinity, incarnation, sin, substitutionary atonement, etc.) are properly basic for many Christians. And, those who hold such religious beliefs are entirely rational, justified, and warranted in doing so.

Some Key Definitions

If we are to understand Plantinga, we must define certain terms he uses. A first is "noetic structure." Plantinga explains that "a person's noetic structure is the set of propositions he believes, together with certain epistemic relations that hold among him and these propositions."[34]

Within each person's noetic structure there are both basic and non-basic beliefs. A *basic belief* is one that a person believes but not on the basis of other propositions.[35] In contrast, a *non-basic belief* is one that a person has on the basis of another or several other beliefs she holds. Ultimately, in a noetic structure put together on a foundationalist model, each non-basic belief will be based on other beliefs which are ultimately based on basic beliefs. A *properly* basic belief is a basic belief one holds which one is justified in holding, and a *properly* non-basic belief is a non-basic belief one justifiably holds on the basis of other beliefs one holds.[36]

Now there are different ways to portray and conceive of a noetic structure. According to a foundationalist conception, there is a foundation to one's noetic structure. This consists of basic beliefs which meet various criteria of basicality (to be explained shortly). Upon the foundation is the "superstructure" of our noetic framework. It consists of non-basic beliefs. Some of those beliefs are closer to the foundational beliefs; i.e., to use Plantinga's terminology, they ingress into one's noetic structure to a greater degree than other beliefs that are further away from the foundation. Each non-basic belief is inferred from other non-basic beliefs which ultimately are inferred from a (or several) basic belief(s).

In contrast to a foundationalist conception of noetic structure, some epistemologists hold a coherentist theory of knowledge. According to this theory, beliefs are held on the basis of other things one believes, but no belief is more basic than any other. Hence, one cannot speak of an ultimate foundation of beliefs that are more certain than others. Rather than portraying knowledge as a building with a foundation and superstructure, a coherentist conception pictures our noetic structure as an interconnected web of beliefs, none more basic than any other.

Plantinga's Answer to the Evidentialist Objection

Evidentialists claim that belief in God is irrational or unjustified, because there isn't sufficient evidence to warrant it. But why think so? Why is it that this challenge even seems credible? Is it because the one who hears it recognizes that the evidential case for God is flimsy? Or is there something else?

While we might think this a substantial objection because we are aware of the evidences for God's existence, and we think the evidence is rather thin, there is something even more fundamental that makes us consider this critique significant. That something is a commitment (tacit or otherwise) to foundationalism. Suppose you held that the evidential case for God's existence is weak, but you didn't hold foundationalism or any other view that says a belief must be supported by evidence for it to be rational. Then, despite the weak evidential case, you might be totally within your epistemic rights in believing anyway.

Given a commitment to foundationalism, however, non-basic beliefs must be supported by evidence—other non-basic beliefs and/or basic beliefs—in order for it to be rational to hold them. So, it certainly seems that Plantinga is right that the evidentialist objection has its bite because of its connection to foundationalism, the dominant theory of knowledge at least in Western thought for centuries. Of course, there are varieties of foundationalism, and Plantinga is concerned with classical ones. The key, as with other forms of foundationalism, is to discern what criteria must be met for a belief to qualify as properly basic.

Plantinga distinguishes between ancient and medieval foundationalists, on the one hand, and modern foundationalists on the other. Ancient foundationalists held that a belief is basic if it is either self-evident or evident to the senses. Modern foundationalists (e.g., Descartes, Locke, Leibniz) affirm as basic beliefs that are either self-evident or incorrigible.[37] Putting these together, beliefs are basic (and properly held as basic) if they are self-evident, evident to the senses, or incorrigible. As Plantinga says, few would deny that a belief that is self-evident, or evident to the senses, or incorrigible is a basic belief. Rather, the problem arises when one holds that *only* beliefs that meet these criteria are basic.[38] Before explaining why that is a problem, however, we must clarify what is meant by self-evident, evident to the senses, and incorrigible.

A *self-evident* belief is one whose truth is immediately obvious to the one who grasps its meaning. One need not build an evidential case before thinking the belief true. The only rational move needed is understanding the proposition. Examples of self-evident truths are found in math and logic, propositions expressing identity, etc. Some are: "3 + 2 = 5"; "there is no such thing as a married bachelor"; "redness is distinct from greenness"; and "the proposition *all men are mortals* is distinct from the proposition *all mortals are men*."[39]

Beliefs that are *evident to the senses* are perceptual beliefs. We can determine whether these beliefs are true or false by using some sense or combination of senses. Examples of this kind of proposition are: "her perfume smells like lilac"; "I just heard a crashing sound in the distance"; "I see a tree before me"; "this meat tastes like chicken." One does not believe such things as a result of some reasoning process. Rather, one knows these propositions are true or false simply by sensory experience, using eyes, ears, nose, or mouth.[40]

Some beliefs are *incorrigible*. This means that it is quite dubious that one could be mistaken about their truth or falsity. While I could be mistaken if I believe I see an elephant on my front lawn, it is hard to imagine how it could be false if it *seems to me* that I see an elephant at that location. Or, I might be wrong that the sky is blue today, but if I'm having a sensory experience of blue, it is hard to imagine how I could be mistaken about having that experience. Hence, as Plantinga explains, propositions of this sort seem immune to error. A proposition p's being incorrigible for someone means that it is impossible for a person to believe p and for p to be false; or that it is impossible for someone to believe not-p and for p to be true.[41]

In sum, the evidentialist objection to theistic belief claims that belief in God is irrational, unwarranted, unjustified, because it isn't supported by sufficient evidence. Sufficient evidence involves beliefs that support God's existence and are either basic beliefs or are inferred from other beliefs that are or stem from basic beliefs. And, those basic beliefs are properly basic (and hence, a sufficient foundation for beliefs like belief in God) as long as they are either self-evident, evident to the senses, or incorrigible. So, belief in God is unwarranted, according to the evidentialist objection, because it isn't a basic belief itself and doesn't stem from beliefs that meet the criteria for proper basicality.

Now, one way to respond to this objection is to argue that there is sufficient evidence to believe in God. Over the centuries of church history, various Christian apologists have offered evidences for belief in God. Even if those evidences weren't themselves basic beliefs nor did they stem from beliefs which meet classic foundationalism's criteria of proper basicality, Christians have deemed them sufficient to warrant belief in God or in some other tenet of the Christian faith.[42]

In contrast, Christians might argue that even if there is sufficient evidence of the sort demanded by classical foundationalism, nonbelievers are so trapped in their worldview that believers can never convince them. Hence, the only hope is to presuppose without proof that God exists and show the critic that only with such a presupposition do the "facts" of reality fit together without logical contradiction. Others might say that despite the lack of tangible evidence of the sort required, they still believe in God because they know he exists in a way that is beyond attack; they have experienced him. This was no ordinary experience but rather an experience so powerful that they just knew it had to be God, and that's why they believe.

Plantinga takes none of these tacks. Instead, he offers two main lines of objection to classical foundationalism, for if he can show it to be wrong, then the evidentialist objection resting upon it collapses. Specifically, classical foundationalism is wrong in that its criteria of proper basicality are objectionable. The first objection is that if we must believe only propositions that are basic (and hence are self-evident, evident to the senses, or incorrigible) or that are traceable to basic ones, then many ordinary beliefs all of us hold turn out to be irrational to hold.

For example, I believe I had breakfast this morning. I also believe the earth has existed for more than ten minutes. Moreover, I believe there are other people distinct from myself, and I believe that my name is John Feinberg. Not only do I believe these propositions, but they are basic for me. Thus, I came to believe none of them through a process of reasoning or proof. Still, I can't see that any of them is either self-evident, evident to the senses, or incorrigible for me, nor are they deduced from propositions that meet those criteria of proper basicality. Likewise, there is a parallel set of sentences that are basic for you and yet fail to meet classical foundationalist criteria of proper basicality.

Do these facts mean that you or I, in believing such things, are actually irrational or that we have failed on our epistemic duties? Not at all! Should we stop believing these propositions because they don't meet classical foundationalist criteria of proper basicality? Of course, not! Instead, we should see that a theory that rejects beliefs about the past, common sense beliefs about the world around us, etc., as irrational and epistemically irresponsible is itself horribly flawed. As already noted, this doesn't mean that beliefs that meet classical foundationalism's criteria for proper basicality don't qualify as basic. Rather, it shows that those are not the *only* beliefs that qualify as basic and rational to hold. To think otherwise just removes too many beliefs as irrational that all of us, including classical foundationalists, hold and are rationally justified in holding.[43]

Plantinga's second argument against classical foundationalism's criteria of proper basicality is that classical foundationalism cannot satisfy its own criteria of proper basicality. Classical foundationalism says that a belief is properly basic if it is self-evident, evident to the senses, or incorrigible. Is this claim itself one that satisfies classical foundationalism's requirements for proper basicality? Well, it can hardly be the case that *the claim* that a properly basic belief is either self-evident, evident to the senses, or incorrigible *is itself* either self-evident, evident to the senses, or incorrigible. Perhaps that is so because the claim in question is a non-basic belief. Perhaps, but then we must ask whether the claim is inferred from and supported by beliefs that meet classical foundationalism's requirements for proper basicality. Again we must answer negatively.

So, then, it appears that if classical foundationalism is right about criteria for proper basicality, then it *cannot* be right and should be abandoned because it fails to meet its own standards. The theory is self-refuting. Or, to use Plantinga's terminology, it is self-referentially incoherent. It contradicts itself, we might say, for it requires every belief to be basic or inferred from basic beliefs, while the proposition about criteria of proper basicality is itself neither properly basic nor does it stem from other propositions that are.[44]

Since the evidentialist objection to belief in God rests on classical foundationalism, and since classical foundationalism is bankrupt, as Plantinga's objections show, the evidentialist objection to belief in God must be dismissed. Plantinga has successfully rebutted the nonbeliever's complaint that belief in God is irrational. But is this all we should say? Plantinga thinks not, for the fact that one line of objection doesn't prove theistic belief to be irrational does not explain *how* and *why* it is rational. Moreover, it doesn't tell us whether belief in God is a basic or a non-basic belief. Plantinga addresses those issues in considerable detail, and to them we turn in the next section.

Plantinga's Modified Foundationalism

Given Plantinga's refutation of the evidentialist objection to theistic belief, one might think that Plantinga rejects foundationalism altogether. However, the remainder of his "Reason and Belief in God" suggests that he still works within a foundationalist framework. In that earlier work he sketches the general contours of his view, but in his trilogy he painstakingly explains his views. Not only does he claim to be a foundationalist, but he offers a detailed explanation of his own criteria of proper basicality, and shows that for many believers a variety of religious beliefs can and do meet those criteria.

In truth, this gets to the heart of Plantinga's answer to the evidentialist objection to belief in God. Rather than agreeing that believers must have sufficiently strong evidence to warrant belief in God (and then trying to show that there is such evidence), Plantinga rejects this whole way of thinking. Many beliefs all of us hold about the world, ourselves, etc., are properly basic for us. Thus, we don't hold them on the basis of an evidential case, and yet no one thinks we are irrational in holding those beliefs. If so, then why can't belief in God also be a properly basic belief for those who hold it? If holding a belief for which we have made no evidential case is acceptable for my perceptual beliefs, memory beliefs, and so on, why not for my belief in God?

Now Plantinga is not requiring all believers to believe in God in a properly basic way without evidence—presumably, some people have found an evidential argument helpful in coming to believe in God. Instead, he argues only that those who do believe in God in a properly basic way are within their epistemic rights and are in no way irrational in doing so. But if belief in God can be properly basic, by what criteria can that be so? Surely, belief in God is neither self-evident, evident to the senses, or incorrigible, nor does it rest on other beliefs that have any such qualities. So how can belief in God be properly basic?

Of course, on *classical* foundationalism's criteria of proper basicality, belief in God can't be properly basic, but Plantinga offers his modified version of foundationalism and its criteria for proper basicality. He doesn't construct these criteria for religious beliefs alone, but does so first for all beliefs that are properly basic. Once having set forth the criteria, he then applies them to religious beliefs. Plantinga suggests that the best way to discover appropriate criteria of proper basicality is to do so inductively. That is, gather together sentences that we believe are properly basic, and ask what it is about each proposition that makes it properly basic. Then abstract from those sentences criteria for proper basicality as we discover them while analyzing each sentence.

Plantinga's Criteria of Proper Basicality

What are Plantinga's criteria of proper basicality? Plantinga presents three main criteria, but each needs explanation.

Beliefs Formed by Properly Functioning Cognitive Faculties. At the heart of Plantinga's account of warrant (and of his criteria of proper basicality) is the notion of proper function. As he explains, each of us has many different bodily organs, and each organ performs a particular function in the body. The heart's purpose is to supply blood to the body. Our digestive system with its various organs is meant to process food so as to store nutrients necessary for living and to remove waste from our bodies. Reproductive organs also have their appointed function.

Thankfully, much of the time our organs function properly, but bodily organs can malfunction. When arteries to the heart are blocked, the results can be heart attacks and strokes. Sometimes we have an upset stomach from the flu. Rather than processing food in preparation for its absorption into our body, the sickness in our stomach causes us to expel the food. Or perhaps an ulcer in our stomach makes it very sensitive to certain foods, or a cancerous growth in our intestines blocks waste from being removed. Then, our reproductive systems can malfunction in various ways (e.g., a wife has blocked fallopian tubes, or a husband has a low sperm count). Most of the time our bodily organs and processes function so well that we overlook possible malfunctions, but malfunctions can happen.

What is true of our bodies is also true of our cognitive faculties. We have eyes, ears, a nose, and a mouth that sense, and a mind that reasons. These organs are usable and useful in acquiring knowledge. Mental faculties include not only our ability to reason, but also our emotions and our will. Though these faculties work wonderfully well on many occasions, they are all subject to malfunction. Cataracts and nearsightedness hamper our vision's proper function. When our hearing is damaged, we may miss information we need to know. Someone suffering with Alzheimer's disease may have a hard time remembering the recent past; someone else inebriated by alcohol finds not only his mind impaired but also many of his senses.

So, cognitive malfunction is something all have experienced at one time or another. Now one of the functions of our cognitive faculties is the formation of beliefs. Given what has been said about malfunctioning abilities, it seems clear that a belief formed by malfunctioning cognitive powers isn't likely to be true, and the one who holds it is not likely warranted in doing so. But human cognitive faculties do function properly much of the time (even most of the time for most of us), and it is abundantly reasonable to conclude that for any belief, basic or non-basic, to be rational to hold, the belief must arise from cognitive faculties that are functioning properly. Without proper function, it is hard to imagine how a belief formed with malfunctioning faculties could qualify as warranted.[45]

Beliefs Formed in an Environment Appropriate for Proper Function of Cognitive Equipment. Proper function is not the only criterion for warranted belief (basic or non-basic), for one's cognitive faculties could be functioning properly but doing so in an environment for which they were not designed. This is also true of other things besides our cognitive faculties. For example, imagine an automobile that has just recently been serviced, so it is in perfect running order. Suppose we transport it by helicopter to the base of Pike's Peak and expect it to work in taking us safely to the top of the mountain and back down again. Although the car is in excellent working order, it was never designed for terrain such as this, so it won't work in that environment. Or consider the person who decides to go skydiving. Suppose he decides not to wear a parachute, because he has arms and legs for moving from one place to another. He figures that if he waves his arms and kicks his feet vigorously enough, he will slowly and gently move from the plane to the ground. Of course, if he actually tries to skydive using only his arms and legs, the result will be catastrophic.

The problem in each example is that the car and the human are using capabilities that are functioning properly but don't work in the environments we've imagined. Just as this is true for the car and human arms and legs, so it is true for human cognitive faculties. Suppose I have perfect vision. Suppose also that on a dark night (stars and moon hidden by clouds), I see two people scuffling with each other a block and a half away. As it turns out, one mugs the other and steals his wallet. The police round up a series of possible suspects, bring them to police headquarters, and bring me in to observe them in a lineup. They ask me to identify the assailant, but I cannot do so with any certainty. I have perfect vision, but the darkness and my distance from what was happening make my belief about which person in the lineup is the attacker unreliable. It would thus be unwarranted for me to firmly believe that I can correctly identify the criminal.[46]

So, for a belief to be warranted for me, I must acquire it through properly functioning cognitive faculties which function in an environment for which they were designed. A belief that fails to meet the standard set by either or both of these criteria couldn't be a basic belief for me, nor should I accept a non-basic belief so formed. But Plantinga notes that while proper function and doing so in an appropriate environment are necessary conditions of a belief's being warranted, these two criteria alone aren't sufficient for warrant. We must add another criterion.

Beliefs Formed according to a Design Plan Aimed at Truth. Everything made is intended to accomplish some purpose or goal. Watches are designed to tell time moment by moment, hour by hour, etc. Eyes and ears in both humans and animals are made so that they can see and hear. A design plan is like a blueprint an architect draws up and uses as his guide for building the structure he is making. Within that overall design plan (the blueprint), the various features of the building have their specific purpose. If the plan is to build a multistory building, there will likely be an elevator in the building. The elevator is designed to move up and down the inside of the building so that people coming to the building can get from one floor to another easily, without much physical stress and strain. If the building is located in a part of the world subject to a lot of earthquakes, the architect and builders will probably include in their design plan some means for keeping the building from collapsing during an earthquake.

So, buildings and other artifacts have a design. This is true for human beings as well. I mentioned various bodily organs and systems; each was made to accomplish some purpose. This is true not only for our physical abilities, but also of our cognitive faculties. As Plantinga explains, human cognitive faculties may have been designed to accomplish different things, depending on the circumstances in which we use them. For example, suppose that someone has cancer, and the prognosis is bad. Still, she is an optimistic person and has beat serious disease before. She also knows that keeping a positive mental attitude is important to have any chance of beating cancer. So, her doctor calls her for an appointment to discuss results from tests recently done. The data suggest that she is losing her battle, but she interprets them as a sign that she is improving. After all, the difference between test results this month and last month shows less deterioration in her condition, so she believes that her disease, if not in remission, is at least slowing down. She leaves the doctor's office with new energy and optimism.

Her beliefs aren't really warranted, but the reason isn't that her cognitive faculties are malfunctioning or operating in an environment for which they weren't designed. Rather, as Plantinga explains, some cognitive faculties may be aimed at helping us survive and cope with difficult circumstances. In this instance, the imagined woman is using properly functioning cognitive faculties in an environment appropriate for their use; it's just that the faculties in use aren't aimed at truth, but rather at survival. Since she will do better if she is optimistic, faculties aimed at survival will lead her to believe that she is getting better. Warranted belief is belief formed by faculties designed to produce true belief, so her optimism isn't warranted. And that is so even if somehow her belief that she will survive turns out, happily, to be true.[47]

Despite instances when we form a belief with cognitive faculties aimed at survival, relief from pain and suffering, etc., each of us has cognitive faculties designed to produce true beliefs in us. Presumably our sense organs are designed to aid in producing true beliefs about the physical, tangible world about us. When they function properly in an environment conducive to formation of true beliefs, there is reason to think those cognitive faculties accomplish the goal for which they were designed. This is so whether the beliefs in question are basic or non-basic.[48]

In sum, how should we understand Plantinga's foundationalism? Plantinga believes that some beliefs are basic and others are non-basic. Moreover, he would surely grant that beliefs which are self-evident, evident to the senses, or incorrigible are properly basic beliefs. Plantinga parts company with classical foundationalists, however, in rejecting the view that all purported basic beliefs must meet the classical foundationalist's criteria of proper basicality. In fact, a given belief might meet none of those standards and yet still be properly basic for a given believer. If the belief is formed using properly functioning cognitive faculties in an environment congenial to the proper function of such faculties, and if the design plan of those cognitive abilities is aimed at truth, then the believer is thoroughly within his epistemic rights in believing what he does. Moreover, if the proposition believed happens to be true, and the believer strongly believes it, it is appropriate to say that he or she knows that proposition. One may come to hold a belief in the way just described if one is merely put in a situation in which the belief naturally arises, or one may acquire the belief as a result of cognitive faculties functioning as mentioned as one reflects on a belief and the evidence that supports it. Having the belief arise in proper circumstances (e.g., when asked what I had for breakfast, I simply remember that it was cereal and fruit) when using my cognitive faculties as noted makes that belief basic for me. No process of reasoning results in my holding the belief. In fact, as Plantinga notes, we often don't have control over what we believe; we simply find ourselves believing something without reason and argument when placed in the proper circumstances.[49] So, a warranted belief is one formed by properly functioning cognitive faculties whose design plan is aimed at truth when one is in circumstances appropriate to the proper functioning of those faculties.

PLANTINGA'S FOUNDATIONALISM AND RELIGIOUS BELIEFS

So far what I have said about Plantinga's foundationalism has focused on beliefs in general. What happens when Plantinga's foundationalism is applied to religious beliefs in general and Christian beliefs in particular? Can those beliefs be warranted, rational, justified? Does one use only the cognitive equipment mentioned in coming to hold nonreligious beliefs, while more intellectual equipment enters into the process of forming religious beliefs? And, are religious beliefs basic or non-basic beliefs? Must one believe them on the basis of evidence, or on some other basis? These are the issues for this part of my chapter.

"Equipment" Relevant to Religious Beliefs

Plantinga holds that the basic cognitive equipment we use for other types of belief is also relevant to religious beliefs. However, everyone has a further "piece" of equipment that specifically relates to belief in God, and those with a personal relation to God through Jesus Christ as Savior have a second source of cognitive information. Plantinga bases these claims not on epistemology per se, but on theological considerations.

First, Plantinga appeals to Reformation theologian John Calvin. He notes that both Aquinas and Calvin held that there is a kind of natural knowledge of God that each human being has. It isn't a complex and complete concept of God, but still, the idea of God is implanted in all of us. Plantinga focuses predominantly on Calvin's expression of this notion. In his *Institutes of the Christian Religion*, Calvin speaks about knowledge that God exists as implanted in us. Calvin refers to this as a *sensus divinitatis* ("sense of deity"). According to Plantinga, the *sensus divinitatis* is the faculty or mechanism "by which we acquire true beliefs about God."[50]

Plantinga links the concept of the *sensus divinitatis* with Romans 1:18–20, and then concludes that "Calvin's basic claim is that there is a sort of instinct, a natural human tendency, a disposition, a nisus to form beliefs about God under a variety of conditions and in a variety of situations."[51] Whether or not this is actually Calvin's position is debatable, but it is certainly Plantinga's.[52] Plantinga sees the *sensus divinitatis* as a kind of faculty or mechanism in us, "which in a wide variety of circumstances produces in us beliefs about God. These circumstances, we might say, trigger the disposition to form the beliefs in question; they form the occasion on which those beliefs arise."[53] As Plantinga adds, we don't typically form these beliefs of our own initiative; rather they are formed in us and we find ourselves holding them in the same way that we find ourselves with various perceptual and memory beliefs.[54]

The circumstances Plantinga has in mind are many and varied. Calvin thinks in terms of the grandeur of nature. Hence, when confronted with the beauty of the Swiss Alps, the Grand Canyon, Niagara Falls, etc., one is overwhelmed with awe and forms a belief about the majesty and power of God who created this. There are many other experiences besides observing the beauty of nature that may trigger belief in God. Plantinga is emphatic, however, that such a belief doesn't arise as the logical conclusion from some multistep argument. As he writes,

> They are *occasioned* by the circumstances; they are not conclusions from them. The heavens declare the glory of God and the skies proclaim the work of his hands: but not by way of serving as premises for an argument. Awareness of guilt may lead me to God; but it is not that in this awareness I have the material for a quick theistic argument: I am guilty, so there must be a God. The argument isn't nearly as silly as it looks; but when the operation of the *sensus divinitatis* is triggered by perception of my guilt, it

doesn't work by way of an argument. I don't take my guilt as *evidence* for the existence of God, or for the proposition that he is displeased with me. It is rather that in that circumstance—the circumstance of my clearly seeing my guilt—I simply find myself with the belief that God is disapproving or disappointed.[55]

Plantinga adds that formation of belief in God using the *sensus divinitatis* parallels or resembles perception, memory, and *a priori* belief. For example, suppose I take a walk on a crisp and sunny fall day. My eyes are bombarded with sensory data from the beautifully colored leaves. Now, Plantinga would say, I don't note that I'm being appeared to in a certain way involving all of these beautiful fall colors and then construct an argument from this experience that concludes that there are trees with beautifully colored leaves. Nor do I further conclude that the colored leaves serve as a good argument that it is autumn. Rather, "upon being appeared to in that way" the belief that the leaves on the trees are beautifully colorful spontaneously arises in me. And Plantinga adds, a belief such as this "will ordinarily be *basic*, in the sense that it is not accepted on the evidential basis of other propositions."[56] The same is true for memory beliefs. Like acquiring the belief that God exists when my disposition to believe is confronted with certain circumstances, my remembering what I had for breakfast when asked by my doctor is formed in me the same way. I don't construct an argument to the effect that I probably had cereal and fruit. When asked, the answer just comes to mind.[57]

In addition, believers and nonbelievers alike have this *sensus divinitatis*, this tendency or disposition to believe in God when confronted by certain circumstances. Of course, Plantinga, along with Calvin and Scripture, grants that many people suppress this knowledge of God because of their sin. In fact, left merely to our own devices, none of us would keep God in our knowledge, nor would we seek further knowledge about God and his relation to us.

There is, however, a further source of information, according to Christian doctrine. Plantinga refers to it as the internal instigation of the Holy Spirit, and he devotes a good deal of discussion to it. What is this internal witness, testimony, instigation of the Holy Spirit of which Scripture, Christian theology, and Plantinga speak? As Plantinga notes, one of the key ministries of the Holy Spirit is to produce faith in us, but faith doesn't arise in an intellectual background where we know little or nothing about

God but throw ourselves on him anyway. Rather, this belief comes in the context of and grows out of our knowledge of the great things of the gospel. But how do we come to agree that the central Christian truths are in fact true? Plantinga answers that this happens by the internal ministry of the Holy Spirit. The Holy Spirit's testimony within us "is therefore a source of belief, a cognitive process that produces in us belief in the main lines of the Christian story."[58]

What Plantinga says about the internal testimony of the Holy Spirit means that what we learn by the Holy Spirit's ministry is actually a form of learning by testimony. This is a special case of learning by testimony, but most things we learn, whether about history, science, literature, etc., are learned by taking them on the testimony of those deemed to be authorities on each topic. Most of us didn't demand argument and evidence for what we learned in math, history, or science classes; we took as true the information supplied by our teachers. Plantinga is saying that the spiritual truth we learn through the internal instigation of the Holy Spirit is really just another instance (albeit a special, supernatural one) of learning things from the testimony of an authority, God himself.[59]

In sum, Plantinga holds that in addition to the "regular" cognitive equipment each of us receives at birth, equipment which lets us get along relatively well in this world, there is further equipment geared or aimed specifically at spiritual or religious truth. On the one hand, all people have the *sensus divinitatis*, an inborn tendency to believe in God when confronted by certain circumstances. On the other, there is the special ministry of the Holy Spirit, who testifies to the verity of the great truths of the gospel. The Spirit's ministry to nonbelievers focuses on their sin and need of a Savior, and urges them to turn to Christ for redemption. In the lives of believers, the Holy Spirit testifies internally to their heart and mind of the truth of the great things of the gospel, constantly urging them to grow deeper in their faith and relationship to Jesus Christ. Of course, these two sources of spiritual and religious belief and knowledge may be thwarted and suppressed by sin, by believers and nonbelievers alike. Finally, the knowledge gained by this additional "equipment" comes in much the same way as do perceptual and memory beliefs. One doesn't make an argument for such beliefs but, rather, finds that they arise in one's mind, having been triggered by a situation conducive to forming those beliefs.

BELIEF IN GOD AS PROPERLY BASIC

If perceptual and memory beliefs are formed without argument and evidence, and religious beliefs are formed in an analogous way, then belief in God and even in the great things of the gospel must also be properly basic, resting neither on argument nor on evidence. This is probably the most controversial part of Reformed Epistemology. Sadly, it is probably also the most misunderstood aspect of Plantinga's views, so we must clarify exactly what Plantinga and his colleagues are saying. I begin with one of the most fundamental errors critics make, namely, thinking that Plantinga is saying that everyone forms and holds (or at least should form and hold) their belief in God in a properly basic way.

One can imagine the dismay of critics, believing that believers cannot meet the demands of the evidentialist objection to belief in God, upon hearing that belief in God is properly basic. Reformed Epistemologists apparently aren't rejecting the evidentialist objection by offering ample proof for God's existence, but instead they reject the whole way of thinking that undergirds that objection. In essence, Reformed Epistemologists are saying that whether or not we have sufficient evidence (according to classical foundationalism's standards) for belief in God is beside the point, for the belief that God exists can be properly basic and hence can be held on the basis of no argument and/or evidence. And, if belief in God is a basic belief for someone, he or she is entirely rational, has met all epistemic responsibilities, and so is justified and warranted in believing.

Not only have nonbelievers been skeptical about these claims; many believers are as well. But we must first explain this view. We must begin with the fact that what Plantinga is saying must be seen as person-relative. That is, Plantinga consistently talks about what is basic or non-basic for himself or for some other specific person. Hence, belief in God may not be a basic belief for you, even if it is for me. This is so in some cases because you don't believe in God at all. It is true in others because you do believe in God but came to that belief upon surveying the evidence for God's existence and concluding that God's existence is more likely than not.

My point is that we must not reject what Plantinga proposes about believing in God without evidence and argument either because 1) we think he is talking about the belief all people hold, or because 2) we think he claims that all theists hold belief in God as a properly basic belief, or because

3) we think Plantinga is stipulating a requirement about the way anyone must come to belief in God. To think any of 1–3 misunderstands Plantinga and ignores the fact that each person's noetic structure is unique (despite similarities to those of others).

Moreover, as we reflect on Plantinga's claim that belief in God is properly basic or can be for various believers, we must remember the objection Plantinga is addressing. He is not offering a positive case for the *whole* of theism or Christianity. Rather, he is responding to the evidentialist complaint that believers in God are irrational because there isn't enough evidence to show that God exists. Plantinga rejects the assumption underlying the objection, namely, that the only way to be rational in holding a belief is to hold it on the basis of evidence. Plantinga responds that there are many beliefs we all hold for which we have never made or heard an evidential case, and yet we hold those beliefs as properly basic (and hence not true on the basis of evidence), and we are thoroughly rational, justified, and warranted in doing so. Moreover, for many theists, belief in God is one of those basic beliefs, and, contrary to evidentialist critics, those theists are thoroughly rational and totally within their epistemic rights in believing in God in this way.

So Plantinga isn't making these claims about every religious belief and every religious believer. In his later work *Warranted Christian Belief*, Plantinga extends his point to the great truths of the Christian faith: the Trinity, the incarnation, sin, substitutionary atonement, etc. However, even here he doesn't stipulate that every Christian does or must hold these beliefs as properly basic. His point is that many Christians do hold them as properly basic, and they are rational, justified, and warranted in doing so.

Some may think this sounds promising but still see it as counterintuitive. For how could one believe in God and in the great doctrines of the Christian faith apart from argument and evidence, and be justified in doing so? Here we must invoke Plantinga's foundationalism with its criteria or conditions for proper basicality. Here we see the ultimate "cash value" in regard to *religious* beliefs of all of his comments about cognitive faculties, proper function, and warrant. We have various cognitive faculties that fit us to interact with our environment. Hence, when one opens one's eyes while in a forest, using those eyes, when properly functioning in an environment suited for their use (vision isn't hindered, for example, by darkness, by evil demons tampering with vision, etc.), functioning in accord with the goal they were designed to achieve (i.e., forming true perceptual beliefs), one will form the belief that he is seeing trees. This belief isn't based on argument or evidence, but on the person being in circumstances in which, relying on the proper functioning of his eyes, he finds himself believing that he sees trees.

Similarly, for belief in God and other religious beliefs, the believer has all the cognitive equipment of the nonbeliever, including the *sensus divinitatis*, plus access to the illumining work of the Holy Spirit. When placed in the appropriate circumstances, the believer's cognitive faculties, functioning as they were designed to function, produce in the individual the belief that God exists, or any of the other great truths of the Christian faith. Now, the fact that one finds herself so believing doesn't guarantee infallibility. In fact, Plantinga has much to say about arguments or evidences that might defeat belief in God or other religious beliefs. If belief in God is formed as suggested, but there is a defeating argument the believer can't answer, then the believer should recognize that her belief isn't likely true and should reject it. However, Plantinga stresses that we must not be too hasty in coming to such a judgment, for there may in fact be very good arguments that rebut the defeater (what Plantinga calls defeater defeater[s]). An example of a potential defeater to belief in God is the problem of evil. A defeater of this defeater would be Plantinga's free will defense or any of a number of other defenses against the problem of evil.[60]

What circumstances or experiences, then, might be appropriate for triggering someone's belief in God's existence or some other Christian doctrine? Earlier I talked about people, upon experiencing the beauty of nature, finding themselves believing in God. This belief may also arise when one reads a portion of the Bible which seems addressed directly to him. Or it may arise while in church listening to a beautiful anthem from the choir, or when hearing something the preacher says. Many such as I were raised in a Christian home. My parents always talked about God, Christ, and the Holy Spirit, though they never offered any arguments for the existence of a supreme being. God was invoked in prayer at mealtimes and bedtime every day. When a family member reported that he or she had escaped a dangerous situation or that something positive and successful had happened on a given day, repeatedly the rescue from danger or the blessing was attributed to God's protection, love, and blessing. Using my cognitive equipment, which was functioning properly (at least I have no evidence of malfunction during those early years of my life) in circumstances of the sort mentioned, it was natural for me to believe in God, even though for the longest time, I never heard of things like the ontological argument or the cosmological argument for God's existence. Plantinga's Reformed Epistemology says that my belief in God is for me a basic belief, and I am thoroughly rational in holding it on the bases explained, and so is anyone else who comes to believe in God in this manner. Later in life I learned about arguments and evidences for God's existence, but none of that invalidates the fact that my belief in God (as well as many other Christian doctrines I first believed when I heard them from the pulpit or the lectern in a seminary class) is basic to my noetic structure, and I am well within my epistemic rights in holding that belief (and many other religious beliefs) on the bases mentioned in this paragraph.

Some readers might still be troubled, for it seems that one could concoct a similar story to justify belief in just about anything, regardless of how reasonable or ridiculous. Plantinga foresaw this problem as it relates to believing the ridiculous and addressed it initially in his "Reason and Belief in God." Plantinga used belief in the Great Pumpkin as a test case.[61] The response to this objection involves a very important distinction Plantinga makes, the distinction between the grounds of and the evidence for a belief. Let me explain and relate it to belief in the Great Pumpkin or other imaginary dignitaries.

Plantinga distinguishes between grounds and evidence most clearly in "Reason and Belief in God," though his later works also seem to presuppose this distinction. According to Plantinga, to believe something on the basis of *evidence* is to believe one proposition on the basis of another. The evidence may be purely propositional, but in some cases memory, sense perception, etc., may also serve as evidential support for the belief's truth. In contrast, the *ground* of a belief is the circumstance(s) in which it is generated. Upon walking in a forest "I am appeared to treely," and the belief that I see trees arises within me. The experience of being appeared to treely isn't evidence to support my belief; rather it is the circumstance in which that belief arises. Hence, my belief isn't supported by evidence, and so it is basic for me, but it is not groundless—it doesn't arise out of thin air. Similarly, if you ask where I grew up, I immediately remember not only that it was southern California, but I begin to recall fond memories of my childhood.

My memory of these things isn't evidence about where I grew up. Rather, your question about my background is the circumstance in which these beliefs about my childhood arise. Here again Plantinga would say that neither your question nor my memory beliefs about my background are evidence for a set of beliefs I have about my upbringing. Instead, the question and the memories it engenders are the ground of my beliefs about my background.

In a similar way, one's religious beliefs may be basic if *in the appropriate circumstances*, one's cognitive faculties, including those relevant to religious belief, properly functioning according to a design plan aimed at truth, lead him to believe that God exists or that Jesus is God incarnate, etc. The circumstances in which such beliefs can arise are many and varied. My being raised in a Christian home where God and Christ were frequently mentioned is the ground of my belief in God and in many other Christian doctrines. But the facts that my parents read the Bible, talked about God and prayed to him, and that my dad was both a well-known Old Testament scholar and a preacher deemed by many to be an authority on such matters, and also my experiences of sensing God speaking to me through a sermon or a reading of Scripture in no way served as evidence for God's existence or for any other religious belief. These experiences and circumstances were the grounds out of which my religious beliefs arose, but if I were asked to offer evidential support for those beliefs, I wouldn't say, "Well, Mom and Dad always prayed to God at mealtime and at my bedtime; that's evidence enough that God must exist." To reason in such a way would be to misunderstand what it means to give an argument or offer evidence. So, many of my religious beliefs were formed as mentioned. They are basic for me, but not groundless. Nor are they a product of wishful thinking or an overly active imagination.[62]

Beliefs formed this way are also warranted, according to Plantinga. It is here that we can return to the Great Pumpkin objection. It may seem that if Christians may believe in God as properly basic and be warranted in doing so, others may also believe in various outrageous things as properly basic and be warranted in their belief. One might think that belief in the Great Pumpkin is warranted as basic; others might think that belief in voodoo is for them properly basic and warranted.

In his "Reason and Belief in God" and in *Warranted Christian Belief* Plantinga offers several answers to this objection. First, belief in God doesn't arise in just any and every situation. Only certain kinds of circumstances trigger this belief.[63] In addition, each person has an inborn faculty, the *sensus divinitatis*, which, in certain circumstances, causes the belief in God's existence to arise. And there is also the internal testimony of the Holy Spirit. These circumstances and the cognitive equipment we bring to them are the ground for many people to believe in God in a basic way.[64]

What about belief in the Great Pumpkin? Are the grounds of properly basic belief in God at work when someone believes in the Great Pumpkin as properly basic? Not at all. Actually, there are no circumstances in which we could expect this belief to arise. This shouldn't surprise us, since as far as we know, no real person has ever believed in the Great Pumpkin—talk of it is all part of a very entertaining cartoon strip by a very creative and imaginative cartoonist. And there is no such cognitive faculty as a *sensus pumpkin*, a tendency to believe in the Great Pumpkin when one is placed in certain circumstances. Nor is there any other cognitive equipment designed to produce true belief in the Great Pumpkin.

Then, Plantinga denies that a belief in the Great Pumpkin as basic would have warrant for the believer, because it would be untrue. Any belief, including belief in the Great Pumpkin, purported to be properly basic must meet the challenge of defeaters. While Plantinga argues in *Warranted Christian Belief* that potential defeaters of belief in God—such as the problem of evil—have defeaters themselves, this is not so for belief in the Great Pumpkin, voodoo, and other such beliefs. Defeaters of such beliefs don't seem to have answers. In addition, to have warrant for a basic belief, the belief must be formed by properly functioning cognitive equipment. If those who believe in voodoo, the Great Pumpkin, etc., came to that belief under the influence of mind-altering drugs or of some psychological problem, their belief wouldn't have warrant. Their malfunctioning faculties make it quite likely that the belief is false, and hence serve as a defeater of these beliefs.

But perhaps there is no cognitive malfunction, and perhaps in the case of voodoo there are some circumstances in which belief in voodoo might arise.[65] Still, there are significant defeaters for these beliefs; hence belief in such things can't be properly basic or warranted, if warrant includes truth of the belief. Think here also of the little girl who believes in the tooth fairy. There is no evidence of cognitive malfunction, and the belief did arise in circumstances with which many of us are familiar. While we might say her belief is justified (in the sense suggested earlier in this chapter), we couldn't say she knows there is a truth fairy, for there is ample evidence that serves as a defeater of her belief in the tooth fairy, and no defeater of that defeater is forthcoming.

Plantinga notes that some may say that belief in voodoo or in some other religion's deity may be grounded in appropriate circumstances. Moreover, they may claim that the *sensus divinitatis* is a disposition in all of us to believe in God; it's just that Christians have misidentified who God is whereas Hindus, Muslims, etc., haven't. And, there are possible defeater defeaters for each of these religions. In such cases, Plantinga would grant that this could be so and that if it were, then the question of whether belief in the god of these religions as basic is warranted ultimately reduces to the question of whether the belief is true. But then, Plantinga argues, the discussion has left *de jure* questions of whether the belief is rational, justified, etc., and moved to *de facto* issues. While Plantinga believes that Christians win the *de facto* debate, presenting the case that Christianity is true goes beyond the bounds of his project.[66]

Some will still think what Plantinga is saying is utterly outrageous, because it seems to allow religious beliefs to be warranted though based on no evidence, while all other beliefs must either be supported by evidence (non-basic) or be basic according to criteria typically associated with classical foundationalism. However, that is wrong for a very important reason. Plantinga believes that what he says about the proper basicality of religious beliefs also applies to many other beliefs we hold. It just isn't true that we espouse most of our beliefs because we have marshaled evidence for each and know that sufficient evidence supports them. Many beliefs are basic for all of us, and no one thinks us irrational in holding them.

This is, I think, quite important, for it means that what Plantinga proposes about belief in God and in the great things of the Christian faith is analogous to the way we come to believe many other things. But Plantinga does more than just assert that holding religious beliefs as properly basic is analogous to the way we believe many other beliefs. In great detail in *Warrant and Proper Function* (readers may consult the pages listed in my endnotes for the details), he considers various categories of beliefs and shows that if those beliefs are formed in appropriate circumstances with properly functioning cognitive faculties designed to produce truth, the beliefs are rational, justified, and warranted for the persons who have them. This is so for knowledge of one's self, including beliefs about whether I'm experiencing pain in my foot, whether I seem to be seeing a computer screen and seem to be typing words, and about the emotional state I find myself in as I reflect on how I'm feeling.[67] Similarly, memory beliefs,[68] perceptual beliefs,[69] beliefs about many *a priori* items,[70] and beliefs that are based on testimony[71] from a teacher, parent, or someone else in an authority position can be properly basic in ways analogous to how religious beliefs may be properly basic and warranted for religious believers.

Some who have read Plantinga's views on belief in God as properly basic are baffled. They have also read Plantinga's magnificent defense against the problem of evil via the free will defense. Moreover, they also know of his careful and stimulating work on arguments for God's existence like the ontological argument. They don't see how all of his work in support of various tenets of theism fits what he says about belief in God as properly basic. Thankfully, we can show that there is no inconsistency between Plantinga's Reformed Epistemology and his other works.

Here we must remember that Plantinga says that whether a belief is basic or non-basic is person-relative. That is, for some people belief in God and the great things of the gospel is basic, but not for others. So, we should look at what reason and evidence offer to those for whom belief in God is properly basic and what they offer to those for whom it is not. Thankfully, Plantinga discussed this issue in "Reason and Belief in God," so we are not left to guess what he would say.

Let us begin with those for whom belief in God is properly basic. What do reason and argument offer them? Plantinga explains that coming to hold a basic belief in the way he describes gives a *prima facie* justification for it. But we still want to know if the belief has *ultima facie* justification. We can distinguish these two types of justification because there are potential defeaters for many beliefs, including our belief in God and other religious beliefs. This is so even if we come to hold such views as basic in the way Plantinga proposes. Such a belief may not have *ultima facie* justification until one defeats its defeater(s). In so doing, reason, argument, and evidence are very important.

Those for whom belief in God is properly basic may, by engaging in the kind of argumentation required to address issues like the problem of evil, shore up their own faith. The theist may have always from childhood onward believed in God without hearing a single argument for his existence. At some time in her life, perhaps while in college, she is likely to hear arguments against God's existence and wonder if God actually exists. If she doesn't find answers, she may abandon belief in God. It is safe to say that in a situation like that imagined it won't suffice to say, "I don't know how to answer the critics, but I just know I must believe." Critics of theism won't allow her such an easy escape. They will likely press her to defend her beliefs, and for the sake of her own faith (and perhaps for that of her nonbelieving friends), she had better have some arguments and evidences.

For believers, reason and argument can also help them understand their own faith. The intellectual rigor demanded, for example, in understanding traditional arguments for God's existence and in understanding how to respond to the many problems of evil is useful not only in answering doubts but also in helping to understand better God's nature and his action in the world. For example, in studying the free will defense against the problem of evil I learn something about divine omnipotence. Despite God's omnipotence, the free will defense says that God can't give humans free will and then control the way they use it so that they never use it to do evil. This allows me to see in a concrete case what it means to say that God, though omnipotent, can't do just anything. That also vividly shows me that there must be a balance between God's action and our action when we act. Thus, I learn something *concretely* about divine sovereignty as it relates to free will which I only previously knew *in theory*.

Reason and argument are also of value for believers for whom belief in God is a non-basic belief. Many of these people did come to believe in God on the basis of other beliefs and information presented in rational arguments. People who come to believe in God this way are also rational. Reason and argument may also be useful to shore up their faith in times of doubt and to help them understand better the faith they have embraced.

What about those who don't believe in God? Some concluded that there is no God as a result of growing up in an environment where God was seldom mentioned (except in swearing) and his existence and interaction in the lives of family members was not assumed. We might say their atheism is a basic belief for them. Others adopted atheism as a result of arguments and evidences against God's existence.

What would Plantinga's Reformed Epistemology say to them about reason and argument? I think there are several roles it can play. First, just as there are potential defeaters for belief in God, there are also defeaters for atheism. Atheists need to use reason and argument to answer those defeaters; otherwise the rationality of their atheism will be suspect.

Second, reason and argument for God's existence may prove to be very important in their deciding to leave atheism and embrace theism. I wouldn't deny the Holy Spirit's activity in moving them to that conclusion, but we must not underestimate the significance of argument and evidence, tools the Holy Spirit uses to help break down barriers to belief in God.

Finally, reason and argument may not convince nonbelievers to believe in God, but it may move them to see theism in a different light. That is, prior to hearing a reasoned defense the atheist may think a compelling case cannot be made for theism and hence to become a theist requires the total sacrifice of intellect. Having heard the theist's defense, they may see how a very intelligent person could be a theist. They gain a new respect for theism and for theists who offer cogent reasons and arguments for belief in God. And, who knows? Perhaps this could be the first step in bringing him or her to belief.

In sum, even if one agrees with everything Plantinga has said about belief in God as properly basic and thus having warrant, there is still plenty of room for reason. Remember, Plantinga deals primarily with *de jure* objections to belief in God, but there are also questions of whether theistic beliefs are true. There is ample room for reason, argument, and evidence when addressing *de facto* questions.[72]

One final point must be addressed. In light of what Plantinga has argued about belief in God and the great things of the gospel, has he answered the charge that belief in God, and religious belief more generally, is irrational? A lot depends on how one defines rationality. In Plantinga's publications on Reformed Epistemology, we find six different senses in which a belief may be rational. Let me summarize them; interested readers can consult his writings for the details.

First, there is what may be called a means-end rationality. "Rationality thus construed is a matter of knowing how to get what you want; it is the cunning of reason."[73] Second, there is what Plantinga calls Aristotelian rationality. According to Aristotle, man is a rational animal. This means that humans are the sort of creatures who can "form concepts, grasp propositions, see relationships between them, think about objects both near and far."[74] What this amounts to, then, is that a creature is rational in this sense if he or she has the power of reason.

A third sense of rationality refers to the deliverances of reason. This sense refers more specifically to reason as the source of *a priori* knowledge, and there are various kinds of such knowledge. The most prominent deliverances of reason are self-evident beliefs and those beliefs which, though not self-evident, follow from beliefs that are. What is true of self-evident beliefs is that once you grasp their meaning, you immediately see that they couldn't be false.[75] In *Warrant and Proper Function* Plantinga details the kinds of beliefs that can be classed as the deliverances of reason. This sense of rationality seems quite significant for apologetics, for the apologist wants to produce the strongest case for Christian belief. If the apologist does construct such a case, then in effect she is making a case that it is rational to believe in Christianity, because on evidence it is the most probable worldview. One should believe what is in accord with the deliverances of reason, and reason tells us to attune our beliefs to the preponderance of the evidence, that is, to believe what is most probable.

Fourth, there is what may be labeled the deontological sense of rationality. In this sense, rationality is linked to epistemic duties. Thus, to hold a belief formed through malfunctioning cognitive faculties, especially if one knows this is so, would be a significant breach of epistemic duty. Since most would think it irrational to disobey duty, including one's epistemic duty, continuing to hold the belief so formed would seem irrational.[76]

Fifth, rationality may be understood in terms of sanity. When we call someone's behavior irrational, we may mean that the person referred to has some sort of psychosis.[77] Finally, Plantinga proposes that to think someone rational means that his cognitive faculties are functioning properly, in an appropriate environment, with the aim of producing true beliefs. Thus, this sense of rationality refers to proper function. As already explained, Plantinga holds that a belief formed in this way is a warranted belief. So, in this sense of rationality, rationality and warrant coincide.[78]

Given these different senses of rationality, I think Plantinga's account of religious beliefs as properly basic fits with rationality in these six senses. Belief in God and the great things of the gospel in no way needs to violate means-end rationality. It may have nothing to do with it. Or someone may hold such beliefs as basic because she thinks that believing in Christianity is the best way to ensure an eternity of blessing rather than punishment. In that case, her beliefs are very rational in light of her intended goal of eternal blessing.

Belief in God and Christianity doesn't violate Aristotelian rationality either. Having read Plantinga or my description of his views, it should be clear that his views evidence the highest sort of reasoning power. Nor do they violate the deliverances of reason. If one grants what Plantinga says about how such beliefs are formed in a basic way, then these beliefs are more probable than not, especially if one can produce defeaters for defeaters of theistic belief. So, such beliefs are rational in this third sense.

Fourth, belief in God and Christianity as basic for the believer doesn't violate any epistemic duties one has. This, of course, is so if one rejects classical foundationalism and its criteria of proper basicality, but if one adopts Plantinga's foundationalism (or something like it), there seem to be no epistemic duties violated by those who believe in God and Christianity as properly basic. Moreover, such religious beliefs are also rational in that there is no evidence that they stem from insanity. Surely, someone could believe in God and Christianity as a result of a psychological disorder, but that would be hard to prove of most or even of many believers.

Finally, rationality in the sense of proper function obviously fits with believing in God and Christianity in the way Plantinga's foundationalism suggests. If these religious beliefs are formed by cognitive faculties that function properly, then, of course, they are rational in this sense of rationality.

Plantinga's Reformed Epistemology is a rich and multifaceted theory. Whether this whole "story" is true is not something for which Plantinga offers evidence and argument, but that doesn't mean it couldn't be done. But what has Reformed Epistemology accomplished? Is it a helpful tool in defending Christian truth? If so, how should we use it? To those issues we turn next.

EVALUATION OF REFORMED EPISTEMOLOGY

When I first read Alvin Plantinga's "Reason and Belief in God," I found much with which I agreed. In particular, I agreed with his rejection of classical foundationalism, but I sensed that he still held some sort of foundationalism. In addition, without details I wasn't entirely convinced that belief in

God could be properly basic for anyone. Of course, many people, myself included, came to believe in God in the general way Plantinga suggests, but I wasn't convinced that I didn't at some point need to construct an evidential case in order to satisfy doubts about whether I really had a right to believe in God. Moreover, I felt certain that few nonbelievers would agree that it is acceptable to believe in God without evidential support. So, I wasn't sure how useful apologetically this would be in a real situation where I was trying to convince a nonbeliever to believe in God, or even trying to fend off complaints that it is irrational to think anyone justified in believing in God without providing evidence that he exists.

As I read critiques of Plantinga's Reformed Epistemology, I saw that I wasn't the only one with questions, and it wasn't just nonbelievers who had questions. Still, knowing Plantinga's work in other areas, I felt it necessary to suspend disbelief until I had read the "complete story." By the time I completed *Warrant and Proper Function*, what Plantinga was arguing and how he was doing so was very clear, and most of my questions were answered. In *Warranted Christian Belief* Plantinga applies his foundationalism to religious belief. I have described it in some detail because I think it is important, and because without clarity on the more significant details, his case isn't as persuasive as it is when one understands the details. My assessment is mainly positive, though I think it is important to understand exactly what Plantinga's project accomplishes.

In this final section of this chapter, I want first to look at some of the most significant objections often raised during the years before *Warranted Christian Belief* appeared. I think it worthwhile to note Plantinga's answers, since readers may still raise these kinds of objections. Then, I want to explain how Plantinga's Reformed Epistemology relates to modern and postmodern epistemology as described in the early chapters of this book. Finally, I shall close this chapter with a final assessment of the value of Reformed Epistemology in defending Christianity.

Objections

Some objections to Reformed Epistemology are more substantial than others, and I want now to address two that seem of greatest significance. A first objection is probably the most significant. As Plantinga makes his case that those who believe in the main tenets of Christianity as basic beliefs are warranted, justified, and rational in doing so, a lot depends on Plantinga's main arguments being arguments based on analogy. That is, he claims that what he says about religious belief is analogous to what anyone would say about a variety of beliefs we take as basic, namely, memory beliefs, many perceptual beliefs, beliefs about various items of *a priori* knowledge, beliefs based on the testimony of others deemed to know, and beliefs often called common sense beliefs. As Plantinga says, even though we have never made an evidential case for any of these, we are still rational in believing them. In the appropriate circumstances, our cognitive faculties, functioning properly, produced them.

Plantinga details the nature of these beliefs because he thinks the way many believers come to believe them is analogous to how they acquire religious beliefs. Various philosophers have objected that there are some significant differences between religious beliefs and these other kinds of beliefs, and those differences ruin Plantinga's argument from analogy.[79]

I am inclined to agree with Plantinga, but I think we must be careful in assessing this discussion. One can always find differences between religious beliefs and these beliefs, for they are analogous, not identical. The issue is whether the differences are critical to the point being made by the argument from analogy. It is especially important here to distinguish between the *content* of all of these beliefs and the *way* some believers come to hold them. Plantinga isn't saying that religious beliefs can be held rationally without argument and evidence because their *content* is analogous to, for example, beliefs of common sense. His point is that the *way* believers come to hold these various beliefs is analogous. Given the analogous way believers come to hold them, if it is rational to hold common sense beliefs derived in the ways described, it should be equally rational to hold religious beliefs that arise in the same way. An example will illustrate this point.

I believe that my first name is John. That belief is basic for me; I have never constructed an evidential case for it, and the only real chance that I ever would do so is if I should suffer from amnesia so badly that I couldn't remember my name, or if someone in an overly skeptical mood told me that he doubted my first name is John. Apart from such situations, I can't imagine even thinking about making an evidential case for this belief. It arose in the ordinary chain of events as I began to learn language, heard the word 'John,' and saw people look at me or point to me when they said my name. As a result, when asked, I've always said my name is John. I have never thought my cognitive faculties were malfunctioning when I've said my name, and no one has ever said that something other than John is my first name.

Similarly, according to Plantinga, belief in God for someone like me is also properly basic. It arose for me in the surroundings and circumstances mentioned earlier in this chapter. But, then, just as I have never made an evidential case for my first name being John and yet am warranted in holding that belief, so I am also warranted in believing in God apart from evidential support. Warrant is granted in both cases because those beliefs were formed in appropriate circumstances by my properly functioning cognitive faculties which are designed to generate true beliefs. Of course, the content of these two beliefs differs, but that's not the point. The cognitive faculties used to form each belief were basically the same (except that, in the case of belief in God, the *sensus divinitatis* was also involved), and the way I came to believe one is analogous to how I came to believe the other. Thus, if one is warranted, so is the other.

Are the two cases of coming to hold a belief analogous enough for the argument to succeed? But what failure of analogy rules out this argument? Surely not the fact that one belief is about myself and the other about another—for that would mean I couldn't be warranted in believing anything about anyone other than myself. Well, perhaps the difference is that it is almost unthinkable that I should ever make a case that my first name is John, but it is not hard to imagine the need to make a case at some time for God's existence. But the problem here is that the objection focuses on the *content* of the belief, not on the *way* it was attained! I grant that there is little controversy surrounding what my first name is, while there is much controversy about whether God exists. Plantinga doesn't deny that, but his point is not about the content of the belief, but about how the believer came to hold such a belief and about whether one is rational in holding a belief that arises in that way. Remember as well that Plantinga is not saying that everyone does or even must come to belief in God in the way described. His point is only that some people believe in God but not on the basis of argument and evidence, and the way they came to that belief is analogous, for example, to the way I came to believe my first name is John.

Perhaps the difference between belief in God and my belief about my first name is that there are more potential defeaters for the former belief than for the latter. Fair enough, but why does that make the way I came to both beliefs disanalogous? If the way I came to both is analogous, then it seems that if one belief is warranted, so is the other. Of course, if I can't defeat the defeaters of belief in God, then I would be foolish to maintain that I am warranted in believing in God's existence. But there are ample responses to defeaters of belief in God.

In light of the above, I believe that the argument from analogy works, so long as the analogy focuses on the way the various beliefs are formed, not on the content of the beliefs. Of course, none of this suggests that skeptics (and there are many) about God's existence have no point to make or that we shouldn't try to present them an evidential case for God's existence. And, of course, my belief about my first name is in no way controversial, while belief in God is. Plantinga would deny none of this. His point is not about skeptics but about believers for whom the various beliefs are basic. If those who hold one kind of basic belief are warranted in so doing, then those who came to believe in God in an analogous way should also be warranted in holding that belief.

A second objection concerns defeaters. Some critics of Reformed Epistemology think Plantinga is far too optimistic about religious beliefs answering defeaters. Plantinga grants that beliefs formed in the properly basic way he details are not exempt from attack by defeaters. In fact, he spends approximately the final one hundred fifty pages of *Warranted Christian Belief* addressing some of the most frequently raised objections to theistic belief. And that is proper, since there are significant defeaters to theistic belief, and many critics of theism believe the defeaters can't be adequately answered. Plantinga has addressed in various places a number of the most significant defeaters, such as the problem of evil. Others also have addressed at length the problem of evil,[80] and of course, various apologists have defended matters like the reliability of Scripture, the possibility of miracles, the resurrection of Jesus Christ, etc. In light of the arguments and evidences supporting each of these, I doubt that it is impossible to defeat these defeaters. For those unsure, I invite you to read the evidences portion of this book.

Some will read the defenses available and deny that they answer the defeaters. It is certainly possible that a better case is needed, but before concluding that the defeaters defeat Christian beliefs, we must agree on the standard an evidential case must meet in order to defeat the defeaters. It is just at this point that some will try to smuggle back into the discussion the criteria of classical foundationalism. If an evidential case must be judged on those standards, I'm not sure that either Christianity or any opposing worldviews can defeat the defeaters. Of course, in light of Plantinga's critique of classical foundationalism, there is no good reason to feel obligated to satisfy the standards of that theory of knowledge.

On the other hand, many critics think Christian belief can't defeat the defeaters because Christian doctrines involve supernatural involvement in our world. We are well aware of contemporary rejections of the supernatural, many of them not based on much besides the notion that any explanation is more probable than one that involves miracles. Of course, this is grossly question begging, but unfortunately that doesn't dissuade critics from holding such a view. Still, if that is the best the critic can do in many cases, then Christians needn't unduly worry that such concerns defeat their beliefs. Those who disagree won't likely be persuaded to be theists, but that alone says nothing about whether the defeaters actually succeed in refuting Christian belief.

Plantinga's Reformed Epistemology and Modernity and Postmodernity

In light of Plantinga's views on belief in God and in the great things of the gospel as properly basic, what might he say to Mo Joe and Pomo Joe? It is safe to say that Plantinga's Reformed Epistemology speaks most directly to epistemological concerns of modern epistemology. After all, it is the modern concept of rationality that generates the evidentialist objection to belief in God, so this should surprise no one. First, Plantinga's attack on classical foundationalism and its criteria of proper basicality is directly relevant to modern epistemology, since so much of modern epistemology is based on classical foundationalism. If the epistemology that undergirds the modern objection to belief in God is wrong, then the objection that rests on it is rebutted.

Second, it is very important that Plantinga not only attacks classical foundationalism, but that he offers something in its place. Without a credible alternative that shows how religious belief can be warranted, rational, and justified, we still wouldn't know whether belief in God as a basic or non-basic belief is warranted. In Plantinga's foundationalism, we have an alternative to classical foundationalism, and in accord with its tenets

Plantinga has shown that belief in God as basic or non-basic can be rationally acceptable and warranted. This means that theists can answer *de jure* objections to theistic belief that for so long have made nonbelievers unwilling to take theists seriously. There may be other accounts of rationality that also answer *de jure* objections to theistic belief, but Plantinga's foundationalism does so very effectively.

Of course, those coming from a modern perspective will likely reply that this is only part of the story. While Plantinga has shown a possible way for theists in general and Christians in particular to be warranted in their religious beliefs, he hasn't demonstrated that his epistemology is correct, nor has he made the case that Christianity is true. Whether or not these things are true is important to all of us, Plantinga included. Without evidence that they are true, there is still much work to be done. But one shouldn't castigate Plantinga for not giving us the rest of the story. His project covers a very specific problem, and he has been one of the few philosophers even asking, let alone answering, the sort of questions he raises in his Reformed Epistemology. For that we should be most thankful!

As to postmodern epistemology, the situation is much different. It is dubious that postmoderns would even raise the *de jure* objections Plantinga handles. Since postmoderns are dubious about the accuracy and value of reason, even if someone thought a belief, including belief in God, were irrational, that alone wouldn't necessarily move a postmodern to reject it. Moreover, I doubt that postmoderns would even raise the evidentialist objection, because it rests on an epistemology they distinctly reject.

This doesn't mean, however, that postmoderns would readily embrace Plantinga's foundationalism. Since it still talks about being rational and about the give-and-take of argument, and holds that there is truth and that it is knowable, postmoderns aren't likely to join the bandwagon. That is, postmodern epistemology would move those who hold it to reject the very questions both *de jure* and *de facto* objections to theistic belief or any other belief raise.

Though Plantinga's main themes aren't really issues many postmoderns care much about, in *Warranted Christian Belief* Plantinga includes a section directly addressed to postmodernism. He offers a list of postmodern doctrines and asks whether any of them are inimical to Christian belief. Some, he notes, are actually positive to Christian themes whereas others don't relate either positively or negatively to key central Christian doctrines. However, at least one postmodern theme is quite significant to Christian claims, namely, the belief that there is no such thing as truth, or if there is, no human is in a position to know it. Since Christianity claims to be truth, if postmoderns are right about truth, that would be devastating to what Christians believe about Christianity.[81]

As Plantinga notes, one frustration in dealing with postmoderns is that they offer so little argument for their views and are often disinterested in the whole mind-set that thinks presenting argument and evidence is important for deciding anything about what is true of our world. Still, there are at least two arguments postmoderns like to raise in defense of their belief that there can't be any absolute truth, and Plantinga addresses them. These two considerations are to a large extent why many postmoderns won't even take seriously the questions (let alone the answers) Plantinga's Reformed Epistemology addresses. Specifically, Plantinga considers the postmodern argument from our historic conditionedness, and the postmodern claim that human beings construct the truth. If either of these postmodern arguments is correct, that would be a significant defeater for Christian belief, let alone for Plantinga's epistemology.

The argument about being historically conditioned notes that who we are and what we believe is largely based on when and where we were born and lived. I was raised in a godly Christian home, but had I been raised in the home of an atheist or agnostic, I might never have believed in God, and my life would likely have followed a very different course. So, postmoderns claim that what a person believes theologically and philosophically is just too dependent upon the specific circumstances of his or her life for such beliefs to be taken as credible and warranted after all.[82]

In response, Plantinga answers first that the argument is self-defeating. This is so because the argument proposes that whatever we believe is a product of our position in time, space, and culture and hence cannot be absolutely true. But if this is so, then the claim that we can't know absolute truth because we are bound by time, place, and culture is itself bound by time, place, and culture, so it cannot be true. Hence, the historical conditioning argument shouldn't bother us, because it refutes itself.[83]

Plantinga's second response asks why we can't know more at one time than another. Suppose Einstein had lived in the eighteenth century. He probably wouldn't have produced the theory of special relativity, but what does that prove about whether relativity theory is or isn't true? Moreover, I now believe that I'm in my study and writing at my computer. I could have been out of town for this whole week and so not believed that I am today in my study. But how, Plantinga would ask, does the fact of where else I might have been this week besmirch as unwarranted my current belief about writing at my computer in my study?[84]

Next, Plantinga turns to the postmodern argument that there can't be absolute truth because truth is something we construct, not something about the world that we just find as it is. His main protagonist is Richard Rorty, who once said that truth is what your colleagues will let you get away with saying. Plantinga shows that if Rorty is serious about this, then we have the troublesome result that all sorts of things that have existed (the Holocaust, the stock market crash of 1929, etc.) didn't really happen. For if truth is what our colleagues let us get away with saying, and if we say that these things never happened, that means they didn't occur. This is obviously absurd and suggests something quite wrong about a view that results in such absurdities.

Rorty has stated his views on truth in a more measured way. Plantinga quotes from Rorty's *Contingency, Irony, and Solidarity* as follows:

> To say that truth is not out there is simply to say that where there are no sentences there is no truth, that sentences are elements of human languages, and that human languages are human creations.
>
> Truth cannot be out there—cannot exist independently of the human mind—because sentences cannot so exist, or be out there.[85]

Plantinga remarks that what this means is by no means easy to say, but it seems to say that human beings create truths. Truths are sentences, parts of languages, and languages are human creations. But if that is so, there wouldn't be truth if there weren't any humans.[86]

Plantinga offers what he considers a fatal objection to this way of thinking. He asks us to grant that the only things that are true in the primary sense are sentences. Since humans are the ones who put sentences together or construct them with the various words, letters, and sounds (if spoken) they convey, and since those sentences can be true or false, there is a sense in which in making sentences we have made truth. But making it the case that there are such things as sentences which can be true or false is not the same as making true or false that which the sentence affirms about the world. Plantinga illustrates beautifully this point and also the problem with the view that truth is something we construct, when he writes,

> We make it the case that the sequence of marks 'There once were dino-saurs' is a sentence and thus capable of being true or false. It doesn't follow that we make it true that there once were dinosaurs. By virtue of our language-making activity, we bring it about that a certain string of marks—'there once were dinosaurs'—is true if and only if there once were dinosaurs. But that is not sufficient for making that sentence true. For the sentence to be true, there must once have been dinosaurs; and that, presumably, is not something we have made to be the case, by our language-making activities or in any other way.[87]

Having dispensed with the major arguments postmoderns offer for there being no absolute truth, Plantinga offers a final assessment of post-modernism. He notes that at least since Descartes there has been a search for certain, unshakable knowledge. While all of us could wish for the sort of Cartesian certainty so many have sought, we know that we are all too ca-pable of error, even in regard to things about which we have great certainty because of a strong evidential case. In such circumstances, we may react at least in one of two ways. The first affirms that there is indeed such a thing as truth (there is a way things are), but also recognizes that we may be wrong at times about what we think the truth to be. A position of this sort requires a strong stomach, for it incorporates a great deal of risk—e.g., suppose I am wrong about the most important things (God's existence, my relation to him, my eternal destiny, etc.); the consequences would be devastating.

On the other hand, one could respond as many postmoderns do. One could remove the risk by claiming that there just isn't absolute truth (only individual truth for each of us), so there shouldn't be any fear of being "wrong." With that view, perhaps the worst one could experience is a sort of bumbling, meandering existence as one goes through life. But nothing involving eternal consequences need be our concern. We can rest easy, even if we rest confused and bewildered about which road to follow through life.

The contrast between these two options is both stark and very signifi-cant: either believe there is absolute truth while admitting that we may often be in error about what the truth is; or reject the idea that there is absolute truth and rest easy, recognizing that though we don't really know our way in life with any certainty, at least there are no devastating eternal consequences to befall us should we make wrong choices along the way (assuming we can know what counts as a *wrong* choice). When you put matters this way, Plantinga says the postmodern problem in choosing the second route turns out to be a failure of epistemic nerve. More importantly, it wrongly assumes that just because I could be wrong about something I hold very dearly and staunchly defend when challenged, that must mean that there actually isn't any such thing as truth. That leap in logic is definitely unwarranted—it is a clear non sequitur. I think these words of assessment of postmodernism are right. Understanding what Plantinga is arguing, we can also understand why he has so little to say, relatively speaking, to postmodernism and is, instead, intent on answering questions that stem from basic commitments of modern epistemology and its adherence to classical foundationalism and evidentialism.

CONCLUDING EVALUATION

In this chapter I have spent much space in presenting, explaining, and defending Plantinga's Reformed Epistemology, not only because I think he is basically right, but because I think he addresses a very important set of objections to theistic and (more specifically) Christian belief. For the most part, I think Plantinga has accomplished what he set out to do. I believe he has shown that it can be completely rational and warranted for someone to hold religious beliefs without having produced argument and evidence to support the beliefs. Since many skeptics of theism have thought theistic believers aren't worth hearing because they don't and even can't offer sufficient evidence for their religious beliefs, what Plantinga argues is, I believe, a strong and correct reply.

But there are limitations to what Plantinga offers. The case he makes that believing in the Christian God as properly basic is warranted, seems applicable across the board to believers in the gods of other religions. It also, in ways explained in this chapter, can show that atheists and agnostics are warranted in their beliefs. Plantinga might say that the cases are different because, for Christian belief, our cognitive equipment includes the *sensus divinitatis* and the internal witness of the Holy Spirit. Non-Christians may reply in one of two ways. First, if one presupposes the truth of Christianity, then of course, in using the cognitive equipment Plantinga outlines, one is likely to come to Christian belief. But why should we believe what Plantinga says about the Christian's cognitive equipment? Members of other religions can say, secondly, that they also have the *sensus divinitatis* and divine light from God as well, but it, along with their life experiences and circumstances, has led them to be Muslims, Buddhists, etc., and given Plantinga's basic line of reasoning, they are warranted and rational in holding such beliefs. It is hard to see how Reformed Epistemology alone can refute this. And unless one presupposes the existence of the special Christian cognitive faculties just mentioned, there seems to be no reason that atheists and agnostics raised in nonreligious settings cannot be thoroughly rational in their atheism and agnosticism.

What seems to be lacking that could answer such questions is evidence and argument that Christian theism is in fact true. If that were forthcoming, there would be reason to think Christian belief is both rational *and* right, whereas believers in other religions without argument and evidence may be rational, but an evidential case against their religious beliefs would show them not to be true. However, to provide such cases moves the discussion to *de facto* issues, and Plantinga has said that his concern instead is to answer *de jure* questions.

In addition, though I think Plantinga convincingly argues that Christians who come to believe in God in the way he describes are warranted in holding that belief, this must not be misunderstood. It doesn't mean that such Christians should never be expected to construct a case for Christianity. Depending on the context in which they work (e.g., an intellectual environment where many coworkers don't believe that the evidence supports belief in God), they may be called upon to "make the case" for Christianity, and should do so. Moreover, those who came to believe in God in the properly basic way Plantinga describes may later in life have doubts, and for reasons explained earlier in this chapter, they will find it necessary and helpful to make an evidential case for the religious beliefs they hold. Both of these tasks are to be expected, because nonbelievers (and even believers themselves) will want to know not only why religious belief is rational and warranted for those who hold it without argument and evidence, they will also want to know whether those beliefs are right. In fact, if believers don't or can't make an evidential case for Christian belief, nonbelievers may agree that we are as justified in our beliefs as is the little girl who believes in the tooth fairy, but as in her case, being justified and warranted isn't enough. Everyone needs to know whether Christian beliefs are true. To establish that they are, *de facto* issues must be addressed, and successfully so.

In conclusion, I do think Plantinga accomplishes the main things he intends to do with his Reformed Epistemology, and I greatly admire and appreciate what he has done. It is no mean feat to make a case that believers who have little or no clue about how to construct an argumentative case favoring belief in God and Christian theism can still be rational and warranted in believing in Christianity. But Reformed Epistemology is basically an exercise in negative apologetics—rebutting objections that Christians are irrational in continuing to believe in God and Christ. It doesn't establish theism or Christianity as a whole as true, nor does it attempt to do so. So, while it establishes something important, it isn't a method for defending the Christian worldview as true. In the next two chapters we turn to ways of defending Christian truth which do address *de facto* concerns about Christian belief and which do offer ways of defending the Christian worldview as a whole and specific doctrines within it.

Chapter 8

Presuppositionalism

During the twentieth century a method of doing Christian apologetics arose that differed from traditional apologetics in how it claimed Christians should argue, and also in its understanding of why it is necessary to use this method. The method is known as presuppositionalism, though some proponents aren't entirely thrilled with that label.[1] The person most associated with this method of apologetics is Cornelius Van Til, though colleagues such as Francis Schaeffer also proposed a version of this approach.

As the twentieth century ended and the twenty-first century has begun, the popularity of this method among Christians has also waned. In addition, many current followers of this approach have so modified some of its main ideas that at times it is hard to detect much difference between their form of presuppositionalism and some forms of Christian evidentialism.[2] Still, within certain circles, especially those of a highly Reformed persuasion, it persists, and it would be unfair to overlook this approach just because its use among Christians is less extensive than at one time. Moreover, Van Til and his followers say some theological and philosophical things that are important for Christian apologists of any era.[3]

Unfortunately, many may think presuppositionalism is just a variant of Reformed Epistemology, and since it is a more primitive form, we need not bother with it. However, this is wrong, for while there are some common terms and concepts between the two approaches, they are quite different in the apologetic questions they address and the methods they employ to defend the faith. We must be careful not to be misled by the fact that both use the term 'Reformed' and both talk about the "noetic effects of the fall."

I'll note significant differences between these two approaches later in this chapter.

One further introductory point is that presuppositional apologetics arose at a time when modernity's epistemology held sway; postmodern epistemology had not yet made its appearance. Once postmodern epistemology came on the scene, presuppositionalists didn't shift their method or emphases to address it. In fact, as we shall see, both postmoderns and presuppositionalists hold some intellectual commitments in common, even though they come to these views on different grounds. Nonetheless, presuppositionalism arose against the backdrop of modern epistemology and continues to be primarily a response to its concerns.

In this chapter I begin with Cornelius Van Til's presuppositionalism. Though many of his followers have modified some of his key ideas, they are still motivated by many of the same theological considerations in particular that moved Van Til to propose this method of apologetics in the first place. Then I want to turn to Francis Schaeffer's version of this approach. My discussion of Schaeffer can be shorter, since he shares many of Van Til's views. However, there are some differences that I want to point out.[4]

As for presuppositionalism itself, I shall argue that what presuppositionalists want us to do in addressing nonbelievers is in part quite helpful to Christian apologetics. Its major value is as a tool for attacking and refuting non-Christian positions. However, Christianity doesn't win by default once non-Christian positions are demonstrably inadequate. We need a positive argument for the truth of Christianity, and it is here that presuppositionalism offers little help. But more on these matters later; we must first understand this approach to Christian apologetics.

THE PRESUPPOSITIONALISM OF CORNELIUS VAN TIL

For many years Cornelius Van Til taught apologetics and theology at Westminster Theological Seminary. He was a very godly man who believed wholeheartedly that human beings are created in God's image and are intended ultimately to bring God glory. Van Til also believed that Christians should honor and glorify God and his word in everything they do, including defending the faith. He believed that apologetic strategy, like all else in life, should be rooted in the Bible. Hence, much of Van Til's rationale for his apologetic method is theological. Thus, one might question Van Til's theological conclusions and the applications he gave them, and that just means that the debate over Van Til's presuppositionalism involves our understanding of Scripture and Christian theology and of how some key doctrinal tenets apply to defending the faith to nonbelievers.

Fundamental to everything else in his apologetics, Van Til stressed that everyone has presuppositions which govern their worldview and ultimately their lifestyle. A presupposition is a belief that is held often without supporting evidence. For Van Til, it is also an ultimate and final reference point.[5] Though one could make a case for it, typically it is held apart from providing evidence for it. While this might sound like one of Plantinga's basic beliefs, that is not necessarily so. A properly basic belief arises in certain circumstances without the knower having made any case for it at all. Its production depends on properly functioning cognitive equipment made to produce true belief. A basic belief is subject to defeaters, counterarguments and evidence that directly attack the truthfulness of the belief. If the belief is to be maintained, the believer must find evidence and argument to defeat the defeater. And, of course, the motivation behind Plantinga's discussion of basic beliefs is to answer questions about the warrant, justification, and rationality of a given belief.

As for a presupposition, it may arise as a basic belief, but it may instead be a non-basic belief. Whereas the key with a basic belief is how it arises (not so much the content), how one attains a presupposition is rather insignificant. One simply chooses a belief as true without proof, because one sees it as foundational to the rest of one's belief system. So the key with a presupposition has nothing to do with what Plantinga says about how one comes to a basic belief, but is rather the content of the belief and how the belief functions in the presuppositionalist's defense of Christianity. Then, as we shall see, not only are presuppositions chosen as fundamental commitments without support from any evidence, neither are those who hold them concerned about potential defeaters that seemingly offer direct evidence against the truth of the assumption. As we shall see, what matters most in disproving a competing worldview is whether its intellectual commitments are internally consistent. And the main thing presuppositionalists are concerned to show about Christianity is that it is internally consistent. Hence, defeaters, as arguments and evidences *outside* a Christian system, are irrelevant to whether or not the Christian position is internally consistent. So, if defeaters are at all dealt with in presuppositionalism, it is indirectly, by showing that systems that contain such evidence are internally inconsistent and by showing that Christianity, which doesn't contain such arguments, is logically consistent with itself. We can also say that Plantinga appeals to properly basic beliefs and how they arise for some people as a way to answer *de jure* questions about Christian belief. The choice of presuppositions and their function as the basis of one's belief system, in contrast, is really about preparing to show that Christianity is true, and thus it is part of the presuppositionalist's method of answering *de facto* questions about Christianity.

As suggested above, a presupposition is usually a belief that undergirds one's worldview so that various elements of the worldview logically flow from it. According to Van Til, no one addresses questions about the ultimate meaning of life and about how things in our universe relate to one another from a purely neutral standpoint.[6] Though nonbelievers often say they are neutral because they begin from impartial, objective reason whereas Christians always begin within the circle of their faith, this is not so. The difference between believer and nonbeliever is not one of faith versus reason (the former thought to be subjective and biased and the latter objective and neutral), but actually one of faith versus faith. The believer's faith in God and his word is set over against the nonbeliever's faith in reason and its ability to know correctly and impartially what is true of our world.

In contrast, Van Til maintained that all people, even those who protest most loudly that they begin from neutral ground, have presuppositions that govern their outlook on the world and their actions. Of course, Van Til's point isn't just that nonbelievers aren't neutral in their outlook, but also that their commitment to reason means that they see it and themselves as autonomous, the final arbiter of truth.[7] The fact, however, that all people have presuppositions should urge believers not to be bashful about holding and stating their presuppositions plainly.

Van Til identifies several presuppositions as key to Christianity. The Christian system begins with belief in God's existence, i.e., a belief in the triune God of Christianity. In addition, Christians also presuppose that God as creator and sovereign over all things has absolute control over everyone and everything throughout all of the universe's history and beyond. This means that God is the ultimate reference point for everything in the universe and that events of our lives and facts of our world make sense only when seen in relation to our sovereign creator.

God's existence is not to be proved using traditional proofs for God's existence; it is assumed as true. "Proof" of God's existence, if one uses such terms, is that facts in the world can be facts and make sense only if God exists. The further main Christian presupposition is that God has revealed himself both in the natural world, including man's very being, and in the Bible, his Word. Christians assume that Scripture is God's Word and hence entirely true. Given its truthfulness, the worldview it teaches offers us God's perspective on all of reality. It is to be accepted as true on its own authority, not as a result of some proof for the reliability of Scripture. In Scripture we learn that humans are made in God's image and that their relation to God gives them great significance and meaning. These, then, are the Christian's non-negotiable presuppositions.[8]

In contrast, nonbelievers presuppose very different assumptions about the world. In particular, atheists assume that ours is a world without God. It is not that he once existed, created this universe, and then either retreated or somehow went out of existence. Rather, atheists typically hold that there never was nor will there ever be a God. If there is no God, then he can't be the ultimate explanation of how things came to exist. Rather, the world was "created" by and has ever since run by blind chance. This, of course, means that there is no ultimate special meaning and dignity of human beings. They are not created as the image of God, but rather are just the products of blind, random chance.

Atheists accordingly also assume that each person is autonomous and is the ultimate authority for himself or herself. In particular, human reason is autonomous and is really the only means by which we can judge what is true or false. While it isn't infallible, reason can discover and judge what is true or not true of the universe. As with Christians and their presuppositions, atheists assume these things as true without proving that they are.[9] In principle, a case could be made for these assumptions, but atheists typically just adopt them as their starting point, without proof.

Clearly, one cannot consistently hold both Christian and non-Christian presuppositions at the same time. Conflict between systems based on such diverse starting points will be inevitable. Clearly as well, there is no neutral starting point that believers hold in common with nonbelievers from which both can engage one another in dialogue and debate. None of this should cause Christians to avoid conversation with nonbelievers, however. They are lost and need to hear the gospel. Since nonbelievers aren't shy about reasoning from their presuppositions, Christians shouldn't recoil from using their presuppositions as their starting point.

Reasoning by presupposition is the preferred method, according to Van Til, for several reasons that appeal to theological principles. First, Van Til has a very healthy respect for the Reformed belief in total depravity and the resultant noetic effects of the fall of the human race into sin. According to total depravity, all aspects of human nature have been touched by sin. While this doesn't remove capacities like reason, bodily movement, and the like, it does hamper their proper and accurate functioning.

Of utmost importance for apologetics and evangelism is the effect of sin on the nonbeliever's mind (i.e., the noetic effects of the fall). Based on Scriptures like 1 Corinthians 2:14, Van Til affirms that when it comes to spiritual matters, people without Christ can't see things the way believers do. They are not just neutral but are negative to spiritual things, including the Christian worldview. In speaking of the effect of sin upon the nonbeliever's mind, Van Til uses a very vivid metaphor to portray the cognitive situation of the unregenerate. He says that sin and the nonbeliever's anti-theistic and anti-Christian presuppositions are like a pair of colored glasses that are cemented to the nonbeliever's face.[10] Those glasses skew everything that the nonbeliever sees and thinks, so he cannot possibly see things as a Christian does.

Of course, the only correct way to understand anything in our world is to see it in light of the ultimate reference point for everything, our sovereign God and creator. This means, according to Van Til, that if human knowledge, including that of nonbelievers, were not actually rooted in the creation and providence of God, there could be no knowledge whatsoever.[11] But how could one prove such a thing, the critic might ask? Van Til replies that "the only 'proof' of the Christian position is that unless its truth is presupposed there is no possibility of proving anything at all."[12]

This has at times been misunderstood to mean that only Christians can know anything at all. Nonbelievers can't even know and understand propositions like "2+2 =4", "there are rocks, trees, and people in the world," and "I'm in pain." This sounds, of course, both arrogant and absurd, but it is not what Van Til and his followers hold. In fact, Van Til emphatically states that, of course, nonbelievers can in a certain sense know such things. His point is that they fail to see that these truths are true in a world created and run by God. Hence, such beliefs as those mentioned are to a degree correct, but they are not entirely correct because they leave out God as the ultimate reference point.[13]

Of course, Van Til does hold that when it comes to spiritual truth, there are many spiritual truths that nonbelievers don't know at all. In addition, even spiritual truths they do grasp intellectually aren't understood in the fullest sense, for that can happen only through the illumining and regenerating work of the Holy Spirit. But left to natural reason alone, regardless of how capable intellectually the reasoner may be, the nonbeliever will never accept the Christian position. We can present to him all the evidence we have and give him the best reasoned arguments we can think of, but if he operates only with autonomous reason and the assumption that there is no God, we can never convince him. Non-Christian presuppositions cannot ultimately yield agreement with the Christian position.[14]

The preceding discussion about the noetic effects of humanity's fall into sin leads to a second major reason that reasoning by presupposition is the preferred method, according to Van Til. In spite of the noetic effects of the fall, some may still think that since reason wasn't ripped out of humans and since we all live in the same world, there must be some points of common ground from which we can begin the conversation with unbelievers and to which we can appeal to support our case for Christianity's truth. However, Van Til disagrees, and does so for several reasons. First, because of spiritual blindness as a result of sin, the nonbeliever simply doesn't see anything dealing with spiritual truths the same way the believer does. That is, there really isn't common ground between the believer and nonbeliever from which the believer can lead a nonbeliever to Christ.

Christian apologists have most often argued for the faith by appealing to the facts of our world to show that Christianity is true. Of course, that assumes that Christians and non-Christians mean the same thing when they talk of spiritual things and agree on what the facts are, and it also assumes that human reason unaided by God is capable of considering the facts and concluding that Christianity is correct. Van Til replies that all of this doesn't take seriously enough the effects of sin on the nonbeliever's mind. Moreover, it grants to human reason the ability and autonomy to determine what is true. However, since nonbelievers, based on their autonomous reason, presuppose that there is no God and that chance rules the universe, how can their unaided reason ever conclude that God exists and controls all things? Since nonbelievers leave God out of their understanding of reality, why should believers think an appeal to facts and commonly held beliefs will lead the nonbeliever to embrace theism of any sort, let alone Christian theism? If one could get to God by autonomous reason alone, then unbelievers probably would have already accepted a theistic point of view. But unbelievers cannot adopt Christianity on the basis of reason alone, and Christians can't argue them into the faith by appealing to commonly held facts, beliefs, and arguments. There simply are no such beliefs that are common ground between believers and nonbelievers.

The idea of no common ground between believer and unbeliever seems unacceptable, but Van Til doesn't make this claim without *any* qualification. He distinguishes between metaphysical and epistemological common ground.[15] Van Til says that, metaphysically, the whole universe is common ground to both believer and unbeliever; we both have access to the same data. Moreover, all facts in the universe, as created by God, reveal God, so revelationally, whatever is available to believers is also available to nonbelievers. In addition, believers and nonbelievers share in common the fact that they are both made in God's image and are his creatures.[16]

In contrast, the epistemological situation is quite different. What facts and beliefs do believers and nonbelievers actually hold in common? Van Til, following Calvin and Scripture, argues that the only spiritual truth that all people know is that God exists. That fact is revealed throughout the universe, including man's very being. However, the natural man deliberately suppresses the knowledge that God exists while the regenerate welcomes and embraces it.[17] Other than the fact of God's existence, believers and nonbelievers share no other common spiritual notions. And, having rejected the truth that ours is a theistic universe, they get every other spiritual truth wrong as well. As a result, the conceptual point of common ground between believers and nonbelievers is a point of both contact and conflict between them. This is so because the nonbeliever has taken the truth of God's existence, plus all other spiritual truths, and has interpreted them according to the naturalistic mind-set that his autonomous reason embraces.[18]

In light of these things, trying to win nonbelievers to Christ by appealing to supposed "common notions" clearly won't ever succeed. Moreover, the facts of the world aren't common ground, for they are not brute, theory-neutral facts. None of us encounters the world as a mere passive mirror that reflects like a snapshot exactly what is seen, heard, etc. Since our mind is active in the knowing process, we know the facts of the world only as our mind understands them. And, Van Til demands that we take most seriously that what our mind understands about the world is dramatically affected by our sinfulness. For the nonbeliever, there is no getting around the influence of sin on his reason, and hence there is no way that his reason can embrace the truth of God's Word. Believers still have the old sin nature and can be controlled by it so as to misunderstand God's revelation in the world and in his Word, but we also have a new nature which isn't bound to sin. When we stay in fellowship with the Lord and follow the dictates of our new nature, we can see things as they really are, according to God's Word. But since the mind is active in the knowing process and sin also influences it, it should be clear that there are no theory-neutral facts on which everyone can and does agree.[19]

In light of what Van Til says about common ground and brute facts, we cannot use the traditional evidential approach to apologetics. We might even conclude that it is hopeless to think there is *any* way to convince the nonbeliever of Christianity's truth. But Van Til tells us not to draw that pessimistic conclusion. There is a method that can succeed in reaching the lost; it is the method of reasoning by presupposition. But what is that method?

Here we could wish that Van Til was much clearer. However, in spite of all the rationale (theological and otherwise) he offers for using a presuppositional method, he says very little about what the method is and how it works. There are also almost no examples in his writings of how to argue presuppositionally in support of Christianity as a whole or for some tenet of the faith in particular. He does, however, offer some explanation of his method, and it would help to quote him and then explain, given his description, what the method must be and how it works. Van Til writes,

> The method of reasoning by presupposition may be said to be indirect rather than direct. The issue between believers and nonbelievers in Christian theism cannot be settled by a direct appeal to "facts" or "laws" whose nature and significance is already agreed upon by both parties to

the debate. The question is rather as to what is the final reference-point required to make the "facts" and "laws" intelligible. The question is as to what the "facts" and "laws" really are. Are they what the non-Christian methodology assumes that they are? Are they what the Christian theistic methodology presupposes they are?

The answer to this question cannot be finally settled by any direct discussion of "facts." It must, in the last analysis, be settled indirectly. The Christian apologist must place himself upon the position of his opponent, assuming the correctness of his method merely for argument's sake, in order to show him that on such a position the "facts" are not facts and the "laws" are not laws. He must also ask the non-Christian to place himself upon the Christian position for argument's sake in order that he may be shown that only upon such a basis do "facts" and "laws" appear intelligible.

To admit one's own presuppositions and to point out the presuppositions of others is therefore to maintain that reasoning is, in the nature of the case, *circular reasoning*. The starting point, the method, and the conclusion are always involved in one another.[20]

Several points are noteworthy and deserve explanation. Van Til's basic point, however, is that his presuppositional method is both circular and indirect. As to circularity, that comes as no surprise, for all along Van Til has said that nonbelievers presuppose the truth of their worldview and then argue from that assumption, and believers should do the same thing. But if you adopt the content of a worldview without any evidence or argument, construct a methodology for discovering truth in accord with the basic principles of the worldview, and then using this methodology, reach conclusions about what is true, certainly this is circular. Ultimately the Christian apologist wants to demonstrate that the Christian perspective is the correct understanding of reality. If you assume its truth and its methodology in thinking about reality, of course you will conclude that Christianity is true. But such reasoning is circular—it assumes as true (Christianity is the correct understanding of reality) what it is trying to demonstrate is true.

Question begging, circularity, *principia petitio*, or whatever else you want to call it, is a logical fallacy or error in reasoning. Normally, when a viewpoint is rightly accused of this kind of argument, participants in the discussion understand that the guilty viewpoint can't be true. However, Van Til sees his apologetic's circularity as unproblematic, because all reasoning—Christian, agnostic, atheist, Buddhist, etc.—is circular in nature.[21]

As Van Til argues, everyone has to begin somewhere, and they rarely demonstrate by reason and argument the correctness of their starting point. So why should Christians hesitate to do what everyone does, especially since there seems to be no way to avoid it?

Van Til also says his method is indirect, not direct. What does that mean? Here Van Til helps somewhat by elaborating what arguing directly means. A direct method hears an objection and points directly to the facts in our world that refute the objection. Or if the Christian wants to demonstrate the truth of Christ's resurrection, for example, he appeals directly to biblical and extrabiblical data from which he constructs a case that Christ's resurrection is a historical fact.

Van Til believes that method won't work. Why not? Isn't this the way most apologists throughout church history have defended Christianity? Indeed, it is, but then, why does Van Til say this is the wrong way to do apologetics? Actually, Van Til already explained why in his theological justification for his method. A direct method won't work, according to Van Til, for several reasons. For one thing, it grants credibility to the nonbeliever's belief that autonomous reason functioning alone can and will come to Christian conclusions. Van Til disagrees, because appeal to autonomous reason makes reason the ultimate reference point that makes sense of everything, and that can't be right, since our world is made and controlled by God. To appeal to the nonbeliever's reason implicitly agrees with his assumptions that humans are alone in a world where chance rules everything, but that view blatantly contradicts the Christian perspective. If so, then we shouldn't point directly to evidences to refute the nonbeliever's criticism of Christianity or to make a positive case for our views.

A direct method is mistaken also because it assumes that the natural man's reason on its own can understand and accept Christian truth. This grossly underestimates the results of sin on the minds of the unregenerate. Other than knowing that God exists (truth which the nonbeliever rejects), the nonbeliever neither understands nor holds any other Christian spiritual concepts as true. Sin blinds him to the truth—remember those colored glasses *cemented* to his face that won't let him see things correctly!

An indirect method, then, is the only reasonable alternative, but what is this indirect method and how does it work? Van Til could have helped us greatly either with more explanation or by offering some examples of real or imaginary apologetic interchanges which illustrate this indirect method. Unfortunately, he didn't, but from what he did say, it is possible to suggest how such a method might look and work.

The key point is his claim that "the Christian apologist must *place himself upon the position of his opponent, assuming the correctness of his method merely for argument's sake*, in order to show him that on such a position the 'facts' are not facts and the 'laws' are not laws"[22] (italics mine). What does it mean to "place oneself on the position of one's opponent"? It means that we assume that the nonbeliever's position is correct in order to examine and evaluate it to see whether indeed it is correct. The Christian doesn't really believe the nonbeliever's views are correct, but if we can't appeal directly to facts to refute his beliefs, we seem to have no alternative but to assess him on his own terms. That means we assume that his views are correct, and then show him what would follow if those views were correct.

Van Til says that once we've assumed the nonbeliever's position as true for the sake of argument, we then show him that his "facts" and "laws" aren't really facts and laws. But how do we do this? Certainly *not* by appealing to data that we think are facts, facts which refute his beliefs in part or wholly—that's the direct method that gets us nowhere since the nonbeliever disagrees with our facts (or at least with our interpretation of them). The most plausible interpretation of Van Til is that once we assume the non-Christian's position as true, we show him that he couldn't in fact continue to hold rationally all the views he claims to hold, because some of his beliefs contradict other things he believes. In other words, the way to use this indirect method is to assume the nonbeliever's position as true, incorporating everything he believes, and then show him that some of the things he believes contradict other things he believes. Since his system is self-contradictory, given the nature of truth, his system must be false.

In using this method in accord with all of Van Til's doctrines, we must remember his comments about no epistemological common ground with the nonbeliever other than that she knows God exists but refuses to acknowledge that as true. Thus, since our task is to show the nonbeliever that she contradicts her own views, the only things we can attack in this part of the conversation are things the nonbeliever actually believes. We must use her facts, concepts, and presuppositions with her definitions and understanding of them if we are to show her that she contradicts *herself*. I can always generate a contradiction in my opponent's views if I'm allowed to impose my facts and assumptions onto her system. But that only shows that things I hold contradict things my opponent holds, and we already knew that—that's why I'm a believer and she isn't. The only way to identify a genuine contradiction in my opponent's system (that is, to show her views to be *self*-contradictory), is to show her that beliefs she actually holds and understands according to her definitions contradict other beliefs she holds.

If that is how Van Til's presuppositional method works, one might wonder, if I have to show my opponent that some of her own views contradict other of her views, how can I know that the contradiction I point out is really a contradiction in her system, not just one of my views that contradicts something she believes? Well, we cannot assume to know what she believes are the facts, their interpretation, or her overall conclusions just because she uses the same terms and appeals to the same data we do. With no common ground between believer and unbeliever, we may think our opponent holds the facts we do and defines terms as we do, but we can't just assume this is so. If we do and then use those concepts and facts against her position, if she doesn't really appeal to the same concepts, facts, and definitions, we haven't shown that she contradicts her own views. We've only demonstrated that her views are incompatible with ours, but we already knew that. That doesn't prove she's wrong.

So, then, when I accuse the nonbeliever of contradicting *herself*, the only way to know that she really holds all the views I'm calling contradictory is at the outset of our conversation to ask what she believes—what are her presuppositions, her facts, the conclusions she derives from the facts and assumptions she holds, and how does she define the terms she uses (if, for example, she uses the term 'miracle' or 'resurrection,' I need to know how she defines those terms)? Ask and listen, and only after considering what she has said do I search for contradictions within the views she has told me she holds.

Once I've shown her the contradictions in her position, turnabout is fair play. I ask my opponent to assume the truth of my position in order for me to show her that my system doesn't contain contradictions, and that therefore it is preferable to her internally inconsistent system.

Given this explanation, it should be clear as to why such a method is indirect rather than direct. Rather than producing evidence and arguments that are not part of the nonbeliever's views and using them to refute directly various tenets in the nonbeliever's system, the strategy is to attack the opponent's view in a less direct frontal assault. I go within her system and show her that things she believes contradict other things she believes. By doing this, I show her that she actually attacks herself by holding views that contradict one another.

As you reflect on Van Til's method, you may be a bit puzzled. If believers and nonbelievers share no common notions and methods, and if nonbelievers are blind to spiritual truth, what hope is there that if I do what Van Til says, my opponent's sin won't get in the way so that he refuses to see as contradictions the inconsistencies in his system that I point out? Van Til answers that in spite of the nonbeliever's sin we can still get through to him, at least in part because he is made in God's image and knows God exists, and because the Holy Spirit stands ready to convince and convict the nonbeliever of the truth of what we say. Undoubtedly, after showing the inconsistencies of the nonbeliever's views and the consistency of the Christian perspective, I'll have an opening to share the gospel. Perhaps he will be devastated psychologically by realizing that all along he has believed things that contradict other things he believes. With such a newly opened mind, the time to present the gospel may be perfect, and believers certainly know what the Holy Spirit can do in convicting sinners and drawing them to Christ when the gospel is preached.[23]

A Sample Conversation

In the preceding paragraphs I have presented Van Til's method of apologetics, along with its theological rationale. Even so, readers may wonder how to use this method in a concrete case. An imaginary conversation will illustrate how one might do so. The imagined conversation is between two university students, Peter (a Christian, committed to Van Til's method) and Steve (a nonbeliever). The topic is the historical reliability of the Gospels, which Peter accepts and Steve rejects. It is 1968, so Peter and Steve are working within the modern understanding of epistemology.[24] Let's listen to their conversation:

> **PETER:** Steve, how are you? I've really been looking forward to our time together today!

STEVE: Me too. I'm just really interested in hearing you explain why you think the Gospel accounts of Jesus's deeds can be believed.

PETER: Well, Steve, fundamentally I believe the Gospel records because they are part of God's Word.

STEVE: How would you know that or prove it?

PETER: I believe in the God of Christianity—Father, Son, and Holy Spirit—and I believe that Scripture is God's revelation to us. Moreover, the Bible tells me it is true, so I believe it.

STEVE: But how can you believe such things? What evidence is there that this is so?

PETER: Steve, the only evidence or proof is that unless Christianity is true, there are no facts and nothing is true. I believe that God created everything and controls everything, and if that is wrong, then there wouldn't be any universe and no one to discuss such things as we are discussing!

STEVE: Wow, that's quite a mouthful! But we're getting a bit off track. I wanted to talk with you about the historical reliability of the Gospels, especially their accounts of miracles that Jesus supposedly did.

PETER: Yes, Steve, let's turn to that topic. Let's begin by you telling me what you think about the Gospels and the history they include.

STEVE: That's just my point, Peter. I don't think the Gospels are reliable historically. I will grant that they are literary masterpieces, but a literary masterpiece can still be a piece of fiction.

PETER: Do you think it's all a piece of fiction?

STEVE: There's probably some accurate history in the Gospels, but not the parts where the writers or editors (whoever finally compiled this) record supernatural events. Everyone knows miracles can't happen in our naturalistic world. Like many other people, I always go with the most probable explanation of things, and the miraculous is never the most probable explanation. That being the case, it is most probable that the writers either lied or were simply mistaken when they recorded miracles. Besides, there's always a naturalistic explanation for every event, and there is always empirical evidence for everything that happens. So, if there's no naturalistic explanation for an event, or if the explanation can't be verified or falsified by evidence, the event didn't occur.

PETER: Wow, Steve, you and I really have a fundamental disagreement here. I presuppose the existence of the Christian God and his control over everything. I take the Bible as true on its own testimony. You also presuppose various things, too. Your comments about our world as purely naturalistic, about probability, and about there always being empirical evidence for whatever happens are your presuppositions. Where's the proof that those presuppositions are right?

STEVE: What do you mean, Peter, by asking for proof? Everyone knows this is how the world works. Each of us has certain intellectual equipment, and we've always used it to gather tangible evidence for whatever is true of the world around us.

PETER: Steve, you've not given me proof; you've merely reaffirmed your belief in those assumptions. That's all right. All of us have our presuppositions. But I want to turn to something you said a few minutes ago. You said there is always a naturalistic explanation for whatever happens. Hence, biblical accounts of miracles can be explained without any reference to the supernatural. How, for example, would you explain away the Gospel account of Jesus walking on water?

STEVE: Well, I haven't thought about that specific alleged miracle, but I suppose something like the following would handle it: what actually happened is that Jesus, a great moral teacher and leader, realized that his cause was losing ground and that his disciples were losing confidence in him. So, he thought he could trick them into renewed confidence by doing something that looked like a miracle. Well, since they were all fishermen, he decided to do something he knew they'd realize was humanly impossible. He would make them believe that he had walked on water. Jesus and his disciples were very familiar with the Sea of Galilee; they had been on it in a boat many times. Actually, Jesus knew where there was a sandbar in the Sea, and so he got up on the sandbar and walked a bit. Jesus's disciples were just simple fishermen—fishermen are quite gullible, you know—so when they saw Jesus, they were fooled. All twelve imagined that he really had walked on water—they were eager to believe, anyway. Actually, they not only believed, but told other people that this had happened, and some of the disciples even wrote up the story and included it in the Gospels. This is a perfect example of an event they wrote about which they had mistaken. For his part, Jesus continued to proclaim such events as divine miracles, and even though such claims were taken by some as blasphemy, many others, like the uneducated, illiterate disciples believed, the movement spread, and the biblical documents remained unchanged. I know it may seem strange to think this is what happened, but I assure you that I'm committed to the rules of reason and believing what's most probable. And what I've told you is the most adequate explanation of the event. Just as Jesus's walking on water has a naturalistic explanation, so do all other alleged miracles. Hence, I don't see how the Gospels can be reliable history.

PETER: Steve, one thing is very clear to me. Either you are right about what happened, or you have quite a fertile imagination. Because I believe in God and the Bible, I think the latter is true. I also think we need a way to decide who's right, but I can tell it will accomplish nothing for me to point to various Scripture verses as evidence that the Bible is true and that Jesus walked on water.

STEVE: That's right, Peter. I'm already aware of those verses, and I've told you what I think they really mean. So where do we go from here?

PETER: Let me offer a suggestion. Just for the sake of argument, let's assume that your assumptions and explanation of what actually happened are correct. If we do that, I think I can then show you that there are logical inconsistencies in the things you say you believe. Then, turnabout is fair play, so after we finish talking about your system, we'll assume for the sake of argument that my views are correct. Then I'll show you that my explanation of what actually happened in no way contradicts other things I believe. How does that sound as a way to see whose views are correct?

STEVE: That sounds fair to me. I think this will be pretty easy for me, because I'm very careful not to incorporate contradictory things into my beliefs. In contrast, I think I know of inconsistencies within your views, so this should just demonstrate what I've been saying all along—my naturalistic explanation is more believable than any account that incorporates miracles.

PETER: We'll see. Let me begin with your views. Steve, you said you always believe what is most probable. Is that right?

STEVE: Yes, I do.

PETER: In your judgment, Steve, how likely is it that people who are uneducated and illiterate could write a literary masterpiece? By "illiterate" do you mean unable to read or write? Could you clarify that for me? I don't want to put words in your mouth—how do you define it?

STEVE: Yes, I define "illiterate" as being unable to read or write, or at best very weak in their reading and writing skills.

PETER: Well, then again I ask how likely it is that uneducated and illiterate people could write a literary masterpiece?

STEVE: It's possible, but I guess it's not very likely.

PETER: Oh my, Steve. I see an inconsistency in what you've said. On the one hand, you said you are committed to believing whatever is most probable. On the other hand, you've said that you think the Gospels are literary masterpieces, and you've also added that you think it's not very likely that uneducated and illiterate people could write a literary masterpiece. And you've called the disciples uneducated and illiterate, even though you've said you think they penned the various Gospels. I'm sure you can see the problem here, Steve. On the one hand, you say that you only believe what is most probable, but then you admit to holding a view about the authors of the Gospels and the value of those Gospels which by your own admission is not very likely. That's a contradiction, Steve!

STEVE: Hmm. I hadn't seen that before, but I guess you have a point. But I doubt you'll find any more problems in my views.

PETER: Actually, Steve, there are other problems. Again, I appeal to your claim that you believe only what's most probable. You also said that you think Jesus was a great moral teacher, but then you later added that you think he tricked his disciples into thinking he walked on water, and then he later lied about what had happened. Is that what you hold, Steve?

STEVE: Yeah, Pete.

PETER: Steve, you said you think Jesus was a great moral teacher. What do you mean by that? How do you understand morality?

STEVE: To be moral means to know the difference between right and wrong, and to do right. Moral rules aren't exactly the same from one culture to another, but there are some basic rules everyone agrees to. Murder, stealing, lying—things like that are considered wrong in most cultures. Those are the kinds of things that make up morality.

PETER: Thanks for clarifying that for me, Steve. Let me ask you a question. How likely is it that someone who is a great moral teacher will trick people into thinking something happened, and then later continue to lie about what happened?

STEVE: It could happen. Just because someone teaches moral rules doesn't mean he always obeys them himself!

PETER: True, it is possible. But how likely do you think it is, Steve?

STEVE: If we're talking about breaking a rule once, then sure, that could happen.

PETER: But are you saying that Jesus only lied about this once? If so, once he started to tell the truth, wouldn't the trick be detected? Wouldn't the disciples know that they shouldn't include this in the Gospels as accurate history? What do you think, Steve?

STEVE: All right, Pete. You've got me. I agree that my explanation could only be true if Jesus repeatedly lied about this event.

PETER: Then, I ask you again, Steve, how likely is it that a great moral teacher would repeatedly lie about something he says he did?

STEVE: I guess it's not very likely after all.

PETER: Then, Steve, there's a contradiction in what you hold. On the one hand, you've admitted that it's not very likely that a great moral teacher would repeatedly lie about something, but on the other hand, you said you think Jesus is a great moral teacher and yet he lied repeatedly about walking on the water. On top of that, you say you only believe what's most probable. So, there's a contradiction, because you say you believe only what's most probable, and yet you turn around and tell me that you believe something that you admit isn't very probable. That's a contradiction, Steve!

STEVE: Well, you got me again, Peter.

PETER: Yes, and there are several others as well. However, let me just mention one more, and then it will be time to look at my system.

STEVE: Okay, I admit I've got some problems in my views, but I'll bet your system is worse.

PETER: We'll see. But first let me raise another problem. Steve, you said that fisherman are quite gullible. What does that mean?

STEVE: That they are easy to fool or trick.

PETER: I thought that's what you meant, but I just wanted to be sure. Don't want to put words in your mouth, Steve—after all, this is about whether your views contradict your views! Let's return to your explanation. You said that all twelve of Jesus's disciples believed he walked on water and that all twelve were quite familiar with the Sea of Galilee. Are you saying that all twelve saw him walking on water?

STEVE: No, I think only three or four saw him walking on water. But they told the rest of the twelve where he had done it, and they, being familiar with the Sea of Galilee, believed that he had walked on water, too.

PETER: That's helpful, Steve. Now, you also said you believe the most probable explanation. And one more thing—you said that it is necessary to abide by the rules of reason like avoiding question begging. What do you mean by question begging, Steve?

STEVE: I'm just talking about the well-known error in reasoning. You know—assuming as true something you haven't proved true; something that needs to be true in order for your argument or explanation to work.

PETER: Good, Steve. Now let me ask you what the evidence is that fisherman are quite gullible. I don't recall hearing your proof of that, but maybe I just missed that.

STEVE: No, you didn't. I just assumed that everyone knows it's true.

PETER: Well, Steve, do you think the view that fishermen are quite gullible is an important part of your explanation of how the disciples were tricked?

STEVE: Yeah, I do. Given their familiarity with the Sea of Galilee, if they weren't so gullible, they probably would have known that Jesus was just fooling them.

PETER: Very good, Steve. I think your assessment is correct, though what really counts here is your assessment, since we're testing *your* views right now for internal consistency. Steve, I can point out two contradictions in what you've been saying.

STEVE: Really? What do you mean?

PETER: Let me explain. On the one hand, Steve, you said that you believe one should avoid question begging in their reasoning. You defined question begging as assuming as true what needs to be demonstrated as true, and you also agreed that it should be proved, not merely assumed, that fishermen are gullible. Presumably, you think it's enough just to say that the disciples were fooled and they were all fishermen. But you've admitted to me that the claim that fishermen are gullible needs proof, and yet you agree that you've not offered proof. Therefore, on the one hand, you say you are committed to avoiding flaws in reasoning like question begging, and yet you essentially admit that you have begged the question in your explanation of what happened when Jesus walked on water. Being committed to avoiding question begging and then engaging in it is inconsistent, Steve.

STEVE: Wow, this is getting to be uncomfortable!

PETER: Stay tuned, Steve. It gets worse! Tell me, Steve, how likely is it that people quite familiar with the Sea of Galilee wouldn't know where there are sand bars in it? How likely is it that all twelve disciples would be quite familiar with the Sea and yet all of them would think Jesus actually walked on water, rather than walking on a sandbar?

STEVE: Well, it did happen at night!

PETER: Yes, but do you think during the day they would have gone back to the Sea of Galilee and figured out where this happened? Wouldn't Jesus probably have come with them? If so, from what you've said, wouldn't he probably try to throw them off by lying about the exact spot?

STEVE: Yeah, I guess they'd try to locate the spot in the daylight.

PETER: Then again, I ask you, how likely is it that twelve people quite familiar with the Sea of Galilee would believe Jesus walked on water if he really only walked on a sandbar?

STEVE: I guess it's not very likely.

PETER: Well, then, I see another contradiction, Steve. On the one hand, you say that you only believe what is most probable. On the other hand, you say it's not very likely that people familiar with the Sea of Galilee could be tricked into thinking there was no sandbar at a place where there was one. That's a problem, for you agree that it's unlikely that all the disciples would have been fooled, but you believe they were, even though at the same time you avow your commitment to believing only what's most probable. That's a contradiction, Steve!

STEVE: I don't know what to say, Peter. I see that my system has some problems. But let's see if your views fare any better.

PETER: Fair enough, Steve. I believe in the Judeo-Christian God of the Bible. I think he is a supernatural being and as such can do things that are supernatural. I also believe that the Bible is God's revelation to us and is true in everything it affirms. As to the account of Jesus walking on the water, I believe there was no sandbar there. He really did miraculously walk on water. That's what Scripture says, and I believe it! I should also add that I believe that Jesus is the Son of God, the second member of the Trinity. So this was no mere man walking on water; it was the God-man. Now, Steve, I trust that you see the consistency of my position. I believe God exists and that he is supernatural. I also believe Jesus is God and hence supernatural. Supernatural beings can do supernatural things, and I believe walking on water is a supernatural event. So, there is no inconsistency in my presuppositions or my explanation of the event. It is totally consistent for a supernatural being (Jesus) to do something supernatural (walk on water). Scripture says Christ did this, and since I believe Scripture is totally true, it is totally consistent for me to believe the Gospel writers when they claim that Jesus walked on water.

STEVE: Wow, you've given me a lot to think about, Pete. I'd like to stay and talk more, but I've got to get to class. Maybe we can talk about this some more tomorrow. Good-bye.

PETER: Good-bye, Steve. Think about what I've said. I'll see you tomorrow.

From this imaginary conversation, it should be clear why this is an indirect method. Peter doesn't appeal directly to any facts he believes are true of the world. Rather, he sticks with Steve's views and facts as Steve understands them. Peter then uses what Steve has said to show him that some things Steve holds contradict other things Steve believes.

As to circularity, that isn't quite so obvious. But neither Steve nor Peter attempt to prove the correctness of their respective presuppositions. Instead, they just assume their presuppositions are true and then use them to present and argue for their positions. So, this whole line of argument is in fact circular, but that isn't as obvious as some of its other features.

Note as well the extreme care that Peter takes to be sure he understands Steve's views before he accuses Steve of contradicting himself. If one holds, as Van Til does, that there is no common ground with nonbelievers other than that everyone is made in God's image and knows there is a God, then one must be very careful to use only things one's opponent has affirmed in making a case that the *opponent* contradicts himself. Exercising care to find out what one's opponent actually holds takes a good bit of time, but it is the only way to ensure that the contradictions one uncovers in the opponent's views really are contradictions in his or her views.

One final note. When Peter turned to his own position, he didn't have a lot to say. This is what we should expect with Van Til's method. Van Til said that we should ask the nonbeliever to assume our views as true for the sake of argument, and then show the nonbeliever that only on our basic assumptions do the facts make sense. But how do we show that? Not by appealing directly to facts that prove that God exists, nor to facts that support the historical reliability of Scripture in general or the Gospels in particular. Instead, one simply states what one believes, and then explains how the various elements in one's position fit together without contradicting one another. Since the nonbeliever contradicts himself and the believer doesn't, the nonbeliever should see that the believer holds the better view.

THE PRESUPPOSITIONALISM OF FRANCIS SCHAEFFER

In addition to Van Til, others like Greg Bahnsen and John Frame have held a presuppositional apologetic. None of them is quite so well known in apologetics as Francis Schaeffer. Because Schaeffer's presuppositionalism is not identical to Van Til's, he serves as a good representative of what we might call a milder form of this apologetic method.

Here I begin by clarifying the similarities between Schaeffer and Van Til. First, both worked out of the Reformed tradition in theology and saw their apologetic as flowing out of it. Hence, Schaeffer fully believed in total depravity and agreed that sin has some very negative effects on the mind. Moreover, both believed that unless the Holy Spirit is involved in apologetics and evangelism, we won't make headway with nonbelievers, regardless of how we argue our case. In addition, Schaeffer agreed that all of us have presuppositions and that those assumptions govern our worldview. Schaeffer doesn't state this as blatantly as Van Til, but he clearly believes it.[25] He does, however, argue that in our time presuppositional argumentation is very necessary. Schaeffer explains that during the twentieth century, many people despaired of finding a way to unify all knowledge. Many lived below what Schaeffer calls the line of despair. Before this happened, people in modern society basically held the same assumptions about truth and reality. Hence there was no reason to challenge the presuppositions of nonbelievers. One could easily defend Christianity by offering arguments and evidence as classical apologists did. However, since many have fallen below the line of despair (key dates for when this began to happen, according to Schaeffer, are 1890 in Europe and around 1935 in the United States), we cannot assume that nonbelievers hold the same assumptions about truth and reality as believers do. Therefore, as Schaeffer says, "*now for us, more than ever before, a presuppositional apologetic is imperative.*"[26] Only such an apologetic will likely challenge the nonbeliever's presuppositions, and that is necessary if we are to show the bankruptcy of the position he holds.

Following a presuppositional approach, Schaeffer argues that nonbelievers cannot live consistently in the real world with their atheism, whereas once one believes in God, then all other facts fall into place consistently, and the Christian can live out his or her views in the real world. In addition, Schaeffer clearly agrees with Van Til that a good bit of the problem with nonbelievers is that they enthrone autonomous reason as the final court of appeal for all things. Schaeffer labels this reliance on human reason rationalism or humanism (he equates the two). He explains what this involves as follows:

> Humanism in the inclusive sense is the system whereby man, beginning absolutely by himself, tries rationally to build out from himself, having only man as his integration point, to find all knowledge, meaning and value. Again, the word rationalism, which means the same as humanism in the wider sense, should not be confused with the word rational. Rational means that the things which are about us are not contrary to reason, or, to put it another way, man's aspiration of reason is valid. And so the Judaistic-Christian position is rational, but it is the very antithesis of rationalism.[27]

Then, like Van Til, Schaeffer also believes it is counterproductive to begin an apologetic by trying to argue for God's existence. Both agree that thinkers like Aquinas and Anselm, though undoubtedly well-intentioned, led Christian apologists astray methodologically. Van Til and Schaeffer don't entirely agree on why this is so, as we shall see, but both agree that a methodology like Anselm's or Aquinas's is not the best way to defend the faith. In sum, some things in Schaeffer's approach definitely echo Van Til, and they are significant enough to warrant considering Schaeffer a presuppositionalist.

On the other hand, Schaeffer differs from Van Til in at least several important respects. These differences are displayed in various of his works, but I can easily uncover them by reference to his *The God Who Is There*. This is a volume whose aim at one level is to explain how contemporary philosophy and especially contemporary theology have deviated from both traditional Christianity and older liberal theology. In particular, existentialism and its theological "cousin" neo-orthodoxy get a good bit of coverage. Schaeffer's basic argument is that during the twentieth century men and women have despaired of making sense of our world as a coherent whole. Rather than abandoning themselves entirely to despair of making any sense of the world, many have taken an existential leap of faith that allows them to go above and beyond reason so as to have some critical experience (presumably with God) which, though it is ineffable, gives meaning to life. The result is what Schaeffer labels a divided field of knowledge.[28] Some things are known in accord with reason, while others are known in ways above reason. The key here is that nothing can be known about true meaning in life according to reason. If one has a way of unifying all of knowledge, it is more likely than not among contemporaries to Schaeffer a way that goes above reason.[29] Schaeffer examines this existential philosophy and its theological counterparts and argues that the assumptions on which it rests (and the existential views themselves) are not ones that allow one to live consistently in the real world. Only Christianity, Schaeffer argues, can be lived out consistently with the way things are in the world.[30]

So how, specifically, do Van Til and Schaeffer differ? The most significant difference is that Schaeffer believes there is common ground to which the believer and nonbeliever can appeal. Throughout his works Schaeffer speaks about various facts of our world but never suggests that nonbelievers have no idea of what those facts are because they are nonbelievers. Rather, the fact that he mentions those data in appealing to nonbelievers suggests that he thinks they can intellectually understand what he is talking about. Moreover, as we shall see, his actual method of argument incorporates the idea that nonbelievers can understand both their own views and also the facts of the world we all live in. Even so, his method is still arguably indirect, though as we shall see, it is a bit different from Van Til's.

Of course, Schaeffer thinks that while nonbelievers can understand various things about our world, they do have the problem Van Til mentions of not seeing the facts against the backdrop of their ultimate reference point. In talking about the task of science, Schaeffer notes that God has given us both natural and special revelation. What God has communicated in these varying forms is true, but it doesn't exhaust all that God knows, nor is it all that we can know about the world through the various academic disciplines. Scientists can study the world around us because the God who exists has created it and revealed himself. If there were no God, there would be no world and no one to study anything. But God has created the world and has revealed himself. Even though the natural man doesn't see all the evidence of a sovereign creator, that doesn't mean that he can't know and learn anything about the facts of the world. Schaeffer sums up his position on this as follows:

> Finite man in the external universe, being finite, has no sufficient reference point if he begins absolutely and autonomously from himself and thus needs certain knowledge. God gives us this in the Scriptures. With this in mind the scientist can understand, in their ultimate relationships, the truths that he is looking at. Thus scientific study in itself can be to the glory of God, for here man is functioning properly in the universe in which God has placed him. He is telling us what is truly there, and he is adding to the store of knowledge of his fellowmen.[31]

Note here that the problem with the nonbeliever is not that he can understand nothing intellectually, but rather that he doesn't understand it fully, because he refuses to see it in terms of its ultimate reference point, the God who created it. What Schaeffer says about science seems to apply as well to other areas of knowledge, including theology. That is, nowhere does he claim that the nonbeliever is unable to grasp the basic intellectual content of the gospel just because he is unsaved. Of course, seeing that the truth relates to him and actually acting in accord with the truth only happens when the Holy Spirit moves the nonbeliever to believe.

The net result of Schaeffer's granting that there is some common ground in addition to the fact that all of us are made in God's image and do know God exists is that he doesn't constantly need to pause and ask the nonbeliever to confirm exactly what he holds. One may simply proceed on the assumption that when presented with some fact about the world, the nonbeliever can understand it intellectually and see that it is true. This, of course, has significant implications for Schaeffer's understanding of facts. Undoubtedly, he would agree with Van Til that we should use facts to challenge the nonbeliever's philosophy of facts. That is, the nonbeliever thinks the facts he knows are true in a world run by blind chance; the believer should challenge that by saying that if there were no God as creator and sustainer of the world, there would be no facts at all.

Schaeffer, however, goes further than this in regard to facts. Nowhere does Schaeffer deny that all of us face the facts with our individual noetic structures, nor does he think that everyone will exhibit pristine objectivity in handling data and arguments. Nor would he deny the negative effects of sin on the mind. Still, he thinks that both believer and nonbeliever can agree intellectually on the various facts of our universe. The nature of the facts of our world (at least empirical data, if not more) is such that within the data themselves is enough information available to all people, believers and nonbelievers alike, so that both can agree on a basic understanding of what is in the world and how it works. In other words, the facts are not so theory-laden that no two individuals can agree about what is true of the world. Granted, using Schaeffer's terminology, they do not understand the facts of the world *exhaustively*, but what they do know, they know *truly*.[32] Because the nonbeliever looks at a tree and doesn't deem it to be a tree in a world created by God, he doesn't know the fact that there is a tree exhaustively. But he does know that there is a tree within his view, and he knows that truly.

Third, there is something that seems true of Schaeffer's apologetic that isn't required by Van Til's. That is not to say that Van Til doesn't incorporate this ever into his apologetic, but only that it need not be part of any and every defense of the faith the presuppositionalist makes. Put simply, both Van Til and Schaeffer are concerned to demonstrate inconsistency in the nonbeliever's views. For Schaeffer, the nonbeliever's views always seem to refer to his whole worldview, not just isolated tenets within it. In contrast, whereas Van Til's method allows the apologist to attack the nonbeliever's whole worldview, one can also use Van Til's method to attack a specific belief (and its presuppositions) in the nonbeliever's system. Perhaps one could adapt Schaeffer's method to this more narrow approach, but the way he seems to use it is to attack the whole worldview of the nonbeliever.[33]

A final set of items show both similarity and difference between Van Til and Schaeffer. Both apologists want to show contradictions in the nonbeliever's viewpoint. Neither, then, places a lot of emphasis on building a case that appeals directly to evidence to support the Christian position or to attack the nonbeliever's system. Of course, with Schaeffer's granting of common ground with nonbelievers, he could very easily incorporate evidential arguments in his apologetic. However, Schaeffer "tips us off" to what is most important for his method when he talks about the nature of proof. He offers what he believes are the steps to proving which viewpoint is true. Once the issue in question is defined, we require two things of a system we test: 1) it must be consistent, i.e., it must not contradict *itself*, and give an answer or explanation to the phenomenon in question; and 2) it must be possible to live consistently with our position.[34]

Now this is most interesting because of what it tells us to do, but also because of what it does *not* include! Any philosopher when testing a system or set of ideas would surely begin by asking if the system contradicts itself. The philosopher should also ask whether what the system proposes is livable in the real world. What is noticeable by its absence is anything about the fit of the system with the facts. A system of ideas could be logically self-consistent and yet fail to correspond to the real world around us. Presumably, neither Van Til nor Schaeffer would be comfortable with a system that failed the test of fit with the facts. But neither emphasized this test, because both use a more indirect method involving pointing out contradictions within the nonbeliever's beliefs. Hence, Schaeffer's belief in common ground between believers and nonbelievers doesn't mean he abandons presuppositionalism for evidentialism.

Are Van Til's and Schaeffer's methods, then, identical? Not really. Schaeffer examines the nonbeliever's whole worldview at once. He contends that this system of beliefs, including its presuppositions, must be forced to confront the facts of reality as we all know them. When that happens, Schaeffer contends that there will always be some point of tension between the nonbeliever's views and the facts of the world. This will not simply be a matter of various propositions in the nonbeliever's belief system contradicting other propositions in his position. It will also result in its being impossible for the nonbeliever to live in the real world in accord with his set of beliefs.[35] As Schaeffer notes, each of us has his or her presuppositions, but those assumptions lead to logical conclusions. It is those logical conclusions that most directly contradict the real world. That creates inconsistency within the nonbeliever's belief system, but it also makes it impossible for him to live consistently with what he believes.[36]

Consider the following as an example. The nonbeliever believes there is no God, or at least that if he exists, he doesn't act in our world. Instead, everything runs by blind chance. These presuppositions have a logical connection to the nonbeliever's adopting evolution as his explanation of the origin and development of the human race as well as all other living things. As Schaeffer shows, however, when you juxtapose these presuppositions and their logical conclusions with the real world, problems arise. Whatever our theory of origins, it must offer an adequate explanation for humans as personal beings. Schaeffer offers four theories that each leave out a personal God and rely upon some purely naturalistic explanation. He shows in each case that each either directly contradicts the facts of the real world or simply cannot be lived in the real world—some of the answers he offers fail on both counts. In contrast, the Christian's answer that human persons are the creation of a personal creator (in whose image they were created) yields consistency of the Christian belief system with the facts of the world and is also an answer that can be lived in the real world.[37]

Given this basic understanding, how exactly might one use Schaeffer's presuppositionalism in a real situation?[38] Schaeffer explains that there is some point(s) of tension with the real world in every nonbeliever's system of thought. The apologist's task is to identify those points of conflict and bring them to the nonbeliever's attention. The point of conflict may be the nonbeliever's presuppositions, the views that logically stem from those assumptions, or both. Invariably humans build defenses around such points of tension; they may bury the inconsistent ideas beneath any number of beliefs, many of which may be innocuous in themselves but serve as a kind of roof to cover the real point(s) of tension. Uncovering these points of tension will not always be easy; it will definitely require the Christian apologist to dialogue with the nonbeliever so as to understand what she believes and why she holds it.

If the logical conclusions of some of the nonbeliever's presuppositions produce tension with the real world, Schaeffer advises apologists not to begin by attacking the presuppositions per se. Rather, the apologist should push the nonbeliever in the direction toward which his presuppositions lead. As he intellectually comes to see the logical conclusions of his beginning assumption, hopefully he will begin to sense the tension between these views and the real world. All of that is very good, for we are gradually leading him to see the futility of anyone actually holding a position such as his. That should suggest that it would be wise to give serious thought to abandoning his current beliefs.

This may give the impression that things will invariably run smoothly when using this argument strategy. However, Schaeffer reminds us that nonbelievers have often buried their assumptions and beliefs that fail to match reality very deeply within their conceptual grid. They have, to use Schaeffer's terminology, "built a roof" over these points of tension so that they won't sense the tension between the real world and these views. It is the Christian apologist's job to "take off the nonbeliever's roof" and show him the inconsistency between the real world and what he believes. This means that in our conversation we will likely need to ask not only what the nonbeliever holds but also to ask why he holds his views. Once we dig down to his most fundamental assumptions and expose them, then as we prod him, he can see that his views don't really match the real world, nor could anyone with such views really live consistently with the world. Schaeffer advises us to be ready for the give-and-take of argument. There is value in dialoguing with the nonbeliever, but it takes time, and nonbelievers will likely have some good arguments and objections to Christianity. So come prepared. Presumably, during this process, we can point to various facts and arguments about the real world. Though neither the Christian nor the nonbeliever is totally neutral to the facts of the real world, there is enough common ground between them that the nonbeliever can see our point about his views being inconsistent with and unlivable in the real world.

This may sound like a very promising methodology, but it does assume that there will be some point or points of tension in the nonbeliever's views. What happens if the nonbeliever has built a system that doesn't contradict the world and is livable? After all, there have been many great philosophers who certainly were good enough logicians to avoid telling a self-contradictory story about reality, so can we be sure we can always do what the method proposes? Schaeffer affirms that we can, because

> No non-Christian can be consistent to the logic of his presuppositions. The reason for this is simply that a man must live in reality, and reality consists of two parts: the external world and its form, and man's 'mannishness', including his own 'mannishness'. No matter what a man may believe, he cannot change the reality of what is. . . .

> Every man, therefore, irrespective of his system, is caught. As he tries intellectually to extend his position in a logical way and then live within it, he is caught by the two things which, as it were, slap him across the

face. . . . Non-Christian presuppositions simply do not fit into what God
has made, including what man is.[39]

In other words, every non-Christian position is inconsistent at some point(s)
with the real world. Hence, it is possible to expose the tension (i.e., point
out the contradiction) between the nonbeliever's views and the real world,
and then to present Christianity as a belief system that is internally consistent with itself and the world and can be lived out.

Assessment of Presuppositionalism

Presuppositionalism has been a major player in twentieth-century Christian
apologetics. We have looked at two of the best-known presuppositionalists,
but there have been and still are many others.[40] How should we evaluate
presuppositionalism's method and its rationale? Some of the comments I
shall make are germane to both Van Til's and Schaeffer's forms of presuppositionalism, whereas many are aimed only at Van Til.

Contributions

I want to mention five contributions of presuppositionalism that are especially helpful. The first was already noted in my description of Van Til's
views, but it bears repeating and elaboration. One cannot read presuppositionalists without taking seriously the whole issue of presuppositions.
They correctly remind us that everyone has presuppositions and that our
assumptions do figure into the worldview we hold and defend. This is important because it helps us respond to nonbelievers who think Christians
blindly hold their beliefs without any proof whereas nonbelievers are driven
by nothing more than reason and the evidence. As already noted, this is not
a case of faith versus reason, but rather one of their faith in reason versus
our faith in God and Scripture. It is important to tell nonbelievers that
though they think they are the only ones who proceed objectively without
presuppositions coloring the results of their reasoning, it is simply not so.

The emphasis on presuppositions is important in another respect.
Presuppositionalists urge us to challenge nonbelievers to look seriously at
their beginning assumptions to see what they lead to and whether such a
worldview can be lived out in the real world. If the nonbeliever's system
of thought ultimately rests upon certain assumptions that he uses as argu-

ments and evidence for the truth of his worldview, somewhere in dealing with him we must challenge him to defend those assumptions. Whether we do so using the indirect method of presuppositionalism or directly marshal evidence to refute those assumptions, they need to be challenged.

A final value of this emphasis on presuppositions is that it reminds us that when we hear the nonbeliever's defense of his system of thought, we must see those arguments as arising from and based on his assumptions. If we don't hold those presuppositions (and we don't accept most, if not all, of the nonbeliever's presuppositions), that should help to explain why we don't find his arguments and evidences compelling. The same is true for nonbelievers as they listen to our arguments for Christianity. But, then, this should help Christians to understand why, despite the excellent arguments and evidences we amass against the nonbeliever's views and in support of ours, we seem to make so little progress with the nonbeliever. Recognizing that nonbelievers start with assumptions that differ from and even contradict those of Christians, we should realize that if we are to make any further headway intellectually with nonbelievers, we must identify their presuppositions and attack them independently from anything else in their worldview.

A second contribution is presuppositionalism's emphasis on the need for the Holy Spirit to be involved in the apologetic enterprise. Before we end this chapter we must discuss whether the Holy Spirit's role is as extensive as at least Van Til suggests, but Christians should quickly recognize the importance of the Holy Spirit's ministry in the apologetic task. It is especially important that Christian evidentialists keep this in mind as they craft their defenses of the faith. Unfortunately, at times their defenses make little or no mention of the Holy Spirit's role, and thereby give the impression that all that is needed to convince and win the opponent is a brilliant set of arguments. I don't think evidentialists really believe they can persuade nonbelievers without the work of the Holy Spirit in their heart, but their lack of reference at times to the Holy Spirit's work can give the impression that they think the Holy Spirit isn't involved or that his involvement is fairly insignificant. This is unfortunate, for while we must indeed offer our best defense, we must also understand that no one will be persuaded to turn to Christ simply because of the cogency of our arguments. And no matter how good the intellectual case for Christianity, it is never so conclusive that there is no room for doubt and no need for faith.

The ultimate quenching of doubt and moving of the will to faith is something only the Holy Spirit can do.

Third, presuppositionalism reminds us that as we "do apologetics" we must take seriously the facts that human reason is finite and has been negatively impacted by sin. We should also remember that Scripture does teach that everyone knows God exists (Rom. 1:19–20) and is held accountable for what they do with that knowledge (Rom. 1:21). It is also true that nonbelievers do suppress the truth of God's existence, as Scripture says and presuppositionalism emphasizes. In fact, some readers of this book undoubtedly know people who have so successfully suppressed the truth that God exists that they seem oblivious and impervious to that and any other spiritual truth. As I shall argue below, it is dubious that sin renders human reason quite as useless as some presuppositionalists propose, but there can be no denying that human finitude and sin do affect the functioning of human reason. When nonbelievers continually reject our defenses, that may not at all indicate that we have made our case poorly. It may instead underscore the fact that sin is taking its toll on the nonbeliever's mind and that we are engaged in spiritual warfare when we witness and defend the faith. In fact, 2 Corinthians 4:3–4 teaches that Satan launches a special attack to keep people from accepting the gospel, an attack that can ultimately be resisted and conquered only by the light of Christ shining in a person's heart (2 Cor. 4:5–6). So, what apologetics does is important. It's just that there is more going on in our interchanges with nonbelievers than just a sharing and evaluating of the cogency of our arguments. Do not overestimate the ability of finite, sin-hardened human reason alone to accept the truth of our defense and turn to Christ as Savior!

A final contribution of presuppositionalism is its method of argumentation. When one sets aside the theological and philosophical "baggage" that comes with presuppositionalism, and just looks at what Van Til and Schaeffer tell us to do in dealing with nonbelievers, one finds a helpful strategy and argument form for defending Christianity. Those without much philosophy background may find this surprising, but those familiar with philosophy and with how philosophers evaluate arguments, systems of belief, and individual beliefs shouldn't be surprised. When confronting a philosophy or system of belief, philosophers typically begin by testing it for logical consistency with itself. If there are contradictions within the set of beliefs under investigation, the philosopher knows the system cannot be true. Even if the system passes the test of internal consistency, it may still be false, but the place to begin evaluating is the matter of self-consistency.

Granting what I have just said about how philosophers operate, there is ample room for presuppositionalism's *method* in the Christian apologist's arsenal of weapons. This is true whether one uses the method as Van Til did or as Schaeffer did. Schaeffer urges us to push the nonbeliever's presuppositions to their logical conclusion. When one does, one finds that the conclusions are absurd; no one could live with such results. What we should understand is that Schaeffer is encouraging us to use a *reductio ad absurdum* argument strategy. Simply put, this strategy assumes the truthfulness of the opponent's beliefs. The apologist shows that if such beliefs are true, they will lead to certain logical conclusions, conclusions that are patently absurd. But if so, then there must be some false belief (or beliefs) somewhere in the opponent's thinking. Similarly Van Til's method tells us to uncover contradictions in the beliefs held by our nonbelieving friend. If we can do that, then the position as a whole can't be true and should be rejected.

Deducing contradictions and making *reductio ad absurdum* arguments are argument strategies in the arsenal of every philosopher. Hence, there can be no objection when Christians (apologists or otherwise) use these argument forms to point out the inadequacies of nonbelievers' views. We have not broken any rules of procedure for evaluating belief systems; we are just doing what philosophers do all the time.

Actually, from a psychological standpoint this kind of argument can be devastating. Most of us don't think of ourselves as geniuses, but on the other hand, we don't think our mental faculties are so benighted that we go around believing things that contradict one another. We know that doing so would exhibit a significant defect in reason. If that is so, then imagine the psychological impact when confronted with the fact that we actually do hold contradictory beliefs! In the imaginary conversation between Peter and Steve, if this were to happen to Steve in a real situation, he would likely be shell-shocked. Sometimes such a shock is needed to get the nonbeliever even to listen to what we say about Christianity. Nonbelievers are often very comfortable in their unbelief, thinking that they have an airtight case for their views. Exposing the fact that they have erred rationally in this most embarrassing fashion (they believe things that other beliefs they hold refute!) may be one of the few ways we can hope to get them to consider the Christianity we present. So, if the nonbeliever's views do contain contradictions, by all means point those out to him or her.

One final point about the usefulness of this method. We must be clear about how and when it is most effective. If my strategy is to destroy my nonbelieving opponent's views before I present a positive case for Christianity, then a presuppositional line of argument is a very helpful weapon. That is, it is most effective in showing nonbelievers that their views can't possibly match the world, because they contain contradictions even though the world they intend to represent doesn't contain contradictory states of affairs. In contrast, if our purpose is to make a case for Christianity, presuppositional apologetics is less helpful, for the most it can show is that Christianity is a logically consistent belief system. What it can't do, because it won't, is point to specific evidences and arguments to build a case for the truth of Christianity. I'll elaborate this point in the next section, but for now suffice it to say that presuppositional argumentation is most helpful when attacking the nonbeliever's views.

Objections to Presuppositionalism

Despite the contributions of presuppositionalism, it has some significant problems. Many of the concerns I'll raise refer specifically to Van Til's form of the method, but some relate to presuppositionalism in general.

An initial objection addresses Van Til's rejection of common ground between believers and nonbelievers. Schaeffer, Frame, and other contemporary presuppositionalists wisely reject this part of Van Til's view. Why is rejecting common ground altogether troublesome? Because if there is no common ground with unbelievers, then it seems impossible for us to communicate with one another, and yet just the opposite is the case. When I tell a nonbeliever my beliefs, he or she may disagree, but they definitely understand what I'm saying. If they really don't grasp what I am saying, it is not impossible to explain my point so that they do grasp what I mean. The same is true when the nonbeliever tells me her beliefs.

Language has both a sense and reference. The sense of a word is what we might call its "dictionary definition." Its reference is the thing, person, or action in the world to which it points. Even if the sense of the language believers and nonbelievers use varies, that doesn't mean the referent of what they say isn't common ground. For example, nonbelievers may say that after Jesus was crucified and buried, he experienced an unusual bodily resuscitation. Believers will call it a resurrection. The sense of "resurrection" isn't identical to that of "unusual bodily resuscitation," but the referent to which both refer is the fact that after his crucifixion Christ was laid in an empty tomb, on Sunday morning the tomb was empty, and later many people claimed to see him alive. Even if nothing else about these events is common ground for believers and nonbelievers, the filled and sealed tomb, then the empty tomb, and later reports of people seeing Christ alive are the set of events to which both believer and nonbeliever point. The referent of our language, then, seems clearly to be common ground.

I must add, however, that even the sense of our language must be common ground or we couldn't communicate with one another. Even if the nonbeliever refers to this event as an unusual bodily resuscitation and I, a believer, don't know what that means, the nonbeliever can explain in language I do understand the sense of what he has said. The same is true if the nonbeliever doesn't understand what I mean when I speak about Christ's resurrection; I can use language the nonbeliever understands to define what I mean by "resurrection," and the nonbeliever can intellectually grasp the sense of what I say.

There is at least one further problem with rejecting common ground between believer and nonbeliever, and it is fatal. The problem is that if Van Til is right about no common ground between believers and unbelievers, then his method won't actually work—it is unusable! Van Til proposes that for the sake of argument, believers should grant the truth of nonbelievers' views so as to then show them the logical inconsistency of their views. After we have finished interacting with the nonbeliever's position, we are to ask him or her to assume the truthfulness of Christianity so that we can show them that Christianity isn't guilty of self-contradiction, the malady that destroys their system of beliefs. But how can this strategy proceed? Presumably there are at least three possible ways all of this could happen.

The first is that we use the nonbeliever's facts and terms and their meanings. Thus, the nonbeliever shares his system using his language, and when we turn to my system, we again use his terms and concepts to understand it. But wait a minute! If the nonbeliever and I share no common terms, facts, etc., how can he teach me his system using his language when

I can't understand it, according to Van Til's views about common ground? Moreover, it would be impossible for him to understand my position using his language, etc., for they have nothing in common.

Well, perhaps we should learn the nonbeliever's position using our language, facts, etc., and then again teach the nonbeliever our position using our language. But that won't work either. If there is as much incommensurability as Van Til believes between the Christian position and a nonbeliever's views, then if I use my language, it should be impossible to teach me the nonbeliever's position, for with my language we get my views, not his. Likewise, I can use my language to teach my system, but since Van Til's claims about no common ground mean that the nonbeliever really cannot understand what I'm saying, I can't teach him my position.

So, what would work? If there were a set of terms and facts which were, so to speak, neutral, or at least neutral enough so that both believers and nonbelievers could use them without begging the question in favor of or against either position, then assuming both sides knew and understood those terms and facts, we could use that common knowledge as a key to unlock one another's views and evaluate whether they are self-consistent or not. This sounds very promising, but it *won't* work! Why not? Because, according to Van Til's rejection of common ground, there are no such neutral terms and facts that we can use to understand and evaluate one another's positions.

The result, then, is that if Van Til is actually right about no common ground, then there is no way for us to use his argument strategy. Thankfully, later presuppositionalists have held that there is more common ground between believers and nonbelievers than just the fact that all are made in the image of God and know that he exists. When one holds that there is common ground between believers and nonbelievers, the impossible situation described above does not result. Presuppositional methodology (Van Til's, Schaeffer's, etc.) can be used, and very effectively so!

A second objection is a corollary of the first. I believe that Van Til is wrong in claiming there are no brute facts, because no one is neutral toward what he or she sees in the world. Hence, a method of apologetics that depends on gathering together facts to support the Christian position is doomed to failure. In reply, I don't believe that the mind passively mirrors the reality that presses in upon it through the senses—there is no need to go back to positions held prior to Kant. However, it is one thing to say that there are no theory-neutral facts (no brute facts), but another to claim that all facts are so theory-laden that, for example, believers and nonbelievers can't come to a common understanding of the facts and cannot even agree what the facts are. The view that facts are so theory-laden that we can't get anywhere with the nonbeliever by simply appealing to facts seems most plausible when the "facts" in question are theological and philosophical views about the nature of reality as a whole, the existence of God, and our relation to this God if he exists. It is rather implausible, however, when it comes to matters of fact about the empirical world around us. While believers and nonbelievers won't be totally impartial to theological claims about reality, that doesn't mean it is impossible for both to understand these data and even to agree on which claims are true and which are false. I have already made this point in discussing objectivity and subjectivity in chapter 4, and I refer readers to that section.

A third objection to presuppositionalism deals with the matter of circularity. Van Til in particular notes that his method is circular in that it assumes the truth of Christian theism and the Bible without offering any proof or evidential support. Van Til doesn't see this as a problem, because he believes all reasoning is ultimately circular. If everyone does it, then there must be no escaping it. Even more, if being circular automatically rules out the possibility that the views supported by such reasoning are right, then no one really knows anything. Surely, we can't be comfortable with such extreme skepticism. But then, the fact that the presuppositional method incorporates circularity shouldn't be seen as a significant problem.

In reply, I begin with a distinction from John Warwick Montgomery between presuppositions of method and presuppositions of content. It is certainly true that everyone must begin somewhere when acquiring knowledge. We can't be expected or required to prove everything we think before we can use it to learn other things about the world. But presuppositions about the best way to go about learning what is true of the world (presuppositions of method) are one thing. We can hardly test the intellectual equipment we have and how it is used in learning without using the equipment itself. So presuppositions of method seem unavoidable, and this isn't damaging because if we don't use our intellectual equipment and its basic ways of interacting with the world, it isn't at all clear how we would learn anything, including whether our equipment functions properly and whether our usual methods of learning are profitable to the end of knowing truth about the world around us.

In contrast, presuppositions of content are assumptions about a whole perspective on reality, assumptions about a worldview. This sort of presupposition accepts without any proof the content of a whole worldview (Christian or non-Christian). Perhaps someone adopts a whole worldview without offering any evidential support for it, because he thinks providing the needed evidence would be too time-consuming (it wouldn't do to withhold belief until all evidence is amassed), and in addition, he's not sure he has evidence for everything he believes. If so, then, adopting a worldview without offering evidence for it is still circular, but at least it is understandable and we might not think the circularity a sufficient reason for rejecting the position as a whole. On the other hand, when there is tangible evidence in bountiful amounts for a worldview and for specific tenets of the worldview—and we shall see in the "evidence chapters" in this book that plenty of evidence of various kinds supports Christianity—then the refusal to offer evidential support at all for one's belief system seems to involve unnecessary circularity. This circularity should count as sufficient evidence for rejecting the position that holds the presuppositions of content.

Van Til might answer that there is no point in presenting evidences supporting the Christian worldview, because human reason alone, infected by sin, will never understand things as Christians do. Nonbelievers won't agree that believers have sufficient amounts and qualities of evidence to warrant belief.[41] Thus, rejecting presuppositions of content in favor of offering evidence for one's position sounds admirable, but it won't work. Since it can't work, one has no alternative but to adopt presuppositions of content. Yes, it is circular, but nonbelievers also adopt their atheistic or agnostic worldviews without proof, and they really have no choice but to do so. So, if this circularity is problematic, then everyone has a problem. If one grants, however, that all must adopt presuppositions of content, then it can't be significant to accuse presuppositionalists of holding assumptions of content.

In reply, however, it seems that this response ultimately rests on the notion that there is no common ground between believers and nonbelievers. If one rejects that dictum, then appealing to evidence in order to convince our nonbelieving friends is not fruitless. Moreover, as we saw in discussing objectivity and subjectivity, the fact of personal involvement in the knowing process does not make it impossible to learn and communicate to others truth about the objective world around us. Hence, my complaint with presuppositionalism is that it adopts presuppositions of content when it could in fact support the Christian worldview with evidence. Refusing to do so involves an unacceptable degree of circularity.

Fourth, presuppositionalists (especially those who follow Van Til) complain about the inability of human reason to discover truth. Because of this inability, we won't get anywhere if we try to convince nonbelievers of Christianity's truth by offering them evidences and arguments to support it. However, presuppositionalists think nonbelievers can at least grasp what is being argued when we show them that their views are self-contradictory; hence presuppositionalism is the preferred apologetic methodology.

But are these claims really correct? I don't think so. If reason is too benighted to be able to grasp and agree with arguments that appeal directly to facts about our world, why should we think reason will work well enough for nonbelievers to understand that their views are self-contradictory? One of the more difficult moves for reason is to identify and describe contradictions in someone's point of view. We do not easily think holistically, nor is it easy to uncover a *genuine* contradiction in someone's position. Hence, it is hard to understand why Van Til and his followers think that reason is inadequate for understanding how specific items of evidence support the truth of a belief, but then think it sufficient to grasp the point when a believer shows a nonbeliever that he contradicts himself. If sin gets in the way of one rational operation (grasping an evidential argument in support of a belief), why should we think it won't also hamper the other operation of reason (deducing a contradiction in a set of ideas), especially since the latter is a more difficult rational maneuver than the former?

Perhaps Van Til would reply that we get through to the nonbeliever when we use the presuppositional method because the Holy Spirit stands ready to help the nonbeliever understand and apply our argument. This is true, but if the Holy Spirit can enable the nonbeliever to understand me when I show her that she contradicts herself, why can't the Holy Spirit also use my evidential argument to convict and convince her to turn to Christ? I don't see any response forthcoming from Van Til and others who decry a method that incorporates a direct appeal to evidences. Indeed, what could the answer be? For these reasons, I reject the idea that an indirect, presuppositional argument form is the only one that will work and that appeal to direct evidence is fruitless.

The previous objection suggests another about the ministry of the Holy Spirit in illumining spiritual truth to the nonbeliever's mind. Van Til's version of presuppositionalism relies very heavily on the ministry of the Holy Spirit to convince the nonbeliever even when he cannot in fact understand what we are saying as we present the Christian position. There is something right about incorporating the Holy Spirit's ministry in one's apologetic, and I have explained what it is. However, I contend that what Van Til implies (by what he says) about exactly what the Holy Spirit does is incorrect. Let me explain.

Remember that for Van Til, there is no common ground between believers and nonbelievers other than that they are all made in God's image and know that God exists. So the nonbeliever can never see things the way believers do. Still, we are urged to use Van Til's indirect method of argumentation. Earlier in my evaluation I explained why, if Van Til is right about no common ground, we can't use his method. Van Til would disagree at least because the Holy Spirit is there to get the point we are making through to the nonbeliever. Presumably, Van Til would classify this ministry of the Holy Spirit under the rubric of illumination.

This has a certain plausibility, but we must look closer. What does this actually mean about the ministry of the Holy Spirit to the nonbeliever when the nonbeliever hears our apologetic and/or our witness? It seems to include at least the following: 1) the nonbeliever doesn't understand the intellectual content of the spiritual truth we state, so for the nonbeliever this material is a virtual foreign language that he doesn't know and so needs to have translated or deciphered; 2) once the nonbeliever grasps intellectually the content of our message, he next must be convinced that this message applies to him, and the Holy Spirit convicts him of that; and 3) the Holy Spirit moves the nonbeliever's will without forcing it to act on—that is, to accept—the truth he now understands intellectually and sees to be relevant to himself. When all three of these things happen, the person, under the ministry of the Holy Spirit, turns from sin and accepts Christ as personal Savior.

Illumination, then, seems to involve these three activities of the Holy Spirit. With what Van Til suggests about how nonbelievers can be won despite their spiritual and moral darkness, it seems that he agrees that the Holy Spirit ministers in all three of these ways. In holding this, Van Til seems to be consistent with much teaching about the Spirit that one hears in the local church. Moreover, there has been a consensus definition of illumination down through the centuries of church history, and it seems to match Van Til's understanding fairly closely.[42] Now I must affirm that Scripture does clearly teach that the Holy Spirit performs the actions listed under items 2 and 3 above. In fact, only the Holy Spirit can perform that kind of persuasion in the heart of the nonbeliever.

My quibble is with item 1. If in fact the Holy Spirit will transfer correctly the intellectual content of the gospel and other theological truths to the mind of the nonbeliever who doesn't understand them because of sin, then what difference does it make as to how good or bad our arguments are, how clearly or confusedly we present them, or what method we use? If the nonbeliever can't understand the intellectual content of what I say no matter how well I say it, but he can still get the right message because the Holy Spirit will save the day by deciphering truth which previously was much like a foreign language to the nonbeliever, then what I say and how I say it make little difference, because it's always up to the Holy Spirit to transfer the correct intellectual content. Well, then, I could perhaps read comic strips from the pulpit or offer a set of arguments that are so confused that I'm not even sure what I'm saying, and it wouldn't matter. It wouldn't matter because, on this theory, the Holy Spirit not only convicts the sinner of sin and moves his will to repent, *but also* clarifies for him the content of the gospel message he needs to intellectually understand to be ready for the Holy Spirit's ministries mentioned in items 2 and 3 above. If this is so, why should anybody worry about training their reasoning skills and homiletical skills so as to be the clearest and most convincing apologist and evangelist as possible?[43] There seems to be little reason to bother.

But does the illumining ministry of the Holy Spirit include item 1? I don't think so, and here I appeal to a doctoral dissertation done at Trinity Evangelical Divinity School by Kevin Zuber on the illumination of the Holy Spirit, for which I was privileged to serve as first reader. First, Zuber does a study of historical as well of contemporary discussions of the doctrine of illumination, from which he constructs what he calls the Christian consensus definition of illumination. Then he turns to every Old Testament and

New Testament text that teaches anything about illumination and presents a careful exegesis of each. On the basis of this study, he affirms that parts of the consensus definition are correct, but not all, and even some parts that are right need some slight adjustment. In particular, he confirms that Scripture does show the Holy Spirit engaged in the ministries associated with items 2 and 3. The real rub comes with item 1. Nowhere is the Holy Spirit seen as the one who intellectually explains to the nonbelievers or transfers to them the intellectual content of what preachers, teachers, evangelists, and apologists are saying. There is, however, something that the Holy Spirit does related to the intellectual element of spiritual truth. He does help people, who already understand the intellectual content of various spiritual truths and facts about the world, to get the ultimate intellectual point all that information is making.

An illustration of this intellectual ministry of the Holy Spirit is easily found in Scripture. Think of Jesus's conversation with his disciples on the road to Emmaus after his crucifixion and resurrection (Luke 24). The disciples are downhearted, because they had believed Jesus was the long-awaited Messiah. They based their hopes on Old Testament prophecies about the coming Messiah and the kingdom he would bring. They understood the intellectual content of those prophecies, because they had studied the Scriptures. However, they were discouraged because they also had seen Jesus die. Somehow they couldn't fit those events together with Jesus's claim to be the Messiah and with Old Testament prophetic teaching about the coming messianic ruler. They knew the information, but just didn't see how it all fit together; they didn't "get it" that everything that had happened was all part of a master plan.

Jesus didn't scold them, nor did he or the Holy Spirit "zap" their brains with information they never knew. Rather, Jesus focuses their attention on something they had studied quite often, the Old Testament. They understood enough of the intellectual content of Old Testament prophecies about the Messiah to become confused as they reflected on the events of previous weeks. Jesus pointed them to various passage that predicted what would happen and then turned their attention to recent events. In the process of doing this, the "light," so to speak, "came on," and they "got it." Their eyes were opened to see that this stranger walking with them was the risen Messiah. And what had he done? Had he put into their minds information they either didn't know or didn't grasp intellectually at all? No, he simply reminded them of things they already knew from their own study, and showed them how all of it fit together with what they had experienced in recent weeks. Similarly, there are times when you and I are so focused on exegesis of individual "trees" that we fail to understand their place in the overall "forest." In fact, sometimes we are so focused on the trees that we don't even sense that there is a forest. The Holy Spirit at times helps us to broaden our vision from individual facts to the whole into which those facts fit. That is a ministry that impacts our intellect, but it presupposes that we have already done the hard work of interpretation that is first required in collecting and understanding data about the world.[44]

So, the Holy Spirit does play a role in relation to our intellect, according to Scripture, but not the one Van Til's presuppositionalism seems to incorporate. Hence, it is important to make the clearest and most cogent arguments we can when dealing with a nonbeliever. Our testimony, message, lesson, apologetic is the intellectual material with which the Holy Spirit works. In light of this, however, we can say that the reason a nonbeliever can grasp our intellectual point when we show him a contradiction in his views is that his mind has the ability to do so. Similarly, if we present direct evidence to refute his beliefs or to support ours, despite his sin, the nonbeliever is intellectually capable of understanding our biblical and theological points. In both cases, the Holy Spirit may need to help the nonbeliever's intellect to finally grasp intellectually what all the arguments and evidences amount to—that is, what message they are sending. But, if the Holy Spirit's role in helping us grasp intellectually how all the data about God, Christ, us, and our relation to them fit together so that we finally "get" what Scripture is saying, that ministry of the Holy Spirit can go on whether we make our case presuppositionally or evidentially.

My final objections relate to both Van Til's and Schaeffer's forms of presuppositionalism. My ultimate complaint with presuppositionalism is that it leaves apologists with nothing to say if there are no contradictions in the opponent's views. But this needs explanation.

I begin by noting that Schaeffer explicitly and Van Til, at least implicitly, have another presupposition that should be identified. It is the belief that every non-Christian system of thought contains at least one contradiction somewhere within it. This, however, is not so. Many philosophers down through the centuries have been extremely proficient logicians. In fact, they are good enough at logic to know how to tell a logically consistent story. And, if they know that we are going to use a method that intends to uncover their contradictions, they also know enough about logic to know how to make slight revisions to their beliefs which will eliminate possible weak spots.[45]

We are less likely to have this problem using Schaeffer's method, because he grants common ground with nonbelievers. Hence, we are allowed to appeal to the data of the world in making our case, and it is likely that if we push the nonbeliever's views hard enough up against the facts of the world, we will find a contradiction. But even here there can be no guarantees. Some people are just very good at logic and hence can quickly make adjustments to their beliefs so that what looked like a genuine contradiction is removed. On the other hand, the problem I'm raising is especially acute with Van Til's method because he allows no common ground. We must work exclusively within the confines of the nonbeliever's views, and we aren't allowed to incorporate into our defense facts from the world around us unless the nonbeliever says he actually holds those data. But, both Van Til's and Schaeffer's methods are in significant trouble because they depend on an assumption (all non-Christian positions are internally inconsistent) that is false.

In light of this, there is another problem. Suppose we use the presuppositional method on a non-Christian position and we can't find any internal inconsistencies. How can we then make our case and win the debate? Given the presuppositional method, the most we can do is show that our views and our facts don't contradict one another. But if this is all our method allows us to say, and if the non-Christian's position is also logically consistent, how can we win this debate? At such a point, it seems that the only way to make any further progress is for each side to point directly to evidences that support their position and refute the opponent's views. But presuppositionalism won't allow us to do this. Suppose, however, that it did allow us to build an evidential case since the situation after presuppositionalism's application is a standoff. I think this would be a decided improvement, but if the presuppositionalist would grant the value of an evidential argument at the end of the discussion, why not begin by dispensing with the cumbersome and time-consuming presuppositional method and go directly to offering direct evidence?

In sum, the believer and the nonbeliever find themselves on the horns of a dilemma if they use presuppositional methodology: either 1) they stick exclusively with presuppositionalism and wind up unable to declare a winner when the non-Christian position happens to be self-consistent; or 2) if both positions are logically consistent, the apologists are allowed to offer an evidential argument for their position and/or against their opponent's views. In situation 1, presuppositionalism won't work, whereas in situation 2 it is unnecessary.

Consider another issue. Suppose that you used presuppositional argumentation (Van Tilian, Schaefferian, or otherwise) in dealing with a nonbeliever, his views do contain contradictions, and you point out those problems (and your friend reluctantly agrees). Then you move to your system and show your friend that the Christian position is self-consistent. Is the debate over and Christianity the winner? Not at all, for the Christian has shown no more than that his friend's non-Christian system can't be true because it contradicts itself and that his Christian system is logically consistent. But that fact—the Christian position is self-consistent—only tells us that Christianity can't be rejected on the grounds of being internally inconsistent. It *does not* tell us that Christianity is true in that it matches what we find in the real world. Even if every non-Christian position *is* internally inconsistent, Christianity (assuming it is internally consistent) would not win the debate by default. This is so because not every logically consistent story is true (in a correspondence sense) to the facts of the world. To show that Christianity corresponds to the facts we need a positive case for the truth of Christianity, and that can be given only by pointing to various evidences that support the various tenets of the faith. Without positive evidential support to confirm the truth of Christianity, our faith may be in nothing more than a logically consistent story, and that isn't enough. So, presuppositional argumentation, even when it works wonderfully well, doesn't go far enough.

CONCLUSION

In concluding this chapter, I remind readers of the valuable contributions of presuppositionalism as well as its problems and limitations. As I have argued, the method itself (whether Schaeffer's version or Van Til's) is usable and appeals to a test philosophers use in assessing a point of view. In cases where the apologist detects contradictions in the nonbeliever's views, by all means the apologist should point out those problems. Moreover, if Christians have doubts about the consistency of Christianity, presuppositional argumentation may help to quell those doubts. My main conclusion, however, is that presuppositional arguments can take us only so far in defending our faith. At some point we must build a positive case for Christianity, and that's where evidential argument takes over.

Presuppositionalism arose against the backdrop of modern epistemology with its evidential objection to religious belief (detailed by Plantinga). It doesn't intend to address postmodern concerns, and it is debatable as to whether postmoderns would find anything attractive in presuppositionalism.

Presuppositionalists have taken very seriously both modern epistemology and the evidential argument against religious belief that flows from it. While not accepting everything modern epistemology has said, presuppositionalism in effect says the following: even granting that we are playing the game of knowledge on the field that you have designed and defined, modern epistemology, we can still beat you with our indirect method of argumentation. To use Plantinga's categories, presuppositionalists are interested in both *de jure* and *de facto* questions about Christianity. But they are more interested in whether Christianity is true, and they believe their method establishes conclusively that Christianity is true. By showing it to be true presuppositionalists would surely believe they have answered any doubts about whether one can be rational, justified, and warranted in believing Christianity.

Chapter 9

Christian Evidentialism

Over the last century the term 'evidentialism' has been used in a variety of ways. Reformed Epistemologists speak of it as detrimental to religious belief in general and Christian belief in particular. In contrast, many Christian apologists use an evidential method in defending the faith. Still other Christian apologists, presuppositionalists, claim that Christian evidentialism has an overly optimistic assessment of the ability of unsaved people to grasp the arguments and evidences presented for Christianity.

The meaning of evidentialism is even harder to understand because of the variety of people who have been listed among the ranks of evidentialists. As Plantinga has shown, many evidentialists have been foundationalists. Hence, W. K. Clifford qualifies as an evidentialist, and so does the skeptic David Hume. On the other hand, Christian thinkers Aquinas and Anselm are also evidentialists, though their arguments for God's existence rest on very different types of evidence—Anselm's ontological argument doesn't appeal to any tangible, empirical evidence. Christian apologists Norman Geisler, William Lane Craig, and John Warwick Montgomery are also evidentialists, but there are significant differences in the way each makes his case for Christianity. And, none of these Christian thinkers would feel comfortable being linked with Hume, nor would they likely agree with W. K. Clifford's version of foundationalism.

Is there any way to make sense of this apparent confusion? I believe there is. We must first distinguish the evidentialism Reformed Epistemologists reject from the evidentialism many Christian apologists embrace. Once that difference is clarified, I want to sketch the main themes and characteristics of Christian evidentialism. Then, I shall present in more detail the evidential approach of Montgomery. His approach has been influential, and he has explained a lot of the philosophical and theological rationale undergirding evidential apologetics. Moreover, his approach offers a strategy for defending the whole Christian worldview at once. The chapter will then conclude with some brief comments about a cumulative case approach to defending the faith. At the outset, I note that evidentialism in its various forms (Christian and non-Christian) is largely a response to the concerns of modern epistemology.[1] Though it is possible to address postmodern themes using evidentialism, that has not been given much attention.

TWO TYPES OF EVIDENTIALISM

The first kind of evidentialism is the type Reformed Epistemology rejects. According to this evidentialism, it is never right to believe a proposition unless one has sufficient evidence to support its truth. Per se Christians might not find this dictum troublesome, especially if they think they can support Christianity's truth claims with ample evidence. Of course, the crucial issue is what counts as sufficient evidence. As Plantinga shows, this sort of evidentialism has most frequently been wedded to classical foundationalism, which requires that beliefs be ultimately supported by basic beliefs which are either self-evident, evident to the senses, or incorrigible. While a Christian apologist might hold foundationalism and its criteria of proper basicality, that would be unwise. It would be unwise, as Plantinga shows, because classical foundationalism is ultimately self-defeating.

In addition, this kind of evidentialism is negative to religious beliefs, because on the basis of classical foundationalism, evidentialists reject religious beliefs as lacking sufficient evidential support to warrant belief. This type of evidentialism is *not* the evidentialism under discussion in this chapter.

There are, however, Christians who adopt an evidentialist approach to defending the faith. These evidentialists may hold foundationalism as their theory of knowledge, but they might instead hold coherentism as their theory of knowledge.[2] If they are foundationalists, they shouldn't hold classical foundationalism (although in earlier centuries some probably did), because, as shown in chapter 7, it is untenable. In addition, it isn't at all clear that the tenets of Christianity either meet the classical foundationalist requirements of proper basicality or are ultimately supported by beliefs that do. A foundationalism with modified criteria of basicality or perhaps a coherentist approach to knowledge would be a better fit for Christian evidentialism.

Christian evidentialists, even if they reject classical foundationalism, take very seriously the dictum that beliefs should be held only if supported by sufficient evidence. In fact, Christian evidentialists believe there is sufficient evidence to support Christianity, and they believe they can prove this to anyone who would consider the evidence they marshal for the Christian faith. Christian evidentialists also believe their method of supporting Christianity is not a matter of special pleading, not an *ad hoc* method of defending Christianity, and doesn't require a special set of rules which apply to no other propositions than the tenets of Christianity. Rather, this method of defending Christianity is the same one Christians and non-Christians have used for centuries to prove or disprove any claim about our world.

In light of these comments about Christian evidentialism, it is clear that this approach to apologetics addresses modern epistemology's conception of knowledge, proof, and evidence. Though Christian evidentialism might also address some or all of the concerns raised by postmodern epistemology, it is seldom so used.

Christian evidentialism is a different way of responding to what Plantinga calls the evidentialist objection to religious belief than is Reformed Epistemology. This doesn't mean that Christian evidentialism can't be wedded to Reformed Epistemology. As long as we remember the distinction between *de jure* and *de facto* issues, we can say that a Christian evidentialist could follow Reformed Epistemology to address nonbelievers' *de jure* objections to Christianity and to religious belief in general. It is, however, in dealing with *de facto* issues that Christian evidentialism, the approach under discussion in this chapter, takes center stage. For Christian evidentialists believe that they can produce sufficient evidence to show that the Christian "story" is indeed true. As we shall see, there are varieties of Christian evidentialism, but certain characteristics seem to be true of most, if not all, forms. To those commonly held elements of Christian evidentialism we turn momentarily. Hereafter in this chapter, unless otherwise noted, I shall use the term 'evidentialism' to refer to Christian evidentialism.

BASIC TRAITS OF EVIDENTIALISM

Typical of evidential apologetics is a belief that human reason can grasp arguments and evidences presented to it. That doesn't mean that evidentialists ignore the fact that we live in a fallen, sinful world. Rather, they believe that while there are negative results for reason from humans' sinful condition, sin has not completely ripped reason from human nature.[3] Hence, when talking about religious beliefs, even the natural man can grasp the intellectual points of our arguments. Nonbelievers can and do know the rules of reason, and they can use those rules correctly in evaluating arguments and evidences. Of course, understanding the intellectual, cognitive point of arguments and evidences in no way guarantees that one will adopt the worldview the arguments support. But at least nonbelievers can understand an evidential case for Christianity.

As to presuppositionalism's method of argument, evidentialists agree that if there are contradictions in the nonbeliever's views, those problems are strong evidence that the nonbeliever's views are false. Evidentialists may point to some of those contradictions in making a case against a nonbeliever's position. But there is no hesitation in pointing nonbelievers directly to the evidence that refutes their views or supports the believer's position.

Second, evidentialists contend that there is common ground between believers and nonbelievers. Evidentialists agree that all people are made in God's image and that everyone does know that God exists. But they see more than this as common ground between believer and nonbeliever. In particular, evidentialists hold that the very facts of the world are common ground. All of us, by using the intellectual equipment with which we were born—reason, sense perception, etc.—can understand the basic data of the world. In addition, there are various concepts that all people hold, and the way believers and nonbelievers use language is by and large the same. Hence, we can understand one another, and if there is misunderstanding, there are ideas and terms that both believers and nonbelievers hold in common so that they can explain to one another (and be understood) what they mean by what they say.

Because evidentialists believe that there is common ground, they also hold that they can point to the facts of reality in building a case for Christianity, and the nonbeliever will understand them and can grant that those facts do support the Christian position or some aspect of it. Of course, this doesn't mean that terms and facts that are common ground with one nonbeliever are common ground with all of them. The apologist must determine through conversation just what facts the nonbeliever knows and accepts, but evidentialists emphatically affirm that there is more common ground with nonbelievers than merely sharing the *imago dei* and knowing that God exists.

It is also worth noting that, just because one believes in common ground between believers and nonbelievers, that doesn't automatically make one an evidentialist. One could believe there is common ground, but still be convinced that showing the nonbeliever that she contradicts herself is a far more effective apologetic than merely pointing to facts about the world in support of Christianity. As we saw in chapter 8, Francis Schaeffer held that there is common ground between believers and nonbelievers; he also believed that the best way to test a nonbeliever's views is to show that they are self-contradictory and can't consistently be lived out in our world. Only if God is the ultimate reference point do the facts make sense. So, belief in common ground doesn't make one an evidentialist. However, it is true that most (if not all) evidentialists affirm that there is substantial common ground between them and nonbelievers. Hence, a direct appeal to the facts makes sense as an apologetic strategy.

A third and related point about evidentialism is its belief about facts. Christian evidentialists are typically metaphysical realists. That means they believe there is a real world outside of the mind which is independent in its existence from the mind. In earlier centuries, many evidentialists might have spoken of the "brute facts" of reality. By this they meant that humans find the world as it is in itself given to them through sense perception. Since Immanuel Kant, it is hard to find an epistemologist who would say that humans know things as they are in themselves, unaltered by the mind's interaction with them. Kant showed that the knowing relation involves two *active* participants, the mind and the world, in the acquisition of knowledge.

Despite the role the mind plays in interacting with and evaluating the data of the external world, evidentialists hold that the mind's activity in this process is not so overwhelming in its applying of one's beliefs to the new data that the mind grossly obscures the truth about the external world. Contemporary evidentialists understand that the term 'brute facts' probably needs to be discarded from the discussion, but that does not mean we can't know and convince others of how things are in the world around us. Evidentialists explain why this is so in various ways, but a typical explanation is that within the facts themselves are adequate criteria to allow the knower to interpret properly what she sees, hears, etc. And, if there are doubts about a particular understanding of the external world, one can always test that understanding against that of others. After all, the empirical, tangible facts of reality are public to all. These features of the world of facts around us make it possible to know what is the case in our universe and also to convince others of our understanding. Though a science teacher, for example, doesn't use the facts of the world to build an apologetic for any religion, in teaching her class about the world, she points her students to various facts in the world that they can test. In a similar way, the apologist points to things in the world not just to explain what the world is like but to use those facts to support the Christian understanding of reality. In appealing to the world in these ways, both the science teacher and the apologist show that they believe not only that the facts are common ground but also that they can be understood for what they are by most people who interact with them—hence science can be taught and learned and worldviews can be defended or attacked by an appeal to the facts.

The points about common ground and about the facts being accessible to all fit a fourth characteristic of evidential apologetics. Evidentialists believe that objectivity in handling facts and arguments is possible. The defense of this point was offered in my interaction with postmodern skepticism (chapter 4). This commitment to objective knowledge does not mean that evidentialists think our previous experiences, preferred ideas, and overall noetic structure never get in the way of grasping the truth about the world. Their point is that despite our subjective preferences, those biases do not inevitably doom us, as we look at arguments and evidences, to see only what we already hold. It is possible to identify our presuppositions and set them aside to an extent that allows us to see the facts for what they are. And, if we err in judging what is the case, it is also possible with argument, evidence, and explanation to correct our misunderstandings. We are not so locked into our ideas that we can't see anything we don't already believe. Thus, there is reason to present argument and evidence in favor of Christianity.

Fifth, evidentialists understand that the evidential case they make is not predominantly a deductive proof. Indeed, they may offer a deductive proof for God's existence, but most of the arguments and evidences they marshal are inductive. As explained in addressing modern skepticism, inductively arrived at truths, because of the nature of induction and the nature of facts about the empirical world, are never considered 100 percent objectively certain; at very best they are 99 percent certain.

Presuppositionalists have complained that with something as important as one's worldview and one's eternal destiny at stake, we need more than a Christianity that is probably true or true with even 99 percent certainty. We need a Christianity that is absolutely true; hence we also need an apologetic methodology that will render Christianity absolutely true. As a result, presuppositionalists believe evidentialism is just not good enough.

Evidentialists respond that because many Christian claims are matters of empirical fact, a case for Christianity can only be 99 percent objectively certain at best. However, that is the nature of empirical, factual matters. Science doesn't deliver 100 percent objective certainty, nor does history or any other empirical discipline, and yet we don't remain skeptical about the deliverances of science or history. Similarly, evidentialists believe there is nothing inadequate with a defense that renders Christianity 99 percent (or thereabout) objectively certain.

In addition, presuppositionalism isn't without problems. Using presuppositionalism, a logically self-contradictory worldview will be absolutely false, but as noted in chapter 8, not every nonbelieving position contains a contradiction. Moreover, if one can show that Christianity is not self-contradictory, that doesn't prove it squares with the facts, but presuppositional methodology won't allow the apologist to make an evidential case that shows that our logically consistent worldview does match the facts.

From my own perspective, the concern about absolute certainty is somewhat misguided. That is so because it fails to distinguish between objective and subjective certainty. As explained in chapter 6, one may be just as subjectively certain about the truth of empirical beliefs as with beliefs of math and logic. If someone were to show a belief (or a system of thought) to be 99 percent objectively certain (or even close to that), there would be no reason to think the method used or the arguments and evidence provided were in any way deficient. For further explanation, see my chapter 6, but we can say that this presuppositionalist concern need not concern us.

Sixth, in earlier chapters I mentioned the differences between offensive and defensive apologetics. I also noted that apologists may need to refute opposing views as well as support their own view. Assuming that there are contradictions in the opponent's views, presuppositionalism can do very well at uncovering them. It doesn't, however, make a positive case for Christianity. Showing that Christianity is self-consistent is important, but more must be shown.

As for evidentialism, it is useful either for attacking the opponent's views or supporting one's own position. That is, evidentialism is useful in both offensive and defensive apologetics. For example, atheists claim that the existence of evil argues against the existence of God. In answering this challenge, theists rebut such claims and thereby defend Christianity—this is defensive apologetics. Another example of defensive apologetics is when Christian apologists answer nonbelievers' claims that there are errors in the New Testament. Sometimes the errors are alleged contradictions within the New Testament. Paul seems to teach that salvation is by faith alone, whereas James stresses works for genuine faith. New Testament Gospel writers apparently disagree on how many times the cock crowed when Peter denied Christ. And, there seem to be factual errors as well. For example, in the parable of the mustard seed, Jesus says that the mustard seed is the smallest seed, but botanists know of smaller seeds. Hence, Jesus appears to be wrong, and if the New Testament writers who quote him think he is right, they are wrong.

In responding to the issues just raised, the Christian evidentialist engages in defensive apologetics. She explains how the existence of an all-loving and all-powerful God can be harmonized with the existence of evil. Further, she offers evidence that Paul and James don't contradict one another, that the Gospel accounts are in fact correct, and that Jesus, in talking about the size of mustard seeds, did not make a mistake. All of this is defensive apologetics, and evidentialism readily embraces the opportunity to produce the evidence to rebut critics' complaints.

Evidentialists also engage in positive apologetics. They offer the traditional arguments for God's existence. They present evidence that the Bible as we have it accurately reflects the books as originally written, and also offer evidence that Scripture's claims are true and reliable. Moreover, they structure positive arguments for the possibility of miracles, and in particular they produce evidence to show that Christ both died and rose from the grave. In constructing these apologetic arguments, evidentialists engage in offensive, positive apologetics. They also present the evidential case that non-Christian beliefs such as evolution are not true.

Seventh, when evidentialists speak of marshaling evidence for Christianity as a whole or for a specific doctrine, they mean any kind of evidence available. The evidence may come from science, archaeology, philosophy, or other disciplines. However, the evidence most frequently adduced in favor of Christianity is historical in nature. Obviously, if one is dealing with creation and evolution, the majority of the evidence relating to evolution will be scientific. But many doctrinal tenets of the Christian faith rest on historical evidence. For example, the authenticity and reliability of Scripture involve many historical evidences. That is, there is a certain history of the writing, copying, and transmission of the biblical text. In addition, many different events and actions recorded in Scripture claim to be historical facts. So, historical evidence is a major emphasis in dealing with Scripture, but it is also a major concern in addressing whether Jesus ever actually died and rose again. Thankfully, there are many historical evidences for these events, and evidentialist apologists do not hesitate to offer them in support of Christianity.

Finally, in discussing presuppositionalism, I noted that evidentialists have not always presented their case in a way that seems to rely on both the work of the Holy Spirit and their own arguments. However, evidentialists believe that no one will be persuaded to accept Christ by the sheer "brilliance" of the evidential case they build in favor of Christianity. The ministry of the Holy Spirit is also imperative in apologetic encounters. To see that evidentialists do emphasize the Holy Spirit's ministry, consider a recent publication (*Five Views on Apologetics*) focusing on apologetic methodology. Three of the five authors hold a form of evidentialism, though all three have distinct emphases. It is of special import that all three of the evidentialists emphasize the need for the Holy Spirit to be involved in the apologetic enterprise if we are to make any real headway in persuading nonbelievers to turn to Christ.[4] While these three authors obviously don't represent all Christian evidentialists, I mention them to show that many evidentialists don't think that making a case for Christianity is only and all about evidence and argument.

VARIATIONS ON A THEME

As just noted, three of the five contributors to *Five Views on Apologetics* are evidentialists in their basic approach. However, there are interesting differences among them which represent many other evidentialists. In this portion of the chapter I want to explore briefly those three variations, and then turn to the evidentialism of John Warwick Montgomery. Montgomery is of interest not only in terms of the importance of his work in apologetics over the last quarter of a century or more. He is also important because of his emphasis on major evidentialist themes and because, using an evidential method that relies heavily on historical evidence, he presents a six-step strategy for establishing the truth of the whole Christian worldview.

Three Varieties of Christian Evidentialism

A first form of evidentialist apologetics is known as classical apologetics. William Lane Craig offers this methodology but includes some twists of his own. For one thing, Craig finds very helpful the work of Reformed Epistemology and its conclusions about the need for evidences to support Christianity. While Craig agrees that one doesn't have to hold Christianity as true on the basis of arguments and evidence in order to be rational, he won't downplay the significance of evidences in apologetics.

So how can one incorporate the insights of Reformed Epistemology with the methodology of classical apologetics in a consistent apologetic strategy? Craig's answer is found in his distinction between *knowing* that Christianity is true and *showing* that it is true.[5] Craig agrees that apart from argument and evidence many people have come to belief in God as detailed by Reformed Epistemology, and that they are rational in doing so. But Craig adds something more, the internal testimony of the Holy Spirit. This is often associated with assurance of salvation, but Craig sees it as a legitimate way to certify the truth of what one believes. Knowing that Christianity is true, then, does not rely on argument and evidence, but rather involves coming to believe in God and Christianity in the way detailed by Reformed Epistemology, plus the inner witness of the Holy Spirit that Christianity is true.

So far, this doesn't sound a whole lot like classical apologetics, but Craig weds these ideas to it. Before we see how, we need to look more closely at what Craig says about the internal witness of the Holy Spirit. He calls it self-authenticating, and goes on to explain that this means:

(1) the experience of the Holy Spirit is veridical and unmistakable (though not necessarily irresistible or indubitable) for the one who has it and at-

tends to it; (2) that such a person does not need supplementary arguments or evidence in order to know and to know with confidence that he is in fact experiencing the Spirit of God; (3) that such experience does not function in this case as a premise in any argument from religious experience to God, but rather is the immediate experiencing of God himself; (4) that in certain contexts the experience of the Holy Spirit will imply the apprehension of certain truths of the Christian religion, such as "God exists," "I am reconciled to God," "Christ lives in me," and so forth; (5) that such an experience provides one not only with a subjective assurance of Christianity's truth; and (6) that arguments and evidence incompatible with that truth are overwhelmed by the experience of the Holy Spirit for the one who attends fully to it.[6]

All of these things for Craig relate to knowing that Christianity is true, but so far nothing has been said about arguments and evidence favoring Christianity.[7] However, when we turn to showing nonbelievers or even doubting believers that Christianity is true, that is where marshaling evidence and argument is appropriate. Here we begin to see the nature of classical apologetics. Craig explains that the strategy of this method is "first to present arguments for theism, which aimed to show that God's existence is at least more probable than not, and then to present Christian evidences, probabilistically construed, for God's revelation in Christ."[8]

So this is a two-step approach. First, one establishes the existence of God, and then the apologist offers argument and evidence that our universe is most likely a Christian theistic one. For Craig the establishment of the first step is best handled by what is known as the *kalam* cosmological argument for God's existence. As to the second step with its emphasis on Christ as God's revelation to us, Craig believes this is best shown by arguing for the resurrection of Christ. Of course, there are other arguments and evidences in support of Christianity, and it will also be necessary to engage in defensive apologetics to answer the objections of critics.[9]

One wonders, of course, whether it is necessary to prove God's existence before proving anything else about Christianity. Craig, in his piece in the *Five Views* book, doesn't claim that this is so. However, some classical apologists have been adamant on this point. For example, Norman Geisler (*Christian Apologetics*), using classical apologetics, complains that a more general evidentialism that doesn't first prove God's existence is inadequate. He explains as follows:

> Facts and events have ultimate meaning only within and by virtue of the context of the world view in which they are conceived. Hence, it is a vicious circle to argue that a given fact (say, the resuscitation of Christ's body) is evidence of a certain truth claim (say, Christ's claim to be God), *unless it can be established that the event comes in the context of a theistic universe.* For it makes no sense to claim to be the Son of *God* and to evidence it by an act of *God* (miracle) unless there is a God who can have a Son and who can act in a special way in the natural world. But in this case the mere fact of the resurrection cannot be used to establish the truth that there is a God. For the resurrection cannot even be a miracle unless there already is a God.[10]

In his response to Craig's essay, Gary Habermas raises this issue, citing various classical apologists who have thought it necessary to prove God's existence before offering arguments for any other tenet of Christianity. In his response to Habermas, Craig questions whether this has been and is really standard procedure for classical apologists. He notes that classical apologists have used both natural theology (arguments for God's existence) and Christian evidences, but says it would be difficult to find a classical apologist who thinks the evidences are useless without the natural theology. So, why does Craig use the arguments for God's existence? He does because these arguments, assuming they are sound (and Craig thinks at least some like the *kalam* argument are sound), only make the case for Christianity stronger, and why would someone prefer a weaker case when a stronger one is possible?[11]

Whether or not the case for Christianity must include arguments for God's existence plus evidences for miracles, Christ's resurrection, and the like, the basic approach of classical apologetics is clear—a "two-step" method for showing that Christianity is true. How does Habermas's form of evidentialism differ?

Gary Habermas's position is simply called evidentialism. He notes that many traits true of most forms of evidentialist apologetics are true of his approach. Moreover, some key emphases of other methodologies are to be found in his system. For example, like many other strategies, he believes that there are no brute, uninterpreted facts. However, he agrees that even though each person has his own noetic structure, it is still possible to agree on what is true of the world, in part because many of the facts we speak about are public. This also means that there is common ground between believers and nonbelievers that goes beyond the fact that we are made in God's image. Similar to other Christian evidentialists and to even Christian apologists who don't use an evidential methodology, Habermas agrees that we must take seriously the pervasive nature of sin and its effects on the mind. He also affirms his belief in the necessity of the Holy Spirit's activity in apologetics if people are to be persuaded to turn to Christ. And his apologetic method engages in both positive and negative apologetics.[12]

So, how does his approach differ from other evidentialists, Reformed Epistemologists, and presuppositionalists? Habermas explains that he does not hold evidentialist *epistemology* (the kind rejected by Reformed Epistemologists) just because he uses an evidential apologetic method. He notes that various epistemologies could be wedded to his evidential apologetic without weakening the credibility and rationality of what he offers.[13] From this portion of his essay, it is clear that he doesn't emphasize a response to what Plantinga calls the *de jure* questions. That doesn't mean he is disinterested in them or that he disagrees with Plantinga's handling of those issues. Rather, it shows that his main concern is with the *de facto* question. Is Christianity true, and how do we show that to be so?

Habermas has much in common, methodologically speaking, with classical apologetics, but there are some differences. Rather than using a two-step methodology which requires the apologist first to establish by argument God's existence and then to look at various evidences for Scripture's truth and the resurrection of Christ, Habermas uses a one-step method. He believes that we can dispense with having to prove God's existence first, and can go directly to evidences which, if true, would establish God's existence anyway. For example, if by presenting historical evidences, the apologist can show that the Bible is reliable historically and that Jesus really rose from the dead, in so doing the apologist would also have shown that God exists. The only credible theory that would explain the nature of Scripture, Christ's resurrection, and the like is one that includes God. Of course, later in one's defense of Christianity, one might add the traditional arguments for God's existence just to strengthen the case, but that isn't necessary to establish the truth of Christianity as a whole or of one of its specific doctrines.[14]

The other distinctive of Habermas's approach is his heavy reliance on historical evidences. He does so in part because many of the tenets of Christianity themselves rest on historical events, but also because historical evidences, while not always immediately available to us and while in essence nonrepeatable, deal with tangible traces of things that happened. These tangible traces are public and hence available for all to observe. This feature of such evidences helps to keep our subjectivity from running rampant in deciding which evidences to choose and in our interpretation of those data. None of this means that Habermas would use only historical evidences. Like other evidentialists, he grants that his approach is somewhat eclectic, i.e., he is happy to gather nonhistorical evidences when they are available and when they help to make the case for Christianity. But for the reasons mentioned, his personal habit is to focus on evidences that are historical.[15]

In addition to explaining the basics of his approach, Habermas gives an example of how one might apply it to defend a tenet of the faith. Though a full defense wasn't possible, given space limitations in a multi-authored book, Habermas shares some of the evidence supporting Jesus's teachings about himself, and some favoring Christ's death and resurrection. For our purposes in this chapter, I note that Habermas employs what he calls a "minimal facts" strategy. Presumably, he would use this approach in dealing with the whole of Christian theism, but he only shows us what it looks like in regard to Christ's teaching about himself and his death and resurrection. Sometimes apologists seem to think that the best way to present an evidential case for something, including a tenet of Christianity, is to gather together any and all evidences and arguments they can find, regardless of how good or bad those arguments are. Habermas prefers his minimal facts strategy which allows him to choose only the strongest and most compelling arguments and evidences.

In choosing the evidences to include in his defense, Habermas uses two main criteria. The first, and most important, is to use data that are well-attested for a number of reasons. The second is to use data that are generally recognized as credible by critical scholars who know the particular issue in view (or the broader area in which the specific tenet of the faith falls). Using such a strategy will be more likely to convince critics than a strategy that simply piles up large amounts of arguments and evidences, regardless of how cogent or feeble they are.[16]

Of course, apologists and critics alike can always argue over which data are the best attested, and they can argue about what those evidences actually prove. None of that per se, however, invalidates either Habermas's evidentialist method or the specific evidences he chooses and the use he makes of them in defending Christianity. In short, this is a position that clearly differs from presuppositionalism, though it has much in common with classical apologetics. The most significant difference between Habermas and classical apologists is the classical apologists' claim that God's existence must first be proved before looking for evidences that support Christianity as the correct form of theism. As already noted, however, even here Craig questions whether this is a *requirement* for all classical apologetic systems.

A final variation of evidential apologetics (in the *Five Views* book) appears in Paul Feinberg's cumulative case approach. He explains that there are various ways to conceive the case for theism. A first way views the apologist's task as offering demonstrably sound arguments that establish theism as true and perhaps, in some apologist's judgment, also Christianity. A sound argument is one whose premises are all true and whose conclusion follows with logical inevitability from the premises. Feinberg states that if we try to confirm Christianity using this strategy, we will probably turn to either the ontological or the cosmological argument for God's existence. Many Christians see these arguments as sound, and hence they believe that the arguments establish God's existence. Unfortunately, nonbelievers don't think all of the premises in these arguments are true; hence, even if they grant that the argument form is valid, they don't agree that the theist has established the truth of Christianity or even theism in general.[17]

Theists may then take an alternate route. They may try to show that theism is probably true; that is, they may offer arguments to show that theism or Christianity is most likely the true worldview. If the apologist takes this approach, Feinberg claims that he will likely use an argument such as the teleological argument or the argument from design. Here the argument's point is to note that there is evidence in our universe of intelligent design and to argue that the existence of an intelligent, purposeful designer (God) is the best explanation of why our world seems designed. Hence, it is probable that theism is true. As with the preceding approach, Feinberg explains that unfortunately, the nonbeliever thinks she can explain evidence of design in a more probable way than can a theist. Specifically, she will point to evolution as the force behind what we observe, and being a nonbeliever (perhaps even an atheist), she will think evolution is the most probable explanation of design in the natural order. Christians will disagree, but, of course, the purpose is to convince non-Christians, so it appears that a strictly probabilistic approach isn't going to succeed in defending Christianity in a way that convinces nonbelievers.[18]

Since neither of the two approaches will likely succeed, what should we do? Feinberg explains that one might use a third approach, a cumulative case approach (sometimes called *inference to the best explanation*). This approach doesn't just appeal to one or two arguments. Instead, it views Christianity and other worldviews as complex systems of belief. In such a system, there are many distinct items, and then there is the question of how they relate to one another in the overall system. One won't likely establish the truth of the whole system with a few arguments. Rather, a whole series of arguments and evidences, aimed at supporting various parts of the system, is required. Following Basil Mitchell's *The Justification of Religious Belief*,[19] we need to think of Christianity and other worldviews along the model of a scientific theory that covers many disparate data, or of the reconstruction of a whole sequence of historical events like the Reformation or the French revolution. We might also view a worldview and its confirmation along the lines of what we do when we offer an interpretation of a complex piece of literature. Seldom is there only one possible interpretation; individual interpreters must marshal a variety of evidences, textual and extratextual, to support their particular interpretation of the text.[20]

Feinberg claims that a cumulative case approach in apologetics has four different characteristics. First, it is not a formal argument with premises that inevitably yield a conclusion, but rather an informal one. It involves gathering various evidences that point to a conclusion in much the same way that a lawyer might construct a legal brief. Second, it appeals to a variety of evidences. These deal with things in our experience that require some sort of overall explanation; that is, we can't make sense of these items in themselves alone, but rather need an overarching theory or worldview that helps us see the role of each element in our world. Third, none of the arguments and evidences amassed is more important than any other. Moreover, no one point in the system must be proved before addressing others. So, unlike many classical apologists who hold that God's existence must be proved first, the cumulative case approach requires no such procedure. The apologist may begin his case at any point in his system, and depending on how the nonbeliever responds may then turn to another item suggested by the nonbeliever or just the next point the apologist wants to tackle. Finally, as Feinberg uses the cumulative case approach, it isn't just a defense of

God's existence or theism, but rather an apologetic intended to establish the truth of the whole of Christianity.[21]

After describing the basics of this approach, Feinberg next turns to various tests for truth by which we can judge the apologist's cumulative case for Christianity or any other worldview. He proposes seven tests for truth (logical consistency, correspondence to fact, comprehensiveness, simplicity, livability, fruitfulness, and conservation[22]), but, of course, one could use the cumulative case approach without adopting all of these tests for truth.

Finally, Feinberg shows us what his cumulative case for Christianity looks like by identifying the types of arguments and evidences that would go into it. He emphasizes the need for the apologist to rely on the ministry of the Holy Spirit, and does so in part by labeling all of the arguments for Christianity as the witness of the Holy Spirit. He divides this "witness" into two broad categories that he labels external aspects (objective) and internal aspects (subjective). Into the former go the traditional arguments for God's existence, arguments from religious experience, evidence from moral behavior, and evidence from revelation. As for revelation, we have arguments that support the reliability of Scripture (fulfilled prophecy being one of those arguments), but from revelation we also get evidence for the deity of Christ and for his resurrection.

As for the internal aspects of this witness, the Holy Spirit ministers differently to believers as opposed to nonbelievers. In the case of believers, the Holy Spirit illumines their minds and helps them understand God's truth, but he also gives believers certitude that they indeed believe the truth in trusting God and Christ. When it comes to nonbelievers, the Holy Spirit's ministry involves convicting the nonbeliever of sin, righteousness, and judgment (John 16:8–11). This involves appealing to the nonbeliever's conscience and to the inborn sense that all people have that there is a God.[23]

Feinberg concludes with a reminder that, just as believers can construct a cumulative case for Christianity, so nonbelievers may do the same in favor of their worldview. How can we then decide which is the preferable cumulative case? The answer, according to Feinberg, rests with the tests for truth. In his judgment the cumulative case for Christianity better fits and passes those tests than does the case for any other worldview. In all of this we see again the general evidentialist characteristics outlined earlier in this chapter, but also a distinct approach to arguing for the faith.

John Warwick Montgomery's Historical Evidential Apologetic

John Warwick Montgomery has written extensively on apologetics and many other topics. Some of his apologetic work, such as "Once Upon an A Priori,"[24] was written specifically in response to Van Til's presuppositionalism, but he has also elaborated his own approach in various publications. As clear and detailed as any are his presentations in *The Shape of the Past* and *Where Is History Going?* Both volumes are subtitled *A Christian Response to Secular Philosophies of History.* In *The Shape of the Past* Montgomery offers a lengthy exposition and analysis of various philosophies of history, beginning with Herodotus and ending with twentieth-century approaches to history and historiography. He then turns to validation of the Christian worldview, and his method is clearly evidential with a hefty emphasis on historical evidences.

Montgomery cites Raymond Aron's claim that belief in God is something that many people hold and that it therefore has a certain value, but many believers think their belief in God touches on issues whose jurisdiction is empirical and sociological study. It is just at this point, according to Aron, that problems arise, for belief, if considered empirically, is not the sort of thing science deals with and hence, empirically, belief in a transcendent being is easily falsifiable.[25]

Montgomery strongly demurs. While non-Christian historians typically reject a Christian interpretation of both classic and contemporary history because they are deemed inaccessible to empirical, scientific study, Montgomery emphatically counters that the Christian worldview is accessible to science and "rests upon an objective foundation which will stand up under the most exacting criticism."[26]

How can this be, one wonders, given the various doctrinal claims of Christianity, many of which seem inaccessible to empirical observation and study? Montgomery says that it is so because Christianity rests on the historical, objective resurrection of Christ from the dead.[27] Montgomery then presents a six-step argument for validating the Christian worldview as a whole. It rests on appeal to empirical evidence with a special emphasis on historical evidence. Because it attempts to confirm evidentially the whole Christian worldview at once, it is worth attending to Montgomery's "resurrection" argument for the truthfulness of Christianity. I offer it in full, pausing here and there to add Montgomery's elaborations and at places my own commentary.

The first step is,

> On the basis of accepted principles of textual and historical analysis, the Gospel records are found to be trustworthy historical documents—primary source evidence for the life of Christ.[28]

Note that Montgomery begins with Scripture, but not all of it—only the Gospels. This is so in part because the direction his argument takes relies heavily on Scriptural data, and because the textual and historical data that relate to the Gospels are so plentiful.

But by whom, one may ask, are these principles accepted? Montgomery's point is that these principles are accepted by people of all sorts and persuasions. They are neither Christian nor atheistic guidelines; hence they favor no worldview in particular, but are useful to anyone in finding the truth about a given document.

The second step in Montgomery's argument is,

> In these records, Jesus exercises divine prerogatives and claims to be God in human flesh; and He rests His claims on His forthcoming resurrection.[29]

Of course, critics have claimed that when we rightly understand which words in the Gospels attributed to Jesus he actually spoke, he didn't claim to be God. Assuming for now that those complaints can be answered, is it true that Jesus exercised divine prerogatives and claimed to be God? In footnotes, Montgomery offers Mark 2:1–12 as an example of the former (Christ forgives sins), and then cites Matthew 11:27; 16:13–17; John 10:30; 12:45; and 14:6–10 as passages where Christ speaks of his divine relation to the Father.

Is Montgomery right, however, about Christ's linking the truthfulness of his claims to his forthcoming resurrection? Indeed, he is, as one can see from passages in the Gospels. Montgomery cites John 2:18–22, but think also of Matthew 12:38–41. In that passage Matthew records the Pharisees' request that the Lord show them a sign, a miracle, to prove that he is who he says he is. This was a frequent request, and the Lord had performed many miracles in their presence, so Jesus was less than thrilled with the request and told his listeners so. However, he did offer one more sign—he appealed to Jonah and remarked that even as Jonah was three days and three nights in the belly of the great fish, so Jesus would be in the earth for three days and three nights. Does this invoke the resurrection? Indeed it does, as we can see when we reflect on the analogy with Jonah. Did Jonah remain in the great fish indefinitely, never to return? Of course not—after three days the fish expelled him back onto land. By analogy, Jesus was predicting his resurrection. Does this passage, however, link the resurrection with Jesus's claims to be the Son of God? Indeed it does, for remember that the Pharisees wanted to see another miracle that would prove that Jesus was who he claimed to be. Though Christ was frustrated by their unbelief in the face of so many miracles already performed, he mentioned Jonah as the sign. But a sign to show what? To show that Christ was who he claimed to be! So, indeed, Jesus's appeal to Jonah does link his resurrection to his claims to be the divine Son of God!

Montgomery then offers a third step:

> In all four Gospels, Christ's bodily resurrection is described in minute detail; Christ's resurrection evidences His deity.[30]

At first glance, this may appear to be question begging. How can Montgomery appeal to Scripture, which is so much at the heart of Christianity, to prove Christ's resurrection, which is also at the core of Christianity? We now see the reason for not making step three the first or the second step in the argument. Montgomery begs no questions here, and he does have a right to appeal to the Gospels because he has already argued on biblical and extrabiblical grounds for their reliability.

Montgomery's fourth step deals with a particular presupposition critics might bring to the study of the evidence. This step shows that if they allow this assumption to color what they see as they assess the evidence for Christ's resurrection, that is logically illegitimate. Step four says,

> The fact of the resurrection cannot be discounted on *a priori*, philosophical grounds; miracles are impossible only if one so defines them—but such definition rules out proper historical investigation.[31]

The assumption the nonbeliever brings to the table is anti-supernaturalism. But what is in part at issue in regard to the resurrection is whether the nonbeliever's assumption that the supernatural can't occur in our world is itself true. Montgomery's point is that you can't legitimately handle the question of whether supernatural events are possible in our world by begging it (by assuming without proof that they can't happen) and think that this is rationally acceptable. The preferred procedure is to have no assumptions pro or con about whether miracles can occur, but simply to "go and see." That is, look at the evidence for Christ's resurrection and see whether it warrants belief that this miracle occurred.

There is another point worth noting, though it is a point for Christian apologists, not for nonbelievers. Through the first four steps of this argument Montgomery has nowhere offered an argument for God's existence. Nor will we find one in the final two steps of his "resurrection" argument. This shows that Montgomery's approach is not that of classical apologists who claim that one must first prove God's existence before doing anything else. As noted earlier, some of these apologists hold that until God's existence is proved, there is no reason to think that miracles can occur, even if one has evidence that something unusual occurred. Though classical apologists certainly don't intend to be anti-supernaturalistic in any way, in essence what they are saying is that unless God's existence is first proved, we must approach any other religious belief (Christian or otherwise) with the presumption of anti-supernaturalism. I know that classical apologists don't intend to do this, but sometimes philosophy makes strange bedfellows (the classical apologist and the anti-supernaturalist).

In this case, if classical apologists reject the whole of Montgomery's six-step argument on the ground that he nowhere proves God's existence, it would be hard to see such a move as not in essence stemming from a presumption of anti-supernaturalism until proven otherwise. On the other hand, what Montgomery is doing gives a concrete example of what Habermas means by a one-step argument that argues directly from the facts about Christ or his resurrection to the confirmation of the whole Christian worldview.

The fifth step in Montgomery's argument is,

> If Christ is God, then He speaks the truth concerning the absolute divine authority of the Old Testament and of the soon-to-be-written New Testament; concerning His death for the sins of the world; and concerning the nature of man and of history.[32]

Montgomery offers various biblical passages that show that Christ does speak about the divine authority of the Old Testament (Matt. 5:17–19) and certifies that he will send the Holy Spirit to guide his apostles into all truth and remind them of Christ's deeds and teaching while on earth (John 14:26–27; 16:12–15; cf. Acts 1:21–26).[33] As to the Holy Spirit's ministry to the apostles, to what end would the Holy Spirit do this? So that when they went to preach and also to write about what they had seen and heard in regard to Christ, they would "get it right!"

The sixth and final step in this argument is,

> It follows from the preceding that all Biblical assertions bearing on phi-losophy of history are to be regarded as revealed truth, and that all human attempts at historical interpretation are to be judged for truth-value on the basis of harmony with Scriptural revelation.[34]

In my opinion, this is a rather compelling argument, though I shall explain later why I think so. For now, I note several further words of expla-nation from Montgomery, and a further point worth noting. Montgomery cautions us not to think of this argument as a deductive demonstration of the truth of Christianity like one we would expect in math or logic. Matters of fact can never have such apodictic certainty when we offer evidence to support them. Rather, his argument "is an empirical argument based upon the application of historical method to an allegedly objective event. Thus it provides no more than probable evidence for the truth of the Christian world-view."[35] In earlier chapters of this book, I explained why this feature of an argument like Montgomery's (empirically and evidentially based) does not by itself make the argument open to suspicion.

Montgomery offers a second caution about his resurrection argument. It is not intended to exclude other apologetic approaches to Christianity. He cites apologists like Pascal and C. S. Lewis whose apologetic work also has value. Still, Montgomery believes his approach is preferable for two reasons. It is the line of argument that was the basis of the apostles' preaching and defending of Christianity in the early church, and Montgomery also prefers it because he believes that it is the ultimate basis or foundation upon which all other defenses rest.[36] In other words, you could exclude other arguments but still succeed in defending the faith if you used only the resurrection ar-gument, whereas other arguments without the resurrection argument would not succeed if the goal is defending Christianity, not just theism in general.

In *Where Is History Going?* Montgomery also presents this six-step resurrection argument. He adds a comment that I think is significant if one is really concerned to convince nonbelievers. Montgomery explains that the methodology and the argument he has presented in no way depends on theological presuppositions (Christian or otherwise). Rather it appeals to commonly used methods of textual and historical analysis that everyone uses, regardless of their worldview.[37] Here we see an example of what Montgomery means when he speaks of presuppositions of method rather than of content. Everyone must start somewhere, but since the methodological assumptions one brings to the task of studying any texts, including Scripture, and any historical event, including Jesus's resurrection, are the same ones used for any other text or event, one can hardly complain that the very "rules of the game," so to speak, that one adopts for investigating these issues predispose anyone who uses them to favor Christianity (or any other worldview, for that matter). No, this will be a "fair fight" as it relates to procedures for investigating the evidence. Equity on this matter won't guarantee that the Christian apologist will win the debate, but it should at least result in his getting a serious hearing.

Let me mention briefly one more item before I close this section. In reading my description of Montgomery's views, you probably sensed that Montgomery seems to believe this method will work because, like other evidentialists, he believes the evidence is public and that objectivity is possible when gathering and evaluating evidence. In fact, some may think his work too optimistic about how objective one can be in evaluating, for example, his resurrection argument.

Indeed, Montgomery does believe that objectivity is possible in historical inquiry and in apologetics. I won't belabor the point, but interested readers can see what he says in an interchange with Gordon Clark (relevant literature is listed in the footnotes).[38] I have covered the issue of objectivity and subjectivity in some detail in chapter 4. Though Montgomery and I wrote about this issue at different times, I believe our responses, though nuanced to the times and audiences we address, are consistent. I raise this issue again, not only to understand Montgomery, but to make a more general point about Christian evidentialism. I raise it to underscore the fact that if one adopts an evidential method of apologetics and builds one's case for Christianity on historical or other kinds of evidences, one must also agree that believers and nonbelievers have common ground, and that it is possible for all involved to exercise enough objectivity in handling arguments and evidences so as to come to an agreement on what is true of reality.

GENERAL ASSESSMENT OF CHRISTIAN EVIDENTIALISM

In this chapter I have discussed various forms of evidential apologetics. My comments now can be brief because I am an evidentialist and agree with much of what I have presented. First, the various forms of evidentialism presented address, in Plantinga's terms, *de facto* questions about Christianity. As such, they don't intend per se to address the *de jure* issues Plantinga raises and handles. But more must be said. In no way do any of these evidentialist positions require rejecting Plantinga's handling of the *de jure* issues. Hence, it is entirely logically consistent to hold Plantinga's answers to whether it is rationally acceptable, justifiable, and warranted for Christians to believe Christianity without evidence, and to wed those answers to an evidentialist method of apologetics when addressing questions about whether Christianity is in fact true. In addition, Plantinga's Reformed Epistemology doesn't make it inappropriate or unnecessary to raise objections to Christianity's truth and to answer those doubts with arguments and evidences. If I came to believe in Christianity in the way Plantinga describes, that doesn't mean that thinking through arguments and evidences that support my beliefs is a waste of time, and certainly I must have responses for non-Christians when they ask why I am a Christian and whether I think anything I believe can be supported by the facts of our world. So, holding some form of evidentialism in no way requires rejection of Reformed Epistemology's program.

Second, though I espouse an evidentialist apologetic, I recognize that it is an apologetic constructed against the backdrop of modern epistemology. In response to the demand for sufficient evidence to hold onto Christian belief, evidentialists offer the evidence they think is required to make the case, even as they reject classical foundationalism and present their modified version of foundationalism, or as they adopt a different theory of knowledge such as coherentism. All of this means, however, that what ultimately drives evidentialism is not a need to answer postmodern epistemology. But can evidentialism be used to address the concerns of postmoderns? In chapters 3 and 4, I addressed postmodern skepticism, and the methodology used was evidentialism.

Finally, though I have explained in this chapter how various evidential systems satisfy the requirements of modern epistemology's concern for adequate evidence, and though I count myself among the company of evidentialists, I have not specified the exact form of evidentialism I would use in defending Christianity. Hence, a few words on that matter are in order. In general, I am most drawn to a cumulative case approach to defending Christianity, and I can share briefly why I think it the best approach and what such a cumulative case might look like.

As to why I find the cumulative case approach most attractive, there are several reasons. First, I am not convinced that one must prove God's existence before anything else is demonstrable. If there is evidence of the required quality and quantity, for example, to warrant belief in the resurrection of Christ, why wouldn't that also show that there must be some supernatural power who performed the deed? Of course, that supernatural being could be evil (Christians do, of course, believe in Satan and demons), but it would be hard to explain the motive for an evil supernatural being to resurrect Christ, especially since Christ is the archenemy of Satan and his minions. Assuming that a malevolent being wouldn't resurrect Christ, and assuming that there is no naturalistic explanation for how a dead Christ can three days after death rise from the dead, what reasonable explanation is there other than that a supernatural good being did it? That alone wouldn't prove the existence of the God of the Bible, but it would surely open the door for belief in him as the agent who raised Christ.

The other reason I wouldn't try to prove God's existence first, if at all, is that I am not convinced that any of the traditional arguments succeeds. That doesn't mean they provide no evidence and support for God's existence and Christianity's truth, but only that I don't find any of them to succeed as a deductive proof. While I am inclined to favor some sort of teleological argument or argument from design, such arguments are probabilistic, and so they don't offer the degree of objective certainty many believers, let alone nonbelievers, would require. Hence, I would use the traditional arguments for God's existence in building a cumulative case for Christianity, but I would rely on other evidences "to carry most of the weight" in an overall defense of Christian truth.

So, what else would I include in a cumulative case defense? Because it seems quite clear that much of the evidence for Christian doctrines (and the historical events they rest upon) resides in Scripture, it is mandatory to give a defense of the reliability of Scripture. Since the most firsthand information about the life and ministry of Jesus is contained in the Gospels, I believe that is the place to begin in defending Scripture. But there are also evidences that can be used to support the reliability of other portions of Scripture. Here disciplines such as ancient Near Eastern studies, secular histories, archaeology, etc., are very helpful.

In addition, following to a large extent Montgomery's rationale, I would include a defense of the resurrection of Christ. There is ample biblical and extrabiblical evidence one might use. A cumulative case approach could also include more generally a defense of miracles.

But a cumulative case can and should do even more. In particular, it should answer major objections to Christianity. For example, the problem of evil is invariably a stumbling block for many in accepting belief in theism, let alone Christianity. Thankfully, there are many defenses that more than adequately answer for many forms of evangelical Christian theology this problem in its logical form, and many answers are also available to address the evidential version of the problem.[39] In addition, whatever evidence one has against evolution and in favor of creationism should be included in a cumulative case. And, in our day with so many committed to the value and equality of all major religions, it would be wise to address the issue of religious pluralism.

Of course, there are other evidences for the truth of Christianity, but the preceding is intended as a general sketch of things I would include in a cumulative case for Christianity. In the previous chapters of this book, I have raised and addressed many methodological issues. As readers have patiently considered those issues with me, I am sure that many have wondered what an actual defense of Christianity or some tenet of it might look like. In the next section of the book, you will get a chance to see. This book is not primarily a book of evidences for every item of the faith. Hence, I won't offer a defense of each Christian tenet. However, to give readers a taste of what all the theory I've presented might look like, in the following portion of the book, I offer a Christian defense related to the following four items: the problem of evil, the reliability of the Gospels, the resurrection of Jesus Christ, and religious pluralism.

PART THREE

Methodology Illustrated—Some Christian Evidences

Chapter 10

The Problem of Evil

The existence of evil in our world presents a challenge that confronts most people at some time in their lives. Whether the evil is experienced by oneself or one's family and friends, dealing with pain and suffering is never easy. Especially in cases where tragedy like the loss of a loved one, diagnosis of a terminal illness, financial ruin, or disintegration of the family through divorce happens, it may take those confronting these evils the rest of their life to recover. In some cases, the afflicted and their friends and families never really get over what has happened. Evil is not something that moderns experience but postmoderns don't. Wrestling with the devastation of evil and affliction in one's life is something true of every society and every generation. Hence, in addressing the issues that evil raises, we are responding to something that everyone will likely confront at some point in their life. In fact, we may have to deal with it on a number of occasions.

The existence of evil poses not only a personal challenge. It raises intellectual questions that at some point need to be answered if there is any hope for a relationship with God to continue. Even if someone has never experienced tragic evil, he will still be aware of the havoc that evil wreaks in people's lives, and he will undoubtedly have questions. The most fundamental question is why God would allow evil to happen, assuming that God exists. In fact, many an atheist came to their atheism in large part because it seemed inconceivable that a loving and powerful God would allow such things to happen. Even if some trials and troubles might be warranted as recompense for the sinful things we do, certainly the amount and kinds of evils that beset people seem to go well beyond what anyone would think is just punishment.

Just as evil has always been with us, it is also true that philosophers, theologians, and ordinary people have raised and wrestled with the problem of evil. For a long time in the history of the debate about this issue the problem was conceived of in one particular way. Since the methodology I have proposed in this book requires that we first understand exactly what the challenge is to theism in general and to Christianity in particular, we must clarify first the nature of the problem of evil.

As traditionally conceived, the problem of evil involves three main claims that many forms of theism do hold. Those affirmations are that 1) God is all-powerful or omnipotent; 2) God is all-loving or omnibenevolent; and 3) evil exists in our world. The complaint against theism is that if any two of these propositions are true, the third must be false. Hence, the set is logically inconsistent. In other words, those who hold all three claims contradict themselves in doing so. If God is omnipotent and yet evil exists, then he must not care enough about us to remove our afflictions. If God does love us and cares enough for us to help us with our trials and yet evil still exists, then he must not have enough power to overcome and remove evil in its many forms. Or, if God is both omnipotent and omnibenevolent, then there seems to be no good reason for evil to be in our world, and yet it is.

J. L. Mackie, a late-twentieth-century atheistic philosopher, explains the complaint well. He says that the problem of evil poses a different kind of problem for theism than does any difficulty theists might have in arguing more generally for God's existence. Mackie believes that the traditional arguments for God's existence don't work, and he thinks that honest theists will agree. Still, one might believe God exists on some grounds other than rational argument. Perhaps one believes that she has experienced God, and that experience is all she needs to support her belief in God.

On the other hand, Mackie believes that the existence of evil poses a much greater challenge to theism than does any inability to prove through traditional proofs that God exists. Why is this so? Because the problem with theism exposed by the problem of evil is not that theism lacks sufficient evidence to maintain belief in God. Rather it is that "the several parts of the essential theological doctrine are inconsistent with one another, so that the theologian can maintain his position as a whole only by a much more extreme rejection of reason than in the former case. He must now be prepared to believe, not merely what cannot be proved, but what can be disproved from other beliefs that he also holds."[1]

This is indeed a robust challenge to theism, so we must be clear about exactly what Mackie and others down through the centuries have been saying. As a Christian, the place to begin is to ask whether in fact we are committed to the truth of the three claims from which the problem of evil is generated. One way to resolve the problem of evil is to deny one of those three propositions. The more intellectually interesting way is to affirm all three and then show how, despite appearances, they do fit together without contradiction. But do evangelical Christians hold all three propositions? Indeed, they do. Though various forms of evangelical theology may define omnipotence and omnibenevolence in different ways,[2] they all agree that God has these attributes.

How about the proposition about the existence of evil? Do Christians hold it? Indeed, they do, and in fact, they had better do so! If there actually is no such thing as evil, then what is the point of Christ's crucifixion? Why should he die to pay for a nonexistent malady? Lest the cross and empty tomb become meaningless, evangelicals must maintain a commitment to the belief that there is evil in our world. In fact, without the existence of evil, much of the impetus behind the incarnation itself is gone. Clearly, the existence of evil is not something Christians can discard without serious disruptions to their doctrines of Christ, sin, and salvation.

But, then, are Christians guilty of the intellectual blunder Mackie outlines? And what exactly does it mean to say that someone holds beliefs that *contradict* one another? Does it mean that there is some way that all claims fit together harmoniously, but we don't now know it? Does it mean that once we die and go to heaven, we'll understand it, but before then we just can't explain how all three propositions can be true? Does it mean that God knows how the three affirmations fit together consistently, but we don't, and since God hasn't told us how, the three appear to contradict one another?

Actually, none of these questions contains the exact complaint. To accuse someone of believing contradictory things (whether religious or nonreligious beliefs) is to say that there is no *possible* way that all of the claims can be true at once. That means that even God cannot explain how all three propositions can be true together. That inability isn't just for now;

it's forever! As you can see, this is an extremely strong objection to theism. It says that it is impossible for God, us, or any other existing being to show that the three claims are all true. And we not only cannot show the propositions to be true *now*; we will *never* be able to do so!

Since the complaint as posed is that there is no *possible* way for all three claims to be true at once, whatever else we must do to respond to this challenge, we must at least propose a *possible* way that all three claims can be true. But before turning to any proposals of a possible way, we must ask a more fundamental question. One gets the impression from reading Mackie's complaint and that of other atheists that there is one and only one problem of evil, the one already explained. This also seems to be the consensus viewpoint among theists. But is that right? Is there just one problem of evil, which confronts every theological position in exactly the same way?

As I have argued repeatedly over the last thirty-five years, this is not the proper way to conceive the problem of evil.[3] The reason is not that there actually isn't any problem that the existence of evil poses for theism. Rather, the reason is that there is no such thing as *the* problem of evil in the sense that there is one and only one problem. "The problem of evil" is actually a rubric for a broad cluster of issues. There are three major reasons for understanding the problem of evil as an issue about many problems of evil.

First, the problem of evil is not just one problem, because we can easily distinguish a number of different problems that evil's existence raises for theism. There is, for example, a theological/philosophical problem of evil which differs from the religious problem of evil. The former is about evil in general. It asks why, if there is an all-loving and all-powerful God, there is any evil at all. You don't have to be suffering to raise this question. In fact, even if there were no God and no evil, we could still pose this problem. The question would be: how, if there were an omnipotent and all-loving God (even though no such deity exists), would the existence of such a God fit with the existence of evil in our world (if evil did exist, even though it actually doesn't)? Such abstract questions delight philosophers and theologians, but they are far from what ordinary people are thinking most of the time.

In contrast, there is the religious problem of evil. This is not an abstract question, but rather a very concrete and personal dilemma. The religious problem stems from some actual evil that someone is experiencing. Moreover, the experience of that evil disrupts the sufferer's relation to God. In fact, in many cases the experience of evil precipitates a crisis of faith. Here the question is not so much how beliefs the sufferer holds can be shown to be logically consistent with one another. Rather, the problem is how the sufferer can continue to worship and serve the God who seems to have abandoned the sufferer to deal with tragedy on his own. The best-known example of someone dealing with the religious problem of evil is the biblical character Job. Job wanted intellectual answers to his theological questions, but even more he wanted an explanation of why God would put him through his trials and do nothing, apparently, to relieve the pain. Until he received reassurance that God still loved him and had a reason (one that God never divulged to Job) for not removing his pain, Job harbored a certain amount of anger toward God, even if Job wouldn't admit it. As Alvin Plantinga says about the religious problem, the person dealing with it doesn't need a philosophical discussion. He needs pastoral care.[4] There are certainly philosophical and theological questions that someone like Job has, and those must at some time be addressed, but not when the pain from the suffering is fresh and intense.

Then, we can distinguish the problem of moral evil from the problem of natural evil. Moral evil is sin, acts that are contrary to precepts of morality. Moral evil refers most specifically to human acts of sin, but angelic sin also qualifies as moral evil. The problem of moral evil is actually the same as the theological/philosophical problem of evil, for when the latter problem is posed, it invariably focuses on moral evil.

In contrast to moral evil, there is natural evil. Some natural evils result from things humans do; for example, pain and disease inflicted by the actions of one person, forest fires or fires in cities that are caused by arson, and so forth. Many natural evils happen when some aspect of the natural order goes awry. These sorts of natural evil include destruction from earthquakes and hurricanes, forest fires that result from a bolt of lightning, genetic defects that are transmitted through natural reproduction, floods, plagues and pestilences, etc. It should be clear that these kinds of events are not caused by the intervention or action of any human agent, and we have no evidence that such things result from the actions of evil angels. The critic of theism may complain that while there may be some reason for allowing moral evil (perhaps to allow humans to use their free will), it is hard to imagine why an all-powerful and all-loving God would allow natural evil in its various forms to beset the world.

Next, there are problems about the amount or degree of evil, the intensity of some evils, the apparent purposelessness of some evils, animal pain and suffering, and the problem of hell. As to the amount of evil, critics complain that while some evil in our world might serve some purpose of God, it is hard to imagine that we need as much evil as there is to accomplish divine ends. For example, whatever God's reason for allowing the Holocaust, could he not have made his point and fulfilled his purpose if only 5 million or even 3 million Jews had been killed? Evils in such huge amounts seem too excessive, if there really is an omnipotent and omnibenevolent God.

The problem of the intensity of some evils asks why some evils are so horrible. Here the point is not how many people are afflicted, but rather why certain instances of evil are so intense. Suppose someone is terminally ill, and the disease is taking its toll rather slowly. Unfortunately, it is also excruciatingly painful, and there don't seem to be any medications that will remove or even reduce the pain. Critics of theism complain that even if God has some acceptable reason for allowing someone to have this disease, it is hard to believe God's purposes require the person to suffer so severely.

Some theists believe they can satisfy atheistic complaints by showing God's purpose or use of evil. In reply, many atheists argue that though some evils may serve a divine purpose, there are still instances of evil which seem to serve no purpose (divine or otherwise) whatsoever. Try as hard as we might to explain their point, we just can't find anything positive that could come from those evils. God should at least remove them. The fact that he hasn't suggests either that God does not exist, or that if he does, he is either impotent or malevolent or both. With any of these options the traditional conception of God is in trouble.

Animal pain and suffering are often cited as unjustifiable. We needn't detail the kinds of things animals suffer either at the hands of humans or from nature. The question is why animals have to suffer at all. Suffering won't aid their spiritual or moral reformation, nor is their suffering punishment for morally evil deeds they have done. Some might reply that God uses animal pain and suffering in concert with afflictions humans experience, and the loss and/or suffering of an animal might be part of an overall set of afflictions sent upon humans in an effort to reform or punish them. Think of Job's case. Satan wanted to prove that Job served God only because God blessed him. God wanted to show Satan that some people serve God not because it pays to do so, but because God is worthy. God allowed Satan to afflict Job. Now someone might say that though they question the nature of the test God allowed Job to undergo, God does have a right to test us, and the point of the test, in part, was to exonerate Job so as to show Satan that Job was a genuinely moral and godly man. The critic might reply that, indeed, the afflictions did have a point, but why couldn't God make that point without all or most of Job's livestock being killed? It just doesn't seem fair that animals should have to suffer and die in order for God and Satan to make their respective points. So when God uses animal suffering to test some human, that seems cruel, unjust, and unnecessary to the animals involved. If one agrees, then one will also likely be disturbed when animal suffering seems to have nothing to do with what God is trying to accomplish in the life of some human being. Surely, an all-loving and all-powerful God should never allow such evils.

A final problem of evil is the problem of hell. As traditionally under-stood by Christians, hell is a place of eternal conscious punishment. It is ex-tremely unpleasant, and it never ends. On the basis of Scripture, Christians contend that everyone who has not accepted Christ as their personal Savior will wind up in hell. That applies to people who have heard the gospel and to those who have never heard and know nothing about Christ. Hell, in contrast to many evils we experience, is clearly an evil that God sends as a punishment upon nonbelievers. But critics of theism, and increasingly in our day those who are theists, complain that if hell is retributive punish-ment, it is a punishment that far exceeds anything humans have ever done. Even the most horrendous sinners have produced only a finite amount of evil (however huge it may be), and so to give them an infinite punishment seems hard to square with the justice of God. Many believe that the only ways to exonerate God's justice are for him to save everyone, or simply to annihilate upon death those who do not respond to Christ. Either of these two approaches would be far more just and benevolent than to send the majority of the human race, as traditional Christian theology holds, to eternal damnation and suffering.

Clearly, there are many problems of evil, not just one. And there is a second sense in which there is not just one problem of evil, but many. This point focuses on the theological/philosophical problem of evil. There are actually as many theological/philosophical problems of evil as there are theologies which claim that God is omnipotent, in some sense of 'omnipotence', God is all-loving, in some sense of 'omnibenevolence', and that evil, in some sense of 'evil', exists in our world.

This may sound odd since we are talking about Christian theology and many might think there is just one version of evangelical theology. However, this is not so. Even among evangelicals, there are different concepts of God and evil. An Arminian theology and a Calvinistic theology have their differences; one of special importance is their respective understandings of how divine sovereignty operates in our world in light of each theology's notion of free will. Moreover, as to divine omnipotence, some evangelicals have construed it to mean that God can do anything whatsoever, including actualizing contradictions and acting contrary to his nature. Others insist that God cannot do anything that would go contrary to his nature and character, nor can he do the logically contradictory. And, not all evangelicals hold the same ethical theory. Some hold theories that determine the morality of a deed on the basis of its consequences. Others believe that something other than consequences (for example, it follows a divine command or it agrees with what one could reasonably will to be a universal law for all people) determines whether an act is morally good or evil. Even among those who hold some form of divine command theory, there is disagreement about whether we should find our moral norms from the law of Christ alone (New Testament) or from both the Mosaic law (Old Testament) and the law of Christ (New Testament).

Each variation of views about God, man, and evil results in a distinct theology. And the existence of evil poses a specific theological/philosophical problem for each theology. Elsewhere I have detailed three broad forms of theism: theonomy, Leibnizian Rationalism, and modified rationalism.[5] Each has its own understanding of metaphysics (its conception of God and his relation to the world) and of ethics. Moreover, the existence of evil, as it confronts each form of theology, raises the problem of evil in a way different from the specific way it attacks other brands of theism. On the contemporary scene, few, if any, would espouse Leibnizian Rationalism. Some evangelicals endorse some form of theonomy, but by far the majority of contemporary evangelicals hold some form of modified rationalism. The theologies (and their respective defenses) that I plan to cover in this chapter presuppose modified rationalism.

There is a third sense in which there is not just one problem of evil. For the longest time, theists and atheists alike posed the problem of evil (and offered defenses against it) as a problem of internal consistency for theists. Uniformly the complaint has been that, however one conceives of God and his relation to the world, of human free will, and of the nature of evil, theistic belief contradicts itself in the way described earlier in this chapter. Currently, one often sees the problem of evil described in the same way.

However, over the last few decades the nature of the discussion (as evidenced in philosophical literature on the topic) has changed. Due in large part to the masterful work of Alvin Plantinga in presenting and defending the free will defense as a way to show how the three propositions in question can all be true at the same time, many atheistic and theistic philosophers have agreed that there is a way to render one's theology internally consistent. However, that doesn't mean the debate about God and evil is over. Rather, atheists have continued the battle on a different front. The complaint now is that the existence of evil provides strong evidence against the likelihood that God exists.

As philosophers discuss the problem of evil in our day, they say that the problem can be posed in one of two different forms. The more traditional form is called the logical form, and the newer form is labeled the evidential, inductive, or probabilistic form of the problem. When the logical form of the problem is at issue, the complaint is that theism contradicts itself in holding the three propositions about God and evil. In contrast, when the evidential problem is in view, the complaint is that evil's existence provides strong evidence that it is improbable that God exists. This distinction also means that many of the problems of evil already outlined may be posed in either a logical or an evidential form.

There are important practical implications of the fact that there are many problems of evil, not just one. The first is that before the debate about God and evil even starts, both sides need to clarify which problem they have in mind and whether they want to discuss it in its logical or its evidential form. Moreover, what one should say in answer to Job is surely different from an appropriate response to the evidential problem of natural evil, for example. And, a defense may be a wonderful answer to the problem of natural evils that are in no way attached to human action, but it may be totally irrelevant to what one should say if answering the logical form of the philosophical/theological problem (which is the problem of moral evil). It would also miss the boat entirely if offered in response to the religious problem of evil, a problem about a specific evil someone experiences which damages his relation to the God who apparently is doing nothing to remove the affliction.

A second implication of there being many problems of evil is that the theist must be careful to choose a defense that actually addresses the problem of evil under discussion with his nonbelieving friend. If not, the defense (our explanation of how God's and evil's existence can both be true of our world) will certainly fail the test of relevance, even if it happens to be true. And it will prove *nothing* about the validity of theism in relation to the specific problem of evil the atheist is raising.

A third implication is one atheists must take seriously. Put simply, it is illegitimate rationally and logically for the atheist to hear a defense and complain that it proves nothing because it only addresses one kind of evil. For an example of a case where this rule is ignored, one need only look at Bertha Alvarez's response to the free will defense. She complains that even if the free will defense explains how an all-loving, omnipotent God might allow moral evil, it says nothing about natural evil. Since it doesn't, the free will defense fails.[6]

While Alvarez is certainly correct that the free will defense as traditionally presented doesn't address natural evil, her conclusion about the free will defense is entirely wrong. Of course, the free will defense doesn't help us with the problem of natural evil. It was never intended to do so. It offers an answer to the problem of moral evil, and as I shall argue, it does satisfy the demands of that problem in its logical form. Alvarez's complaint ultimately amounts to saying that because the free will defense doesn't solve *every* problem of evil, it doesn't solve *any* problem of evil. But this complaint is cogent only if there is only one problem of evil and only if a defense could be adequate if it explains how every type and instance of evil squares with divine benevolence and omnipotence. Unfortunately, Alvarez doesn't seem to understand that there are many distinct problems of evil and that, therefore, you don't have to account for *every* kind of evil in order to answer *any* problem of evil. In other words, the "flip side" of the point that *theists* must offer an answer that actually addresses the problem of evil in question is the point that *atheists* cannot legitimately complain that the theist's defense against one type of evil doesn't work because it doesn't address other forms of evil.

The implications of there being more than one problem of evil are more than just practical implications. They also serve as "ground rules" for addressing the problem of evil as an atheist or as a theist. There are two further ground rules worthy of note that relate specifically to the problem of evil in its logical form. The first is that the logical problem is always and only about whether the theological system of the theist *contradicts itself.* Hence, in evaluating the theist's defense against a problem of evil, if the atheist doesn't personally think the theist's answer is very plausible, that is irrelevant. The point of the logical problem is not plausibility but internal consistency of a given theology. If the problem in view is the evidential problem, then how plausible the theist's answer is does matter. But when dealing with the logical problem, the only question that matters is whether, if one adds the defense to the theist's theology, the result is that the theology as a whole is internally logically consistent. If the theology with the defense shows how God and evil can coexist without generating a contradiction in the theology, then the defense is successful and the theology in question is exonerated.

This must not be misunderstood. Reading this, some might conclude that they can offer any answer they want, regardless of how ridiculous it is, so long as it produces a logically consistent theology. While taking such an approach does work within the rules for handling the logical problem, theists should seek to offer a defense that not only resolves the apparent contradiction, but that also is plausible. The reason is that ultimately the theist will want to do more than simply prove his theology is logically consistent. He hopes that the atheist will find his views attractive as an instrument in moving him to adopt a theistic point of view. Choosing a defense that has little or no plausibility, even if it meets the demands of the logical form of the problem, won't likely result in the atheist seriously considering belief in God as a viable option.

A final "ground rule" is that when dealing with the logical form of the problem of evil, both theist and atheist must recognize that this is a problem about the internal consistency of a theology. That means that what is in question is *not* the *atheist's* concepts of divine power and goodness or the *atheist's* understanding of evil. Rather, the only viewpoint that matters when dealing with this problem is the *theist's theology*. Hence, the theist must be careful to clarify for herself and for the atheist exactly what she (the theist) holds about God and evil. And she must be sure that her defense actually does fit the concepts of God, evil, and freedom that she actually holds. Otherwise the discussion will not be a test of the *internal* consistency of her theology.

It also goes without saying that in order for both theist and atheist to test the theologian's views, they must know what those views are. Theists should not assume that atheists will automatically know how theists define concepts like omnipotence and evil. Nor should atheists assume that they know this. Clearly, in order for the discussion to proceed, the theist must tell the atheist what her metaphysics and theory of ethics are.

For the atheist, the fact that the logical problem is always about the internal consistency of the theist's views has an important implication. It means that it is illegitimate for the atheist to attribute *his* views of God, evil, and/or freedom to the theist and then inform the theist that the theist has a problem of logical consistency that is *internal to the theist's beliefs*. If the views in question are the atheist's, not the theist's, then they will generate a contradiction, but it won't be *internal* to the beliefs the theist actually holds. Sadly, atheists often transgress this rule. Mackie again serves as an example. In discussing the free will defense, Mackie has a major objection. He notes that free will defenders argue that God cannot both give humans free will and then ensure that they never use it for evil. But Mackie disagrees, because he believes it is possible for God to give us free will and still guarantee that we never use it for evil. What Mackie has in mind presupposes a certain concept of free will. If free will defenders are required to incorporate his view of freedom into their theology, then they can't answer his objection. The problem with Mackie's objection is that free will defenders do not hold his notion of free will. Hence, he has not shown at all that God can give humans the type of free will that free will defenders have in mind and at the same time guarantee that they never use it for evil.[7]

With what I have shared so far, it is now possible to specify exactly what is at issue when someone raises a problem of evil as an objection to theistic belief. One must first decide which of the many problems of evil is in view, and also whether it is to be considered in its logical or its evidential form. If the evidential problem is in view, it would be *helpful* for the theist to clarify his views about God and evil so that both the theist and the atheist know which conception of God and evil is under scrutiny. However, if the logical form of the problem is under discussion, then it is *imperative* for the theist to state clearly his views of God and evil, and then both the theist and the atheist must be scrupulous in keeping the debate focused on views the theist actually holds. Moreover, if the logical problem is in view, the theologian's defense must meet the requirement that it renders his theology internally consistent, regardless of how plausible or implausible the defense is. Hopefully, the theist will offer a plausible explanation, but the requirement is only that the theist's defense shows a possible way for propositions about God's nature and evil's existence to be conjointly true.

Choosing a Problem and Clarifying the Theology

While there is great value in addressing the evidential problem of evil, for our purposes it would be best to handle the logical problem of evil. Those who are interested in pursuing the evidential problem are welcome to consult my *Many Faces of Evil*, chapters 8–12 for a detailed discussion of the current debate and my responses to the evidential problem.

In the remainder of this chapter, I shall offer two defenses against the logical problem of moral evil. Both presuppose the same broad form of theism, and both espouse the same basic account of ethics. The first of these defenses is the free will defense, which fits well an Arminian theology. While I believe the free will defense does solve the logical problem of moral evil for Arminian theologies, my theology is Calvinistic. Hence, the second defense I'll present is my own defense, which has at times been called the integrity of humans defense. Since we are dealing with the logical form of the problem of evil, what is at issue is whether the free will defender's theology is internally consistent and whether my theology is internally consistent. My contention is that both defenses render their theology internally consistent and hence solve their logical problem of moral evil. In what follows, I'll explain how they do so.

A Word about the Strategy of Defenses

Before turning directly to these theologies and their defenses, a word about the strategy of most defenses will help readers understand the logic that underlies them. Elsewhere I have detailed this basic strategy, and it would help to articulate it here.[8] The four-part strategy[9] I shall present doesn't apply to the religious problem of evil, but seems implicit in handling the logical form of the problem of evil for Christian theologies other than theonomy.[10]

The theologian begins by defining divine omnipotence to mean that God can do whatever is logically possible and does not contradict his divine nature. Thus, he cannot actualize a world with contradictory states of affairs. Nor can he sin. Though sinning is not a logical impossibility, i.e., the very idea doesn't contain a contradiction as does the idea of a married bachelor, God cannot do it because of his absolutely holy nature. If the theist holds a view of divine omnipotence which allows God to actualize contradictory states of affairs, then the theist's theology may in fact contain a contradiction. So, in order for theists to meet the critic's charge that the existence of evil makes their theologies internally inconsistent, it would be best to hold a notion of divine omnipotence which doesn't allow God to actualize contradictions.

The second step in the strategy of defense and theodicy-making invokes a commonly held ethical principle. That principle is that no one can be held morally accountable for failing to do what they couldn't do or for doing what they couldn't fail to do. In other words, no one is morally accountable unless they act freely. As we shall see, most theologies claim that God is not free both to remove evil and to accomplish some other positive goal in our world. Hence, he isn't guilty for failing to do both.

Third, the theist argues that in creating a world, God had to choose between including in it either one or the other of two good things. The two goods are mutually contradictory, so God couldn't include both, because the theist's definition of omnipotence won't allow God to actualize a contradiction. Regardless of the particular theology, one of the two options will be removing evil. As to the other option, each theology presents some other valuable thing God could do in creating a world. For Leibniz, it is creating the best of all possible worlds. The free will defender says God's second option was to create a world with incompatibilistically free creatures. John Hick (*Evil and the God of Love*)[11] holds that the second option was to create a world suitable for building souls. For my theology, the second option is creating a world with non-glorified human beings.

Once the theist presents these two options, he argues that God cannot do both conjointly. If he removes evil, he can't also create the best of all possible worlds. If he gives us libertarian free will, he can't remove evil.

Hick claims that to build souls there must be evil, so God can't both build souls and remove evil. My defense says that if God removes evil, he can't also create non-glorified human beings and let them function in our world as God intended. In each case, one option logically excludes the other. Since the theist's concept of divine omnipotence doesn't allow God to actualize contradictions, God can't both remove evil and include the other valuable thing in our world.

Someone might agree that God isn't guilty for failing to actualize both options, but still wonder why God chose the one he did, rather than removing evil. If God chose something evil (or at least a lesser good than removing evil), then it still seems that God did something wrong. This brings us to the final step in the strategy. The theist agrees that if God had chosen to remove evil, he would have done something very good. However, the theist argues that the option God chose is a value of such magnitude that it is at least as valuable as removing evil. It either counterbalances or overbalances the evil present in our world. Hence, in choosing this option instead of removing evil, God has done nothing wrong.

In sum, the basic strategy of theodicy and defense-making is to argue that God is a good God, despite the evil in our world, because he can't remove it. He can't, because even an omnipotent God can't actualize a contradiction. God could either remove evil or do something else of value with our world, but not both conjointly, because the two contradict each other. Since he can't do both, he isn't guilty for failing to do both. Moreover, what he did choose put a value of the highest order into our world. God has fulfilled his moral obligation; he is a good God. In the upcoming discussion of two defenses, this four-part strategy is implicit.

Two Modified Rationalist Defenses

Given the strategy just outlined, how would a Christian theist solve the problem of evil? Here we must first specify which problem is in view and also articulate the essentials of the theology under consideration. We have already decided to handle the problem of moral evil in its logical form. Now I need to describe the metaphysics and account of evil for the theologies under consideration.

I have already mentioned three forms of Christian theism: theonomy, Leibnizian Rationalism, and modified rationalism. The two theologies I shall discuss in more detail are both forms of modified rationalism, so I must recount the metaphysics and ethics of that broad form of theism.[12]

Modified rationalism is a metaphysical system that holds that God isn't required to create anything, for his own existence is the highest good. However, creating a world is a fitting thing for him to do, but not the only fitting thing he can do. There is an infinite number of finite, contingent possible worlds that God could create. Some are intrinsically evil, so God had better not create any of them, but at least more than one is a good possible world. There is no best possible world. God is free either to create one of the good possible worlds or not to create at all. Finally, in the modified rationalist's universe, some things are known by reason and/or revelation, whereas others can be known only through divine revelation.

Modified rationalist theologies incorporate one of two broad accounts of ethics: consequentialism or nonconsequentialism. Consequentialist ethical theories hold that what makes an action morally right is its consequences. Whatever deeds produce a desired non-moral value (like increasing pleasure and removing pain) are both morally good and obligatory to do. In contrast, nonconsequentialist theories contend that what makes an act morally right or wrong is something other than its consequences. An act may be right and obligatory because duty demands it or God prescribes it, for example, but then, what makes it morally right is something besides its results.

Consequentialism and nonconsequentialism apply to the problem of evil in very specific ways. According to consequentialist ethics, the world as created from God's hand contains evil, but that results in no moral stain on God, because he will ultimately use this evil to maximize good. Clearly, with this account of ethics, God has acted morally despite the evil in our world, if God uses that evil to produce some counterbalancing or overbalancing good. In contrast, nonconsequentialist systems say that the world as created from God's hand contains no evil in it. Evil is introduced into the world by the actions of God's creatures. On this account of ethics, God has acted morally despite the evil in our world, if the world as created contained no evil, and if he placed in it some value of the first order. If so, then, even though God's creatures do evil, God in creating our world did nothing wrong.

In light of this account of metaphysics and ethics, how would a problem of evil arise for a modified rationalist theology? The problem can be stated in the form of the following question: is our world one of those good (in the sense the modified rationalist defines 'good') possible worlds that the modified rationalist believes God could have created? In addressing this question, modified rationalist theologians will point to some valuable feature of our world and claim that it makes our world one of those good worlds. Note that the modified rationalist's God isn't required to create the best of all possible worlds, for the modified rationalist doesn't believe there is such a thing. Nor must this God create a good world which is better than other good worlds he might have created. The modified rationalist maintains that there are good and evil possible worlds. If God decides to create a world, his moral obligation is to create one of the good ones. So long as modified rationalists can explain why our world is a good world, despite the moral evil in it, their God isn't guilty of failing to meet his moral obligation.

The Free Will Defense

Is our world one of those good possible worlds? Many Christian theists have held that it is because it contains human beings with free will, a value deemed to be of the first order. In fact, even many Calvinists have appealed to the free will defense in answer to the problem of evil. Unfortunately, making such an appeal generates a contradiction in the Calvinist's theology. The reason, as we shall see, is that the free will defense presupposes incompatibilistic or libertarian free will. However, Calvinists are determinists. Determinists who believe humans have free will hold compatibilism and reject libertarian free will. Hence, Calvinists should look elsewhere to solve their problem of evil.[13]

Though soft determinists such as I cannot use the free will defense to solve their problem of moral evil, it is still worthwhile to examine this defense. After all, the Calvinist knows there are various forms of evangelical theology. Atheists claim that none of them can solve their problem of evil. If an Arminian theology can solve its problem of evil, that only helps Christian theists, regardless of their views on free will, to make the overall point that atheists are wrong when they claim that no form of theism can solve the problem of evil. Similarly, Arminian theologians should rejoice when Calvinists present a defense that shows their form of theism is internally consistent. In the debate about God and evil, Christian theists, regardless of their exact views on free will, etc., must see that the enemy is not other Christian theists. The enemy is the atheist and the agnostic who don't believe in God and think the existence of evil justifies their rejection of God.

The free will defense, of course, is a defense for any theist committed to libertarian free will. The defense also presupposes a modified rationalist metaphysic. Moreover, it is fundamentally nonconsequentialist in its ethics; hence, it claims that the world as created by God is good, but moral evil is introduced into the world by God's creatures, humans in particular.[14] Augustine is one of the free will defense's earliest proponents, and we can see in his work the essentials of this defense.

Augustine begins book 1 of *On the Free Choice of the Will* by asking whether God is the cause of evil, and he answers that God is not. Instead, each of us causes the evil we willfully commit.[15] In the rest of book 1, Augustine discusses God's nature, and then he turns to a lengthy consideration of various kinds of evils (how they arise and how they relate to the will). As to how evils arise, Augustine says the problem stems from our desires. Desires in themselves needn't be problematic, but we get into trouble when we desire temporal things rather than eternal things, and when we do so excessively.[16] Once excessive desires are present in us, we exercise our will in accord with them and bring evil into the world.

Toward the end of book 1 Augustine asks why God gave us free will, if he knew we could and would abuse it.[17] Augustine begins book 2 with his basic answer, and in the rest of books 2 and 3 he fills in further details. He writes of various types of goods as follows:

> Therefore the virtues, by which men live rightly, are great goods, while all kinds of physical beauties [*species*], without which no one can live rightly, are the intermediate goods [*media bona*] between these two. No one uses the virtues for evil. However, the other goods, the lowest and the intermediate ones, can be used not only for good, but also for evil.[18]

According to Augustine, all of these goods come from God, and free will is an intermediate good, because it can be used to produce either good or evil.[19]

Since free will is an intermediate good that can be used for evil, should God have given it to us? Augustine answers that God was right in doing so, because we can use it to do good. If we abuse our free will, that isn't God's fault, and the possibility of abusing free will is worth it in view of the possibility of using free will to do good.[20]

Another question still remains, however. Isn't God still responsible for the evil we do with free will, because he must have foreknown that we would use our freedom to do evil? In book 3 Augustine emphatically argues that God's foreknowledge of our sins does not make them necessary. Moreover, we are responsible for our sin, because we could have done otherwise; our decision to sin is voluntary.[21] In addition, free will defenders add that God also knew that though we would use this freedom for evil, many would use it to do good and love him. God reasoned that it was worth putting up with the possibility and actuality of our using freedom to do evil, because he preferred to have creatures who would love and obey him because they wanted to, not because they were forced to do so.

So, free will is a value of the first order that shows that ours is one of those good possible worlds God could have created. But, he cannot both give us free will and guarantee that there will be no moral evil in our world. Sadly, we have used our freedom to sin, but ours is still a good world, and many use their freedom to do good as well.

On the contemporary scene, no one has defended the free will defense as vigorously and ably as Alvin Plantinga. But it has also had its detractors, and it would be worth noting one of the major objections raised against the defense. I maintain that the complaint is misguided, but hearing it and seeing how it is problematic is very instructive. I shall summarize the main thrust of the objection that J. L. Mackie has raised against the free will defense. We may call it Mackie's "good choosing argument."[22] Mackie writes:

> I should ask this: if God has made men such that in their free choices they sometimes prefer what is good and sometimes what is evil, why *could he not have made men such* that they *always freely choose the good*? If there is no logical impossibility in a man's freely choosing the good on one, or on several occasions, there cannot be a logical impossibility in his freely choosing the good on every occasion. God was not, then, faced with a choice between making innocent automata and making beings who, in acting freely, would sometimes go wrong: there was open to him the obviously better possibility of *making beings who would act freely but always go right*. Clearly, his failure to avail himself of this possibility is inconsistent with his being both omnipotent and wholly good[23] (italics mine).

Mackie's objection sounds cogent in part, because free will means that a person can do either good or evil. If so, on one occasion a person might use his freedom to do good. Moreover, it is at least *possible* that someone would use his freedom on every occasion to do good. If it isn't impossible for us to do good on every occasion, and if God is omnipotent, why can't he make it the case that we always freely do what is right? In essence, Mackie rejects the underlying assumption of the free will defense, namely, that if God creates a world with free creatures, he cannot at the same time so control them that the world has no moral evil. Mackie argues that God can do both, and hence, the free will defense fails.

Alvin Plantinga and numerous other free will defenders have responded as we might expect. What Mackie proposes may sound reasonable, but it actually isn't. If God *makes it the case* or *brings it about* that we do anything, then we don't do it *freely*! Hence, God can't guarantee that there will be no moral evil and give us free will at the same time.[24]

As one reflects on this response, it certainly seems to make sense. In essence, doesn't it imply that Mackie misunderstands the very meaning of free will? That seems to be the underlying message of this rejoinder. But how likely is it that a seasoned philosopher like Mackie doesn't know how to define free will? Not very likely, but neither is it even remotely thinkable that a philosopher as astute as Alvin Plantinga would be wrong about the definition of free will.

But then what is going on in this interchange between the free will defender and his critic? The answer is that we have before us two different concepts of free will. According to libertarian free will, genuine free human action is incompatible with causal determinism. Thus, regardless of how many and what kind of causes impact the will as the agent chooses, no individual cause nor all of them collectively are strong enough to move the will to choose one option over another. Hence, regardless of what the agent chooses to do, he could just as easily have done otherwise. With this definition of libertarian free will, it should be clear that God cannot guarantee ("make it the case" or "bring it about") that anyone will do anything *freely*, for guarantees invoke causal determinism, but libertarian free will cannot coexist with causal determinism. It is this kind of free will that the free will defense incorporates.

In contrast, there is another notion of free will which some determinists hold. It is known as compatibilism or soft deterministic free will. According to compatibilism, genuine free human action is compatible with causal conditions that decisively incline the will without constraining it. This means that there can be guarantees about what someone will do, because the causes playing upon his will when he chooses are strong enough to move him to choose one option over the others. According to compatibilists, so long as the causes don't constrain the will, the agent chooses freely. To act under constraint is to act contrary to what one wishes to do. So, according to compatibilism, an action is causally determined but still free so long as the agent does what she wishes/wants to do.[25]

Even the casual observer should see that compatibilism blatantly contradicts incompatibilism. Moreover, it should also be clear that Mackie's objection to the free will defense makes sense only if one defines free will as do compatibilists. Thus, the free will defense and Mackie's objection rest on competing notions of human freedom.

What does this mean, however, for whether the free will defense solves the problem of moral evil for its theology? When we remember the "ground rules" of the logical form of the problem of evil (and that is the form under discussion now), we see that Mackie's objection is misguided. The logical problem of evil accuses theists of contradicting *themselves*, and that just means that to succeed in destroying the theist's system, the critic must show that views the theist actually holds contradict other beliefs the same theist espouses. Now, it is clear that Mackie holds compatibilistic free will, but the free will defender doesn't. But then, Mackie is generating a problem in the free will defender's system by attributing to it compatibilism, and of course, any free will defender who incorporates compatibilism in her system contradicts herself. Since free will defenders hold libertarian free will, not compatibilism, Mackie hasn't shown any inconsistency *internal* to theologies that solve their logical problem of moral evil by appealing to the free will defense. But the requirements of the logical form of the problem of evil demand that the alleged contradiction between God and evil must be shown to exist *within* (*internal to*) the theology under consideration. Mackie's objection fails to meet this requirement! In short, his objection does not demonstrate that God could both give humans *libertarian* free will *and* guarantee that our world would be rid of moral evil. The free will defense does render free will theologies internally consistent on this matter. Traditional Arminians and open view theists (even some process theists) use the free will defense to solve this problem of evil, and they succeed.

As a Calvinist, I welcome this result, for it shows that atheists who claim that no theist can solve the problem of evil are wrong. Nonetheless, I have argued in chapters 11 and 13–15 of *No One Like Him* that there are good reasons for rejecting libertarian free will and the theologies that incorporate it. Hence, while I agree that the free will defense renders these theologies internally consistent, I think these theologies as a whole are deficient. My objections, however, in no way show that the free will defense doesn't succeed in resolving this particular problem of alleged internal inconsistency.

There is a price to pay for rejecting theologies with libertarian free will in favor of a theology committed to compatibilistic free will. The price is that what Mackie proposes seems totally possible with compatibilism. That is, with compatibilism, it appears that God can make it the case that we always freely (compatibilistically) do what is right. But then, why hasn't he done so? As a compatibilist, my answer cannot appeal to the free will defense, for that assumes a different notion of freedom than I hold. I must offer an answer that incorporates compatibilism and at the same time explains why God cannot remove moral evil. To that defense I now turn.

Integrity of Humans Defense

My soft determinist Calvinist theology also presupposes a modified rationalist metaphysic. As to ethics, I am a nonconsequentialist. In particular, I hold a modified divine command theory. That is, I believe moral norms are prescribed by God, but I don't believe God prescribes arbitrarily. Instead, his precepts reflect his character.[26]

My defense against the logical problem of moral evil has three stages.[27] I ask first what sort of beings God intended to create when he made humans. Here I refer to the basic abilities and capacities God gave humans. At minimum, I believe he intended to make creatures with ability to reason (that ability varies for each person), beings with emotions, beings with wills that are compatibilistically free (although freedom isn't the emphasis of my defense), beings with desires, beings with intentions (formed on the basis of desires), and beings with the capacity for bodily movement. Moreover, he intended us to use these capacities to live and function in a world suited to beings like us. Thus, he created our world, which is run according to natural laws, and he evidently didn't intend to annihilate creation once he made it.

In addition, God didn't want each of us to be identical in respect to these capacities. For example, some might have certain desires to the same degree other humans do, but in no two people would all these qualities of human nature be conjoined so as to obliterate individuality. In other words, character traits wouldn't be so similar in any two people that they would be stereotypes of one another. Finally, God intended to make beings who are finite both metaphysically and morally (as to the moral aspect, our finitude doesn't necessitate doing evil, but means only that we don't have God's infinite moral perfection). In sum, God intended to create non-glorified human beings, not glorified humans, subhuman or superhuman beings, or even gods.

I don't believe any of these qualities were lost by the race's fall into sin. Of course, I believe that sin has affected us and our world, but my point is that sin didn't result in the removal of desires, intentions, free will, bodily movement, and the like. Because of our fall into sin, these capacities don't function as well as they would without sin, but that doesn't mean we no longer have them. Likewise, the fall didn't overturn the basic laws of nature and physics according to which our world runs. The fundamental features of humanity and of our world are still as God created them.

How do I know this is what God intended? By looking at the kind of beings he created when he formed us, and by noting also that the world in which we live is suited to our capacities. Someone may reply that this same line of reasoning could be used to say God also intended to create moral evil, because we have it, but that is not so. Moral evil isn't something God created when he made other things. It isn't a substance at all. God created substances, including the world and the people in it. God intended that we could act, for he made us able to act. But he neither made our actions, nor does he perform them. Hence, we can't say God intended there to be moral evil because we have it in our world. God intended to create and did create agents who can act; he didn't create their acts (good or evil).

How do we know by looking at what God did that he really intended to do it? Don't others at times act without fully understanding their own intentions? It is true that humans don't always know what they intend to do, but that can't be true of an omniscient being's awareness of his intentions. By seeing what he did, we can be sure we know what he really intended to do.

If humans are the kind of creatures I have described, how do they come to do moral evil (sin)? This brings me to the second stage of my defense, a consideration of the ultimate source of evil deeds. My answer isn't free will, although I agree that free exercise of will is instrumental in bringing about moral evil. However, as a compatibilist, I dare not use the free will defense.

In accord with James 1:13–15, I hold that morally evil deeds stem from human desires. Desires in and of themselves aren't evil nor do they perform the evil. James says, however, that desires (*epithumia* is the word for desire, and it can refer to any desire) are carried away (*exelkomenos*) and enticed (*deleazomenos*) to the point where sin is actually committed (conceived).[28] Many moral philosophers would agree that the point of "conception" is when a person wills to do the act if she could. Once that decision is made, it remains only for her to translate that choice into overt public action.[29]

Morally evil acts, then, ultimately stem from our desires. When desires are aroused so as to lead us to disobey God's prescribed moral norms, then we have sinned. Desires aren't the only culprit, however, for will, reason, and emotion, for example, also enter into the process. But James says temptation and sinful deeds start with our desires.

If humans are the sort of creatures described, and if moral evil arises as I have suggested, what would God have to do to get rid of moral evil? This brings me to the final stage of my defense. If removing evil is God's only goal, he certainly can accomplish it. However, my view of divine omnipotence doesn't allow God to actualize contradictions, so if I can show that by removing evil God would contradict some other goal(s) he wants to accomplish, then I will have shown why God can't remove evil. Of course, if he *can't* create a utopia without producing further and greater problems, he isn't required to do so.

It is my contention that if God did what is necessary to rid our world of moral evil, he would either contradict his intentions to create human beings and the world as he has, cause us to wonder if he has one or more of the attributes ascribed to him, and/or do something we wouldn't expect or desire him to do, because it would produce greater evil than there already is. To see this, let us consider how God might get rid of moral evil.

Some may think all God needs to do to remove moral evil is just arrange affairs so that his compatibilistically free creatures are causally determined to have desires only for the good and to choose only good without being constrained at all. For each of us, God should know what it would take, and he should be powerful enough to do it.

However, this isn't as simple as it sounds. If people are naturally inclined to do what God wants, God may need to do very little rearranging of our world to accomplish this goal. If people are stubborn and resist his will, it may take a great deal more maneuvering than we think. God would have to do this for everyone every time we resist his will. Moreover, changes in circumstances for one of us would affect circumstances for others, for we don't live in isolation. But what might be needed to get us to do good might disrupt others' lives, constrain them to do something that serves God's purposes in regard to us, and perhaps even turn them toward doing evil.

Consider, for example, what God might have to do to move even one person to choose good freely. To convince that person to do right would probably require rearrangements in other people's lives, changes that would require them to do things they don't want to do. If God wants those other people to do what he wants unconstrainedly, he may need to rearrange even other people's lives. To get that third group of people to do unconstrainedly what he wants may require yet more people to do something they don't want to do. I could continue, but the picture is clear. To uphold everyone's freedom may be much more difficult than we suppose. It is more likely that the free will of some will be abridged as a result of God's attempts to convince certain people to do good.

There is further reason to believe it may be harder than we think for God to get us to do right. God didn't create us with an inclination toward sin, but even Adam in ideal surroundings and circumstances did sin. According to Scripture, the race inherited from Adam a sin nature that disposes us toward evil. In light of that sin nature, it isn't at all clear that a minimal rearranging of events, actions, and circumstances would achieve the goal of getting us to do good without constraining us. It might turn out that God would need to constrain many people to do things he needed done in order to organize circumstances to convince a few of us to do the right thing without constraining us. Of course, that would contradict compatibilistic free will for many of us, and would likely do so more frequently than we might imagine. Moreover, one begins to wonder how wise this God is if he must do all of this just to bring it about that his human creatures do good. Why not at the outset just make a different creature who couldn't do evil? But, of course, that would contradict God's decision to make humans, not subhumans or superhumans.

There is a further problem with getting rid of evil this way. This method also assumes that if God rearranged the world, all of us would draw the right conclusion from our circumstances and do right. Our desires, intentions, emotions, and will would all fall into place as they should without abridging freedom at all. This is most dubious, given our finite minds and wills as well as the sin nature within us that inclines us toward evil. Hence, it isn't clear that we can coherently conceive all the changes God would have to make to ensure that we got the right message and acted morally.

Perhaps there is a simpler, more direct way for God to get rid of evil. Although we might wonder what other avenue is open to God, there are at least eight other ways God might get rid of evil. However, none of them would be acceptable. First, he could remove moral evil by doing away with mankind. Not only is this a drastic solution all of us would deem unacceptable, but it would also contradict God's intent to create humans who live and function in the world he made.

A second way to remove moral evil is for God to eliminate all objects of desire. Without objects of desire, it is hard to see how our desires could be led astray to do moral evil. However, to eradicate all objects of desire God would have to destroy the whole world and everything in it, including human bodies. Minds alone would remain, unless minds could be objects of desire that might lead someone astray.

Objections to this option are obvious. Its implications for human life and well-being make it unacceptable. Moreover, the God I have described would have to reject it, because adopting it would contradict his intentions to create humans and put them in a world which he didn't plan to annihilate once he created it.

Since sin ultimately stems from desires, a third way for God to rid the world of moral evil would be to remove human desires. Problems with this solution again are obvious. God intended to create creatures who have desires, but if he removes all human desires, that contradicts his plans about the creature he wanted to create. Moreover, removing desires would also remove the ultimate basis of action so that people wouldn't act, and that would contradict God's decision to create beings who perform the various actions necessary to remain alive. Of course, if that happened, the ultimate demise of the race would result. Surely, that would be less desirable than our world is now.

A fourth possibility seems to be one of the more likely things God could do. He could allow us to have desires but never let them be aroused to the point where we do moral evil (perhaps not even to the point where we would form intentions to do evil). Now, since any desire can lead to evil, this means that we would retain all our desires, but God would eliminate or neutralize them once they approach or reach a degree of arousal that would result in intending or willing an act of moral evil. If God chose this option, he could accomplish it in one of two ways. He could make us with the capacity for our desires to run rampant, but then perform a miracle to stop them whenever they start to do so. Or, God could make us so that our desires would only be aroused to a certain degree, a degree that would never be or lead to evil. I shall address the former option when I discuss more generally God removing evil by performing a miracle. The latter option concerns me now.

As for that option, there are several problems. For one thing, it contradicts God's intent to create people who aren't stereotypes of one another. I do not mean that people would always desire the same things. Rather, whenever someone's desires were allured to something forbidden, those desires could be enticed only up to a point, a point that wouldn't be evil or lead to it. What would be true of one person would be true of all. This might appear to leave much room for individuality, but not necessarily. Any desire can lead to evil, and God knows when a given desire, if pursued, would do so. In every such case, we would need to be preprogrammed to squelch the desire before it went too far. That would seem to make us stereotypes of one another more often than we might think.

There is another problem with God making us this way. Imagine what life would be like. Whenever a desire would start to run amuck, we would have to stop having the desire (or at least not follow it), change desires, and begin a new course of action. The picture that comes to mind is one where our daily routines are constantly interrupted (if not stopped altogether) and new courses of action are implemented only to be interrupted and new ones implemented and interrupted ad infinitum. Life as we know it would probably come to a standstill. The world envisioned would be a different world (perhaps radically different), but not necessarily better or even as good as our world. Moreover, it would seemingly contradict God's intent to create us so as to function in this world.

Perhaps the greatest objection to this fourth option is that to make us this way God would have to make us superhuman both morally and intellectually. We wouldn't have to be divine or angelic, but we would have to be much different morally and intellectually than we now are. In order to make us so that our desires wouldn't get out of hand, God would have to make us willing to squelch them whenever they would lead to evil (a hard enough thing to do). To do this we would also need to *know* when desires would lead to evil, so that we could stop them from being overly enticed. Whatever God would have to do to make us this way, it seems it would involve making us more than human. If so, God would contradict his decision to make human beings, not superhuman beings.

Fifth, God could allow all desires and allow us to form intentions for actions based on those desires, unless the intentions would lead to evil. God could remove these intentions in either of the ways mentioned for handling evil-producing desires (by miracles or by making us so we would never develop intentions that lead to evil). However, removing evil by handling intentions this way faces the same problems raised in regard to desires.

Sixth, God might remove moral evil by erasing any willing that would produce evil. We could will good things freely (compatibilistically), but whenever we might will evil, the willing would be eliminated. God could do this either by miraculous intervention (to be discussed later) or by making us so that we would never will evil. However, removing evil this way faces the same kinds of objections that confront the desire and intention options.

Seventh, God could eliminate the public expression of moral evil by stopping our bodily movement whenever we try to carry out evil. He could do this either by miracle or by making us so as to stop bodily movement when it would lead to evil. Bodily movement would probably be interrupted and stopped quite often. However, this option faces the same kinds of objections the desire, intention, and will options face.

If all of these ways are problematic, perhaps God could still rid the world of moral evil by miraculous intervention at any of the various mental and physical phases of action. Several problems, however, beset this method of removing moral evil. First, if God did this, it would greatly change life as we know it. At any moment, God would miraculously stop desires, intentions, willing, or bodily movement if he knew they would lead to evil. Since we wouldn't always know when our actions would lead to evil,[30] we often wouldn't know when to expect God to interfere. We might become too afraid to do, try, or even think anything, realizing that at any moment, our movements or thoughts could be eliminated. Under those circumstances, life as we know it might come to a standstill, and that would contradict God's desire to create people who live and function in this world. Moreover, it isn't at all clear that a world in which there is a constant threat of remov-

The Problem of Evil

ing our thoughts, willing, or bodily movements would be a better world or even as good a world as the one we have.

Second, it is one thing to speak of God miraculously intervening to eradicate desires, intentions, willing, or bodily movements that lead to evil. It is another to specify exactly what that means. As for bodily movement, God would probably have to paralyze a person as long as necessary (perhaps indefinitely) to stop bodily movements that would carry out an evil act. Of course, stopping bodily movement this way even momentarily would alter the nature of life altogether. Every few moments, series of people would be paralyzed while trying to carry out an action. Once they agree to change their actions, they would begin to move again while yet other people would be paralyzed. It isn't clear that this would be a better world than ours, and it would apparently contradict God's intention to make creatures who can live and function in this world.

In addition, it is difficult to imagine what miracle God would have to do to remove a desire, intention, or act of willing that would lead to evil. It hardly makes sense to talk about paralysis of intention, desire, or will. God would probably have to knock us unconscious or cause us to lose our memory for as long and as often as needed in order to remove evil-producing thoughts. The picture one gets is of a world of people who fall in and out of consciousness and undergo periodic spells of amnesia. Wouldn't that virtually bring life to a standstill and thereby be inconsistent with God's intention to make us so that we can live and function in this world?

Up to this point in my defense, I have been discussing evil that is voluntarily produced. If a world where God removes those sorts of actions is problematic, then there is even more reason for concern when one realizes that involuntary and reflex actions can also produce evil. If it would be disruptive to normal life to remove our evil-intentioned acts, it would be even more disruptive to remove our good-intentioned actions and reflex actions that produce evil. Regardless of someone's intentions, God would know when an act would bring evil to someone else. In order to rid our world of evil, God would have to remove those actions as well.[31] If life would likely come to a standstill if we knew evil-intentioned acts would be interrupted, think of how much more paralyzing it would be to know that *any* action could be stopped![32]

A final objection to removing evil miraculously is that it would give reason to question God's wisdom. If God goes to all the trouble to make human beings as he has, but then must perform these miracles to counteract them when they express that humanness in ways that would produce evil, there is reason to ask about God's wisdom in making us as he did. Of course, had God made us differently so that he wouldn't have to remove evil by miracles, that would contradict his desire to make the sort of beings he has made. So, either God must perform miracles and thereby raise questions about his wisdom, or he must change our nature as human beings, something that would contradict his goal of making humans, not superhumans or subhumans.

This discussion about what God would have to do to remove moral evil shows that God *cannot* remove it without contradicting his desires to make the kind of creature and world he has made, causing us to doubt the accuracy of ascribing to him attributes like wisdom, or making a world we wouldn't want and would consider more evil than our present world. Someone may suggest that God could avoid all these problems if he made different creatures than human beings. In other words, why not make creatures without desires, intentions, will, and/or bodily movement?

God could do this, and if he did, it would likely remove moral evil, but it would also remove human beings as we know them. It is hard to know what to call the resultant creature since it would neither move nor think— even "robot" seems too complimentary. Anyone who thinks there is any worth in being human would find this unacceptable.

Someone else might object that God shouldn't make us subhuman, but moral evil could be avoided if he made us superhuman. I agree that God could do this, but I contend that humans as we know them are a value of the first order. Scripture says humans are created in God's image (Gen. 1:26–27); it never says this of angels, animals, or any other creature. Moreover, when God completed his creative work, he saw that all of it, including human beings, was very good (Gen. 1:31). Psalm 8:5–8 speaks of God crowning us with glory and honor and giving us dominion over the other parts of his creation. In light of this evaluation by God, who are we to say that humans as created by God aren't valuable? As a modified rationalist, all I need to show is that our world is one of those good possible worlds God could have created. Clearly, a world with human beings in it is a good world.

Another objection confronts not only my theology, but many other evangelical Christian systems. Theists, including myself, often say our world is a good world because of some feature in it, but we also believe in a future state (call it the kingdom of God or the eternal state) in which there will be no evil. It is agreed that, morally speaking, this will be a better world than our present world. Since God not only can create this better world but will some day, why didn't he do it in the first place? Since it will be a better world and God could have created it, the fact that he didn't suggests to some that something is wrong with him.

I respond initially that this objection demonstrates no internal inconsistency in my theology or in any other evangelical Christian system. Critics of theism might reject all evangelical theologies on this ground, but that wouldn't be a rejection on grounds of inability to solve a logical problem of evil, a problem of internal inconsistency.

More directly to the point, this is a significant objection, but it contains a confusion. The confusion centers around what a modified rationalist theology is required to do to solve its logical problem of evil. Modified rationalists don't claim there is a best world, but they do claim there is more than one good possible world. Moreover, modified rationalism doesn't demand that God create the best world or even a better world than some other good world. It only requires God to create a good possible world. The task for a modified rationalist, then, is to look at the world God *did* create and explain why it is good in spite of the evil in it.

Since this is the requirement, neither I nor any other modified rationalist needs to show that our world is the best or even better than some other good world God might have created. We need only to show that ours is one of those good worlds God could have created. I have done that by pointing to human beings, and arguing that God cannot both create them and remove evil. Hence, I have solved my theology's logical problem of moral evil.[33]

Can God remove moral evil from our world? I believe he can, if he creates different creatures than human beings. He also can if he creates humans and then removes evil in any of the ways imagined. But we have seen the problems that arise if God takes any of those options.

Has God done something wrong in creating human beings? Not at all, when we consider the great value human beings have and the great worth God places upon us. As an empirical fact, we can say that moral evil has come as a concomitant of a world populated with human beings. Still, it is one of those good possible worlds God could have created. God is a good God; our world with human beings demonstrates his goodness. This defense against moral evil renders my theology internally consistent, and hence solves its logical problem of evil.

CONCLUSION

Both a Calvinistic and an Arminian theology can solve their problem of moral evil in its logical form. There are other problems of evil, and other theists and I have addressed them elsewhere.[34] Some may still reject either Arminianism or Calvinism (or both) altogether, because they believe it has an inadequate account of God, man, sin, or salvation. However, from what I have shown in this chapter, one cannot legitimately reject either an Arminian theology that uses the free will defense or a Calvinistic system like mine with its defense on the ground that they can't solve their respective problems of moral evil in their logical form.

Some may complain that at most I have shown a way to make these theologies internally consistent, but that still doesn't tell us whether they and their defenses are true. Hence the problem of evil hasn't been solved by either. However, if one understands the "ground rules" for handling the problem of evil, one sees that the preceding discussion handles the logical problem of moral evil for an Arminian and a Calvinistic theology successfully.

This complaint, however, shows the importance of clarifying at the outset the nature of the attack on theism. As we saw, the complaint that atheists raise initially is that theologies committed to the existence of an omnipotent, omnibenevolent God and evil contradict themselves. This, of course, poses the problem of evil in its logical form. Since the charge of contradiction means that there is no *possible* way that the theology in question can resolve the apparent contradiction, all that is required of the theist is that she show a possible way all the relevant claims could be true. Now it may turn out that the free will defense or my defense offer the actual reason(s) God had for not removing evil, but that is not at issue when dealing with the logical problem of moral evil. Both the free will defense and my defense offer a possible way that God can be both all-powerful and all-loving and at the same time there can be evil in our world. I believe both of these defenses also suggest *plausible* answers, but demonstrating that is for another time and place. It is not true that Christians committed to the three propositions with which we began are guilty of holding a self-contradictory theology.

Chapter 11

The Reliability of
the Gospels

Many religions have a holy book, so Christianity is not unique in that respect. However, few, if any, portray the lives of individuals at the heart of that religion in such careful detail as we find in the Bible. This is especially so in regard to Jesus, whose life, ministry, death, burial, and resurrection are presented with much detail. Events like the incarnation, the transfiguration, Christ's miracles, and his death and resurrection are not merely the basis for various Christian doctrines. The Scriptures present these events as happening within space and time, and if the events portrayed are not facts of history, then the most fundamental doctrines of Christianity are suspect. It is safe to say that in no other religion (with the possible exception of biblical Judaism) does the credibility of the religion's essential doctrines rely so heavily on the events involving that religion's main character(s) being actual historical events.

In the New Testament, the Gospels and Acts contain most of the historical data about the life and ministry of Christ and the beginning of the church through the ministry of the apostles. While the emphasis of the Epistles is not so much historical as doctrinal and practical, there are various historical elements in them, too. Even the book of Revelation contains some history and relies on the foundation of certain facts of history in order to understand its look into the future (beyond the letters to the seven churches [Revelation 2–3]).[1]

For many centuries of church history there was little debate about whether the New Testament is historically reliable. The Gospels and Acts seem intentionally written as documents whose purpose in part is to recount the history of Christ's life, death, and resurrection, and the history of the early church. Over the last few centuries, with the rise of biblical criticism and a general entrenching of an anti-supernaturalist mind-set in Western cultures, the veracity of the events recorded in Scripture has been under severe and repeated attack. If the portrait offered of Christ's words and deeds corresponds to his actual life and ministry, there are significant implications about our beliefs and about how we must live. On the other hand, if the "historical Jesus" is quite different from the one portrayed in the New Testament, then who can say that we even know Jesus's moral and theological teachings (as traditionally understood from the New Testament), let alone that we are bound to live by them?

Clearly, much is at stake in examining the reliability of Scripture. Part of this topic's importance is that most of the basis for Christian doctrine and practice is set forth in Scripture. There aren't lengthy secular historical accounts of the life of Christ and his followers. There aren't even much shorter treatises detailing the events of Jesus's life and ministry. So, while there are many extrabiblical evidences that support a Christian worldview, unquestionably, the Bible contains most of the evidence for it. Hence, in defending a Christian worldview, defending Scripture's reliability is mandatory.

Whole books have been written on this topic, but in this book I must limit my coverage to a manageable size and focus. Thus, my focus is the historical reliability of the Gospels. Some arguments and evidences will be relevant to other parts of Scripture, but the Gospels are the main focus. If the Gospels can be shown to be reliable, that "sets the table," so to speak, for the discussion of the resurrection of Jesus Christ.

In addressing this topic, I must clarify what we are not doing as well as what we are. Some Christians have thought that significant evidence for Scripture's truth is the impact it has had on so many lives over the centuries. Others point to the fact that though many political regimes have sought to obliterate copies of the Bible and punish those who possess copies, the Bible still survives and continues to be a best seller. Yet others have commented on the unity of Scripture, despite its having been written at so many different times and places and by many different authors. While I appreciate these items, I don't think they tell us much more than that the Bible is a unique book, and that many people have found it to be significant. These qualities are also true of other books, but even if Scripture alone had these qualities, that still would not tell us that what it says is true. Hence, I won't use those arguments in support of Scripture's reliability.

Next, I should distinguish a theological defense of Scripture's reliability from an apologetic one. The theological doctrine most closely associated with this concept is inerrancy, and of course, inerrancy and inspiration go together. In theology classes on the doctrine of Scripture, as an evangelical, my concern is to set forth what Scripture teaches about its own inspiration and truthfulness. Questions about whether texts that speak of inspiration and inerrancy are themselves reliable are not the focus of the discussion. Rather, the theologian assumes that the philosophers and apologists have made the case that Scripture is reliable and should be believed, regardless of the topic. So, the task of the apologist is to make the case that the Bible is reliable in what it teaches about any topic. The usual starting point of such a defense is the historical claims the Bible makes. It is only after the apologist has made the case that Scripture is to be trusted in whatever it says that evangelical theologians can set forth what Scripture teaches, including what it teaches about itself.

This means that if one is defending apologetically the reliability of Scripture, one should not make the case by saying that Scripture is to be trusted, because it says it is true. That argument will carry no weight with skeptics, and it shouldn't satisfy Christians who would like to know whether there is evidence in and outside of Scripture for trusting Scripture when it deals with any topic. The sort of defense I am proposing adopts an evidential approach to apologetics. Presuppositionalists (at least of Van Til's sort) would think it unnecessary and fruitless to offer such a defense to a nonbeliever. Instead, we should tell him or her that we presuppose without argument the truth of Scripture, just as nonbelievers prefer without argument to rely on reason as the arbiter of truth. In contrast, I am saying that nonbelievers will ask why anyone should believe anything Scripture says about any topic, and "because it says so" won't be an acceptable reply. Hence, believers must present a case for Scripture's reliability. While we, of course, must point to certain features of Scripture if we are to assess its reliability, at no point will we simply cite passages like 2 Timothy 3:16–17, 2 Peter 1:19–21, and John 17:17 as proof of Scripture's reliability.

This last comment suggests something else I won't address in this chapter: Scripture's inspiration. Though I am fully committed to Scripture's complete inspiration, that isn't my focus. If Scripture is not historically reliable, it cannot be inspired. But it could be historically (and otherwise) reliable without being the inspired Word of God. Many other books tell the truth; that alone doesn't make them God's Word. In a complete defense of the evangelical notion of Scripture, one should offer evidence that it is both historically reliable and inspired. The task more accessible to tangible, non-biblical evidence is its historical reliability. Given space limitations, that is my focus.

At the outset, I must also clarify what the historical reliability of the Gospels means and how one would go about proving it. As to meaning, it is very helpful to distinguish two separate concepts. The first concept is the authenticity or genuineness of Scripture. The second is the reliability of Scripture. Though many apologists and biblical scholars use these two terms synonymously, I want to distinguish between two related but distinct concepts that must be at the heart of our discussion, regardless of the terms we use for these concepts. In this chapter, I shall use the terms 'authenticity' and 'reliability' for two key concepts.

'Authenticity' (as I use it) refers to several things. First, it refers to whether the words of the document we have are in fact the words the author originally wrote. If not, how far from the original is the wording of the document we have? Authenticity also deals with who the author is and, to an extent, the date of the original. So, for example, in regard to the Gospel of Matthew, we want to know whether the copies we have approximate closely or are even identical to what the author originally wrote. We also want to know who wrote it and the original date of its writing. No one possesses the actual documents the authors themselves wrote; rather, we have copies of them. Hence, we need to know, for example, the oldest date of the copies we possess. Regardless of that date, it indicates that the original was written beforehand. Once we have an idea of when the original was written, we are also in a better position to say whether it was written at a time when Matthew was alive and could have written it.

As it turns out, none of the Gospels explicitly names its author.[2] Rather, tradition assigned them to Matthew, Mark, Luke, and John. Thus, there is reason to try to discern whether the original was written at a time when these men could have written it. Of course, a key in all of this is to establish that the books could have been (and likely were) written at a time when the writers either were themselves eyewitnesses to what they recorded, or at least could have contacted people who were eyewitnesses.

In contrast to authenticity, reliability relates to whether the documents tell the truth. It is, of course, possible for a document to be authentic but unreliable. It is also possible for a document to be inauthentic and yet reliable. And, a document could be both authentic and reliable or lack both qualities. Reliability focuses on the truthfulness of what the authors say. That does not mean that Satan's lies, for example, become true, just because they are contained in Scripture. Rather, reliability means that whatever the author affirms is so. Thus, in Genesis 3, the author does not claim that Satan's lie to Eve ("You shall not surely die") is true after all. Instead, the author affirms that Satan said "You shall not surely die." The reliability of that claim does not rest on Satan's lie somehow being true. Its reliability rests on Satan actually having said that.

From what I have just said, it follows that in determining the reliability of a text it is crucial first to clarify what the text means. We can always introduce error into Scripture through poor exegesis, but that is our error, not Scripture's. Biblical inerrancy/reliability means that "when all facts are known, the Scriptures in their original autographs and properly interpreted will be shown to be wholly true in everything that they affirm, whether that has to do with doctrine or morality or with the social, physical, or life sciences."[3]

Strategy of the Defense

We can now present a strategy for defending the reliability of the Gospels. I propose that our strategy should focus on history as it relates to the Gospels, and I note that history in two different respects is important to this defense. First, the Bible is a book written by different authors at various times and places in history. That should allow us to make a judgment about who each author was and when he wrote, and it should help us determine whether and to what extent the manuscripts we possess accurately reflect what the author actually wrote. We can address these issues by what is known as the bibliographic test. This test looks at the various manuscripts and their likely date in order to determine, if possible, when the original book was written and what it actually said. In proposing that we use this test to determine Scripture's authenticity, I am not suggesting a procedure that is unique (and perhaps, special pleading) to Scripture. This test can be and is applied to any book, ancient or contemporary.

There is a second way that history is important in defending Scripture. In addition to being written at different times in history, the Bible also records a number of historical events. We want to know whether those historical claims are actually true. Thus, once it is established that the documents are authentic or genuine, we must test them for their reliability or truthfulness. Someone could be an eyewitness of various events, but misunderstand what he saw and heard and hence report it incorrectly. Or an eyewitness might deliberately lie about what he saw and heard.

How do we test a document's truthfulness? Typically, literary critics, in dealing with any book, not just Scripture, employ two tests. The first is the test of internal evidence. Here we ask whether an author intends to tell us things that actually happened or whether he is writing a work of fiction. Sometimes it is very difficult to make that assessment, while in other cases, it is easy. In addition, we want to see whether the author contradicts himself, or, if multiple authors write about the same topic, whether he contradicts the other authors. Moreover, there can also be signs in a document of whether the author is making things up or telling the truth. For example, if the author is one of the people mentioned in the book, and he includes embarrassing incidents about himself, it is more likely that he is telling the truth than not—when given an opportunity to tell a story that includes oneself, the storyteller often paints himself in a very positive light.

In addition to various evidences internal to a document, a second test focuses on evidence external to the text. It is important to see whether evidence from outside the text confirms and/or corroborates things said in the document in question. Such evidence can either lower or raise the credibility of the claims made in the text. Sources of external evidence include things like secular histories, archaeological discoveries, and in the case of the Gospels, comments from various church fathers who affirm that what a given text says is in fact true (the church father in question may even say why he knows a particular event actually happened). In addition, if a text makes any scientific claims, those claims can be confirmed or rejected by consulting the findings of whatever branch of science (biology, paleontology, geology, etc.) is relevant.

Before turning to actual evidences for biblical reliability, we must ask an initial question whose answer will determine our exact strategy for defending the Gospels. Specifically, in defending Scripture's reliability, is it necessary to make the case for both its authenticity and reliability, or can we go directly to its reliability? I maintain that while it is not necessary to do both when dealing with some history books, *both* the authenticity and reliability of *Scripture* must be defended.

But why this difference? Let me explain by way of an illustration. Historian Edward Gibbon wrote a mammoth work entitled *History of the Decline and Fall of the Roman Empire*. The book first appeared in an English translation in 1750. I don't believe there has ever been a question about whether Gibbon wrote this, what the date of the book is, or whether we can be sure that the copies we have accurately reflect the words Gibbon wrote. Regardless, I contend that even if there were some question about any of these items, in investigating the reliability of the work, we could skip the step of making a case for the work's authorship, date, and contents, and go directly to defending (or critiquing) the reliability of its history.

In contrast, with Scripture, we must begin with the issue of authenticity and then move to reliability. In fact, if the case for authenticity cannot be made, it is hardly worth trying to defend reliability. Such a case, no matter how good we think it is, will be plagued with questions about whether the author was actually in a position to know the things he wrote about and questions about whether what we have represents the text the author actually wrote. So, with Gibbon's *Decline and Fall* we can forego establishing authenticity and go directly to reliability, but with Scripture we must prove both. Why?

The answer is not, for example, that many New Testament writers claimed to be an eyewitness or claimed to talk to eyewitnesses of the events they record, whereas Gibbon makes no such claims. While some New Testament writers were eyewitnesses or knew eyewitness, that isn't why both Scripture's authenticity and reliability must be defended. The answer stems from the relation of the documents in question (Gibbon's work and Scripture) to other primary source documents. By a primary source, I mean a document written by someone who was an eyewitness to the events he records (or written at least by someone who claimed to have talked with people who were eyewitnesses). Despite Gibbon's massive contribution to our understanding of Rome's decline and fall, Gibbon was neither an eye-witness of the events he wrote about, nor could he have talked with anyone who was. That fact, however, does not mean we should be suspicious about the reliability of his work. Even if the authenticity of *Decline and Fall* cannot be established, the book could still be reliable and could be shown to be so. This is so, because we have other primary source documents about the history of the Roman Empire. So, if we wanted, we could compare the contents of Gibbon's work to other primary source documents (presumably, Gibbon did this sort of research in preparing to write his book—he couldn't have talked to any eyewitnesses).

With Scripture, the situation is different. If Scripture was not written by eyewitnesses (or by people who knew eyewitnesses), we have no eyewitness accounts of the events of Israel's history, the life of Christ, and the founding of the church. It isn't that there is no extrabiblical material to help us at all, but only that what is available in no way approaches the level of detail we have in Scripture. Many of the events recorded in the Gospels aren't discussed at all outside of Scripture, and when extrabiblical works of the time do mention something, it is very general. So, the Gospels are the *only* primary source documents we have for the life of Christ. Hence, if the Gospels can't pass the bibliographic test so as to show that they were likely written at a time when the authors could have been eyewitnesses or could have consulted eyewitnesses, we have no primary source documents of the events they record. And, if there are no eyewitness accounts, then the likelihood that the Gospels record what actually happened is highly suspect.

As a result, in order to defend the reliability of the Gospels (or of any other part of Scripture), we must begin by establishing that the books are authentic. Even if they are authentic, that doesn't mean the authors told the truth, so after establishing the Gospels' authenticity, we must then present the evidence for reliability. In the rest of the chapter, I shall offer a sampling of the evidences available to support the Gospels' authenticity and reliability.

THE AUTHENTICITY OF THE GOSPELS

Kinds of Manuscript Evidence

The key to establishing the authenticity of any book is the kind and number of copies available. The great news in dealing with the New Testament, and the Gospels in particular, is that there is more than ample evidence to support traditional beliefs about these books. Manuscript evidence falls into four categories. With each type of document, we move further from the original, and so each kind of document is of a lesser value in establishing authenticity than the types mentioned before. I shall first list the four kinds of manuscripts available, and then focus on a few key manuscripts relating to the authenticity of the Gospels.

First, there are papyri and codices of portions of the Greek New Testament. These copies are written in Greek, so there are no questions about whether a translator has properly rendered the original. There is an overwhelming number of these documents, more than 5,600.[4] Second, there are early versions of the New Testament. Since these are translations, the textual scholar must try to reconstruct the Greek text by translating the language used in the version in view. Of course, the original translation was based on some version of the Greek text, so the exact wording of the version depends both on the Greek text from which the translator worked and on the skills of the translator in rendering the Greek text into the language of the version involved. The copies of these documents contain parts or all of the New Testament. While there are many of these different versions, some of the more significant are those in Latin, Syriac, and Coptic.

Third, there are quotes of parts of the New Testament in works by early church fathers. Just as people today write commentaries, sermons, and even devotionals that incorporate verses or parts of Scripture, this was also true of the church fathers. These manuscripts are of lesser value than the two types already mentioned, because they don't contain lengthy portions of Scripture, as the others do. Moreover, passages quoted are often excerpted for the purposes of the one using them, just as we sometimes quote or paraphrase a portion of a verse when we are making a sermonic or exegetical point.

Finally, there are also lectionaries. In our day it is common to have hymnbooks with reading selections at the end. These portions typically focus on one theme and bring together verses from a variety of passages that relate to the topic in question. The result is a concise and focused set of verses on a particular subject which can be used in corporate worship. The same thing was done in the ancient church. Obviously, those who compiled these lectionaries were using either a Greek manuscript or manuscripts of some translation of the various New Testament books. While these reading selections don't usually have lengthy segments from any given passage, they still help us to determine what the original Greek text must have been.

Setting Out the Context: Dates and Authorship of the Gospels and Acts

In setting the context for this discussion, several facts help to grasp the proper perspective for considering the manuscripts to be discussed. The first deals with a key date in the life of Christ. Scholars generally agree that Christ's crucifixion occurred in either 30 or 33 AD.[5]

Second, there are the dates and authorship of the four Gospels. As for Matthew, D. A. Carson argues that the most likely date is sometime during the sixties AD.[6] As to authorship, Carson notes that the early church unanimously held the author to be Matthew. A case can be made to the contrary, but the case for Matthean authorship is the most defensible.[7] As for Mark, after discussing various possibilities, Walter Wessel opts for a date sometime during the latter half of the sixties AD. Such a date would allow for the death of Peter in about AD 64, and would also allow for John Mark, who was closely associated with Peter, to be its author.[8]

In turning to Luke, we should also consider Acts, which seems to have been intended as a companion volume to the Gospel (see Acts 1:1–3 and Luke 1:1–4). Walter Liefeld sets forth the grounds for attributing this third Gospel to Luke, the close companion of the apostle Paul, and there seems to have been universal attestation to this in the early church. This also means that Luke was the author of Acts, and that makes abundant sense in light of the "we passages" in Acts (16:10–17; 20:5–15; 21:1–18; 27:1–28:16) that speak of Paul and his traveling companions, including Luke, on various missionary journeys.[9] As for the date of Luke and Acts, the presumption, of course, is that the former preceded the latter. Given that assumption, Liefeld explains that Acts ends with a reference to Paul's two-year imprisonment at Rome, which happened around AD 60 to 62. In addition, there is no hint of the persecution of Christians under Nero in AD 65 or the destruction of Jerusalem in AD 70. Paul's death is considered to have coincided with the Neronian persecutions. Given these facts, one arrives at a date of somewhere between AD 63 or 64 for Acts, which would, of course, place the composition of Luke earlier. Liefeld argues that when all considerations are taken into account, we arrive at a date for both books somewhere between AD 60 and 70.[10] Richard Longenecker offers a detailed discussion of the major theories about the date of Acts, but in the end opts for an early date around AD 64 for the composition of this book.[11]

Finally, there is the Gospel of John. Merrill Tenney sets forth the case that John the son of Zebedee—the beloved disciple—was its author.[12] As to the date of this Gospel, there have been many suggestions, but in light of manuscript evidence (to be discussed) it is likely to have been composed no later than the late first century or the early second century (perhaps sometime during the first decade). Though not necessarily espousing this himself, Tenney explains that it is also possible that the Gospel was written much earlier—perhaps even prior to AD 70, but only "published" or widely circulated much later.[13] Though he does not state his own preference about the date of John, Tenney notes that most conservative scholars (at the time Tenney wrote the commentary) place the date of John between AD 85 and 90.[14]

In comparing these proposed dates for the composition of the Gospels and Acts with the death of Christ no later than AD 33, it is clear that between his death and the writing of each of these books, except John, there is no more than 30 to 35 years. In the case of John, if we go with the AD 85 to 90 dates, then there is a time gap of 50 to 60 years. This is significant, because it means that the people we traditionally associate as authors of these books would likely have been alive at the times these books were written. Moreover, between Christ's death and the composition of these books, the authors would have had ample opportunity to talk with many people who had lived during Christ's life and ministry, so the things they wrote could very likely have been based on eyewitness testimony—their own, but also that of many others who witnessed these events but never wrote about them. Certainly, the dates of the Synoptic Gospels (Matthew, Mark, and Luke) and Acts are such that many people who lived during the events chronicled in these books would have been alive. And that means there would have been an ample number of people who could have refuted the contents of these books, if the accounts were wrong. It is significant that we have little, if any, evidence that anyone tried to do this. While it is possible that there were many eyewitnesses who disagreed with the contents of these books and sought to refute them, one would think that at least some of their attempts (in written form or passed down through oral tradition) would have survived, but the evidence is to the contrary. The evidence we have from church fathers and the like confirms what we have seen about the authors of these books and their contents.

Some Key Manuscripts

With so many different manuscripts available, it is impossible in this chapter to mention all of them. However, some are of special importance, and I must at least mention them. The ones I shall consider are either very old and/or contain large portions of the Gospels and even of the whole New Testament. Let us begin with some papyrus manuscripts.

A first manuscript is p[52]. It contains a few verses from the Gospel of John (18:31–33, 37–38). It was acquired in Egypt, in a town along the Nile, even though the book of John is thought to have been written while John was in Ephesus, a good distance from Egypt. This papyrus contains so few verses that one might think it inconsequential. But it would be a significant mistake to conclude that. The reason is the manuscript's date. Its date is around AD 125. If we accept the later date of the composition of the Gospel of John (AD 85 to 90), then in (at most) forty years this document had already been circulated quite a distance. What is most important about this, however, is its closeness to the time of composition and to the time of Christ's life. All of this is of special importance for a further reason. During the late-nineteenth and early-twentieth century, liberal New Testament scholars claimed that the Gospel of John was written at earliest after the midpoint of the second century AD, and possibly later. If so, then it couldn't have been written by John or any of his contemporaries. Those who proposed the late date believed that the early church had written it to spread abroad and legitimize their version of theological propaganda. The acquisition of and (later) the recognition of this fragmentary manuscript in the early twentieth century put to rest liberal proposals of the sort just mentioned.[15] Merrill Tenney notes the significance of upholding an early date for the composition of the Gospel of John. He writes that "if the Gospel were written before the end of the first century, or even by 85, it would still have been read by men only one generation removed from the contemporaries of Jesus. Thus it could have been verified or contested by those who had authentic information concerning him."[16]

Another important manuscript of the Gospel of John is p[66]. It contains much more of the book (John 1:1–6:11; 6:35–14:26, 29–30; 15:2–26; 16:2–4,

6–7; 16:10–20:20, 22–23; 20:25–21:9), and is dated around AD 200. It was acquired by Martin Bodmer, founder of the Bodmer Library of World Literature at Cologny, a suburb of Geneva, Switzerland.[17] Then p[64] +[67] contains various portions of the Gospel of Matthew (3:9, 15; 5:20–22, 25–28; 26:7–8, 10, 14–15, 22–23, 31–33), and is dated at about AD 200.[18] As we shall soon see, manuscripts such as these which are, relatively speaking, very close to the time when the original was written, are unusual for books of the ancient world.

In addition, p[75] is a very important manuscript. It contains portions of the Gospel of Luke (3:18–22, 33–4:2; 4:34–5:10; 5:37–6:4; 6:10–7:32; 7:35–43; 7:46–18:18; 22:4–24:53) and of the Gospel of John (1:1–11:45, 48–57; 12:3–13:1, 8–9; 14:8–30; 15:7–8). This manuscript was acquired by Martin Bodmer, and its editors (Victor Martin and Rodolphe Kasser) date it between AD 175 and 225. As Metzger says of its date, "It is thus the earliest known copy of the Gospel according to Luke and one of the earliest of the Gospel according to John."[19] Another early manuscript related to the Gospels is p[4] which also dates from the third century AD. It contains some of the early chapters of Luke (1:58–59; 1:62–2:1, 6–7; 3:8–4:2, 29–32, 34–35; 5:3–8; 5:30–6:16).

There are, of course, many manuscripts of one Gospel or another that have a later date, but I have presented these because they are some of the very earliest. Interestingly, none of the early manuscripts mentioned contain part of the Gospel of Mark. This is interesting because there are so many New Testament scholars who think Mark was written first and that it is "foundational" to the Synoptic Gospels (Matthew, Mark, and Luke). If one takes that view, then, of course, with or without early manuscripts of Mark, it must have been composed before the other Gospels.

Two other papyri are of special note, though they are of other portions of the New Testament. They are p[32] and p[46]. The former is in the John Rylands Library in Manchester, England, and the latter is one of the Chester Beatty papyri; both are dated at around AD 200. p[32] contains part of Titus (1:11–15; 2:3–8), whereas p[46] contains portions of many Pauline Epistles and Hebrews. The books represented are Romans (5:17–6:14; 8:15–15:9; 15:11–16:27), 1 Corinthians (1:1–16:22), 2 Corinthians (1:1–13:13), Galatians (1:1–6:18), Ephesians (1:1–6:24), Philippians (1:1–4:23), Colossians (1:1–4:18), 1 Thessalonians (1:1; 1:9–2:3; 5:5–9, 23–28), and Hebrews

(1:1–13:25).[20] My reason for mentioning these two manuscripts is that p[46] includes 1 Corinthians. A manuscript of this early date only makes it more likely that the original was written at a time when the apostle Paul would have been alive and would likely have authored it. As we shall see in the chapter on the resurrection of Jesus Christ, 1 Corinthians 15 as a whole, and verses 1–4 in particular, are significant in making a case for the historicity of the resurrection.

Several other manuscripts are of great significance in helping us piece together the New Testament and portions of the Old Testament as well. Each is a codex, as follows: Codex Sinaiticus, Codex Alexandrinus, Codex Vaticanus, and Codex Bezae Cantabrigiensis. There are, of course, many other codices, but these are of special import.

Codex Sinaiticus contains the whole of the Bible in Greek, with parts of the Old Testament missing. The whole of the New Testament, however, is still intact. Its date is placed during the fourth century, but it wasn't discovered until the nineteenth century, by Constantin von Tischendorf. He found the codex at the monastery of St. Catherine on Mt. Sinai—hence the name Sinaiticus. Eventually Tischendorf was able to acquire the manuscript. As Metzger notes, the "definitive publication of the codex was made in the twentieth century when Oxford University Press issued a facsimile from photographs taken by Professor Kirsopp Lake (New Testament, 1911; Old Testament, 1922)."[21] The story of what happened to this codex between the time von Tischendorf found it and was later able to bring it to Europe is a fascinating one.[22] It didn't, however, end until the discovery in 1975 of a sealed room in the monastery of St. Catherine. In that room were found art treasures and more than 1,000 manuscripts, of which 836 were written in Greek. Among the Greek manuscripts were twelve complete leaves from Codex Sinaiticus.[23] Codex Sinaiticus contains not only the whole of the Bible, but also part of the extrabiblical works the Epistle of Barnabas and the Shepherd of Hermas.[24] In comparing this Codex with early papyri documents, scholars have been able to trace different text traditions, but they can also see the continuity between earlier documents and Sinaiticus.

Codex Alexandrinus (known as A) contains most of the Old Testament and most of the New Testament, a notable exception being the majority of the Gospel of Matthew. The Codex is dated by scholars from about the fifth century AD. As to its quality, Aland and Aland say that "the text is of uneven value (based on exemplars of different types in its different parts), inferior in the Gospels, good in the rest of the New Testament, but best in Revelation . . ."[25] To explain this a bit more, in the Gospels it follows the Byzantine type of text which scholars consider to be of inferior form, while the rest of the New Testament, like Sinaiticus, offers a sample of the Alexandrian type of text.[26]

Codex Vaticanus (B) is in the Vatican Library at Rome, where it has been since sometime before AD 1475.[27] It contains the whole Bible, with several gaps in both the Old Testament and the New Testament. It dates from the middle of the fourth century AD. Metzger opines that the lack of ornamentation of this document may suggest an older date than Codex Sinaiticus. However, "some scholars believe that these two manuscripts were originally among the 50 copies of the Scriptures that the Emperor Constantine commissioned Eusebius to have written."[28]

Finally, there is Codex Bezae Cantabrigiensis (Codex D) which dates from the fifth century. It has this name because in 1581 Theodore Beza, an important reformer who followed Calvin at Geneva, presented it to Cambridge University. This text contains most of the four Gospels and Acts, and a small fragment from 3 John. It has the unusual characteristic of having the Greek text written on one page, and the Latin equivalent on the page facing the Greek. Metzger explains as well that it is unique in that "no known manuscript has so many and such remarkable variations from what is usually taken to be the normal New Testament text. Codex Bezae's special characteristic is the free addition (and occasional omission) of words, sentences, and even incidents."[29] This Codex is taken to be the main representative of the Western text. In light of its penchant for variation from the traditional text, one might think this Codex and manuscripts like it are of little use. However, that is not so. For one thing, as noted, it helps us to understand the Western text type, but equally important is that by comparing it with manuscripts following the Alexandrian text tradition, textual critics are better able to judge what the original actually said.

There are, of course, numerous other manuscripts, but even these few suggest that the New Testament, and the Gospels in particular, were very likely written during the first century AD. In my original summary of the kinds of manuscript evidence available, I mentioned references to parts of the New Testament in the writings of early church fathers. These church fathers not only quoted parts of the New Testament for sermonic purposes or as part of theological or exegetical treatises they were writing. They also made comments about the origin of some of these New Testament books. Many of these confirm that those traditionally taken to have authored the Gospels are in fact the ones who did. An especially important statement to this effect appears in *Adversus haereses*, written around AD 180 by Irenaeus, bishop of Lyons. Irenaeus writes,

> Matthew published his Gospel among the Hebrews [i.e., Jews] in their own tongue, when Peter and Paul were preaching the gospel in Rome and founding the church there. After their departure [i.e., death, which strong tradition places at the time of the Neronian persecution in 64], Mark, the disciple and interpreter of Peter, himself handed down to us in writing the substance of Peter's preaching. Luke, the follower of Paul, set down in a book the gospel preached by his teacher. Then John, the disciple of the Lord, who also leaned on his breast [this is a reference to John 13:25 and 21:20], himself produced his Gospel, while he was living at Ephesus in Asia.[30]

This statement from Irenaeus is quoted for a very specific reason. Irenaeus was a student of Polycarp, bishop of Smyrna, who was martyred in AD 156. And Polycarp had been a follower of the apostle John. "Irenaeus had often heard from Polycarp the eyewitness accounts of Jesus received from John and others who had been personally acquainted with Jesus."[31]

This is a truly remarkable statement from Irenaeus. Of course, it is possible that he misunderstood Polycarp or that Polycarp misunderstood John, but on matters of this significance, it is extremely unlikely. This is especially so because, in making these comments, Irenaeus is clearly identifying himself with the traditional understanding of the origin of the Gospels, and by these comments, as well as others, he aligns himself with the Christian church, as did Polycarp and John before him. The implications of this are especially significant, because during the lifetime of all three (John, Polycarp, and Irenaeus) Christianity was illegal in the Roman Empire. Many early Christians refused to bow the knee to Caesar, preferring death in an open arena to denying their Lord and Savior Jesus Christ. So, associating oneself with Christ and these Gospels written about him was risky business. Why would people such as Polycarp and Irenaeus pass on as firmly true information whose truth they were unsure of, if as a result of believing such things they opened themselves to persecution and ultimately death? That just wouldn't make sense. Realizing the implications for one's personal well-being of believing such things, anyone would do whatever they could to confirm the truth of such beliefs, and repeat them only if they were sure that the claims were true. So, the connection of Irenaeus to John through Polycarp is valuable not only because it is such an early witness to the authenticity of the Gospels but also in that, given the danger one would face for believing such things, it is unreasonable to think this information would have been passed to Polycarp and Irenaeus, and to anyone reading Irenaeus's treatise. The most reasonable explanation of why these men said these things is that they knew they were true.

The manuscript evidence I have presented is impressive support for the authenticity of the Gospels, but it is even more impressive than one might suppose. This is so because it is most instructive to compare the New Testament with other documents of the ancient world. That comparison can be made on several grounds. First, we should compare the sheer volume of manuscripts available. We have already seen that manuscripts of parts or all of the New Testament written in Greek number more than 5,600. In contrast, the writings that come in "second place" are those of Homer. There are some 643 copies of his works. We have, by comparison, 200 copies of the works of Demosthenes, only 10 copies of the writings of Caesar, 20 copies of the works of Livy, 20 of the works of Tacitus, and 8 each of Thucydides's and Herodotus's writings. Among scholars of these secular works, there is little question about whether they are genuinely from the authors we think wrote them. But if that is so, then why should the genuineness of the New Testament books be doubted, when the amount of manuscript evidence we have is so much more?

A second feature of these documents is also significant. As already noted, the earliest copy of any of the Gospels is the fragment from the Gospel of John, dated around AD 125. If we adopt AD 85 as the date of composition of John's Gospel, the earliest manuscript of it appears within 40 years. We also saw that p[66], which contains most of the Gospel of John, is dated around AD 200, some 115 years after its composition. That sounds like a long time until you compare it with other works of the ancient world by authors already noted. The shortest time gap between the writing of their original works and the earliest copy we possess is about 1,000 years.

Caesar's works were composed in the first century BC, and the earliest copy we have is dated AD 900, about 1,000 years after the original was written. Tacitus's works were written around AD 100, and the earliest copy of any of his work dates from AD 1100, a 1,000-year time gap. For others the time gap is even greater. Thucydides composed his works in the fifth century BC, and so did Herodotus. The earliest copy of either of these historians' works dates AD 900, a gap of 1,400 years. Even the works of Demosthenes (200 copies) have a lengthy time gap between their origin and the date of the earliest copy we possess. Demosthenes wrote during the fourth century BC and the earliest copy of any of his writings dates AD 1100, about 1,500 years later. Despite the huge time gaps, there are few who would doubt the authenticity of the works of these writers. Simple fairness requires belief in the authenticity of the New Testament as well.

A third matter of comparison deals with accuracy of the copies. Given the paucity of copies of these ancient secular works and the time gap between composition of the original and the making of the copies, it is hard to know whether we have the equivalent of the documents the authors first wrote. In fact, it is only with the works of Homer that we have an estimate, and that estimate is 95 percent accuracy. Though this is indeed very high, the New Testament does even better at 99+ percent. New Testament textual critics affirm that while there are some variant readings, "no Christian doctrine is founded solely or even primarily on textually disputed passages."[32]

When the New Testament documents are compared with other works of the ancient world on the bases of the three items mentioned, there really is no comparison. But since the authenticity of these other works is not disputed, why should the authenticity of the New Testament be in question? One suspects that if the New Testament didn't record various miracles and other supernatural phenomena, there would be little question of its authenticity. However, to assume the New Testament is deficient on the matter of authenticity because it records miracles begs the question. And you don't have to be an evangelical Christian to come to that conclusion. In light of the overwhelming manuscript evidence for the New Testament, and in particular for the Gospels, there is ample reason to believe that the texts we have, if translated well from the best Greek texts of the Gospels, are authentic. The further confirmation from the statement by Irenaeus only makes more secure a conclusion that is already very objectively certain.

THE RELIABILITY OF THE GOSPELS

There is ample evidential support for the authenticity of the Gospels. Hence, we have good reason to think that they were written by eyewitnesses to the events they record, or at least by people who had contact with eyewitnesses. Still, just because we know the author, date, and contents of these books, that doesn't prove that the authors told us the truth or even knew the truth. Sometimes even eyewitnesses of the same event give different accounts of what they saw and heard.

Is there reason, then, to believe that the Gospels and Acts tell us the truth? I believe there is, and I want to present what seem to me to be the strongest evidences that this is so. Typically, in defending the reliability of a document, two kinds of evidence are invoked: internal evidence and external evidence. Internal evidence points to features of the document itself that make it believable. External evidence points to different sources than the work in question, which sources corroborate various claims of the document under study. I shall try to divide my discussion of internal and external evidences into two distinct parts, though in some instances I must appeal to both to make a given point.

Internal Evidence of the Reliability of the Gospels

We begin with a principle for handling a literary work that goes back at least as far as Aristotle. The principle is that as the interpreter addresses the text, he or she should give the writer the benefit of the doubt as to whether the writer is being accurate in what is reported (assuming that the work intends and claims to give an accurate account of various events).[33] This, of course, doesn't preclude ultimately rejecting the document's accuracy in the face of evidence that shows it to be wrong. It only says that each document has its basic "situation," and as we begin to read the book, we should suspend disbelief of what the writer purports to be doing, at least until there is reason to believe that what the author includes doesn't fit with the rest of his work or that it is untrue (if the document claims to tell the truth). This means that for a work that appears to give a historical account of various persons and events, that work should be presumed innocent of error until proven guilty. While this may not seem very important, it makes a substantial difference as to how, for example, one approaches the historical reliability of the Gospels. Are these documents at the outset to be presumed guilty of error, or innocent? If the former, it will be an uphill grind to demonstrate that the document reports the truth, even if many things recorded in the document are deemed trustworthy. If the document is presumed innocent, however, then when various details are shown to be reliable, we don't have to wait until all details, regardless of their nature, are shown to be true in order to believe any of it.

Critics of the historical reliability of the Gospels may be willing to grant this rule, but may still feel that there is good reason to be suspicious of the truthfulness of these books. That reason is that the Gospels record the occurrence of various miracles. When we move to Acts, it is no longer Jesus doing the miracles, but rather the disciples (though apparently less frequently than Jesus did). The accounts of miracles in these books, say the critics, automatically show that the books cannot be reliable historical documents. To draw such a conclusion, however, is odd on several accounts. One is that even if an account of a miracle is suspect as non-naturalistic, why does that also make the rest of the historical claims (which don't report miracles) false? The other odd point about this denial of reliability is that it seems to go contrary to normal historical procedure. That is, when a reported event is doubted, before concluding that the event didn't occur, usually investigators withhold judgment until the matter has been investigated. To reject as unreliable an account of an event just because one doesn't think such events are possible is question begging. The question being begged is whether it is possible for a miracle to occur. Logic requires that whatever one's answer, one must offer evidential support for the answer, rather than just assuming that one's answer is correct without investigating the evidence. No one is arguing here that miracles are frequent occurrences so that none of us should doubt the possibility of their happening. Rather, the argument is that being an extremely unusual event allegedly performed by a supernatural being doesn't make it impossible that the event happened. Instead of prejudging the event as impossible and short-circuiting any serious research, the wiser approach (and the one required by logic and intellectual fairness) is to withhold judgment about whether such an event is *possible* or *impossible*, and to conduct a fair investigation of the evidence that a given miracle *actually* occurred.

Even if one grants that the author must be allowed his "given" and that we cannot reject *a priori* his document as untrustworthy just because it reports a miracle, that doesn't automatically make his writing reliable. There may be other grounds than suspicion about the miraculous for doubting the work's truthfulness, but there should also be other grounds for believing it to be reliable. And those grounds can be within the document itself. In what follows I shall offer a variety of features about the Gospels and Acts that strongly suggest that they are reliable.

An initial question we should ask of these texts is whether their authors give any evidence that they intend to recount truthfully what has happened. Of course, even if an author states this as his intention, he could either intentionally or unintentionally report events that never happened, or at least didn't happen exactly as he reports them. But it would help to know whether he intends to be historically accurate in what he reports. The answer to this question is that the authors of the Gospels and Acts both implicitly and explicitly show that this is exactly what they intend to do and what they believe they have done. The prologue of Luke's Gospel (1:1–4) says,

> Inasmuch as many have undertaken to compile an account of the things accomplished among us, just as those who from the beginning were eyewitnesses and servants of the word have handed them down to us, it seemed fitting for me as well, having investigated everything carefully from the beginning, to write it out for you in consecutive order, most excellent Theophilus; so that you might know the exact truth about the things you have been taught.

It is hard to imagine a more explicit statement of authorial intent about the book that follows these words. Luke sees himself as recounting what actually happened in the lives of Christ and his disciples. At the start of Acts, Luke refers back to the Gospel of Luke. He does not make an explicit claim as he did in the prologue to Luke, but the reference to the Gospel suggests that this "new" work will be more of the same. If we have any serious doubts about Luke's intent, we need only to read the book of Acts. Sometimes Luke includes himself in the stories he reports and sometimes not, but the whole book has the ring of recounting history. Though critics would undoubtedly question the reliability of stories that involve the supernatural, it is hard to see how they could deny Luke's intent to relate what happened in the lives of the apostles and of those to whom they ministered.

The apostle John also tells us his intent in writing his Gospel, though in John's case the statement comes near the very end, not at the beginning. John writes (20:30–31),

> Many other signs therefore Jesus also performed in the presence of the disciples, which are not written in this book; but these have been written that you may believe that Jesus is the Christ, the Son of God; and that believing you may have life in His name.

How could John expect his readers to conclude from his book that Jesus is the Messiah, the Son of God, if John's intent had been merely to relate some entertaining stories about imaginary people and imaginary events? Clearly, John sees himself as telling the truth about Jesus's life, much of which he saw and heard as an eyewitness.[34]

While Matthew and Mark do not make such explicit claims about recounting the facts of Jesus's life, the tone and tenor of their works is that the events they recount happened. Either they personally were there, or others were. Here it is important to note the connection between Peter and Mark, and to note as well what Peter says in 2 Peter 1:16: "For we did not follow cleverly devised tales when we made known to you the power and coming of our Lord Jesus Christ, but we were eyewitnesses of His majesty." In verses 17–18 Peter explains specifically that he saw Christ's majesty on the Mount of Transfiguration (cf. Mark 9:2ff.). It is hard to believe, however, that Peter's comments about not telling his readers fables applies only to the Mount of Transfiguration event. Surely, Peter isn't thinking that he was an eyewitness to that event but that the rest of what he preaches and writes is based on fables which the apostles imagined but never witnessed. It is also hard to believe that anything other than eyewitness accounts of Christ's life, death, and resurrection are the intent of Mark's Gospel, considering Mark's heavy dependence on Peter.

So the authors of the Gospels and Acts intend to recount events from Christ's life, but are there evidences internal to the documents that show they are telling the truth? I believe there are and want to present that evidence in what follows. First, if, as some critics have claimed, the disciples concocted all of the stories about Christ's miracles, or if the second- or third-century church made up the supernatural elements of the Gospels, then we would expect to see not only Christ but his followers portrayed as noble heroes of the faith. Or if not, we would at least not expect to see them depicted negatively. The portrayal of the disciples in the Gospels, however, is far from complimentary. In fact, fairly uniformly they are depicted in a bad light. Frequently, in their interactions with one another and with Jesus, their main concern seems to be who will be greatest in the kingdom—in other words, what's in it for me, given that I have followed you? And think as well about the reaction at the Last Supper when Jesus says one of them will betray him. The main issue on their mind is not to comfort or reassure Jesus of their loyalty, but rather to learn whether they will be the guilty one.

In addition, they are portrayed as people who don't quite have the faith required to meet the occasion. Think of Peter's attempt to walk on water; it started out well, but then he took his eyes off of Jesus and began to sink. Think also of Thomas's reaction upon hearing the reports that Christ had risen. And think of their reactions at the time of Jesus's trial and crucifixion. Peter's denial of Christ is notorious, but it isn't clear that all of the disciples were even present at the crucifixion. After Christ's death, they are fearful and go and hide in fear of what the authorities might do to these "followers" of Christ if they should be found. The portrayal of the disciples during the last days of Christ's life is far from positive. At Gethsemane they can't stay awake while Jesus prays. When the officials come to take Jesus, Peter cuts off the ear of Malchus, the high priest's slave (John 18:10; Matt. 26:51; Mark 14:47), only to be rebuked by Jesus. It's almost as though Jesus is saying to Peter that his act is outrageous. Has he been with Jesus all this time and still doesn't understand the resources at Jesus's disposal, nor does he understand that Jesus has to die? This incident is far from Peter's most shining moment; it's actually quite embarrassing!

Even on occasions when they seem to be magnanimous in their attitudes, they are shocked when they hear Jesus's response to them. In other cases, when Jesus explains the true meaning of the law and offers a higher standard than anyone at the time lives up to, rather than affirming Jesus's teaching, they are just as shocked as others who hear what he says. Two incidents illustrate the point. In Matthew's Gospel (Matt. 18:21–35) we find the parable of the merciless slave. This is a parable about the need to forgive those who have wronged us and then ask for our forgiveness. But notice the context. The incident begins with Peter coming to Christ and asking how often he is required to forgive his brother who sins against him. Peter asks if he should do so as many as seven times? On the surface, this may sound very magnanimous. After all, rabbinic thinking at that time said that one should forgive one's brother three times for a repeated sin; on the fourth recurrence, there was no need to forgive. So, in effect, Peter must have thought his suggestion was quite generous, for he was willing to forgive an erring brother four more times than the rabbis of the day thought was necessary. Jesus's response, however, is hardly congratulatory to Peter. Jesus replies that seven times isn't enough; one must be willing to forgive up to seventy times seven (v. 22). In essence, Jesus is saying we should always be willing to forgive an erring brother. Jesus then illustrates his point about the need for forgiveness by telling the parable of the merciless slave. The main point of the parable is that in light of all that God has forgiven us, how can we justify failing to forgive those who wrong us and ask for forgiveness? In light of the message of this parable, Peter's offer to go four times better than the rabbis required hardly sounds as noble as it might at first glance.

Consider as well the incident recorded in Matthew 19. In the first 12 verses of this chapter, Matthew records Jesus's teaching on divorce and remarriage. Many Jews in Jesus's day thought the Mosaic teaching about divorce (Deut. 24:1–4) allowed people to divorce on grounds of ʿerwat dabar (translated "something indecent"). There were two schools of thought on what that included. One group, the Hillel, took it loosely to mean anything a husband might find disagreeable about his wife. As you can imagine, this was a popular view among Jewish men. On the other hand, the Shammai, the more conservative group, argued that ʿerwat dabar referred only to adultery, so adultery was the only ground for divorce. While this may sound much more conservative, it was still problematic, because the Mosaic law said that adulterers and adulteresses were to be stoned to death. There was no point in thinking about whether remarriage was allowed, because it is irrelevant to debate whether people who are supposed to be executed can be remarried. The Pharisees posed a test to Jesus; they asked him to comment on the meaning of ʿerwat dabar. They thought they had him trapped. If he sided with the Shammai, he could appear to take the law seriously, but the Shammai position was not very popular in that day. If he held the Hillel position, many people would be pleased with him, but then the Pharisees could complain that he didn't take the Mosaic law seriously enough.

Rather than falling into the Pharisees' trap, Jesus pointed them to

God's original design for marriage as set forth in Genesis 1 and 2. Eventually, in verse 9, Jesus offered his assessment of what one is doing when one divorces his wife on grounds of any old thing that is disagreeable to him. Jesus says that when that happens and the husband marries another wife, by the divorce and remarriage he commits adultery. As recorded in Matthew 5, Jesus teaches that when a wife was divorced on such grounds and then was forced into another marriage (women in that culture had few rights and few options as to how to support themselves and their children—marriage was clearly the best option), she also became an adulteress by that remarriage.

This was a very serious thing that Jesus was saying. Up to that time no one had ever said that if one divorces his wife on insufficient grounds and then remarries, he commits adultery. But that was Jesus's fundamental teaching, and he knew and his hearers also knew what the Mosaic law required of adulterers and adulteresses. In Matthew 19:10, Matthew records the response of the disciples: "The disciples said to Him, 'If the relationship of the man with his wife is like this, it is better not to marry.'"

This is a truly outrageous response! Having heard Jesus's teaching on divorce and remarriage, and realizing that it entails that you cannot get in and out of marriage on any old grounds without committing adultery and thus deserving execution, rather than asking the Lord to help them live up to this standard, they react as you might expect any nonbeliever or immature believer to do. In essence, their response is that, if that's the rule that governs marriage and divorce, well, then it would be better just not to marry at all. In other words, if getting out of a marriage and into another is going to be as hard as you are suggesting it to be, then who in their right mind would ever get married? Rather than commit themselves to the high standard that Jesus presents, in effect, they immaturely say, "If we can't play by any rules that we want, then we might as well take our ball and go home." Such language hardly presents the disciples as moral paragons!

We could multiply these embarrassing accounts of the disciples' thoughts and deeds as depicted in the Gospels, but I am sure you get the picture. What, however, is my point? My point is that if, when you write one of these Gospels, you're just making up stories to deceive people into thinking highly of Jesus, why would you include in it all of these stories that are quite embarrassing to yourself and other leaders of the movement? If historical accuracy is not an issue for you, why portray yourselves in such a bad light, especially if you are hoping to attract other people to Christ? If you want to win people to your movement, then show that Christ has made a positive difference in the lives of his followers. Don't show them to be as immature and unspiritual as they are depicted in the Gospels—that sort of story is hardly a good advertisement to attract new people to the movement. The fact that the Gospels and Acts record so many things that portray the disciples in a very bad light on many occasions can only reasonably be explained by saying that the people who wrote this are telling the truth about what happened. The depiction of the disciples as less than noble and less than moral exemplars is internal evidence that these books tell us the truth.

Relatedly, though a distinct point, if you are making up stories about a miracle, and you really want to convince your readers that the miracle happened, make the story as credible as you possibly can. That said, think of the accounts of the resurrection. The first people to come to the tomb and then report the resurrection to the disciples are women. This is significant, because women in that day had few rights and were not taken seriously. A woman's testimony in a court of law counted as nothing. Surely the authors of the Gospels knew that. Why would they give women such an important place in their stories about the resurrection, if their intent was just to make up a story that includes things that would make it believable? The only answer that makes sense is that the authors included these details about the women because that's the way it really happened. The inclusion of women, not only in the story about the death and resurrection of Christ but also at other points in the Gospels, makes little sense unless they were actually involved! The inclusion of women is internal evidence of the truthfulness of these accounts.

Craig Blomberg helps us with several specific items internal to the text. Blomberg notes that many skeptics have developed a series of criteria to use in determining whether various texts are likely telling the truth. Though these are labeled criteria of authenticity, they actually deal with the truthfulness of the text, so they are, to use my terminology, criteria of reliability. The four criteria are 1) dissimilarity, 2) multiple attestation, 3) Palestinian environment, and 4) coherence.[35] Let us examine each in turn.

According to the criterion of dissimilarity, elements of a document which are distinctively different from either a first-century Jewish or an early Christian perspective are likely to be authentic and so are taken as such.

Hence they can't be explained away as arising out of either of these sources. As an example, Blomberg points to the kingdom parables of Jesus. Jewish leaders often told a parable to help in the exegesis of a passage of Scripture but rarely if ever used parables to speak of the reign of God breaking into our world. On the other hand, neither the rest of the New Testament nor early Christian practice often, if at all, uses a parable to teach the concepts they want to convey. In light of this, Blomberg rightly concludes that these parables most likely originated with Jesus, and the Gospel writers are correct in attributing them to him. Blomberg also notes that while the Jews were concerned about and spoke of the kingdom of God, their conception of it was largely as a future phenomenon. In the teachings of Jesus, the kingdom is seen both as a present reality and yet as future in some important senses. Given the uniqueness of these concepts and literary forms, it is most likely that the parables originated with Jesus.[36]

The second criterion is multiple attestation. According to this criterion, details that appear in more than one independent source are likely to be true. Blomberg offers several examples that clarify the point. First, the story of the feeding of the five thousand appears in all four Gospels (Matt. 14:13–21; Mark 6:32–44; Luke 9:10–17; and John 6:1–13). Then the story of the commissioning of the Twelve after Jesus first called them appears in each of the Synoptic Gospels (Mark 6:7–11; and in a different form common to parts of Matt. 10:1–16 and Luke 9:1–6). A third example is the recounting of Jesus's words about the rejected stone becoming the head of the corner, said in conjunction with the parable of the wicked tenants (Matt. 21:33–46; Mark 12:1–12; and Luke 20:9–19).[37]

Blomberg then turns to the criterion of Palestinian environment and explains that this criterion "admits as more likely authentic those traditions which seem to require an early Palestinian Jewish-Christian milieu for their genesis."[38] As examples, Blomberg offers the Lord's "Son of Man" sayings, and his use of the Aramaic "Abba" for Father. Blomberg adds to this Christ's "concern for the outcasts of his society, rejection of the purity laws, frequent conflicts with the religious authorities over the law (especially the Sabbath). And many of these details receive dual corroboration by the dissimilarity criterion."[39]

The fourth criterion of coherence holds that we may accept as accurate "traditions which are not immediately suggested by an application of the previous three criteria but which are profoundly consistent with the meaning and significance of those which do."[40] An example of this is Jesus's changing water to wine as an illustration of "the newness of the kingdom taught by the parable of the wineskins (compare John 2:1-11 with Mark 2:19-20)."[41]

These four criteria, developed by scholars who are greatly skeptical of the truthfulness of many things recorded in the Gospels, when applied to the contents of the Gospels, actually affirm that the authors are telling the truth. Then, we have already noted that when multiple eyewitnesses record the same event, that makes it increasingly likely that all of them are telling the truth. Certainly that seems to be the commonly used approach toward testimony in a court of law. However, some skeptics will reply that multiple attestation of certain events may mean that there aren't multiple accounts, but rather only one account which several authors copied, even though they weren't all eyewitnesses or associated with an eyewitness.

In response, it is important to note that even though multiple eyewitnesses recount the same event, there is evidence within each account that they are writing independently of one another, not just repeating a common story. The point is not simply that some of the Gospels omit events that others include, but also that even when two Gospels include an account of the same event, each author chooses to relate his own set of details about the event. An example will illustrate this point.

Consider the accounts of the betrayal and capture of Jesus, recorded in all four Gospels (Matt. 26:47–56; Mark 14:43–49; Luke 22:47–53; and John 18:1–11). Matthew, Mark, and Luke all mention the betrayal kiss by Judas; John says nothing about it. Matthew and Mark say that Judas actually kissed Jesus, whereas Luke says that Judas approached Jesus to kiss him, but Jesus asked him whether he was betraying "the Son of Man" with a kiss, and Luke does not actually say that Judas kissed Jesus (though nothing Luke says precludes Judas from doing so). As for John, he refers to Judas and shows that he was there when Jesus was arrested, but John says nothing whatsoever about the kiss. Then all three Synoptics say that the servant of the high priest's ear was cut off, but they don't say who did it. Only John tells us it was Peter, and only John tells the name of that slave. Finally, Jesus's response to all of this differs in each Gospel. In Matthew, Jesus tells the one who cut off the servant's ear to put away the sword. He then asks if the one who did this doesn't know that his Father has legions of angels ready to protect him.

Jesus then turns to those who came to arrest him and asks them whether they have come with swords and clubs to arrest him as though he were a robber. He reminds them that every day he used to sit in the temple teaching, but they never seized him then. In Mark's account, once the servant's ear is cut off, Jesus's only response is to ask those who came to arrest him whether they have come to take him as a common criminal, a robber. In Luke's Gospel, after the servant's ear is cut off, Jesus simply says, "Stop! No more of this." He then heals the servant's ear, and turns to those who have come to arrest him and asks if they have come with swords and clubs to arrest him as they would a robber. He reminds them that they could have laid hands on him when he was in the temple, but "this hour and the power of darkness are yours." And in John's Gospel, once Peter cuts off the high priest's servant's ear, Jesus turns to Peter, tells him to put up his sword, and then asks, rhetorically, whether or not he must drink the cup the Father has given him. There is no word that Jesus healed Malchus. Nor does John record Jesus as saying anything to his captors, and John doesn't relate that Jesus says anything about his Father having legions of angels at his disposal.

Upon minimal reflection, it isn't hard to see how all of these accounts can be true and harmonizable. Clearly, the way each tells the story is distinctive. It doesn't square with the idea that there was really only one account of the story, and the others just copied it. This is the kind of evidence of the independence of the eyewitnesses that lends credibility to what they say.[42]

Another internal evidence of the reliability of the Gospels is the amount of details they include in relating the various incidents of Jesus's life. John and Luke in particular do this, but Matthew does as well. Consider the birth narratives of Jesus. Only Matthew and Luke include a genealogy, and it isn't the same one. Matthew alone records the visit of the wise men, Herod's attempt to kill the baby Jesus, and the flight of Jesus, Mary, and Joseph into Egypt. Luke includes the annunciation to Zacharias of the forthcoming birth of John the Baptist and the announcement to Mary that she would give birth to Jesus. In both cases, Luke includes extensive details about the announcement and the reactions of Zacharias and Mary. It is also Luke who tells us about the decree of Caesar to take a census, and then he adds the detail that this was the first census taken when Quirinius was governor of Syria (Luke 2:1–2). In chapter 3 Luke tells us of John the Baptist's ministry, but he begins the chapter with details that pinpoint exactly the time of these events—surely those who first read this would know whether Luke was remembering correctly who was politically in power and who was in the high priesthood of Israel. Luke (3:1–2) writes,

> Now in the fifteenth year of the reign of Tiberius Caesar, when Pontius Pilate was governor of Judea, and Herod was tetrarch of Galilee, and his brother Philip was tetrarch of the region of Ituraea and Trachonitis, and Lysanias was tetrarch of Abilene, in the high priesthood of Annas and Caiaphas, the word of God came to John, the son of Zacharias, in the wilderness.

As you read the story of John the Baptist that follows this, you have to wonder why we needed all of this information recorded in verses 1–2 in order to understand what Luke tells us about John the Baptist. Such details are hardly necessary if this is a work of fiction, and even as a work of non-fiction, all of these details aren't necessary.

It is also interesting to note the number and variety of parables to be found in the Gospels. Matthew, Mark, and Luke include various parables, but both Luke and Matthew include parables that are found nowhere else (e.g., only Luke tells the parable of the prodigal son [15:11–32] and the parable of the good Samaritan [10:25–37], and only Matthew [20:1–16] tells the parable of the landowner and the workers in the vineyard, and the parable of the ten virgins [25:1–13]). One may wonder what this has to do with the historical reliability of these books, and the answer is much. Matthew and Luke not only tell us these parables, but they affirm that Jesus taught them, and usually they explain the circumstances in which Jesus taught these parables.

Then, John's Gospel is a treasure trove of details. As already noted, it is only John who tells us the name of the disciple who cut off the ear of the high priest's servant, and only John who tells us the victim's name. Moreover, it is only John who tells us about Nicodemus being present at the burial of Christ, and John makes a specific point to tell us how many pounds of spices Nicodemus brought. Then, it is also only John who tells us that at the crucifixion the Jews were worried that Christ's body would be on the cross on the Sabbath. Because this was a special Sabbath (John 19:31) they were especially concerned to have Jesus's body removed. It is also only John who tells us that because of this they went to Pilate and asked that the legs of the three men being crucified be broken so that they would die quickly and their bodies could be removed. John alone continues the story by telling us that the Roman soldier didn't need to break Jesus's legs because he was already dead. And only John tells us that the soldier thrust a spear into Jesus's side and as a result blood and water came out. As we shall see in the chapter on the resurrection, this last comment about the blood and water has great significance, but not a significance that John would have known. Still, he includes all of these details about Jesus's last moments on the cross that none of the other Gospel writers tell us.

While we could offer further examples of the specific details the writers relate, I think the point is well enough illustrated from what I have said. The question you are probably asking, however, is how any of this relates to the reliability of the text. The point is that we have one of two possible explanations for the inclusion of all of these details. Either the Gospel writers are incredibly creative storytellers who could embellish their tales of fiction with all sorts of specific details to make them seem more realistic, or all of these details are included because things actually happened this way. While we have little evidence that the Gospel writers lacked imagination altogether, it is much more reasonable to explain, for example, the sort of details noted in Luke's birth narrative and in John's account of the crucifixion by saying they included those details (and they knew to do so; they didn't need to make them up), because that is the way it actually happened. The inclusion of details such as those mentioned only serves to give the account the ring of truthfulness.

Let me turn next to two final indicators of reliability from within the texts of the Gospels. If authors aren't really telling the truth, for whatever reason, they may include things in their works that contradict other things they have written, or several authors telling basically the same set of stories may contradict one another. As we saw in the chapter on presuppositionalism, if a set of ideas (in this case, ideas and events contained in a narrative about various persons and events) is internally consistent, i.e., the individual points made don't contradict other things that are said about the same topic or event, that isn't proof that the one holding those views or relating those stories is getting everything right. It is possible for someone to be good enough at logic so as to set forth a system devoid of contradictions, but it is also possible that the system presented is an internally consistent system of error when one compares what is said with the world around us. So, avoidance of contradiction alone can't prove that a set of ideas or stories is true. But, if authors contradict themselves or other authors who speak of the same things, those contradictions prove that one or more of the writers are wrong in what they relate.

Do the Gospel writers contradict themselves or other Gospel writers? Many critics are certain they do and, hence, are just as certain that the Gospels cannot be reliable in what they record. Examples of alleged inconsistencies in the Gospels aren't hard to find. For example, what did Jesus actually say about divorce and remarriage? Matthew records Jesus as including an exception clause, while Mark and Luke only include the basic rule which prohibits divorce and remarriage. Who is right? As I wrote above about the differing accounts of Jesus's betrayal, I am sure that readers noticed inconsistencies in what the various writers recorded. And then there is the question about how many times the cock would crow before Peter denied Jesus. Mark records Jesus as telling Peter that before the cock crows twice, Peter would deny him three times (14:30). Later Peter does deny Jesus three times (Mark 14:66–71) and then the cock crowed a second time (14:72). Matthew records Jesus as saying that "before the cock crows, you shall deny me three times" (Matt. 26:34). Matthew then records that a cock crowed after Peter denied Jesus three times (26:69–75). Luke says (22:34) that Jesus told Peter that the cock would not crow that day until after Peter denied Jesus three times. He then shows Peter denying Christ three times, and tells us that while Peter was denying Christ the third time, a cock crowed (Luke 22:56–60). And finally, John (John 13:38) records Jesus as telling Peter that a cock would not crow until after Peter denied him three times. In John 18:15–27 John records Peter's three denials of Christ and says that the cock crowed after Peter denied Jesus (given John's account of the times Peter denied Jesus) the third time. How many times did Jesus say the cock would crow, and how many times did it crow? Which Gospel writer's account is true?

And what about the accounts of the tomb on resurrection morning? Luke says (24:4) the women saw two men in dazzling apparel in the tomb, while John says (20:12–16) they saw two angels dressed in white and that Jesus also appeared to Mary, who initially thought he was the gardener. Matthew says (28:2–7) they saw one angel, whose appearance was like lightning and his garment as white as snow, and Mark says (16:5) there was just one young man dressed in a white robe. Which is correct?

Other examples are easy enough to find. The key question, however, is whether the writers contradict one another. If so, then someone (perhaps all of them) either doesn't know the truth or isn't telling the truth. How shall we respond to this challenge to the reliability of the Gospels? I believe several things can be said in response, but I begin with a reminder of what one is charging when one accuses someone of contradicting himself or someone else. A contradiction is the affirmation and denial of one and the same thing at the same time and in the same way. It asserts that there is no *possible* way that all the claims made can be true at once. This is so not just for us but for God as well. It applies not only now but will always be the case that all the claims involved can't be true at once. So, if there are genuine contradictions in the Gospels, that means there is no possible way all the claims involved could be true at the same time. But if the complaint is that there can be no *possible* way, the apologist needs only to offer an answer which would make it possible for all claims involved to be true. Hopefully, the answer given will be plausible (and we should surely seek the most plausible answer to the charge of contradiction), but even if not, given the nature of the complaint, the apologist's only requirement is to offer an explanation that would remove the alleged contradiction so that all claims in question would be true.

Second, the principle with which I started this whole discussion of internal evidence for reliability must be remembered. It demands that we begin with the presumption that the writers are innocent of contradiction until proven otherwise. This does make a difference, because those who are sure that Scripture is guilty until proven innocent typically turn up their noses at various possible answers to the charge of contradiction, because they don't see the answers as very plausible. But if Scripture is guilty until proven innocent, when the critic rejects various answers to the charge of contradiction, what happens to Scripture? In the eyes of the critic it is guilty of a contradiction. On the other hand, if Scripture is assumed innocent until proven guilty, then even if one or two answers to explain an apparent contradiction don't work (i.e., they don't really remove the contradiction), while we await a satisfactory answer—a possible way that all claims in question could be true—Scripture is still assumed innocent until proven guilty.

And, to prove Scripture is truly guilty of contradicting itself, one would have to raise all possible explanations of how the claims could all be true, and would have to show that none of them actually removes the contradiction before we could decisively say that the claims in the text actually do contradict one another.

Third, we must remember the difference between modern and ancient conventions about the use of language. I raise this point because often the Gospel writers offer Jesus's teaching at one time or another. They begin their account by saying that "Jesus said" and then they report what he said. In our modern translations, these words of Jesus are usually set off with quotation marks. Modern conventions about the use of quotation marks in English when relating what someone said demand that we give a verbatim account of what the person said. Hence, if two witnesses tell us what someone said, and they set off those comments with quotation marks, we expect both accounts of what was said to be identical. Now if we impose such standards on Scripture, then surely we can see contradictions in it, for the Gospel writers do not always report that Jesus used exactly the same words when he gave a particular message. However, it would be mistaken to treat these accounts that way. In biblical times there were no such conventions about the meaning of quotation marks as we have today. In fact, the inclusion of quotation marks, chapter and verse divisions, etc., were not there in the original or in many copies—they are more modern insertions into the text. Because people in the time of Jesus didn't think in terms of exact verbatim quotes, it was assumed that if someone reporting what another said got the gist of the comments, that was sufficient. Hence, when two Gospel writers recount the same teaching from Jesus and don't match one another verbatim, that doesn't mean the authors contradict one another. As long as the gist of what they report Jesus saying is the same or at least consistent with other accounts so as not to contradict them blatantly, the differences in wording of a teaching as recorded in two or more Gospels is not an error, and certainly not a contradiction.

While I contend that it is crucial to remember these things in answering complaints about contradictions, none of it suggests how one might remove the apparent contradictions I've mentioned. The good news is that we don't have to withhold judgment that the Gospels are reliable until we identify and resolve every apparent contradiction (an impossible task). But I do think we need to offer answers to alleged contradictions a given nonbeliever might raise in a conversation with us. In that spirit, I want to address the apparent contradictions I have mentioned.

What about the different contents in Jesus's teaching on divorce and remarriage? Only Matthew includes the exception clause, but does that mean he is wrong or that the other Gospel accounts are wrong? Actually, it means neither. Matthew, Mark, and Luke all include the basic teaching that if a man divorces his wife and marries another, he commits adultery. It is only Matthew who adds the exception clause, and only Mark who tells us that the basic rule applies to a woman if she divorces her husband and marries another man (Mark 10:11–12). Let me first address this difference in Mark's account. Mark doesn't say that the rule applies to wives divorcing husbands, but not to husbands divorcing wives. In fact, Mark states the rule in two forms, one with the husband doing the divorcing, and the other with the wife doing it. Matthew's and Luke's accounts only speak of the husband divorcing his wife. But they don't say that *only* a husband can divorce his wife, nor do they say that *only* when a husband divorces and remarries he commits adultery (suggesting that maybe a wife could divorce her husband and remarry without her committing adultery). Mark's relating that Jesus applied the rules to husbands and wives alike in no way contradicts the other Gospel writers; it just shows that the rule applies to both husbands and wives.

What about the exception clause in Matthew alone? Here we must remember the nature of rules (and even ethical evaluations of conduct) and the nature of exceptions to those rules and evaluations. To say that a rule or an evaluation of conduct has an exception doesn't mean that the rule is thrown out altogether so that it never applies to anyone. Rather, the exception applies only in the exceptional cases. In non-exceptional cases, the basic rule or evaluation of conduct still applies. So, unless Mark and Luke tell us that there is no exception (and that there cannot be an exception) to what Jesus says about divorcing and remarrying, there is no contradiction between the three Gospel writers. Mark and Luke say no such things about an exception. All three Gospels state the basic evaluation of conduct; Matthew adds an exception, but it doesn't throw out the rule altogether as recorded in Matthew, Mark, and Luke. It only overturns it in exceptional cases. So, all three Gospels can be correct in the ways just explained. There is no contradiction in the accounts of Jesus's teaching on divorce and remarriage.

How shall we handle the differences in the accounts of Christ's betrayal? I note initially that there will be trouble only if one Gospel, for example, records Jesus's comment to Peter after healing Malchus's ear, and adds that Jesus said nothing further to anyone else at the betrayal. Of course, no such language is used by any of the Gospel writers, so there is no reason that Jesus could not have made comments to Peter and to his captors that are recorded in the Gospel. Moreover, the fact that only John records the name of the person who cut off the ear of the high priest's servant, and only John tells us the name of that servant, in no way contradicts what the other Gospels say. They claim that one of the men with Jesus cut off the ear of the high priest's servant. When John tells us it was Peter, indeed he was one of the men with Jesus. When John tells us that the victim was named Malchus, that too contradicts nothing. There would be a contradiction only if someone other than Peter had done the deed and someone other than Malchus was the victim, or if Matthew, Mark, and Luke say we don't know who did it or who the victim was, or if they tell us that Peter didn't do it, and the servant of the high priest wasn't the victim. But none of these things are said anywhere in the Gospels. Hence, there is nothing inconsistent about the different accounts.

What should we say about Peter's denial of Christ and the number of times the cock crowed? I note first that all four Gospel writers record Jesus as telling Peter that he would deny him three times, and each Gospel records Peter denying Jesus three times. In addition, each Gospel says that a cock crowed after Peter's third denial. The "rub" is with Mark's claim that the cock would crow a second time after Peter denied Christ, and Luke's recording of Jesus saying that a cock wouldn't crow that day until Peter had denied Jesus three times. Here I think it is important to note that the prediction in each case is that Peter will first deny Christ three times, and then the cock will crow. Luke's account requires that the cock not crow at all on the day Peter denies Christ before Peter does deny him. While in Mark's account Jesus says the cock will crow twice, he is very clear that Peter will deny Christ three times before the cock crows twice. Hence, the cock won't crow the first time after the first or second denial; he will crow at all only after the third denial. Moreover, it is Luke who says that while Peter was denying Jesus the third time, the cock crowed. The other Gospel writers suggest that the cock crowed after Peter completed his third denial.

From the preceding, I think it is quite possible to show that there is no contradiction among the Gospel accounts. Here is how. Jesus, according to Mark, told Peter that the cock would crow twice after his denial. Luke tells us that as Peter was speaking the cock crowed. Hence, Peter had already denied Jesus twice and was in the process of doing so a third time. Luke 22:60 records his third denial as well as the fact that the cock crowed while Peter was denying he knew Christ. Now if this had happened in our day, someone might have been keeping track of the exact timing of the cock crowing—perhaps even using a stopwatch to determine how far into Peter's third denial it was that the cock crowed. But it would be ridiculous to impose such methods on the text or on the situation itself (had we been there to witness it). Since the cock crowed while Peter was speaking, that means he had begun this third denial before the cock crowed, and surely it is possible to see how this sequence fits with the claim that the cock would not crow until after the third denial.

But there is more, because in Mark's account Jesus says that the cock would crow twice after Peter denied Jesus. Since Luke says the cock starting crowing while Peter was denying Christ a third time, it is possible to see that the cock also crowed a second time, but did so *completely after* Peter finished denying Jesus the third time. This would fit with the requirement from Mark's Gospel that the cock crow twice after the third denial. It would also fit with Luke 22:34 that the first crowing of the cock on that day wouldn't happen until Peter denied Jesus three times. Since the cock first crowed while Peter was denying Jesus a third time, and the second crowing was completely after Peter finished, nothing in Luke about the cock not crowing on that day until Peter denied Jesus three times is contradicted. Both crowings can be seen as happening after Peter's third denial, and they can surely be the first time that day the cock crowed. Matthew and John record Jesus as saying that a cock will crow after Peter denies Jesus three times, and both Gospels record Peter denying Jesus three times and then the cock crowing. What Jesus says in Matthew, Luke, and John in no way precludes the cock from crowing more than once after Peter's denial. The only stipulation is that the crowing comes after the third denial, but none of the Gospels says that the cock couldn't start crowing while Peter is denying Christ the third time. That being so, I have suggested above how all of what we see in Matthew, Luke, and John can be consistent with Mark's account

of Jesus predicting the cock would crow twice after Peter's third denial. Neither Matthew's, Luke's, nor John's account of Jesus's prediction records
him as saying that the cock will crow once and *only* once after Peter's third
denial. I should also add that it is quite possible that when Matthew, Luke,
and John speak of the cock crowing, they are referring to the second crowing that happened *completely after* Peter finished denying Christ a third
time. Or, they may be referring to the crowing that Mark tells us happened
while Peter was denying Jesus the third time. We can't be absolutely sure
to which of the two crowings Matthew, Luke, and John refer, but that is
really irrelevant to the issue of whether the Gospels contradict one another
on this matter. My explanation shows how what all four Gospels say about
this matter can be true at the same time.

Finally, what about the post-resurrection appearances of the angel(s)/
man (men) at the tomb? I think we run into difficulty because of the way
we conceive of angels. We are inclined to believe that they all have wings
and that whenever someone sees an angel, he will see those wings. Hence,
it will always be abundantly clear that one is seeing an angel, not a human
being. While such a conception is understandable, it isn't correct. Angels
are spirit beings. They are able, however, to make their presence known to
human beings by taking on some physical form to manifest their presence.
On some occasions that physical form includes wings; on others it doesn't
have to. Hence, there is really no inconsistency between the Gospel accounts
that call this individual an angel and those that call him a man. If an angel
takes on the form of a man, he is still an angel. Hence, all accounts can be
correct, i.e., the women truly saw angel(s) at the tomb, but they came in the
form of a human being. What about their apparel? Was it a mere, ordinary
white robe, or something bright and shining (dazzling apparel)? Why must
it be either/or rather than both/and? There is no impossibility that those
involved were wearing a white robe that was bright and shining so that it
appeared dazzling to those who saw it. When Mark says the women saw a
young man dressed in a white robe, nothing in the text says that the robe
couldn't be bright, shining, or dazzling.

As to whether there was one or two, that is a bit more difficult, but not
impossible to explain. If there were in fact two angels at the tomb, then
certainly there was at least one. Matthew only speaks of one angel, but
that may be because he was the only one who spoke to the women. Since

the other one didn't say anything, Matthew need not mention him. Only if Matthew says there was one and only one is there a problem, but Matthew doesn't say that. As to Mark, the same explanation applies. It is only the one young man who speaks to the women. He tells them that Jesus has risen and shows them the place where Jesus had lain. Mark doesn't say there was one and only one young man in the tomb. He simply says (16:5) that when the women entered the tomb they saw a young man and they were amazed. Mark 16:6 then tells us what the man said to the women. None of this means there couldn't have been another man there who isn't mentioned, perhaps because he remained silent.

What I have just said seems to be refuted by Luke's and John's accounts. Not only do they say there were two men/angels, but the text says "they said to them," "they" referring to the angels/men and "them" referring to the women. The verb for "said" in Luke 24:5 and in John 20:13 is third person *plural*. This suggests that Luke and John say not only that there were two rather than one individual in the tomb, but that they both spoke to the woman. If so, then my claim that Matthew and Mark can be right because only one of the angels/men spoke seems doomed. However, this is not necessarily so. For often times several people come to deliver someone news and yet only one of them speaks—he or she serves as the spokesperson. When you read what the angels/men ask the women and then tell them, there is clearly no need for them both to say this in unison. One of them could serve quite adequately as spokesperson for both. If so, then my explanation of why Matthew and Mark only mention one angel/man can stand.

Though readers will vary in their judgment of how plausible this explanation is, that isn't the point. Rather the point is whether this explanation, if adopted, would remove the apparent contradiction, and the answer to that is clearly affirmative. It is *possible* that the accounts of all four Gospels are correct on this matter in accord with the explanation I have offered. And remember, all that is required to meet the charge of contradiction is a *possible* way all claims can be true.

As noted previously, it is not mandatory that the apologist explain away every apparent contradiction the nonbeliever raises in order for Scripture to be considered reliable. What would be problematic is if the apologist offers answers to none of the alleged contradictions. But then, having answered the problems raised, it is not wrong to claim that there is reason to think others can be answered as well. And hence, there is no need to withhold judgment that the Gospels are reliable until all possible contradictions are shown to be only apparent.

External Evidences of Reliability of the Gospels

In the previous section, I offered many indications from within the texts of the Gospels that they are reliable. I wrote extensively on that, because I believe most of the evidence for reliability is internal to the Gospels. That should surprise no one because of what I said when I explained why we need to establish both authenticity and reliability of the Gospels. There simply are not secular historical accounts that go into the kind of detail we find in the Gospels. While non-canonical "Gospels" like the Gospel of Thomas may speak about many of these events, invariably those books were not considered canonical because there are clear mistakes in them. Having granted that there are errors in such non-canonical works, there is dubious value in appealing to them for confirmation of what the Gospels teach. This must not be misunderstood. I am not suggesting that there is nothing in the non-canonical works that is true. I am only saying that there are errors or other problems that rule them out as canonical, and that being so, it is debatable as to how helpful they are in confirming the truthfulness of the Gospel accounts.

What sort of extrabiblical evidence for the reliability of the Gospels is there? Here we can point to four basic kinds of evidence, but we needn't go into as much detail as in the previous section in order to make the point. Those four sources of evidence are comments in writings of church fathers who knew eyewitnesses (or knew those who had a connection with eyewitnesses) of the events contained in the Gospels, comparison of the Gospels with other ancient biographies, evidence from secular historical accounts of the times, and evidence from archaeology. Let us discuss each in turn.

As for writings of the early church fathers, we have already seen the statement from Irenaeus. Blomberg also notes that testimony from Papias is helpful. It dates from the early second century, and it was preserved and cited by the historian Eusebius, writing in the early 300s. In his *Historia Ecclesiae* (3:39.14–16) Papias claims that Matthew "originally compiled the oracles or sayings of Jesus in the Hebrew (or Aramaic) language and that Mark was Peter's interpreter, writing accurately though 'not in order' what he learned from that apostle."[43]

Let me offer another example, from the writings of Clement of Rome. Clement of Rome wrote a letter to the Corinthians which is dated around AD 95. In this letter, one finds confirmation of various historical facts that relate to the events chronicled in the Gospels and the book of Acts. Clement writes,

> The Apostles received the Gospel for us from the Lord Jesus Christ; Jesus Christ was sent forth from God. So then Christ is from God, and the Apostles are from Christ. Both therefore came of the will of God in the appointed order. Having therefore received a charge, and having been fully assured through the resurrection of our Lord Jesus Christ and confirmed in the word of God with full assurance of the Holy Ghost, they went forth with the glad tidings that the kingdom of God should come. So preaching everywhere in country and town, they appointed their firstfruits, when they had proved them by the Spirit, to be bishops and deacons unto them that should believe.[44]

As Habermas explains, in this one quote Clement relates that the good news of the kingdom of God was the major Christian message, the gospel came from God and was given to the disciples by Jesus himself, Christ's resurrection (which is assumed as having occurred) provided assurance that his teachings were true, the disciples spread the gospel, and wherever people responded to the gospel and started local congregations, leaders were chosen to minister in these congregations.[45]

Second, one might wonder whether the Gospels should be seen as historical, because most history of the times wasn't about the life of some person, and when the lives of specific people were mentioned, the author didn't include the amount of detail we find in the Gospels about various events in Jesus's life. Moreover, ancient historians and their histories deal mostly with political or military rulers and their exploits. So, we might initially wonder whether the Gospels and Acts should be seen as history.[46] However, when you compare the Gospels with the styles of ancient biographies, there are many similarities, and scholars consider those biographies as generally trustworthy. As Blomberg explains,

> Giving disproportionate attention to someone's birth and death, particularly if they were seen to have religious significance, grouping material topically as well as chronologically, paraphrase rather than exact quotation, summarizing and digesting long speeches or stories, and a general

freedom to describe events from a variety of perspectives, all regularly characterized ancient biographies, including those which historians of antiquity classify as generally historically trustworthy.[47]

While this sort of evidence doesn't prove that the Gospels are historically reliable, it lends credibility to such claims. Even if the Gospel writers used a literary genre that had never before been seen or heard of, that wouldn't in itself make them historically unreliable. On the other hand, when we see that this genre (Gospel) was not so different from the way biographies of the time were written, it helps to confirm what the Gospel writers saw themselves to be doing.

Third, there is some evidence in secular history about details of the Gospels and Acts. A prime example is found in Josephus's *Jewish Antiquities*, which was written in the last third of the first century. Josephus wrote,

> About this time there lived Jesus, a wise man, if indeed one ought to call him a man. For he was one who wrought surprising feats and was a teacher of such people as accept the truth gladly. He won over many Jews and many of the Greeks. He was the Messiah. When Pilate, upon hearing him accused by men of the highest standing amongst us, had condemned him to be crucified, those who had in the first place come to love him did not give up their affection for him. On the third day he appeared to them restored to life, for the prophets of God had prophesied these and countless other marvelous things about him. And the tribe of the Christians, so called after him, has still to this day not disappeared.[48]

As Blomberg notes, Josephus's works were preserved and edited in Christian circles. And because Josephus wasn't a Christian, "there is reason to believe that the references to Jesus's dubious humanity, Messiahship, and resurrection were added or altered by later Christian scribes. But there is a fair consensus that the rest of the testimony is what Josephus originally wrote, since it closely fits his style of writing elsewhere."[49]

Blomberg adds that in Josephus there are references to "Herod the Great, Herod Archelaus, Antipas's execution of John the Baptist, a summary of the Baptist's message, the reign of the ethnarch Aretas, the death of Agrippa I, the famine in Judea, Gallio in Corinth, the accessions of Felix, Festus, and Agrippa II, and various other details which all basically support the parallel narratives in the gospels and Acts."[50]

Gary Habermas's *Ancient Evidence for the Life of Jesus* and *The Historical Jesus* are extremely helpful in citing various secular sources that speak of things mentioned in the Gospels. One such example is especially noteworthy: a portion from the writings of the Roman historian Tacitus (c. AD 55–120). Here is a very important passage in his *Annals*, written about AD 115. It is about the fire in Rome during Nero's reign:

> Consequently, to get rid of the report, Nero fastened the guilt and inflicted the most exquisite tortures on a class hated for their abominations, called Christians by the populace. Christus, from whom the name had its origin, suffered the extreme penalty during the reign of Tiberius at the hands of one of our procurators, Pontius Pilatus, and a most mischievous superstition, thus checked for the moment, again broke out not only in Judaea, the first source of the evil, but even in Rome, where all things hideous and shameful from every part of the world find their centre and become popular. Accordingly, an arrest was first made of all who pleaded guilty; then, upon their information, an immense multitude was convicted, not so much of the crime of firing the city, as of hatred against mankind.[51]

It is indeed interesting to see the number of things this passage affirms. It affirms among others that Christ was a historical person, that Christians derived their name from Christ, that he was put to death during the reign of Tiberius under the authority of Pontius Pilate, and that belief in Jesus was checked momentarily by his death, but then reasserted itself in Judaea and even as far as Rome. Tiberius is known to have ruled from AD 14 to 37.

Finally, there is external evidence confirming various historical aspects of the Gospel accounts from archaeology. There are many examples, so let me offer a few. In 1961 an inscription was found in Caesarea that referred to Pilate during the time of Tiberius. This extrabiblical evidence corroborated the biblical claims about the existence and rule of the person who sentenced Christ to death. Then there was also the discovery of a bone-box of a man named Johanan crucified in the first century. His bones confirm that nails were driven into his ankles, so the claims about Jesus and the two thieves having this done in preparation for hanging on the cross are most likely correct. In addition, in 1992 the burial grounds of Caiaphas, the Jewish high priest at the time of Christ's trial and crucifixion, were found in Jerusalem.[52] And then, coins have been found which were minted to honor Pontius Pilate's rule. These coins are dated AD 30–31.[53] These coins as well as the inscription at Caesarea are significant, because at one time not so long ago skeptics doubted that there ever lived such a person as Pontius Pilate.

The Gospel of John seems to contain more references to things like chronology, geography, and topography than do the Synoptic Gospels. As Blomberg explains,

> These have been demonstrated to be highly accurate, particularly in light of modern archaeological discoveries: the five porticoes of the pool of Bethesda by the Sheep Gate (5:2), the pool of Siloam (9:1-8), Jacob's well at Sychar (4:5), the "Pavement" . . . where Pilate pronounced judgment on Jesus (19:13), Solomon's porch (10:22-23), and so on.[54]

The point here is not that archaeological finds have proved that the events described in John actually happened. Rather they prove that the items mentioned in relation to the various events described actually existed. Since John has been shown to be right about these details, that increases one's faith that he has accurately reported the things that Jesus, the disciples, etc., actually said and did.

Then, Luke's reputation as an accurate historian is based on what we see both in his Gospel and also in the book of Acts. In particular, many of the details included in his stories of the apostles' exploits are well known. Many of the details can be confirmed by extrabiblical sources which, of course, include archaeological finds. Blomberg summarizes the point well when he writes,

> The plethora of names Luke uses to describe the different kinds of political rule in the various cities of the Roman empire—procurators and proconsuls, magistrates and legates, governors and prefects, even the "chief man" on the island of Malta, all have been shown, despite earlier skepticism, to correspond to precisely the legislative setup in the respective communities into which Luke places them. The detailed references to places through which Paul traveled on his missionary journeys all correspond to the actual terrain. Names of provinces fit the Roman administration of the day, even though some of these were then relatively recent and short-lived. Although some of the dates remain a little uncertain, a synthesis of the events of Acts with the historical information Paul supplies in his epistles enables us to reconstruct a harmonious and relatively detailed chronology of events in the life of the early church, especially related to Paul's travels.[55]

Another example of Luke's accuracy as a historian (and there are many of these) appears in the book of Acts. In Acts 19:23ff. Luke writes about a riot that occurred in Ephesus as a result of Paul's preaching the gospel and the conversion of many Ephesians. Verses 29–30 explain that in the midst of this riot the city was filled with confusion, and the people rushed to a theater. They dragged along with them Paul's traveling companions from Macedonia, Gaius and Aristarchus. Paul wanted to go to this meeting, but the disciples wouldn't let him. This mention of a theater refers to an amphitheater. But did such a place exist, and was it likely that there were assemblies that met there at one time or another? Archaeological excavations unearthed a theater at Ephesus that was large enough to hold 25,000 people. In addition, an inscription was found that speaks of silver statues of Artemis (known also as Diana) to be placed in the "theater during a full session of the Ecclesia."[56] The Greek word *ekklesia* is the word used in the New Testament for the church, but it is also used to refer to a meeting for purposes other than religious services. While these archaeological finds don't prove that what Luke says happened in Ephesus actually did occur, it at least shows that there was a large place where there could be and certainly would be public assemblies. What Luke says happened there is in no way implausible.

Luke's historical abilities are very well known and respected. Famed late-nineteenth- and early-twentieth-century British archaeologist Sir William Ramsey originally believed that Acts was written in the second century AD, and he intended to prove that. If so, then Luke couldn't have written it. As Ramsey began to investigate available archaeological evidence, he repeatedly found it to match the historical details of the book of Acts. Though he began his research project as a skeptic, by the time he finished, he had changed his mind. In his book *St Paul the Traveler and the Roman Citizen* (first published in 1895), he explained that he had come to conclude that "in various details the narrative showed marvelous truth."[57]

In sum, if we had only the information from these external evidences, it would be hard to be sure that all the details of the stories the Gospel writers and the author of Acts wrote could be trusted. Of course, none of the external evidence suggests that the Gospels are historically unreliable. But when the external evidence is coupled with the internal evidences presented, a very strong case can be made that the Gospels and Acts offer reliable history. If a predisposition to disbelieve in the supernatural were removed from critics, it is hard to see how they could make a good case that these works are unreliable. And, of course, rejecting as true the history of the Gospels just because of an anti-supernatural bias is question begging and cannot serve as adequate grounds for rejecting the claim that these books are reliable in the history they present.

FINAL THOUGHTS AND CONCLUSION

What I have presented as evidence for the reliability of the Gospels is not all there is to say on the topic. Indeed, it alone doesn't prove that the rest of Scripture is reliable. But I believe it is a very important step in an apologetic for the reliability of all Scripture. I am inclined to use Montgomery's strategy (as detailed in the chapter on Christian evidentialism) for defending the entirety of Scripture's truthfulness, but making that case goes beyond the space limitations in this chapter.

In reflecting on the kinds of arguments and evidences presented in this chapter in defense of the Gospels, one may be surprised at the lack of any mention of fulfilled prophecy as evidence for Scripture's reliability. Though I have a warm response to such an argument because of the role prophecy played in my own spiritual journey, I have omitted such arguments here for specific reasons. As with many collegians who grew up in a Christian home, I had some spiritual problems during my undergraduate college years. These went on for several years and were troublesome. Other Christian friends were going through similar experiences, and I saw them turn from the faith. I was raised in the home of a prominent biblical scholar and professor. Among other things, biblical prophecy, especially messianic and end-time prophecy, were his specialties. I was privileged to hear many of his sermons on prophecy, as he was a frequent guest speaker in many churches and Bible conferences. Over the years of listening to these sermons, I was amazed at how detailed and accurate many of these prophecies were. As a result, when I had spiritual problems in college, I asked myself whether the problem was more likely with me or with Christianity. Repeatedly, I told myself that the problem must be with me. After all, it can hardly be a matter of chance or coincidence that so many biblical prophecies have been fulfilled. A book and religion with that kind of "track record" could not easily be dismissed. Rather than jettisoning my faith, I continued to search for answers which, thankfully, in time the Lord provided.

So, in light of these experiences I am sympathetic to arguments from fulfilled prophecy in support of Scripture's truthfulness. However, in later years as I began to teach apologetics, I came to see that there are some difficulties with this kind of argument. First, there is always the question of whether the one using this argument has accurately interpreted the meaning and fulfillment of any given prophecy. Perhaps he has, but that doesn't mean proving so is all that easy, especially if you are dealing with a skeptic who wants to show you that you can't even get this argument off the ground, let alone succeed with it. Now, this point doesn't mean that your interpretation of the meaning and fulfillment of a given prophecy is wrong. It only suggests that if you intend to use this sort of evidence, you must be ready not only to show that the prophecy has been fulfilled, but also to defend your interpretation of the prophecy and its fulfillment. One senses that very quickly this sort of argument involves a lot more than one originally bargained for and a lot more than one can likely persuade the skeptic of anytime soon.

But there is another problem that is more logical than practical, and this is the one that makes me hesitate to use this sort of argument at all. The problem is as follows: How many prophecies do you think there are in Scripture? Regardless of the number, have they all been fulfilled? Certainly Old Testament prophecies about things that would happen during the span of the Old Testament era have been fulfilled, and prophecies about the first advent of Christ have been fulfilled. But there are still many prophecies about the second advent of Christ and the events before and after it that have not yet been fulfilled. The sheer volume of such prophecies is quite large. If, then, fulfilled prophecies are evidence *for* Scripture's reliability, then don't unfulfilled prophecies have to count as evidence *against* its truthfulness? It would certainly seem so, especially when we remember that a lot of these prophecies were given two thousand years and more ago. If some modern-day astrologer made a prediction that didn't come to pass even in a hundred years, would we still believe the prediction was correct? I doubt it, but then the skeptic is likely to tell us that if these prophecies about the end times were really true, they would have been fulfilled by now. Certainly, these prophecies can't be used as evidence that Scripture is reliable.

This must not be misunderstood. I am not saying that end-time prophecies are false or that they will forever go unfulfilled. I am only commenting on the logic of such an argument in building a case for Scripture's reliability. And my point is that there are too many of these prophecies which are not yet fulfilled for us to claim that the fulfillment of biblical prophecies proves that Scripture is reliable. There are still so many unfulfilled that it would not be surprising that, if we were to make an argument from fulfilled prophecy, the skeptic would respond that we have made an unwarranted inductive generalization. That is, even if the skeptic grants that we are right about all the prophecies we believe have been fulfilled, he has a right to say that those fulfilled ones aren't a large enough sampling of all the biblical prophecies there are for us to have a right to make the inductive leap that all prophecies will be fulfilled because of the ones already fulfilled. And, if we can't (logically don't have a right to, that is) claim that it is certain the rest will be fulfilled, then how can we think that it will be compelling if we say fulfilled prophecy shows that Scripture is reliable? Of course, if you disagree with me on this point you are welcome to use fulfilled prophecy to try to convince doubters of Scripture's reliability. Just be ready to defend your interpretation of the prophecy before you even get to making the case that the prophecy has been fulfilled as you understand what it predicts.

Thankfully, the case for the reliability of the Gospels doesn't rest on just one argument. What has been presented to satisfy the bibliographic test and the tests of internal and external evidence is sufficient. The evidence is true (as has been shown), and the evidences used at each step of the way are relevant to the point at issue—first to show authenticity, but then later arguments to show reliability. When all of these arguments and evidences are taken together, there is still room for faith, but I maintain that the case has been made for reliability beyond a reasonable doubt!

Chapter 12

The Resurrection of Jesus Christ

The apostle Paul wrote to the church at Corinth about the resurrection of Christ. The Corinthians didn't believe in resurrections, but they did think Christ had risen from the dead. In 1 Corinthians 15 Paul addresses these issues directly. He argues that if resurrections cannot occur, then even Christ hasn't risen from the dead. If Christ is risen, then other resurrections are possible. Paul then entertains the notion that Christ didn't actually rise from the dead, and he spells out the consequences. What he offers in 1 Corinthians 15:12–19 is a classic example of a *reductio ad absurdum* argument. This argument strategy grants for the sake of argument the truth of a particular belief that one doesn't really hold. Assuming that the belief is true, one then lays out the consequences. The consequences are absurd, so something must be wrong in the overall chain of ideas. The critic of the claim explains that the culprit is the original idea that was granted for the sake of argument. Once it is rejected, the absurd consequences don't obtain.

In 1 Corinthians 15 the idea that Paul grants for the sake of argument is that Christ didn't actually rise from the dead. Paul says that if the Corinthians are right in rejecting resurrections in general, then Christ must not be risen. But if he hasn't risen, all sorts of absurdities result. The culprit in this line of reasoning must be the idea that Christ didn't rise from the dead. When that idea is rejected, none of the absurdities can possibly be true.

But there is more. If Christ really rose from the dead, then we cannot, generally speaking, say that resurrections are impossible. By the latter part of chapter 15 Paul picks up the theme of resurrections other than Christ's. Not only is there no impossibility about such resurrections occurring; we can even talk about the nature of the glorified body of those resurrected. Paul tells us that our resurrection will follow the pattern of Christ's. That is, just as his resurrected human body is immortal and incorruptible, so ours will be as well.

But what if Christ actually never rose from the dead? Paul offers in 1 Corinthians 15:12–19 a series of negative consequences, including the fact that those who preach Christ's resurrection from the dead (including Paul) are liars. The Greek actually says they have been "detected as liars"; that is, we have caught them in the act of lying. At the time Paul wrote 1 Corinthians, there were plenty of people still alive who had witnessed the events at the very end of Christ's life. Such people would know whether those who preached the resurrection were liars, and at least some of them would surely have exposed the apostles as liars. We have no record of that ever being seriously attempted, let alone succeeding.

There is something even worse, however, than detecting phonies preaching a lie. If Christ has not been raised, then as Paul says, no one's sins are forgiven. Those of us who think we have God's forgiveness and assurance of life eternal with him are seriously deluded. If Christ could not completely conquer the power of sin and its consequence death, he cannot defeat it for any of us. Yet we believe that he has, and many of Paul's first readers and hearers were persecuted for believing in Christ and his resurrection; many of them gave their life rather than recant their belief in Christ. But if Christ hasn't risen from the dead, those Christians endured persecution and even death for nothing. Indeed, as Paul says, if the resurrection of Christ never happened, then those who believe it did and have adjusted their lives accordingly are of all people most miserable!

The resurrection of Jesus Christ is no minor or nonessential doctrine of the Christian faith. We cannot abandon it and still have true, biblical Christianity. Like the doctrines of the Trinity and the hypostatic union of Christ, the doctrine of Christ's resurrection is unique to Christianity—no other religion has such a doctrine and none of them needs it. But if the resurrection of Christ is nothing more than a doctrine, then belief in it may at times give us a warm feeling toward God and Christ, but it won't accomplish anything really essential (like forgiveness of sins now and eternal life beyond the grave). Thankfully, we need not believe that the resurrection is true without having any way of confirming or disconfirming the belief. This is so because the resurrection is not just a Christian doctrine; what the doctrine claims requires that it also be a historical event. And thankfully there are plenty of historical data with which to assess whether this doctrine is mere wishful thinking or something true.

In this chapter my intent is not to handle the resurrection from the perspective of its doctrinal content and place in an overall Christian theology. Instead, my concern is whether the event the doctrine speaks of actually happened. As already noted, we have ample historical evidence to make a decision about that matter. So, what exactly is at issue in this chapter? What are we trying to prove and critics trying to disprove?

In answering these questions, we should specify both what we are and are *not* trying to prove. I begin with the latter. First, what is not at stake is whether miracles in general are *possible*. The possibility of miracles often *is the point* of the discussion when defending miracles in general. But something more specific is at issue in this chapter. Of course, one way to defend miracles as possible is to demonstrate that we possess the evidence needed to prove that one actually happened. Thus, if we succeed in showing that the resurrection actually occurred, we will also have shown that miracles in general are possible, even though miracles as possible isn't our main point.

Second, when defending the resurrection of Christ, one way to approach the topic is merely to refute the naturalistic explanations of what actually happened to Christ's body. Beyond the evidence to refute those explanations, a positive case would not be offered. Here I must emphatically say that this is neither my strategy nor my intent in this chapter. My concern is to offer the positive case for the resurrection. In so doing, I believe ample evidence will be presented to refute naturalistic alternative explanations. The reason that our task is not simply to refute competing explanations is that if this is all we do, we will have shown naturalistic explanations of the resurrection to be wrong, but we won't necessarily have presented ample evidence to show that the resurrection actually happened. That is, if all other explanations of the resurrection are proved wrong, belief that the resurrection really occurred doesn't win by default. It may be that no current explanation, including the one that Christ actually rose, is adequate. Hence, at some point the Christian apologist must offer the evidence for the resurrection.

Third, the point of the defense I shall offer is not to prove that God exists. For the purposes of this chapter, I am assuming that an adequate case has already been made for his existence. But even if that case has not been made, I am not convinced that God's existence must first be proved before one can prove the resurrection. Many believe otherwise, reasoning that if ours isn't a theistic universe, resurrections are impossible. While I appreciate this point of view, I have never found it conclusive for several reasons. One is that we must remember what must be proved to establish a resurrection. There must be clear and convincing evidence that someone who was alive died a physical death. Then, there must be further evidence that some time after physical death, the same person was seen alive. Now if there is overwhelming evidence that both of these things happened, why would you have to deny or withhold judgment that the person was dead and later alive until you could prove God's existence? Remember, we are not asking who brought him back to life or how he did it—such evidence may not be available, empirically speaking. What is available empirically is evidence that he was dead and then later was alive.

Even so, some will claim that, depending on one's worldview, their interpretation of these events may differ. A committed anti-supernaturalist can grasp the evidence, but because of his anti-supernaturalism, the most he will likely say is that we have here a phenomenon that he cannot explain in naturalistic terms. A committed theist will likely see the evidence and conclude that a genuine resurrection has occurred, and will probably think that God performed this miracle.[1]

I am more than willing to grant that one's worldview impacts one's interpretation of the data. My claims are that, regardless of one's worldview, there are two facts that must be explained: 1) someone physically alive later showed clear evidence of being physically dead, and 2) that same person who was physically dead later was seen as alive again. This is ultimately what we are trying to establish in proving Christ's resurrection. Call these events a resurrection or a naturalistically inexplicable phenomenon, we can still agree on whether the facts show that someone alive died, and that the same person was later seen physically alive.

Hopefully, if evidence of such things were available, anti-supernaturalists would take such evidence as counterevidence to their disbelief in the supernatural. The evidence might not convince them to be theists, but it should surely help them to see that their case for anti-supernaturalism is not 99 percent objectively certain. In fact, it is possible, though we shouldn't expect it, especially since we aren't trying to prove it, that the naturalist will see the evidence for the resurrection as hard to contest and will reconsider his or her naturalism and atheism. Similarly, if conclusive evidence were found that Christ is still dead, that wouldn't shake theists' belief in God (that belief doesn't rest solely on the resurrection of Christ), but it would at the very least have to count as evidence against what Christians believe about God. Still, if an atheist wanted to convince a theist of naturalism, she would have to do more than merely present evidence that Christ is dead and then conclude that this fact proves theism is wrong.

It is in the sense just explained that I mean we are not arguing for God's existence when we make a case for the resurrection of Christ. As to whether evidence for the resurrection counts if we don't first prove the existence of God, I think it does, because proper historical method requires suspended judgment about the interpretation of evidence so as to view as objectively as possible what the facts require. But that is a discussion for another place. For our purposes, I contend only that arguing for God's existence and for Christ's resurrection, though relevant for one another, are not the same thing. In this chapter we are making the case for Christ's physical death at one time and his live appearances at a later time. Who raised Christ and how it was done go beyond the scope of this chapter.

Finally, I think it helpful to see that, interpreted one way, Christ's resurrection actually involved two miracles, not just one. Christ's resurrection is not the only one recounted in Scripture. Jesus raised Lazarus, the apostles raised a few people from the dead, and there is even some indication in the Old Testament that a very few people were resurrected. However, Christ was the only person resurrected who did not later die a natural death. Christ was not only bodily resurrected, but his body also was transformed into a glorified body so that he could never die physically again.[2] When Paul speaks of the resurrection of the church at the rapture (1 Cor. 15:55ff.; 1 Thess. 4:13–18), he makes it clear that we will be given glorified bodies, just as Christ was.

In light of the fact that Christ's resurrection involved a double miracle, one might think I am going to defend both miracles, resurrection *and* glorification (by glorification I do not mean Christ's ascension; I mean the changes to Christ's physical body upon resurrection, changes that happened when he arose from the dead—certainly well before his ascension). While I am inclined to think that each of these miracles deserves and needs its own defense, because of the brevity of space my intention is only to offer support for the resurrection. However, as we shall see, one line of evidence crucial to the case for his resurrection will cover most of the bases, so to speak, if not all in establishing that his resurrected body was also glorified.

Since none of the items I have enumerated above are what I am defending in this chapter, then what exactly is the focus of my apology? It is my intent to offer evidence to establish that someone who was physically dead, namely Jesus Christ, came back to life. Here, when I speak of being physically dead, I am thinking in contemporary terms of what it means to be dead. Some years ago an Ad Hoc committee from Harvard Medical School set forth four criteria to define physical death. Those criteria are: 1) unreceptivity and unresponsivity (no stimuli of any sort evoke any kind of response); 2) no movements or spontaneous breathing for at least an hour; 3) no reflexes, and fixed dilated pupils; and 4) a flat brain wave (flat EEG) for at least ten minutes, preferably twenty. All four of these criteria must be at once true of the person, and they should still be true some twenty-four hours later.[3]

From this definition it becomes clear that we are not talking about someone in a coma whose heart and lungs still function and who several months in the future wakes up. This definition of physical death wouldn't even fit someone deemed to be in a persistent vegetative state. Though there is no way to go back in time and check Jesus for these four criteria, the descriptions offered in the Gospel accounts suggest more than someone in a coma. And his state remained that way for more than twenty-four hours. Our task, then, is to offer evidence that someone (Jesus) who would likely meet the four criteria for physical death enumerated above later came back to life so that none of the four criteria were then true of him.

POSSIBLE STRATEGIES

If this is our task, how might we go about achieving it? Since much of the case for Christ's resurrection relies heavily on information from the New Testament, especially the Gospels, one might think the defense has to begin with a defense of the reliability of the New Testament. For the sake of this chapter, I am assuming that the reliability of the New Testament, especially the Gospels, has already been established. In chapter 11, I presented evidence to that effect.

Even if we grant the reliability of the New Testament, that doesn't automatically seal the case for the resurrection. That is so because it is possible to interpret the events recounted in a different way than would require a resurrection. In fact, some of the best-known naturalistic explanations of the event claim that those who think the Gospel accounts require a resurrection have misinterpreted the texts. So, there is work for us to do, and there are several ways we might go about offering a defense of the resurrection. For example, we might assume that in response to whether Christ was dead and then arose, the options are only two—yes or no. Those who answer as agnostics don't really add a third option to the question at hand. Christ either did or didn't die and rise again. Agnosticism about these events tells us something about our knowledge and understanding of what happened, but it doesn't change the fact that Christ either did or did not die and rise again.

Since there are only two answers about whether Christ died and rose again, we could adopt a strategy that just listens to critics' objections to the resurrection and answers them. If objections can be answered, we might think that means Christ must have arisen. Perhaps if all possible objections could be stated and refuted, that would be enough to defend the resurrection, but we are obviously not in a position to be certain that we know all possible objections. Anyway, even if it were possible to answer all the critics' objections, we would still be expected to offer positive evidence that the resurrection actually occurred. So this strategy, while of some value, is probably not the best way to proceed.

A second strategy does not try to answer objections directly. Rather it presupposes that if Christ did not die and rise again, there must be a naturalistic explanation of what actually happened. Perhaps, then, the best strategy for the apologist is to present each naturalistic explanation of what happened and then offer evidence to refute them one by one. This, like our first strategy, has some value. After all, regardless of the strategy taken, one must address naturalistic counter-explanations at some point. In fact, the strategy I shall propose will implicitly, if not explicitly, refute alternate explanations. Still, I am not entirely convinced that merely refuting counter-explanations is enough. If it succeeds, it demonstrates that the naturalistic explanations available are wrong, but that alone doesn't prove the resurrection is a historical fact. There may be a better naturalistic explanation that is currently not on the horizon but that beats all theories, including the resurrection conclusion. Even if there isn't a better naturalistic explanation, refuting the theories we know of still doesn't make a positive case *for* the resurrection. So, I think a different strategy is likely better.

Third, even if one decides that the best strategy is to offer a positive case for the resurrection, where does one begin? One might begin with the fact of the empty tomb and then consider the possible ways it might have become empty. In considering the various options, one could hopefully show that the most probable explanation is that the tomb was empty because Jesus had risen. While I think such an approach has merit, I suspect it would wind up doing little more than a strategy that simply considers the naturalistic counter-explanations and refutes them.

In light of these concerns, I want to propose an alternate approach. I think we need to present the positive case for the resurrection. I think such a case has four major things it must establish. First, the apologist must present the evidence that shows that *Jesus really died*. This seems obvious but is worth noting anyway. Unless it can be conclusively established that Jesus was actually physically dead, it is impossible to talk about a resurrection. If Jesus only fainted (or "swooned," as various naturalistic explanations have claimed), or if he was in a coma, then at most we can speak about a bodily resuscitation or reawakening, but not a resurrection.

The second step in defending the resurrection is to show that Jesus was *buried in a known tomb*. If Jesus was never buried, or if he was buried but no one remembered where, then one can hardly speak about a resurrection as the best explanation of an empty tomb. Of course, if his body were burned (even cremated), no evidence of an empty tomb would prove anything about a resurrection. But it is highly unlikely in that day and culture that there would be cremation rather than a burial. Then, because Jesus was crucified with two criminals and was blamed for blasphemy by the Jewish leaders and those they incited, it is unlikely that the Jews would have given him a separate tomb. He would more likely have been placed in a common grave with other convicted and executed criminals. Of course, if that was the destiny of Jesus's physical remains, it would be very hard to prove that anyone in the grave arose—who would want to count the bodies every few hours so as to be on the alert lest one of them arose from the dead?

On the other hand, if Jesus was buried in a distinct tomb, it is important to establish that the exact location of that tomb was known. And, it would be preferable if its location was known not only by the disciples but also by the Jews and Romans. If only the disciples knew where Jesus was buried, and then three days after the crucifixion they began pointing people to an empty tomb and began preaching the resurrection, those who saw the tomb would agree that it was empty. But surely they would doubt that it was Christ's tomb, and they wouldn't agree that Christ was placed dead in *that* now vacant tomb.

So, it is important to show that Jesus was buried. This will help to discredit claims that he merely swooned on the cross but never actually died. And it is just as important to show that more than just a few people, and definitely more than just the disciples, knew where he was buried. If everyone went to the wrong tomb on that first Easter morning, then people may have found an empty tomb, but it wasn't Christ's, and *that* empty tomb didn't mean he was alive again.

The third major step in arguing for the resurrection is to show that *the body was missing but not stolen*. This, of course, means that we must first prove that the tomb where Jesus was buried was empty. But we must prove even more. If all we can show is that a tomb, purported to be Christ's, was empty, then it will be difficult to prove a resurrection. There are a number of reasons why the tomb might be empty. It might be empty because Christ never really died, and later in the tomb revived and then slipped past the guards on duty. Or the tomb might be empty because everyone went to the wrong tomb and concluded that since Jesus wasn't there, he must have arisen. But, of course, we already would have foreclosed the chance of these two possible explanations being true by establishing first that Jesus really died and secondly that he was buried in a known tomb.

An empty tomb, however, could be explained by Christ's body being stolen. And, we must remember that there were many different candidates for the task of theft. The obvious choice is that the disciples did it, but it could have been the Jews, the Romans, or grave robbers. Hence, at this third stage of the defense, we must discredit the notion that any of these groups stole Christ's body. If the body is missing but cannot be explained away by the supposition that Jesus didn't really die, or that everyone went to the wrong tomb, or that someone or some group of people stole the body, what other option is there than that the tomb was empty because Jesus had arisen? If there are other options, let the critic suggest them, and the apologist for the resurrection can explain why those further explanations are unlikely and invalid.

Though you might think that nothing more is needed to show that Christ arose, there actually is. When we finish step three, we will likely claim that the most plausible explanation of the empty tomb is that Jesus rose from the dead. Since such an event would be a major miracle, if we offer no further evidence, the critic will likely think that any other naturalistic explanation is still more plausible than a resurrection. I can certainly sympathize with such thinking, and that is why it would really help if there were some further evidence to support the claim that the tomb was empty as a result of a resurrection. Thankfully, there is. If Jesus actually rose from the dead, it would surely help to confirm that by his appearing to people after he arose. Hence, the final phase of our apologetic turns to *post-resurrection appearances*. Many people claimed to see Christ alive after he died and was buried. What are we to make of these claims? Were those people hallucinating? Were they seeing visions of Christ, but not Christ himself? And how many people and how many sightings are we talking about? Offering evidence that these post-resurrection appearances were genuine encounters with the risen Christ will only serve to confirm that a resurrection is the best explanation of the empty tomb.

In sum, to defend Christ's resurrection from the dead, we must show four things: 1) Jesus really died; 2) Jesus was buried in a known tomb; 3) Jesus's body was missing, but not stolen; and 4) a living Jesus appeared to many people after he had died and was buried. Each of these four items has its own arguments and evidences, and the apologist must present the relevant arguments at the appropriate stage of the defense. Now, some may complain that they have other evidences that help make the case, even though those data don't relate specifically to any of the four items mentioned. I'm not denying that there might be other evidences of value; I'm only saying that to show that Jesus rose from the dead, one must establish as probable the four items set forth in this section.

EVIDENCE THAT CHRIST ACTUALLY DIED

Here I begin with a couple of arguments that one sometimes hears. Those who present them think they are helpful in proving that Jesus really died, but I disagree. Once I address these weak arguments, I shall turn to what seem to me much better arguments that Christ actually died.

Some apologists believe that the fact that Jesus was flogged during the events leading up to the crucifixion is a good argument to show that Christ really died. Those who offer this argument often claim that Jesus was whipped with a flagrum or cat-o'-nine-tails. This was a whip that had pieces of metal and bone embedded in it. When the victim was flogged using this whip it would lacerate his body. It was so destructive that on occasions it laid bare the victim's muscles, sinews, and bowels. While the Jews had rules that limited scourging to forty lashes, the Romans had no such rules. So, it is argued, Jesus's flogging offers good evidence that he died.[4]

Using our three tests (is it true, is it relevant, and how much does it prove?), I can say that this is actually a weak argument. First, as to its truth, a careful reading of the Gospel accounts of Christ's trial and crucifixion shows that he was flogged, but nothing is said about the instrument used or the number of lashes he received. In fact, the Gospels say that Pilate had Christ scourged and then released him to the crowd to crucify him. Since Pilate publicly noted his failure to find fault with Jesus, it is certainly possible that he told those who whipped Jesus not to scourge him as ruthlessly as they might normally flog a criminal. Of course, we can neither confirm nor disconfirm this supposition, but that is also the case in terms of the instrument used to scourge Jesus and the number of lashes given. So, it is not clear that the argument as stated is true.

Second, as to the relevance of this argument, it has some significance, but probably not as much as those who propose it suggest. At this stage of the defense the intent is to prove that Jesus actually died. Pointing to his scourging is relevant to his death, not because he died from the scourging but because it contributed to his overall weakened state. But since we don't know what was used to flog him, or how many lashes he received, we cannot say exactly how much it weakened him. One thing is clear, however. Regardless of how bad off Jesus was after the flogging, it didn't kill him. If it had, there would have been no need to crucify him.

What I have just said about the relation of the flogging to the crucifixion also helps us to answer how much this line of argument actually proves. The answer is that as currently stated, it proves very little. It certainly doesn't prove that Jesus died. The most we can say—if I used this argument at all,

I would nuance it as follows—is that if Jesus was whipped using the instrument that was typically used, a cat-o'-nine-tails, and depending on how many lashes he received, it is likely that he was in a weakened physical state even before he was crucified. But the flogging didn't kill him, and since we are attempting to prove that Jesus actually died, this is not an argument that helps much to make that case.

Consider next another argument one sometimes hears. Apologists know that many who doubt that Jesus actually died hold some form of the swoon theory. According to this naturalistic explanation, Jesus didn't actually die. Instead, there was a plot to make it look like he died, but he only fainted. Later in the coolness of the tomb he revived, got up, and escaped from the tomb without being noticed by the guards, or if noticed, he was able to overpower or at least elude them.

Now apologists who interact with the swoon theory believe they see a major problem with it. How, they ask, could someone in as bad shape as Christ was after the whole ordeal of the trial and crucifixion revive in a cool tomb, push away the huge stone, elude the soldiers, and later appear to the disciples as the conqueror of death? Wouldn't the cool tomb send him into shock and likely kill him, given what he'd already been through? If he wasn't dead already, placement in the tomb would have likely killed him, and if so, then he couldn't then escape from the tomb and proclaim his resurrection in any convincing way. The swoon theory cannot be true.

What shall we say to this argument? There are some who find it convincing, but I note initially that it actually contains elements that are contrary to fact. When an argument is based on a hypothetical scenario, that doesn't mean it can't be true, but there should at least be hope that the claims made in the conditional part of the scenario are actually true or at least could be true. And here is where we run into trouble. A good bit of the force of this argument turns on the notion that Christ was placed in a cool tomb. But if the tomb is not "cool enough" (whatever "cool enough" means), then the thought of its refreshing and reviving Jesus is in trouble. Moreover, the claim that the cool tomb would likely send Jesus into shock and kill him, if he wasn't already dead, is also in trouble. But here is where the difficulty arises. All of this is happening in the spring of the year. Since it was Passover time when this occurred, we are likely talking about some time in April. In addition, from what we know about tombs that were not mass graves, it is likely that Jesus's tomb was not one that was dug deep in the ground. In fact, because there was a stone rolled in front of the entrance, it is likely that this tomb was at ground level or slightly below.

How cool do you think a ground-level tomb in the month of April in a Mediterranean climate would be? I was raised in a similar climate, and April in that kind of climate is not freezing. I am raising these issues because the line of argument we are considering turns on the idea that the tomb was cold. No one I have read who uses this argument speaks of the tomb as though it were as cold as a refrigerator, but at times you do wonder if that isn't their thought. If so, or if they are counting on the tomb being quite cool, it is dubious that conditions at that time of year would be as this argument requires. So, I am somewhat skeptical about this matter of fact, and if I am right, the hypothetical scenario suggested is less likely to be the case.

As to the rest of the argument—moving the stone, getting past the guards unnoticed, appearing as hale and hearty—I think what this argument claims is believable. My concern here is that this whole line of thinking makes some sense if all we are trying to do is refute one aspect or another of the swoon theory. The three items just mentioned show it would be hard for Jesus to escape the tomb, not that he was actually dead. The aspect of this argument that does more directly address whether he actually died is the part about the coolness of the tomb, and there is reason to question the factualness of that matter. All of this also helps us answer our second question about the relevance of the argument. It is surely relevant to elements of various swoon theories, but that doesn't mean it proves that Jesus really died. Hence, I wouldn't be inclined to use it, if the intent is to prove that Jesus actually died.

All of the above also means that this argument doesn't prove a whole lot about Christ's death. Assuming that the flogging left him in a terribly weakened condition, and that the crucifixion ran its course and killed him, then, assuming that the tomb in which he was placed was quite cool, it is likely that being placed in the tomb would kill him if he wasn't already dead. But such an argument contains a lot of "ifs" whose answers we don't actually know. So, it is dubious that this part of the argument helps us much to prove that Christ died. On the other hand, if one is trying to *disprove* that Jesus, under his own natural powers (not the powers we would associate with a resurrected Christ), moved the stone and snuck past the guards, this line of argument is helpful. But as proof that Christ actually died, this argument doesn't help us very much.

Despite these and other weak arguments, there are strong reasons to think that Jesus actually died on the cross. First, the Gospel writers Matthew, Mark, and Luke inform us that a Roman soldier who was at the cross heard Jesus's last words and saw that he had died. In fact, John tells us that it was getting late in the day, and the Jews didn't want the bodies left on the cross on the Sabbath day, so they went to Pilate to request that the victims' legs be broken so that they would die and could be removed (John 19:31). When the soldiers went to break Christ's legs so that he could no longer push up on his legs so as to gather air into his lungs, they saw that it was unnecessary because Jesus was already dead.[5]

But this is not the whole argument, for we must ask about the knowledge level of the soldiers involved. If these were new recruits who hadn't seen many or even any crucifixions, perhaps they were just wrong in thinking Christ was dead. While this is possible, it is in no way probable. Matthew (27:54), Mark (15:39), and Luke (23:47) tell us that a key soldier who concluded that Christ died was a centurion. Such a military officer was no "rookie." It is likely that he had seen many men die, and probably had been involved in other crucifixions. As to the soldiers who came to break Jesus's legs, John doesn't tell us their rank (John 19:32–33). Nor does he tell us whether the centurion was the one who looked at Jesus and decided he was dead. If it was the centurion, it is extremely unlikely that he was wrong about this.

But even if the soldier was of lesser rank, there is no reason to think he was a "rookie" and would make an error. I maintain this for some very specific reasons. First, Jesus had caused quite a stir among the people. Remember that on the Sunday prior to the crucifixion (less than a week before), Jesus had made his triumphal entry into Jerusalem. The crowds hailed him as the long-awaited Messiah and deliverer. Though Palestine was firmly in Rome's control, that didn't mean it was the easiest place to rule. The Jews hated their Roman overlords, and the Romans had to keep a tight grip on the reins of government and military power to convince the Jews that it would be a disaster if they revolted. Surely, Christ's wildly enthusiastic reception on Palm Sunday must have captured the attention of the Roman rulers and military in Jerusalem.

In addition to fears about Jesus, the Romans were also sensitive to the desires of the Jews. The last thing they would want was a revolt started by Jesus's followers, a revolt which the Jews, sensing a chance to throw out the Roman overlords, would then join. In fact, the Roman rulers were so concerned to pacify the Jews that even though Pilate and Herod found no cause to crucify Christ, they handed him over to be crucified anyway, to satisfy the Jewish leaders and those they incited.

What is the point of the last two paragraphs? It is that Jesus's crucifixion was not the death of some unknown, unimportant individual. He had caused quite a stir among the inhabitants of Jerusalem, and the Romans knew that the Jewish leaders would not be satisfied until Christ was dead. In such a historical context, how likely is it that the Romans would have used raw recruits unfamiliar with and unskilled in crucifixion? It seems quite clear that the Romans had a significant stake in making sure that Jesus was dead. It is unthinkable that they would have sent new or recent recruits on this detail, or that the soldiers would not check carefully the condition of Jesus before they took him down from the cross.

It is also highly probable that Jesus was dead because the Jewish leaders had a major stake in this crucifixion. We are told that it was because of envy of Jesus that the Jewish religious leaders determined to kill him (Matt. 27:18; Mark 15:10). In other words, Jesus was attracting too many people, the Jewish leaders saw that they couldn't compete with him, and so they decided to kill the competition. As noted above, the Jews, concerned about the requirements of the Mosaic law about leaving a dead person unburied on the Sabbath, asked Pilate to speed up the death and remove Jesus before sundown. Now how likely is it, given the Jewish leaders' desire to remove the competition and their concern to follow ceremonial ritual, that the Jewish leaders would let the body be taken without being sure that Jesus was dead? It is highly probable that they would demand to know that he was dead.

Then, we must also ask how likely it is that those who actually went to the tomb to bury Jesus would think he was dead, if he was actually alive? It is surely possible that they were mistaken, but improbable, and there is no evidence to support the notion that they made a mistake. Furthermore, it is hard to believe that, given the already mentioned furor surrounding Jesus, plus his comments about rising from the dead, the Romans would not check to see that his body was in the tomb and that he was dead before sealing the tomb and placing a guard there to protect the tomb from tampering. The evidence we do have suggests that they knew he was in the tomb and knew he was dead before they sealed it.

All of these arguments and evidences make it extremely difficult to imagine that Christ didn't actually die. However, there is one further piece of evidence that should remove any lingering doubt. John tells us something further about the soldiers entrusted with breaking the legs of those crucified that day. John 19:34 says that one of the soldiers did something more than just check to see if Christ was alive. He thrust a spear into Christ's side, and that resulted in blood and water separately coming out of his side. Medical science tells us that this was a sure sign of death—likely death from a ruptured heart.[6] What is especially significant about the inclusion of this detail in John's Gospel is that John would not have known the medical significance of what he reported—probably no one else at that time would have known either. I mention this because if this fact were known at that time, we might think John included it in order to make his account more believable when he recorded that Christ was dead. Because the medical significance of this fact wasn't likely known at the time, we are left to conclude that John included this detail because it was part of what he actually saw and what happened. But from what we now know about the medical significance of this fact, it seems totally wrongheaded to propose that, even so, Christ hadn't really died.

Before moving to the second stage in this defense, we should test what I've said by our three criteria. Are the arguments true? Given that we are granting that the Gospels are in general historically reliable, it seems that the details I've noted in the accounts are in fact true. Moreover, since Jesus's death involves no miracle whatsoever, it is hard to imagine that critics would have any significant grounds to claim that despite everything mentioned, Christ was still alive.

Are the arguments offered relevant? Indeed they are. Every one of the arguments offers a reason (or reasons) why it is most likely that Christ died. Regardless of whether critics will agree with the evidences and arguments proposed, it gives away nothing to theists to agree that these arguments are relevant to whether Christ died and to whether there was anyone who witnessed the crucifixion (or was otherwise involved in this case) who could confirm that he was dead.

How much do the arguments prove? The arguments prior to the one about the spear all make it quite likely that Christ was dead as a result of the crucifixion. The argument about the spear removes any lingering doubt. As a result, I can confidently say that even if we remove as weak the two arguments I mentioned at the very beginning of this section, we are still able to establish with a very high degree of objective certainty that Jesus actually died. A consequence of this, though not the whole point of this line of argument, is that the swoon theory, in one version or another, really has little, if any, support.

Evidence that Christ Was Buried in a Known Tomb

A good place to begin this second phase of the defense is Paul's comments in 1 Corinthians 15:4. As various scholars note, verses 3–4 were likely taken from an old Christian saying that summarizes the substance of early Christian preaching. William Lane Craig offers evidence that the date of this saying, given the date of 1 Corinthians around AD 55, may well have been within five years or so of the crucifixion itself.[7] Regardless of the exact date, commentators agree that Paul is quoting from a very early saying that sketches the basics of the gospel. The saying clearly states that Christ was buried. Though this might seem obvious, it is significant. As noted above, it was not uncommon for crucified criminals to be thrown into a common grave. If that happened to Jesus, the apostles, especially those who wrote the Gospels and the Epistles, might have had no contact with anyone who saw where the body was placed. If so, that would only complicate making the case that the women and the disciples whom the Gospels say were the first to go to the tomb actually knew where Jesus's tomb was.

That Christ was buried is significant for another reason. As some have noted, it was not unusual after a crucifixion for victims to be left on the cross so that birds could feast on the dead corpses. In such instances, there might be nothing left to bury.[8] Of course, if that happened to Jesus, the results for arguing for a resurrection, let alone a known tomb, would be devastating.

So, it is helpful to confirm that there was a burial, but that alone doesn't show that those who claimed on Sunday morning that Christ had arisen actually went to the right tomb, or that they had any idea of where it was. Thankfully, we have ample evidence to establish that Jesus was buried in a known tomb. Consider several of these indicators. First, the Gospel writers themselves describe the tomb in terms that suggest that they knew where it was. John tells us (John 19:41) that the tomb was a newly hewn tomb that had never been used, and that it was located in a garden near where Jesus was crucified. Matthew (Matt. 27:60), Mark (Mark 15:46), and Luke (Luke 23:53) confirm that it was a newly hewn tomb. Matthew and Mark also say that there was a stone that was rolled to the opening of the tomb to seal it. All four Gospels tell us that it was Joseph of Arimathea who requested Jesus's body for burial and that he was given it. It is Matthew alone (Matt. 27:60) who says the tomb actually belonged to Joseph.

If we grant the traditional view about who wrote these Gospels (see the chapter on the reliability of the Gospels for details), then we have four independent accounts about the tomb which concur without being identical. Both the concurrence of the testimony as well as the individuality of each account give the distinct impression that there wasn't just one eyewitness whom others copied. Rather the evidence suggests independent accounts of the same thing.

If what I have said about the authorship of these accounts and the Pauline comment in 1 Corinthians 15 are correct (and other than doubting the reliability of any of the accounts, there seems to be no good reason to think my claims are incorrect), then we should see what the writers recorded. I note initially that Matthew (27:61), Mark (15:47), and Luke (23:55) all say that women accompanied Joseph when he buried Jesus, and they saw where Christ was buried. Matthew and Mark specifically name Mary Magdalene and the other Mary (Matthew), the mother of Joses (Mark) as present. All four Gospels name one or more of these same women as part of the group of women who went to the tomb on Sunday morning. Mark and Luke specifically say that they came with spices, etc. to anoint Jesus's body.

There are two reasons for mentioning the involvement of the women. First, to claim that everyone went to the wrong tomb on Sunday morning is to claim that between Friday late afternoon (before sundown) and Sunday morning, not even two full days later, the women forgot where the tomb was, or for some other reason couldn't find it. To suppose that the women didn't know where to go so soon after the burial is hard to imagine with any credibility. Jesus was no ordinary person to them, and it is not as though there was urban sprawl in this part of Jerusalem, with great congestion on the roads leading to the garden, so it is hard to see how the women would have forgotten or become so disoriented that they went to an entirely incorrect location.

There is another reason, however, for mentioning the women. As many have noted, in those times women had few rights and even less respect. They were not allowed to serve as witnesses in a court trial. So if the Gospel writers (or other early Christians) were trying to "manufacture" a story about Jesus rising from the dead, it would not lend credibility to the story to pin so much emphasis on any woman, including those who saw Jesus's burial and came to the tomb on Sunday morning. The only reason to report that these same women were present on Friday evening and also were the first to the tomb on Sunday morning is that this is what actually happened.

There are other reasons to believe that Jesus was buried in a known tomb. Matthew writes (27:62ff.) that on Saturday, the chief priests and Pharisees came to Pilate and requested that a guard be set at the tomb. They reminded Pilate that Jesus had predicted that he would rise from the dead on the third day, and they were worried that before the third day the disciples might come and steal Christ's body and then claim that he had risen. Hearing their request and the rationale for it, Pilate gave them a guard to seal the tomb and watch it. Now the question that must be asked is the following: given the nature of the commotion caused in Jerusalem related to Jesus, and given the reason for the Jewish leaders' request, how likely is it that the guard sealed a tomb and guarded it without ever checking to be sure that Christ was its occupant? It is unthinkable that such a thing would happen. Certainly the soldiers and the Jews would be sure that the guard was posted at the right tomb. The idea that no one knew where the right tomb was simply isn't believable, for surely the guard and those who requested it would be sure about the contents of the tomb being guarded.

At this point I can also mention an argument that one might be tempted to make, even though it is actually a bad argument. Some might say that if the women really didn't know where the tomb was, they could always ask the guards who were there to guard it, and surely the guards would know where it was. Unfortunately, this argument doesn't work. For one thing, what happens if the women were so disoriented and confused about the location of the tomb that they went to a part of Jerusalem that wasn't near the tomb at all? In that case they wouldn't find the tomb, but they wouldn't see any guards either. Hence, they wouldn't be able to ask the guards to verify the location of the tomb.

But there is an even more fundamental problem with this argument. It seems to presuppose that the women, as they set off for the tomb on Sunday morning, could reassure themselves that they could find the tomb, since if all else failed, they could ask the guards for the location. But for that to be true, they would have to know that there were guards at the tomb, and it is debatable that they did. The women came to the tomb late on Friday afternoon and saw where Jesus was buried. The guard wasn't set until the next day. Nothing in any of the accounts of the events on Friday through Sunday morning suggests that any of the women or disciples went near the tomb on Saturday. So, when the women set out on Sunday morning to go to the tomb, it is highly unlikely that they knew anything about a guard having been set. They must have gone simply trusting their memory of where the tomb was, and as argued above, that would likely have been all they needed to find it. So, if one is tempted to claim that the women knew that if they couldn't find exactly where Jesus was buried, the guards around his tomb could help them, one should resist that temptation.

A final argument that the tomb's location was known should remove any lingering doubts. Even if the women and disciples couldn't find the tomb on Sunday morning, and even if the Romans and Jews couldn't find it either, how can we believe that between late Friday afternoon and Sunday morning Joseph of Arimathea wouldn't remember where the tomb was? Joseph was a secret follower of Christ; he didn't want the Jews to know. But he wanted to give Christ a proper burial, so he went directly to Pilate and asked for the body. Granted, the events of that Friday would have been emotionally wrenching, but even so, is it really believable that Joseph would ask for the body without knowing where he would put it? It's possible, but not very likely. It seems then, that even if no one else would remember where the right tomb was (hard as that is to believe), surely Joseph would know. The preponderance of the evidence presented suggests that Jesus was buried in a known tomb.

In evaluating the arguments offered, it seems that all are relevant to the issue of whether Jesus was buried, and if so, relevant to whether the tomb was known to the women and the disciples. As to the truth of the evidence presented, the Gospel writers and Paul certainly don't contradict one another on these matters. It seems that the main reasons for doubting the evidence are either that one recognizes that the evidence helps make the case for a resurrection, and on *a priori* grounds one rejects any supernatural explanation of the event in favor of a naturalistic one, or one believes that the Gospels themselves are unreliable. But we have seen, in the chapter on Scripture, reasons for thinking the Gospels are reliable. As to how much these arguments prove, it is hard to imagine what further argument or evidence would be the "clinching" argument if those presented don't satisfy reasonable doubt. As we shall see shortly, after the resurrection, the soldiers came and told the chief priests what had happened. After the chief priests and elders of the Jews conferred, they bribed the soldiers to say that the disciples stole the body (Matt. 28:11–15). This is very interesting, for even though the chief priests and elders hadn't been to the tomb, they believed the soldiers. Moreover, they offered the first naturalistic explanation ever offered against a genuine resurrection. It is important that there is no hint that a wrong tomb theory was even considered, let alone considered a serious alternative to the stolen body theory. Perhaps they did discuss that as an option, but it is clear that they rejected it. But why? It seems at least reasonable to think they rejected it, because they didn't find it plausible. At any rate, if it was considered at all, they thought the stolen body story the better way to explain away the resurrection.

In light of the preceding, it is safe to conclude that Jesus was buried in a known tomb, and that the evidence offered establishes that with a high degree of objective certainty. And, when you think about it, it really doesn't make sense for those who reject the resurrection to try to refute it at this stage of the argument. If they were to grant that Jesus was buried in a known tomb, that in itself wouldn't establish that Jesus rose from the dead. So, critics can afford to be charitable to this line of argument, since little, if anything, of significance is lost if they grant that Jesus was buried in a known tomb.

Evidence that Jesus's Body Was Missing, but Not Stolen

Scripture says that when the women arrived at Jesus's tomb on Sunday morning, it was empty. Matthew, Mark, and Luke report that there were angels or men in the tomb who told the women that Jesus had risen from the dead. John simply says that the stone that sealed the tomb was taken away from the tomb. Mary Magdalene ran to tell Peter, and she said that Christ was not in the tomb and she didn't know where "they" had taken him (John 20:1–2). When various disciples went to the tomb they, too, saw that it was empty. We also learn that members of the guard set at the tomb came to the chief priests and told them that the body was gone. From what Matthew says, the chief priests and elders didn't tell them to go back and look again for the body. Nor did they go to the tomb themselves to confirm that it was empty. Rather, they concocted the story about the disciples stealing the body. Of course, if Jesus was still in the tomb, there was no need for such an explanation, which would make sense only in the face of an empty tomb.

Indeed, that the tomb was empty has been granted by friend and foe of the resurrection alike. Evidence that this is so stems from the various naturalistic explanations of how and why Jesus's body could not be found. Why bother to offer a naturalistic interpretation of what happened if you know that the body is still in the tomb? Similarly, if the tomb had Jesus's remains when the disciples began to preach his resurrection, their message could have been quickly refuted. Preaching the resurrection in Jerusalem and its environs couldn't have lasted very long with any credibility attaching to it if Jesus's dead body was in the tomb. As we have already shown, friend and foe alike knew (or could easily have learned) where the tomb was, so if Jesus was still dead, there were many who could easily prove this to be so.

These considerations show that the tomb was empty. The key question is how it became empty. One explanation is that Jesus never really died, but later revived in the tomb, slipped out and returned to the disciples, and convinced them that he had risen from the dead, but we have already seen ample evidence that this is false. Another way the tomb might have been empty is if no one knew where Jesus's tomb was, so that the tomb they found was empty, but it wasn't Jesus's tomb. But we have also seen the evidence against that explanation. So, why was the tomb empty? Undoubtedly, the most plausible naturalistic explanation is that someone stole the body. This must have been the reasoning of the chief priests and elders. They had every reason to squelch the story that Jesus rose, and no reason to allow it to persist. If the stolen body explanation was not the best explanation, then whatever was better surely would have been spread abroad as the answer as to why the tomb was empty. Evidently, the story that the disciples stole the body was persuasive enough and believed enough that Matthew says that even to the time of his writing the Gospel, this was the story most held among the Jews (Matt. 28:15).

So, it makes most sense to believe that Jesus's tomb was empty after he had been placed there lifeless. And, the most likely naturalistic explanation of what happened to the body is that someone stole it. Though focus is invariably placed on the disciples as the culprits, they are not the only ones who could have stolen the body. It might also have been taken by the Jews, by the Romans, or even by grave robbers. We should consider each of these options separately. But before I turn to them, it would be worth noting several weak or clearly false arguments that are sometimes used to answer the possibility that the body was missing because someone stole it.

First, some would say that it isn't believable that the body was stolen, because no one would have a motive to do it. This is simply false, and it is false not just because the disciples might have had a motive. It is possible to offer a motive for the Jews, the Romans, and grave robbers, and when we address each of these options independently, I'll explain what their motive might have been. For now, let me just say that if any of these groups had engaged in such bizarre activity as stealing a body while it was under a guard intended to prevent such a thing, it is believable that they would have some motive, regardless of how bizarre the motive might be.

Second, sometimes I have heard defenders of the resurrection say that from what we know about the disciples, they just didn't have the psychological makeup to attempt such a theft. During the trial and crucifixion, various ones showed themselves to be cowardly even to the point (as in Peter's case) of denying that they had any connection to Jesus at all. After the crucifixion, they stayed in hiding in their homes out of fear that they might be caught and crucified as well. How could people with such a mind-set put aside their fears, challenge and overcome the guards at the tomb, and take Christ's body away?

Though some elements of this line of argument are helpful (e.g., how could the guards at the tomb be beaten?), the argument has significant flaws. It is true that the disciples were scared and acted in a cowardly way. It is also true that they were emotionally distraught over what had happened to Jesus. It is also true that it would have been irrational to think they could overcome the guard and to try to do it. The problem with all of this is that none of it proves they didn't try. Sometimes distraught people act in very irrational ways. Moreover, if they had a motive for stealing the body, then despite their fears they might well have tried to do it. So, while this line of argument does underscore the fact that the disciples were greatly mentally and emotionally troubled, sometimes people who are that upset do things we would never expect them to do in more normal and less stressful circumstances. Thus, this argument isn't as compelling as it might at first glance seem.

A final weak argument is heard quite often. It says that if someone did actually steal the body, when the disciples began preaching the resurrection and people believed, the thieves could have squelched all of this by producing the body. This could be the case, but it is not necessarily so. If the thieves were grave robbers, they would likely have no concern about the message being preached. Moreover, to have produced the body would be to admit that they stole it. Why would they subject themselves to the potential punishment from the authorities that would come once it would be known that they stole the body? If grave robbers stole the body, it would make sense for them to say nothing once the resurrection began to be preached.

And, there are other reasons that the body might not be accessible. Suppose the Jews or the Romans decided that Jesus and his disciples had created enough unrest in Palestine. If the disciples began preaching a resurrection (one that many of them knew Jesus had predicted), that would only foment more unrest. One way to guarantee that a resurrection wouldn't occur would be to take Jesus's body while it lay dead in the tomb and burn it. If either the Jews or the Romans (or anyone else) had done this, and then later the disciples began preaching the resurrection, no one could produce the body to disprove the claim that he arose. And yet the reason they couldn't show his body would have nothing to do with a resurrection. The ultimate point here is that if someone or some group had a motive for stealing the body in the first place (strange as that would be for most potential thieves), we cannot rule out the possibility that they would also have a reason to keep it hidden once the disciples began to preach the resurrection. When you open the door to bizarre things happening in the first place, who is to say that something equally or more bizarre might not happen once the initial oddity occurs?

Of course, if Jesus's body was still in the tomb and then the disciples began to preach his resurrection, it would be easy for his opponents simply to show people his body. But that's not what this weak argument claims. It grants that the tomb *is empty*, and once you grant that, how can you be sure that those who took it (if someone had a reason to take it and did) wouldn't also have a reason to keep the body hidden once the resurrection was preached?

Despite these weak arguments, there are many good reasons to think Jesus's body was not stolen. Let's first consider the disciples as the thieves. Several things weigh heavily against their doing this. First, let us consider their motive for doing it. Perhaps they feared that Jesus's body would be desecrated if left in the tomb, so they stole it and placed it where no one could find it. Or perhaps the events of the prior week, leading up to and including the crucifixion, had so disturbed them mentally and emotionally that they irrationally decided they would steal Christ's body, and so they tried it. Or perhaps they saw themselves as being involved in a new religious movement. As long as Jesus was alive, the movement could grow, but once he died, the movement was at death's door as well. Suppose that the disciples didn't want that to happen, so they stole the body so as to be able to go out and preach Christ's resurrection and thereby keep the movement going. This would allow them to say, if they wished, that the Romans and Jews thought they could kill Jesus and the growing movement around him, but this resurrection story proves that they couldn't. This might have given them a sense of satisfaction as they made the point that their opponents may have "won the battle" by crucifying Jesus, but they had not "won the war" of totally squelching the movement that had arisen around him.

Perhaps there are other possible motives they might have had, but let us consider the three mentioned. As to the first, we must look at the guard set at the tomb. There is debate over whether the guard was a temple guard set by and made up of Jews, or whether it was a Roman guard. Matthew's account of the setting of the guard (27:62–66, esp. v. 65) is ambiguous enough to allow for either possibility, if all we are considering are the words in verse 65. But I think it is possible to say that the guard would have been a Roman guard. As to why: if they meant a temple guard, why would they need to ask Pilate to set this sort of watch? Couldn't they have set the watch themselves, supplying the needed men? And, what about the seal placed on the stone? Commentators believe that this refers to a Roman seal, a sign that the contents of the tomb were not to be tampered with, and that if the seal was broken, those who did it would incur the wrath of the Roman rulers. Now, it is possible that the guards stationed at the tomb were temple guards while the seal was placed on the tomb by the Romans, but it makes more sense to think that if the Romans placed a seal on something, they would be sure that it was a Roman guard that would stand watch as well.

Finally, note Matthew 28:14. The chief priests gave money to the members of the guard to say the disciples stole the body while the soldiers were sleeping. Of course, if these were Roman soldiers and their superiors learned that they had slept on their watch, there would be serious trouble. Hence the chief priests said that if this story came to the governor's ears, the chief priests would persuade the governor and protect the members of the guard. This makes no sense if the guards are temple guards. What would they fear from the Roman authorities, and why would the chief priests have to protect these temple guards if the governor heard the story that the guards fell asleep on their watch? None of this makes sense if we are dealing with a temple guard. On the other hand, if the guard is a Roman guard, it makes abundant sense to promise that if the members of the guard get in trouble with the governor, the chief priests would protect them. If the concocted story really were true and the Roman officials learned of it, those soldiers placed to guard the tomb would be in deep trouble.

So, it makes most sense to see the guard as a group of Roman soldiers. But that leads to my point about the first alleged motive the disciples might have had for stealing the body. If there really was a guard of Roman soldiers and a seal had been placed on the tomb, it is dubious that the disciples would have an actual reason to worry about someone getting into the tomb and desecrating Jesus's body. It is highly unlikely that anyone or even a group would have even tried to get by the guards, and the disciples surely should have known all of this. There is no reason to think they didn't know it.

Of course, we are assuming that the disciples decided to steal the body themselves so as to assure that it wouldn't be desecrated. But this makes no sense. Assuming for the sake of argument that they could get past the guards, wouldn't unwrapping the grave clothes and removing a naked body desecrate it? Why, then, think you can keep a body from being desecrated by doing something which itself desecrates the body?

What about the second possible motive for the disciples to steal the body? Perhaps the disciples were just so distraught and demoralized that they became mentally unstable and tried to do this very irrational thing. The problem with this supposition is that, first, there is no evidence that the disciples were insane, even temporarily. Even more, if they tried to steal the body, how could they overcome the Roman guards? It is possible, I suppose, but extremely unlikely. Moreover, if they had to contend with the soldiers—and of course, they would have had to do so if they tried to steal the body—why, once they got in the tomb, would they take the time to unwrap Jesus's body and leave the grave clothes? And what would they want or do with his naked body? I raise these questions because Scripture says that while Jesus was not in the tomb on Sunday morning, his grave clothes were there (John 19:38–20:7).[9] None of this makes sense, even if the disciples, being emotionally devastated and mentally disturbed, actually tried to steal the body.

But what about the motive of wanting to keep the movement going and protecting Jesus's and their credibility? Here is a motive that makes some sense. At least it makes sense as long as the disciples are allowed to preach the resurrection without any persecution for doing so. However, once the persecution started, and it definitely did, there was no reason for them to continue to preach a message that they knew wasn't true, especially when the results of preaching that Jesus rose was their own persecution and threat of death. Surely they wanted to keep the movement going, but unless they were insane or incredibly stupid, it is hard to explain why, once persecution came for preaching this message, they wouldn't have told the truth and produced the body (assuming that they still had it). None of the evidence we have in the New Testament or in extrabiblical material suggests that the disciples were either insane or incredibly stupid. Nor is there any evidence from any source that any of the disciples broke down under persecution, went and got the body, or simply admitted that they had stolen it. You would think, for example, that under the terrible persecutions the apostles suffered (described in the book of Acts) at least someone would have broken the silence and admitted that the body was stolen and that Jesus never rose from the dead. The fact that no one did admit this or produce the body in the face of all this persecution (nor did they stop preaching the resurrection) suggests that they didn't steal the body just to maintain the movement.

There are other arguments against the disciples stealing the body. For-getting anything said about motive and their own mental framework after the crucifixion, is it realistic that they actually could have overpowered the guards at the tomb? It is possible, but unlikely, and there is no evidence that this happened. When the soldiers came to the chief priest to relate what had happened at the tomb, they didn't say the disciples had overpowered them and then had taken the body. The story that the chief priests then concocted was that the disciples had stolen the body while the guards slept. That story isn't very believable, given what we know about the discipline and training of Roman soldiers, but a story that would say the disciples actually defeated the soldiers would be even less believable, and everyone knew that.

Finally, let us focus again on the story the chief priests and elders paid the soldiers to tell. The fact that they decided to make up this story and to pay the soldiers to tell it argues against the story being true. If the disciples had stolen the body, no story needed to be made up. The religious leaders could simply have told the truth about what happened, and then the idea that the tomb was empty because Jesus arose would be squelched.

Though the disciples are the most likely to have stolen Jesus's body, the evidence shows that they didn't do it. What about the Jews? Again, we begin with the issue of motive. They might have been so afraid that something would go wrong (like the disciples stealing the body and claiming Christ arose) that they decided to take matters into their own hands. They might have decided that if they took the body and buried it somewhere else, they could produce it if the disciples started preaching the resurrection. Or maybe they thought that if they stole the body and burned it, that would put an end to any possibility of resurrection. If the disciples then started preaching the resurrection, the Jews couldn't show everyone the body to disprove the disciples' claims, but the Jews could simply explain what they did with the body.

Though the Jews might have had such motives for stealing the body, why did they ask for guards at the tomb? If they believed guards could ward off any thieves and so asked for guards, why then would the Jews try to steal the body? On the other hand, if they didn't think the guards would be adequate to fend off any grave robbers, then why not ask the authorities for something more to ensure that the contents of the tomb would remain un-touched? In either case, it doesn't make sense to try to steal the body. Since a guard was set as requested by the Jewish leaders themselves, in order for any Jews to try to steal the body it seems that they would have had to think that stealing the body would be a better way to disconfirm a resurrection than simply to leave the body in the sealed tomb with the Roman guard. But why would they believe that they could handle the situation better than the guards posted at the tomb?

Thus, while the Jews might have had a motive to steal the body, it is dubious that it would have been a good enough motive for them actually to attempt a theft. And they likely would have known that. But even if one thinks the imagined motives would be sufficient to move the Jews to action, where is the evidence that they actually tried to steal the body? None is forthcoming from the New Testament, nor is there any evidence of a theft attempt in non-biblical literature of the time.

Some of the other arguments against the Jews stealing the body are the same as those against the disciples doing it. For example, if they tried to do this, they would still have to overcome the guards. Moreover, why would they take time to unwrap Christ's grave clothes, and if they did, what would they do with a naked body? Answers here are no more convincing than they were in regard to the possibility of the disciples stealing the body. And, if they did steal the body but didn't destroy it, when the disciples began to preach that Christ had risen, why didn't the Jews just show everyone the body and/or the tomb to which they had taken it?

Next, let us consider the Romans as those who stole the body. Arguments about unwrapping grave clothes and dealing with a naked body are problems here as well. Moreover, it is more difficult in this case to explain a motive for the theft than in either of the previous two cases. If the Romans saw Jesus as a potential threat to their control over Jerusalem, then the Roman authorities had Jesus exactly where they wanted him—dead and lying in a tomb guarded by Roman soldiers. If those who took Jesus's body were Romans who were secret followers of Christ, then we are really back to the option of disciples taking the body. Surely, Roman citizens and even Roman governmental leaders would realize the futility of trying to get past the guards at the tomb.

If the Romans involved in the theft were some of the soldiers in the guard, would they have been able to ward off all of their comrades? Is it likely that all or even most of the contingent of soldiers chosen for guard duty happened to be secret followers of Jesus, so that they would have out-numbered the rest of the guards? Perhaps some of the soldiers would have been secret disciples, but it is hard to believe that most of the soldiers chosen just happened to be secret disciples.

Then, for Roman soldiers to steal Jesus's body would mean that they had shirked their duty. They would certainly have known the penalty for doing that, and that would have been a major deterrent. Only if they had some motive that was stronger than their fear of punishment for failing to protect the tomb from theft would it make sense for them to try to steal Jesus's body. But where is the evidence that any of the guards at the tomb tried to steal Jesus's body? And where is the evidence that Romans who weren't soldiers either had a motive for stealing the body or actually tried to do it? It is fine to raise all sorts of possible ways for the body to have been stolen, but granting that something is possible doesn't prove that it actually occurred. In order to draw that conclusion we need evidence, and there is none.

Final "candidates" as those who stole Jesus's body are grave robbers. As to motive, they definitely had one. They might have chosen this particular tomb because it was common knowledge that such tombs were owned by the rich. Hence, they might have chosen this tomb, thinking that inside it there would be various "treasures" that wealthy people might put in their tombs, treasures worth stealing. Even if they didn't know this tomb belonged to Joseph of Arimathea or that he was a wealthy man, this sort of tomb could offer quite a temptation. So, there clearly could have been a motive for grave robbers to open this tomb.

Still, too much evidence argues against this option. An initial problem is that the robbers would have had to contend with the guards at the tomb, and though they might be more than willing to fight, it is hard to see that even such a group of thieves could overpower a Roman guard. Then, if the purpose of robbing the tomb was to steal possessions and wealth, why would they take Jesus's naked body? What would a dead, naked body be worth? Moreover, it is also extremely hard to explain why they would have taken the time and effort to unwrap the grave clothes and then leave them. If they took time to do this, it seems that their only reason could have been that they thought that either the body or the grave clothes were worth something. But the body was gone, and the grave clothes were still there.

Perhaps the reason for bothering with the grave clothes is that this group of thieves hadn't robbed a grave before and so, initially, they thought the grave clothes might be worth something, but by the time they unwrapped Jesus they realized they really couldn't sell used grave clothes to anyone, and that's why they left them in the tomb. While this suggestion is possible, where is the evidence that this was a first-time job? In fact, there simply isn't any evidence that ordinary grave robbers were the ones who stole the body. If grave robbers actually stole the body, why then would the Jewish leaders tell the soldiers to say the disciples stole it? A true story about grave robbers would serve the purpose of squelching a belief in the resurrection just as well as a bogus story about the disciples stealing it.

In evaluating the arguments and evidences presented, can we say that the arguments are true? From what we learn from the Gospels and from common sense, the various arguments and evidences offered don't seem to be based on faulty reasoning or falsehoods. Moreover, the evidence presented is relevant to whether the body was missing and to whether it is believable that any of the possible thieves actually succeeded in stealing the body. The only substantive evidence that someone stole the body is the fact of the empty tomb and the story that the Jewish leaders concocted and spread abroad. As to the empty tomb, it is agreed that it was empty, but there is more than one way it could have become empty. Available evidence that we have considered doesn't make it likely that it became empty as a result of someone stealing the body. Then, we have evaluated the respective cases for one group or another stealing the body, and we have seen that while it is possible that someone or some group actually tried it, it is highly unlikely that any could have succeeded. Hence, it is not unreasonable to hold that the best explanation of how the tomb became empty is that Christ miraculously rose from the dead and left the tomb empty.

EVIDENCE THAT A LIVING CHRIST APPEARED TO PEOPLE AFTER THE TOMB WAS EMPTY

If the story ended with the empty tomb and there was no further evidence related to Jesus's body, we might suspect a resurrection but would definitely have a difficult time proving it. If we are inclined to reject all naturalistic explanations of the empty tomb and to suspect a resurrection happened, it would be a whole lot easier to argue for a resurrection if someone saw Christ alive after he died and was buried. After his resurrection, Christ could have appeared to no one and just directly ascended to heaven. Thankfully, that didn't happen. After his resurrection, Scripture tells us that Jesus appeared to many people on various occasions.

For the benefit especially of those who think there were just a few people who claimed to see Jesus alive after his death, it would be worth noting his post-resurrection appearances. The list is long, but it underscores that this did not happen "in a corner" (see Acts 26:26) where few if any could see what was happening. Christ appeared after his resurrection to Mary Magdalene (John 20:14; Mark 16:9); to women returning from the tomb (Matt. 28:9–10); to Peter later, on resurrection Sunday (Luke 24:34; 1 Cor. 15:5); to the disciples on the road to Emmaus (Luke 24:13–33); to the apostles when Thomas was not there (Luke 24:36–43; John 20:19–24); to the apostles again but when Thomas was present (John 20:26–29); to seven people by the Lake of Tiberias (John 21:1–23); to a group of more than five hundred believers (1 Cor. 15:6); to James (1 Cor. 15:7); to the eleven (Matt. 28:16–20; Mark 16:14–20; Luke 24:33–52; Acts 1:3–13); at the ascension (Acts 1:3–12); and to Paul (Acts 9:3–6; 1 Cor. 15:8).[10]

It would be understandable if someone looked at this list and said, "This is great; we have the independent testimony of more than five hundred people who claimed to have seen Jesus alive after he was dead." But such a claim wouldn't be quite right. The Scriptures listed above all appear in one of six New Testament books: Matthew, Mark, Luke, John, Acts, and 1 Corinthians. Assuming that the authors were the people traditionally associated with these books, we know that Luke and Acts were written by the same person, so we actually have the written biblical witness of only five New Testament writers. Even so, it is hard to imagine that the uniform testimony of five independent witnesses in a court of law wouldn't be sufficient to settle a case.

On the other hand, the writers record that more than five hundred people claimed to have seen Jesus alive after he died. At the time when the Gospels, Acts, and 1 Corinthians were written, many of the people mentioned were still alive. Hence, it was possible to ask them whether, as the New Testament authors said, they actually saw Jesus alive after he died. In fact, in 1 Corinthians 15:6 Paul says that many of the five hundred who saw Jesus all at the same time were still alive at the time Paul wrote 1 Corinthians. It's as if Paul is saying, "If you don't believe me, go and ask the people I'm mentioning. If I'm wrong, they will tell you."

So, there is a sense in which we do have more than five hundred eyewitnesses who saw Christ alive after he had died, and there is a sense in which we really have just the five biblical authors who recorded the various appearances of Jesus to one person or another. But if the New Testament writers were wrong about this, readers could confirm that by asking many of the people mentioned in the list. If Jesus really wasn't alive, we would expect someone or some group of people to refute the claims that they had seen him. If his body was still in the tomb, or if it had been moved to a place that some people (the ones who moved him, at least) knew about, it is likely that the claims of post-resurrection appearances would have been rejected. But we don't find evidence of any attempt to refute the idea that people actually saw Jesus alive after his death. The main attempt to discredit the resurrection was the story the Jewish leaders concocted about the disciples stealing the body, and clearly few, if any, thought *that* story "trumped" all the eyewitnesses' testimony to have seen the risen Christ.

How do nonbelievers answer these claims of seeing Jesus alive? The most commonly heard response is that all of these people were just hallucinating. They thought they saw Jesus, but they really didn't. But how likely is it that all of these post-resurrection sightings were hallucinations? I think we can make the most knowledgeable response if we see what is most typical of hallucinations. For one thing, hallucinations tend to be linked to a person's subconscious and its recollection of past experiences. They are also more likely to occur when people are expecting something to happen.

How does this fit with Jesus's story? Not well. During his earthly ministry Jesus had surely mentioned his death and resurrection many times, but it is clear from the Gospels that his listeners didn't understand what he meant. When Jesus died there is no sign of his followers encouraging one another with the prospects of his forthcoming resurrection. The disciples are portrayed after the crucifixion as disconsolate, depressed, demoralized, and quite scared of what might happen to them. Such a mind-set is not fallow ground for hallucinating that one sees Jesus alive.

In addition, psychologists tell us that hallucinations are very individualistic. It is extremely unlikely that any two people would have the same hallucination, let alone more than five hundred people all at once. And, it is dubious that a hallucination would recur again and again in different places and circumstances to different people. Moreover, many who saw Christ not only claimed to have seen him, but they touched him and talked with him. It is surely possible for one having a hallucination to think such things are actually happening, but it is hard to believe that all eleven disciples, for example, would be having that same hallucination at once.

So, it is possible that everyone who claimed to see Jesus alive after his death was hallucinating, but that is highly improbable when you consider the number of different people involved, their frame of mind, the different circumstances in which they claimed to see Jesus, etc.[11] If someone gave testimony in a court of law and said that there are five hundred people, most of whom are alive today, who could corroborate their testimony, anyone would be inclined to believe the person making such a statement. Given that he is testifying that he saw a resurrected person, before we believed, we would naturally be inclined to find some of those five hundred mentioned to ask them what they saw. It is reasonable to think, therefore, that people who read 1 Corinthians 15 did go and ask people who claimed to have seen Jesus. It is also reasonable to think that readers of the Gospel accounts would question the people whom the Gospel writers said saw Jesus alive after his death. And we would also expect, given the dates of the four Gospels, Acts, and 1 Corinthians, that during the last half of the first century AD there would be many refutations of the alleged sightings of Jesus, if they never happened. So, it would have been difficult for the apostles' preaching of the resurrection to carry any credibility with listeners. And yet, we don't find refutations of these appearances, and we don't find large numbers of people who heard the apostles preach the resurrection both rejecting their message and also offering counterevidence against Christ's resurrection.

In evaluating these evidences, we begin with the question of whether they are true. If only one or two people saw Christ alive after he died, we might chalk it up to wishful thinking. But there were more than five hundred people who saw Jesus over a forty-day period. Some of them saw him on more than one occasion, and saw him in varying circumstances and situations. How many people have to see the living Christ in order to believe that he actually was alive again after being dead? Critics will likely respond that it's not the number of people who saw him that counts; it's the credibility of the witnesses. Fine, but why should we disbelieve the witnesses unless our disbelief is driven by an anti-supernaturalistic bias that says, no matter how many people claimed to see Christ alive after his death, it wouldn't be enough, because that would mean a miracle occurred, and any explanation is more believable than a miracle? To respond this way to the evidence of many sightings of Christ alive after he died is nothing more than illegitimate question begging. It is just as bad as would be a group of Christians who said that, of course the witnesses are right, because we know miracles can occur. Proper historical method suggests that both sides put their biases aside, look at the evidence, and decide what is the most likely explanation of the evidence we have. If more than five hundred people testified that some naturalistic event occurred, wouldn't that be sufficient evidence? Of course, but then why should we discount and discredit the testimony of all of these people who claimed to see a living Christ after he had died? An anti-supernaturalistic bias may make it impossible for someone to feel subjectively certain about the historicity of Christ's resurrection, but that can in no way invalidate the fact that a case with very high objective certainty supports the belief in the resurrection.

So, there is ample reason to think the arguments and evidences offered about the post-resurrection appearances are true. Are they relevant? It's hard to see why they wouldn't be relevant to the claim that Christ was seen alive after he died and was buried. How much does it prove? If this were the only line of evidence we had, it alone wouldn't warrant belief in a resurrection. Jesus might well have been seen by many if he never died and then escaped the tomb. Merely seeing Jesus doesn't prove he rose from the dead. But when we take these appearances together with the case we have made that in fact he really died, that he was buried in a known tomb, and that his body was missing from the tomb but not stolen, the probability that people who saw Christ alive after he had died were seeing the *risen* Christ is very high. Moreover, the evidence offered to support the view that these were genuine appearances of Christ after his death does seem adequate to support such a claim.

SEVERAL CONCLUDING THOUGHTS

The case presented in this chapter for the resurrection of Christ is a very strong one. It is not so strong as to be infallible or to rule out any need for faith. But it does offer ample grounds for believing in the resurrection. Some may be skeptical, because they think I have ignored a major objection to the resurrection. Others may be unhappy because I have omitted one of their favorite arguments in favor of the resurrection. Let me address both concerns in turn.

As to the objection, there are skeptics who are unimpressed because they believe the Gospel accounts (and the New Testament documents in general that speak of the resurrection) can be explained away as legends or myths. The only reason Christians are so willing to believe in the resurrection is that they think the New Testament is reliable history. Critics believe it is legend. They note that legends arise and attach to many notable people. When we hear those legends, we realize that while such people probably lived, they certainly didn't do what the legends say.[12]

In contrast, some Christian apologists have argued that the documents lying behind the Gospels and the Epistles, and the New Testament books themselves were written so soon after the life of Christ that there simply wasn't sufficient time for legend to arise around them.[13] Critics disagree, for they think either that the books of the New Testament were written much later than conservative Christians believe, or that it is impossible to rule out legend arising shortly after someone's life.

From my own perspective, this objection is just a specific extension of the complaint that the Gospels, etc., aren't historically reliable. If one can't show that they are reliable, then of course, everything presented in this chapter in favor of the resurrection is questionable. But we have seen in chapter 11 that there is good reason to think the Gospels were written when they are traditionally held to have been written, and there is good reason to think the authors told the truth. As to the debate over how long it takes for legend to arise, I am inclined to side with those who think it takes longer than the dates of the New Testament books would allow. However, when dealing with such a fantastic person as Jesus, who allegedly did so many miracles and who was so loved by his followers and deemed to be the long-awaited Messiah by many, I don't think it is impossible for legends about such a person to grow quickly. But I don't think this issue is really worth debating, because in a way both sides are relying upon their own psychological reconstruction of what was going through people's minds when they heard and told the stories about Jesus. We simply aren't in a position to affirm or deny causal connections between what people heard and thought, and what they then said about Jesus. Thankfully, we don't have to rely on speculations about how long it takes to build a legend; the data available about the date and content of the New Testament books show them to be early enough that many of the people spoken of in these books were still alive when the books were written and were also alive during Christ's life and had contact with him. When you have such testimony from so many people, and the authors invite the skeptics to go ask those who are still alive, that doesn't sound like the authors are trying to run away from the facts and hide behind the cloak of legend and myth. One's decision, however, on the matter of legend and myth ultimately depends on the authenticity and reliability of the New Testament.

As to evidences not used in my defense, some may be troubled that I make little or no reference to the changed lives of the disciples after seeing Jesus, and no mention is made of the beginning and growth of the church. Some apologists believe that these are strong evidences for the resurrection. While I do think there is an argument to be made here, I don't believe it is the one we most frequently hear. We are typically told that demoralized, despondent disciples couldn't have been changed into the confident and bold apostles we read of in the New Testament unless the resurrection actually occurred. We are also told that neither the phenomenal growth of the church in its earliest days, nor its impact for the last two thousand years could have occurred without the resurrection being true.

The problem with these arguments as stated is that at most they show that people have believed that Jesus rose. But believing it happened doesn't prove it to be true. Other religious leaders (Muhammad, Buddha, Joseph Smith) and even non- or anti-religious leaders (e.g., Marx, Lenin, Mao Tse-tung) have attracted a large number of devoted followers. That fact, however, Christians would claim, does not make their philosophies and religions true. But then, the same must be true in regard to the resurrection. Unquestionably, many people have believed that Jesus rose. The key questions are why they believed, and whether the evidence supports their belief. Hence, I see the evidence presented at the four stages of defense used in this chapter as much more compelling than simply pointing to the change in the disciples' mind-set and their resultant deeds, and more persuasive than merely pointing to the growth of the church.

But I do think there is an argument in all of this that is of value. It relates most directly to the apostles and early Christians. The demeanor and deportment of the disciples after they claimed to see the risen Christ was indeed different from that on Good Friday, Saturday, and even Sunday morning before the women came back from the tomb. That shows that something changed their outlook and their actions, but was their belief that Jesus rose correct? This question brings me to what I think is an argument of value.

The disciples went about preaching and teaching about the risen Christ, and they performed miracles in his name. In response, some believed, but many others persecuted them. One has only to read the book of Acts and accounts in secular histories of the centuries prior to Emperor Constantine to see that in response to preaching the resurrection, these men were persecuted severely. Likewise, many early Christians refused to recant their belief in Jesus, because they believed so strongly in Christ, given what they had heard about his resurrection. Now it makes abundant sense for people riding the crest of popularity because of the message they preach to continue preaching that message all the more loudly. That is so even if they know the message to be false. What does not make sense is to persist in preaching a message *which results in your own suffering and affliction*, when you know that message is *false*.

Sure, the disciples believed in the resurrection; that's why they made it the centerpiece of their presentation. But doesn't it make sense that once persecution came as a result of preaching that message, those preaching it would confirm that the message was in fact true? Why wouldn't they confirm the message's truth if, in response to preaching it, they received nothing but trouble? Unless the apostles and the earliest Christians were insane (and there is little evidence of that), they would not have continued to preach and hold a belief they knew to be false—especially if the results of preaching and holding that belief were persecution and, in many cases, death. And, a crucial point to remember is that these people were in a position to know the truth of what they were preaching, while others were in a position to refute it. But the nonbelieving contemporaries of the apostles did not refute it, and the apostles and earliest Christians continued to preach and believe in the resurrection in spite of the persecution that followed them and others who believed it.

While we don't have all the evidence before us that they had, it is assuring to know that those who were most in a position to know what happened said that Jesus did in fact rise from the dead. Because of their testimony, especially as recorded in Scripture, and their fidelity to Christ amidst persecution for their beliefs (as we learn from Scripture and secular history), we can make a compelling objective case for the resurrection of Christ. Given the evidence presented and the evaluation of those arguments and evidences (using our three criteria of truth, relevance, and how much is proved), we can say with assurance that Jesus Christ rose from the dead!

Chapter 13

Religious Pluralism

We are living in very strange times! If you are a Christian, you are more likely to get a hearing for the gospel than at other times. On the other hand, it is less likely that what you say about Christ and the gospel will be taken seriously by those who hear it. How could this be so?

We live in a time of great uncertainty. That doesn't refer just to the economy, or global, national, and local politics, or our own personal physical, mental, and financial well-being. It refers to our understanding of the world and our place in it, and most fundamentally to our ability to know whether that understanding is true or false. As noted in this book, we live in a time of great skepticism about worldviews, grand narratives, and the like. If there is just one "right" way of understanding reality (and there is reason to question whether such a thing as one right understanding exists), how can anyone ever be sure that he or she has found "it"? Isn't what someone else believes just as likely to be close to the "truth" as what we believe? Even more, perhaps everyone we meet knows more about "the truth" than we do.

Because of this great uncertainty about "correct" answers to life's most ultimate and important questions, the prudent attitude is one of openness to new ideas. Hence, rather than rejecting what others have to say about God and religion, we should listen respectfully, even if not entirely attentively, to what they have found to be "true" about these matters. If others have different views than we do, we should be tolerant of what they think and say. Who knows, we might benefit from what they tell us. So, in principle, the Christian gospel could contain some useful information, and hence, we may find others willing to listen when we tell them about Christ and what he has done for us. Rather than retreating behind the "fortress of their own world-view" which they "know" to be "right," they are open to hear what we say.

On the other hand, is there real hope that they will take seriously what we tell them about Christ? Undoubtedly, they will be intrigued to hear of the changes in our life that a relation to Christ has made, and they will be happy for us that our beliefs give us peace, serenity, and even security in the midst of the overwhelmingly challenging times in which we live. But when we tell them that Christ is for them, too—in fact, he is for everybody, because no one can have a relation with God except through Christ—the conversation will soon be over. In an age of so much intellectual uncertainty, how can one tolerate such unbridled dogmatism? How can it be true that unless they trust Christ, not only is their thinking wrong, but they will also spend eternity in conscious punishment? How can it also be true that an eternity of torment is in store for people who might have believed in Christ if they had ever heard of him, but they never heard? Will an all-loving God abandon for eternity most of his human creatures who have ever lived? If that was his intent, why did he bother creating a world at all?

Some of the most fundamental beliefs of Christianity seem utterly absurd to our contemporaries, and so while they may listen politely for a time to what we say, they are really not open to taking what we say seriously at all. Even though means of mass communication make it possible for more people than ever before to hear the gospel, and while intellectual uncertainty about truth makes people willing to listen, that same uncertainty makes it unlikely that anyone who claims to know "the truth" and proclaims it in a way which leaves no other viable answers to life's most important questions will be taken seriously.

Indeed, we live in very strange times! Welcome to the culture of relativism in all things! Welcome to the age of religious pluralism!

To illustrate the sense of uncertainty so many feel today, consider the following imaginary scenario. Imagine that someone is adrift on a raft in a huge body of water—maybe an ocean, but maybe a sea or just a very large lake. Everywhere he looks he sees nothing but water. He senses that there is land out there somewhere, but he can't see any and has no idea of what direction he needs to travel to find land. He doesn't have a compass, or if he does, he isn't sure that it works. It might work, but he doesn't know how to read a compass and there is no one he can ask. The one thing he has always believed is that the sun rises in the east and sets in the west, so that gives him a point of reference as to where he might be and what direction he might be going. But even so, after many days adrift with no change in his situation, he isn't even sure of the sun's location when it rises and sets. Perhaps it rises in the north and sets in the south, or rises in the west and sets in the east. How can one be sure when all one sees is endless water?

His raft is relatively small; there is only room for him. Actually, that isn't a problem, because it has been days since he has seen anyone or heard from anyone. He can, of course, speak, and someone might actually hear him, but he gets no reply, so for all he knows there is no one anywhere close to him. As to his raft, so far, it has kept him out of the water, but it might sink at any moment and then he would drown. It has "worked" for him to this point, but he can't be sure about the future.

In this imaginary story, the man adrift represents each human being. The body of water represents the vast number of ideas about the nature and meaning of the universe. Like the water, there are many competing worldviews, or conceptions of reality, but nowhere can there be found directions about which direction to travel and where one might find land (God, ultimate and absolute truth, etc.). The raft represents the man's own set of beliefs and values, his "truth." He has lived his life by this mind-set, and it has "worked for him so far," but no one can say whether his truth is truth for all. He can't even say whether in the end his raft will carry him to land or whether it will fall apart and he will drown. If a huge wave comes, will his raft be able to withstand it, or will it capsize and sink, leaving him to flounder in the water and ultimately drown? No one knows for sure. In such a world, of course, some things (like the direction of the sun's rise and set) have always been taken for granted as certain, but in the face of so much uncertainty about life's ultimate meaning and purpose, he has begun to doubt even these certainties.

If someone told him the way to go to find land, what they say might sound counterintuitive, but he should be respectful and listen. Perhaps this other person is just as lost as he is. Perhaps this person's raft is no sturdier than his, but perhaps this other person might be saying something that will help him find his way to shore. One can never be sure about such things, so one should listen and consider all viewpoints.

Given the skepticism about knowledge that is adrift in today's cultures, many who embrace religious pluralism would have us believe that everyone is really like that man adrift in a vast body of water. We are searching for something, even someone (a god), and that something or someone might be out there, but nobody knows for sure. In such a context, how wrong it seems for someone to tell the lost man to follow him because he knows the way to land; or even worse, that his way is the only way to land!

How we arrived at such a state of affairs has been explained to some extent in earlier chapters of this book. Certainly, the rise in epistemological skepticism has much to do with it, and so does our gradually "shrinking" world which has given us easy and quick access to peoples and religions whom in earlier centuries we only heard about. These previously unfamiliar peoples, cultures, and religions are now easily accessed by contact with people who are literally our neighbors and populate our communities.[1]

But our focus in this chapter is not to explain how we arrived at a point where commitment to religious pluralism is increasingly more popular. Rather, it is to understand what pluralists are saying and to answer their objections to believing that only one religion is true and is the only way to God. Before turning to any of those objections, we first need some basic definitions and then a clarification of what in this chapter is being defended and what is under attack.

Basic Definitions

In contemporary discussions about religious pluralism, three main positions are typically identified: *exclusivism*, *inclusivism*, and *pluralism*. There are, of course, variations of each view, but we can still get a basic definition of each. For many centuries exclusivism was the position of choice of traditional Christians. That is still the case for many, but in recent decades there have been Christians, even some who are otherwise rather theologically conservative, who have said that while Christ is unique and crucial for salvation, it is possible that people who are faithfully following another religion and may never have heard of Christ will in fact be saved and wind up in heaven for eternity. As opposed to both of these positions, religious pluralists typically believe that all religions are equally valid, and no religion possesses *the* truth. The particular religion one follows is more a result of one's geographical and cultural location and one's upbringing than a result of being convinced by argument and evidence that one's religious beliefs are true.

But these are general definitions, and we can be more specific. *Religious exclusivism* is usually understood to hold that religious truth and salvation are restricted to one religion alone. Though it is possible for those of other religions to be exclusivists, typically the label is attached to traditional Christianity, both Roman Catholic and Protestant. Since the notion of religious exclusivism is often linked to intolerance, arrogance, and narrow-mindedness, some writers prefer the term *religious particularism*.[2]

Regardless of the choice of terms, as Harold Netland explains, the key to Christian exclusivism is a set of theological commitments. Three are especially essential. First, Christian exclusivism holds that the Bible is God's inspired and authoritative Word. Thus, where the Bible and other religious books disagree, the latter are wrong and should be rejected in favor of biblical teaching. Second, Jesus Christ is God incarnate, fully human and fully divine, and there are no other incarnations of God. Moreover, it is only through the person and work of Christ that salvation is possible. Finally, divine salvatory grace is "not mediated through the teachings, practices, or institutions" of any other religion or religions.[3]

Though these three claims of Christian exclusivism do not entail that nothing of value is available in any other religion, they do entail the belief that those who don't accept Christ as personal Savior will forfeit a blessed eternity with God. This might happen by their experiencing eternal conscious punishment. Or it might come to pass by nonbelievers being annihilated at physical death. The former end is better supported by biblical teaching and has been the majority position of conservative Christians down through the centuries, but belief in annihilation of those outside of Christ is also consistent with an exclusivist position.[4]

Since the group of nonbelievers includes most people who have ever lived, exclusivist beliefs have served as a major stimulus to Christian missions for many centuries. In our own time, when there is so much easy interchange with peoples of other cultures and religions, these beliefs are taken by many as embarrassments. How can one really believe, for example, that his or her kind and generous neighbor will reside in hell, tormented unremittingly for eternity, just because the neighbor, though appreciative of and respectful to Christ, follows another religion? Why, if there is only one way to be saved, would a loving God inform so few of his human creatures of the path of salvation?

Because of considerations like those just mentioned, in the nineteenth and twentieth centuries a more open view to other religions became widespread. This perspective, which can encompass a variety of views, is known as *religious inclusivism*. As Netland explains, this approach is committed to three main principles. First, proponents of this view maintain that there is a sense in which Jesus is unique and superior to other religious figures. In addition, in some sense it is through Christ that salvation is available to anyone. Still, it is secondly the case that the salvation and grace based on Jesus are both available and efficacious to people through other religions. Finally, as a result of the second point, other religions should be viewed positively as part of God's purposes for the human race.[5]

Such commitments are, of course, vague, and so varieties of inclusivism abound. Some inclusivists still hold to belief in the Trinity, the incarnation, and the need for substitutionary atonement, while others jettison one or more of these traditional Christian beliefs. Regardless, the key to religious inclusivism "is the desire to maintain in some sense the uniqueness and normativity of Jesus Christ while simultaneously acknowledging that God's saving grace is present and effective in and through other religions."[6]

In contrast to religious exclusivism and inclusivism is *religious pluralism*. Here there are variations on the pluralist theme, but there are also some general characteristics common to all or most versions. According to pluralist thinking, each religion is a product of the time and culture in which it arose and continues to exist. A religion is an attempt to crystallize a culture's understanding of and response to ultimate reality. Obviously, each religion has its own set of beliefs, and those beliefs do not necessarily square with the views of other religions. Nonetheless, each religion's views have a certain validity, but no religion can legitimately claim to have "the right conception" of God, and it would be hard to make a case that any of the more major religions is either more or less "true" than the others. This is true in part because the object of religious devotion is not empirically observable, but also because of the grounds for epistemological skepticism (especially of the postmodern variety) discussed in earlier chapters of this book.

In light of the above description of pluralism, it also follows that neither Christ nor Christianity is normative for evaluating religious truth claims, nor is Christ a more effective means of salvation than any other religion's method of salvation. As Netland aptly writes, the result of this point about salvation is that "although Christians can hold that Jesus is unique and normative *for them*, they cannot claim that Jesus is unique or normative in an objective or universal sense. Jesus may be the savior for Christians, but he is not the one Savior for all peoples."[7]

How, then, should humans respond to the diversity of religions? With respect and tolerance, say the pluralists. There is certainly no need for others to convert to a different religion, and debates and arguments about religions and their specific beliefs are unnecessary and unwarranted.[8]

THE VARIETY OF ISSUES RELATED TO PLURALISM AND THE FOCUS OF THIS CHAPTER

Though the preceding definitions are general, those familiar with the topic of religious pluralism will know that "religious pluralism" is a label for a host of different issues. It would be helpful to mention a number before narrowing the focus of this chapter. Discussions on religious pluralism can involve such matters as whether there is such a thing as absolute truth and if so, whether humans are in any position to know what it is. More specifically, is there such a thing as religious truth (if so, what sort of thing is a *religious* truth?), and are humans able to discern which religious claims are true or false (in a correspondence sense of truth, for example)? And, is there a true religion, and what does it even mean to talk of a "true religion"?

Coordinate to these issues about truth are questions about whether Christ is a distinctive savior (and in what sense distinctive), and whether Christianity or any other religion is superior to its counterparts. If Christ is in any way deemed essential to human salvation, then what should we conclude about the fate of those who never heard the Christian gospel or even the name of Christ? If, on the other hand, Christ is in no significant way normative or unique, then are not all religions at root really the same, and don't they all actually produce the same result(s)? Even if Christ has some special significance, couldn't it be true that each religion offers a sufficient path to a relation with God and to salvation?

Then, in response to religious exclusivists or inclusivists who insist that their religion is a better vehicle to a relation with God, or who claim that their religion is "more true" than any other, many pluralists would ask how anyone could know such things. It seems at the very least that there would have to be criteria for evaluating individual religious truth claims and for evaluating the truthfulness of a complete religion and its worldview. But what could such criteria be, and how likely is it that there are criteria independent of every worldview? And how, in a non-worldview-dependent way, can we identify what such criteria might be or convince others that those criteria are the "correct" ones for assessing worldviews? Such questions are, of course, critical, because there is no sense in claiming any religion and its beliefs victorious over any other, if all criteria for making that judgment presuppose the worldview of one religion or another. But if no worldview-independent criteria exist, then there is no point in talking about which religion is best or truest. And if that is so, then there is no reason to divide people groups and even individuals on the basis of their religion.

These last points raise a further issue. Put simply, is it intolerant and bigoted to reject religions other than one's own as false? What exactly does it mean to be religiously tolerant or intolerant? Is it even possible to be religiously tolerant if one disagrees with religious views and religions one doesn't hold?

It should also be said that a discussion on religious pluralism may at times focus on the question of whether any god exists, or the question of how such a god, assuming that he exists, should even be conceived. This isn't an exhaustive list of topics, but it is clearly a diverse set. In a single chapter we cannot cover all things, so which should we address and how should we proceed?

As with all issues of Christian evidences, it is important first to talk about the different things one might defend and to explain the strategy involved in doing so in each case. Once that is clarified, the apologist can choose the item or items for defense and then use the relevant strategy to make his or her case. Given the many issues involved in religious pluralism, it seems that there are at least three major strategies one might use in arguing against it. But we should first introduce two distinctions that are helpful in understanding what we are trying to do.

Apologists and philosophers of religion often distinguish between negative and positive apologetics. The basic idea of negative apologetics is to rebut the attacks hurled at a particular position or idea. If one succeeds in answering the attacks, that won't "prove" that the position attacked is correct, but it will show that objections against it can be answered and that therefore, those who hold the view aren't irrational in so doing. A good example of an issue where the main emphasis of one's apologetics, if one is a theist, is negative apologetics, is the problem of evil.

The apologetic posture just described is essentially a defensive one. But there is another form of negative apologetics a Christian might use. The Christian might leave his defensive strategy and go on the offensive against the views of the nonbelieving opponent. This would involve raising objections to the nonbeliever's view. If those objections cannot be answered, that would show the nonbeliever's view to be untenable. It wouldn't, however, show that the *believer's* position is correct.

In contrast to negative apologetics, a positive apologetic approach attempts not so much to answer objections to a belief but to amass positive evidence in favor of it. If the apologist succeeds, he or she will have shown not only that the views held are possibly true but also that they are likely true. A good example of an issue where the main focus is building a strong case to support a belief is the case typically built in support of the resurrection of Christ.

As to the offensive/defensive apologetics distinction, positive apologetics is definitely apologetics on offense. In this case, the apologist reasons that the best defense is the positive case in favor of his or her position, and so the apologist builds that case. It is also fair to say that attacking the opponent's position might be done not just by raising a few objections to it (the apologist goes on the offensive against the opponent's view), but also by building the positive case against it. Such a maneuver would be apologetics on offense; whether it is positive or negative apologetics I leave to the reader's reflection.

My main concern is to distinguish negative from positive apologetics. Within the scope of each kind, the apologist might also adopt a defensive or an offensive strategy. Netland aptly summarizes the notions of positive and negative apologetics, especially as they relate to the pluralism issue. He writes that with negative apologetics the concern is with

> responding to direct attacks upon the truth or rationality of Christian faith, trying to show that such criticisms are unjustified. The objective here is to show that the believer is justified or is not violating any rationality norms or is within his or her "epistemic rights" in accepting Christian belief. . . . But there is no attempt to go beyond this to demonstrate that the unbeliever ought to accept the Christian claims as well. Positive

apologetics . . . goes beyond merely responding to critiques and is concerned to show, in an appropriate manner, that non-Christians too ought
to accept the truth claims of Christianity.[9]

From this description, we can also say that negative apologetics in relation
to religious pluralism will require Christian apologists to adopt mainly a
defensive posture, while positive apologetics will require a more offensive
stance or strategy.

While these distinctions are helpful, they do not name any particular
arguments, nor do they suggest any specific strategy one might follow in
addressing religious pluralism. But it is possible to identify various strategies one might adopt for this discussion. In particular, I offer three different
possible approaches. First, the Christian apologist might present a positive
case *for exclusivism*. No doubt this would involve at least positive proof
that Christian doctrine is true (objectively so for everyone) and that Christ
is the one and only way to salvation and an eternal relation with God. If the
apologist takes this first strategy and shows that Christianity is the one true
religion, then other religions cannot as a whole be true. That is, religious
pluralism with its belief that no religion is "the truth" could not be true.

A second strategy requires apologists to identify the objections that
pluralists raise against exclusivism, and to refute them. Since these objections are often used by pluralists as positive evidence *for* pluralism, if the
apologist can answer these objections, he can say first that the pluralist
hasn't succeeded in refuting exclusivism and *hasn't* made the case *for* pluralism. If one follows this second strategy (and uses it successfully), he or
she will have undercut the case for pluralism, but the pluralist might still
have other positive evidences favoring pluralism. Whether or not this is so,
by answering these supports for pluralism (i.e., the pluralist's objections
to exclusivism), the apologist will have shown that exclusivism cannot be
rejected on the grounds the pluralist has offered. But that in no way will
show that exclusivism is true—only that it is not rendered impossible by
the pluralist's objections. To show that exclusivism is not only possible but
probable, a convincing positive case for the exclusivist's religion must be
presented and defended against pluralists' objections.

There is yet a third strategy one might adopt in handling religious pluralism. It involves the apologist building a case against pluralism to show
that it cannot be true. This means that rather than offering isolated objec-

tions to one tenet or another held by pluralists, the apologist would present a sustained argument which would show that as a whole pluralism is wrong. Of course, this strategy might instead involve building a case against several pluralist notions that are so foundational to pluralism as a whole that if those key items are wrong, the whole approach collapses. If this third strategy is the apologist's preferred approach, it would remove, should it succeed, pluralism as a correct approach to the world's religions. That would mean that exclusivism *could* be right, but it wouldn't prove that it is right. In order to show that exclusivism is in fact correct, a positive case for it would have to be presented.

Strategies one and three require the apologist to adopt an offensive stance. The first is also positive apologetics; the third could be construed as a form of either positive or negative apologetics. Strategy two is both negative and defensive apologetics. While it would be wonderful if the apologist, using strategy one, could make the positive case for exclusivism, this strategy seems to be the most difficult of the three to "pull off." Strategy three is also difficult, but probably not as hard as the first because a string of cogent arguments aimed at the main concepts in the pluralist's position isn't impossible to imagine. It seems to me, however, that the most significant concern with the third strategy is that it does not necessarily require the apologist to answer any of the pluralist's major objections to exclusivism. I suspect that unless those objections are honestly, clearly, and cogently addressed, there is little chance of pluralists taking exclusivism seriously. Of course, even if the key objections to exclusivism are answered, pluralists may remain unimpressed, but at least they cannot say that exclusivists hold their views without even considering any evidence against them.

Because the second strategy takes most seriously the pluralist's objections to exclusivism, it seems the most fruitful route to use, especially in a short chapter like ours. I also happen to think that of the three strategies, it is the easiest with which to succeed. But again we must remember what "success" is with this strategy. "Success" involves rebutting objections that would, if unrefuted, make exclusivism impossible and pluralism more probable.

In the rest of this chapter, then, I propose to discuss a series of issues that pluralists raise and turn into objections against exclusivism. Since pluralists believe these objections cannot be adequately answered, they believe that by raising them, they are also offering evidence in support of pluralism. Specifically, we need to discuss a set of issues surrounding the question of truth. Then, we must assess the claim that all religions are really the same and accomplish the same thing for their adherents. Then, some pluralists note that for every claim of truthfulness found in one religion there are similar claims in other religions. Hence, they conclude, with such parity of conflicting truth claims, the wise person should simply respect all views involved rather than try to declare a "winner" among the conflicting claims. This issue needs to be addressed. Then we must handle the matter of tolerance for other religions and the question of criteria for evaluating religions and religious claims within various belief systems. Finally, I think it appropriate to go on the offensive against pluralism by offering some arguments which, if correct, offer significant reasons to reject pluralism.

Though this agenda may appear to be too much for one chapter, I note that many of the issues to be raised in the following pages have already been addressed in some detail in previous chapters of this book. Hence, we can refer to those discussions briefly without going into the detail otherwise necessary to discuss the issues in question.

The Question of Truth

Several questions should be addressed in this section. However, because several of them have already been handled earlier in this book, we can move rather quickly through the questions.

An initial question is about what truth means in discussions of religious pluralism. In response, there are several different notions of truth we can identify before noting which one(s) are relevant to the discussion of pluralism. First, it is possible to speak of a person as true, as in the sentence "he is a true friend," or as in Jesus's claim to be the way, the truth, and the life. Generally, this notion of truth focuses on the reliability or dependability of the one said to be true. Jesus's claim is, of course, more complex, for his comment can be taken to mean that he is the embodiment of everything true, that he is dependable, that he is the only deity who matches the ideal notion of deity, etc. While the claims of Christ about himself are indeed often under discussion when pluralism is the topic, truth in a person is not the most basic sense under consideration in religious pluralism.

Then, there is *personal truth*, which isn't the same thing as truth of or in a person. Personal truth refers to truth that seems right and/or has proven to be helpful to some individual. Those who speak of personal truth do not typically think their truth is for all; no such notion of absolute truth is in view. Rather, this sort of truth is relative to the one who holds it, and is more pragmatic in nature than anything else. That is, it is an idea or ideas that the holder has found useful.[10] Those who deny that there is absolute truth typically think personal truth is all that is available. Hence, if asked whether any religion is the one true religion, they say no.

Finally, we can identify propositional truth or the truth of a proposition or affirmation. Affirmations are typically thought to be true according to one or another theory of propositional truth. The best known theory is the correspondence theory of truth. According to this notion, truth of a proposition is a relationship between word and world. If the state of affairs affirmed in the claim matches or corresponds to the way the world is, the sentence is said to be true in a correspondence sense. Another theory of propositional truth is the coherence theory. It sees propositional truth as a relation between word and word. That is, if two claims do not contradict one another, they are said to be true in a coherence sense of truth. Of course, propositions true in a coherence sense may be false in a correspondence sense. That is, even though they do not contradict one another, they don't match the way the world is.

Of the different notions of truth discussed, it is the correspondence sense that is most in view in discussions of pluralism. Typically, pluralists believe that truth in a correspondence sense would be nice, but we just are not in a position to know whether religious claims (or a whole religion) are true in this sense. Reasons for thinking this to be so were discussed in the chapter on postmodern skepticism and need not be repeated here. Or, a pluralist might believe that humans can know truth in a correspondence sense, but there just isn't enough evidence to affirm any specific religion as true. And, there may not be enough evidence to affirm individual religious truth claims either.

In contrast, religious exclusivists typically think there is such a thing as truth in the correspondence sense, and that we can know it. This is so for nonreligious claims and for religious beliefs as well. Exclusivists are not saying that all religious claims are equally verifiable in a correspondence sense, but they do believe it is possible to show conclusively that the key claims of their religion are true in this sense. Sentences that are true in a correspondence sense do not contradict other sentences that are true in a correspondence sense. Otherwise, there could be contradictory states of affairs in the world, just as there could be contradictions in language. Since it is absurd to think there are genuinely contradictory states of affairs in the world, our language about the world shouldn't contain contradictions either. Hence, if claims of other religions contradict those of the religion deemed to be true in a correspondence sense, those other religious claims cannot be true. Hence, if one religion is true in a correspondence sense, other religions must be excluded as false.

We have, then, uncovered the sense of truth most in question when the question of truth is raised in discussions of religious pluralism. Whatever is said about any religion's truth, it is understood that what is most under consideration is whether the religion's claims correspond to the way things actually are in the world outside our minds. But some may wonder how there could be such things as religious truths in this sense, since religious truths are presumably about "religious entities" and "religious actions," and those kinds of things and deeds are so unlike things and deeds that are empirically observable. Despite the difference between religious entities, etc., and physical entities, it seems that the only ways we humans have of verifying or falsifying claims about such things are the same ways we have for verifying or falsifying claims about things that are empirically observable. As a result, many have thought that it really is impossible to verify or falsify religious claims. Those who use religious language must not actually be making claims intended to correspond to anything, since there seems to be no way for humans to test whether such claims do or do not correspond to states of affairs they affirm.

On the other hand, many who use religious language believe they are making assertions about states of affairs in the world outside our minds. They believe that it is not nonsensical to think of religious claims in this way, because they believe there are either empirical and/or nonempirical ways such statements can be verified or falsified. Hence, they think not only that it makes sense to say that their religion is the one true religion. They think there are ways to prove that this is so.

The main questions about truth in discussions of religious pluralism are whether there is absolute truth (even absolute religious truth), and if so, are humans in any position to know what it is. In discussing postmodern epistemology, we saw reasons why many are dubious about there being absolute truth. The main one is that no one can have more than his or her own perspective on the world at any time, and of course, our "take" on reality is largely impacted by the time, place, and culture we live in and by our own life experiences. There just isn't a "God's-eye" view of everything available to any mere human, and even if there were, it would need to be constantly adjusted as time and history move on, and as human knowledge of the world continues to grow and change. If this is true of empirically observable things, how much more are religious entities and their actions hidden from ordinary human beings! Even those who think we can know some things as absolutely true must exercise a healthy skepticism about knowing religious truth claims as true or false.

The appropriate responses to such views are those we employed in addressing both postmodern and modern epistemological skepticism. Especially significant are the comments on how to go about demonstrating things to be true, my comments on certainty, and the discussion of whether any kind of meaningful objective knowledge is possible. Though it is true that religious truth claims are about things that are more difficult than many nonreligious beliefs to verify or falsify, because they speak of things that aren't empirically observable, that doesn't mean there is no way at all to verify such claims. In fact, some lines of evidence to support such claims are empirically observable, but as we have also seen, empirical evidence isn't the only kind of support that can be marshaled in favor of religious claims. Of course, some religious claims are less open to testing for truth than others, but that is also true for nonreligious beliefs. Such claims should be held, of course, with less dogmatism than we have in holding claims that are more thoroughly verifiable and have conclusive evidence to support or refute them. The argumentation for these epistemological claims is contained in my responses to postmodern and modern skepticism and needn't be repeated here.

The net result is that we need not embrace all religions as equally valid because we have no way of knowing which are true. Granted, it may be easier to falsify a religious truth claim (and a religion) than to verify its truth, but even so, that is progress in evaluating religions. We needn't remain totally agnostic about which religion(s) is(are) true. That this is so means that a major reason for adopting religious pluralism (i.e., there isn't absolute truth, or if there is we can't know it) is answered. That doesn't tell us which religion is "the right one" (evidence for and against each religion needs to be examined carefully), but it does say that we don't have to reject exclusivism on the ground that it requires only one religion to be true and we just aren't in a position to make and prove such a claim.

But Aren't All Religions the Same, Anyway?

Even if one grants that there is absolute truth (in a correspondence sense) and that humans can know it, pluralists will likely claim that this doesn't matter, because all religions are really the same and actually produce the same result. Hence, there is no need to reject any religion or to favor any one over the others. Is this so?

When pluralists make this claim, they are not denying that each religion has its unique characteristics. Rather, they are saying that despite certain differences, religions are all basically about the same thing, and if you follow any one religion, the result for you as a person will be essentially the same as what any other religion will do for its adherents.

When this objection to exclusivism is raised, it may actually contain two distinct objections, one explicit and the other implicit. The explicit one is that all religions are really about the same thing and produce the same results. The more implicit point for many pluralists is that even if two religions have significant differences, both of them could still be true. The fact that claims in competing religions may even contradict one another doesn't show either religion to be false. Thinking that it does shows a dependence on the law of noncontradiction, but there is no reason to think we must be bound by such rules of rationality. So, whether religions' truth claims do or don't conflict really doesn't matter; all of them could be true.

Clearly these are significant arguments for pluralism, and they must be answered. The place to begin is with the claim that all religions are really the same. Is it true that, in their most fundamental and important commitments, all religions are really the same and aim to produce the same results? I think not, but this needs proof and explanation.

An initial and very significant difference between Christianity and other religions, for example, is Christianity's relation to history. If there had been no Muhammad, or if he had existed but didn't do many of the things attributed to him (e.g., take his ride to heaven, leaving from the rock located in Jerusalem), Islam could still be true, for many of its most central beliefs are not about Muhammad but about Allah and what he expects of his human creatures. Moreover, if Siddhartha Gautama had never existed, or had just been an ordinary person, the central tenets of Buddhism might still be true, because those beliefs are taken to be eternally true and don't depend on the history of Gautama.[11] Even Judaism's major beliefs could be true if there were no Moses or King David. Moreover, while the promises made to Abraham, Isaac, and Jacob are important, many of those promises could have been made to other people without the core tenets of Judaism being false or in need of being changed. No Jew, for example, has a right relation to God by believing that Moses, David, and the patriarchs existed.

In contrast, Jesus is not just the central teacher of Christian truth. He claims to be the truth, the Messiah and Savior of the world, and the divine Son of God. If none of these things is true, then his death cannot pay for anyone's sins. And, if he never rose from the dead, his most crucial teaching about the conquest of sin and its results are false. As Paul wrote, "If Christ has not been raised, . . . you are still in your sins" (1 Cor. 15:17). The identity of Jesus and the history of his birth, life, and death matter to the truth of Christianity's central tenets in a way that is not true of other religions. If the tomb of Jesus were found on the outskirts of Jerusalem with human remains in it that could be identified as those of Jesus of Nazareth, there would be no reason to believe in the truth of Christianity. This is not true of other religious leaders like Moses, Muhammad, Buddha, Confucius, etc.[12]

Closely related to, but distinct from, the above is the conception of God or the religious ultimate one finds in various religions. While it is true that Judaism, Islam, and Christianity believe in only one God, neither Judaism nor Islam hold anything close to the Christian doctrine of the Trinity. Multiplicity of any sort in the godhead is ruled out altogether in these non-Christian monotheisms. And it is wrong to think that the Greco-Roman pantheon of gods, for example, is parallel to Christianity because it postulated a multiplicity of divine beings. This is so because each of the gods was understood to have his or her distinct divine essence. In Christianity, however, while there are three persons who are deity, all three share the one and only divine essence. So, Christianity is not like other forms of monotheism, and it isn't really, after all, a form of polytheism.

When we move to other world religions, the diversity in the conception of the divine only increases. Netland compares Buddhism, Hinduism, and Shintoism on this matter. In the former two at least, there are variations in the different branches of these religions. Theravada Buddhism speaks of *nirvana* as the religious ultimate, but *nirvana* isn't a being, but rather "a complete cessation of attachment." Mahayana Buddhism might proffer *Dharmakaya*, "the ultimate, all-inclusive Law Body of the Buddha essence," as that which is religiously ultimate. For Zen Buddhists, emptiness may be thought of as the religious ultimate, and Pure Land Buddhists "tend to think in quasi theistic terms of the Amida Buddha, a being with definite personal characteristics, as the religious ultimate."[13]

As to Hinduism, there are again various conceptions of the ultimate, such as *nirguna* Brahman, Vishnu, Shiva, or Krishna. In contrast, atheistic Hindus "will tend to regard the entire cosmic process as ultimate."[14] In Shintoism there is belief in various deities known as *kami*, but they are thought of neither as ontologically transcendent nor as distinct from the world around us. Hence, in some sense they are thought to be continuous with the experiential world outside our minds. As Netland explains, "the difficulty we have in identifying religious ultimacy in Shinto is in itself instructive, for it underscores the great difference in worldview between polytheistic religious traditions such as Shinto and monotheistic faiths such as Christianity and Islam."[15]

The above offers only some examples of the diversity of conceptions of the divine in various religions. It should be clear that the pluralist claim about the sameness of all religions is hard to sustain in view of this evidence. We can hardly say that these religions are after all worshiping the same divine being. John Hick, of course, has famously argued that these conceptions are in fact distinct, but that they are only culturally conditioned responses to the one ultimate reality which he labels *the Real*.[16] At this point we cannot go into all of the details of Hick's theory, but at least some response is needed. Critiques of Hick's theory are legion,[17] and interested readers should consult them. Thankfully as well, Hick has responded to his critics and they have offered counterresponses, so we don't have to imagine how the various parties in this debate might respond.

For our purposes, I note simply that it is rather hard to believe what Hick says about there just being one ultimate reality, *the Real*, when Hick gives us so little information about the nature of *the Real*, and when he adds that the various gods of various religions (about which we can say a lot of things—and perhaps even verify or falsify some claims about them) don't actually exist. If deities which peoples down through the centuries have held as ultimate reality and have described with various characteristics are nonexistent, how are we to believe Hick when he tells us that there actually is a religious ultimate, *the Real*, about which we can offer few positive predications, and when he tells us, anyway, that the various gods of world religions actually point to the one ultimate reality, *the Real*? It seems that this belief in *the Real* with little or no way to verify or falsify that *the Real* exists (or is truly distinct from the gods of various world religions) is in fact a form of religious exclusivism itself! Even worse, for all the information Hick offers and in light of its being unclear as to how we could ever verify existence of *the Real*, belief in *the Real* may be nothing more than belief in something that is actually nothing. If the various gods of world religions are culturally conditioned projections of human responses to the divine ultimate, those gods may point more to the humans who "created" them than they point beyond themselves to some ultimate reality beyond everything in the empirical world. Put differently, when we have little idea of the content of the referent of the term *the Real* and little or no way to confirm that this referent exists, belief in *the Real* may be nothing more than believing in nothing.

There are other significant differences between world religions. For example, they do not all agree on the human situation. Muslims see humans as having free will and being able to do God's will in history. Humans are coworkers with God and have dignity as such; they don't need a savior, as sin is seen as a defect or imperfection, not as a radical problem that binds the human will so that it cannot in itself obey God.[18]

In contrast, Buddhism and Hinduism generally hold that humans are trapped in the cycle of rebirths through which they must migrate in accord with *karma*. Buddhism especially emphasizes that the various life cycles are filled with pervasive suffering. For both of these religions, the fundamental problem with humanity is not willful rebellion against God's will but "a profound ignorance, blindness or confusion regarding the true nature of reality."[19]

In contrast to all of these religions and to Christianity, Shintoism does not portray the current order as fallen. Rather, the problem, if one chooses to call it a problem, is that somehow the *kami* have been offended and this results in a cosmic imbalance. "Evil is rooted in defilement or contamination from association with what is impure. But contamination does not stem from sin (rebellion against a holy God) but rather from association with what is undesirable, especially death."[20]

It should be quite clear that for any of these religions, the notion of Jesus as the divine-human savior who has paid for the sins of all humanity (no mere human could ever pay for even his or her sins so as to satisfy God) in order to make peace between God and humans is unnecessary and irrelevant. Of course, the good news of salvation in Christ really makes sense only if one understands and agrees with the "bad news" that requires Christ's sacrifice. If the "bad news" of a given religion has little or nothing to do with humans being radically alienated from God by disobedience and unable to do anything to remove this alienation, then it is easy to dispense with the Christian good news of Christ's atoning sacrifice for sin.[21]

Another pluralist argument claims that differences in religious beliefs such as those already mentioned don't really matter, anyway. Typically, pluralists argue that religions stem from the religious experiences of the divine among their adherents and produce in their followers the same result(s). Of course, with what different religions believe about the being and nature of God, it is understandable if adherents to a given religion have one sort of experience of the divine while those from other religions have a different kind of experience. Pluralists note that it is extremely difficult, if not impossible, to make a judgment as to which religious experiences are genuine, and which are not experiences of the divine. Hence, it would seem arbitrary to reject a given religion on the grounds that its adherents don't really "connect" with the divine. And besides, when we see that religions tend to produce the same results in their followers, what difference does it make if we can't decide exactly which religious experiences are most genuine? Most religions have the goal of moving their followers from being self-centered to being God- or ultimate reality-centered. The exercise of compassion is also a goal of most major religions.[22]

This argument actually contains several arguments. The first is that there is no way to rule out others' religious experiences as not really being experiences of the divine. A second is that doctrinal differences don't really matter, because any religion can get you connected with the divine. A third is that all religions bear (or at least intend to bear) the same fruit in their followers. As to the first, exclusivists don't claim that people who follow another religion have never had a genuine experience of God. The Bible, for example, speaks of various forms of natural revelation that are available to all people, and it also shows that God may use some form of special revelation (direct speech, a dream, a vision, for example) to speak to people who aren't Christian.[23] So, rejecting pluralism doesn't mean that only "my religious experiences" are veridical while those of people from other religions are illusory. What it does mean is that the perceptions of and responses to the divine among those who experience God cannot all be correct when the account of the religious ultimate in various religions is so different and even contradictory of accounts of the religious ultimate in other religions.

As to whether doctrine really matters, it matters much more than pluralists claim. Adherents to Christianity believe they are led by the Holy Spirit or that one or more members of the Trinity has met them and urged them to adopt a certain course of action. How can this be the "same" or even "same kind of" experience as that of the person whose religion views God as an impersonal force or basically holds that there is no divine religious ultimate? These various experiences may "feel" the same to all who have them, but given contradictory beliefs about the source of the experience, it is hard to see these experiences as truly stemming from the same origin. And, given the specific religion the believer holds, the believer may go away from the experience with a renewed sense of his own sin and defilement and with a need to repent and obey God's law better (think of Isaiah's experience of God, as recorded in Isaiah 6). But if one's religion has no place for the concept of sin, or if it does believe there is sin but that man is fully able to conquer it himself so there is no need to repent, seek God's forgiveness, and seek his aid in following righteousness, the responses to the religious experience of the divine will be quite different. It seems impossible for them to be the same. But then, what one believes about God, human nature, and sin, and the need for and nature of salvation makes a huge difference in one's interpretation of one's religious experience and responses to that experience.

And what should we say about the claim that all religions produce the same fruit in their followers? Here we should not dismiss this claim on the ground that there are adherents to various religions who don't show its fruits. That is true, but it doesn't prove that religions are different; it may show only that there are adherents to all religions who are spiritually mature and others who are rather immature and relatively unchanged by the religious beliefs they espouse.

More to the point is whether all religions really intend to produce the same thing in their followers. Even if this were so, the various religions tell quite contradictory stories about how this is to happen and how capable human beings are of making it happen. For example, Muslims should follow Allah, even as Christians should obey God, but the two religions give a very different account of how and whether this is possible. As we saw above, Muslims think that humans have free will that allows them to follow the wishes of Allah. There is temptation to sin, but humans can resist that temptation under their own power. In contrast, Christian doctrine says that people who don't know Christ as Savior are in bondage to sin. They are able to make free choices, but they have such a positive propensity to sin, that without divine help, the spontaneous, free thing to do is always to fall to temptation and sin. To correct this problem, humans need to accept Christ as Savior and then, with the enablement of the Holy Spirit, obey the commands of the Lord. Despite salvation, the old sin nature remains, and there will invariably be a struggle between the old and new nature within the believer. But once one is saved, sin no longer has such a stranglehold that it is impossible to obey God. With the Holy Spirit's enablement we can obey. In contrast, most of humanity has no such relation to God and no such power. Hence, developing Christian virtues, let alone a heart for God, is not even possible in our own power, according to Christianity. This is certainly a much different story than the one told by Islam.

And, the idea that all religions intend to move their followers away from self-centeredness to God-centeredness is simply false. For example, New Age religion, with its heavy emphasis on Eastern religions, urges its followers to move toward self-realization and fulfillment. What exactly does that mean? Among other things, it means that each person needs to discover the divine in himself or herself. But that doesn't mean that we should see that we have within us traits that are like God's attributes. It means that we must see that we are all really gods ourselves, and we need to develop our potential to achieve the highest goals we can and thereby have a sense of self-worth and fulfillment. Such goals are certainly quite different from the notion that the fruit of all religions is to be compassionate to others and to move from self-centeredness to God-centeredness (God being understood as distinct from oneself).

Other examples could be offered, but the point is clear enough. Doctrine does matter, and the intended fruits of each religion are not necessarily the same. But even if the intended fruits were all the same, how one goes about reaching those goals and whether one, in only one's own power, is even capable of achieving them is not at all agreed on by the various religions. So, contrary to what pluralists want us to believe, it just isn't true that all religions are the same. And, what one religion says about God, human nature and the human situation, salvation, etc., is not just contrary to what other religions say. In many cases, it blatantly contradicts what other religions profess!

In response to this portrayal of the differences between religions, pluralists may offer one of two answers. They may, on the one hand, grant that there are differences between religions and that those differences do matter. However, they might reply that such differences suggest that it would be wisest to withhold judgment as to which truth claims (and which religions) are correct, since there are noble, moral followers of each religion and since it is so difficult to determine which religion's claims (that contradict other religions' beliefs) are true.[24]

In reply, what this pluralist claim suggests seems to be very good advice, especially if there is no such thing as absolute truth, or if absolute truth exists but humans are in no position to know what it is. However, as argued throughout this book, there is reason to think that there is absolute truth, and that humans can know it. This doesn't mean that the task of evaluating various religions' truth claims for accuracy will be easy. It is only to say that the human situation with respect to evaluating truth claims and knowing what is true is far from hopeless. Arguments in support of this claim have been offered throughout this book and need not be repeated again.

Pluralists may offer a second reply to the fact that truth of claims of various religions contradict those of others. They may answer that this is so, but that does not mean all the claims cannot be true. One only concludes that some claims can't be true if others contradict them if one persists in following the law of noncontradiction. But adherence to the law of noncontradiction is a peculiar feature of Western logic and need not be a requirement imposed on everyone. If we don't need to follow the law of noncontradiction, then there is no need to reject any religion's truth claims as false because they contradict the claims of other religions.

Though this seems to be a rather popular belief of many religious pluralists, its popularity doesn't prove its correctness. If we must adopt this rejection of the law of noncontradiction, then everything said in the previous paragraph *and claims that blatantly contradict what the paragraph says* can both be true. But then how should we proceed, for if the previous paragraph and its contradictory are both true, that would mean that contradictory claims both do and do not matter? Thus, contradictory religious claims both are and are not all true, and we should then hold both religious pluralism and exclusivism at the same time.

Don't think too long and hard about what has just been said; it is absurd, and trying to make sense of it is futile and may well give you a headache. Convinced pluralists may agree but may ask "so what?" What difference does it make whether or not we follow the law of noncontradiction? Here I must refer readers to my discussion of this issue in the first chapter dealing with postmodern skepticism. There it was clearly explained why the law of contradiction matters. We saw that the law of noncontradiction is not just a matter of "Western" logic. Rather it relates to something true of the world, all languages, and all thinking. So, whether you rely on this law or not is not just a "Western thing." It's a "human thing"—more specifically, it's a "thing" about the world in which humans live and about all human language and knowledge. And, as we also saw, whether you follow the law of noncontradiction or not makes a huge difference as to what you should do and even as to whether you have any idea of how, in a given instance, to act.

If what is at stake in the debate over which religion's claims are true (in a correspondence sense of "true") were of minimal significance, then we might simply say that we need to agree to disagree about the import of the law of noncontradiction. But that is hardly true, for religions address how one should live this life, and they give a vision of the afterlife. They also have different accounts of how to establish and maintain a relation with God, and they disagree in their understanding of the eternal destiny (or destinies) that are possible for human beings. Such matters are hugely significant and need to be addressed directly. It may be for a time "liberating" to think that all religions are the same and will lead everyone to a blissful eternity, but at some point in their life most people should and will want to know whether that is true or is only wishful thinking. To be wrong about this matter has eternal consequences, and unfortunately, if you get the answer wrong, there will come a time when you cannot correct the error. For those who respond that this last claim is itself just one religion's take on the matter of eternal destiny, my reply is: are you sure? Following a pluralist approach to religion gives little or no ground for certainty about such matters. And that should be quite disturbing to anyone who thinks about it for any length of time!

ARE THERE WORLDVIEW-INDEPENDENT CRITERIA FOR EVALUATING RELIGIONS?

To one degree or another, proponents of religious pluralism will likely be unimpressed with what I have written so far. They may agree, for example, that there are significant differences between religions and that the truth claims of various religions contradict those of others. They may even be a bit sympathetic to the idea that we can know things that are true of the world (in a correspondence sense of "true"), especially claims that are based on simple observation of the empirical world.

Despite such agreement (assuming pluralists will agree), pluralists will respond that this doesn't matter, because even if we would like to have a way to decide which religion and religious claims is/are true, we cannot. The reason is that we need criteria for testing religious truth claims that are independent of all religions, and there are no such criteria. The reason criteria should be independent of all religions is that if they are part of a religion, they will automatically presuppose the truth of the religion of which they are a part even before any claim of any religion is evaluated. Of course, if criteria presuppose the truth of a given worldview, those with a different worldview will reject the criteria, because they know that to accept the criteria will inevitably lead to the conclusion that their religion is false. Presupposing that a religion is true by choosing criteria (criteria already part of a religious worldview) for testing religious truth claims is to beg the question. Question begging (assuming as true without proof what you need to prove is true) is a logical error, and no one should accept the evaluations of a process that incorporates logical mistakes.

These are, of course, significant issues, but those who have read my chapters on postmodern and modern skepticism will also recognize that the objections have a familiar ring. In particular, what is at stake (though not the only thing) is ultimately the matter of objectivity and subjectivity. That is, are our intellectual perspectives so colored by our culture, upbringing, and prior learning that it is impossible for us to evaluate things we believe and things we reject in a fair and unbiased way? If the answer is no, then we must simply retreat to our own intellectual worldviews and commit to relativism. Clearly, this is an important issue, but it is not one peculiar to evaluating religions and religious claims alone. It is a problem that besets any intellectual enterprise.

So, how should we approach this issue? First, we should realize that this issue raises at least two fundamental questions. One is whether there are in fact any criteria independent of all worldviews which can be used to evaluate conflicting truth claims (including those about religion). Second, if it is possible to identify such criteria, that doesn't tell us whether those criteria can be applied in evaluating religions in a way that is not so filled with subjectivity that such evaluations are doomed to the complaint of question begging. In answer to the first question, I believe that there are such criteria, and I intend to present them below. As for the second question, we have already discussed this issue at length, so only a brief reminder will be necessary.

Before addressing either of these questions, however, I must raise an even more fundamental issue. We must ask whether humans even possess the intellectual, perceptual, etc. equipment needed to allow them to recognize criteria for evaluating truth claims and to do so in an objective and unbiased way. If we don't have such equipment, or if we have intellectual equipment for the task but it is "theory-laden" (and hence predisposed to one viewpoint or another before any claims and evidence for or against the claims are even confronted, let alone evaluated) even before it gets used, then there is no need to address the other two questions raised above. The situation is hopeless; we might as well commit to relativism and embrace religious pluralism.

Thankfully, there is such equipment, and there are ways of using it which, if not infallible, are reliable enough to think that commitment to relativism is not the only sane option. In fact, throughout the chapters of this book which discuss the questions of truth, certainty, and evidence, I have identified that equipment and explained how it can be used to discern what is true of our world and to mount a compelling proof of such beliefs. A brief review of those answers is in order at this point.

As to the intellectual equipment, it includes our minds and our senses. Granted, some people are more intelligent than others and some people's sensory equipment doesn't function as well as it might (e.g., vision is not 20/20 and some have suffered some loss of hearing). Granted, as well, some people are born significantly depleted (e.g., some are severely mentally retarded, and others are blind or deaf from birth). My point is that most people are born with minds which, as the person grows, become able to think and reason, and their sensory organs function well enough so that they can correctly observe sensory objects in the world. In addition, as we grow we come to recognize that certain kinds of arguments contain fallacies, and we learn how to support or refute with evidence various beliefs. Moreover, as we use our sensory organs and our mind, we learn how to identify the sensory objects that confront us.

It would be very hard to make a case that this equipment comes at birth already "loaded" with the content of one worldview or another. In fact, such an idea hardly makes any sense. If we are born with the content of a worldview on or in our minds, there is no way to verify this with newborn infants. Moreover, I suspect that there are few who later in life would claim to remember that at birth or even in the early months of life they were already committed to Christian, Muslim, Hindu, etc. beliefs, or that they already could identify the size, shape, taste and texture, or the odor of various perceptual objects. If someone made such claims, it is hard to know how they could possibly be verified. Would they also be able to tell us about life in their mother's womb during the last few days before birth, or could they relate what it was like to travel down the birth canal and be born?

Considerations like the preceding lead me to conclude that human beings in general are born with the intellectual equipment to attain knowledge about the world. They are also able to learn how to use that equipment so as to grow in knowledge of the world around them. This equipment and these capacities to learn are true of all people at all times, regardless of geographical location and of the culture in which they are born.

Even so, some may protest, particular argument forms and the recognition that certain types of reasoning are guilty of committing logical fallacies is a peculiarly Western phenomenon. Easterners typically reject such thought forms. Here the words of Harold Netland are instructive as he notes that rejecting some idea or principle of reason is not the same thing as refuting it.[25] As I demonstrated in answering postmodern skepticism, there are many people who would deny that we are bound to avoid logical fallacies such as question begging, the *post hoc* fallacy, and the genetic fallacy. On the other hand, put them in an actual situation where someone discounts their credentials with reasoning that begs the question, or in a situation where, committing the *post hoc* fallacy, their discoveries are rejected as stolen from someone else and a lawsuit is filed against them, and they will cry foul. They may never have heard of the logical fallacies mentioned above, nor could they define any of them if asked, but when those errors in reason are committed and the results are used against them, they will understand that some rational mistake is being made. Neither our intellectual equipment nor the rules by which it works are so culturally dependent that members of one culture cannot even discuss their views with members of another because each culture has its own separate intellectual equipment with its own particular rules. As argued earlier in this book, these are not "Western things"; they are "human things." And it is hard to see how the equipment prejudices the case for or against any particular religion. This would seem especially so when one considers that people in various locations and cultures, using the same equipment in the same basic ways, come to different religious beliefs.

Establishing that humans have "theory neutral" equipment and methods for learning about the world is an important step. But we must next see whether there are in fact any criteria that are worldview-independent. If not, then we still have no way to judge between conflicting truth claims, which are correct and which incorrect. As Netland argues, various philosophers such as Ninian Smart, William Wainwright, Keith Yandell, and Paul Griffiths (each quite familiar with at least one non-Christian religious tradition) have argued that there are such independent criteria. Examples include such things as "demanding internal consistency within a set of beliefs, freedom from ad hoc hypotheses, congruence with what is known to be true in other domains of study such as history and the sciences, explanatory power in accounting for fundamental aspects of human experience and so on."[26] Others have added a moral criterion, which holds that to be an acceptable religion, a religion "should satisfy some basic moral and aesthetic intuitions and provoke and inspire persons to live morally responsive and responsible lives."[27]

A word about these is in order. The demand for internal consistency as applied to religious claims means that a claim must not be self-contradictory (as the notion of a married bachelor is), and it must not contradict other claims made by the same religion. Moreover, if one were to incorporate into one's set of beliefs other beliefs from other religions, those new claims must not contradict religious claims already held. Obviously, the notion of internal consistency invokes along with it the law of noncontradiction. Some will reject this as part of "Western logic," but as noted above, rejection is not refutation. In my chapters on postmodern skepticism, I explained why attempts to refute the law of noncontradiction are futile; that explanation fits here as well.

But why is internal consistency so important? The answer harkens back to our discussion of truth. As we saw, what we really want to know is whether our statements are true in a correspondence sense of "true." A sentence is true in that sense if what it asserts matches the world outside the mind. But then, we must ask whether the world in which we live contains contradictory states of affairs. Is it possible, for example, that at the very moment I am writing this in a suburb of metropolitan Chicago, I am also sunbathing on the French Riviera? Or do we need to do a worldwide door-to-door survey before we can affirm that there are in fact no married bachelors? Obviously, such notions are absurd! But then, if in our world there are no genuinely contradictory states of affairs, our language about the world had better not itself contain contradictory claims. If it does, then it can't be true, because what it says about the world does not match the way the world is. Internal consistency and the law of noncontradiction are not peculiarly Western. These rules and concepts apply to all people at all places and times, regardless of whether they like it or not. And, I note that adopting such a criterion in no way prejudices the case in favor of or against any particular religion. That is so at very least in part because it does not belong to any religion as a tenet of that religion.

As to freedom from ad hoc hypotheses, it depends on what this means. If it means that one is not allowed to propose a theory (without offering any proof of the theory, and even if there isn't any possible evidence to support it) just to support a belief or set of beliefs which otherwise have little or no support, then I can agree. In other words, no religion should be adopted or rejected just because someone proposes a theory which would refute a central claim of the religion, especially when there is no compelling reason for believing that the theory is true. Though there might be some possible world in which the ad hoc theory might be true and demonstrable as such, to conclude that our world is that world (without any proof that this is so) is to engage in question begging, a mistake in reasoning. It is hard to see how such a criterion would prejudice the case for or against any particular religion. Hence, it seems to be genuinely worldview-independent and acceptable in that regard.

The third proposed criterion amounts to fit with known facts. This, too, seems to be a basic rule of reasoning. Why should one accept any claim, religious or otherwise, that contradicts some known fact? For example, if someone should claim that Jesus never existed, that would fly in the face of too much historical evidence for us to take it seriously. Or if someone's religion required the belief that the sun rotates around the earth, there is too much evidence to the contrary for this to be taken seriously. Of course, this criterion does come with some caveats. For one thing, it does not assume that everyone will agree with the content of allegedly "known facts." What is to be taken as common knowledge by all may need some discussion and debate. Moreover, this criterion does not mean that each purported fact is 100 percent objectively certain, and that there are no reasons for reasonable doubt nor could there be. In short, this criterion (and the use of it) has to assume as its background everything I argued in the chapters on modern skepticism about truth, certainty, and demonstrating a claim to be true. But with that material included in one's understanding of what counts as a "known fact," this criterion seems acceptable. It is hard to imagine that such a criterion prejudices the case in favor of or against any specific religion, unless one holds a religion that claims that nothing is real—everything is an illusion. But such a religion would be self-defeating, for if everything is illusory, then so is the claim that everything is illusory. We needn't spend time dealing with something that doesn't exist, and of course, if a belief that all is illusion is correct, then we cannot consider that claim since, if the claim is true, we ourselves do not exist.

As to a claim's having explanatory power of aspects of human experience, here I find myself less convinced. On the one hand, if a claim or a religion explains nothing about human experience, we would all likely be suspicious of its truth. On the other hand, if this criterion is to be used it must leave room for any given religion at certain points in its beliefs to appeal to mystery. Even Christianity doesn't purport to explain everything, and at certain points in Christian doctrine explanation does end and appeal is made to mystery.

So, if this criterion is to be used, it must be used so as to make room for a religion to appeal to mystery. But at this point, we must admit that there can certainly be differences of opinion about which beliefs in a religion need explanation and what is and is not an appropriate place for the religion to appeal to mystery. I suspect that it may not be possible for people from different religions to agree on that matter, in part because depending on where the line is drawn between what must be explained and what is "acceptable mystery," that might just rule out their religion as false even before any evidence is produced and evaluated. In addition, how much should a religion explain in order to qualify as true, and how would we know when a religion has met the requirement? I'm not at all optimistic about getting agreement from the various religions on non–question-begging answers to such questions. Hence, there is something that seems right about this proposed criterion (a religion that doesn't explain much or even anything should be doubted), but I'm not optimistic about agreeing on the rules governing the use of this criterion or optimistic about whether this criterion can actually be used in a non–question-begging way.

That brings us finally to the moral criterion. This is perhaps the most contentious of all the proposed criteria, and that is understandable. There is so much ethical diversity *within* cultures, let alone *between* different cultures that many would be inclined to argue that common principles of morality held by all cultures just are not available. The problem isn't just that specific 'dos' and 'don'ts' vary from culture to culture, but that ethicists know that there is more than one possible way to define ethical terms like 'good,' 'evil,' 'right,' and 'wrong.' That is, normative ethics cannot be entirely disconnected from meta-ethical issues such as the meaning of ethical terms and one's method of justifying one's set of ethical norms.

In contrast, those who favor invoking a moral criterion for evaluating religions argue that despite the great variety and diversity in ethical norms and practices from culture to culture, the basic notion that some things are right and others are wrong seems universal, as do certain commonly held moral "dos" and "don'ts." Part of the argument for such views is the evident connection between morality and religion. It is quite typical for a culture's metaphysical views to be connected somehow to its view of ethical norms. That is not to say that each culture and religion has the same metaphysical commitments as do others, but rather that a culture's metaphysical views (and hence, its religion or religions) are typically connected to whatever the culture subscribes to as matters of moral right and wrong. And we could even add that a culture's sense of moral right and wrong is often embodied in its laws. So, for example, a country that is primarily atheistic is likely to have conventions about moral "dos" and "don'ts" and even laws that differ from cultures where religious beliefs (and the moral rules and laws that stem from them) are widely held. But even in countries that one might think are predominantly atheistic, there seem to be (claim those who support the idea of a moral criterion for evaluating worldviews) certain widely held ethical norms that match basic ethical rules of other cultures. Ronald Green sees enough commonality in morality across cultural boundaries to support the idea of a moral criterion as a worldview-independent criterion for evaluating the truth of various religions. He writes,

> One of the most striking impressions produced by comparative study of religious ethics is the similarity in basic moral codes and teachings. The Ten Commandments of Hebrew faith, the teachings of Jesus in the Sermon on the Mount and of Paul in his epistles, the requirements of *sadharana*, or universal *dharma*, in Hinduism (*Laws of Manu*, 10.63), Buddhism's Five Precepts, and Islam's decalogue in the Qur'an (17:22-39) constitute a very common set of normative requirements. These prohibit killing, injury, deception, or the violation of solemn oaths. C. S. Lewis has called basic moral rules like these "the ultimate platitudes of practical reason," and their presence and givenness in such diverse traditions supports his characterization.[28]

What should we say about a moral criterion? Anyone who has ever read C. S. Lewis's *Mere Christianity* and found Lewis's moral argument for God's existence at all compelling will likely be sympathetic to the notion of universal moral norms and a moral criterion. While I am sympathetic, I see some rather significant problems as well. For one thing, there is so much variety possible in answering meta-ethical questions about the meaning of ethical terms like 'right' and 'good,' and so much variation in approaches to justifying a set of moral norms as correct that one wonders if it is really possible to generate a set of ethical norms which everyone would argue are objectively true. My point isn't just the diversity one finds in ethical norms (despite the commonalities Green mentions), but also that there are disagreements about what moral terms mean and disagreements even about whether there is such a thing as an objective moral law or whether instead moral norms are simply a product of subjective social construction intended to produce an orderly society even though such norms don't define what is objectively morally right and wrong.

Second, the very fact that morality is so closely tied to religious beliefs and to a society's laws makes one wonder whether moral rules can be truly independent of all worldviews, for that is really the issue, not just whether societies happen to hold similar ethical rules. Certainly, none of the criteria I have already affirmed have such a connection to any religion or worldview in the way moral rules do. Hence, the argument that moral rules are worldview-independent seems difficult to support.

Then, I am also dubious about how we can confirm such moral rules as "the moral criterion" by which all religions should be and can be objectively judged. That is, how are we to determine that a set of rules (even a set common to many cultures) is correct? Do we judge it by seeing whether people who adhere to a given religion obey the moral rules that stem from it? Given the tendency of all of us to break moral rules (even if only occasionally), deciding on whether a set of moral rules is the "right set" on the grounds of whether its adherents obey the rules is very risky business. Or do we make this decision by building a case to support the worldview which ultimately supports these ethical norms? But that isn't likely to work, because there appear to be a number of worldviews which support these norms (at least one per culture), and yet we have already seen that these different worldviews contain truth claims that conflict with those of other worldviews. But then how should we build a case to confirm that a set of moral rules (perhaps we can agree on specific norms) is the correct set to use as the moral criterion? If we can't make such a case, then regardless of which moral rules we choose to use to evaluate religions, what will our evaluation actually be worth? In dealing with the other criteria I've supported, there was a case that could be made and that was made to support these as correct criteria. There is good reason to think that people with different worldviews could still agree on those criteria. My problem with the notion of a moral criterion is that there is so much that needs to be proved (and I'm dubious about whether people of varying worldviews would agree with the case built) in order even to determine what the criterion should be that this seems like a lot of work with little hope of agreement. My further problem is that it just isn't clear that in order to make a case for a particular set of moral rules, it won't be necessary to adopt a given worldview just to make the case; that certainly isn't so with the other criteria I have supported. And finally, it also isn't clear that when those moral rules (whatever they turn out to be) are applied to the task of evaluating worldviews, proponents of a worldview that is disqualified as invalid by the moral criterion will agree that the rules chosen are the correct and proper "measuring tools" for judging which worldviews are right and which are wrong.

Hence, though I am sympathetic to what the moral criterion proposes, I think that in our ethically relativistic cultures it will be hard to convince many that any set of moral rules is worldview-independent. And, if that can't be done, then the moral criterion won't be a worldview-independent criterion for judging the truth of religions. Some will likely find this troubling, but I don't agree. The reason is that I think, as I've argued throughout this book, that the criteria I have supported are sufficient to make a judgment about which religions are false and which are true.

One further issue remains before we leave this discussion of criteria for judging worldviews. Even if there were general agreement on the criteria for judging religions, that doesn't mean that those criteria will be applied in a fair and objective way when judging whole religions or even specific truth claims within a religion. Thankfully, this is an issue we have met and dealt with already in this book. It is the question of objectivity and subjectivity and the implications of that issue for whether humans can actually know what is true. We needn't repeat that discussion again. It should suffice to remind readers that we concluded that while it is impossible to know anything without using our noetic structure, our presuppositions, prior training, and experiences do not make it impossible to determine what is true of the world. And if we disagree with others about matters of fact, it is not impossible to present evidence that can convince them that their views are wrong. Of course, when the "facts" in question are *religious* truth claims, verifying or falsifying those claims becomes more challenging than verifying or falsifying empirical observation claims. In some cases, the objective case we can make for a religious truth claim will not even be, for example, 80 percent objectively certain. That doesn't mean that this will be the case for every religious truth claim. Nor does it necessarily mean that a claim that is only 80 percent objectively certain is unworthy of our belief. As argued in earlier chapters, one needs to assess what needs to be proved in order to support a belief, and one needs to assess the quality (not the quantity) of the evidence available to support or reject the belief in question. As also argued in this book, the case for a religious belief (and for a whole religion) is never so strong as to remove entirely the need for faith. On the other hand, the case for many religious beliefs will seldom be so weak as to warrant a refusal to believe at all. Some religious beliefs and religions can be demonstrably falsified. Hence, there is reason to think we shouldn't embrace pluralism because all religions are equally valid. But that doesn't mean there is no religion for which there is sufficient reason to believe. Of course, where the evidence is weaker in support of a view, we should be less dogmatic. In this book (the methodological parts and the chapters on Christian evidences) I have argued that we are not in a position of having either to deny all religious claims or even having to be agnostic about the truth of all religious claims. I leave to readers' evaluation the degree to which I have made the case for the claims mentioned in the preceding sentence.

Is Any Position Other than Religious Pluralism Intolerant?

Religious pluralists typically answer this question affirmatively. Moreover, in light of skepticism about our ability to know absolute truth, pluralists affirm that it is just arrogant to think our religion alone is true. Such an attitude rules out mutual understanding and makes it impossible to live together in harmony and community. Besides, if we weren't so arrogant about our own views, we might actually learn something of value by listening to and tolerating other perspectives.[29]

In response, we should begin with a clear understanding of what it means to be tolerant. As Moses Oke explains, tolerance is often viewed as a negative concept in that it is taken to refer to putting up with or enduring a person or view with which one disagrees. Of course, this sort of tolerance may stem from any of several things. It may stem from one's realization that there is nothing he or she can do to change things that are disagreeable. Rather than constantly fight battles that one cannot win anyway, it is often just simpler to let others be. A second reason for this negative type of tolerance might be indifference. That is, you might disagree with someone's views but believe the issues in question just aren't important enough to bother contesting them, and so you put up with the views or practices. A third form of negative tolerance is compromise with the objectionable belief.

As Oke explains, this sort of tolerance really means that you accept what you really don't hold. But in such cases, the disagreements won't go away, especially if they are about religious beliefs and practices or about anything else that really matters to people. This kind of tolerance won't likely promote genuine understanding of other religions and won't be easy to maintain.[30]

Even so, Oke's paper underscores an important point: before addressing whether religious exclusivism, for example, is intolerant, we need a clear definition of what we mean by tolerance. It is here that Netland helps us understand what is really at stake. As he shows, there are different senses of tolerance, and only some rule out making judgments that another person's views are false. Netland discusses three separate contexts in which we can speak of religious tolerance.

The first is tolerance in a *legal context*. In this case the governing laws of a country guarantee all people the right to practice their own religion as they please. This is a basic human right, and even though there are some places around the world where it is denied, it should be upheld. As Netland explains, however, Christian exclusivism in no way seeks to deny people of other religions the legal right to worship as they please.

Second, there is tolerance in the *social context*. In this context, tolerance dictates that we treat people of other religions with respect. We do not discriminate against them solely on the basis of their religious beliefs. Christians should show this kind of tolerance on the grounds that all people are made in God's image and thereby deserve respect. But giving this kind of tolerance to those with whom we disagree does not mean we cannot talk with them about matters of religion and cannot even try to persuade them that their views are wrong and that they need Christ. In other words, it is possible to have significant disagreements with people of a different faith and still be good friends with them, even including them in various parties and social outings your family has. Religious exclusivism doesn't rule out such things. In fact, many Christian missions have as part of their strategy for evangelism making friends of those with whom we want to share the gospel.

Then, there is tolerance in the *intellectual context*. This is the context in which exclusivists are thought to be intolerant and bigoted. The intellectual context focuses on whether the belief or beliefs in question are true. The common complaint today is that if one says anything negative about someone else's belief, one is intolerant. To be truly tolerant intellectually is not to reject anyone's views as false.[31]

How should we respond to the charge that religious exclusivists are intellectually intolerant and that the only way to escape this is to embrace religious pluralism? Several answers seem appropriate. First, imagine that everyone, including exclusivists, decided not to disagree with the views of any other religion, regardless of how much those views oppose one another. If so, then it is hard to know why anyone would adhere to any one religion as opposed to another. About the only reason for holding one's beliefs would be that one was "brought up to believe in that religion." But such a response is going to be extremely unsavory to many religious believers. The reason is that it admits that anyone's religious tradition obligates its adherents to follow certain rules of conduct, but there is no way to show that those rules are anything other than arbitrary. And it also means that what any given religion says about salvation and eternal life has nothing to do with why someone became a believer. Even worse, we can't say that any religion can guarantee salvation and eternal life, because we know that other religions have different and even contradictory (to our religion) views on these matters, and it would be intolerant to think those other religions are wrong. For someone who has fears about displeasing God or fears about his or her final destiny, such a stance seems religiously inadequate. If this is the best any religion can do in addressing these matters, why would anyone want to follow any religion? Why obligate yourself to follow a religion's rules when there is no way of saying that religion and its rules are right, and when it is impossible to say that following the religion will guarantee a pleasant, comfortable eternity?

Of course, many religious believers did not adopt their beliefs just because "they were raised to do so." They have studied their religion and reflected at length on its claims, and have concluded that their religion is right on key doctrinal matters. That is, they have reasons (many good ones) for following a particular religion; their choice to be a believer was not based solely on indoctrination or on anything arbitrary, but rather they made a rational judgment in light of the facts that support their religion. However, pluralists will complain that all of this is just intolerant intellectually, because it means these believers think other people's religious views are wrong.

My second point about intolerance (and an answer to the pluralist challenge just raised) takes its cue from a distinction Netland raises. As he writes, "it is one thing to accept someone's holding a particular belief but quite another matter to accept the content of the belief itself. Religious tolerance does imply the former, but not the latter."[32] Or put differently, "Tolerating a religious belief, then, does not involve a half-hearted acceptance or endurance of the belief *in itself*, but rather it involves acceptance or endurance of *someone's holding* that belief, that is, of a certain case of believing."[33]

Not only do I believe this is correct, but I think an illustration will confirm this and will show that most people who really think about what is being argued would actually agree. Consider the following imaginary (yet not impossible) scenario.

Suppose that you have a MasterCard credit account, and in one month's statement you find a charge for something you never purchased. You call up MasterCard to ask about this. The agent informs you that on a certain date you purchased a particular item. She tells you that she has a copy of the charge receipt with your signature on it. She compares that signature with your signature on other charge slips and says they look identical. Hence, she believes the charge is legitimate. But the fact is that you were out of town on the day the purchase was made, so you could not have charged the item on your statement. Moreover, there is only one copy of your MasterCard, so your wife (who was in town on the day in question) couldn't have made the purchase using the MasterCard.

Now, there are several ways you can respond. A first option would be as follows: believing that it is intolerant to disagree with someone whose beliefs are different from yours, you kindly thank the agent for her time, agree that she's probably right, hang up, and pay the bill. Or, you could choose a second response. Knowing that you are right about this, you become angry with the agent for not believing you. You "read her the riot act" for not believing you, telling her how stupid she is and perhaps raising questions about her ancestry. In addition, you tell her that her belief about the charge is dead wrong, you give her the evidence, yell that there is no way you will pay the bill, and then slam the phone down. But there is also a third option: you know that your belief is correct, but you also agree that it is important to treat people with respect. Hence, you explain calmly and patiently the facts that will convince her that the charge is not legitimate. Regardless of how many further questions she asks about this, you patiently respond. Then, you thank her for her trouble, wish her a good day, and end the conversation.

Of the three possible responses, which would you think best? Would you agree that the third choice is the best but then insist that you have no right to use that approach because disagreeing with someone else's views (even agreeably doing so) is intolerant? Are you required to ask her to dialogue with you a bit more so that the two of you can come to a better understanding of one another's views on this and other matters? Or are you required to adopt the first strategy for handling the situation, because any response that involves telling the agent that she is wrong is intolerant?

If such suggestions sound silly, I would add that they are no sillier than the notion that we are intolerant unless we agree with or say nothing negative about another person's religious beliefs. I certainly grant that deciding whether a belief about religion is true or false can be considerably harder than deciding who's right about the charge on your MasterCard statement. But the point is still the same. If it is intolerant to disagree with someone else's beliefs (regardless of what they are about—religion, politics, credit card charges, etc.), then only the first response mentioned above seems open to us in any situation. The fact that we are not likely to agree with that does not suggest that we are all just money hungry and hence are unable to let the issue about the charge go. Rather, it reflects the fact that intuitively we all agree that when something is wrong, we have a right to say so, though at the same time we should agree that we should respect someone else's right to believe otherwise. Respecting that right, however, in no way obligates us to refrain from trying to change his mind. Being tolerant does, however, seem to rule out the second kind of response, because it is disrespectful of the other person as a person.

We have every right to say that what we believe is true and to explain why we believe it. Intolerance enters the situation not when we merely state our views and the support for them. It enters when we present the views in a condescending manner, showing either by word, deed, or attitude that we think those who disagree with us are intellectually deficient. It also enters the situation when we refuse to listen to our friend's reply or we respond to it in ways that are demeaning to him or her. But such intolerant attitudes, words, and deeds do not automatically come with the stating of one's own views as correct. Not only does religious exclusivism not logically entail intellectual intolerance, but it is also true that religious pluralists need to watch that they don't treat with disdain those who disagree with their views on pluralism. Holding religious pluralism does not make it impossible to be intellectually intolerant of people of other persuasions!

CONTRADICTIONS WITHIN PLURALIST THINKING

So far in this chapter we have addressed supports for pluralism that are actually objections to exclusivism. In this final section I want to "go on the offensive" by presenting some arguments against pluralism. All of them note some internal inconsistency in pluralistic thinking. Since logical consistency is a worldview-independent criterion for assessing truth claims of various viewpoints, it should be acceptable to use it to assess the logical cogency of pluralism itself!

Jan Van Wiele is especially helpful on this matter. He grants that there are varieties of religious pluralism, but argues that at root its various forms seem to hold three key commitments: epistemological skepticism about knowledge in general and especially about religious knowledge, the non-normativity of Christ, and a commitment to religious pragmatism (i.e., one's vision of religion and what is true in religion should be determined by praxis in order to root out social oppression and injustice, for example—that is, a deemphasizing of theology in favor of a focus on action).[34]

After describing these three pillars of pluralist thinking, Van Wiele then argues that pluralism is actually guilty of a number of internal inconsistencies (Van Wiele calls them paradoxes, but as you will see, they are actually contradictions internal to pluralist thinking). He divides them into three groups which he labels: an epistemological paradox, methodological paradoxes, and ethical paradoxes.[35] It is worth rehearsing at least some of these.

Van Wiele initially turns to an epistemological inconsistency. On the one hand, pluralists claim that each religion and each religious truth has been mediated to us through the cultures out of which it arose. Hence, we are agnostic at best and skeptical at worst about knowing whether these truths rest on any actual facts. On the other hand, when some pluralists address the question of the Jesus of ordinary history, for example, they still believe they can strip away the religious vision of the divine son of man who is God's savior and crystallize an accurate picture of the historical, earthly Jesus of Nazareth. That picture removes any divine character of Jesus and turns him ultimately into a mere end-time prophet.

But how can this be so? If the crystallized picture of Jesus is taken from the Gospels and the later New Testament writings and even the confessions of the Christian community, then they are taken from documents which themselves were socially constructed pictures of Christ. Even more, the "demythologized" version of Jesus as just a historical man is itself a culturally conditioned portrait painted by those who constructed their vision of the Jesus of history. As Van Wiele explains, "the 'cleaned-up' historical Jesus *wie es eigentlich gewesen*, which pluralists believe themselves able to distill, is nothing more than the results of a specific individual culturally determined projection."[36]

The point seems clear enough. Either all knowledge is culturally constructed, including the knowledge we claim to attain by studying some historical figure and events, and so we cannot get at the historical truth of the matter, or it is possible to discover the historical truth about events and persons. But then the theory that we can know nothing more than what we believe from our social construction of reality is just wrong. If "knowledge" of someone and some events is purely a reflection of the societies and cultures in which the beliefs arose, who is to say that the resultant picture (like the biblical picture) of someone like Christ is actually true? Given pluralist epistemological commitments, we simply are not in a position to rule this out. On the other hand, if it really is possible to "get at the facts" of history because they aren't just social constructions, then what Christians say about Christ can be not only true, but demonstrably so.

Van Wiele turns next to what he labels methodological paradoxes, and he delineates five of them. An initial one centers on the pluralist belief that there are no worldview-independent criteria for evaluating the truth of religious beliefs. But if this belief is taken seriously, it also is true of pluralist accounts of religion. As Van Wiele explains, "if, in line with the pluralistic paradigm, one claims that there is no single transcultural ground for granting the truth content of religious or cultural expressions, then pluralism cannot claim that its relativistic concept of truth has any universal standard of truth which could be applied to whatever religion and/or culture."[37]

A second methodological inconsistency is related to the first, but distinct. Pluralists believe, and want us to believe, that the truth claims of each culture and religion are absolutely relative to the cultures and peoples that hold them. But then, pluralists like John Hick turn around and claim that all religions are really about the same thing and actually have many common elements, so that it is possible to make claims about various religions, which claims are transculturally and transreligiously true. Our ability to do this is said to demonstrate that all religions are just culturally conditioned responses to the same ultimate reality and are actually in many ways the same.[38]

Van Wiele illustrates the inconsistency he is describing. Given the relativism that pluralists embrace, each religion has its own conception of reality and its own symbols, which differ from those of other religions. This seems to imply that it is logically inconsistent to abstract symbols from one religion, compare them with symbols of other religions, and conclude that they are analogous. And yet to adopt the belief that religious worldviews with their symbols are really all the same as they point to ultimate reality, is to do exactly what pluralist thinking denies can be done, given the belief that religions are absolutely relative to culture, time, and place.[39]

Two more of Van Wiele's methodological paradoxes are worth noting. The first relies on the fact that many versions of pluralism claim that it is the best view to adopt about which religion is true, because there is so much mystery surrounding our understanding of transcendent reality. In fact, some pluralists have claimed that "no human ideas are capable of saying anything definitive about the transcendent."[40] But if pluralists are right in holding this view, it defeats their own position that human ideas can't say anything definitive about the transcendent. The claim that human ideas can't say anything definitive about God because he is shrouded in so much mystery is itself a definitive claim about the transcendent. This is a significant inconsistency on the part of pluralists who hold such a view.

The other *methodological* inconsistency stems from the pluralist belief that the truth value of all knowledge is only preliminary, since we are not in a position to know what is finally and absolutely true. If pluralists are right about this, then the truth value of religious pluralism itself must be preliminary. And, as Van Wiele argues, any argument about whether and why the truth value of any religion is only preliminary would itself be preliminary, and hence of little use. But pluralists repeatedly affirm that their belief that all religious truth claims are only preliminarily true or false is a belief that is definitively correct. But this just means, as Van Wiele says, that on this point pluralists are actually exclusivists, and that is radically contradictory to pluralism![41]

Finally, there are ethical inconsistencies that pluralism raises, and from the standpoint of the practical details of how people live, Van Wiele argues that these inconsistencies have the gravest of consequences. They are not just problems that need to be worked through to produce an internally coherent conceptual understanding of reality. They are also problems that have a practical impact on what must be tolerated about seemingly intolerable and immoral living conditions in various social contexts around the world.

Put simply, pluralist thinking necessitates adopting a certain ethical relativism when evaluating the ethical rules and conduct of various cultures and their religions. On the other hand, it is often religious pluralists who take an adamant stance on matters of human rights and social oppression. In various societies, one finds a variety of what has been called demonic and discriminating forms of oppression. Examples abound, so only a few are needed to make the point. In Islam, for example, one man is allowed to have many wives. Others would say this discriminates against women's rights and dignity (often these wives become mere slaves to do their husband's bidding while also being consigned to function as little more than "baby-producing factories"). In Afghanistan, under Taliban rule, women have been severely restricted. They were not allowed to attain an education, practice a profession, or render public service, and they have generally been banned from public life. Moreover, they have been forced to follow strict rules about dress in public; they have to be covered completely from head to toe. Failure to comply with clothing laws could lead to legal prosecution and beating as a punishment.[42]

Further examples of violations of human rights abound, but those just presented are sufficient to make the point. Religious pluralists (like many non-pluralists) denounce such violations of human rights as clearly and conclusively immoral. And yet in many cases, the cultures involved are merely living out their version of what is ethically right and wrong. According to pluralist principles, there can be no universal agreement on ethics, even as there cannot be agreement about matters of religion. That means that their pluralistic, relativistic mind-set should lead them to be silent about practices like the ones described. But they are not silent; they do not say all ethical norms are equally acceptable when it leads to the abuses and discrimination described. Hence, their protest of oppression and discrimination, while admirable from the perspective of many pluralists and even non-pluralists, blatantly contradicts their pluralist principles, which require that no set of ethical rules or conduct is absolutely correct and so all peoples of all cultures must simply be tolerant of, for example, Taliban treatment of women.[43]

Clearly, pluralists cannot have it both ways. They cannot legitimately demand tolerance of any and every ethical rule and practice because no one knows which rules are absolutely correct (assuming it even makes sense to talk about absolutely correct rules), and then denounce as transculturally and uniformly immoral practices that oppress individuals and societies. Adopting such a stance generates not only a contradiction between what they think and how they act; it also turns them into "narrow" exclusivists who are *absolutely certain* that the oppressions they denounce are morally wrong.

What should we conclude from this study of a variety of logical inconsistencies in pluralist thinking and practice? I think we must conclude that pluralist thinking is easier to believe than to live. This is a serious criticism. It is common among philosophers to test a given conceptual scheme for three things: 1) internal consistency; 2) fit with known facts; and 3) practical livability. What I have shown in this chapter is that there are problems with items 1 and 3 (though I haven't shown every problem that these tests uncover) as these tests are applied to religious pluralism. To a certain extent I've also shown problems with item 2, though that hasn't been the main thrust of the chapter.

So, in conclusion, what exactly has been shown? Most of the chapter has engaged in defensive, negative apologetics. Charges and complaints that pluralists typically level against exclusivists have been raised and answered. Hence, pluralists haven't shown exclusivism to be wrong, and since their arguments against exclusivism were intended also as supports for pluralism, pluralists haven't made their case for pluralism. Pluralists may have other positive evidences to support their views, but while not covering anywhere near all pluralist arguments, we have examined many of its supports and found the position wanting. In addition, at the end of the chapter I have enumerated various objections to pluralism that add further reason to doubt that it is a correct account of the truthfulness of religion and of religious claims.

Does this mean that religious exclusivism has won the day? Absolutely not. I have only shown that exclusivism is not guilty of many of the problems pluralists attribute to it. What I have done in this chapter leaves open the possibility that exclusivism is correct. But we need a positive evidential case in support of exclusivism to confirm that it is correct. That is a task for another time and place.

Readers should not despair at these conclusions, for we have accomplished much. Significant reasons to doubt that pluralism is correct have been offered. Moreover, we have answered objections to exclusivism, which, had they been correct, would make it impossible for exclusivism to be right. Not a bad chapter's work; not a bad start at all! There is no need to think that Christianity cannot be shown to be true. No need to think that Christianity is just one of many acceptable roads to God. No need to think that proclaiming the gospel is intolerant. No need to fear that it is impossible to get non-Christians to accept Christ, because all of us have just a very limited perspective on reality, and so no one knows which religion is correct or even has any idea of how to go about showing which religion is true! And no need to be silent! Proclaim the gospel. Defend the faith when needed. Do so as clearly and convincingly as you can. It is unquestionably truth you can believe. And then rely on the Holy Spirit to take the seed you have planted and make it bear fruit!

Notes

1. See my *No One Like Him: The Doctrine of God* (Wheaton, IL: Crossway, 2001), chapter 5.

Chapter 1: Introduction

1. Bertrand Russell, "Why I Am Not a Christian," in *Why I Am Not a Christian* (New York: Simon & Schuster, 1957), 3ff. Also Wesley Salmon, "Religion and Science: A New Look at Hume's Dialogues," *Philosophical Studies* 33 (1978): 176.
2. W. K. Clifford, "The Ethics of Belief," in *Lectures and Essays* (London: Macmillan, 1879), 186.
3. Ibid., 184.
4. W. V. O. Quine, "Two Dogmas of Empiricism"; cited in Nancey Murphy and James W. McClendon, Jr., "Distinguishing Modern and Postmodern Theologies," *Modern Theology* 5 (April 1989): 200. This essay is anthologized in W. V. O. Quine, *From a Logical Point of View: Logico-Philosophical Essays* (New York: Harper, 1963).
5. Diogenes Allen, "Christianity and the Creed of Postmodernism," *Christian Scholar's Review* 23 (1993): 119.
6. I am indebted to comments by Harold Netland for some of the details on this point. A good resource supporting these points about skepticism is Richard Popkin's *History of Skepticism from Erasmus to Spinoza* (Berkeley: University of California Press, 1979).
7. See my *No One Like Him: The Doctrine of God* (Wheaton, IL: Crossway, 2001) for a presentation and evaluation of the ontological, cosmological, teleological, and moral arguments (in various forms) for God's existence.
8. See Alvin Plantinga, *God and Other Minds* (Ithaca, NY: Cornell University Press, 1967); William Lane Craig, *Reasonable Faith: Christian Truth and Apologetics*, 3rd ed. (Wheaton, IL: Crossway, 2008), especially chapters 3 and 4; and William Lane Craig, *The Kalaam Cosmological Argument* (Eugene, OR: Wipf & Stock, 2000).
9. William Lane Craig, "The Absurdity of Life without God," in *Reasonable Faith*.

Chapter 2: Modernity and Postmodernity

1. For a fuller description of modern and postmodern themes, see my *No One Like Him: The Doctrine of God* (Wheaton, IL: Crossway, 2001), chapter 3.
2. To show how complicated it can be to specify precisely the beginning of modernity, I note Philip Clayton's discussion. Some see the beginning with Descartes's *Meditations*; others point to Copernicus, making his discovery in astronomy the key to

humans' sense of "homelessness" in the universe, while yet others point to Pico della Mirandola's *Ode to Humanism*, which appeared in the fifteenth century and made centeredness on the human subject the basis of modernity. See Philip Clayton, "On Holisms: Insular, Inclusivist, and Postmodern," *Zygon* 33 (September 1988): 470.

3. William Beardslee, "Christ in the Postmodern Age: Reflections Inspired by Jean-François Lyotard," in David Griffin, William Beardslee, and Joe Holland, *Varieties of Postmodern Theology* (Albany: State University of New York Press, 1989), 63.

4. I am indebted to Harold Netland for these historical distinctions relating to modernity and the Enlightenment. As Netland notes, Peter Gay (*The Enlightenment* [New York: W. W. Norton, 1969]) has argued that Hume, not Descartes, was the key exemplar of Enlightenment thinking.

5. Perez Zagorin, "History, the Referent, and Narrative: Reflections on Postmodernism Now," *History and Theory* 38 (Fall 1999): 5.

6. Thomas Jovanovski, "Postmodernism's Self-Nullifying Reading of Nietzsche," *Inquiry* 44 (2001): 429 fn. 1.

7. Clinton Collins, "Using Critical Thinking in Postmodern Ways: Elbow's Methodological Believing," *Inquiry* 19 (Summer 2000): 36.

8. Jared Hiebert, "Shaping Evangelical Theology in the Postmodern Turn," *Didaskalia* (Spring 2002): 7 fn. 3. Various authors emphasize one trend or another in describing modernity. Langdon Gilkey, in speaking of the theological ferment in the late 1960s as Western cultures moved away from the modern mind-set, characterized the mood of the times (and hence, the general mood of modernity) as one of secularization. He identified four general characteristics of the secular spirit: contingency, relativism, the temporality or transience of all things, and the autonomy and freedom of man. See his *Naming the Whirlwind: The Renewal of God-Language* (Indianapolis: Bobbs-Merrill, 1969), 32–34, 40, 48, 53, 57–58. Though this is true of the modern era, it is even more true of the postmodern era. Nancey Murphy and James McClendon also help in capturing the mood of the times. They identify modern thought as describable along three separate axes, each focusing on a key issue for the modern era. One axis is epistemological; it moves between foundationalism and skepticism as its two extremes. A second axis focuses on theories of meaning in philosophy of language. The two extremes are what Murphy and McClendon label a representational (referential) theory of language and an expressivist (emotivist) theory of language. The third axis, more ontological in nature, focuses on whether reality should be understood in atomistic, individualistic terms or in relational, collective terms. The two extremes of this axis are individualism and collectivism. For further details see Nancey Murphy and James W. McClendon, Jr., "Distinguishing Modern and Postmodern Theologies," *Modern Theology* 5 (April 1989): 192–199. See also Nancey Murphy, "Philosophical Resources for Postmodern Evangelical Theology," *Christian Scholar's Review* 26 (1996).

9. Immanuel Kant, *Critique of Pure Reason* (New York: St. Martin's, 1965), 257–275.

10. Ibid., 41.

11. Alvin Plantinga, "Reason and Belief in God," in Alvin Plantinga and Nicholas Wolterstorff, eds., *Faith and Rationality* (Notre Dame, IN: University of Notre Dame Press, 1984), 24–34. See also Kelly James Clark, *Return to Reason* (Grand Rapids, MI: Eerdmans, 1990), 5.

12. Laurence Bonjour, *The Structure of Empirical Knowledge* (Cambridge, MA: Harvard University Press, 1985), 26, 28. For further discussion of the forms of foun-

dationalism see Noah Lemos, *An Introduction to the Theory of Knowledge* (New York: Cambridge University Press, 2007), chapter 3; and J. P. Moreland and Garrett DeWeese, "The Premature Report of Foundationalism's Demise," *Reclaiming the Center: Confronting Evangelical Accommodation in Postmodern Times*, eds. Millard Erickson, Paul K. Helseth, and Justin Taylor (Wheaton, IL: Crossway, 2004), 81–108. I am indebted to Harold Netland's comments on an earlier draft of my chapter for these points.

13. Plantinga, "Reason and Belief in God," 55–59; and Clark, *Return to Reason*, 134–135.

14. David Griffin, "Postmodern Theology as Liberation Theology: A Response to Harvey Cox," in *Varieties of Postmodern Theology*, 85.

15. Metaphysics traditionally includes topics like God, freedom, and immortality; none of these is an object of sense, so according to Kant's classification, they would all be noumena and hence not objects of knowledge.

16. Murphy and McClendon, "Distinguishing Modern and Postmodern Theologies," 193. See also A. J. Ayer, *Language, Truth, and Logic* (New York: Dover, Prentice-Hall, 1964), chapters 1 and 6.

17. See Ludwig Wittgenstein, *Tractatus Logico-Philosophicus* (London: Routledge & Kegan Paul, 1971), 5.6 (p. 149); 7 (p. 189); and 6.522 (p. 187).

18. Here I am thinking of Jean François Lyotard's comment in *The Postmodern Condition: A Report on Knowledge*, trans. Geoff Bennington and Brian Massumi (Minneapolis: University of Minnesota Press, 1984), xxiii–xxiv, that postmodernism involves the "incredulity toward metanarratives."

19. Michael Murray, "Reason for Hope (in the Postmodern World)," in Michael J. Murray, ed., *Reason for the Hope Within* (Grand Rapids, MI: Eerdmans, 1999), 6; see also J. Richard Middleton and Brian J. Walsh, "Facing the Postmodern Scalpel: Can the Christian Faith Withstand Deconstruction?" in Timothy Phillips and Dennis Okholm, eds., *Christian Apologetics in the Postmodern World* (Downers Grove, IL: InterVarsity Press, 1995), 137.

20. This is just the opposite of what Keith Yandell says typifies anti-realism. See his "Modernism, Post-Modernism, and the Minimalist Canons of Common Grace," *Christian Scholar's Review* 27 (Fall 1997): 18.

21. See, for example, Raymond Boisvert, "Philosophy: Postmodern or Polytemporal?" *International Philosophical Quarterly* 40 (September 2000): 319; and John MacQuarrie, "Postmodernism in Philosophy of Religion and Theology," *International Journal for Philosophy of Religion* 50 (2001): 10.

22. For some, a proposition is the thing a sentence is about. Hence, in this ontology there exists between language and the world the proposition which links the two. Even if a sentence isn't an assertion, it is still about some propositional idea, and it is possible to see what the sentence says about the proposition and to see whether the proposition matches things in our world.

23. Murphy and McClendon ("Distinguishing Modern and Postmodern Theologies," 194) call such theories expressivist or emotivist theories. See their whole discussion (193–196) of the various theories of language used by moderns. See also Murphy, "Philosophical Resources for Postmodern Evangelical Theology," 188–190.

24. See, for example, R. B. Braithwaite, "An Empiricist's View of the Nature of Religious Belief," in Basil Mitchell, ed., *The Philosophy of Religion* (Oxford: Oxford University Press, 1971), 79–80.

25. See, for example, the helpful discussion of postmodern themes in art, architecture, literature, and more broadly in popular culture, in Todd Gitlin, "The Postmodern Predicament," *The Wilson Quarterly* 13 (Summer 1989).

26. Lyotard, *Postmodern Condition*, xxiii–xxiv.

27. David Griffin, "Introduction to SUNY Series in Constructive Postmodern Thought," in *Varieties of Postmodern Theology*, xii.

28. For a very helpful overview of postmodernism and the "postmodern God," see Graham Ward, "Introduction, or A Guide to Theological Thinking in Cyberspace," in Graham Ward, ed., *The Postmodern God* (Malden, MA: Blackwell, 1997).

29. John MacQuarrie, "Postmodernism in Philosophy of Religion and Theology," 9–10; Murray, "Reason for Hope," 4–5; James Sire, "On Being a Fool for Christ and an Idiot for Nobody: Logocentrism and Postmodernity," in *Christian Apologetics in the Postmodern World*, 116–119; and Jerold J. Abrams, "Aesthetics of Self-Fashioning and Cosmopolitanism: Foucault and Rorty on the Art of Living," *Philosophy Today* 46 (Summer 2002): 185–186.

30. Murray, "Reason for Hope," 6; see also J. Richard Middleton and Brian J. Walsh, "Facing the Postmodern Scalpel," 137.

31. Keith Yandell, "Modernism, Post-Modernism," 18.

32. Ibid.

33. In a fascinating article, Perez Zagorin presents the implications of postmodern anti-realism (and postmodernism more generally) for history and historiography. As he shows, given our distance temporally (and perhaps spatially as well) from past historical events, plus the postmodern understanding of human reason and the type of contact it has with reality, the past cannot be the object of historical knowledge. Any historian chooses certain details and overlooks others as he or she constructs an account of what happened. So any given piece of historical writing is actually a fiction which constructs in language a story about what happened. Hence, all of us, historians included, must be anti-realists with respect to past events and actions. See Perez Zagorin, "History, the Referent, and Narrative," 13–15. See also Robert Anchor, "On How to Kick the History Habit and Discover that Every Day in Every Way, Things Are Getting Meta and Meta and Meta . . . ," *History and Theory* 40 (February 2001): 107–109; and Richard J. Evans, "From Historicism to Postmodernism: Historiography in the Twentieth Century," *History and Theory* 41 (February 2002).

34. The preceding material is my presentation of the basics of how the mind works, based on key ideas from Kant's *Critique of Pure Reason*.

35. Richard Rorty, *Philosophy and the Mirror of Nature* (Princeton, NJ: Princeton University Press, 1979), 12.

36. My discussion of this point about language structuring our world was greatly helped by the following: Brendan Sweetman, "Postmodernism, Derrida, and *Differance*: A Critique," *International Philosophical Quarterly* 39 (March 1999): 7–8; Jared Hiebert, "Shaping Evangelical Theology," 8–9; Douglas Groothuis, "Postmodernism and Truth," *Philosophia Christi* 2 (2002): 275–277; Stefan Eriksson, "Refining the Distinction between Modern and Postmodern Theologies: The Case of Lindbeck," *Studia Theologica* 56 (2002): 156ff.; Sire, "On Being a Fool," 104–105; and Roger Lundin, "The Pragmatics of Postmodernity," in *Christian Apologetics in the Postmodern World*, 28ff.

37. Ludwig Wittgenstein, *Philosophical Investigations* (New York: Macmillan, 1968), 7 (p. 5e); see also 19 (p. 8e).

38. Ludwig Wittgenstein, *Lectures and Conversations on Aesthetics, Psychology, and Religious Belief*, ed. Cyril Barrett (Oxford: Basil Blackwell, 1966), 61–62; see also 56 and 57.
39. Wittgenstein, *Philosophical Investigations*, 23 (pp. 11e–12e).
40. Ibid., 11 (p. 6e).
41. Wittgenstein, *Lectures and Conversations*, 61–62.
42. See Wittgenstein, *Philosophical Investigations*, 224e.
43. W. V. O. Quine, "Two Dogmas of Empiricism"; cited in Murphy and McClendon, "Distinguishing Modern and Postmodern Theologies," 200. This essay is anthologized in W. V. O. Quine, *From a Logical Point of View: Logico-Philosophical Essays* (New York: Harper, 1963).
44. Hiebert, "Shaping Evangelical Theology," 8.
45. Macquarrie, "Postmodernism in Philosophy of Religion and Theology," 10.
46. Ibid.
47. Thomas Kuhn, *The Structure of Scientific Revolutions*, 2nd ed. (Chicago: University of Chicago Press, 1970). See chapters 3–4 and especially chapter 5, where Kuhn discusses the role of scientific paradigms in the work of the scientist.
48. Ibid., chapters 7–10.
49. How well I remember, during doctoral studies in philosophy at the University of Chicago in the early 1970s, sitting in classes and hearing professors critique Kuhn's work, pointing out its many flaws. Hearing such clear-cut objections, one takes it for granted that others will see the same problems and reject it. Much to my surprise and consternation, however, within a decade of finishing my doctoral work I could tell that this view was deemed "orthodox" by a large segment of the philosophical community.
50. A very helpful article on the alleged subjectivity of science is Gerald Holton's "The Rise of Postmodernisms and the 'End of Science'," *Journal of the History of Ideas* 61/2 (April 2000): 327–341.
51. Groothuis, "Postmodernism and Truth," 275.
52. James Danaher, "Toward a Postmodern Correspondence Theory of Truth," *Sophia* 41 (October 2002): 56.
53. Ibid.
54. Ibid., 57.
55. Ibid., 58–59.
56. See my article on theories of truth for further explanation of these various theories of truth: "Truth: Relationship of Theories of Truth to Hermeneutics," in Earl Radmacher and Robert Preus, eds., *Hermeneutics, Inerrancy, and the Bible* (Grand Rapids, MI: Zondervan, 1984).
57. See the interesting discussion of truth between Richard Rorty, Alvin Plantinga, and Nicholas Wolterstorff. In *Philosophy and the Mirror of Nature*, Rorty, in rejecting foundationalism and the correspondence notion of truth, said in defining truth that "truth is what your peers will let you get away with." Plantinga takes him to task for this. Rorty replies, "I do not think that you can define 'truth,' either as what your peers will let you get away with, or as correspondence with the intrinsic nature of reality, or as anything else. 'True,' like the word 'good,' is a primitive predicate, a transcendental term which does not lend itself to definition"; see page 180 in Stephen Louthan, "On Religion—A Discussion with Richard Rorty, Alvin Plantinga, and Nicholas Wolterstorff," *Christian Scholar's Review* 26 (Winter

1996). This certainly is of little help, but it also suggests why the door is so open to pragmatism, and Plantinga continues to chide Rorty, in light of his retraction, for saying that "truth is what your peers will let you get away with" (180). For further discussion of postmodernism and truth see Rolf Hille, "Transition from Modernity to Post-Modernity: A Theological Evaluation," *European Journal of Theology* 11 (2002): 94–100; Sire, "On Being a Fool," 102–104; MacQuarrie, "Postmodernism in Philosophy of Religion and Theology," 14–15; and Yandell, "Modernism, Post-Modernism," 22–24.

58. Brian Trainor, "The Origin and End of Modernity," *Journal of Applied Philosophy* 15 (1998): 135–136.

59. Ibid., 136.

60. Ibid.

61. In an interesting article, Wentzel van Huysteen asks whether postmoderns are postfoundationalists. The gist of the article is that postmoderns should be post-foundationalists, but that doesn't mean they all are. Van Huysteen offers some examples of theologians who claim to be postmodern but still hold onto some form of foundationalism. See J. Wentzel van Huysteen, "Is the Postmodernist Always a Postfoundationalist? Nancey Murphy's Lakatosian Model for Theology," in J. Wentzel van Huysteen, *Essays in Postfoundationalist Theology* (Grand Rapids, MI: Eerdmans, 1997).

62. Ken Gemes, "Postmodernism's Use and Abuse of Nietzsche," *Philosophy and Phenomenological Research* 62 (March 2001): 341–342.

63. Lyotard, *Postmodern Condition*, xxiii–xxiv.

64. Lyotard, cited in William Edgar, "No News Is Good News: Modernity, the Post-modern, and Apologetics," *Westminster Theological Journal* 57 (1995): 373–374. Huston Smith argues that among postmoderns there are three versions of how to view narratives. What he calls *minimal* postmodernism claims that today no accepted worldview exists. *Mainline* postmodernism argues that we will never again have such an authoritative metanarrative, for now that we understand how the mind works, we recognize the impossibility of an accurate universal worldview. Finally, *hardcore* postmodernism not only agrees with the mainline position but adds that it is "good riddance" that worldviews are gone, for they absolutize and in doing so oppress and marginalize minorities who don't fit the predominant structures the worldview puts in place. In contrast, Smith argues that worldviews are something we need, it is possible to form valid ones, and valid worldviews already exist in the world's great enduring religious traditions. See Huston Smith, "The Religious Significance of Postmodernism: A Rejoinder," *Faith and Philosophy* 12 (July 1995).

65. In my thinking and in my writing of this section I found especially helpful the following: Trainor, "The Origin and End of Modernity"; Gemes, "Postmodernism's Use and Abuse of Nietzsche"; Hiebert, "Shaping Evangelical Theology"; MacQuarrie, "Postmodernism in Philosophy of Religion and Theology"; Thomas Jovanovski, "Postmodernism's Self-Nullifying Reading of Nietzsche," *Inquiry* 44 (2001); Raymond D. Boisvert, "Philosophy: Postmodern or Polytemporal?" *International Philosophical Quarterly* 40 (September 2000); Brendan Sweetman, "Post-modernism, Derrida, and *Differance*"; and Robert Koch, "Metaphysical Crises and the Postmodern Condition," *International Philosophical Quarterly* 39 (June 1999).

66. Jan-Olav Henriksen, "Creation and Construction: On the Theological Appropriation of Postmodern Theory," *Modern Theology* 18 (April 2002): 154.

67. Ibid., 155.
68. Ibid.
69. Ibid., 156.
70. Ibid.
71. Ibid., 156–157.
72. Ibid., 157.
73. Ibid.
74. Ibid.
75. Ibid.
76. Ibid.
77. Ibid.
78. I have devoted a good bit of space to Henriksen's description of relativism/plurality. Henriksen notes that he doesn't agree with everything he is describing but only intends to clarify the nature of postmodernism. I have appealed to his description because it rather extensively and clearly portrays the postmodern thinking and rationale on this issue. I also found the following articles helpful on this point: Hille, "Transition from Modernity to Post-Modernity," 97–98; Murray, "Reason for Hope," 5–6; Hiebert, "Shaping Evangelical Theology," 8; MacQuarrie, "Postmodernism in Philosophy of Religion and Theology," 12–13; and Diogenes Allen, "Christianity and the Creed of Postmodernism," *Christian Scholar's Review* 23 (1993): 118–119.
79. Elisabeth Schussler Fiorenza, *In Memory of Her* (New York: Crossroad, 1983), chapter 1, details the essentials of feminist hermeneutics.
80. For further discussion of how postmoderns handle authors and texts, the following are very helpful: Hiebert, "Shaping Evangelical Theology," 10–11; Sweetman, "Postmodernism, Derrida, and *Differance*," 10–11; Steven Kepnes, "Ethics after Levinas: Robert Gibbs's *Why Ethics? Signs of Responsibilities*," *Modern Theology* 19 (January 2003): 104–106; Richard Evans, "From Historicism to Postmodernism: Historiography in the Twentieth Century," *History and Theory* 41 (February 2002) on history and historical texts; Mark Bevir, "What Is a Text? A Pragmatic Theory," *International Philosophical Quarterly* 42 (December 2002); Sire, "On Being a Fool," 102; Christina Hendricks, "The Author['s] Remains: Foucault and the Demise of the 'Author Function'," *Philosophy Today* 46 (Summer 2002); and David Guretzki, "Barth, Derrida, and *Differance*: Is There a Difference?" *Didaskalia* (Spring 2002): 54–57, 63–64.
81. MacQuarrie, "Postmodernism in Philosophy of Religion and Theology," 19–20. For further discussion of deconstructionism see Sweetman, "Postmodernism, Derrida, and *Differance*"; Hiebert, "Shaping Evangelical Theology," 10; Middleton and Walsh, "Facing the Postmodern Scalpel," 136–138. The most comprehensive work on hermeneutics, including deconstruction, is Kevin Vanhoozer's *Is There a Meaning in This Text? The Bible, the Reader, and the Morality of Literary Knowledge* (Grand Rapids, MI: Zondervan, 1998).

Chapter 3: Answers to Postmodern Skepticism (I)

1. See the discussion of Alvin Plantinga and Reformed Epistemology in chapter 7.
2. Of course, this example about meeting for lunch includes another complication. Since Nice, Rio de Janeiro, and Sydney are located in significantly different time zones, 11:30 a.m. in one of those locations won't be 11:30 a.m. in the other two. But

if we can ignore the law of noncontradiction, none of this should bother us. The envisioned scenario is definitely absurd, but that only underscores the absurdity of thinking the law of noncontradiction is disposable.

3. Here I must clarify what I am saying. I am not saying that different cultures all have identical thought patterns, nor that all cultures express their ideas in exactly the same way, nor that the same concepts are understood and emphasized in the same way in all cultures. Rather, I am saying that all people have the same intellectual equipment, and there are certain rules for how to use it correctly. In this case, the equipment is the mind and its ability to reason. Various logical fallacies show us things to avoid when using our equipment. These rules about how reasoning should or should not work are so fundamental to all uses of our intellectual equipment that they cannot be ignored without serious negative consequences (as my examples in the text show).

Chapter 4: Answers to Postmodern Skepticism (II): Objectivity, Subjectivity, and Apologetics

1. Jose Luis Bermudez, "Skepticism and Subjectivity: Two Critiques of Traditional Epistemology Reconsidered," *International Philosophical Quarterly* 35 (June 1995). Bermudez contrasts the Cartesian and the postmodern understanding of the subject. For Descartes, humans are to be viewed as disinterested and disconnected subjects who need arguments and evidence of claims about the world, because they are detached from it and so could be wrong about what is going on in it. In contrast, the postmodern understanding of the subject's relation to the objects of knowledge is very much connected, and whatever he knows about the world is related to the fact that he is immersed in the world. What he understands about the world is intimately tied to the fact that he brings his past experiences and ideas to his interaction with the world. Because of his subjective connection with the world, Bermudez explains that it is the postmodern who has fewer questions about the existence of things in the world (and the world as a whole) than does someone following the Cartesian notion of the subject as an unconnected observer of the world around him.

2. See here Philip D. Kenneson, "There's No Such Thing as Absolute Truth, and It's a Good Thing, Too," in Timothy R. Phillips and Dennis Okholm, *Christian Apologetics in the Postmodern World* (Downers Grove, IL: InterVarsity Press, 1995), 156–157. Kenneson offers a clear explanation of this sort of objectivity. Kreeft and Tacelli explain this sense of 'objective' in even greater detail. They note that it doesn't refer to an unemotional, detached attitude, nor does it mean 'known by all', or 'publicly proved', for you might know something is true but be unable to offer good arguments and evidence for it, or you might just keep the fact known a secret. See Peter Kreeft and Ronald K. Tacelli, "Objective Truth," in *Handbook of Christian Apologetics* (Downers Grove, IL: InterVarsity Press, 1994), 363–364. Also Maben Poirier, in an article about Michael Polanyi and objective knowledge, offers some helpful definitions and distinctions. Polanyi distinguishes between focal knowledge and tacit knowledge. Focal awareness is the kind of awareness we have when we focus our attention directly on some object or concept. Normally, this happens when the thing or concept is directly before us as a thing distinct from us, and we attend to it. On the other hand, tacit knowledge refers to what might simply be called background knowledge that is relevant to the thing or concept

attended to in focal awareness. Background knowledge comes from everything we have learned through focal awareness throughout our life. In any given instance of focal knowledge, the degree to which tacit knowledge impacts our understanding is unpredictable. Poirier explains the relation of focal and tacit knowledge to objectivity and subjectivity, according to Polanyi. For details see Maben Poirier, "Michael Polanyi and the Question of 'Objective' Knowledge," *Philosophy Today* 32 (Winter 1988): 314–315.

3. Israel Scheffler, *Science and Subjectivity* (Indianapolis: Bobbs-Merrill, 1967).

4. Peter Kosso, "Science and Objectivity," *The Journal of Philosophy* 86 (1989): 245, referring to Scheffler's book.

5. A good example of this kind of independence is the experiments of Jean Perrin at the start of the twentieth century, experiments designed to measure the number of molecules in one mole of material, Avogadro's number. Perrin measured the same physical quantity in a variety of different ways, thereby invoking a variety of different auxiliary theories. Perrin's results are so believable, and they provide good reason to believe in the actual existence of molecules, because he used a variety of *independent* theories and techniques and got them to agree on the answer. See Kosso, "Science and Objectivity," 246–247.

6. H. E. Longino, "Scientific Objectivity and the Logics of Science," *Inquiry* 26 (1983): 94.

7. Ibid., 94–100. As Longino notes, this feature of science is also true of other disciplines, such as literary or art criticism and philosophy.

8. Mark Bevir, "Objectivity in History," *History and Theory* 33 (1994): 332.

9. Ibid., 333.

10. Ibid. This sounds good, but how can this guarantee objectivity? Can't two scientists appeal to the same facts to support different conclusions? Bevir agrees that they can, but answers that when historians debate different interpretations of the same event, they do so in accord with rules of debate that everyone recognizes must be followed if the work is to embody intellectual honesty. Bevir claims that objectivity "is principally a product of our intellectual honesty in dealing with criticism." Bevir offers three rules of thumb to delineate what comes with intellectual honesty: 1) a willingness to take criticism seriously; 2) a preference for established standards of evidence and reason backed by a preference for challenges to these standards which themselves rest on impersonal and consistent criteria of evidence and reason; and 3) a preference for positive speculative theories, that is, speculative theories postulating exciting new predictions, not speculative theories merely blocking off criticisms of our existing interpretations. See Bevir, ibid., 335.

11. Amartya Sen, "Positional Objectivity," *Philosophy and Public Affairs* 22 (Spring 1993): 126–127.

12. Ibid., 128.

13. Ibid., 127–130. Sen argues in the rest of his article that the notion of positional objectivity can be used as well to assess things such as subjectivism and cultural relativism, decision theory, and the ethical acceptability of a person's actions.

14. Fred D'Agostino, "Transcendence and Conversation: Two Conceptions of Objectivity," *American Philosophical Quarterly* 30 (April 1993): 87–88.

15. Ibid., 87.

16. Richard Rorty, *Philosophy and the Mirror of Nature* (Princeton, NJ: Princeton University Press, 1980).

17. Scheffler, *Science and Subjectivity*.

18. Ibid., 37–40 are the pages in which Scheffler most specifically discusses this distinction and how it relates to intellectual matters, including our understanding of and articulating of observation experiences.

19. Frank Morison, *Who Moved the Stone?* (1930; repr., Grand Rapids, MI: Zondervan, 1987).

20. In addition, I am not suggesting that the handling of observational and non-observational claims is totally identical. While there are similarities, there are significant differences. Non-observational claims at times receive indirect support from observational propositions. But often, if a non-observational belief has evidential support, the kind of evidence will not be empirical and observational in nature. For example, it is hard to imagine what observational evidences would directly prove that Jesus is right when he says of heaven, "In my Father's house are many mansions: if it were not so I would have told you. I go to prepare a place for you, and if I go and prepare a place for you, I will come again, and receive you unto myself; that where I am, there ye may be also" (John 14:2–3, KJV). Probably the best chance of defending such claims as true will come in an overall apologetic for the reliability of all of Scripture.

21. Some readers will undoubtedly note that my response to this complaint about objectivity does not include a remark that such objections are self-refuting. That is, if everything we believe is riddled with bias and prejudice so that we cannot treat argument and evidence fairly, then the belief that everything we believe is riddled with subjectivity is not a belief that we came to in a fair handling of the issue. Thus, the critic's claim, if true, defeats itself. I agree that this is a good argument. My reason for not including it is that this is the sort of rejoinder to postmodern skepticism that one most frequently hears. In fact, most of the time it is the only type of rebuttal offered. I left it out of the text because I want to show that there are other substantial reasons for rejecting postmodern skepticism.

22. D'Agostino, "Transcendence and Conversation," 87.

23. Ibid.

24. Ibid. D'Agostino takes this basic statement from Zygmunt Bauman's *Legislators and Interpreters* (Oxford: Polity, 1987).

25. Ibid., 89.

26. Ibid., 90–91. These labels and description of positions are D'Agostino's.

27. Ibid., 91–92. In these pages, further objections to both forms of absolutism are offered.

28. Ibid., 92.

29. Ibid.

30. Ibid. See pages 92–95 for further objections to essentialism.

31. Ibid., 99–100.

Chapter 5: Answers to Modern Skepticism (I)

1. Such a view could be held by evangelical Christians, and in fact is held by those who understand Genesis 1 and 2 and the seven days of creation according to the literary framework view.

2. See my "Truth: Relationship of Theories of Truth to Hermeneutics," in Earl D. Radmacher and Robert D. Preus, eds., *Hermeneutics, Inerrancy, and the Bible* (Grand Rapids, MI: Zondervan, 1984).

3. See ibid. for my espousal of the semantic theory of truth, which is related to the correspondence theory.

4. See Robert Holyer's discussion of this distinction in his "Religious Certainty and the Imagination: An Interpretation of J. H. Newman," *Thomist* 50 (1986): 395–396. It is Newman who uses the certainty/certitude terminology. Holyer calls it the difference between *epistemological certainty* and *psychological certainty*. All of these labels are helpful in one way or another. The terminology may vary, but the concepts are basically the same.

5. Ibid., 396.

6. Ibid.

7. Antony Flew, "Theology and Falsification," from the "University Discussion," in Antony Flew and Alasdair MacIntyre, eds., *New Essays in Philosophical Theology* (New York: Macmillan, 1973), 96. Flew's complete presentation of this argument with its implications appears on pages 96–99.

Chapter 6: Answers to Modern Skepticism (II): Doubt and Certainty

1. Wittgenstein rejects the theory of meaning he held in his earlier philosophy. For that theory of meaning, see his *Tractatus Logico-Philosophicus*, with its picture theory of meaning. The picture theory is a heavily referential theory of meaning according to which words are the names of objects and sentences refer to states of affairs. As such, the state of affairs tells us the meaning of individual words and whole sentences. As the names of such things, meaning was seen as invariant, regardless of the context in which language was used.

2. For these ideas, see Ludwig Wittgenstein, *Philosophical Investigations* (New York: Macmillan, 1968), 7 (p. 5e); and 23 (p. 11e).

3. Ibid., 43 (p. 20e); and 23 (pp. 11e–12e).

4. Students of postmodernism should see how totally amenable these claims are to postmodern rejection of some underlying metanarrative that makes sense of all lesser narratives and to the adoption of a thoroughgoing commitment to perspectivism. I am not saying that Wittgenstein here is teaching perspectivism with its skeptical outcome; I'm only noting one of the reasons Wittgenstein's later philosophy is so often referred to in support of postmodern perspectivism. Also worth noting here is Wittgenstein's assessment of the nature of religious and theological language-games. In his *Philosophical Investigations* and *Lectures and Conversations on Aesthetics, Psychology, and Religious Belief*, he makes it very clear that whatever religious believers are doing when they make claims about their beliefs, they are not making assertions of facts about the world outside the mind. Hence, to think that phrases like "God is a loving Father" or "Jesus of Nazareth is Israel's Messiah and the Son of God" are making assertions about the way things are in the world and that they could be verified or falsified in the same way a scientist goes about testing a scientific hypothesis or a historian supports his interpretation of a given historical event is to make a huge intellectual mistake. The problem is that one shows he or she hasn't fully understood the language-game of religion nor what one is actually doing when offering statements of religious belief.

5. Wittgenstein, *Philosophical Investigations*, 420 (p. 126e).

6. Ibid., p. 223e.

7. Ibid., 84 (p. 39e).

8. Ludwig Wittgenstein, *On Certainty* (New York: Harper & Row, 1972), 71 (p. 11e).

9. Ibid., 72 (p. 11e).
10. G. E. Moore, "In Defence of Common Sense," in J. H. Muirhead, ed., *Contemporary British Philosophy* (2nd series) (Sydney, Australia: Allen & Unwin, 1925).
11. Wittgenstein, *On Certainty*; sections 111, 112, and 114 are on page 17e.
12. Ibid.; section 115 is on page 18e. See relatedly but not identically, section 141 (page 21e).
13. Wittgenstein, *Philosophical Investigations*, 226e.
14. Wittgenstein, *On Certainty*, 558 (p. 73e).
15. Ibid., 559 (p. 73e).
16. Wittgenstein, *Philosophical Investigations*, 249 (p. 90e).
17. Ibid., 250 (p. 90e).
18. See also in the *Investigations* the comment about a lion speaking, and Wittgenstein's response that lions don't speak.
19. Sections in *On Certainty* where one can find these points about doubting our whole way of looking at the world are 61–75, 83, 92–94, 102–105, 185, 188, 209–211, 217, 225, 233–235, 246–248, 255–257, 262, 274, 279.
20. Wittgenstein, *On Certainty*, 257 (p. 34e).
21. Ibid., 273–274 (p. 35e).
22. In the *Philosophical Investigations*, 87 (pp. 40e–41e), Wittgenstein makes a somewhat related point about someone asking for an explanation and challenging everything said so as to require the person making the explanation to heap more explanation upon explanation. At some point, the explanation has gone as far as it can and explanation needs to end. I am not saying that Wittgenstein makes the exact point I'm making in my text about doubting, but only that his comments on explanations are helpful to me in considering the matter of doubt and certainty.
23. Wittgenstein, *Philosophical Investigations*, 224e.

Chapter 7: Reformed Epistemology

1. Alvin Plantinga, "Reason and Belief in God," in Alvin Plantinga and Nicholas Wolterstorff, eds., *Faith and Rationality* (Notre Dame, IN: University of Notre Dame Press, 1983).
2. Alvin Plantinga, *Warranted Christian Belief* (Oxford: Oxford University Press, 2000), xiii.
3. In preparing to write this chapter, I found the following literature (most of it secondary) helpful: Stewart C. Goetz, "Belief in God Is Not Properly Basic," *Religious Studies* 19 (1983); Julie Gowen, "Foundationalism and the Justification of Religious Belief," *Religious Studies* 19 (1983); Alvin Plantinga, "The Foundations of Theism: A Reply," *Faith and Philosophy* 3 (1986); Mark McLeod, "The Analogy Argument for the Proper Basicality of Belief in God," *Philosophy of Religion* 21 (1987); James G. Hanink, "Some Questions about Proper Basicality," *Faith and Philosophy* 4 (January 1987); David Wisdo, "The Fragility of Faith: Toward a Critique of Reformed Epistemology," *Religious Studies* 24 (1988); David Basinger, "Hick's Religious Pluralism and 'Reformed Epistemology': A Middle Ground," *Faith and Philosophy* 5 (October 1988); John Hick, "A Concluding Comment," *Faith and Philosophy* 5 (October 1988); Donald Hatcher, "Some Problems with Plantinga's Reformed Epistemology," *American Journal of Theology and Philosophy* 10 (January 1989); Terrence W. Tilley, "Reformed Epistemology and Religious Fundamentalism: How Basic Are Our Basic Beliefs?" *Modern Theology* 6 (April

1990); John Zeis, "A Critique of Plantinga's Theological Foundationalism," *International Journal for Philosophy of Religion* 28 (1990); Richard Grigg, "The Crucial Disanalogies between Properly Basic Belief and Belief in God," *Religious Studies* 26 (1990); Hunter Brown, "Alvin Plantinga and Natural Theology," *International Journal for Philosophy of Religion* 30 (1991); Clifford Williams, "Kierkegaardian Suspicion and Properly Basic Beliefs," *Religious Studies* 30 (1994); Derek S. Jeffreys, "How Reformed Is Reformed Epistemology? Alvin Plantinga and Calvin's 'Sensus Divinitatis'," 33 (1997); John Beaudoin, "Evil, the Human Cognitive Condition, and Natural Theology," *Religious Studies* 34 (1998); William Hasker, "The Foundations of Theism: Scoring the Quinn-Plantinga Debate," *Faith and Philosophy* 15 (January 1998); and Evan Fales, "Reformed Epistemology and Biblical Hermeneutics," *Philo* 4 (Fall–Winter 2001).

4. Plantinga, *Warranted Christian Belief*, 3; see also x–xi; and Alvin Plantinga, "Afterword," in James F. Sennett, ed., *The Analytic Theist: An Alvin Plantinga Reader* (Grand Rapids, MI: Eerdmans, 1998), 355.

5. Plantinga, *Warranted Christian Belief*, viii–ix.

6. Ibid., ix.

7. Ibid., 498–499.

8. Alvin Plantinga, "Christian Philosophy at the End of the Twentieth Century," in *Analytic Theist*, 336.

9. See my *The Many Faces of Evil: Theological Systems and the Problems of Evil*, rev. ed. (Wheaton, IL: Crossway, 2004), chapters 10–12.

10. Plantinga offers several other examples of issues where the believer's response requires negative apologetics: 1) the positivistic claims that propositions of religious belief are meaningless; 2) the objections of thinkers like Freud, Marx, and Nietzsche that belief in God is mere wish fulfillment, or the result of cognitive malfunction, or the result of a weak, sniveling, and disgusting sort of character; and 3) the claims of religious pluralists that no single religion like Christianity has all the truth or is the only road to God. See Alvin Plantinga, "Christian Philosophy at the End of the Twentieth Century, 337–338.

11. Plantinga, "Christian Philosophy at the End of the Twentieth Century," 338–340.

12. Alvin Plantinga, *Warrant: The Current Debate* (Oxford: Oxford University Press, 1993), 7–11, quotes various contemporary philosophers on the matter of justification, demonstrating thereby a rather diverse understanding of this important concept.

13. Ibid., 10.

14. Ibid., 5.

15. Ibid.

16. Ibid., 6. In contrast, Plantinga defines epistemic externalism as follows: "The externalist, by contrast, holds that warrant need not depend upon factors relevantly internal to the cognizer; warrant depends or supervenes upon properties to some of which the cognizer may have no special access, or even no epistemic access at all" (6).

17. Ibid., 10.

18. Ibid.

19. Ibid., 10–11.

20. Ibid., 11.

21. Ibid.

22. Plantinga, *Warranted Christian Belief*, 177–178.

23. Edmund Gettier, "Is Justified True Belief Knowledge?" in A. Phillips Griffiths, ed., *Knowledge and Belief* (Oxford: Oxford University Press, 1967), 144. The article originally appeared in the journal *Analysis* 23 (1963) but has been anthologized in a number of places such as the one I'm citing.

24. Ibid., 145.

25. Ibid.

26. Ibid.

27. Ibid. On pages 145–146 Gettier offers a second example, but this time the key sentence in question is a disjunct rather than a conjunct. Again, the result is an instance of an imagined person having justified true belief and yet not having knowledge.

28. Plantinga, *Warranted Christian Belief*, xi.

29. Ibid., 79.

30. John Locke, *Essay* 4.19.1 (p. 429). Quoted in Plantinga, *Warranted Christian Belief*, 79.

31. W. K. Clifford, "The Ethics of Belief," in *Lectures and Essays* (London: Macmillan, 1879), 186.

32. Plantinga, *Warranted Christian Belief*, 82. For a description of the kinds of evidences (besides propositional evidence) one might marshal in building an evidential case, see Plantinga, *Warrant and Proper Function* (Oxford: Oxford University Press, 1993), 185–193.

33. Plantinga cites Michael Scriven, Bertrand Russell, J. L. Mackie, Antony Flew, and W. K. Clifford. See Plantinga, "Reason and Belief in God," 24ff.

34. Plantinga, "Reason and Belief in God," 48.

35. Ibid., 46.

36. In ibid., pages 49–55, Plantinga offers more details about the nature of a noetic structure, and in so doing amplifies the various definitions I have offered.

37. Plantinga, "Reason and Belief in God," 58–59.

38. Ibid., 59.

39. Ibid., 55–56. Some of the examples are taken directly from Plantinga; others are my own but follow the basic pattern of examples he sets forth.

40. Ibid., 57–58. Again, some of these examples are Plantinga's and others are mine.

41. Ibid., 58. Here I'm paraphrasing Plantinga's more formal account of incorrigibility. As Plantinga notes, an incorrigible truth is probably what Descartes had in mind in searching for one indubitable truth upon which to build what he knew.

42. One thinks here, for example, of the argument that all the eyewitnesses who claimed to see Christ alive after he had definitely died must count as sufficient evidence that the resurrection occurred. Surely, beliefs expressing what the eyewitnesses claimed to see are neither self-evident, evident to the senses, nor incorrigible (nor is it clear that their testimony can be ultimately traced back to beliefs that meet such criteria for proper basicality). Hence, though many apologists might think eyewitness testimony of Christ's post-death appearances sufficient evidence to warrant, on a classical foundationalist view, belief in the resurrection, such a conclusion is unjustified. The case hasn't been made.

43. Plantinga, "Reason and Belief in God," 59–60, 62.

44. Ibid., 61.

45. Plantinga, *Warrant and Proper Function*, 4–11. See also Plantinga, *Warranted Christian Belief*, 146, 154–155. My text summarizes the main ideas in these pages, but for details consult the two works cited.

46. Plantinga, *Warrant and Proper Function*, 7, 18.
47. Ibid., 16. See also 11–17.
48. For further details on beliefs being formed according to a design plan see Plantinga, *Warrant and Proper Function*, 21–31, 195–199, and Plantinga, *Warranted Christian Belief*, 154–155.
49. Plantinga, "Reason and Belief in God," 34.
50. Plantinga, *Warranted Christian Belief*, 170.
51. Ibid., 171.
52. Plantinga (ibid., 171) quotes Calvin's *Institutes* 1.3.1 (p. 44) on this matter, but a closer look at the passage quoted shows that Calvin is talking about an inborn or innate knowledge of God. Plantinga notes that Calvin seems to be talking about innate knowledge of God, but dismisses this as not Calvin's position. However, we must remember that while Locke's critique of innate ideas dealt a devastating blow to that conception, Calvin never read it. The reason is quite simple: Calvin died in 1564 and Locke wasn't born until 1646. Hence, it is likely that Calvin really did hold to innate ideas, as did many others prior to Locke. Having said this, however, the exact history of Calvin's view doesn't really matter to Plantinga's point. For whether the idea is innate at birth or the capacities or disposition to form the idea are innate, the result is the same for both Plantinga and Calvin, viz., all people at all times know that there is a God.
53. Plantinga, *Warranted Christian Belief*, 172.
54. Ibid., 172–173.
55. Ibid., 175.
56. Ibid.
57. Ibid., 175–176. For more on Plantinga's views on the *sensus divinitatis*, see ibid., pages 172–176, 182–184, 334–335, 485, and 490–492.
58. Ibid., 206.
59. Ibid., 251. For more on the internal testimony of the Holy Spirit and Plantinga's use of this doctrine, see pages 180, 201, and 249–252.
60. Here see my *Many Faces of Evil*, rev. ed.
61. For those unfamiliar, the Great Pumpkin is an imaginary figure that kids in the comic strip *Peanuts* believe in. They believe that on Halloween the Great Pumpkin rises out of a pumpkin patch and gives candy to good little boys and girls.
62. Plantinga, "Reason and Belief in God," 79–82.
63. Ibid., 74–78.
64. Ibid., 78ff.
65. Plantinga, *Warranted Christian Belief*, 346–349.
66. Ibid., 348–350.
67. Plantinga, *Warrant and Proper Function*, 48ff.
68. Ibid., 57–64.
69. Ibid., 89–101.
70. Ibid., 102–116.
71. Ibid., 77–82ff.
72. My discussion of this issue takes its cue from Plantinga, "Reason and Belief in God," 82–86. Those familiar with Plantinga's essay will recognize that I have embellished what he says, but I think what I have said is consistent with the basic points Plantinga makes about the role of reason, argument, and evidence in religious belief.

73. Plantinga, *Warrant: the Current Debate*, 133.
74. Ibid., 134.
75. Ibid., 134–135.
76. Ibid., 135–136.
77. Ibid., 136–137.
78. Ibid., 137; Plantinga lumps sanity and proper function into one category. However, it seems better to distinguish the two, for someone's cognitive faculties could malfunction without their being in the least bit insane. If I have an eye exam and the doctor dilates my pupils, for awhile afterward it will be hard for me to open my eyes unless they are shaded with sunglasses, and even if I do wear sunglasses I may make mistakes about what I think I'm seeing. Surely this isn't proper function in appropriate circumstances, but it certainly isn't any form of insanity either. So insanity and cognitive malfunction may coincide in some cases, but they don't in all instances of malfunction. See also Plantinga, *Warranted Christian Belief*, 110–113. In the section from *Warranted Christian Belief*, Plantinga makes a further distinction between internal and external proper function, but the specific details go beyond the point I am making in the text.
79. See Richard Grigg's "The Crucial Disanalogies between Properly Basic Belief and Belief in God"; and Mark McLeod, "The Analogy Argument for the Proper Basicality of Belief in God," *International Journal for Philosophy of Religion* 21 (1987).
80. Such as myself in *Many Faces of Evil*, rev. ed.
81. Plantinga, *Warranted Christian Belief*, 423–425.
82. Ibid., 427–428.
83. Ibid.
84. Ibid., 428–429.
85. Richard Rorty, *Contingency, Irony, and Solidarity* (Cambridge: Cambridge University Press, 1989), 5; cited in Plantinga, *Warranted Christian Belief*, 434.
86. Plantinga, ibid.
87. Ibid., 435.

Chapter 8: Presuppositionalism

1. For example, see John Frame, *Apologetics to the Glory of God* (Nutley, NJ: Presbyterian & Reformed, 1994). Even Cornelius Van Til was not entirely comfortable with that label. See Van Til, *The Defense of the Faith* (Phillipsburg, NJ: Presbyterian & Reformed, 1980).
2. See, for example, John Frame, "Presuppositional Apologetics," in Steven B. Cowan, ed., *Five Views on Apologetics* (Grand Rapids, MI: Zondervan, 2000), 207–231.
3. For those interested in more contemporary discussions of presuppositionalism, see K. Scott Oliphant and Lane G. Tipton, eds., *Revelation and Reason: New Essays in Reformed Apologetics* (Nutley, NJ: Presbyterian & Reformed, 2007).
4. Originally, I had planned to cover Frame's form of presuppositionalism, but one can't cover everything. I chose Van Til and Schaeffer because in them we see presuppositionalism in its "purest" form. But interested readers would benefit as well by reading Frame on presuppositionalism. See his *Apologetics to the Glory of God*.
5. Van Til, *Defense of the Faith*, 101.
6. Ibid., 100.
7. Ibid., 77.
8. Ibid., 94–95.

9. Ibid., 96–102 passim.

10. Ibid., 77.

11. Cornelius Van Til, "My Credo and Apologetics," in E. R. Geehan, ed., *Jerusalem and Athens* (Nutley, NJ: Presbyterian & Reformed, 1977), 17.

12. Ibid., 21.

13. Van Til, *In Defense of the Faith*, 77–84, 103.

14. Ibid., 96ff.

15. Ibid., 168, and passim in chapters on common grace, common notions, and common ground.

16. Ibid., 101.

17. Ibid.

18. Ibid., 98–99.

19. For example, ibid., 67; and Van Til, "My Credo," 19–20.

20. Ibid., 100–101; reprinted in Van Til's syllabus "Apologetics" (Westminster Seminary), 62.

21. Here we must distinguish a circular *argument* from circular *reasoning* in general. Van Til espouses the latter, not the former. The point in part is that all reasoning starts somewhere. Those starting points are carried along as reasoning proceeds, and so are conclusions reached along the way. I wish to thank William Edgar for pointing out this distinction.

22. Van Til, *In Defense of the Faith*, 100.

23. Ibid.

24. Given postmodern disavowals of the value of reason and argument plus their rejection of the notion of absolute truth, it is dubious as to how one might use Van Til's presuppositional method when talking with a postmodern. But Van Til worked within the context of modern epistemology and its demands, and his presuppositional methodology is one way to respond to the demands of modern epistemology, especially with its commitment to classical foundationalism.

25. See, for example, pages 13–15 in *The God Who Is There* (Downers Grove, IL: InterVarsity Press, 1968).

26. Ibid., 15.

27. Ibid., 17.

28. Ibid., 44ff.

29. Ibid., 13–18.

30. This is, of course, a brief summary of Schaeffer's book. A more detailed reading shows how Schaeffer goes about arguing his case.

31. Schaeffer, *God Who Is There*, 93.

32. This is Schaeffer's way of referring to God's revelation in our world and in his Word, and it seems appropriate to use those terms here. See ibid.

33. Ibid., 121–130, in which Schaeffer explains the basics of his strategy for arguing against the nonbeliever's position. Repeatedly, it is the nonbeliever's whole worldview with its presuppositions, not just a small piece of that view, that is held up to the world around us.

34. Ibid., 109.

35. Ibid., 119–125.

36. Ibid.

37. For details, see ibid., 109–111.

38. The next few paragraphs are built upon Schaeffer's explanation in ibid., 119–130.

39. Ibid., 121–122.

40. One of the better-known contemporary presuppositionalists is John Frame. His major work on apologetics is *Apologetics to the Glory of God*. A shorter piece by Frame appears in *Five Views on Apologetics*. In these works one finds familiar presuppositionalist themes. However, Frame not only agrees that there is common ground with the unbeliever, but he also (especially in the more recent piece) seems to treat evidence and argument in a way much akin to that of Christian evidentialism. The result is that the shorter piece seems hard to distinguish from the evidentialist contributions to that volume.

41. By quality of evidence I refer to whether evidence passes the three tests set forth in earlier chapters: Is it true? Is it relevant? And how much does it prove? In each case, how do I know?

42. Here I'm relying on Kevin Zuber's doctoral dissertation at Trinity Evangelical Divinity School for an understanding of what he calls the consensus Christian definition of the Holy Spirit's illumination (Kevin Zuber, "What Is Illumination? A Study in Evangelical Theology Seeking a Biblically Grounded Definition of the Illuminating Work of the Holy Spirit" (PhD diss., Trinity Evangelical Divinity School, 1996).

43. I am not suggesting that Van Til holds that whatever you tell the nonbeliever, the Holy Spirit can transfer to his mind the correct intellectual content. Rather my point is first that illumination does not involve activity 1); nonbelievers can grasp the intellectual content of what we say, so either presuppositionalism or evidentialism can achieve that. My further point is that if the Holy Spirit must actually do what is described in 1), then the "absurdities" I mention in the rest of the paragraph seem to follow.

44. See ibid. for Zuber's exegesis of the various verses on illumination and for the theological conclusions they require in our understanding of illumination.

45. Here I'm thinking of some of the great philosophers like Leibniz, Spinoza, and Hegel. I don't believe their systems are correct, but am only saying that it is hard to show how and where any of these thinkers' system contradicts itself.

Chapter 9: Christian Evidentialism

1. This, of course, does not refer to thinkers like Aquinas and Anselm, who lived long before the advent of the modern mind-set. Though they don't work within that framework, many of the assumptions and procedures used by Aquinas and Anselm fit with what we find in more contemporary evidentialists.

2. According to foundationalism, beliefs are supported by other beliefs that ultimately can be traced back to beliefs that are properly basic and hence rest on no other beliefs. Various forms of foundationalism adopt different criteria of proper basicality, but all at least require that there be some non-basic beliefs and some basic beliefs in a person's noetic structure. In contrast, a coherentist theory of knowledge agrees that beliefs are to be held on the basis of other beliefs one holds, but according to this theory no belief is more basic than any other belief in one's noetic structure.

3. Here I point to Calvin's claims about the noetic effects of the fall upon the human race. Calvin clearly acknowledges that sin has not removed reason from human nature. He affirms that in non-spiritual matters like government, the liberal arts, fine arts, and various practical fields of endeavor, reason works quite well for nonbelievers. However, when it comes to spiritual matters, nonbelievers, according to Calvin, are "blinder than moles." However, Calvin doesn't take this to mean

that nonbelievers can't even have a basic understanding of the facts of the gospel. Even the demons believe and understand some theological truth (James 2:19). The problem with the natural man is that he doesn't see spiritual truth as important for him, and he cannot accept spiritual truth so as to change his life and live within a relation to God. Moving his will to decide to abandon his sinful life and follow God is accomplished only through the ministry of the Holy Spirit. For Calvin's views on fallen men's intellectual and moral powers, see my "The Doctrine of Human Freedom in the Writings of John Calvin" (ThM thesis, Trinity Evangelical Divinity School, 1972).

4. See Steven B. Cowan, ed., *Five Views on Apologetics* (Grand Rapids, MI: Zondervan, 2000). William Lane Craig, Gary Habermas, and Paul Feinberg are the three evidentialists in this volume. All of them place heavy emphasis on the role of the Holy Spirit in apologetics and evangelism.

5. William Lane Craig, "Classical Apologetics," in *Five Views on Apologetics*, 28ff.

6. Ibid., 29–30.

7. This is indeed a somewhat strange viewpoint on at least two accounts. First, it sounds a bit as if it is in the same neighborhood as neo-orthodox views about the nonverbal revelatory encounter with God. If you've had the encounter, you just know it is God and you know what he has said, even though the encounter didn't include God verbally speaking to you. One wonders about how one just knows, even as one wonders how Craig can be sure that the believer just knows that what he is thinking about the truth of Christianity comes from the Holy Spirit's assurance. Second, as Craig presents this internal witness, it gives the impression that every believer has this experience, and so at least should have no doubts, even if one does. Perhaps some Christians have this sense of Christianity's truth, but I doubt that all believers do.

8. Craig, "Classical Apologetics," 48.

9. Ibid., 48–53.

10. Norman Geisler, *Christian Apologetics* (Grand Rapids, MI: Baker, 1976), 95. See also his claims on page 139.

11. William Lane Craig, "A Classical Apologist's Closing Remarks," in *Five Views on Apologetics*, 316.

12. Gary Habermas, "Evidential Apologetics," in *Five Views on Apologetics*, 94–99.

13. Ibid., 92–94.

14. Ibid., 92.

15. Ibid.

16. Ibid., 100.

17. Paul Feinberg, "Cumulative Case Apologetics," in *Five Views on Apologetics*, 148–149.

18. Ibid., 150.

19. Basil Mitchell, *The Justification of Religious Belief* (New York: Macmillan, 1973).

20. Paul Feinberg, "Cumulative Case Apologetics," 150ff.

21. Ibid., 151–152.

22. Those interested in the details for each of these tests can consult ibid., 154–156.

23. Ibid., 158–166.

24. This essay was part of a *festschrift* honoring Van Til. That volume is E. R. Geehan, ed., *Jerusalem and Athens* (Nutley, NJ: Presbyterian & Reformed, 1977).

25. Raymond Aron, ed., *L'histoire et ses interpretations* (Paris: Mouton, 1961); cited

in John Warwick Montgomery, *The Shape of the Past* (Minneapolis: Bethany Fellowship, 1975), 138.

26. Montgomery, *Shape of the Past*, 138.
27. Ibid.
28. Ibid., 138–139.
29. Ibid., 139.
30. Ibid.
31. Ibid.
32. Ibid.
33. See Montgomery's footnote 117 on pages 171–172 of *Shape of the Past*.
34. Montgomery, *Shape of the Past*, 139.
35. Ibid.
36. Ibid., 140.
37. John Warwick Montgomery, *Where Is History Going?* (Minneapolis: Bethany Fellowship, 1972), 53–54. Montgomery writes, "the most irritating aspect of the line of argumentation that I have taken is probably this: it depends in no sense on theology. It rests solely and squarely upon historical method, the kind of method all of us, whether Christians, rationalists, agnostics, or Tibetan monks, have to use in analyzing historical data."
38. Gordon Clark, *A Christian View of Men and Things* (Grand Rapids, MI: Eerdmans, 1952), 56–57 and 92; quoted in Montgomery, *Where Is History Going?* 149–150. See also Montgomery, *Where Is History Going?* 150, 164, and 181. See also J. W. N. Watkins, "Philosophy of History: Publications in English," in *La Philosophie au milieu du vingtieme siecle*, ed. Raymond Klibansky, 4 vols., 2nd ed. (Florence: La Nuova Italia, 1961–1962), 3:174; quoted in Montgomery, *Where Is History Going?* 171.
39. For details see my *The Many Faces of Evil: Theological Systems and the Problems of Evil*, rev. ed. (Wheaton, IL: Crossway, 2004).

Chapter 10: The Problem of Evil

1. J. L. Mackie, "Evil and Omnipotence," in Basil Mitchell, ed., *Philosophy of Religion* (Oxford: Oxford University Press, 1971), 92.
2. For a discussion of these divine attributes in Christian theology, see my *No One Like Him: The Doctrine of God* (Wheaton, IL: Crossway, 2001), chapters 6–8. For different forms of theism and how their conceptions of God generate a distinct problem of evil, see my *The Many Faces of Evil*, rev. ed. (Wheaton, IL: Crossway, 2004).
3. See, for example, my *Theologies and Evil* (Lanham, MD: University Press of America, 1978); *Many Faces of Evil* (first published by Zondervan and currently by Crossway); "God, Freedom, and Evil in Calvinist Thinking," in Bruce Ware and Thomas Schreiner, eds., *The Grace of God, The Bondage of the Will*, vol. 2 (Grand Rapids, MI: Baker, 1995), 459–483; and "Why I Still Believe in Christ, in Spite of Evil and Suffering," in Norman Geisler and Paul Hoffman, eds., *Why I Am a Christian* (Grand Rapids, MI: Baker, 2001).
4. Alvin Plantinga, *God, Freedom, and Evil* (New York: Harper & Row, 1974), 63–64.
5. See my *Many Faces of Evil* for a description of each of these forms of theism.
6. See Bertha Alvarez, "How the Problem of Evil Poses an Obstacle to Belief in God," *Dialogue* 41 (April 1998): 23.

7. See my discussion of the objection and my answer to it in *Many Faces of Evil*, chapter 4.

8. Here I use the term *defense* as opposed to *theodicy*. In contemporary discussions philosophers distinguish between offering a possible reason for God allowing evil and explaining the actual reason for God doing so. The former explanation is referred to as a defense, while the latter is called a theodicy. Given the charge of contradiction, it should be clear that all theists need to do is offer a possible explanation (defense) of how evil fits with the existence of an omnipotent, all-loving God. A case can be made that my defense offers God's actual reason for allowing evil, but for purposes of solving the logical problem of evil, it isn't necessary to prove that one has specified God's actual reason for allowing evil. Hence, I offer my explanation as a defense rather than a theodicy.

9. The remainder of this chapter is taken, with a few wording changes here and there, from chapter 16 of my *No One Like Him*.

10. It may be possible to show that this strategy is implicit in defenses of theonomy. However, because that theology so heavily emphasizes God's power to do whatever he wants (even act arbitrarily in some cases), different approaches to solving theonomy's problem of evil are possible. For example, the theonomist's God might reveal that categories of good and evil apply to us but not to God. Hence, typical strategies theists use to show that God is good, despite the evil in our world, don't necessarily apply to theonomy.

11. John Hick, *Evil and the God of Love* (New York: Harper & Row, 1966).

12. For a description of theonomy and Leibnizian Rationalism plus their problems of evil and answers to those problems see chapters 2–3 of my *Many Faces of Evil*.

13. For detailed proof that the free will defense rests on incompatibilism and that this contradicts compatibilism, see *Many Faces of Evil* (chapter 4) and my article "And the Atheist Shall Lie Down with the Calvinist: Atheism, Calvinism, and the Free Will Defense," *Trinity Journal* 1 NS (1980): 142–152.

14. I must note here that Arminians committed to consequentialist ethics cannot use this defense. Instead, they might well turn to the soul-building theodicy. This defense incorporates consequentialist ethics, and at least as John Hick presents it, it also espouses libertarian free will.

15. Augustine, *On Free Choice of the Will*, trans. Anna Benjamin and L. H. Hackstaff (New York: Bobbs-Merrill, 1964), 1.1 (p. 3).

16. Ibid., 1.3 (pp. 6–8); ibid., 1.15 (pp. 29–33).

17. Ibid., 1.16 (p. 34).

18. Ibid., 2.19 (pp. 80–81).

19. Ibid., 81.

20. Ibid., 2.1 (p. 36); and 2.18 (p. 79).

21. Ibid., 3.3 (pp. 90–93).

22. Bennett refers to Mackie's argument this way in Philip W. Bennett, "Evil, God, and the Free Will Defense," *Australasian Journal of Philosophy* 51 (May 1973): 39–50.

23. Mackie, "Evil and Omnipotence," 100–101.

24. Those familiar with Plantinga's defense of the free will defense immediately recognize that it is much more complicated and sophisticated than this brief summary of one of its key points. For details of Plantinga's presentation see his *God, Freedom, and Evil*.

25. For much more on the different senses of free will, see my *No One Like Him*, chapter 13.

26. For explanation of this and other ethical theories, see John S. Feinberg and Paul D. Feinberg, *Ethics for a Brave New World*, 2nd ed. (Wheaton, IL: Crossway, 2010), chapter 1.

27. Here I note that I am addressing the philosophical/theological problem of evil, which is really the problem of moral evil. This isn't peculiar to my system, for most defenses address that problem. Unfortunately, many theists and atheists don't see that there are other problems of evil that must also be addressed and that a defense against moral evil doesn't answer all problems of evil, nor need it do so.

28. Joseph B. Mayor, *The Epistle of St. James*, in the Classic Commentary Library (Grand Rapids, MI: Zondervan, 1954), 54–55.

29. This interpretation of the point of sin's conception certainly squares with the tenor of Jesus's teachings, when he claimed that sin is committed in a person's thoughts first and made public later. Think, for example, of Matthew 5:27–28, where Jesus teaches that if a man desires a woman in his heart, he has already committed adultery with her before doing any overt act.

30. In this case, people wouldn't have to be able to have such knowledge, since God would take care of any possible problems by means of miracles.

31. My point here is similar to Dilley's response to Steven Böer's proposal (see chapter 4 of my *Many Faces of Evil*). See Steven E. Böer, "The Irrelevance of the Free Will Defence," *Analysis* 38 (1977); and Frank B. Dilley, "Is the Free Will Defence Irrelevant?" *Religious Studies* 18 (1982). For God to get rid of evil in any of the ways imagined would produce a much more different world from ours than we might imagine.

32. This must not be misunderstood. Were I a consequentialist, the decision about which actions are evil would depend on the consequences of those actions. But even here, I might intend to do an act whose consequences would be beneficial to others, and yet there might be unforeseen consequences that turn out otherwise. In this case, the evil is unintentional, but it is still real. God would have to stop those acts, too. Moreover, reflex actions which are preceded by neither good nor evil intentions but lead to evil consequences would have to be stopped. As a nonconsequentialist, I determine rightness or wrongness of an act otherwise than by consequences. The point about involuntary and reflex actions, however, still applies. I may intend to do and perform an act which obeys God's command. Even so, there may be unforeseen results that are negative toward the well-being of others. Hence, God would have to stop my good-intentioned act in that case. Likewise, reflex actions which attach to neither good nor evil intentions but produce evil for others would have to be stopped.

33. I agree that this other world would be better morally, because there would be no moral evil in it. But God cannot make that world and also make the non-glorified human beings he has made. Was God wrong in making non-glorified humans? Only if making such creatures is evil in itself, and it isn't. Is God obligated to create this other world, anyway? According to modified rationalism, God is free either to create or not create at all. If he creates, he is free to create any good possible world available. He isn't obligated to forego our world in favor of the eternal state, so long as our world is a good world, and I have shown why ours is a good world.

34. See my *Many Faces of Evil* as well as the vast amount of literature on this topic in books and philosophical and theological journals.

Chapter 11: The Reliability of the Gospels

1. Here one thinks of Revelation 17 and the beast with many heads that the woman rides; or the scene in Revelation 12 when the dragon is thrown to earth and then persecutes the woman who gave birth to the child.

2. It is, of course, true that commentators take John's descriptive comments about one of Jesus's disciples in John 19:26 and 21:24 to be a reference to himself (21:24 seems to name this person as the writer of the words we are reading). My point is only that none of these references uses the name 'John' and identifies him as writer of this Gospel.

3. Paul D. Feinberg, "The Meaning of Inerrancy," in Norman Geisler, ed., *Inerrancy* (Grand Rapids, MI: Zondervan, 1979), 294.

4. Eckhard Schnabel, "Textual Criticism: Recent Developments," in Scot McKnight and Grant Osborne, eds., *The Face of New Testament Studies: A Survey of Recent Research* (Grand Rapids, MI: Baker, 2004), 60.

5. Craig Blomberg, "The Historical Reliability of the New Testament," in William Lane Craig, *Reasonable Faith: Christian Truth and Apologetics* (Wheaton, IL: Crossway, 1994), 195.

6. D. A. Carson, *Matthew*, Expositor's Bible Commentary, vol. 8 (Grand Rapids, MI: Zondervan, 1984), 21. See his whole discussion of the date, pages 19–21.

7. Ibid., 19. See his complete discussion of the authorship issue, pages 17–19.

8. Walter Wessel, *Mark*, Expositor's Bible Commentary, vol. 8 (Grand Rapids, MI: Zondervan, 1984), 605–608. In these pages Wessel discusses both the authorship and date of the Gospel.

9. Walter Liefeld, *Luke*, Expositor's Bible Commentary, vol. 8 (Grand Rapids, MI: Zondervan, 1984), 798–799.

10. Ibid., 807–809.

11. Richard Longenecker, *The Acts of the Apostles*, Expositor's Bible Commentary, vol. 9 (Grand Rapids, MI: Zondervan, 1981), 235–238.

12. Merrill C. Tenney, *The Gospel of John*, Expositor's Bible Commentary, vol. 9 (Grand Rapids, MI: Zondervan, 1981), 5–9.

13. Ibid., 9.

14. Ibid.

15. Bruce Metzger, *The Text of the New Testament*, 4th ed. (New York: Oxford, 2005), 55–56. See also Kurt Aland and Barbara Aland, *The Text of the New Testament*, 2nd ed., trans. Erroll F. Rhodes (Grand Rapids, MI: Eerdmans, 1989), 99.

16. Tenney, *Gospel of John*, 9–10.

17. Metzger, *Text of the New Testament*, 56–57. See also Aland and Aland, *Text of the New Testament*, 100.

18. Ibid., 55. See also Aland and Aland, *Text of the New Testament*, 100.

19. Ibid., 58. See also Aland and Aland, *Text of the New Testament*, 101.

20. Aland and Aland, *Text of the New Testament*, 98–99. See also Metzger on p[46], *Text of the New Testament*, 54–55.

21. Metzger, *Text of the New Testament*, 64.

22. Here see Metzger, *Text of the New Testament*, 62–65, for the details.

23. Ibid., 65.

24. Aland and Aland, *Text of the New Testament*, 107.

25. Ibid., 109.

26. Metzger, *Text of the New Testament*, 67.
27. Ibid., 67–68.
28. Ibid., 68.
29. Ibid., 71. See also Aland and Aland, *Text of the New Testament*, 109–110.
30. Irenaeus, *Adversus haereses* 3.1; cited in John Warwick Montgomery, *Where Is History Going?* (Minneapolis: Bethany Fellowship, 1972), 48. The comments inserted in brackets are Montgomery's.
31. Montgomery, *Where Is History Going?* 48–49. For this information Montgomery cites no less an authority than Eusebius's *Historia ecclesiastica* 5.20.
32. The data for comparing manuscripts in relation to the three items comes from a chart in Geisler's *Christian Apologetics* (Grand Rapids, MI: Baker, 1976). For the claim that no doctrine is involved in the variant readings where textual critics haven't decided conclusively which is the best reading, see Blomberg, "Historical Reliability of the New Testament," 194.
33. Aristotle, *Art of Poetry*, 1460b–1461b; cited in Montgomery, *Where Is History Going?* 46.
34. The same is true in terms of the way John starts 1 John. What he says there surely applies to his Gospel as well.
35. Blomberg, "Historical Reliability of the New Testament," 222–223.
36. Ibid., 223. Though much of this point does relate to matters I'm including in authenticity, it is important that there is a strong likelihood that Jesus actually said them. Otherwise, they are not his parables and the text is wrong in attributing them to him.
37. Ibid. On the third example, Blomberg also includes a reference to the apocryphal Gospel of Thomas (65–66).
38. Ibid.
39. Ibid., 224.
40. Ibid.
41. Ibid.
42. Other examples are plentiful. For example, not all Gospels record Jesus saying the same things while on the cross. John gives us far more details than the other Gospels about the spices brought to the tomb for Jesus's burial. It is only John who tells us about Nicodemus being there, and that Nicodemus brought about 100 pounds of spices (John 19:39–40).
43. Papias, quoted in Blomberg, "Historical Reliability of the New Testament," 204.
44. As quoted in Gary R. Habermas, *Ancient Evidence for the Life of Jesus* (Nashville: Thomas Nelson, 1984), 141–142.
45. Ibid., 142.
46. Blomberg, "Historical Reliability of the New Testament," 214–215.
47. Ibid., 216. See also Blomberg's further comments on this matter on 218.
48. Josephus, *Jewish Antiquities* 18.63–64; quoted in Blomberg, "Historical Reliability of the New Testament," 215.
49. Blomberg, "Historical Reliability of the New Testament," 215.
50. Ibid. These references are largely undisputed by critics.
51. Habermas, *Ancient Evidence for the Life of Jesus*, 87–88.
52. Blomberg, "Historical Reliability of the New Testament," 216. As a source of this information, Blomberg cites Rainer Riesner, "Archeology and Geography," in *Dictionary of Jesus and the Gospels*, ed. Joel B. Green, Scot McKnight, and I. Howard

Marshall (Downers Grove, IL: InterVarsity Press, 1992), 33–46; and E. M. Blaik-lock, *The Archaeology of the New Testament* (Nashville: Thomas Nelson, 1984).

53. Gary Habermas, *The Historical Jesus* (Joplin, MO: College Press, 1996), 184.
54. Blomberg, "Historical Reliability of the New Testament," 219.
55. Ibid., 220.
56. F. F. Bruce, "Archaeological Confirmation of the New Testament," in Carl Henry, ed., *Revelation and the Bible* (Grand Rapids, MI: Baker, 1969), 326; cited in Josh McDowell, *Evidence That Demands a Verdict* (San Bernardino, CA: Campus Crusade for Christ, 1972), 74.
57. Ramsey, quoted from the Baker Book House edition of this work, published in 1962; quoted in McDowell, *Evidence That Demands a Verdict*, 73.

Chapter 12: The Resurrection of Jesus Christ

1. For an interesting interchange regarding this matter and others about the rationality of believing in the resurrection see Michael Martin, "Christianity and the Rationality of the Resurrection," *Philo* 3 (Spring–Summer 2000): 52–62; and Stephen T. Davis, "The Rationality of Resurrection for Christians: A Rejoinder," *Philo* 3 (Spring–Summer 2000): 41–51.
2. Robert Greg Cavin makes this point in the most detail. He shows that to support fully everything Christians believe about the resurrected Christ, one would need to show much more than merely that someone who was physically dead regained physical life. For details see Cavin's "Is There Sufficient Historical Evidence to Establish the Resurrection of Jesus?" *Faith and Philosophy* 12 (July 1995). The "occasion" of this essay is a response to apologists like Gary Habermas and William Lane Craig who claim that there is sufficient historical evidence to establish the resurrection of Jesus (and his glorification) from the dead.
3. For this information see John S. Feinberg and Paul D. Feinberg, *Ethics for a Brave New World*, 2nd ed. (Wheaton, IL: Crossway, 2010), 222.
4. Josh McDowell, citing Michael Green, Eusebius, et al., on pages 196–197 in *Evidence That Demands a Verdict*, rev. ed. (San Bernardino, CA: Here's Life, 1979).
5. The Roman method of crucifixion actually involved asphyxiation. People nailed to a cross had their legs crossed and nails driven through their ankles. This was done so that as they hung on the cross, they could push down on the nails and raise their chest so as to inhale. If the legs were not crossed, the weight of their body hanging would make it impossible to raise their chest so that their lungs could inhale another breath. When the Romans thought the criminal had suffered enough, they would break the legs of the victim so that it would be impossible for him to push down on the nails to lift his body to take in another breath of air. The result was that the victim would die from asphyxiation.
6. McDowell, *Evidence That Demands a Verdict*, 198–199.
7. William Lane Craig, *Knowing the Truth about the Resurrection: Our Response to the Empty Tomb* (Ann Arbor, MI: Servant, 1988), 39–40.
8. See McDowell, *Evidence That Demands a Verdict*, 200. He quotes W. J. Sparrow-Simpson's comments on the burial given Jesus.
9. Some have thought the text means that the grave clothes were still wrapped up as they would have been when Jesus was in them. While this is possible, commentators suggest that it isn't absolutely certain. See Merrill Tenney, *The Gospel of John*, The Expositor's Bible Commentary, vol. 9 (Grand Rapids, MI: Zondervan, 1981),

186–188; and J. H. Bernard, *A Critical and Exegetical Commentary on the Gospel according to St. John*, vol. 2, The International Critical Commentary (Edinburgh: T & T Clark, 1963), 652–661.

10. McDowell, *Evidence That Demands a Verdict*, 224. McDowell also includes appearances to Stephen (Acts 7:55), to Paul (Acts 22:17–21; 23:11), and to John on Patmos (Rev. 1:10–19). I have not included these in the list because one could easily argue that these appearances came in visions, and sometimes in a vision one sees things that don't necessarily exist in the world outside the mind (see, for example, Ezek. 37:1–14, the vision of the valley of dry bones).

11. For further objections to the hallucination theory in light of the fact that hallucinations are quite different from the nature of what all the witnesses saw, see Peter Kreeft and Ronald K. Tacelli, "The Resurrection," in *Handbook of Christian Apologetics* (Downers Grove, IL: InterVarsity Press, 1994), 186–187.

12. See Robert M. Price, "Is There a Place for Historical Criticism?" *Religious Studies* 27 (September 1991): 380–388.

13. William Lane Craig in particular has argued long and hard for this point. As an example see his "On Doubts about the Resurrection," *Modern Theology* 6 (October 1989): 63–75.

Chapter 13: Religious Pluralism

1. This, of course, is only a very small part of the reasons for the rise in religious pluralism. A careful and thorough analysis of the various factors that have brought us to this place is available in Harold Netland, *Encountering Religious Pluralism* (Downers Grove, IL: InterVarsity Press, 2001), especially chapters 3–4.

2. Ibid., 46–49.

3. Harold Netland, "Religious Exclusivism," in Paul Copan and Chad Meister, eds., *Philosophy of Religion: Classic and Contemporary Issues* (DeKalb, IL: John Wiley, 2007), chapter 5; and Netland, *Encountering Religious Pluralism*, 48.

4. I am indebted to comments by Harold Netland for the clarification that exclusivism alone does not entail eternal conscious punishment and that exclusivism can be wedded either to that view or to annihilationism.

5. Netland, *Encountering Religious Pluralism*, 51–52; and his "Religious Exclusivism."

6. Netland, "Religious Exclusivism," and *Encountering Religious Pluralism*, 52 (which uses slightly different wording but amounts to the same thing).

7. Netland, *Encountering Religious Pluralism*, 53.

8. For further presentation of the basic definition of religious pluralism see Netland, *Encountering Religious Pluralism*, 53–54; and "Religious Exclusivism"; Timothy O'Connor, "Religious Pluralism," in Michael J. Murray, ed., *Reason for the Hope Within* (Grand Rapids, MI: Eerdmans, 1999), 176–177; and Jan Van Wiele, "The Constitutiveness of Christ in Christian Theology of Religions," *Studies in Interreligious Dialogue* 12 (2002): 184–188.

9. Netland, *Encountering Religious Pluralism*, 260.

10. An example of someone who believes that religious claims are nothing more nor less than expressions of personalistic truth is W. Cantwell Smith in his *The Meaning and End of Religion* (Minneapolis: Fortress, 1991). As Netland explains, Smith doesn't offer a clear definition of personalistic truth, but his basic idea is that "personalistic truth does not reflect correspondence with reality so much as it signifies integrity and faithfulness in a person, or authenticity in one's life" (Harold

Netland, "Religious Pluralism and Truth," *Trinity Journal* 6 [Spring 1985]: 78). Netland goes on to explain the problems with seeing religious truth claims as nothing more than assertions of personalistic truth.

11. Netland, *Encountering Religious Pluralism*, 339. Netland quotes Robert E. Wood's claim of this point in Wood's "Tillich Encounters Japan," *Japanese Religions* 2 (May 1962): 48–50.

12. The basic point made in these paragraphs is raised by Netland, *Encountering Religious Pluralism*, 338ff.

13. See Netland, *Encountering Religious Pluralism*, 183–184 for these varieties of Buddhism.

14. Ibid., 184.

15. Ibid.

16. John Hick, *God Has Many Names* (Philadelphia: Westminster, 1982); and *An Interpretation of Religion* (New Haven, Conn: Yale University Press, 1989).

17. For discussion of different conceptions of God in world religions and how they compare with Hick's notion of God, see Harold Netland, "Religious Pluralism and Truth," 84–86. For further discussion of Hick's notion of God see J. Andrew Kirk, "John Hick's Kantian Theory of Religious Pluralism and the Challenge of Secular Thinking," *Studies in Interreligious Dialogue* 12 (2002): 26–28.

18. Scott Yakimow, "Bridging the Gap: Sharing the Gospel with Muslims," *Concordia Journal* 28 (July 2002): 278 fn. 24; and Netland, *Encountering Religious Pluralism*, 185.

19. Netland, *Encountering Religious Pluralism*, 184.

20. Ibid.

21. In light of these different understandings of the human condition, it also goes without saying that different religions disagree about whether salvation is necessary, and if so, how one finds salvation. For details see ibid., 185–186.

22. For this argument in favor of pluralism see Timothy O'Connor, "Religious Pluralism," in Michael J. Murray, ed., *Reason for the Hope Within* (Grand Rapids, MI: Eerdmans, 1999), 167–170.

23. Ibid., 169.

24. For this sort of support for pluralism see Netland, "Religious Pluralism and Truth," 74–75; Netland, "Religious Exclusivism"; O'Connor, "Religious Pluralism," 172–175; and John Hick, "A Response to Andrew Kirk on Religious Pluralism," *Studies in Interreligious Dialogue* 12 (2002): 226–227.

25. Netland, *Encountering Religious Pluralism*, 295.

26. Ibid., 291.

27. Michael Peterson, William Hasker, Bruce Reichenbach, and David Basinger, *Reason and Religious Belief: An Introduction to the Philosophy of Religion*, 2nd ed. (New York: Oxford University Press, 1998), 274; quoted in Netland, *Encountering Religious Pluralism*, 291.

28. Ronald M. Green, "Morality and Religion," in *The Encyclopedia of Religion*, ed. Mircea Eliade, 16 vols. (New York: Macmillan, 1987), 10:99; quoted in Netland, *Encountering Religious Pluralism*, 299–300.

29. Timothy O'Connor raises this objection in the form of an argument that religious exclusivists are arrogant in holding that their views alone are correct. For his explanation of and answer to this objection, see O'Connor, "Religious Pluralism," 170–172.

30. Moses Oke, "A Philosophical Approach to Positive Religious Tolerance," *Asia Journal of Theology* 16 (2002): 362–363. Though we might agree that such religious tolerance is hardly the answer, Oke's proposal for positive religious tolerance involves incorporating the Wittgensteinian notion that religions are language-games of the sort specified in Wittgenstein's later philosophy. Using that notion, Oke offers what he calls the language-game approach to religious tolerance. See 367–373. Those unmoved by Wittgenstein's understanding of the language-game of religion won't find Oke's proposal for positive religious tolerance palatable.

31. Harold Netland, *Dissonant Voices: Religious Pluralism and the Question of Truth* (Grand Rapids, MI: Eerdmans, 1991), 300–313 passim.

32. Ibid., 307.

33. Jay Newman, cited in Netland, *Dissonant Voices*, 307.

34. Jan Van Wiele, "The Constitutiveness of Christ in Christian Theology of Religions," *Studies in Interreligious Dialogue* 12 (2002): 185–188.

35. Ibid., 188–195.

36. Ibid., 189. This epistemological paradox is explained on 188–189. Readers will hopefully note that one of the fundamental problems here is that the line of reasoning presented is question begging, for it argues that all knowledge is culturally constructed while using arguments for that thesis which are assumed not to be culturally conditioned. That is, if you claim that all knowledge is a product of time and culture, you cannot then assume that some things you know fall outside this description.

37. Ibid.

38. Ibid.

39. Ibid., 189–190.

40. Ibid., 190.

41. Ibid.

42. Ibid., 192–193.

43. Ibid., 193. Van Wiele offers further examples (193–195) of how pluralists, despite espousing tolerance for each culture's ethical codes and practices, denounce various forms of social and political oppression wherever they are found.

General Index

Scripture Index

The Bible's Answers to Today's Ethical Dilemmas

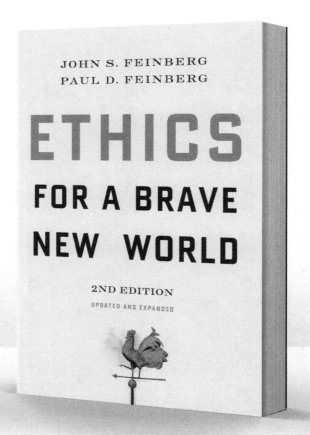

This updated and revised second edition analyzes the current literature on various complex ethical issues. Includes a new chapter on stem cell research and expanded material on other topics.